THE
MACMILLAN
VISUAL
ALMANAC

Bruce S. Glassman, editor

Text by
Jenny Tesar

Computer Graphics by
David C. Bell

A BLACKBIRCH PRESS BOOK

Macmillan•USA

P9-DFG-557

T

MACMILLAN
A Simon & Schuster Macmillan Company
1633 Broadway
New York, NY 10019-6785

Library of Congress Cataloging-in-Publication Data

Tesar, Jenny.
    The Macmillan visual almanac: more than 2,000 charts, graphs, maps, and visuals that provide essential information in the blink of an eye / Bruce S. Glassman, editor; text by Jenny Tesar; computer graphics by David C. Bell.
        p.   cm.
    Originally published for children as: The new view almanac. Woodbridge, Conn. : Blackbirch Press, c1996
    Includes index.
    ISBN 0-02-861247-7
    1. Almanacs, American. 2. United States—Statistics. I. Glassman, Bruce. II. Tesar, Jenny E. New view almanac. III. Title.
AY64.T47   1996
031.02—dc20   96-5857
                                                  CIP

Printed in the United States
1   2   3   4   5   6   7   8   9   10

TABLE OF CONTENTS

1

HEALTH
AND
NUTRITION

THE AMERICAN DIET

A well-balanced diet consists of a wide variety of important nutrients, including carbohydrates, proteins, fats, vitamins, and minerals. The lack of any one of these—or too much of any one—can cause malnutrition and possibly disease.

No single food can supply all the important nutrients in the amounts you need. To have a nutritious diet, you must eat a variety of foods. In 1992, the U.S. government introduced what it called a "food pyramid." This diagram shows what proportions of foods are recommended for good health. It helps people make healthy dietary choices. Today, nutrient information can be found on almost every kind of food package in the U.S. Many packages display the food pyramid.

What people eat has changed drastically over the last 30 years. Americans have improved their diets by eating more fruits and vegetables and by avoiding fats. For example, Americans reduced the amount of fat in their diets from 42% in the mid-1960s to 34% in 1994. Health experts recommend that daily sodium intake be no more than 3,000 milligrams. They also recommend that sugars be eaten only in moderation. A diet with lots of sugar has too many calories and too few nutrients for most people.

Food alone does not make a person healthy or unhealthy. One's state of health also depends on other factors, such as heredity, environment, medical care, and lifestyle. In that food supplies fuel for the body, though, food choices are certainly a critical element of our health that is well within our control.

FINGERTIP FACTS

- Americans are eating less fat and cholesterol. In 1994, the American adult's average fat consumption had dropped to 34% of calories. This trend has helped to reduce the risk of heart disease.

- Despite the drop in fat consumption, the American diet has seen an increase in calorie consumption. In 1994, Americans were eating an average of 231 more calories per day than they did in 1984.

- In 1994, more than 12.4 million Americans—7% of the population—said they were vegetarians. That's almost 10 times as many as in 1978.

- Vegetarians are 28% less likely than meat-eaters to die of heart disease and 39% less likely to die of cancer.

- Yogurt consumption was 4 times greater in 1991 than in 1971.

- Egg consumption has dropped considerably during the past 20 years. In 1970, the average American ate 309 pounds of eggs in a year. By 1993, the consumption had fallen to about 225 pounds.

- Soft drinks are Americans' favorite beverage. Water ranks #3, and milk is #5—after coffee and beer.

- The average American drinks about 44 gallons of soft drinks per year.

- In 1994, Snackwell's—a reduced-fat cookie line—replaced Oreos as America's favorite cookies.

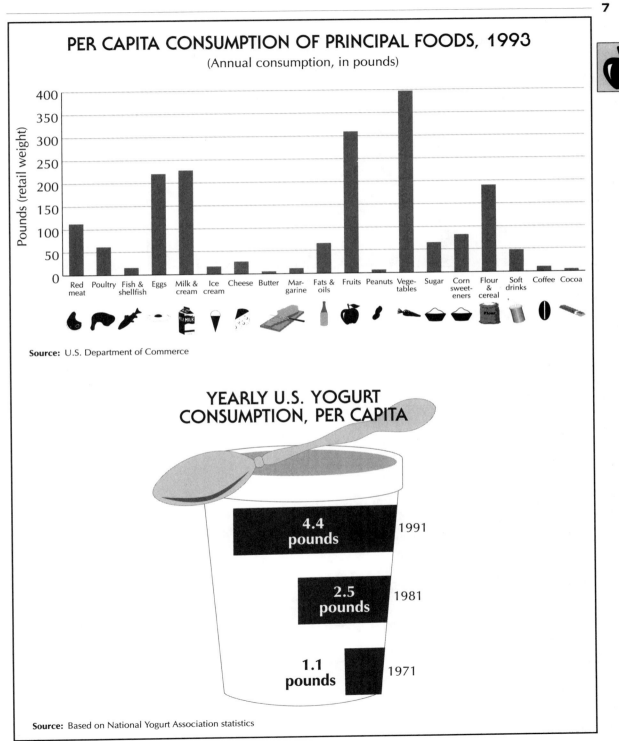

PER CAPITA CONSUMPTION OF PRINCIPAL FOODS, 1993
(Annual consumption, in pounds)

Pounds (retail weight)

400
350
300
250
200
150
100
50
0

Red meat · Poultry · Fish & shellfish · Eggs · Milk & cream · Ice cream · Cheese · Butter · Margarine · Fats & oils · Fruits · Peanuts · Vegetables · Sugar · Corn sweeteners · Flour & cereal · Soft drinks · Coffee · Cocoa

Source: U.S. Department of Commerce

YEARLY U.S. YOGURT CONSUMPTION, PER CAPITA

4.4 pounds — 1991

2.5 pounds — 1981

1.1 pounds — 1971

Source: Based on National Yogurt Association statistics

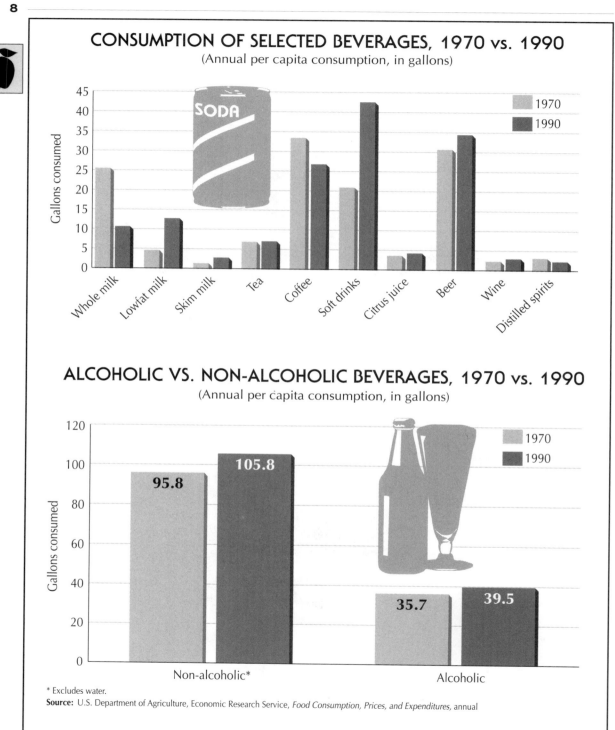

CONSUMPTION OF SELECTED BEVERAGES, 1970 vs. 1990
(Annual per capita consumption, in gallons)

ALCOHOLIC VS. NON-ALCOHOLIC BEVERAGES, 1970 vs. 1990
(Annual per capita consumption, in gallons)

* Excludes water.

Source: U.S. Department of Agriculture, Economic Research Service, *Food Consumption, Prices, and Expenditures,* annual

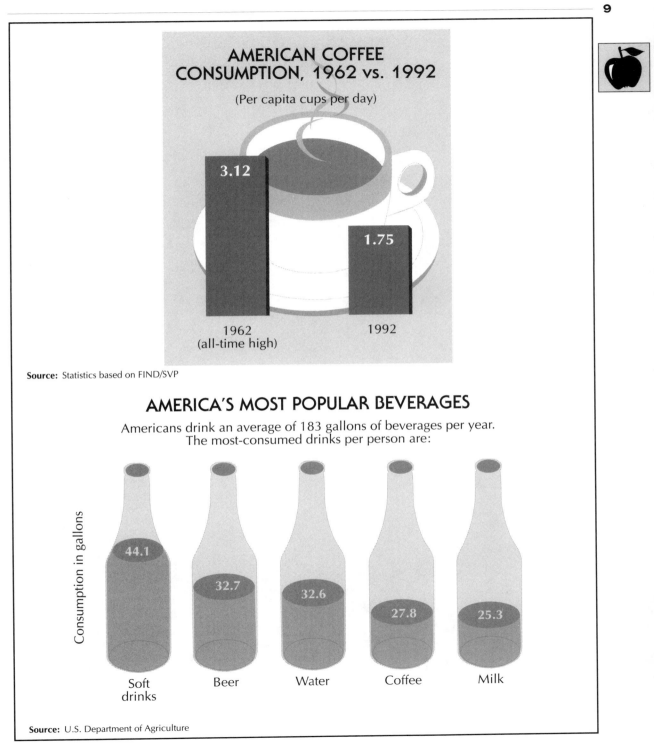

AMERICAN COFFEE CONSUMPTION, 1962 vs. 1992

(Per capita cups per day)

3.12

1.75

1962
(all-time high)

1992

Source: Statistics based on FIND/SVP

AMERICA'S MOST POPULAR BEVERAGES

Americans drink an average of 183 gallons of beverages per year.
The most-consumed drinks per person are:

Consumption in gallons

44.1

32.7

32.6

27.8

25.3

Soft
drinks

Beer

Water

Coffee

Milk

Source: U.S. Department of Agriculture

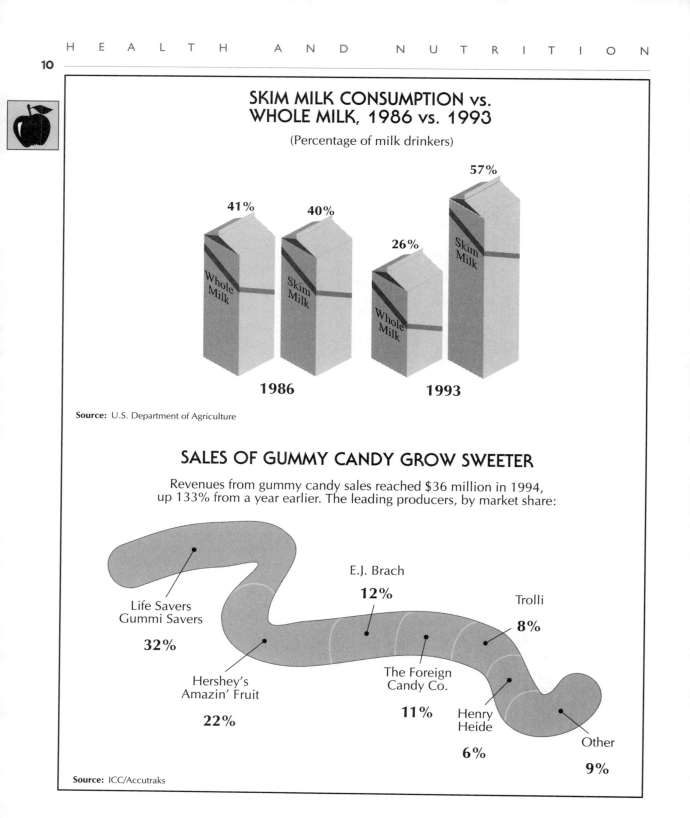

SKIM MILK CONSUMPTION vs. WHOLE MILK, 1986 vs. 1993

(Percentage of milk drinkers)

57%

41%   40%

26%

Whole
Milk

Skim
Milk

Skim
Milk

Whole
Milk

1986   **1993**

Source: U.S. Department of Agriculture

SALES OF GUMMY CANDY GROW SWEETER

Revenues from gummy candy sales reached $36 million in 1994,
up 133% from a year earlier. The leading producers, by market share:

Life Savers
Gummi Savers

32%

Hershey's
Amazin' Fruit

22%

E.J. Brach

12%

The Foreign
Candy Co.

11%

Henry
Heide

6%

Trolli

8%

Other

9%

Source: ICC/Accutraks

COKE CONSUMPTION: U.S. vs. THE WORLD, 1992

(Average per capita consumption, 8-ounce servings of any Coca-Cola soft drink)

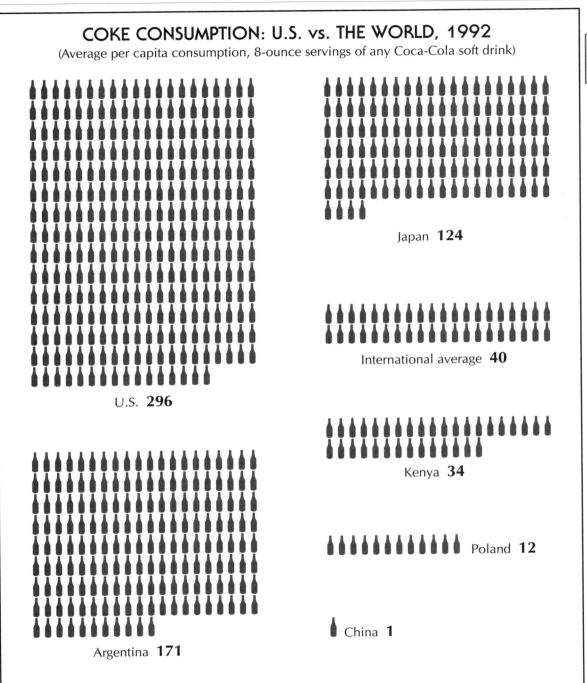

U.S. **296**

Japan **124**

International average **40**

Kenya **34**

Poland **12**

China **1**

Argentina **171**

Source: Coca-Cola

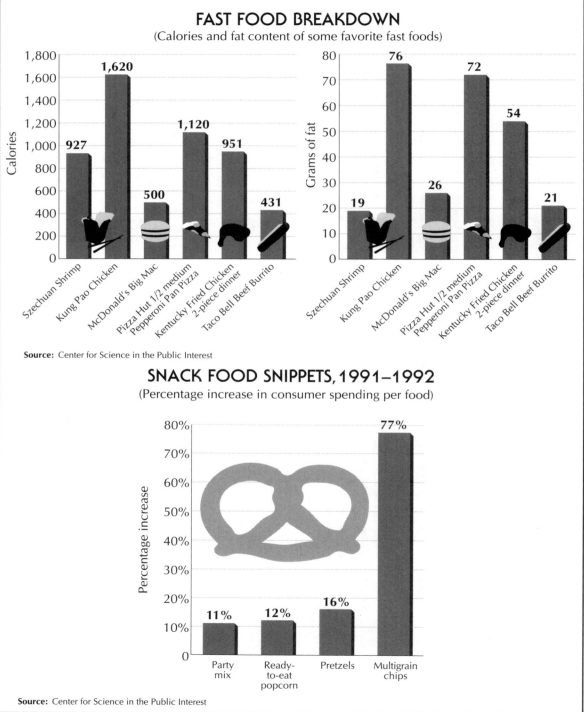

FAST FOOD BREAKDOWN
(Calories and fat content of some favorite fast foods)

Calories

Food	Calories
Szechuan Shrimp	927
Kung Pao Chicken	1,620
McDonald's Big Mac	500
Pizza Hut 1/2 medium Pepperoni Pan Pizza	1,120
Kentucky Fried Chicken 2-piece dinner	951
Taco Bell Beef Burrito	431

Grams of fat

Food	Grams of fat
Szechuan Shrimp	19
Kung Pao Chicken	76
McDonald's Big Mac	26
Pizza Hut 1/2 medium Pepperoni Pan Pizza	72
Kentucky Fried Chicken 2-piece dinner	54
Taco Bell Beef Burrito	21

Source: Center for Science in the Public Interest

SNACK FOOD SNIPPETS, 1991–1992
(Percentage increase in consumer spending per food)

Percentage increase

Snack	Percentage increase
Party mix	11%
Ready-to-eat popcorn	12%
Pretzels	16%
Multigrain chips	77%

Source: Center for Science in the Public Interest

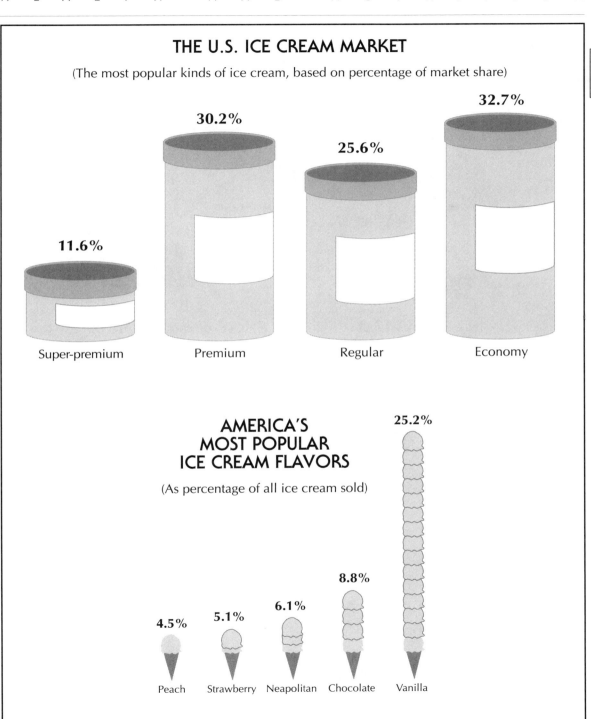

THE U.S. ICE CREAM MARKET

(The most popular kinds of ice cream, based on percentage of market share)

11.6% Super-premium
30.2% Premium
25.6% Regular
32.7% Economy

AMERICA'S MOST POPULAR ICE CREAM FLAVORS

(As percentage of all ice cream sold)

4.5% Peach
5.1% Strawberry
6.1% Neapolitan
8.8% Chocolate
25.2% Vanilla

Source: Information Resources, Inc.

PERSONAL HEALTH PRACTICES OF THE AVERAGE AMERICAN ADULT, BY SELECTED CHARACTERISTIC

(Percentage of population, ages 18 and older)

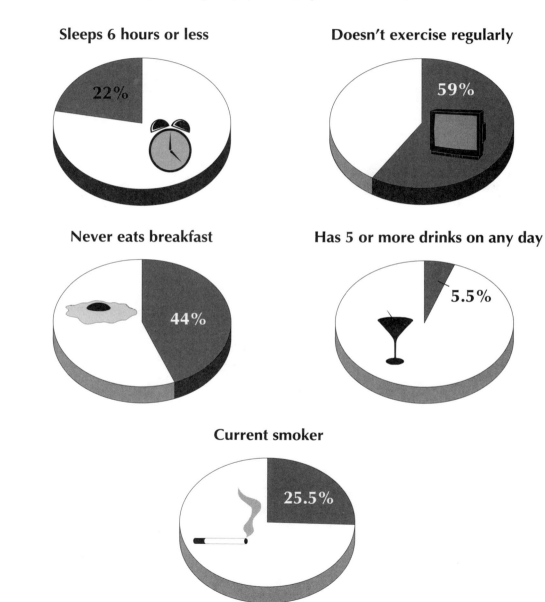

Sleeps 6 hours or less

22%

Doesn't exercise regularly

59%

Never eats breakfast

44%

Has 5 or more drinks on any day

5.5%

Current smoker

25.5%

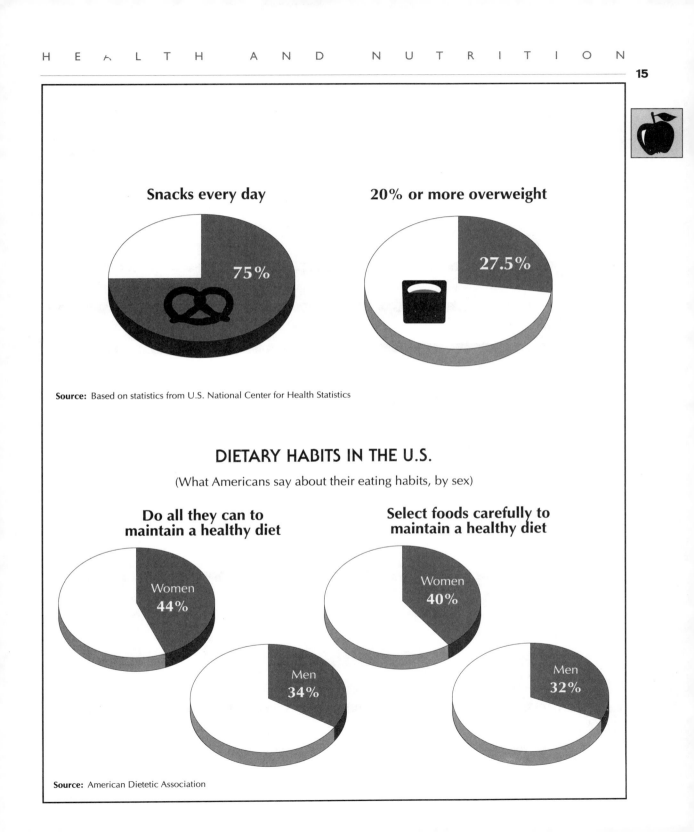

Snacks every day

75%

20% or more overweight

27.5%

Source: Based on statistics from U.S. National Center for Health Statistics

DIETARY HABITS IN THE U.S.

(What Americans say about their eating habits, by sex)

**Do all they can to
maintain a healthy diet**

Women
44%

Men
34%

**Select foods carefully to
maintain a healthy diet**

Women
40%

Men
32%

Source: American Dietetic Association

SELECTED CHARACTERISTICS OF COMMON FOODS, PER PORTION

Food	Measure	Grams (weight)	Calories	Fat (grams)
DAIRY PRODUCTS				
Cheese, cheddar	1 oz.	28	115	9
Cheese, cottage, small curd	1 cup	210	220	9
Half-and-half	1 tbsp.	15	20	2
Cream, sour	1 tbsp.	15	25	3
Milk, whole	1 cup	244	150	8
Milk, nonfat (skim)	1 cup	244	85	T
Milkshake, chocolate	10.6 oz.	300	355	8
Ice cream, hardened	1 cup	133	270	14
Sherbet	1 cup	193	270	4
Yogurt, fruit-flavored	8 oz.	227	230	3
EGGS				
Fried in butter	1	46	85	6
Hard-boiled	1	50	80	6
Scrambled in butter (milk added)	1	64	95	7
FATS & OILS				
Butter	1 tbsp.	14	100	12
Margarine	1 tbsp.	14	100	12
Mayonnaise	1 tbsp.	14	100	11
MEAT, POULTRY, & FISH				
Bluefish, baked with butter or margarine	3 oz.	85	135	4
Clams, raw, meat only	3 oz.	85	65	1
Crabmeat, white or king, canned	1 cup	135	135	3
Fish sticks, breaded, cooked, frozen	1 oz.	28	50	3
Salmon, pink, canned	3 oz.	85	120	5
Shrimp, French-fried	3 oz.	85	190	9
Tuna, canned in oil	3 oz.	85	170	7
Bacon, broiled or fried crisp	2 slices	15	85	8
Ground beef, broiled, 10% fat	3 oz.	85	185	10
Roast beef, relatively lean	3 oz.	85	165	7
Beef steak, lean and fat	3 oz.	85	330	27
Lamb, chop, lean and fat	3.1 oz.	89	360	32
Liver, beef	3 oz.	85	195	9
Ham, light cure, lean and fat	3 oz.	85	245	19
Pork, chop, lean and fat	2.7 oz.	78	305	25
Bologna	1 slice	28	85	8
Frankfurter, cooked	1	56	170	15
Sausage, pork link, cooked	1 link	13	60	6
Veal, cutlet, braised or broiled	3 oz.	85	185	
Chicken, drumstick, fried, bones removed	1.3 oz.	38	90	4
Chicken, half broiler, broiled, bones removed	6.2 oz.	176	240	7
FRUITS				
Apple, raw, 2 3/4 in. diam.	1	138	80	1
Apricots, raw	3	107	55	T
Banana, raw	1	119	100	T
Cherries, sweet, raw	10	68	45	T
Grapefruit, raw, medium, white	1/2	241	45	T
Grapes, Thompson seedless	10	50	35	T
Cantaloupe, 5 in. diam.	1/2	477	80	T
Orange, 2 5/8 in. diam.	1	131	65	T
Peach, raw, 2 1/2 in. diam.	1	100	40	T
Raisins, seedless	1 cup	145	420	T
Strawberries, whole	1 cup	149	55	T
Watermelon, 4 by 8 in. wedge	1	926	110	T
GRAIN PRODUCTS				
Bagel, egg	1	55	165	2
Bread, white, enriched, soft-crumb	1 slice	25	70	1
Bread, whole wheat, soft-crumb	1 slice	28	65	1
Oatmeal or rolled oats	1 cup	240	130	2
Bran flakes (40% bran), added sugar, salt, iron, vitamins	1 cup	35	105	1
Corn flakes, added sugar, salt, iron, vitamins	1 cup	25	95	T

Food	Measure	Grams (weight)	Calories	Fat (grams)
Rice, puffed, added iron, thiamin, niacin	1 cup	15	60	T
Wheat, shredded, 1 biscuit or 1/2 cup	1	25	90	1
Cake, angel food, 1/12 of cake	1	53	135	T
Cupcake, 2 1/2 in. diam. with chocolate icing	1	36	130	5
Boston cream pie with custard filling, 1/12 of cake	1	69	210	6
Brownie, with nuts, from commercial recipe	1	20	85	4
Cookies, chocolate chip, from home recipe	4	40	205	12
Crackers, graham	2	14	55	1
Crackers, saltine	4	11	50	1
Doughnut, cake type	1	25	100	5
Muffin, corn	1	40	125	4
Noodles, enriched, cooked	1 cup	160	200	2
Pizza, cheese, 1/8 of 12 in. diam. pie	1	60	145	4
Popcorn, popped, plain	1 cup	6	25	T
Pretzels, stick	10	3	10	T
Rolls, enriched, brown & serve	1	26	85	2
Rolls, frankfurter & hamburger	1	40	120	2
Spaghetti with meatballs & tomato sauce	1 cup	248	330	12
LEGUMES, NUTS, & SEEDS				
Beans, Great Northern, cooked	1 cup	180	210	1
Peanuts, roasted in oil, salted	1 cup	144	840	72
Peanut butter	1 tbsp.	16	95	8
Sunflower seeds	1 cup	145	810	69
SUGARS & SWEETS				
Candy, caramels	1 oz.	28	115	3
Candy, milk chocolate	1 oz.	28	145	9
Fudge, chocolate	1 oz.	28	115	3
Candy, hard	1 oz.	28	110	T
Honey	1 tbsp.	21	65	0
Jams & preserves	1 tbsp.	20	55	T
Sugar, white, granulated	1 tbsp.	12	45	0
VEGETABLES				
Asparagus, canned, spears	4 spears	80	15	T
Beans, green, from frozen cuts	1 cup	135	35	T
Broccoli, cooked	1 stalk	180	45	1
Cabbage, raw, coarsely shredded or sliced	1 cup	70	15	T
Carrots, raw, 7 1/2 by 1 1/8 in.	1	72	30	T
Celery, raw	1 stalk	40	5	T
Collards, cooked	1 cup	190	65	1
Corn, sweet, cooked	1 ear	140	70	1
Lettuce, iceberg, chopped	1 cup	55	5	T
Mushrooms, raw	1 cup	70	20	T
Onions, raw, chopped	1 cup	170	110	T
Peas, frozen, cooked	1 cup	160	110	T
Potatoes, baked, peeled	1	156	145	T
Potatoes, frozen, French fried	10	50	110	4
Potatoes, mashed, milk added	1 cup	210	135	2
Potato chips	10	20	115	8
Potato salad	1 cup	250	250	7
Spinach, chopped, from frozen	1 cup	205	45	1
Sweet potatoes, baked in skin, peeled	1	114	160	1
Tomatoes, raw	1	135	25	T
MISCELLANEOUS				
Cola-type beverage	12 fl. oz.	369	145	0
Ginger ale	12 fl. oz.	366	115	0
Gelatin dessert	1 cup	240	140	0
Olives, pickled, green	4 medium	16	15	2
Pickles, dill, whole	1	65	5	T
Popsicle, 3 fl. oz.	1	95	70	0
Soup, tomato, prepared with water	1 cup	245	90	3

T = Trace

Source: *Home & Garden* Bulletin No. 72, U.S. Government Printing Office

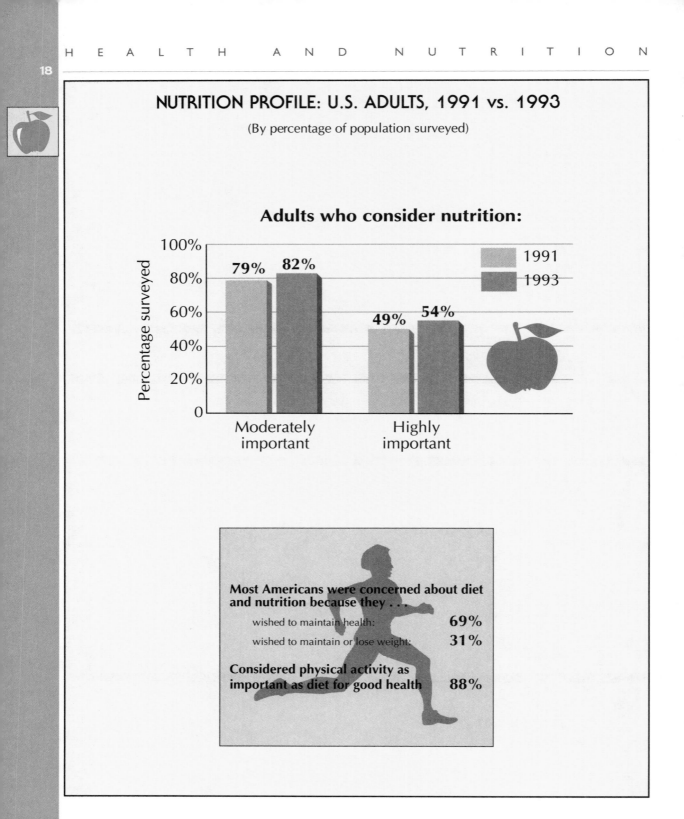

NUTRITION PROFILE: U.S. ADULTS, 1991 vs. 1993

(By percentage of population surveyed)

Adults who consider nutrition:

Percentage surveyed

100%
80%
60%
40%
20%
0

79% **82%**

49% **54%**

1991
1993

Moderately
important

Highly
important

**Most Americans were concerned about diet
and nutrition because they . . .**

wished to maintain health: **69%**

wished to maintain or lose weight: **31%**

**Considered physical activity as
important as diet for good health** **88%**

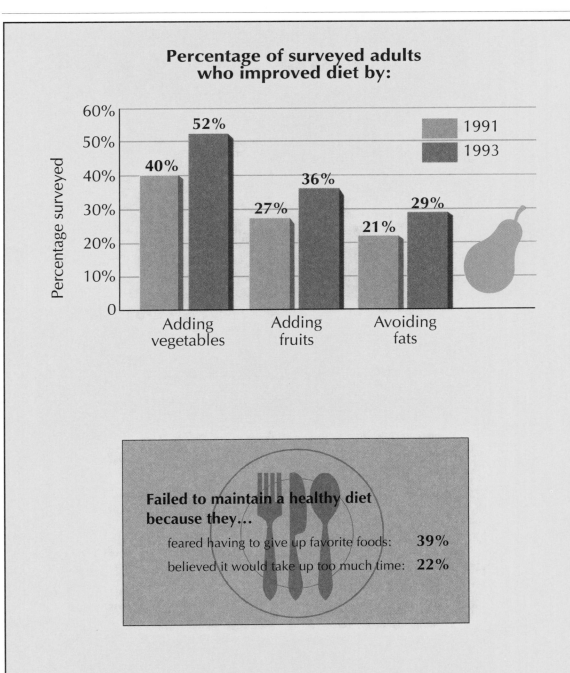

Percentage of surveyed adults who improved diet by:

- 1991
- 1993

Percentage surveyed

	Adding vegetables	Adding fruits	Avoiding fats
1991	40%	27%	21%
1993	52%	36%	29%

Failed to maintain a healthy diet because they...

feared having to give up favorite foods: **39%**

believed it would take up too much time: **22%**

Source: American Dietetic Association

PERSONAL HEALTH

Americans are getting heavier. In 1992, approximately 31% of adult men and 35% of adult women in the U.S. were estimated to be overweight. This was a 31% increase since 1980. Equally problematic is the fact that 21% of U.S. teenagers are overweight. Excess weight has been linked to a number of serious health problems, including cancer, cardiovascular disease, diabetes, and gallbladder disease.

There are two main reasons why people gain weight: they eat too much food and get too little exercise. On average, Americans are consuming more calories than their bodies can burn. They are sitting in front of television sets for hours on end, and jumping into automobiles for short trips instead of walking. A 1993 survey reported that only 33% of Americans engaged in strenuous exercise at least 3 days a week. Many do not exercise at all.

Many people need to change their lifestyles if they want to maintain good health. They need to engage in regular physical exercise, with at least 20 minutes of continuous aerobic activity 3 to 5 days a week. Any kind of regular physical exercise can improve health. Some people prefer vigorous exercise, such as skiing and running. Others prefer less strenuous activities, such as walking and biking. Of course, more strenuous activities burn calories more quickly.

The benefits of keeping fit are many. A good diet and regular exercise help to build bones and fight disease. They also improve one's mental outlook—another important factor in one's overall health.

FINGERTIP FACTS

- Obesity is defined as being 20% or more above your desirable weight.

- In the 1970s, about 15% of U.S. teenagers were overweight. By 1991, the rate had jumped to 21%.

- About 70% of children who are overweight at ages 10 to 13 will become overweight adults.

- The U.S. diet industry (diet foods, books, programs, etc.) has total estimated annual revenues of $40 billion to $50 billion.

- Only 37% of high school students say they exercise regularly.

- Boys are more physically active than girls. Statistically, white high school students exercise more regularly than African-American students.

- Americans spend more than $2 billion per year on exercise equipment alone.

- The more money people make, the more likely they are to exercise regularly. More than half of all people who earn $50,000 or more exercise; only 35% of people who earn $15,000 or less exercise.

- Aerobics is a heavily female-dominated form of exercise; 84% of all aerobic sessions are done by women.

IDEAL WEIGHTS FOR ADULTS

108 109 **110** 111 112 113 114 1

Height	Weight, in pounds	
	19–34 years	35 years and over
5'0"	97–128	108–138
5'1"	101–132	111–143
5'2"	104–137	115–148
5'3"	107–141	119–152
5'4"	111–146	122–157
5'5"	114–150	126–162
5'6"	118–155	130–167
5'7"	121–160	134–172
5'8"	125–164	138–178
5'9"	129–169	142–183
5'10"	132–174	146–188
5'11"	136–179	151–194
6'0"	140–184	155–199
6'1"	144–189	159–205
6'2"	148–195	164–210
6'3"	152–200	168–216
6'4"	156–205	173–222
6'5"	160–211	177–228
6'6"	164–216	182–234

Source: National Research Council

CALORIES USED PER MINUTE, ACCORDING TO BODY WEIGHT

Activity	Weight, in pounds					
	100	120	150	170	200	220
Volleyball (moderate)	2.3	2.7	3.4	3.9	4.6	5.0
Walking (3 mph)	2.7	3.2	4.0	4.6	5.4	5.9
Table tennis	2.7	3.2	4.0	4.6	5.4	5.9
Bicycling (5.5 mph)	3.1	3.8	4.7	5.3	6.3	6.9
Calisthenics	3.3	3.9	4.9	5.6	6.6	7.2
Skating (moderate)	3.6	4.3	5.4	6.1	7.2	7.9
Golf	3.6	4.3	5.4	6.1	7.2	7.9
Walking (4 mph)	3.9	4.6	5.8	6.6	7.8	8.5
Tennis	4.5	5.4	6.8	7.7	9.1	10.0
Canoeing (4 mph)	4.6	5.6	7.0	7.9	9.3	10.2
Swimming (breaststroke)	4.8	5.7	7.2	8.1	9.6	10.5
Bicycling (10 mph)	5.4	6.5	8.1	9.2	10.8	11.9
Swimming (crawl)	5.8	6.9	8.7	9.8	11.6	12.7
Jogging (11-min. mile)	6.1	7.3	9.1	10.4	12.2	13.4
Handball	6.3	7.6	9.5	10.7	12.7	13.9
Racquetball	6.3	7.6	9.5	10.7	12.7	13.9
Skiing (downhill)	6.3	7.6	9.5	10.7	12.7	13.9
Mountain climbing	6.6	8.0	10.0	11.3	13.3	14.6
Squash	6.8	8.1	10.2	11.5	13.6	14.9
Skiing (cross-country)	7.2	8.7	10.8	12.3	14.5	15.9
Running (8-min. mile)	9.4	11.3	14.1	16.0	18.8	20.7

Source: *Home & Garden* Bulletin No. 72, U.S. Government Printing Office

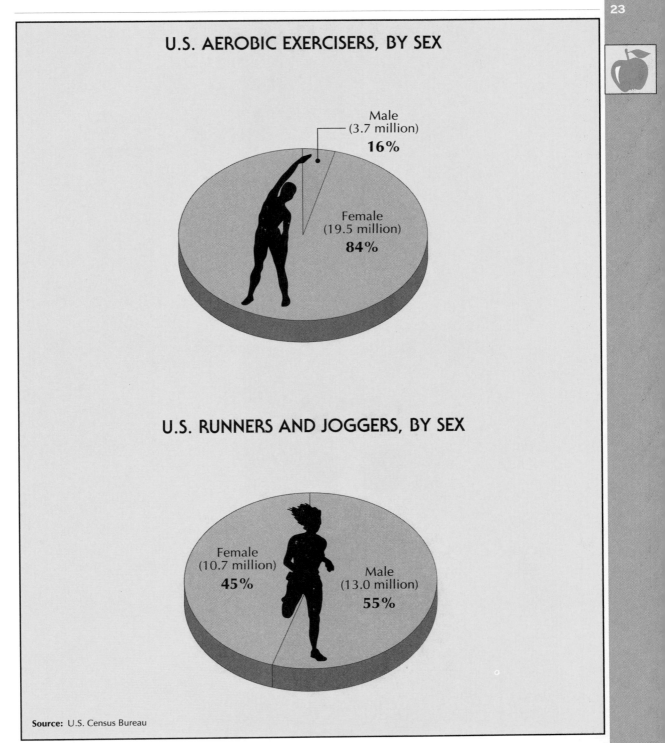

U.S. AEROBIC EXERCISERS, BY SEX

Male
(3.7 million)
16%

Female
(19.5 million)
84%

U.S. RUNNERS AND JOGGERS, BY SEX

Female
(10.7 million)
45%

Male
(13.0 million)
55%

Source: U.S. Census Bureau

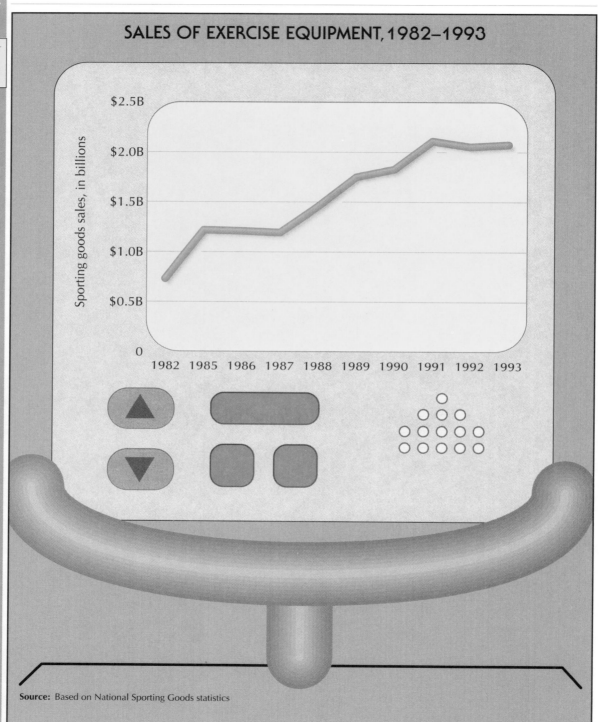

SALES OF EXERCISE EQUIPMENT, 1982–1993

Sporting goods sales, in billions

$2.5B
$2.0B
$1.5B
$1.0B
$0.5B
0

1982 1985 1986 1987 1988 1989 1990 1991 1992 1993

Source: Based on National Sporting Goods statistics

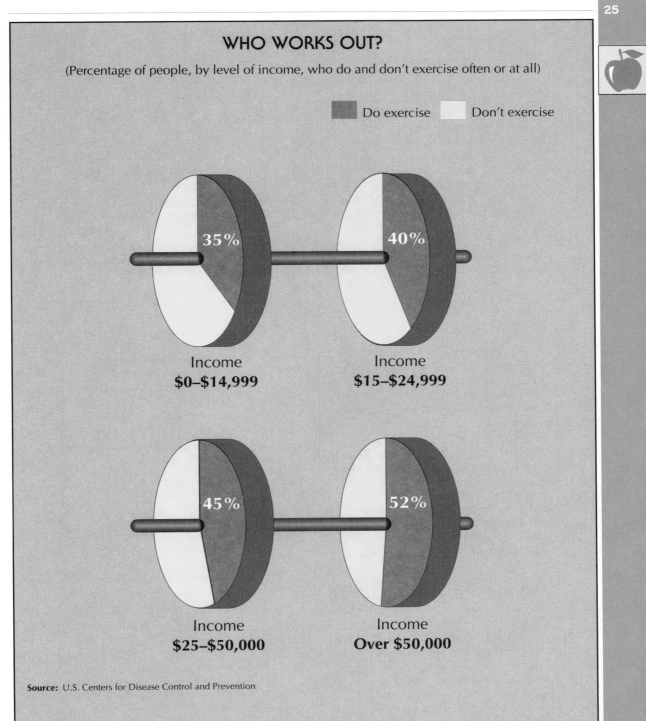

WHO WORKS OUT?

(Percentage of people, by level of income, who do and don't exercise often or at all)

Do exercise · Don't exercise

35%

Income
$0–$14,999

40%

Income
$15–$24,999

45%

Income
$25–$50,000

52%

Income
Over $50,000

Source: U.S. Centers for Disease Control and Prevention

SMOKING

Each year, more than 400,000 people in the U.S. die as a result of smoking. Most of these people were smokers. But almost 50,000 people die because they inhaled second-hand smoke—that is, other people's tobacco smoke.

Smoking increases the risk of many serious and deadly diseases, especially heart disease, cancers (including lung, mouth, throat, breast, colon cancers), emphysema, pneumonia, and bronchitis. Smoking robs the body of vitamins, weakens bones, interferes with sleep, and doubles the risk of eye cataracts.

Smoking is more than a dangerous habit. It is an addiction. People who smoke become addicted to a chemical in tobacco called nicotine. Many smokers report that they want to quit but are unable to do so. They experience physical withdrawal symptoms as they try to break their addiction to this powerful drug. The majority of studies show that women have a harder time quitting than men.

There are major benefits to be gained from quitting smoking, regardless of a person's age. Within 24 hours of quitting smoking, the chance of a heart attack decreases. Within 48 hours, nerve endings begin to regrow. Within 3 months, lung function improves up to 30%. Within 5 years, the risk of cancer declines sharply.

In general, smoking is no longer fashionable in the U.S. Anti-smoking campaigns and bans on smoking in many public places have encouraged many people to "kick the habit." In many other parts of the world, however, smoking is commonplace and still growing in popularity. Experts predict that if current trends continue, smoking will cause 10 million deaths worldwide each year by the year 2020.

FINGERTIP FACTS

- Smoking is the most preventable cause of death in the U.S.

- Smokers are twice as likely as nonsmokers to have strokes.

- Worldwide, smoking kills 3 million people each year. That's 1 person every 10 seconds.

- Each year in the U.S, there are twice as many deaths from second-hand smoke as from murder.

- The number of pregnant women who smoke has been declining. In 1992, about 17% smoked.

- In 1964, when the government released its first report warning that smoking was unhealthy, 40% of Americans smoked. In 1991, some 25% smoked.

- About 75% of U.S. adults who smoke regularly had their first cigarette before they were 18 years old.

- Over 3 million U.S. teenagers smoke cigarettes. More than 1 million teen males use smokeless tobacco.

- One out of 4 teenagers uses tobacco by age 18.

- People who start using tobacco as young teenagers are most likely to develop long-term nicotine addiction.

- Each year, more than 4 million U.S. smokers use nicotine patches in efforts to stop smoking.

- Worldwide, 5.45 trillion cigarettes were sold in 1991—enough to give every person on Earth about 3 cigarettes each day.

- It is estimated that smoking costs the nation more than $100 billion per year in lost productivity, medical bills, insurance, and other health-related expenses.

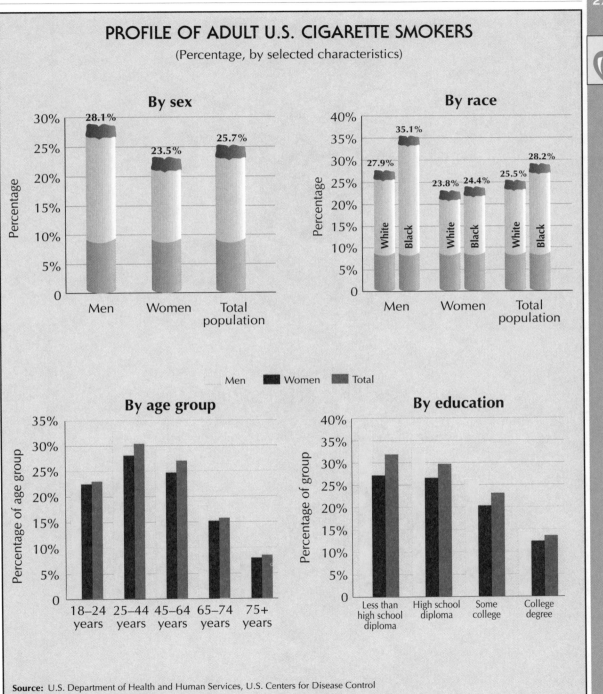

PROFILE OF ADULT U.S. CIGARETTE SMOKERS
(Percentage, by selected characteristics)

By sex

- Men: 28.1%
- Women: 23.5%
- Total population: 25.7%

By race

- Men: White 27.9%, Black 35.1%
- Women: White 23.8%, Black 24.4%
- Total population: White 25.5%, Black 28.2%

Men   Women   Total

By age group

- 18–24 years
- 25–44 years
- 45–64 years
- 65–74 years
- 75+ years

By education

- Less than high school diploma
- High school diploma
- Some college
- College degree

Source: U.S. Department of Health and Human Services, U.S. Centers for Disease Control

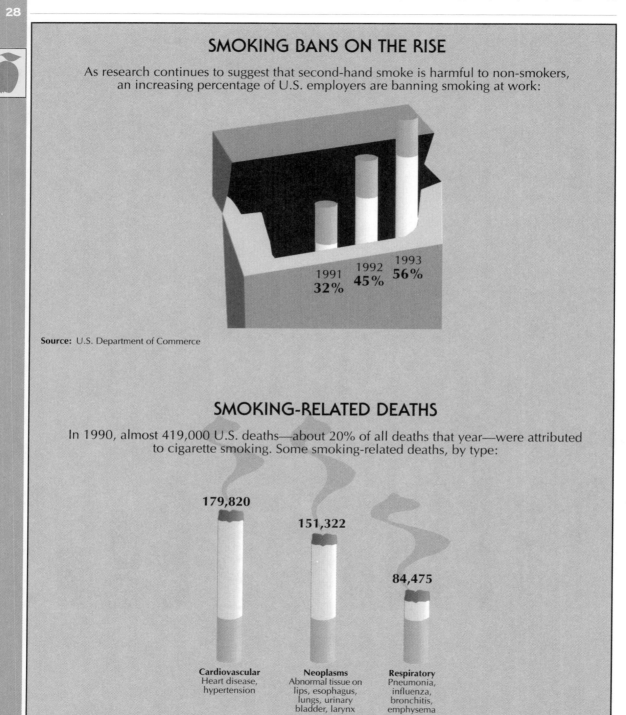

SMOKING BANS ON THE RISE

As research continues to suggest that second-hand smoke is harmful to non-smokers, an increasing percentage of U.S. employers are banning smoking at work:

1991
32%

1992
45%

1993
56%

Source: U.S. Department of Commerce

SMOKING-RELATED DEATHS

In 1990, almost 419,000 U.S. deaths—about 20% of all deaths that year—were attributed to cigarette smoking. Some smoking-related deaths, by type:

179,820

151,322

84,475

Cardiovascular
Heart disease,
hypertension

Neoplasms
Abnormal tissue on
lips, esophagus,
lungs, urinary
bladder, larynx

Respiratory
Pneumonia,
influenza,
bronchitis,
emphysema

Source: U.S. Centers for Disease Control

CHILDREN WHO SMOKE

(Percentage of U.S. kids in
each age group who smoke)

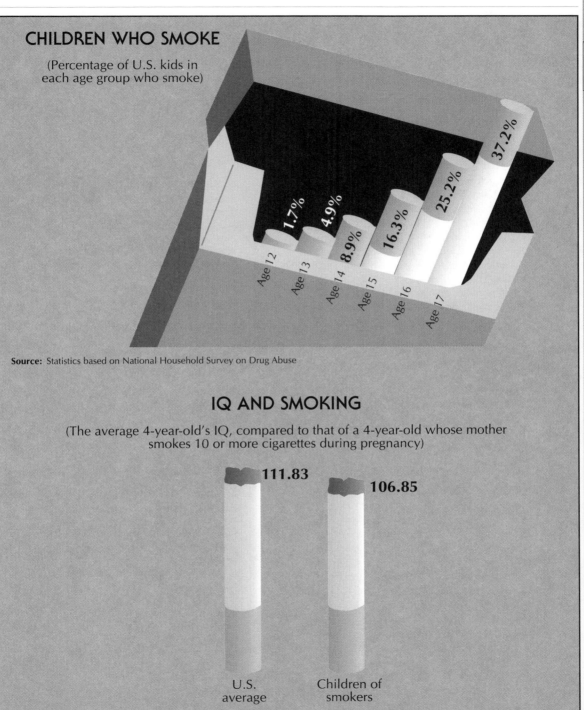

1.7% — Age 12
4.9% — Age 13
8.9% — Age 14
16.3% — Age 15
25.2% — Age 16
37.2% — Age 17

Source: Statistics based on National Household Survey on Drug Abuse

IQ AND SMOKING

(The average 4-year-old's IQ, compared to that of a 4-year-old whose mother
smokes 10 or more cigarettes during pregnancy)

111.83 — U.S. average

106.85 — Children of smokers

Source: Cornell University/University of Rochester

DRUGS AND ALCOHOL

A shockingly large number of Americans use illegal drugs. A 1992 survey estimated that 11.4 million people ages 12 and older used illegal drugs in the month prior to the survey. The good news is that this represents a significant decline from peak U.S. drug use, in the late 1970s. The bad news is that drug abuse causes tremendous health and social problems. Addiction—a physical or psychological dependency—is a common result. Cocaine addiction, for example, can result in convulsions, heart attacks, and sudden death.

The most commonly abused illegal drug is marijuana, followed by cocaine. People also abuse legal drugs, such as alcohol, cold medicines, amphetamines, and tranquilizers. Alcohol is the most commonly abused legal drug in America. A 1992 survey concluded that approximately 98 million Americans ages 12 and older had used alcohol in the previous month. Alcohol is the "drug of choice" among adolescents, with more than 75% of high school seniors reporting current use.

Alcohol is a factor in more than 100,000 deaths annually. Some of these deaths are from diseases, such as of the heart and liver. Even moderate drinking can be dangerous. For example, some studies suggest that a woman who has only a few drinks a week has a significantly greater risk of developing breast cancer than do non-drinkers.

The consumption of alcohol is also associated with accidents—in homes, workplaces, and on the road. Almost half of all traffic fatalities in the U.S. are alcohol related. These statistics mean that one alcohol-related traffic death occurs in the U.S. every 26 minutes. More than one-third of these deaths occur among people ages 25 or younger.

FINGERTIP FACTS

- Use of illegal drugs peaked in 1979, when there were 24.3 million drug users in the U.S. By 1992, the number had dropped to 11.4 million. It rose to 11.7 million in 1993.
- People ages 18 to 25 are the biggest users of illegal drugs. People age 35 and older are the lowest users.
- Most users of illegal drugs are white, but the rate of use per capita is somewhat higher among blacks than whites.
- Males are heavier users of illegal drugs than females. People who have not completed high school are heavier users than people with more education.
- Marijuana is the most commonly used illegal drug, taken by about 78% of drug users.
- People who start to drink before age 15 are more likely to use marijuana or cocaine.
- Since the early 1980s, Americans have been drinking fewer distilled spirits. Per capita consumption fell from 2.76 gallons in 1980 to 2.31 gallons in 1991.
- A government study estimated that alcohol abuse costs the U.S. about $85 billion a year; drug abuse costs another $58 billion.
- Deaths caused by drunk driving are declining. In 1982, more than 30% of the drivers in fatal accidents were drunk. By 1992, the number had dropped to 22%.
- Men ages 21 to 35 are responsible for more than 50% of all alcohol-related car fatalities in the U.S.
- About 40% of all people in the U.S. will be involved in an alcohol-related traffic crash during their lifetimes.
- By mid-1994, some 44 states mandated prison time for drivers with 2 convictions for drunken driving.

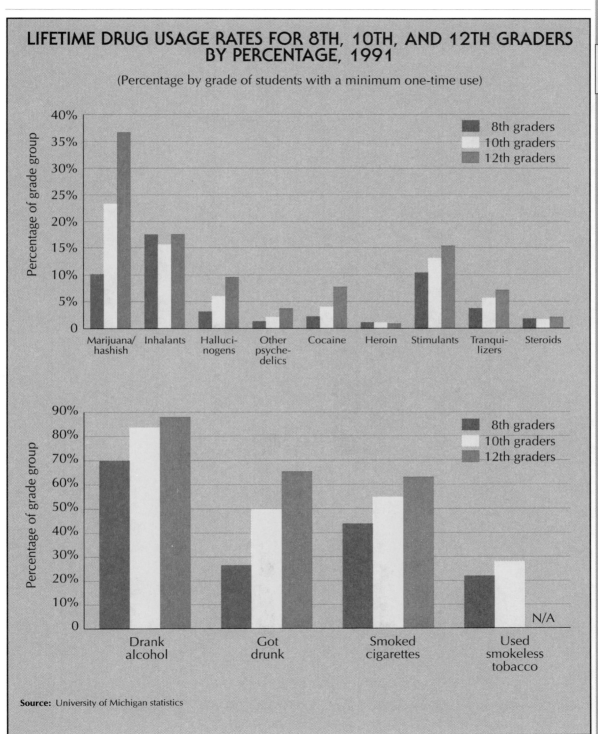

LIFETIME DRUG USAGE RATES FOR 8TH, 10TH, AND 12TH GRADERS BY PERCENTAGE, 1991

(Percentage by grade of students with a minimum one-time use)

Source: University of Michigan statistics

PROFILE: DRUG USE BY U.S. HIGH SCHOOL STUDENTS

(Percentage of student population who used drugs
during the 30 days before survey)

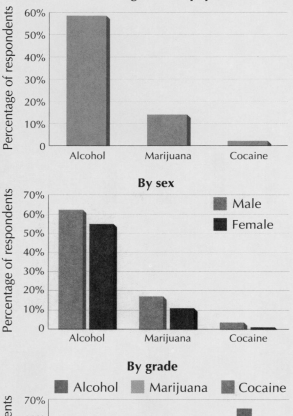

Total high school population

By sex

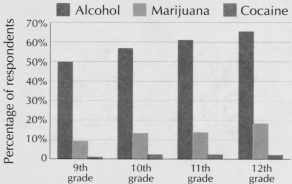

By grade

Source: U.S. Department of Health and Human Services, U.S. Centers for Disease Control

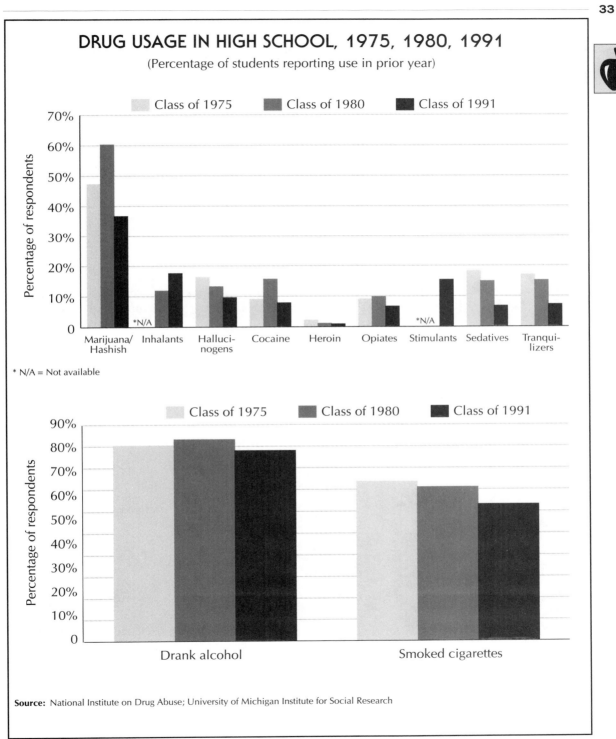

DRUG USAGE IN HIGH SCHOOL, 1975, 1980, 1991

(Percentage of students reporting use in prior year)

Class of 1975   Class of 1980   Class of 1991

*N/A = Not available

Source: National Institute on Drug Abuse; University of Michigan Institute for Social Research

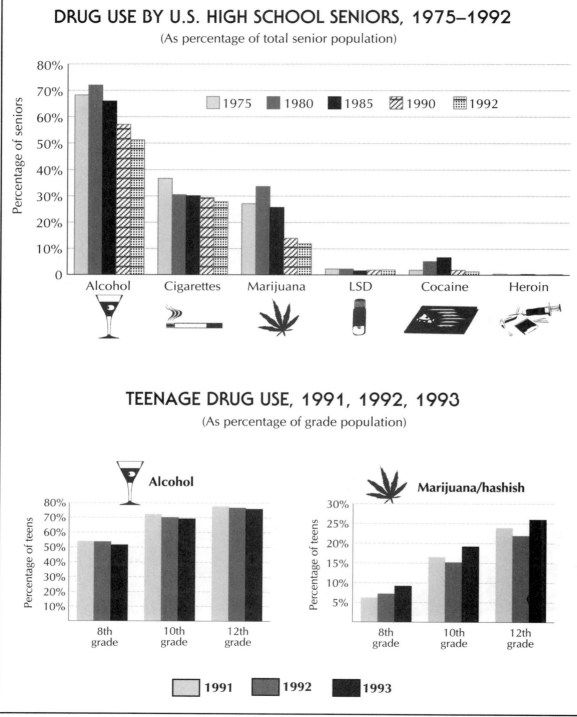

DRUG USE BY U.S. HIGH SCHOOL SENIORS, 1975–1992
(As percentage of total senior population)

Percentage of seniors

☐ 1975 ■ 1980 ■ 1985 ▨ 1990 ▦ 1992

Alcohol Cigarettes Marijuana LSD Cocaine Heroin

TEENAGE DRUG USE, 1991, 1992, 1993
(As percentage of grade population)

Alcohol

Percentage of teens

8th grade 10th grade 12th grade

Marijuana/hashish

Percentage of teens

8th grade 10th grade 12th grade

☐ 1991 ■ 1992 ■ 1993

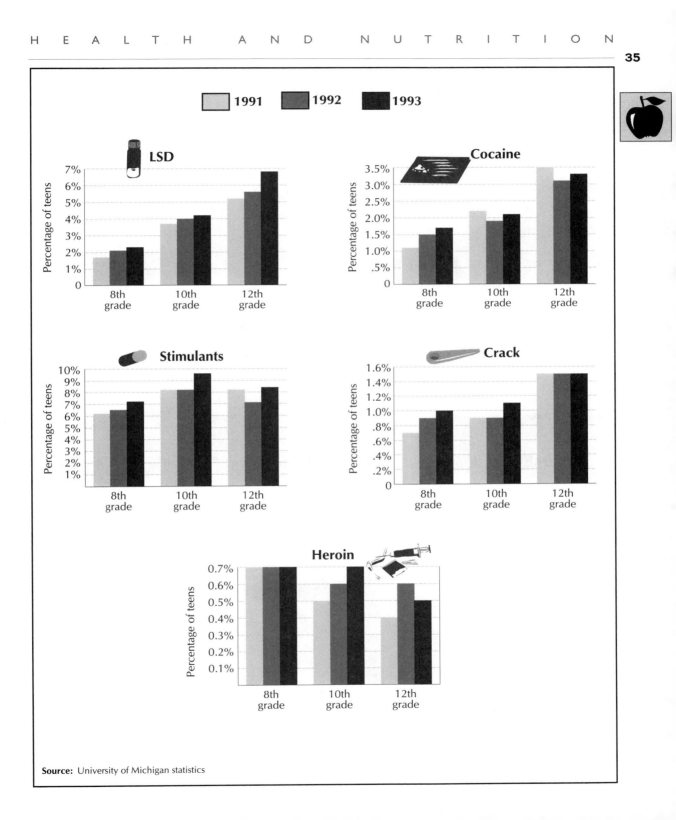

Source: University of Michigan statistics

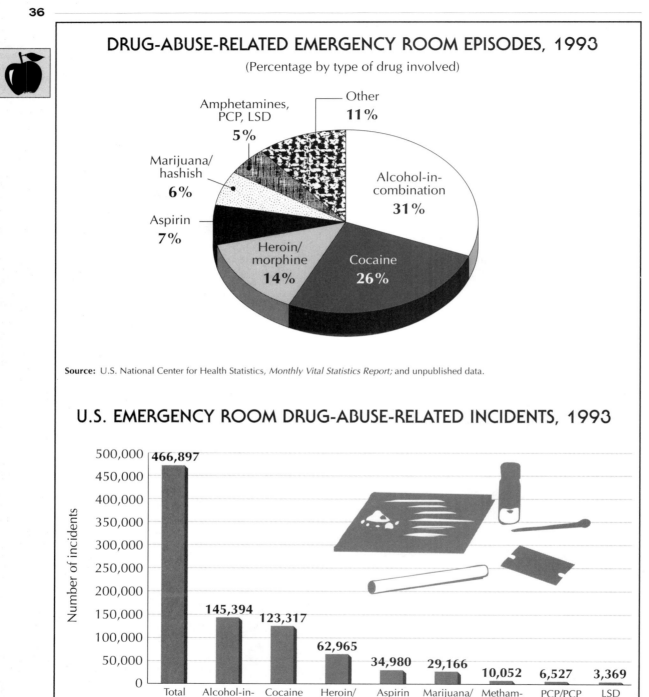

DRUG-ABUSE-RELATED EMERGENCY ROOM EPISODES, 1993
(Percentage by type of drug involved)

Other **11%**

Amphetamines, PCP, LSD **5%**

Marijuana/ hashish **6%**

Aspirin **7%**

Heroin/ morphine **14%**

Cocaine **26%**

Alcohol-in-combination **31%**

Source: U.S. National Center for Health Statistics, *Monthly Vital Statistics Report;* and unpublished data.

U.S. EMERGENCY ROOM DRUG-ABUSE-RELATED INCIDENTS, 1993

Number of incidents

Total episodes	466,897
Alcohol-in-combination	145,394
Cocaine	123,317
Heroin/morphine	62,965
Aspirin	34,980
Marijuana/hashish	29,166
Methamphetamine	10,052
PCP/PCP combinations	6,527
LSD	3,369

Source: U.S. Department of Health and Human Services, National Institute on Drug Abuse; Drug Abuse Warning Network

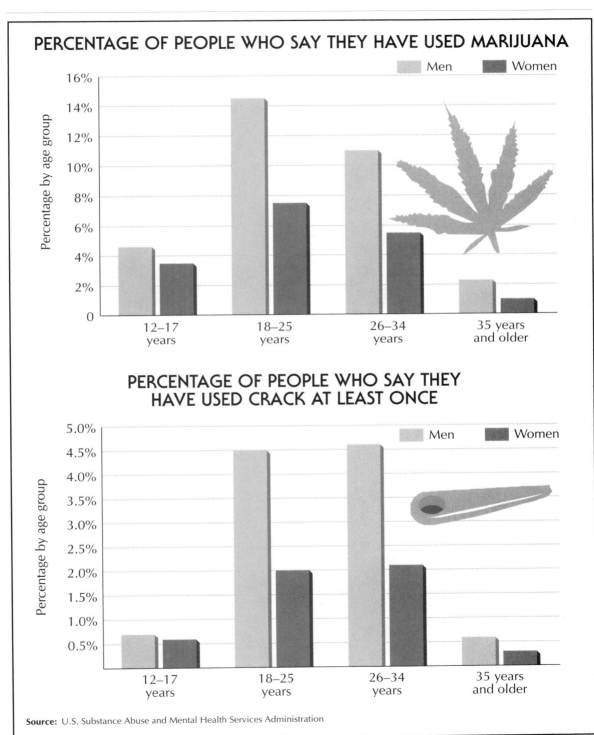

PERCENTAGE OF PEOPLE WHO SAY THEY HAVE USED MARIJUANA

Men   Women

Percentage by age group

16%
14%
12%
10%
8%
6%
4%
2%
0

12–17 years   18–25 years   26–34 years   35 years and older

PERCENTAGE OF PEOPLE WHO SAY THEY HAVE USED CRACK AT LEAST ONCE

Men   Women

Percentage by age group

5.0%
4.5%
4.0%
3.5%
3.0%
2.5%
2.0%
1.5%
1.0%
0.5%

12–17 years   18–25 years   26–34 years   35 years and older

Source: U.S. Substance Abuse and Mental Health Services Administration

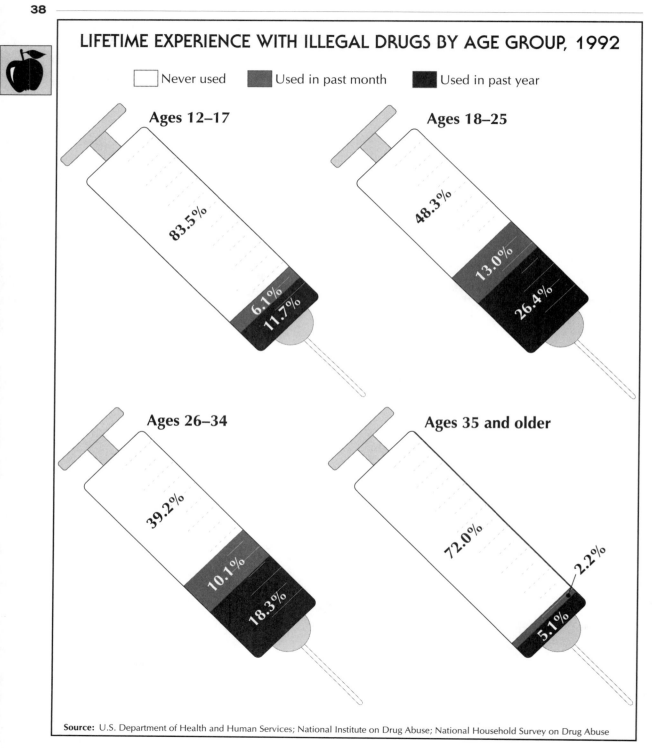

LIFETIME EXPERIENCE WITH ILLEGAL DRUGS BY AGE GROUP, 1992

Never used   Used in past month   Used in past year

Ages 12–17

83.5%

6.1%

11.7%

Ages 18–25

48.3%

13.0%

26.4%

Ages 26–34

39.2%

10.1%

18.3%

Ages 35 and older

72.0%

2.2%

5.1%

Source: U.S. Department of Health and Human Services; National Institute on Drug Abuse; National Household Survey on Drug Abuse

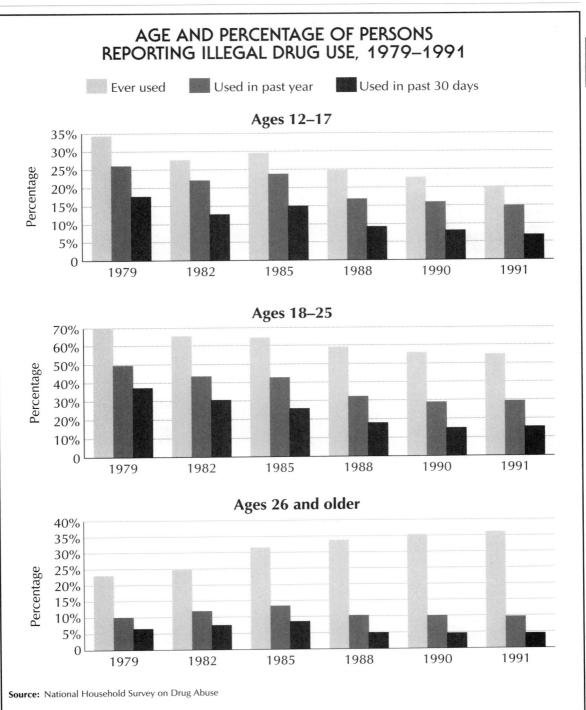

AGE AND PERCENTAGE OF PERSONS REPORTING ILLEGAL DRUG USE, 1979–1991

■ Ever used ■ Used in past year ■ Used in past 30 days

Ages 12–17

Ages 18–25

Ages 26 and older

Source: National Household Survey on Drug Abuse

PROFILE: HEAVY ALCOHOL CONSUMPTION, BY AGE, RACE, AND SEX

Heavy users are defined as those drinking 5 or more drinks per day for
5 or more days within past month:

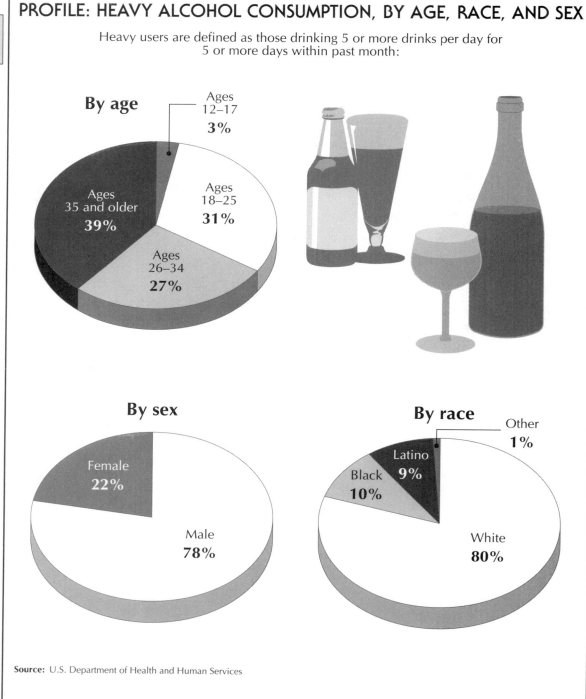

By age

Ages
12–17
3%

Ages
18–25
31%

Ages
35 and older
39%

Ages
26–34
27%

By sex

Female
22%

Male
78%

By race

Other
1%

Latino **9%**

Black
10%

White
80%

Source: U.S. Department of Health and Human Services

ALCOHOL DEPENDENCE AND ABUSE IN THE U.S., BY AGE AND SEX

By age

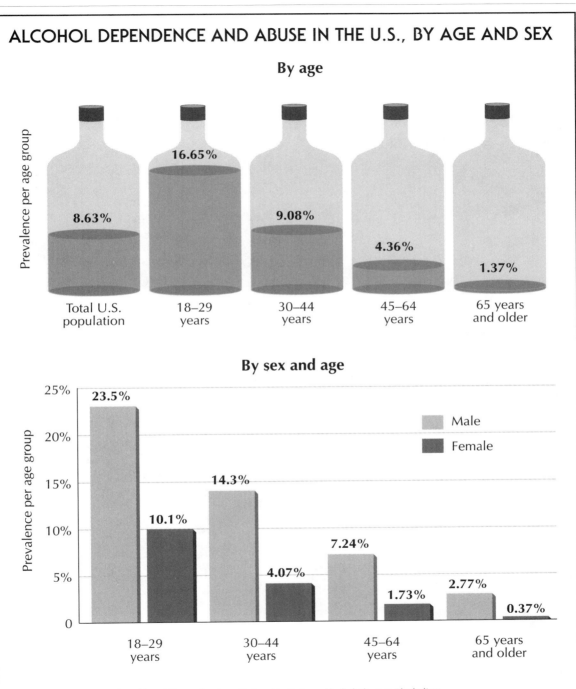

Prevalence per age group

| 8.63% | 16.65% | 9.08% | 4.36% | 1.37% |
| Total U.S. population | 18–29 years | 30–44 years | 45–64 years | 65 years and older |

By sex and age

Prevalence per age group

- Male
- Female

	18–29 years	30–44 years	45–64 years	65 years and older
Male	23.5%	14.3%	7.24%	2.77%
Female	10.1%	4.07%	1.73%	0.37%

Source: U.S. Department of Health and Human Services, National Institute on Alcohol Abuse & Alcoholism

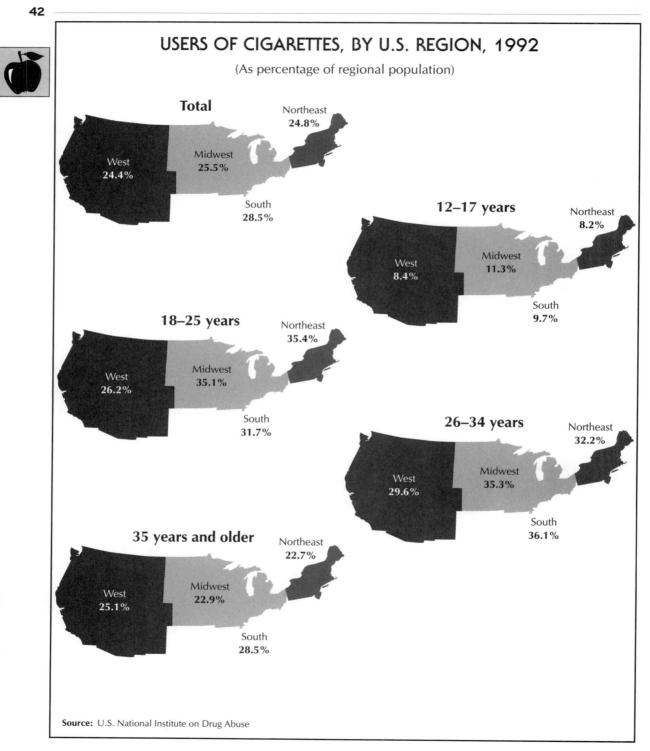

USERS OF CIGARETTES, BY U.S. REGION, 1992

(As percentage of regional population)

Total

Northeast
24.8%

West
24.4%

Midwest
25.5%

South
28.5%

12–17 years

Northeast
8.2%

West
8.4%

Midwest
11.3%

South
9.7%

18–25 years

Northeast
35.4%

West
26.2%

Midwest
35.1%

South
31.7%

26–34 years

Northeast
32.2%

West
29.6%

Midwest
35.3%

South
36.1%

35 years and older

Northeast
22.7%

West
25.1%

Midwest
22.9%

South
28.5%

Source: U.S. National Institute on Drug Abuse

USERS OF ALCOHOL, BY U.S. REGION, 1992

(As percentage of regional population)

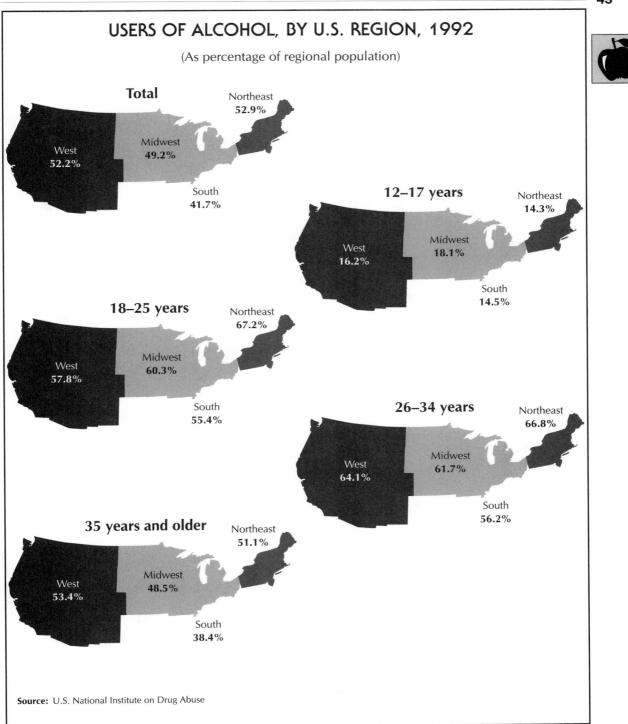

Total

Northeast
52.9%

West
52.2%

Midwest
49.2%

South
41.7%

12–17 years

Northeast
14.3%

West
16.2%

Midwest
18.1%

South
14.5%

18–25 years

Northeast
67.2%

West
57.8%

Midwest
60.3%

South
55.4%

26–34 years

Northeast
66.8%

West
64.1%

Midwest
61.7%

South
56.2%

35 years and older

Northeast
51.1%

West
53.4%

Midwest
48.5%

South
38.4%

Source: U.S. National Institute on Drug Abuse

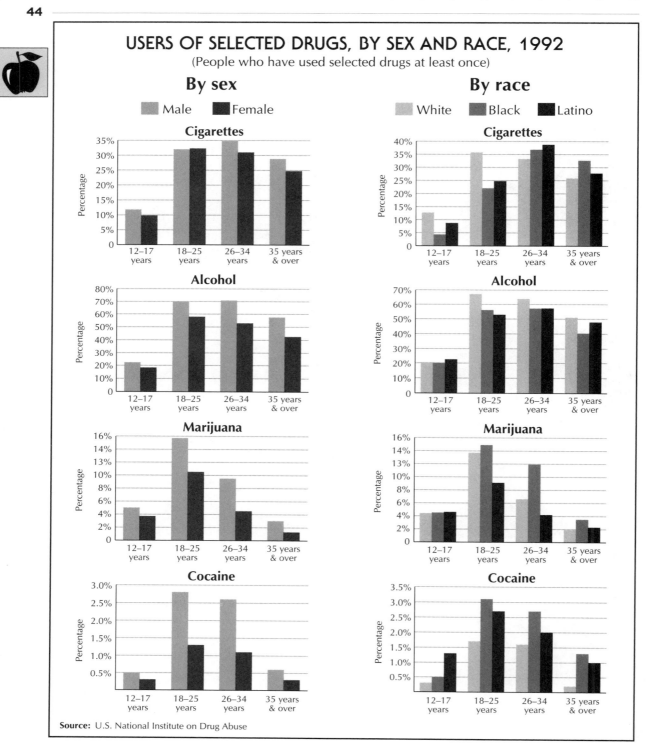

USERS OF SELECTED DRUGS, BY SEX AND RACE, 1992
(People who have used selected drugs at least once)

By sex
Male   Female

By race
White   Black   Latino

Source: U.S. National Institute on Drug Abuse

USERS OF SELECTED DRUGS, BY SEX AND RACE, 1992

(People who have used selected drugs at least once)

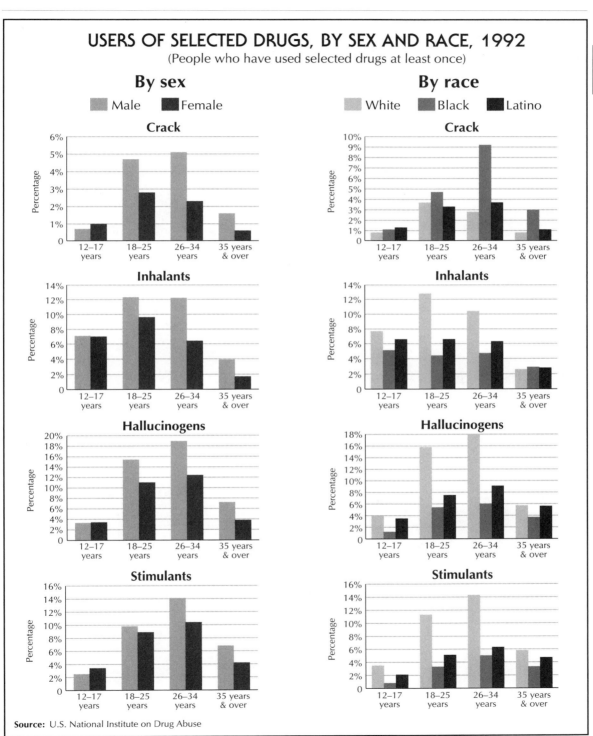

Source: U.S. National Institute on Drug Abuse

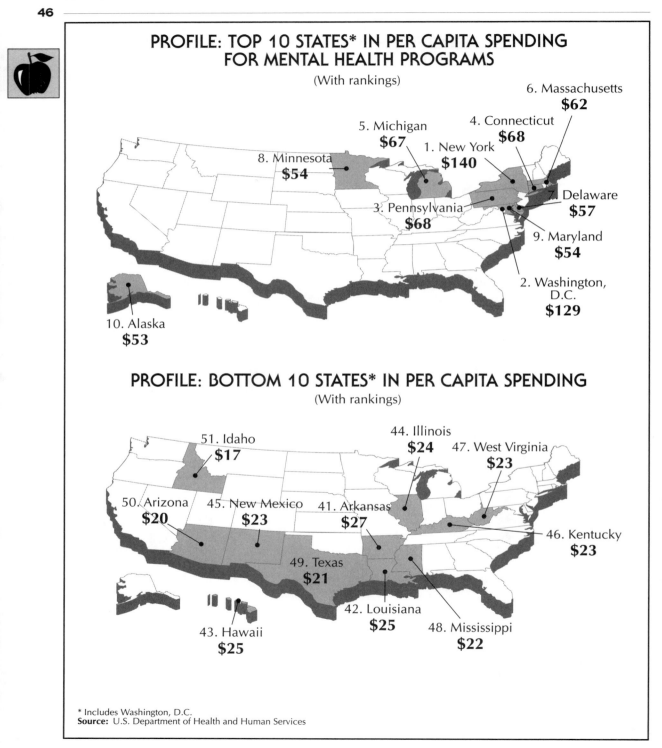

PROFILE: TOP 10 STATES* IN PER CAPITA SPENDING FOR MENTAL HEALTH PROGRAMS
(With rankings)

6. Massachusetts **$62**

4. Connecticut **$68**

5. Michigan **$67**

1. New York **$140**

8. Minnesota **$54**

7 Delaware **$57**

3. Pennsylvania **$68**

9. Maryland **$54**

2. Washington, D.C. **$129**

10. Alaska **$53**

PROFILE: BOTTOM 10 STATES* IN PER CAPITA SPENDING
(With rankings)

51. Idaho **$17**

44. Illinois **$24**

47. West Virginia **$23**

50. Arizona **$20**

45. New Mexico **$23**

41. Arkansas **$27**

46. Kentucky **$23**

49. Texas **$21**

42. Louisiana **$25**

48. Mississippi **$22**

43. Hawaii **$25**

* Includes Washington, D.C.
Source: U.S. Department of Health and Human Services

MENTAL ILLNESS IN AMERICA, BY DISORDER, 1990

Millions of cases

Anxiety: phobia, panic, obsessive-compulsive	23.3M
Depressive: manic, major depression	17.6M
Substance abuse disorders	17.5M
Severe cognitive impairment	5.0M
Anti-social personality	2.8M
Schizophrenia	2.0M

Source: National Institute of Mental Health; estimates based on 1990 census of 184 million people 18 and older

PROFILE: TREATMENT FOR DRUG DEPENDENCY

Most drug-dependent people are not in treatment. Only about 15% of people with a chemical dependency are actively involved in treatment programs. People in treatment, by race:

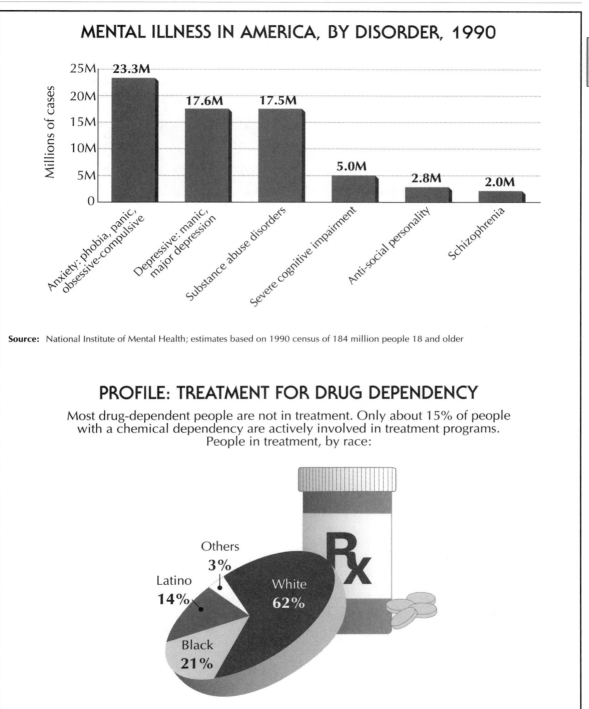

Others 3%
Latino 14%
White 62%
Black 21%

Source: National Drug and Alcoholism Treatment Survey

LIFE EXPECTANCY AND BIRTH RATE

People are living longer. An American born in 1900 could expect to live 47.3 years. An American born in 1992 could expect to live 75.6 years. Life expectancy has increased because death rates have fallen. Better health care, sanitation, and nutrition account for much of the drop in death rates.

Infants are at risk of dying from pregnancy complications, premature birth, low birthweight, respiratory ailments, and other causes. But infants' chances of surviving have steadily improved.

The infant mortality rate—the number of infant deaths per 1,000 live births—has fallen dramatically. But it has fallen much faster, and much further, for whites than for African-Americans. From 1980 to 1991, the rate of white infant deaths in the U.S. fell 33%, from 10.9 to 7.3 per 1,000 births. The rate for blacks fell 20.7%, from 22.2 to 17.6 per 1,000 births.

The U.S. birth rate has also fallen. The birth rate is the number of births per 1,000 people. In 1910, the U.S. birth rate was 30.1. It fell to 14.6 in 1975. Then it rose gradually, reaching 16.3 in 1991.

Because people are living longer, there are more older people than ever before. Between 1980 and 1990, the number of people ages 85 or older increased by 35%, to 3 million.

Many factors affect life expectancy and birth rates, including age, sex, race, occupation, and nutrition. Life expectancy and birth rates also vary from one country to another. Japan has the world's highest life expectancy; a Japanese child born in 1992 could expect to live 87.6 years. Poor countries have the lowest life expectancy. In most African countries, life expectancy for children born in 1992 was less than 60 years.

FINGERTIP FACTS

- Life expectancy in the U.S. is higher among whites than blacks. A white male born in 1992 could expect to live 5.4 years longer than a black born the same year.
- Females live longer than males. A white female born in 1992 had a life expectancy of 79.7 years. A white male's life expectancy in the U.S. was 73.2 years.
- More education means longer life. Death rates are lower among college graduates than among people who did not complete high school.
- Life expectancy for older people is up. In 1970, a 65-year-old American could expect to live another 15.2 years. In 1990, that same person had a life expectancy of 17.2 years.
- U.S. death rates are higher in cities than in rural areas.
- U.S. infant deaths for 1988-1990 ranged from 6.7 per 1,000 births in Maine to 22.2 per 1,000 in the District of Columbia.
- The number of births to unmarried mothers has increased. In 1990, a total of 20.4% of white mothers and 66.5% of black mothers were unmarried.
- In the U.S., there is one birth every 8 seconds and one death every 14 seconds, for a net gain of 4,400 people per day.
- In 1991, approximately 143.5 million babies were born in the world.
- Every 2 seconds around the world, 9 babies are born and 3 people die. This results in a net increase of 3 people every second, or 10,600 people per hour.
- In 1992, the U.S. ranked #18 in average life expectancy. Canada ranked #7. Japan ranked #1.

YEARS OF LIFE EXPECTED AT BIRTH IN U.S., 1920–1992

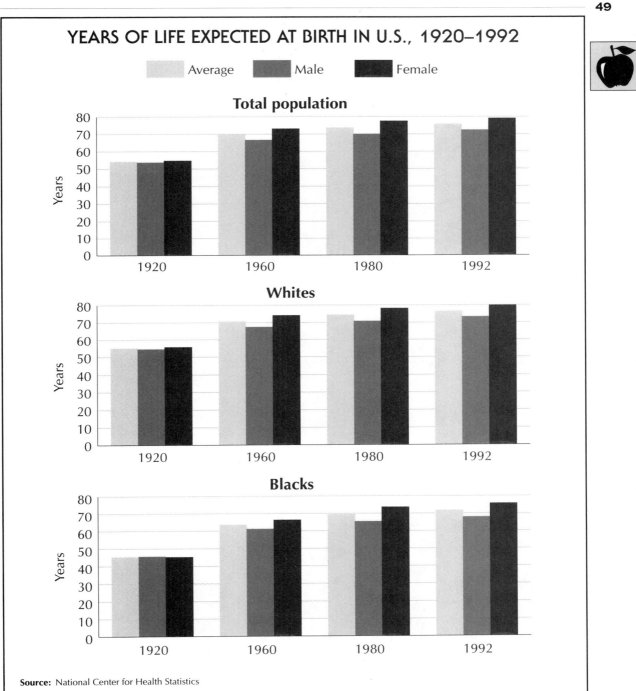

Legend: Average | Male | Female

Total population

Whites

Blacks

Source: National Center for Health Statistics

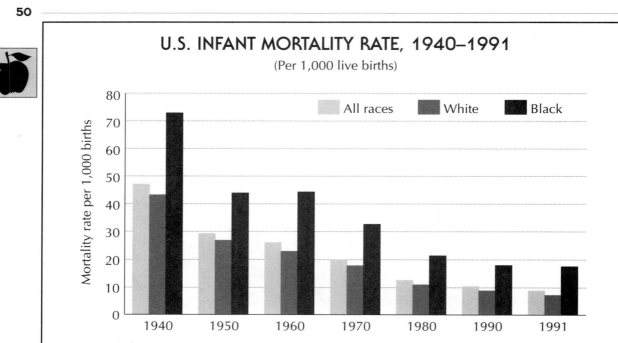

U.S. INFANT MORTALITY RATE, 1940–1991
(Per 1,000 live births)

Legend: All races | White | Black

Mortality rate per 1,000 births

1940 | 1950 | 1960 | 1970 | 1980 | 1990 | 1991

Sources: U.S. Department of Health and Human Services; National Center for Health Statistics; U.S. Centers for Disease Control

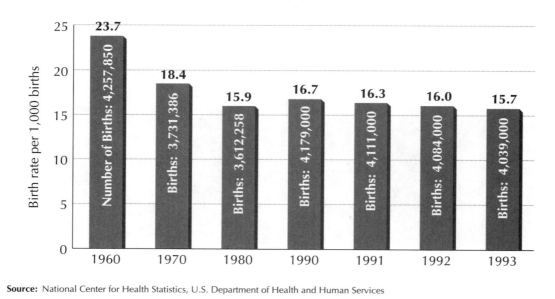

U.S. BIRTH RATE, 1960–1993
(Per 1,000 population)

Birth rate per 1,000 births

Year	Rate	Births
1960	23.7	Number of Births: 4,257,850
1970	18.4	Births: 3,731,386
1980	15.9	Births: 3,612,258
1990	16.7	Births: 4,179,000
1991	16.3	Births: 4,111,000
1992	16.0	Births: 4,084,000
1993	15.7	Births: 4,039,000

Source: National Center for Health Statistics, U.S. Department of Health and Human Services

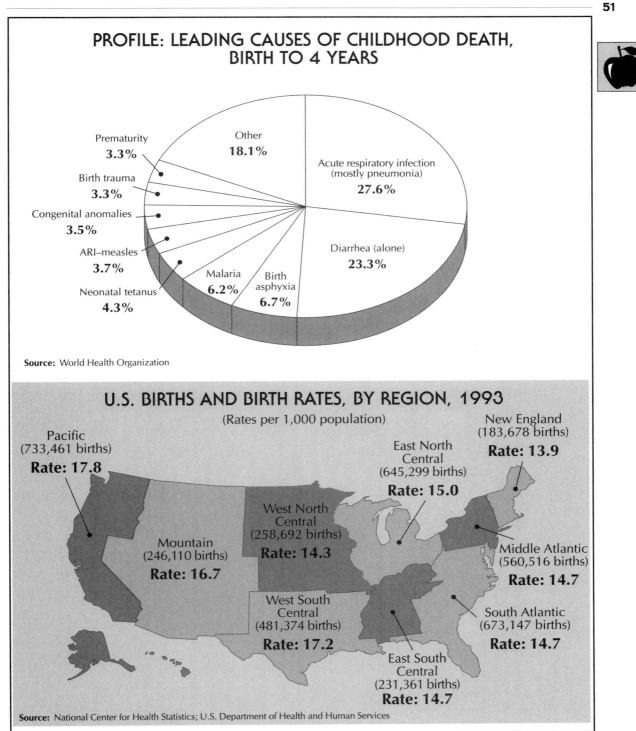

PROFILE: LEADING CAUSES OF CHILDHOOD DEATH, BIRTH TO 4 YEARS

Prematurity
3.3%

Birth trauma
3.3%

Congenital anomalies
3.5%

ARI–measles
3.7%

Neonatal tetanus
4.3%

Malaria
6.2%

Birth asphyxia
6.7%

Other
18.1%

Acute respiratory infection (mostly pneumonia)
27.6%

Diarrhea (alone)
23.3%

Source: World Health Organization

U.S. BIRTHS AND BIRTH RATES, BY REGION, 1993

(Rates per 1,000 population)

Pacific
(733,461 births)
Rate: 17.8

Mountain
(246,110 births)
Rate: 16.7

West North Central
(258,692 births)
Rate: 14.3

West South Central
(481,374 births)
Rate: 17.2

East North Central
(645,299 births)
Rate: 15.0

New England
(183,678 births)
Rate: 13.9

Middle Atlantic
(560,516 births)
Rate: 14.7

South Atlantic
(673,147 births)
Rate: 14.7

East South Central
(231,361 births)
Rate: 14.7

Source: National Center for Health Statistics; U.S. Department of Health and Human Services

HEALTH INSURANCE

Health insurance promises to pay specified health care costs—such as hospital charges, doctors' fees, and medicine bills—to a covered person. Which costs are covered depends upon the person's insurance policy. Insurance coverage in the U.S. is quite uneven. Most people are covered for most hospital care, and many are covered for at least some doctors' bills. But only a minority of people are covered for such costs as dental services, medicine, home care, and other, more common but expensive medical needs.

In 1993, about 30% of personal health care costs were paid for by insurance companies. The remaining 70% of costs were paid for either by the patients themselves or by the U.S. government. The two main government health insurance plans are Medicare and Medicaid. Medicare covers severely disabled people and people ages 65 and older. Medicaid covers poor people.

Most Americans' health insurance is paid for by their employers. As the cost of insurance has risen, however, companies are limiting the insurance coverage they provide for their workers. People who lose their jobs typically lose their health insurance, too.

Many Americans cannot afford to pay for health insurance on their own. According to a 1994 Census Bureau report, 60 million Americans were without health insurance for at least one month during the early 1990s. Half of those people went without coverage for 6 months or longer. Only 47% of people ages 18 to 24 were continuously covered during the 32 months evaluated in the survey.

FINGERTIP FACTS

- The percentage of Americans without health insurance has been steadily increasing. Between 1990 and 1994, a reported 60 million Americans were without health insurance for one month or more.

- Whites are more likely to be insured than blacks. Hispanics have the lowest percentage of insured individuals.

- Women are more likely to have health insurance than men.

- The percentage of insured people rises as education levels rise.

- In 1992, there were 9.8 million children—14.8% of all U.S. children—who were uninsured.

- Coverage varies among regions. The Northeast has the lowest percentage of uninsured people. The South has the highest percentage.

- The percentage of workers who are covered by employer-sponsored health care plans varies with the industry. Most high-technology workers are covered by such plans; most retail workers are not.

- In a 1994 poll, 80% of the people surveyed said it was very important that all Americans have health insurance coverage.

- The number of people covered by Medicare increased from 19.5 million in 1967 to 36.3 million in 1993.

- Medicaid recipients increased from 10.0 million in 1967 to 32.6 million in 1993.

PROFILE: PERCENTAGE OF U.S. POPULATION WITHOUT HEALTH COVERAGE, BY SELECTED CHARACTERISTICS

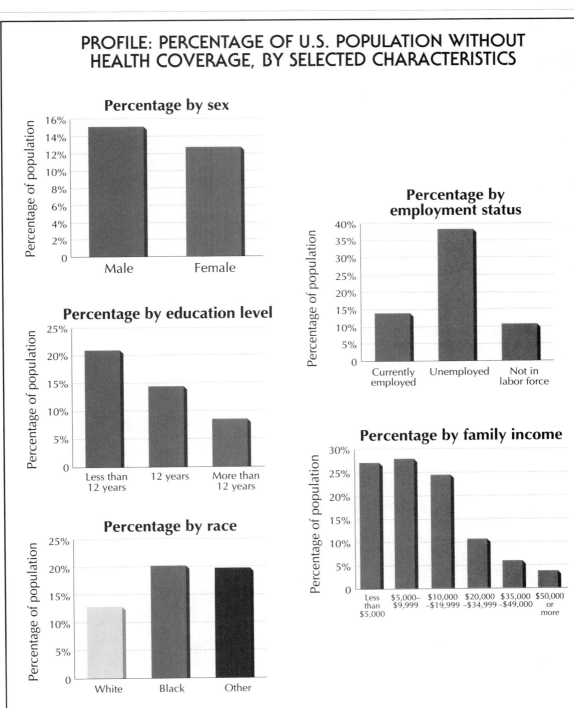

Percentage by sex

Percentage by employment status

Percentage by education level

Percentage by family income

Percentage by race

Source: National Center for Health Statistics

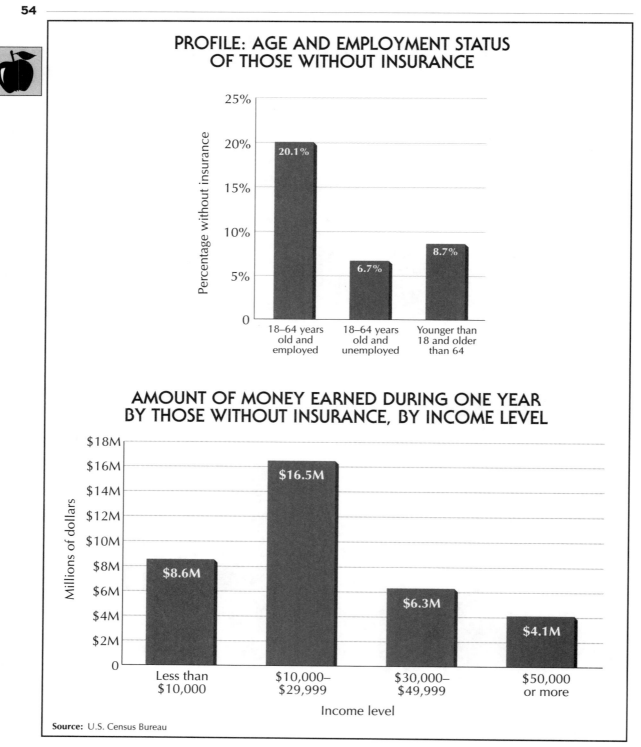

PROFILE: AGE AND EMPLOYMENT STATUS OF THOSE WITHOUT INSURANCE

Percentage without insurance

- 18–64 years old and employed: 20.1%
- 18–64 years old and unemployed: 6.7%
- Younger than 18 and older than 64: 8.7%

AMOUNT OF MONEY EARNED DURING ONE YEAR BY THOSE WITHOUT INSURANCE, BY INCOME LEVEL

Millions of dollars

- Less than $10,000: $8.6M
- $10,000–$29,999: $16.5M
- $30,000–$49,999: $6.3M
- $50,000 or more: $4.1M

Income level

Source: U.S. Census Bureau

HEALTH COVERAGE FROM U.S. EMPLOYERS, 1991

About 74% of U.S. employees are covered by employer-sponsored health care plans in companies with 200 or more employees. The percentage of coverage, however, by industry varies:

Percentage of industry

High technology	Manufacturing	Services	Transportation/ communications	Retailing
89%	82%	80%	78%	39%

Source: Based on statistics from KPMG

AMERICANS LIVING WITHOUT HEALTH INSURANCE, BY SEX, 1991

16.0 million

19.4 million

Female

Male

Source: U.S. Census Bureau

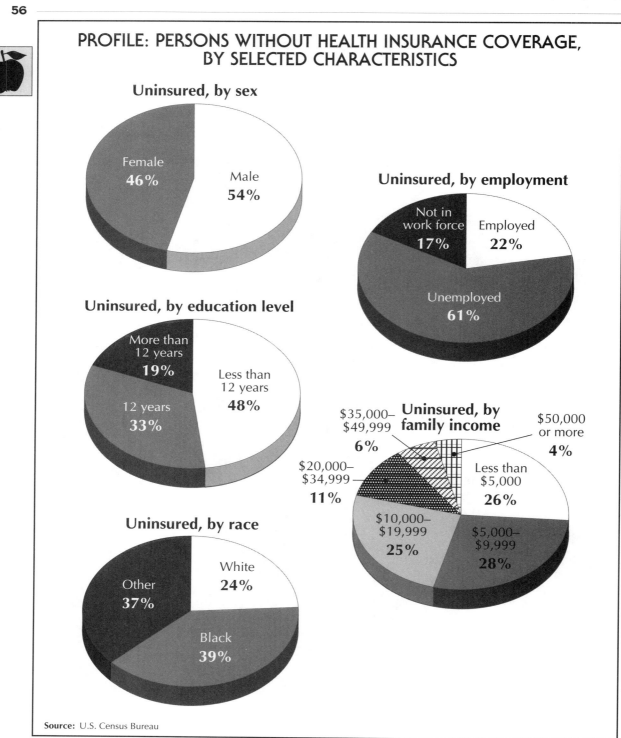

PROFILE: PERSONS WITHOUT HEALTH INSURANCE COVERAGE, BY SELECTED CHARACTERISTICS

Uninsured, by sex

Female 46%
Male 54%

Uninsured, by employment

Not in work force 17%
Employed 22%
Unemployed 61%

Uninsured, by education level

More than 12 years 19%
Less than 12 years 48%
12 years 33%

Uninsured, by family income

$35,000–$49,999 6%
$50,000 or more 4%
$20,000–$34,999 11%
Less than $5,000 26%
$10,000–$19,999 25%
$5,000–$9,999 28%

Uninsured, by race

Other 37%
White 24%
Black 39%

Source: U.S. Census Bureau

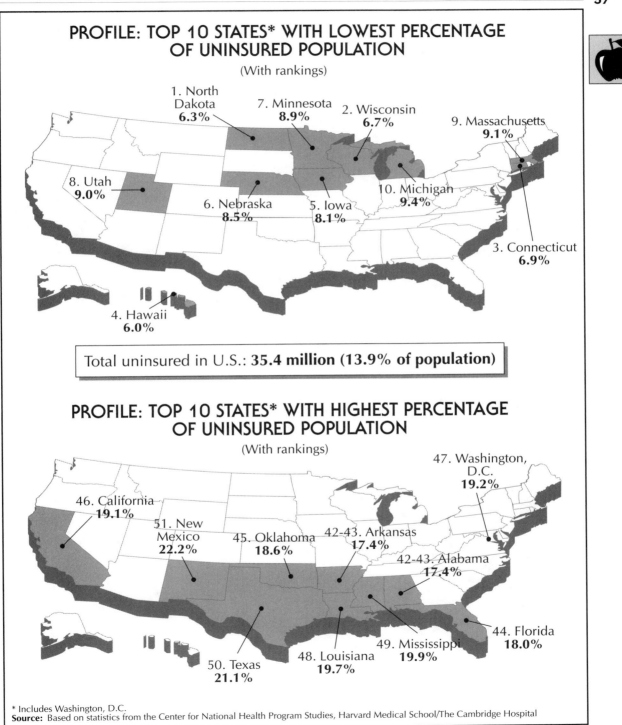

PROFILE: TOP 10 STATES* WITH LOWEST PERCENTAGE OF UNINSURED POPULATION

(With rankings)

1. North Dakota **6.3%**

7. Minnesota **8.9%**

2. Wisconsin **6.7%**

9. Massachusetts **9.1%**

8. Utah **9.0%**

6. Nebraska **8.5%**

5. Iowa **8.1%**

10. Michigan **9.4%**

3. Connecticut **6.9%**

4. Hawaii **6.0%**

Total uninsured in U.S.: **35.4 million (13.9% of population)**

PROFILE: TOP 10 STATES* WITH HIGHEST PERCENTAGE OF UNINSURED POPULATION

(With rankings)

47. Washington, D.C. **19.2%**

46. California **19.1%**

51. New Mexico **22.2%**

45. Oklahoma **18.6%**

42-43. Arkansas **17.4%**

42-43. Alabama **17.4%**

44. Florida **18.0%**

49. Mississippi **19.9%**

48. Louisiana **19.7%**

50. Texas **21.1%**

* Includes Washington, D.C.
Source: Based on statistics from the Center for National Health Program Studies, Harvard Medical School/The Cambridge Hospital

U.S. RESIDENTS WITHOUT HEALTH INSURANCE, 1980–1991

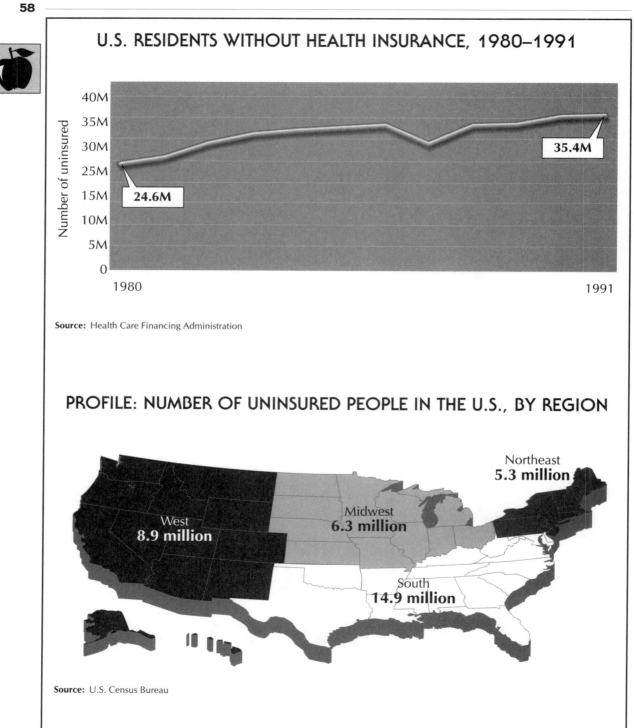

24.6M

35.4M

Number of uninsured

40M
35M
30M
25M
15M
10M
5M
0

1980

1991

Source: Health Care Financing Administration

PROFILE: NUMBER OF UNINSURED PEOPLE IN THE U.S., BY REGION

Northeast
5.3 million

West
8.9 million

Midwest
6.3 million

South
14.9 million

Source: U.S. Census Bureau

HEALTH MAINTENANCE ORGANIZATIONS (HMOs) IN THE U.S., 1980–1992

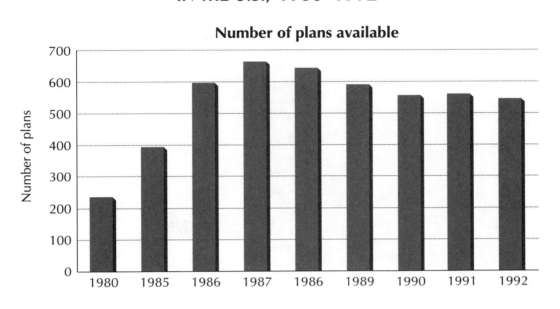

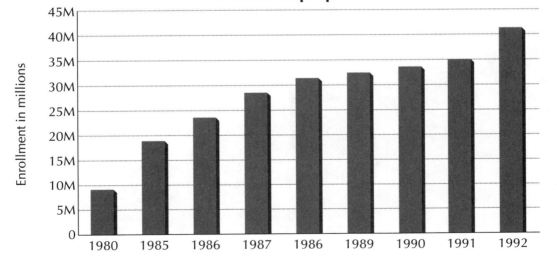

Source: Group Health Association of America, Inc.

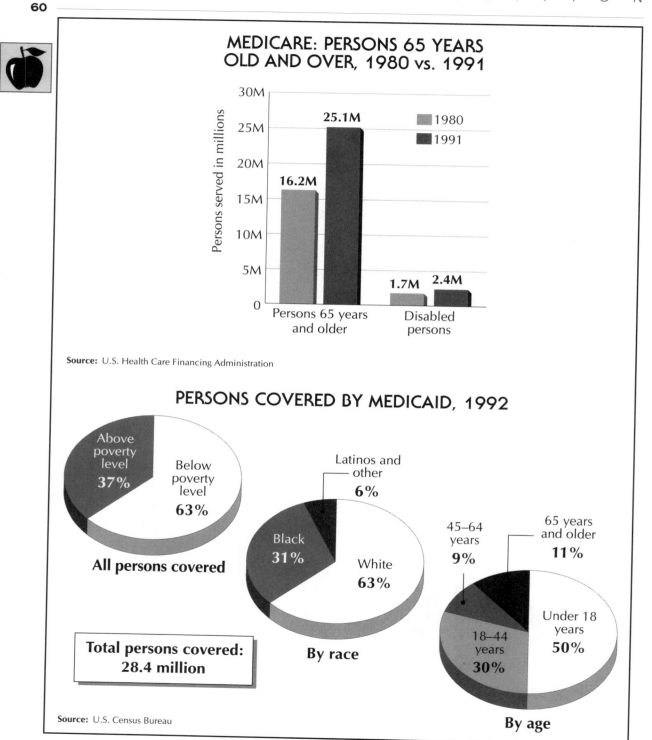

MEDICARE: PERSONS 65 YEARS OLD AND OVER, 1980 vs. 1991

Persons served in millions

- 1980
- 1991

16.2M
25.1M
1.7M
2.4M

Persons 65 years and older

Disabled persons

Source: U.S. Health Care Financing Administration

PERSONS COVERED BY MEDICAID, 1992

Above poverty level **37%**

Below poverty level **63%**

All persons covered

Latinos and other **6%**

Black **31%**

White **63%**

By race

45–64 years **9%**

65 years and older **11%**

18–44 years **30%**

Under 18 years **50%**

By age

Total persons covered: **28.4 million**

Source: U.S. Census Bureau

MEDICARE ENROLLMENT AND PAYMENTS IN THE U.S., 1970–1993

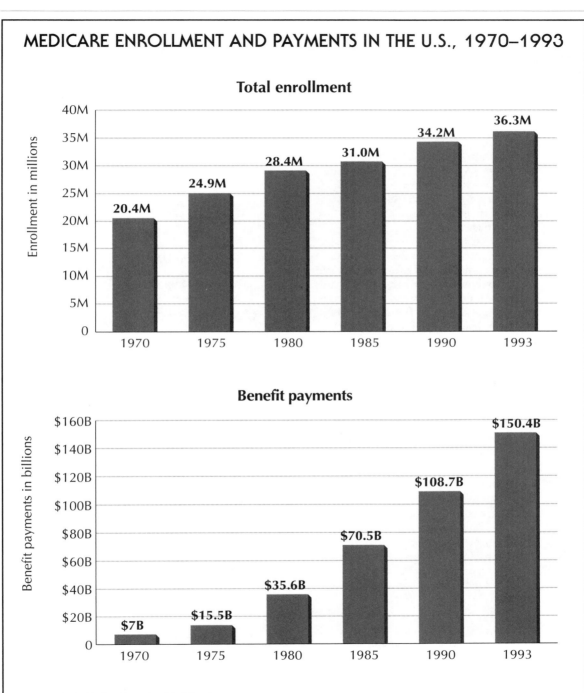

Total enrollment

Enrollment in millions

20.4M	24.9M	28.4M	31.0M	34.2M	36.3M
1970	1975	1980	1985	1990	1993

Benefit payments

Benefit payments in billions

$7B	$15.5B	$35.6B	$70.5B	$108.7B	$150.4B
1970	1975	1980	1985	1990	1993

Source: U.S. Health Care Financing Administration

HEALTH CARE COSTS AND REFORM

The United States spends more money on health care than any other country in the world. In 1993, health care cost the U.S. an estimated $903 billion. This industry accounted for 14.4% of the U.S. economy, or gross domestic product. In contrast—in 1967—the U.S. only spent a total of $51 billion, or 6.3% of the gross domestic product, on health care.

Various factors have fueled the dramatic increase in health care costs. New technologies and procedures, such as CAT scans and organ transplants, are expensive. People demand more health care than in the past. There are more elderly people today, and these people generally require more medical care than younger people. Salaries of health care professionals have also risen, and the cost of malpractice insurance has skyrocketed in recent years. In addition, it costs many millions of dollars to develop and test new medicines.

Medical costs vary significantly from area to area. For example, the average daily hospital room charge in 1990 was $297. In Arkansas, it was only $170. In California, however, it was $453.

There is widespread feeling that the U.S. health care system needs to be reformed, both to control costs and to provide better coverage to all citizens. However, exactly what reforms are needed is a matter of considerable debate.

Meanwhile, the health care industry is making significant changes in an effort to control costs. For example, hospitals are shortening patient stays and performing more procedures on an outpatient basis. There is also increasing consolidation within the industry of hospitals, pharmaceutical companies, and other key health care providers.

FINGERTIP FACTS

- ☞ U.S. health expenditures are projected to reach $1.74 trillion in the year 2000. This would represent 18.1% of the gross domestic product.
- ☞ In 1991, there were 9.8 million workers in the health care industry. About half were employed in hospitals.
- ☞ In 1992, there were 22.4 patient-care physicians for every 10,000 people in the U.S. (excluding military personnel). The ratio was lowest in Idaho (12.9) and highest in Massachusetts (35.3).
- ☞ Between 1980 and 1990, hospital inpatient admissions fell 14%, but outpatient visits jumped 49%.
- ☞ Emergency rooms at urban hospitals treated 104% more patients in 1990 than in 1980.
- ☞ Health care is expensive, regardless of who is paying the bill. In 1992, General Motors spent $3.7 billion for employee health care.
- ☞ Americans spent $1.5 billion on nursing home care in 1960. In 1990, they spent $53.1 billion.
- ☞ It costs an average of $60,000 to $110,000 to make a "test tube" baby. In comparison, the average cost of a normal delivery is $10,000.
- ☞ A 1993 study indicated that administrative expenses account for almost 25% of U.S. hospital costs.
- ☞ Drug companies often charge more for prescription drugs in the U.S. than elsewhere. A U.S. government study found that 77 commonly prescribed drugs cost an average 60% more in the U.S. than in Britain.
- ☞ Health care expenditures vary tremendously among nations. Most sub-Saharan African countries, where annual incomes are $100 to $600, spend less than $40 per person.

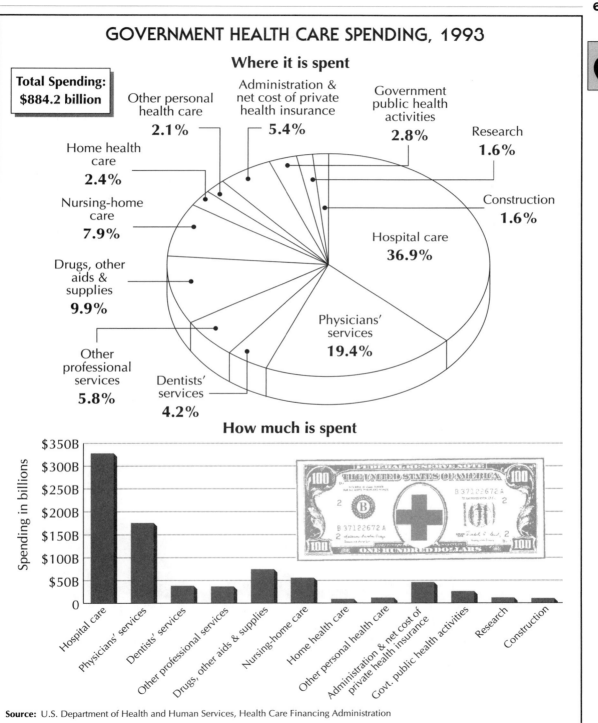

GOVERNMENT HEALTH CARE SPENDING, 1993

Where it is spent

Total Spending: $884.2 billion

Other personal health care
2.1%

Administration & net cost of private health insurance
5.4%

Government public health activities
2.8%

Research
1.6%

Home health care
2.4%

Nursing-home care
7.9%

Drugs, other aids & supplies
9.9%

Other professional services
5.8%

Dentists' services
4.2%

Construction
1.6%

Hospital care
36.9%

Physicians' services
19.4%

How much is spent

Spending in billions

$350B
$300B
$250B
$200B
$150B
$100B
$50B
0

Hospital care · Physicians' services · Dentists' services · Other professional services · Drugs, other aids & supplies · Nursing-home care · Home health care · Other personal health care · Administration & net cost of private health insurance · Govt. public health activities · Research · Construction

Source: U.S. Department of Health and Human Services, Health Care Financing Administration

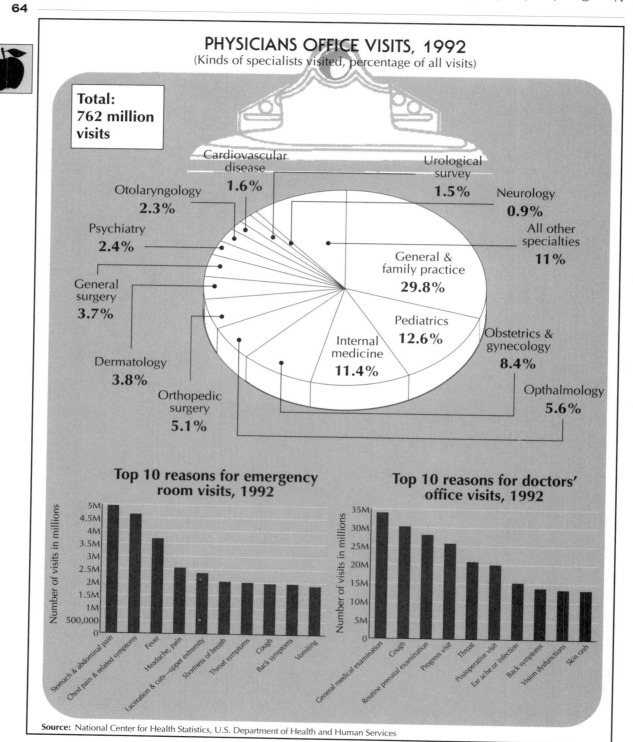

PHYSICIANS OFFICE VISITS, 1992
(Kinds of specialists visited, percentage of all visits)

Total:
762 million
visits

Cardiovascular disease **1.6%**

Otolaryngology **2.3%**

Psychiatry **2.4%**

General surgery **3.7%**

Dermatology **3.8%**

Orthopedic surgery **5.1%**

Urological survey **1.5%**

Neurology **0.9%**

All other specialties **11%**

General & family practice **29.8%**

Pediatrics **12.6%**

Internal medicine **11.4%**

Obstetrics & gynecology **8.4%**

Opthalmology **5.6%**

Top 10 reasons for emergency room visits, 1992

Number of visits in millions

5M
4.5M
4M
3.5M
3M
2.5M
2M
1.5M
1M
500,000
0

Stomach & abdominal pain
Chest pain & related symptoms
Fever
Headache, pain
Laceration & cuts—upper extremity
Shortness of breath
Throat symptoms
Cough
Back symptoms
Vomiting

Top 10 reasons for doctors' office visits, 1992

Number of visits in millions

35M
30M
25M
20M
15M
10M
5M
0

General medical examination
Cough
Routine prenatal examination
Progress visit
Throat
Postoperative visit
Ear ache or infection
Back symptoms
Vision dysfunctions
Skin rash

Source: National Center for Health Statistics, U.S. Department of Health and Human Services

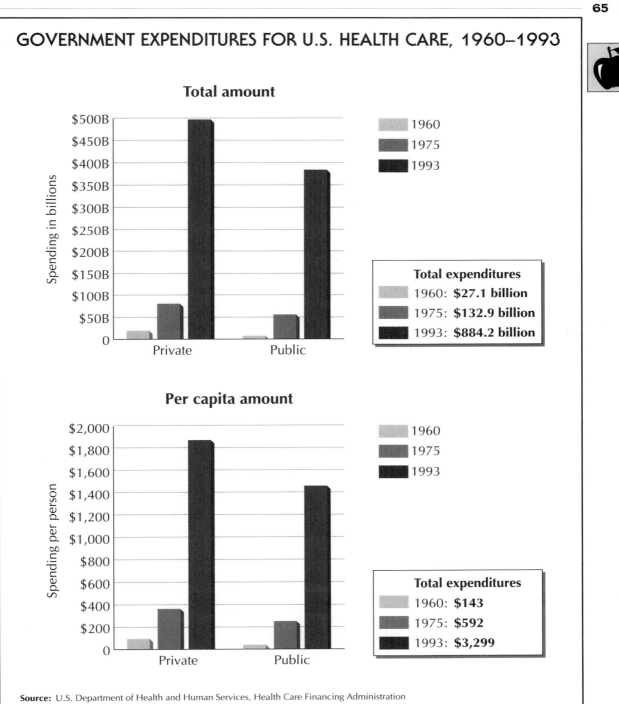

GOVERNMENT EXPENDITURES FOR U.S. HEALTH CARE, 1960–1993

Total amount

Spending in billions

- 1960
- 1975
- 1993

Private   Public

Total expenditures
1960: **$27.1 billion**
1975: **$132.9 billion**
1993: **$884.2 billion**

Per capita amount

Spending per person

- 1960
- 1975
- 1993

Private   Public

Total expenditures
1960: **$143**
1975: **$592**
1993: **$3,299**

Source: U.S. Department of Health and Human Services, Health Care Financing Administration

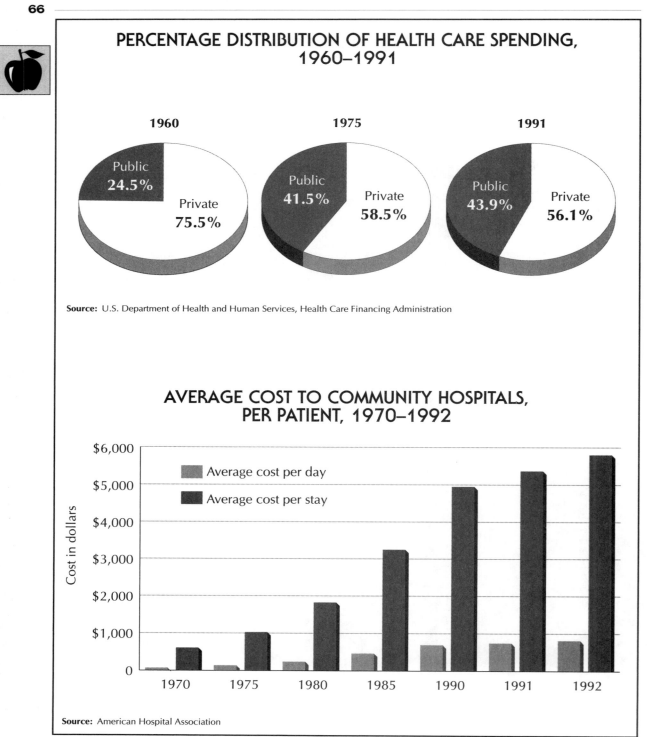

PERCENTAGE DISTRIBUTION OF HEALTH CARE SPENDING, 1960–1991

1960

Public
24.5%

Private
75.5%

1975

Public
41.5%

Private
58.5%

1991

Public
43.9%

Private
56.1%

Source: U.S. Department of Health and Human Services, Health Care Financing Administration

AVERAGE COST TO COMMUNITY HOSPITALS, PER PATIENT, 1970–1992

Cost in dollars

- Average cost per day
- Average cost per stay

$6,000
$5,000
$4,000
$3,000
$2,000
$1,000
0

1970   1975   1980   1985   1990   1991   1992

Source: American Hospital Association

TOP 10 STATES* WITH THE MOST EXPENSIVE HOSPITAL COSTS, 1992
(With rankings)

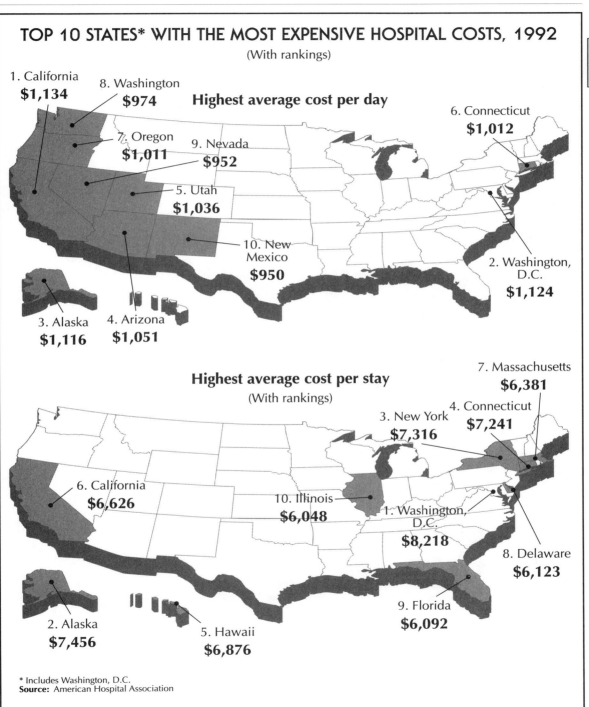

Highest average cost per day

1. California
$1,134

8. Washington
$974

7. Oregon
$1,011

9. Nevada
$952

5. Utah
$1,036

6. Connecticut
$1,012

10. New Mexico
$950

2. Washington, D.C.
$1,124

3. Alaska
$1,116

4. Arizona
$1,051

Highest average cost per stay
(With rankings)

7. Massachusetts
$6,381

3. New York
$7,316

4. Connecticut
$7,241

6. California
$6,626

10. Illinois
$6,048

1. Washington, D.C.
$8,218

8. Delaware
$6,123

2. Alaska
$7,456

5. Hawaii
$6,876

9. Florida
$6,092

* Includes Washington, D.C.
Source: American Hospital Association

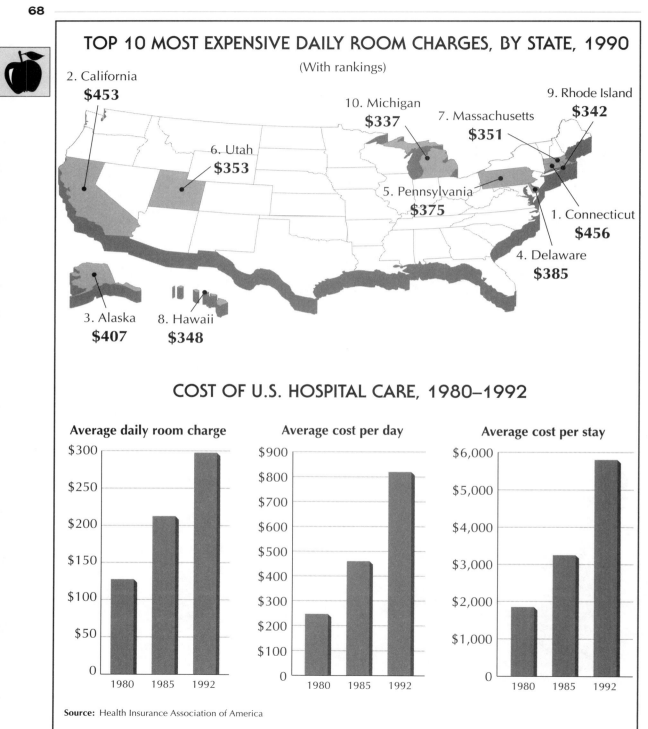

TOP 10 MOST EXPENSIVE DAILY ROOM CHARGES, BY STATE, 1990

(With rankings)

2. California
$453

10. Michigan
$337

7. Massachusetts
$351

9. Rhode Island
$342

6. Utah
$353

5. Pennsylvania
$375

1. Connecticut
$456

4. Delaware
$385

3. Alaska
$407

8. Hawaii
$348

COST OF U.S. HOSPITAL CARE, 1980–1992

Average daily room charge

Average cost per day

Average cost per stay

Source: Health Insurance Association of America

MOST COMMON SURGICAL PROCEDURES, 1980 vs. 1990

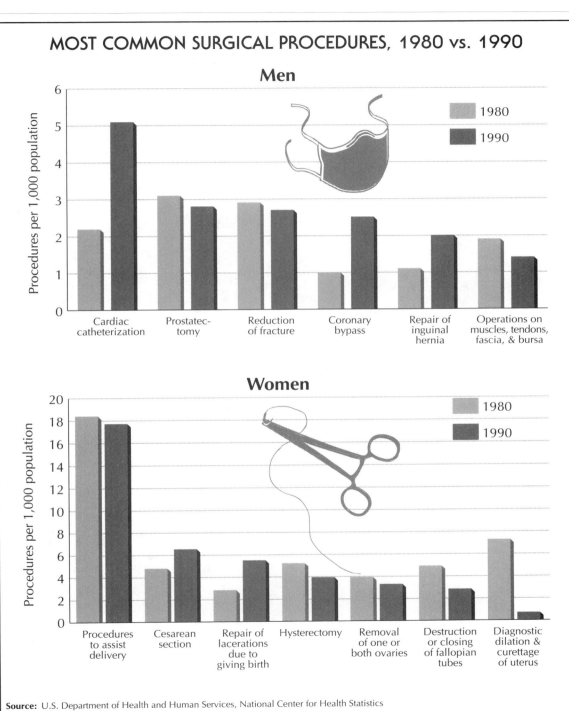

Men

Procedures per 1,000 population

1980 / 1990

- Cardiac catheterization
- Prostatectomy
- Reduction of fracture
- Coronary bypass
- Repair of inguinal hernia
- Operations on muscles, tendons, fascia, & bursa

Women

Procedures per 1,000 population

1980 / 1990

- Procedures to assist delivery
- Cesarean section
- Repair of lacerations due to giving birth
- Hysterectomy
- Removal of one or both ovaries
- Destruction or closing of fallopian tubes
- Diagnostic dilation & curettage of uterus

Source: U.S. Department of Health and Human Services, National Center for Health Statistics

VISITS TO ALTERNATIVE PRACTITIONERS, 1993

In 1993, people made 425 million visits to unconventional practitioners, such as herbalists, massage therapists, acupuncturists, and chiropractic physicians. Percentage of people with the following ailments who visited one or more of these care providers:

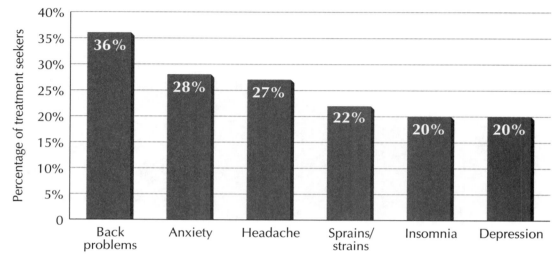

Source: *New England Journal of Medicine* survey of 1,539 adults

PROFILE: SPENDING ON PRESCRIPTION DRUGS

(Annual spending on pharmaceuticals per person, by country)

Source: Pharmaceutical Manufacturers Association

SPENDING ON HEALTH CARE: ELDERLY vs. NON-ELDERLY HOUSEHOLDS, 1984 vs. 1991

(Percentage of income spent annually on health care)

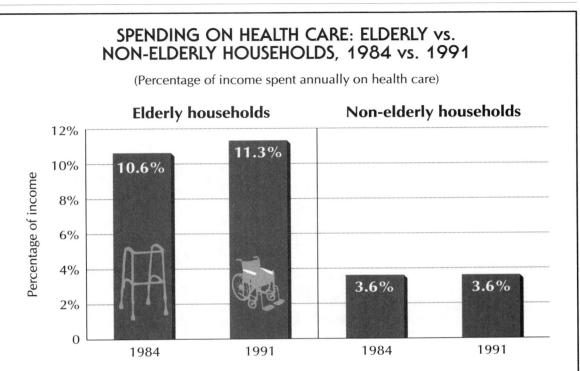

Source: U.S. Department of Health and Human Services

THE STEEP RISE IN U.S. HEALTH CARE COSTS, 1975–1990

From 1975 through 1990, U.S. health care costs increased from $132 billion to $671 billion:

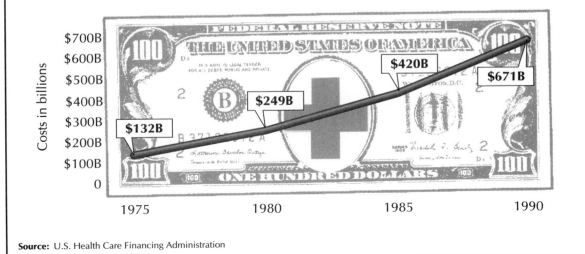

Source: U.S. Health Care Financing Administration

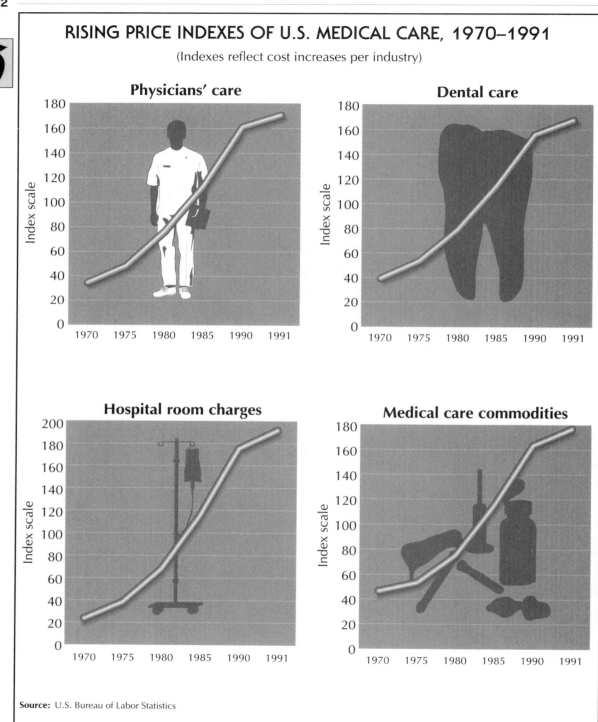

RISING PRICE INDEXES OF U.S. MEDICAL CARE, 1970–1991

(Indexes reflect cost increases per industry)

Source: U.S. Bureau of Labor Statistics

MOST-HEALTHY AND LEAST-HEALTHY STATES*, 1992

(Based on number of medical problems and insurance claims per capita, with rankings)

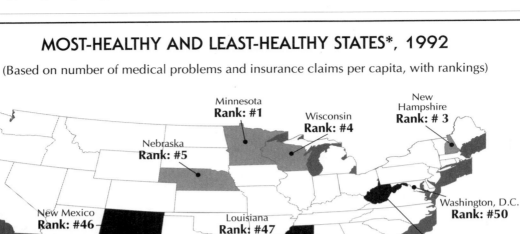

Minnesota
Rank: #1

Wisconsin
Rank: #4

New Hampshire
Rank: # 3

Nebraska
Rank: #5

New Mexico
Rank: #46

Louisiana
Rank: #47

Washington, D.C.
Rank: #50

West Virginia
Rank: #48

Mississippi
Rank: #49

Hawaii
Rank: #2

Top 5 most-healthy states
Bottom 5 least-healthy states

Source: American Medical Association

MONEY U.S. RESIDENTS SPENT ON HEALTH CARE, BY ITEM, 1992

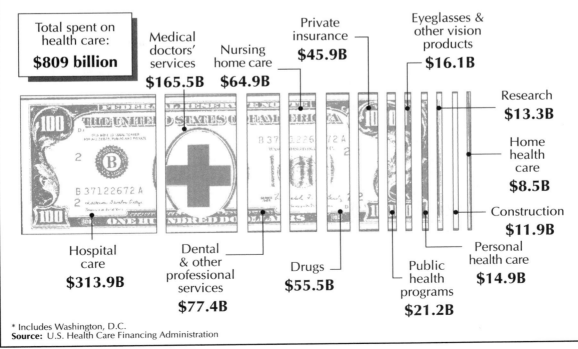

Total spent on health care:
$809 billion

Medical doctors' services
$165.5B

Nursing home care
$64.9B

Private insurance
$45.9B

Eyeglasses & other vision products
$16.1B

Research
$13.3B

Home health care
$8.5B

Construction
$11.9B

Personal health care
$14.9B

Hospital care
$313.9B

Dental & other professional services
$77.4B

Drugs
$55.5B

Public health programs
$21.2B

* Includes Washington, D.C.
Source: U.S. Health Care Financing Administration

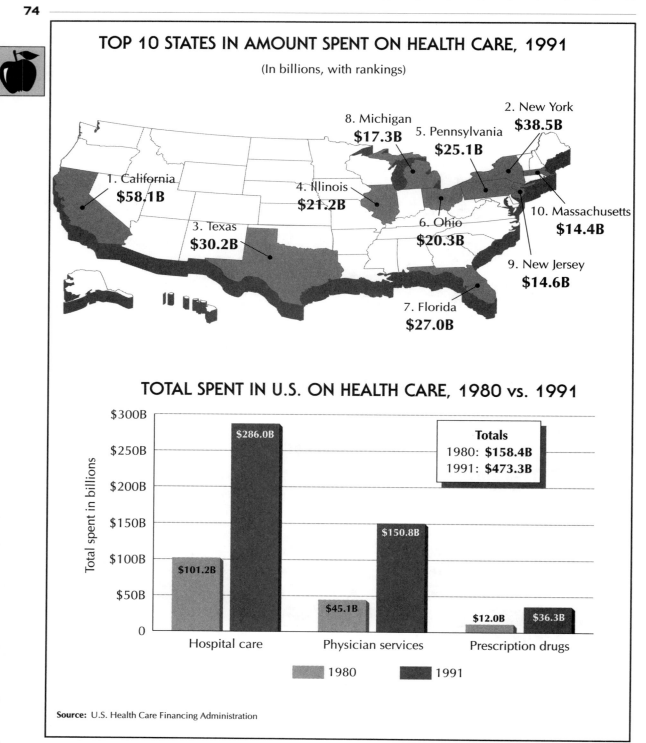

TOP 10 STATES IN AMOUNT SPENT ON HEALTH CARE, 1991

(In billions, with rankings)

2. New York
$38.5B

8. Michigan
$17.3B

5. Pennsylvania
$25.1B

1. California
$58.1B

4. Illinois
$21.2B

10. Massachusetts
$14.4B

3. Texas
$30.2B

6. Ohio
$20.3B

9. New Jersey
$14.6B

7. Florida
$27.0B

TOTAL SPENT IN U.S. ON HEALTH CARE, 1980 vs. 1991

Total spent in billions

$300B
$250B
$200B
$150B
$100B
$50B
0

	Totals
1980:	**$158.4B**
1991:	**$473.3B**

Hospital care: **$101.2B** (1980), **$286.0B** (1991)

Physician services: **$45.1B** (1980), **$150.8B** (1991)

Prescription drugs: **$12.0B** (1980), **$36.3B** (1991)

☐ 1980   ☐ 1991

Source: U.S. Health Care Financing Administration

PHARMACEUTICAL COSTS INCREASE MORE THAN OTHER GOODS, 1980–1990

(Percentage by which 1990 prescription drugs or health care prices were greater than 1980 prices)

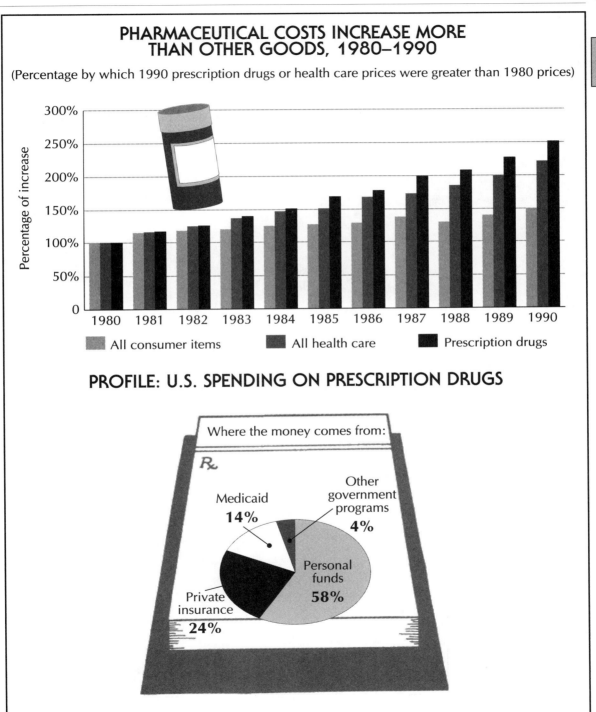

PROFILE: U.S. SPENDING ON PRESCRIPTION DRUGS

Where the money comes from:

Medicaid **14%**

Other government programs **4%**

Personal funds **58%**

Private insurance **24%**

Source: U.S. Health Care Financing Administration

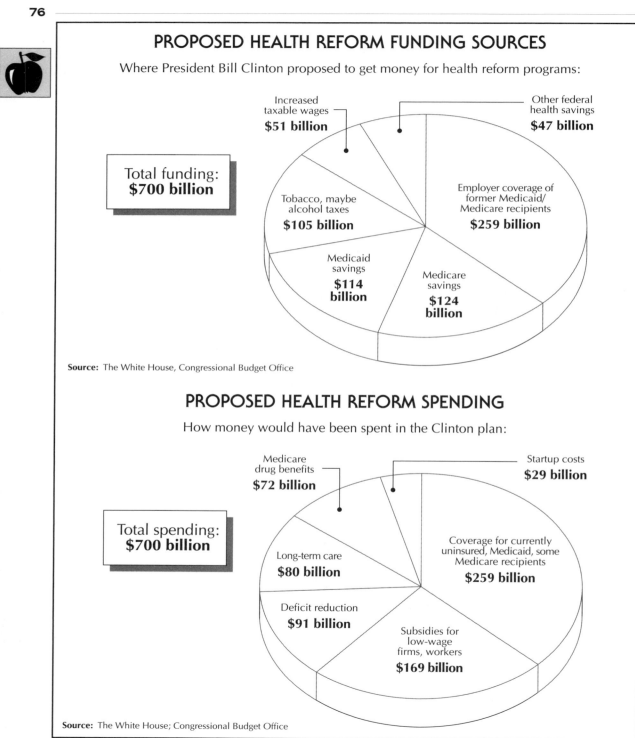

PROPOSED HEALTH REFORM FUNDING SOURCES

Where President Bill Clinton proposed to get money for health reform programs:

Increased taxable wages **$51 billion**

Other federal health savings **$47 billion**

Total funding: **$700 billion**

Tobacco, maybe alcohol taxes **$105 billion**

Employer coverage of former Medicaid/ Medicare recipients **$259 billion**

Medicaid savings **$114 billion**

Medicare savings **$124 billion**

Source: The White House, Congressional Budget Office

PROPOSED HEALTH REFORM SPENDING

How money would have been spent in the Clinton plan:

Medicare drug benefits **$72 billion**

Startup costs **$29 billion**

Total spending: **$700 billion**

Long-term care **$80 billion**

Coverage for currently uninsured, Medicaid, some Medicare recipients **$259 billion**

Deficit reduction **$91 billion**

Subsidies for low-wage firms, workers **$169 billion**

Source: The White House; Congressional Budget Office

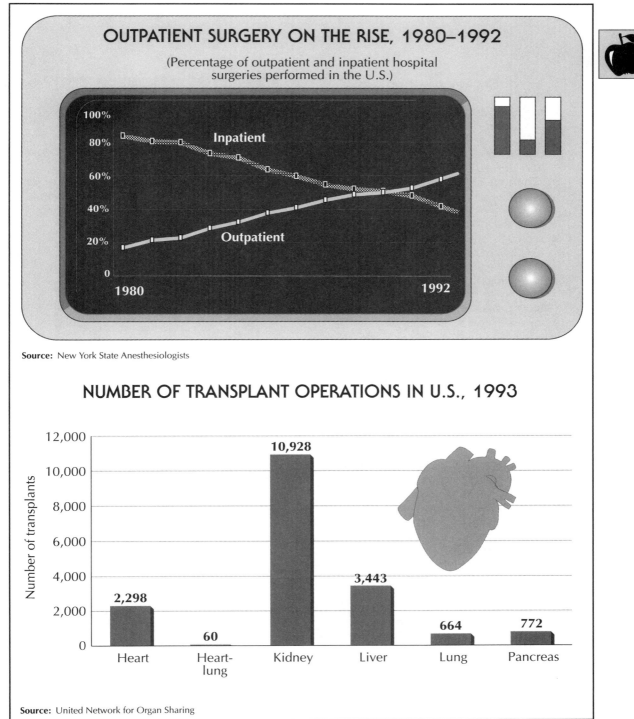

OUTPATIENT SURGERY ON THE RISE, 1980–1992

(Percentage of outpatient and inpatient hospital surgeries performed in the U.S.)

Inpatient

Outpatient

1980   1992

Source: New York State Anesthesiologists

NUMBER OF TRANSPLANT OPERATIONS IN U.S., 1993

Number of transplants

Heart	2,298
Heart-lung	60
Kidney	10,928
Liver	3,443
Lung	664
Pancreas	772

Source: United Network for Organ Sharing

T U B E R C U L O S I S

In 1880, tuberculosis, or TB, was one of the most common—and most deadly—diseases in the U.S. By 1980, it had almost disappeared. Public health officials hoped they could eliminate the disease completely in the U.S., but then TB returned with a vengeance. The number of new cases jumped from a low of 22,201 in 1985 to 26,673 in 1992. There was a slight decline in 1993 and 1994, due mainly to more aggressive surveillance and treatment.

Tuberculosis is caused by rod-shaped bacteria called tubercle bacilli. It is named for the tubercles, or lesions, that form wherever the germs destroy body tissues. In most cases, TB germs invade the lungs. But they also can infect the bones, kidneys, skin, and other parts of the body.

People can be infected with TB germs without having an active case of the disease. The bacilli may remain hidden in their bodies for their entire lives. More than 10 million Americans carry TB germs, but only about 10% of carriers will actually develop active cases. Usually, the bacilli become active when a person's immune system is weakened by illness or malnutrition.

The most obvious symptom of active pulmonary (lung) tuberculosis is a persistent cough. Other symptoms include loss of energy, fatigue, night sweats, and loss of weight. Active tuberculosis is extremely contagious. The germs are easily spread by coughing and sneezing.

Tuberculosis can almost always be cured. Treatment usually involves taking medicines for a period of 6 to 9 months. Without adequate treatment, however, a person may develop drug-resistant tuberculosis, which is very difficult to treat.

FINGERTIP FACTS

- Overcrowding increases the spread of TB. TB is more common in cities than in rural areas.

- Outdoors, ultraviolet radiation from the sun quickly kills TB germs.

- In 1900, the tuberculosis death rate was 194.4 per 100,000. In 1947, it was 33.5. In 1990, it was 0.7.

- In 1992, there were 1,400 TB deaths reported in the U.S.

- People infected with tuberculosis who have AIDS are up to 40 times more likely to develop active cases of TB than people without AIDS. AIDS weakens people's defenses against TB germs.

- Worldwide, the World Health Organization estimates that 1.7 billion people—almost one-third of the world's population—are carriers of TB germs. TB causes 3 million deaths each year—more than all other infectious diseases combined.

- Tuberculosis is one of the world's oldest diseases. Some ancient mummies found in Egypt and Peru had tuberculosis.

- People can acquire tuberculosis by drinking unpasteurized milk from infected animals. During pasteurization, milk is heated, which effectively kills tuberculosis bacilli and other harmful microorganisms in the milk.

- A tuberculosis vaccine has been injected in an estimated 3 billion people worldwide, but is not widely used in the U.S.

TUBERCULOSIS INCREASES IN U.S., 1960–1993

(Number of people with tuberculosis)

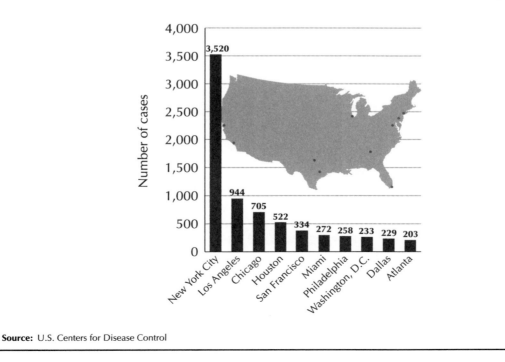

Number of people infected

60,000
50,000
40,000
30,000
20,000
10,000
0

25,313

1960   1970   1980   1990   1992   1993

TOP 10 U.S. CITIES IN NUMBER OF CASES OF TUBERCULOSIS, 1992

Number of cases

4,000
3,500
3,000
2,500
2,000
1,500
1,000
500
0

New York City — 3,520
Los Angeles — 944
Chicago — 705
Houston — 522
San Francisco — 334
Miami — 272
Philadelphia — 258
Washington, D.C. — 233
Dallas — 229
Atlanta — 203

Source: U.S. Centers for Disease Control

PROFILE: TUBERCULOSIS IN THE U.S., BY AGE, RACE, AND SEX

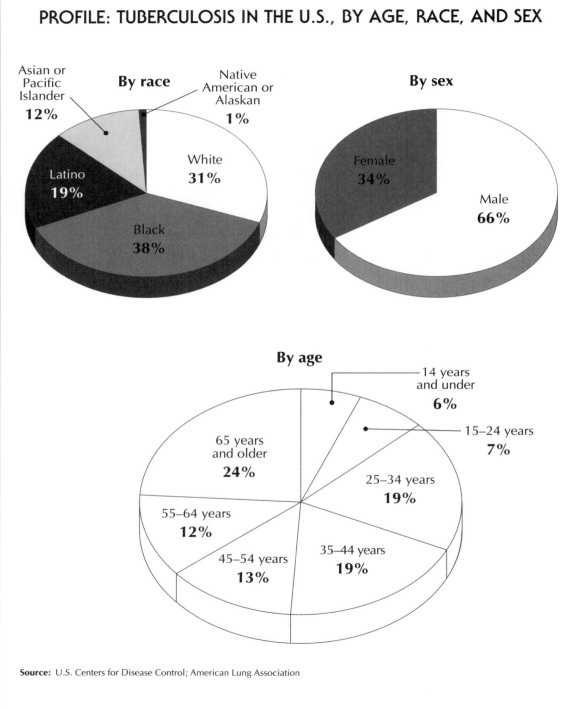

By race

Asian or Pacific Islander **12%**

Native American or Alaskan **1%**

White **31%**

Latino **19%**

Black **38%**

By sex

Female **34%**

Male **66%**

By age

14 years and under **6%**

15–24 years **7%**

25–34 years **19%**

35–44 years **19%**

45–54 years **13%**

55–64 years **12%**

65 years and older **24%**

Source: U.S. Centers for Disease Control; American Lung Association

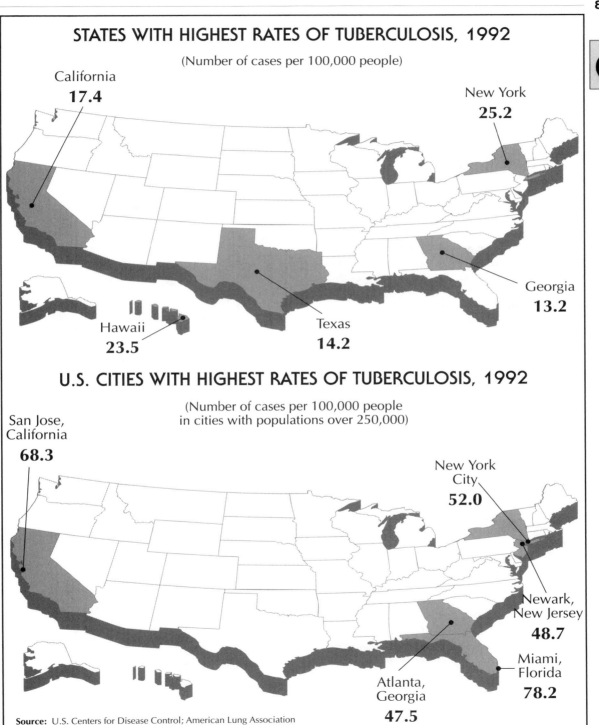

STATES WITH HIGHEST RATES OF TUBERCULOSIS, 1992

(Number of cases per 100,000 people)

California
17.4

New York
25.2

Georgia
13.2

Hawaii
23.5

Texas
14.2

U.S. CITIES WITH HIGHEST RATES OF TUBERCULOSIS, 1992

(Number of cases per 100,000 people
in cities with populations over 250,000)

San Jose,
California
68.3

New York
City
52.0

Newark,
New Jersey
48.7

Miami,
Florida
78.2

Atlanta,
Georgia
47.5

Source: U.S. Centers for Disease Control; American Lung Association

HEART DISEASE, CANCER, AND OTHER DISEASES

Heart disease and cancer are the main causes of death in the U.S. Annually, they account for 57% of all deaths. Strokes are the third main cause, accounting for 6.6% of all deaths.

Often, heart disease and cancer develop slowly, over many years. This is why they are more common among older people than among the young. A variety of factors increases the risk of developing these diseases. For example, some people have inherited genes that cause or increase the risk of heart disease or cancer. But many risk factors can be avoided or changed. Cigarette smoking is the biggest preventable cause of heart disease and cancer.

In the early 1900s, few people with heart disease or cancer lived very long. Today, with better detection and treatment, many lives are prolonged. About 40% of people who get cancer today will be alive 5 years after diagnosis.

Some kinds of cancer are deadlier than others. For example, 79% of women who get breast cancer and 77% of men who get prostate cancer have 5-year survival rates. But the 5-year survival rate for lung cancer is 13%, and for pancreatic cancer it is only 3%.

A number of other less threatening but serious diseases plague hundreds of thousands of Americans each year. Sexually transmitted diseases (STDs), the most common of which are gonorrhea and syphilis, afflicted more than 614,000 Americans in 1993. Aseptic meningitis and meningococcal infections struck more than 15,000 people in that year. While annual cases of other diseases, such as typhus, typhoid fever, toxic shock syndrome, and leprosy, number only in the hundreds, some serious illnesses—such as encephalitis and malaria—threaten more than 1,000 lives each year.

FINGERTIP FACTS

- Cardiovascular diseases—diseases of the heart and blood vessels—are the #1 cause of death in the U.S. Each day, they claim the lives of more than 2,500 Americans.

- Death rates from cancer and heart disease increase with age. Death rates are higher among blacks than among whites.

- Death rates from heart disease are falling. In 1960, the U.S. death rate from heart disease was 286.2 per 100,000. By 1990, it had dropped to 152.0 per 100,000.

- Up to 50 million Americans ages 6 and older have high blood pressure (hypertension). Many people die from heart attacks and strokes caused by high blood pressure.

- Smokers are twice as likely as non-smokers to have heart attacks.

- Death rates from cancer are increasing. In 1960, the U.S. death rate from cancer was 125.8 per 100,000. By 1990, it had increased to 203.2 per 100,000.

- In 1994, about 538,000 Americans died of cancer—more than 1,400 per day.

- Cancer causes more deaths among U.S. children ages 1 to 14 than any other disease.

- Lung cancer is the leading cause of U.S. cancer deaths. Smoking is responsible for 87% of the lung cancer deaths.

- About 700,000 skin cancers were diagnosed in the U.S. in 1994. About 90% of these could have been prevented by avoiding exposure to the sun's rays.

HEART DISEASE AND CANCER DEATH RATES, BY REGION, 1992

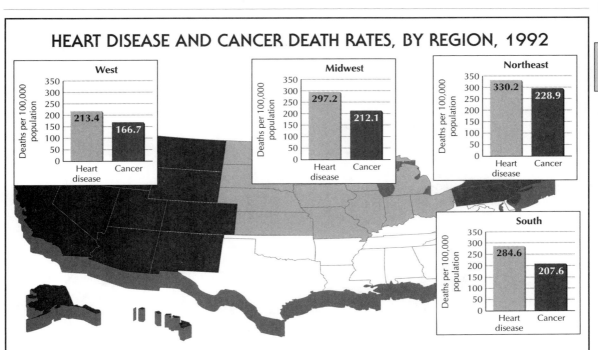

West
Deaths per 100,000 population
- Heart disease: 213.4
- Cancer: 166.7

Midwest
Deaths per 100,000 population
- Heart disease: 297.2
- Cancer: 212.1

Northeast
Deaths per 100,000 population
- Heart disease: 330.2
- Cancer: 228.9

South
Deaths per 100,000 population
- Heart disease: 284.6
- Cancer: 207.6

Source: U.S. National Center for Health Statistics, *Monthly Vital Statistics Report;* and unpublished data.

ESTIMATED PERCENTAGE OF U.S. POPULATION WITH HYPERTENSION, BY RACE AND SEX, AGES 18–74

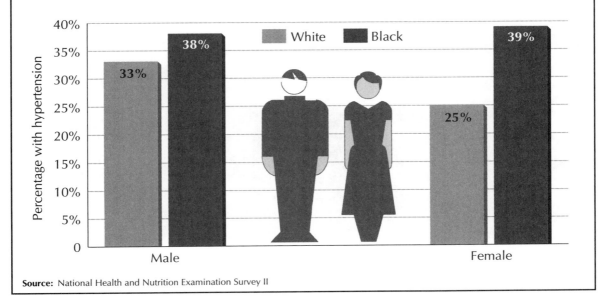

Percentage with hypertension

- White / Black

Male: White 33%, Black 38%
Female: White 25%, Black 39%

Source: National Health and Nutrition Examination Survey II

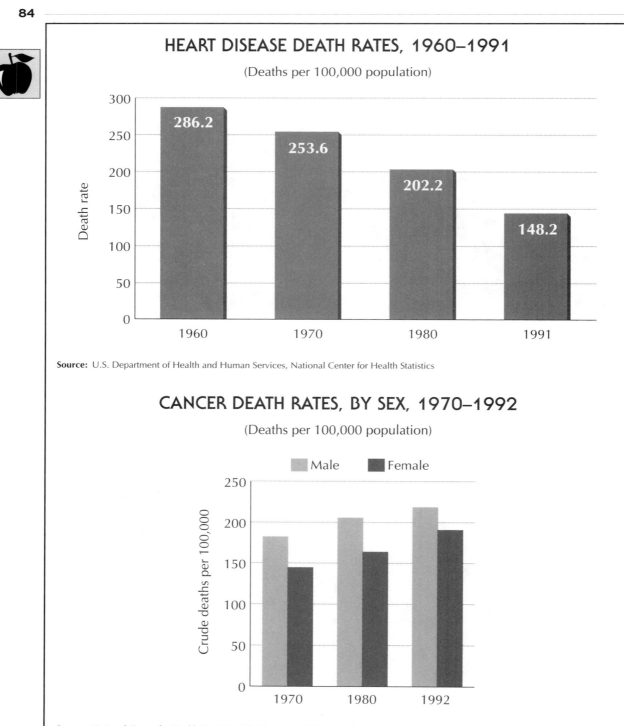

HEART DISEASE DEATH RATES, 1960–1991

(Deaths per 100,000 population)

Death rate

- 286.2 (1960)
- 253.6 (1970)
- 202.2 (1980)
- 148.2 (1991)

Source: U.S. Department of Health and Human Services, National Center for Health Statistics

CANCER DEATH RATES, BY SEX, 1970–1992

(Deaths per 100,000 population)

Male Female

Crude deaths per 100,000

1970   1980   1992

Source: National Center for Health Statistics, *Vital Statistics of the United States*, annual

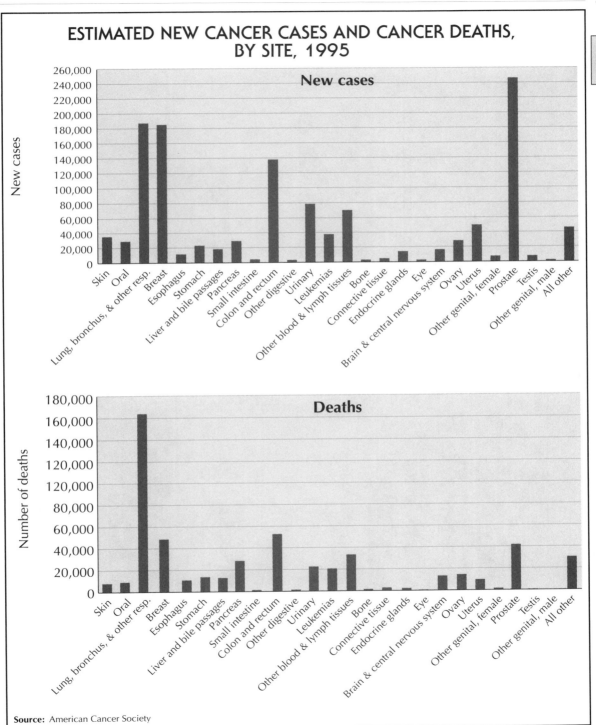

ESTIMATED NEW CANCER CASES AND CANCER DEATHS,
BY SITE, 1995

Source: American Cancer Society

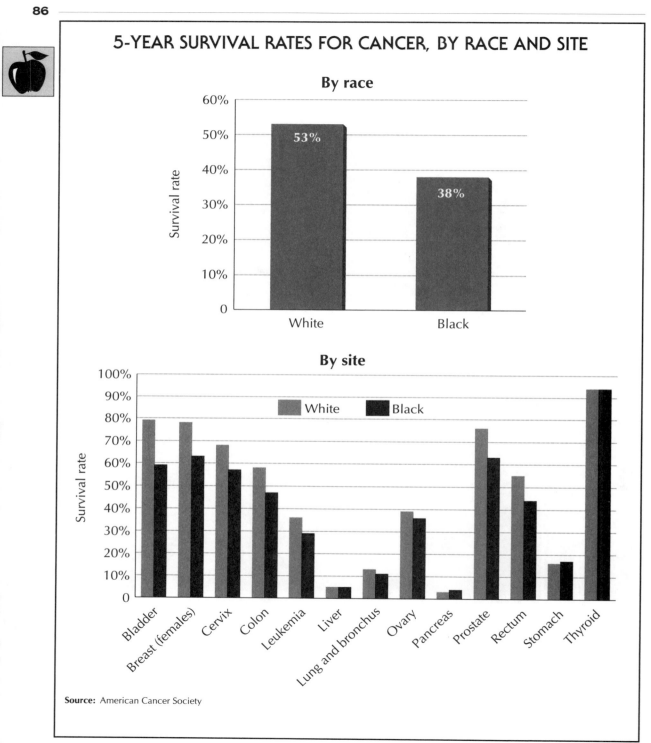

5-YEAR SURVIVAL RATES FOR CANCER, BY RACE AND SITE

By race

By site

Source: American Cancer Society

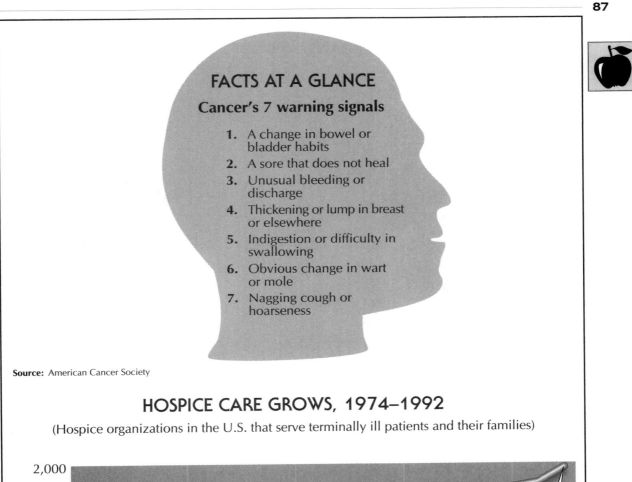

FACTS AT A GLANCE

Cancer's 7 warning signals

1. A change in bowel or bladder habits
2. A sore that does not heal
3. Unusual bleeding or discharge
4. Thickening or lump in breast or elsewhere
5. Indigestion or difficulty in swallowing
6. Obvious change in wart or mole
7. Nagging cough or hoarseness

Source: American Cancer Society

HOSPICE CARE GROWS, 1974–1992

(Hospice organizations in the U.S. that serve terminally ill patients and their families)

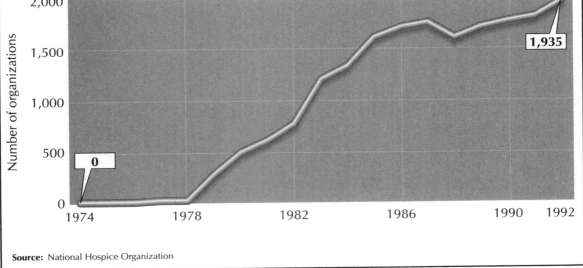

Source: National Hospice Organization

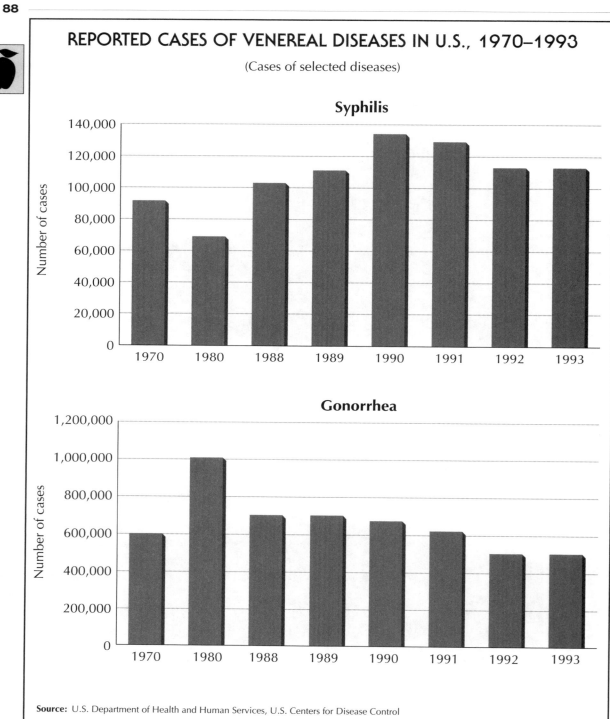

REPORTED CASES OF VENEREAL DISEASES IN U.S., 1970–1993

(Cases of selected diseases)

Syphilis

Number of cases

140,000
120,000
100,000
80,000
60,000
40,000
20,000
0

1970   1980   1988   1989   1990   1991   1992   1993

Gonorrhea

Number of cases

1,200,000
1,000,000
800,000
600,000
400,000
200,000
0

1970   1980   1988   1989   1990   1991   1992   1993

Source: U.S. Department of Health and Human Services, U.S. Centers for Disease Control

RABIES IN U.S. ANIMALS ON THE RISE

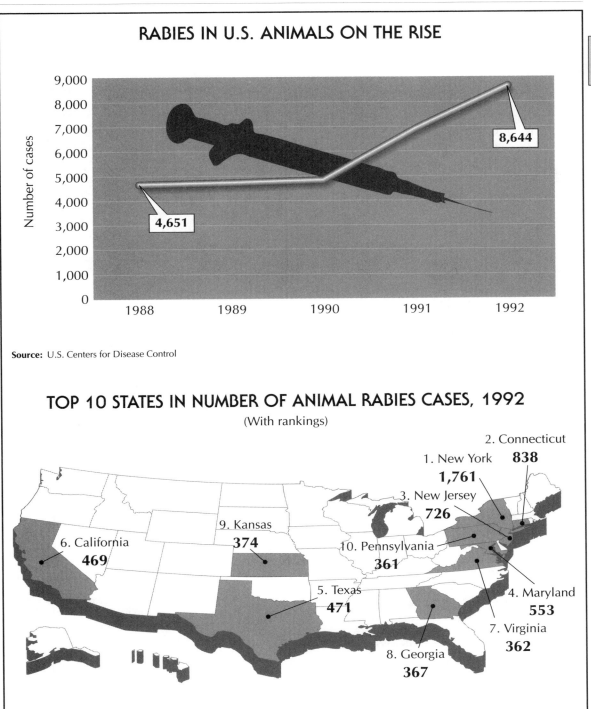

Source: U.S. Centers for Disease Control

TOP 10 STATES IN NUMBER OF ANIMAL RABIES CASES, 1992
(With rankings)

2. Connecticut **838**

1. New York **1,761**

3. New Jersey **726**

9. Kansas **374**

6. California **469**

10. Pennsylvania **361**

5. Texas **471**

4. Maryland **553**

7. Virginia **362**

8. Georgia **367**

Source: U.S. Centers for Disease Control

A I D S

Acquired immune deficiency syndrome (AIDS) was first publicly recognized in 1981. Since then, it has claimed the lives of more than 243,000 Americans. An additional 1 million Americans are estimated to be infected with human immunodeficiency virus (HIV), which causes the disease.

HIV is spread from one person to another through the exchange of body fluids, such as semen and blood. Most people become infected during sexual intercourse. The sharing of drug needles and syringes with infected people is the second most common route of transmission. Infected women can also transmit the virus to their babies during pregnancy or at birth.

HIV-infected people may feel fine and look fine. The virus may reside in their bodies for 10 years or more before AIDS symptoms actually develop. The illness weakens the body's immune system and, therefore, its ability to fight disease. People who have AIDS are vulnerable to "opportunistic diseases." These kinds of diseases are caused by microbes that usually are harmless in people with healthy immune systems. Opportunistic diseases include certain cancers as well as infections of the lungs and brain.

Scientists have not found a cure for AIDS. At present, the disease is fatal. Some drugs, however, fight the opportunistic diseases and help AIDS patients live longer. The drug AZT dramatically reduces HIV transmission from infected women to their babies. Scientists are hard at work trying to develop vaccines that would protect people from getting the disease. This is a difficult challenge, because HIV changes, or mutates, rapidly. In this way, it escapes the killing power of most drugs.

FINGERTIP FACTS

- More than 400,000 people in the U.S. have been diagnosed with AIDS since the disease was first identified.

- More than 243,000 people in the U.S. have died as a result of AIDS.

- AIDS is among the top 10 causes of death in the U.S. It is the leading cause of death of 25- to 44-year-old African-American and Latino men.

- The great majority of people with AIDS live in large cities. In the U.S., New York City has the largest number of AIDS patients.

- In 1994, the U.S. government spent $2.4 billion on AIDS research.

- In the U.S., homosexuals and bisexuals who don't use drugs make up 53% of all adult and adolescent AIDS patients. Drug abusers—both men and women—make up 31% of the total.

- The World Health Organization estimates that 17 million people worldwide have been infected with HIV. By the year 2000, an estimated 30 to 40 million people will have been infected.

- The majority of people infected with HIV are in Africa.

- Worldwide, women are becoming infected as often as men. Most become infected through sexual intercourse with infected men.

- About 25% of HIV-infected women transmit the virus to their babies during pregnancy or at birth.

PROFILE: AGES OF PEOPLE LIVING WITH AIDS

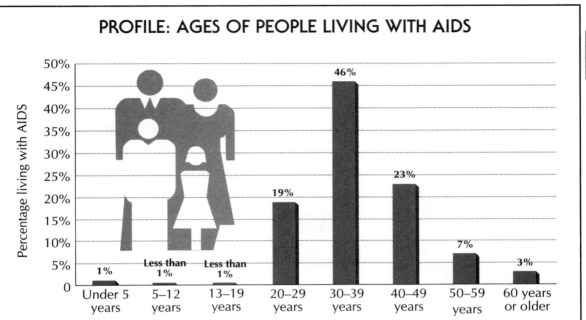

Source: U.S. Centers for Disease Control

PROFILE: MOST COMMON MODES OF AIDS TRANSMISSION

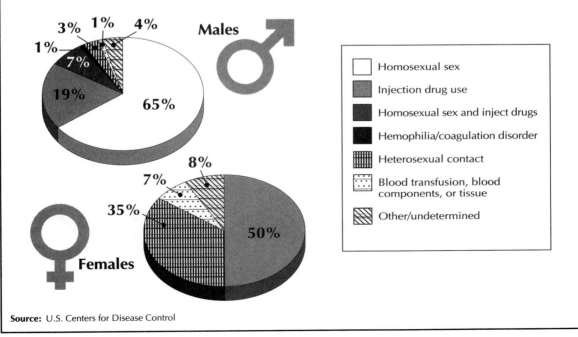

Source: U.S. Centers for Disease Control

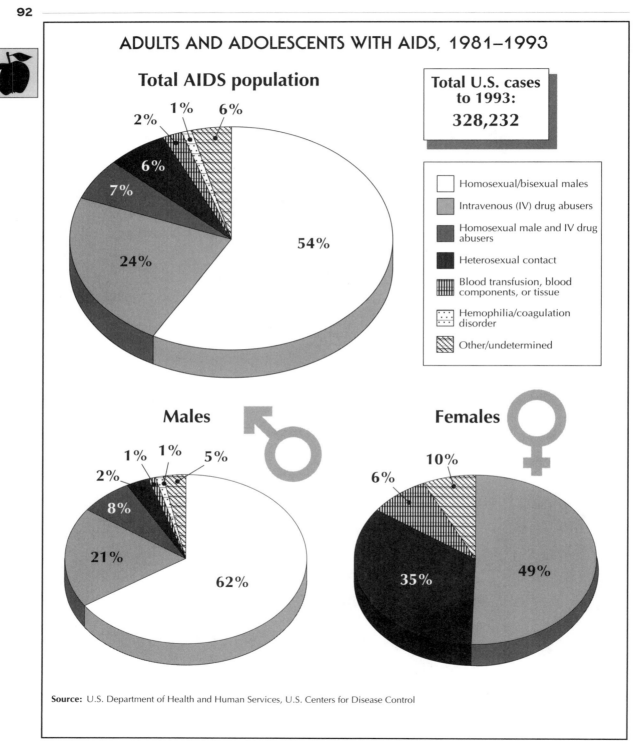

ADULTS AND ADOLESCENTS WITH AIDS, 1981–1993

Total AIDS population

1% 6% 2% 1% 6% 7% 6% 24% 54%

Total U.S. cases to 1993: 328,232

- Homosexual/bisexual males
- Intravenous (IV) drug abusers
- Homosexual male and IV drug abusers
- Heterosexual contact
- Blood transfusion, blood components, or tissue
- Hemophilia/coagulation disorder
- Other/undetermined

Males

1% 1% 5% 2% 8% 21% 62%

Females

10% 6% 35% 49%

Source: U.S. Department of Health and Human Services, U.S. Centers for Disease Control

AIDS CASES AMONG 13- TO 24-YEAR OLDS, 1989 vs. 1992

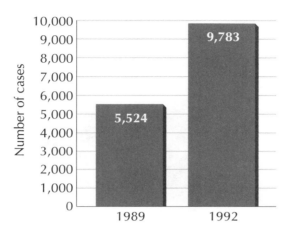

HIV INFECTION AND AIDS IN PEOPLE AGES 13–19, BY SEX AND RACE, 1992

(Percentage of AIDS population by age group)

By sex   **By race**

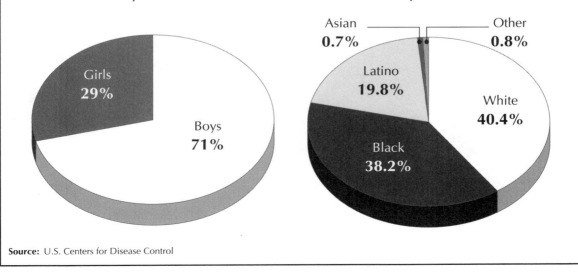

Source: U.S. Centers for Disease Control

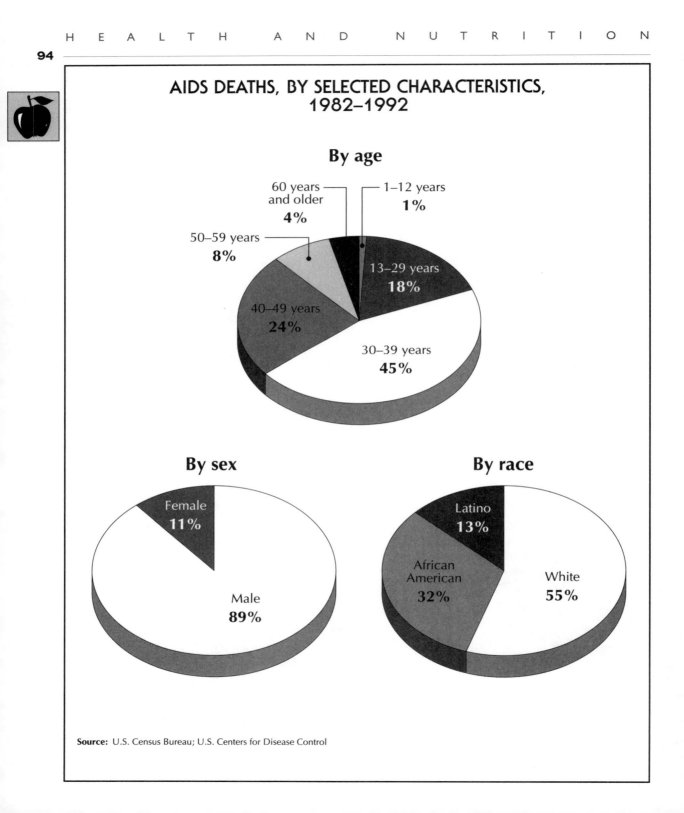

AIDS DEATHS, BY SELECTED CHARACTERISTICS, 1982–1992

By age

1–12 years **1%**

60 years and older **4%**

50–59 years **8%**

40–49 years **24%**

13–29 years **18%**

30–39 years **45%**

By sex

Female **11%**

Male **89%**

By race

Latino **13%**

African American **32%**

White **55%**

Source: U.S. Census Bureau; U.S. Centers for Disease Control

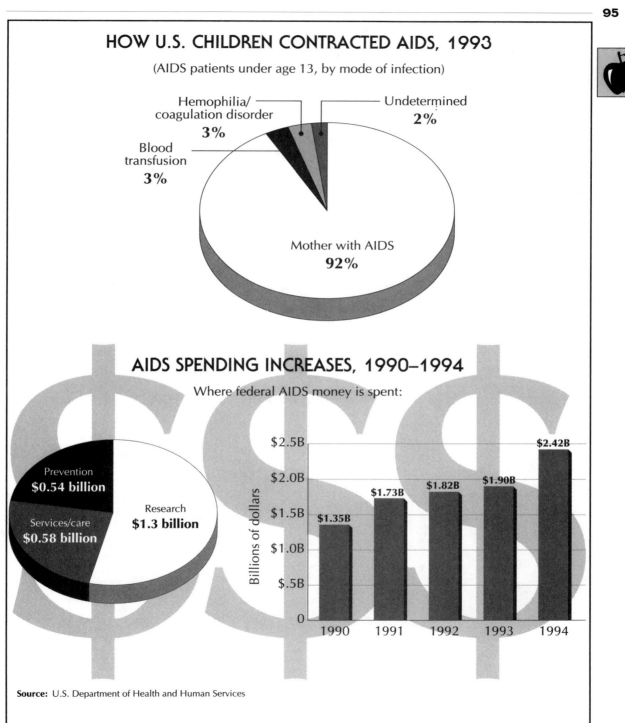

HOW U.S. CHILDREN CONTRACTED AIDS, 1993

(AIDS patients under age 13, by mode of infection)

Hemophilia/
coagulation disorder
3%

Undetermined
2%

Blood
transfusion
3%

Mother with AIDS
92%

AIDS SPENDING INCREASES, 1990–1994

Where federal AIDS money is spent:

Prevention
$0.54 billion

Research
$1.3 billion

Services/care
$0.58 billion

Billions of dollars

$2.5B   **$2.42B**

$2.0B   **$1.82B**   **$1.90B**

$1.73B

$1.5B   **$1.35B**

$1.0B

$.5B

0

1990   1991   1992   1993   1994

Source: U.S. Department of Health and Human Services

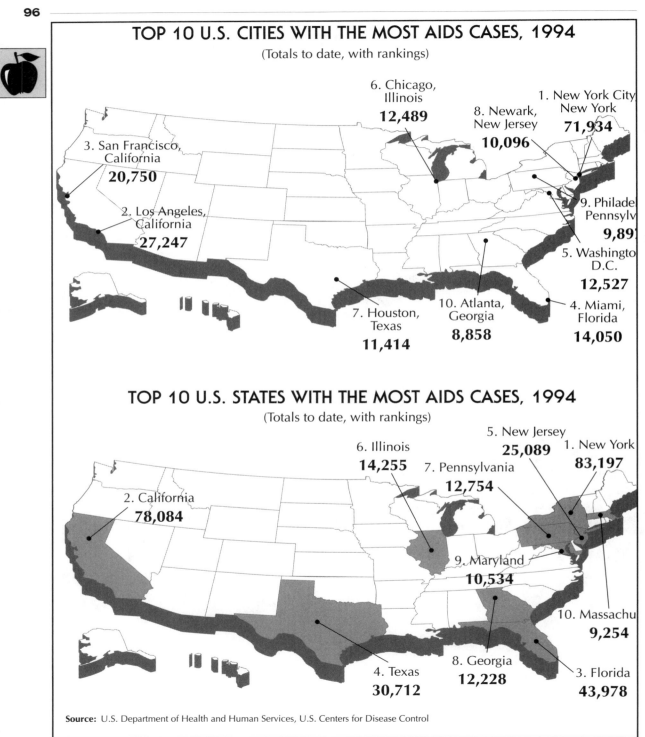

TOP 10 U.S. CITIES WITH THE MOST AIDS CASES, 1994
(Totals to date, with rankings)

6. Chicago, Illinois
12,489

8. Newark, New Jersey
10,096

1. New York City New York
71,934

3. San Francisco, California
20,750

2. Los Angeles, California
27,247

9. Philade Pennsylv
9,89

5. Washingto D.C.
12,527

7. Houston, Texas
11,414

10. Atlanta, Georgia
8,858

4. Miami, Florida
14,050

TOP 10 U.S. STATES WITH THE MOST AIDS CASES, 1994
(Totals to date, with rankings)

5. New Jersey
25,089

1. New York
83,197

6. Illinois
14,255

7. Pennsylvania
12,754

2. California
78,084

9. Maryland
10,534

10. Massachu
9,254

4. Texas
30,712

8. Georgia
12,228

3. Florida
43,978

Source: U.S. Department of Health and Human Services, U.S. Centers for Disease Control

AIDS CASES AND DEATHS IN THE U.S., 1981–1993

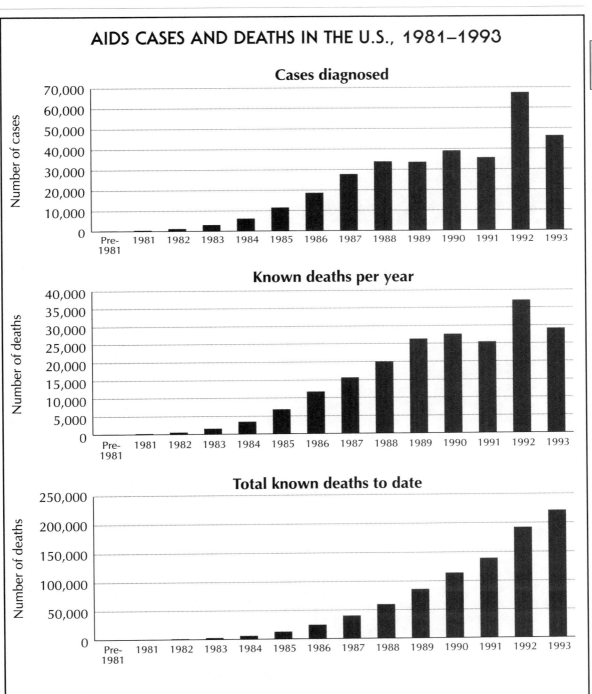

Cases diagnosed

Number of cases

70,000
60,000
50,000
40,000
30,000
20,000
10,000
0

Pre-1981 | 1981 | 1982 | 1983 | 1984 | 1985 | 1986 | 1987 | 1988 | 1989 | 1990 | 1991 | 1992 | 1993

Known deaths per year

Number of deaths

40,000
35,000
30,000
25,000
20,000
15,000
10,000
5,000
0

Pre-1981 | 1981 | 1982 | 1983 | 1984 | 1985 | 1986 | 1987 | 1988 | 1989 | 1990 | 1991 | 1992 | 1993

Total known deaths to date

Number of deaths

250,000
200,000
150,000
100,000
50,000
0

Pre-1981 | 1981 | 1982 | 1983 | 1984 | 1985 | 1986 | 1987 | 1988 | 1989 | 1990 | 1991 | 1992 | 1993

Source: U.S. Department of Health and Human Services, U.S. Centers for Disease Control

A B O R T I O N

Abortion is one of the most controversial issues in the U.S. The purpose of an abortion is to end an unwanted pregnancy. There are many different reasons why women have abortions. Sometimes the pregnant woman's life is in danger. Sometimes a woman does not want to bear a child that is the result of incest or rape. At other times, a woman feels she is unable to accept the tremendous responsibility of having a child.

Abortion is opposed by most major religions, and many countries have laws prohibiting it. In the U.S., however, a 1973 Supreme Court ruling called *Roe v. Wade* formally guaranteed a woman's right to end an unwanted pregnancy through abortion. The Supreme Court reaffirmed this right in 1992.

A normal pregnancy lasts about 9 months. Almost 90% of all abortions are performed within the first 3 months of pregnancy. In 1972, before abortion was legal in the U.S., there were about 587,000 illegal abortions. Today there are about 1.4 million legal abortions a year. The majority of women who have abortions are white, unmarried, and under 25 years of age.

Abortion is a surgical procedure. In the 1980s, however, scientists in France developed a drug, RU-486, that induces abortion if used in the early stages of pregnancy. RU-486 is administered in combination with another drug called prostaglandin. Opponents of abortion pressured the government to keep RU-486 out of the U.S. In 1994, however, the first nationwide study of RU-486—also called mifepristone—began at U.S. clinics under the direction of the Population Council. This may make RU-486 available to American women in 1996.

FINGERTIP FACTS

- In 1992, women under age 20 accounted for 25% of U.S. patients having abortions.

- The Alan Guttmacher Institute estimates that about 25% of U.S. women under age 45 have had at least one abortion.

- There were 339 abortions for every 1,000 live births in the U.S. in 1991.

- Most abortions in the U.S. are performed in clinics that are separate from hospitals, on an outpatient basis.

- Abortion rates vary enormously from state to state. In 1992, there were 46.2 abortions for every 1,000 women ages 15 to 44 in New York, and 4.3 for every 1,000 women of that age group in Wyoming.

- In 1994, only 17% of U.S. counties had a clinic, hospital, or doctor who performed abortions. As a result, many women who wanted abortions had to travel to other parts of the country.

- A study reported in 1994 suggested that women who have abortions may increase their risk of breast cancer.

- In the 1960s, illegal abortions caused about 20% of all U.S. deaths related to pregnancy and childbirth.

- Some abortions are spontaneous; they are called miscarriages or stillbirths. As many as 75% of all conceptions may be spontaneously aborted.

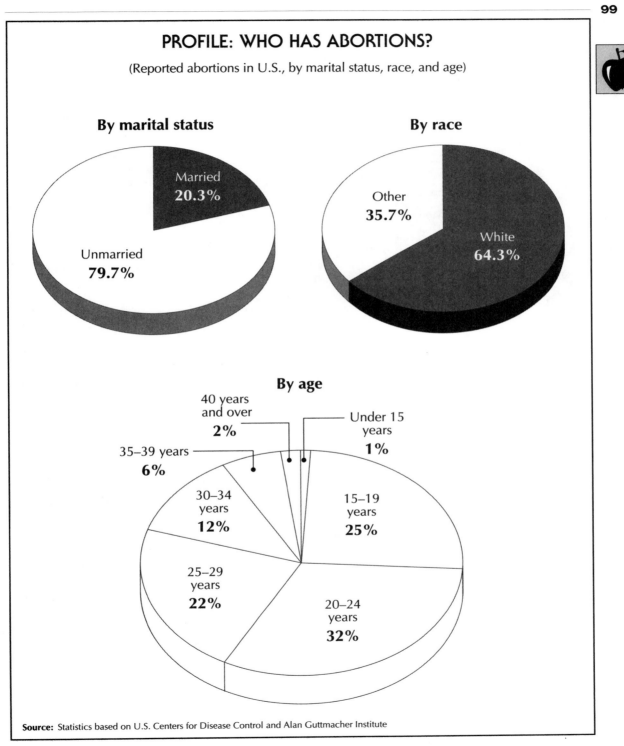

PROFILE: WHO HAS ABORTIONS?

(Reported abortions in U.S., by marital status, race, and age)

By marital status

Married
20.3%

Unmarried
79.7%

By race

Other
35.7%

White
64.3%

By age

40 years
and over
2%

Under 15
years
1%

35–39 years
6%

30–34
years
12%

15–19
years
25%

25–29
years
22%

20–24
years
32%

Source: Statistics based on U.S. Centers for Disease Control and Alan Guttmacher Institute

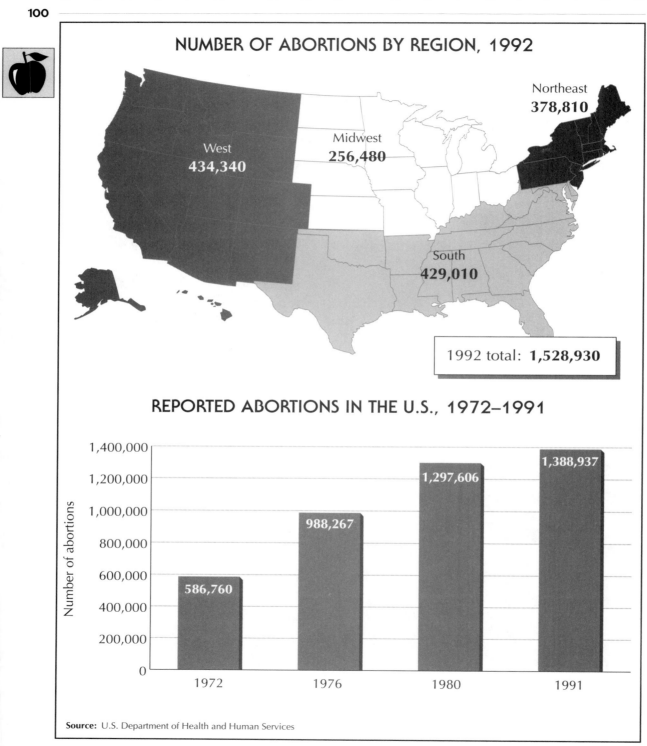

NUMBER OF ABORTIONS BY REGION, 1992

Northeast
378,810

West
434,340

Midwest
256,480

South
429,010

1992 total: **1,528,930**

REPORTED ABORTIONS IN THE U.S., 1972–1991

Number of abortions

- 1,400,000
- 1,200,000
- 1,000,000
- 800,000
- 600,000
- 400,000
- 200,000
- 0

586,760 (1972)
988,267 (1976)
1,297,606 (1980)
1,388,937 (1991)

Source: U.S. Department of Health and Human Services

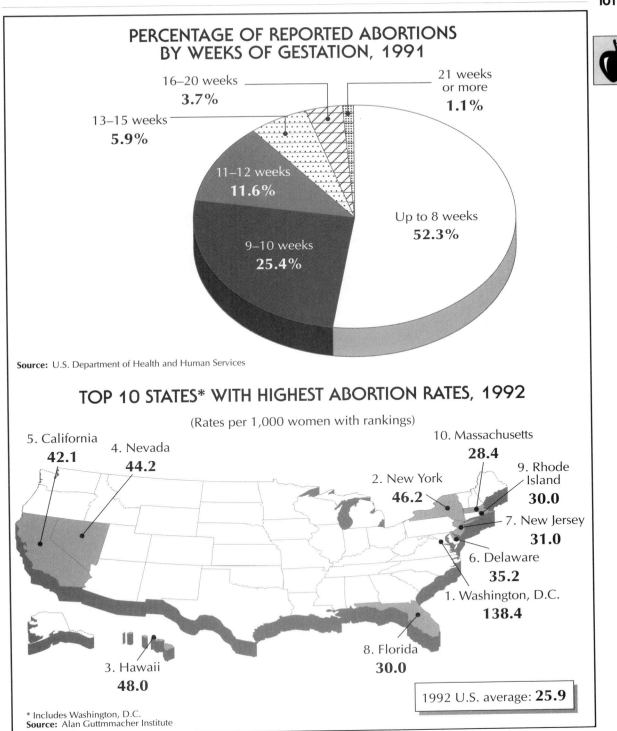

PERCENTAGE OF REPORTED ABORTIONS BY WEEKS OF GESTATION, 1991

16–20 weeks
3.7%

21 weeks or more
1.1%

13–15 weeks
5.9%

11–12 weeks
11.6%

Up to 8 weeks
52.3%

9–10 weeks
25.4%

Source: U.S. Department of Health and Human Services

TOP 10 STATES* WITH HIGHEST ABORTION RATES, 1992

(Rates per 1,000 women with rankings)

5. California
42.1

4. Nevada
44.2

10. Massachusetts
28.4

2. New York
46.2

9. Rhode Island
30.0

7. New Jersey
31.0

6. Delaware
35.2

1. Washington, D.C.
138.4

8. Florida
30.0

3. Hawaii
48.0

1992 U.S. average: **25.9**

* Includes Washington, D.C.
Source: Alan Guttmmacher Institute

2

LIFESTYLES
AND
PASTIMES

SEX AND LOVE

Although they are highly personal parts of our lives, the sexual and romantic habits of America's citizens seem to be a source of never-ending interest. Scientific research—plus anecdotal evidence displayed in tabloids and on TV talk shows—indicates that a number of dramatic sexual behavioral changes have occurred over the past few decades. For example, people are having sexual relations at an earlier age but are marrying later than ever before. Divorce, contraceptive use, unwed motherhood, and homosexuality are no longer taboo subjects; nor, in the minds of many, are they taboo behaviors. Other previously "hidden" issues, including child pornography, rape, spousal violence, and sexual abuse, have come to the forefront of the news and of political debate.

Many myths about the sexual lives of Americans were contradicted in 1994 when a team of researchers based at the University of Chicago released the results of a survey of nearly 3,500 people between the ages of 18 and 59. Among many surprising things, the survey found that married couples actually reported the highest rates of sexual satisfaction—and the most frequent sex. They also found that most married people were faithful to their spouses.

Better understanding of sexual behavior and its consequences affects the lives of individuals as well as the formation of public policy. The growing threat of AIDS, for example, has led to increased monogamy and condom use. Peer pressure among teens to have sex (and even to become pregnant) has also decreased as more teens have become more educated about the realities of sexual relations and its potential consequences.

FINGERTIP FACTS

- The majority of teens ages 12 to 17 say they believe in abstinence. However, before age 18, at least 73% of American boys and 56% of American girls have had intercourse. Fewer than 20% remain virgins throughout their teenage years.

- The number of teenagers who say they have had sex before age 16 is going up. In 1990, some 44% of teens said they had sex by age 16. By 1994, that percentage had risen to 53%.

- People are getting married at a later age. In 1970, the median age at which women first married was 20.8 years; by 1993, it had risen to 24.5 years. The median age for men rose from 23.2 to 26.5 years.

- More children are being born out of wedlock. In 1960, more than 94% were born to married women. By 1990, that percentage had shrunk to 72%.

- Americans are generally monogamous. Almost 75% of married men and 85% of married women report that they are faithful to their spouses.

- The majority of Americans (83%) have one or no sexual partners during a year. Over a lifetime, men average 6 partners, while women average 2.

- The rate of unmarried cohabitation has grown tremendously in the past 2 decades. In 1970, unmarried heterosexual couples made up about 0.5 million households; by 1993, they accounted for 2.6 million households.

PROFILE: HAPPY IN LOVE

(Percentages of married and single people in the U.S. who say their current "significant other" will be their one and only partner for the future)

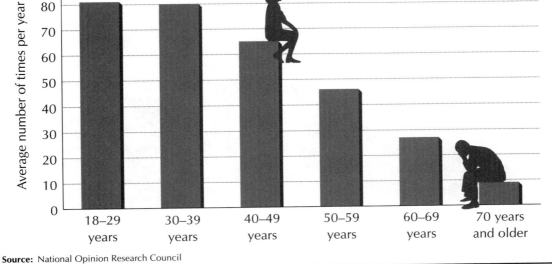

85%

70%

Percentage of partners

Married people

Single people

Source: Based on *USA Today* statistics

SEX THROUGH THE YEARS, BY AGE

(As self-reported, the average number of times U.S. adults have sex per year)

Average number of times per year

18–29 years

30–39 years

40–49 years

50–59 years

60–69 years

70 years and older

Source: National Opinion Research Council

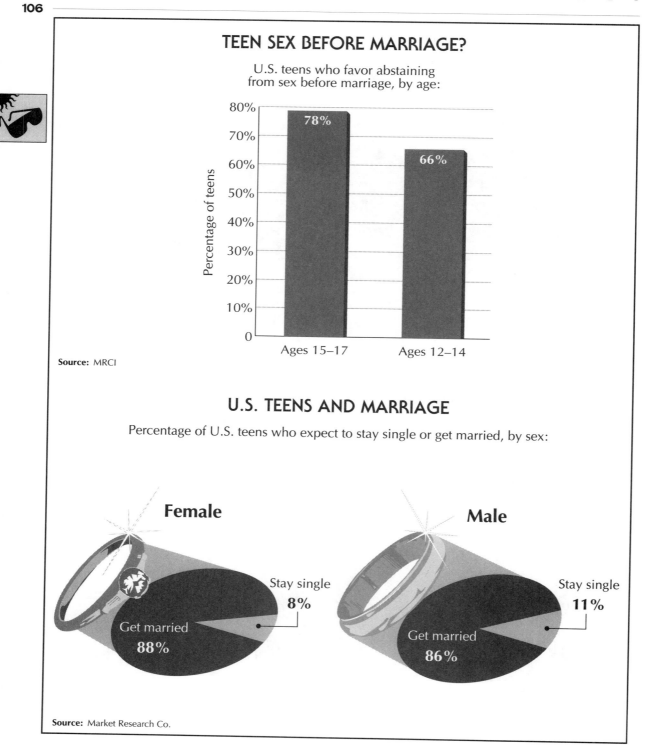

TEEN SEX BEFORE MARRIAGE?

U.S. teens who favor abstaining
from sex before marriage, by age:

Percentage of teens

78%

66%

Ages 15–17   Ages 12–14

Source: MRCI

U.S. TEENS AND MARRIAGE

Percentage of U.S. teens who expect to stay single or get married, by sex:

Female

Stay single
8%

Get married
88%

Male

Stay single
11%

Get married
86%

Source: Market Research Co.

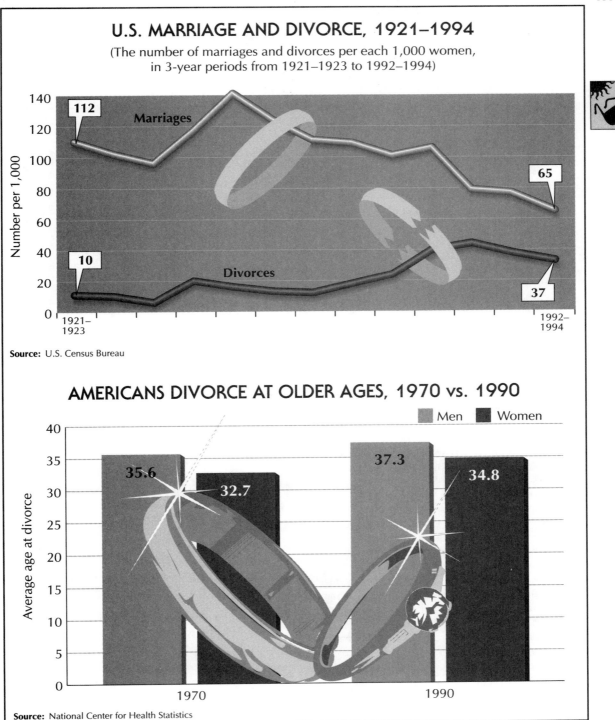

U.S. MARRIAGE AND DIVORCE, 1921–1994
(The number of marriages and divorces per each 1,000 women,
in 3-year periods from 1921–1923 to 1992–1994)

Number per 1,000

112

Marriages

65

10

Divorces

37

1921–1923

1992–1994

Source: U.S. Census Bureau

AMERICANS DIVORCE AT OLDER AGES, 1970 vs. 1990

Men   Women

Average age at divorce

35.6

32.7

37.3

34.8

1970

1990

Source: National Center for Health Statistics

E A T I N G

Food is a major topic of interest for Americans. Through the centuries, eating has evolved from an activity undertaken for biological necessity into one of the nation's most popular—and most social—pastimes. While some people limit food intake to the traditional 3 meals a day, others "graze" their way through life, nibbling, snacking, and dining on everything from abalone steaks to zucchini bread.

Researchers at Rockefeller University estimate that approximately 500 foodstuffs were available to Americans 100 years ago. Today, there are more than 50,000. Advances in agriculture and food processing give us an ever-growing array of fresh, packaged, and prepared items; improved transportation has put fresher strawberries and more exotic mushrooms on menus everywhere year-round.

Eating habits have also changed for economic reasons. Women who in previous generations would have stayed at home now leave for work and thus lack the time to prepare elaborate meals. Although some 60% of all U.S. food sales—more than $320 billion per year—originate in grocery stores, including supermarkets, the remaining 40% is purchased in restaurants and other food-service establishments.

Overconsumption of fats and sugars in American diets has led to obesity, heart disease, and other health problems. But while many Americans gobble down weighty, artery-clogging foods, others have adopted healthier eating habits. Each day, more people are cutting back on red meats, avoiding fatty foods, and turning to vegetarianism and other macrobiotic, or plant-based, diets.

FINGERTIP FACTS

- A typical grocery store in 1928 stocked about 870 items. Super-size supermarkets of the 1990s carry up to 15,000 items.

- A typical trip to the supermarket lasts about 44 minutes; shoppers spend an average of $45.54 per trip.

- The price of eating out varies from place to place. In 1994, a restaurant meal in Atlanta averaged $18.49; in Los Angeles, $22.95; and in New York $29.38.

- People are eating more cheese—consumption has risen from 11.4 pounds per capita in 1970 to 26.0 pounds in 1992. American cheese is the most popular type.

- A 1992 survey estimated that 12.4 million adult Americans were vegetarians, which was more than double the 1985 number of 5.4 million.

- On average, a person consumes about 5 gallons of frozen desserts each year; 63% of this is ice cream.

- Guacamole is America's most popular snack; on Super Bowl Sunday alone, people consume an estimated 12 million pounds of this avocado dip.

- Each year, the typical American child sees about 10,000 food ads on television.

- The U.S. government allots $50,000 to each state annually to teach children about healthy diets and nutrition.

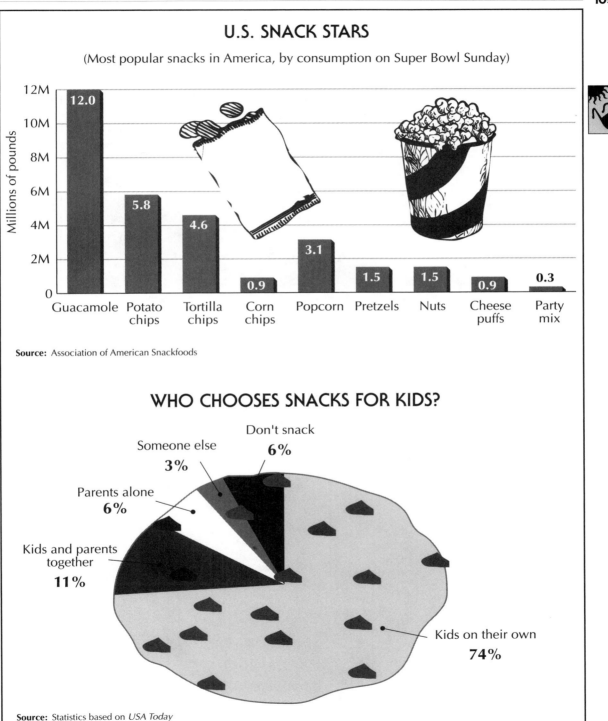

U.S. SNACK STARS

(Most popular snacks in America, by consumption on Super Bowl Sunday)

Millions of pounds

Guacamole	Potato chips	Tortilla chips	Corn chips	Popcorn	Pretzels	Nuts	Cheese puffs	Party mix
12.0	5.8	4.6	0.9	3.1	1.5	1.5	0.9	0.3

Source: Association of American Snackfoods

WHO CHOOSES SNACKS FOR KIDS?

Don't snack
6%

Someone else
3%

Parents alone
6%

Kids and parents together
11%

Kids on their own
74%

Source: Statistics based on *USA Today*

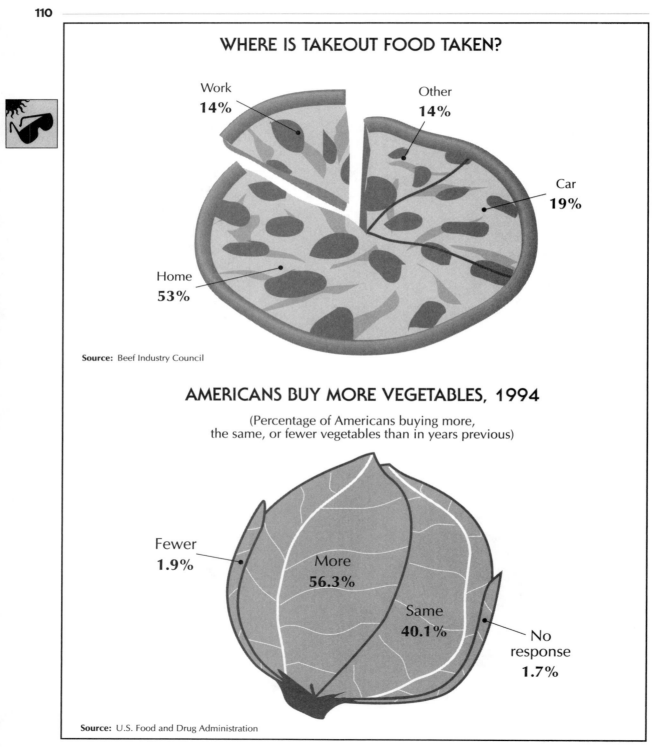

WHERE IS TAKEOUT FOOD TAKEN?

Work
14%

Other
14%

Car
19%

Home
53%

Source: Beef Industry Council

AMERICANS BUY MORE VEGETABLES, 1994

(Percentage of Americans buying more,
the same, or fewer vegetables than in years previous)

Fewer
1.9%

More
56.3%

Same
40.1%

No
response
1.7%

Source: U.S. Food and Drug Administration

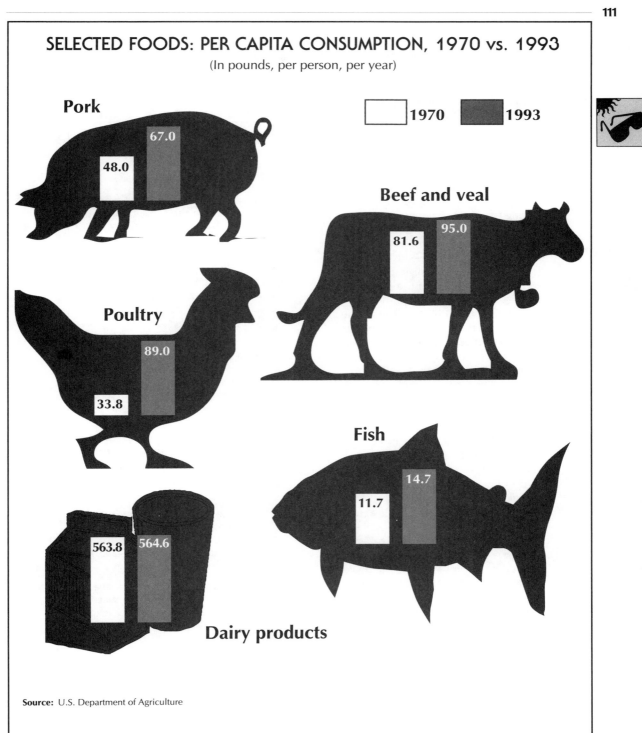

SELECTED FOODS: PER CAPITA CONSUMPTION, 1970 vs. 1993

(In pounds, per person, per year)

Pork

67.0

48.0

1970   1993

Beef and veal

81.6   95.0

Poultry

89.0

33.8

Fish

14.7

11.7

563.8   564.6

Dairy products

Source: U.S. Department of Agriculture

R E L I G I O N

Religion has always been an important part of American life. Today, the most widely practiced religions in America are Judaism, Christianity, and Islam. Additional thousands of Americans are adherents of Far Eastern religions, such as Buddhism, Shintoism, and Taoism.

The percentage of Americans who belong to religious groups has remained relatively stable in recent decades. In 1960, a total of 114.4 million people—64% of the population—belonged to churches and other religious groups; in 1990, a total of 63% of the population—156.3 million—were members. The apparent depth of people's commitment to their religion, however, is less than devout. For instance, fewer than half of Americans attend services 4 or more times a month. Despite their somewhat lax attendance record, Americans are generous when it comes to donations, giving their congregations some $39 billion a year.

In addition to serving as centers of worship and religious education, religious organizations perform a broad range of other functions. Many provide marriage and family counseling, meal services, and alcohol and drug abuse prevention programs.

Rapid social change and other factors have led to numerous changes in traditional religious services, and even to new religious movements. "Mainline" churches, for example, saw their congregations shrink during the 1970s and 1980s as television evangelists drew the faithful to "electronic church" ministries. A small percentage of Americans, many of them young and well educated, have increasingly embraced cults, which have a diverse variety of ideologies and practices.

FINGERTIP FACTS

- In 1980, there were 797 non-profit religious organizations in the U.S.; by 1993, the number had jumped to 1,230.

- Islam is the most rapidly growing religion in the U.S. It currently has about 5 million adherents. About 12% of U.S. Muslims are people of Arab ethnicity; 25% are people of South Asian origin; and 42% are African Americans.

- Some 40.7% of Americans say they attend religious services 4 or more times a month; 46.5% attend less than once a month.

- In a 1994 poll, 20% of Americans said they had had a revelation from God during the previous 12 months; 13% saw or sensed the presence of an angel.

- Revenues of U.S. religious congregations in 1991 totaled an estimated $48.4 billion, of which $39.2 billion came from individuals.

- Of the major religious groups in the U.S., Mormonism has the highest percentage of married members—73.1%; Islam has the most single members—39.0%.

- The highest percentage of Americans who say they are not religious live in the western states; Oregon residents lead, with 17.2% saying they have no religion.

- Roman Catholics make up more than a third of all people in the U.S. who are religiously affiliated.

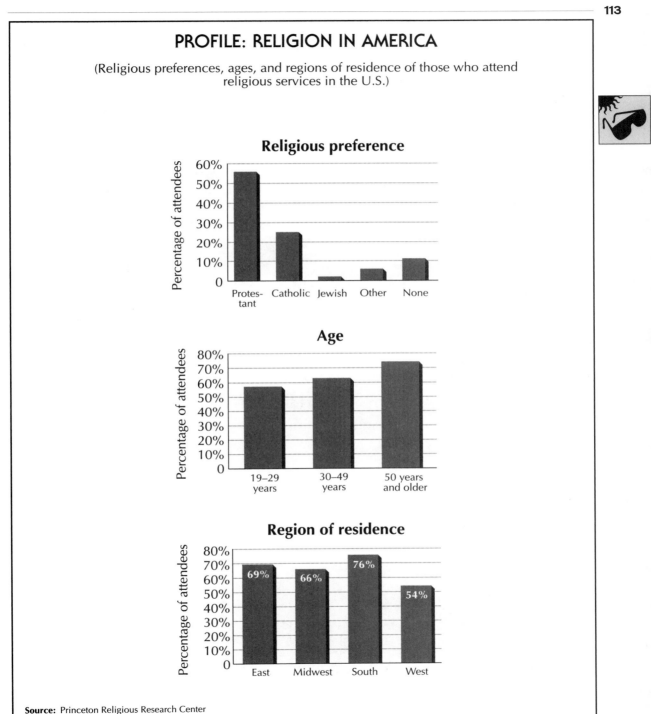

PROFILE: RELIGION IN AMERICA

(Religious preferences, ages, and regions of residence of those who attend religious services in the U.S.)

Religious preference

Percentage of attendees

Protes-tant | Catholic | Jewish | Other | None

Age

Percentage of attendees

19–29 years | 30–49 years | 50 years and older

Region of residence

Percentage of attendees

East 69% | Midwest 66% | South 76% | West 54%

Source: Princeton Religious Research Center

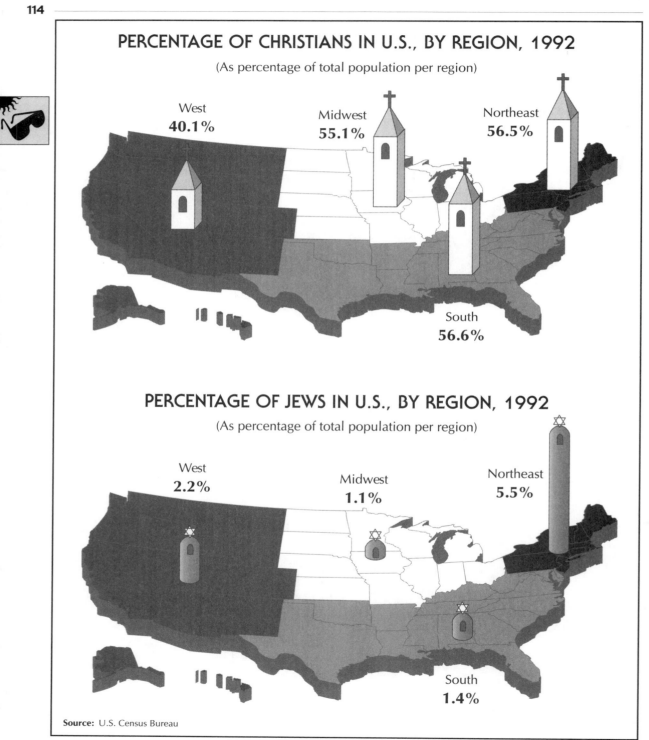

PERCENTAGE OF CHRISTIANS IN U.S., BY REGION, 1992

(As percentage of total population per region)

West
40.1%

Midwest
55.1%

Northeast
56.5%

South
56.6%

PERCENTAGE OF JEWS IN U.S., BY REGION, 1992

(As percentage of total population per region)

West
2.2%

Midwest
1.1%

Northeast
5.5%

South
1.4%

Source: U.S. Census Bureau

MAJOR RELIGIOUS AFFILIATIONS IN THE U.S.
(By percentage of total religiously affiliated population)

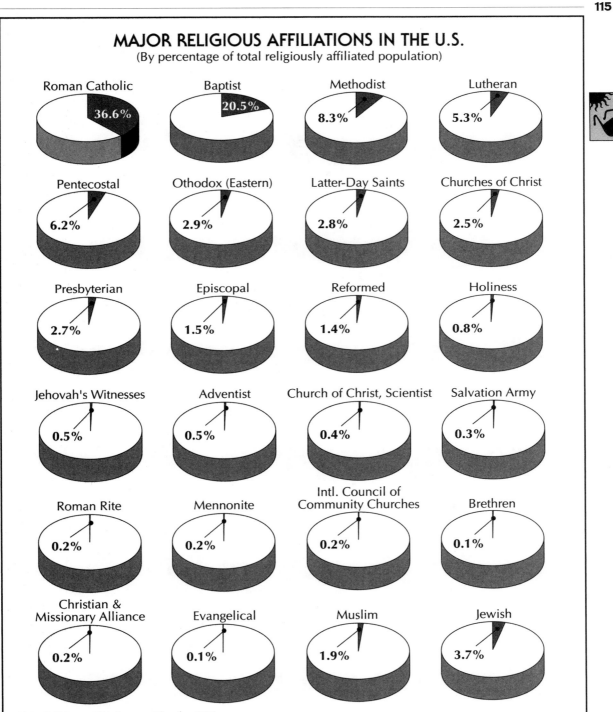

Roman Catholic — 36.6%

Baptist — 20.5%

Methodist — 8.3%

Lutheran — 5.3%

Pentecostal — 6.2%

Othodox (Eastern) — 2.9%

Latter-Day Saints — 2.8%

Churches of Christ — 2.5%

Presbyterian — 2.7%

Episcopal — 1.5%

Reformed — 1.4%

Holiness — 0.8%

Jehovah's Witnesses — 0.5%

Adventist — 0.5%

Church of Christ, Scientist — 0.4%

Salvation Army — 0.3%

Roman Rite — 0.2%

Mennonite — 0.2%

Intl. Council of Community Churches — 0.2%

Brethren — 0.1%

Christian & Missionary Alliance — 0.2%

Evangelical — 0.1%

Muslim — 1.9%

Jewish — 3.7%

Note: Religions not listed represent less than 0.1%
Source: *Yearbook of American and Canadian Churches*

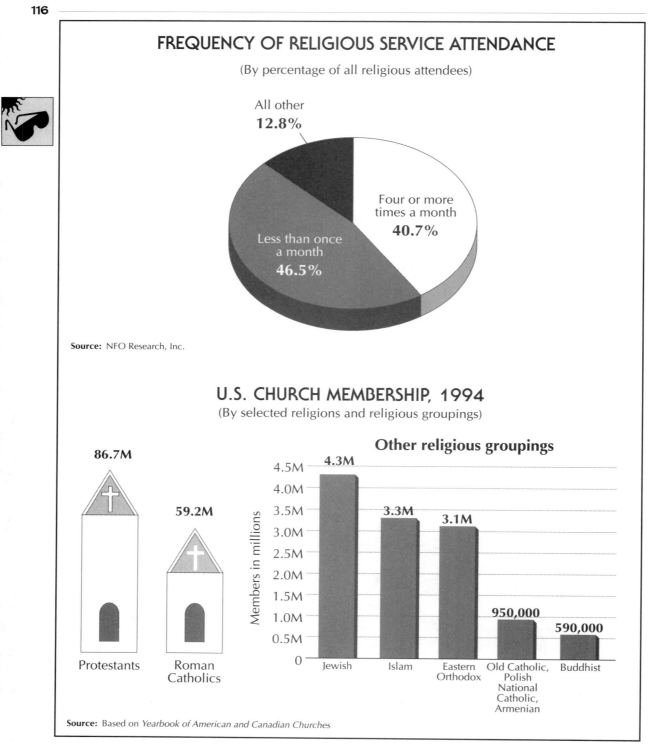

FREQUENCY OF RELIGIOUS SERVICE ATTENDANCE

(By percentage of all religious attendees)

All other
12.8%

Four or more
times a month
40.7%

Less than once
a month
46.5%

Source: NFO Research, Inc.

U.S. CHURCH MEMBERSHIP, 1994

(By selected religions and religious groupings)

86.7M

Protestants

59.2M

Roman
Catholics

Other religious groupings

Members in millions

4.5M — **4.3M**
4.0M
3.5M — **3.3M**
3.0M — **3.1M**
2.5M
2.0M
1.5M
1.0M — **950,000**
0.5M — **590,000**
0

Jewish | Islam | Eastern Orthodox | Old Catholic, Polish National Catholic, Armenian | Buddhist

Source: Based on *Yearbook of American and Canadian Churches*

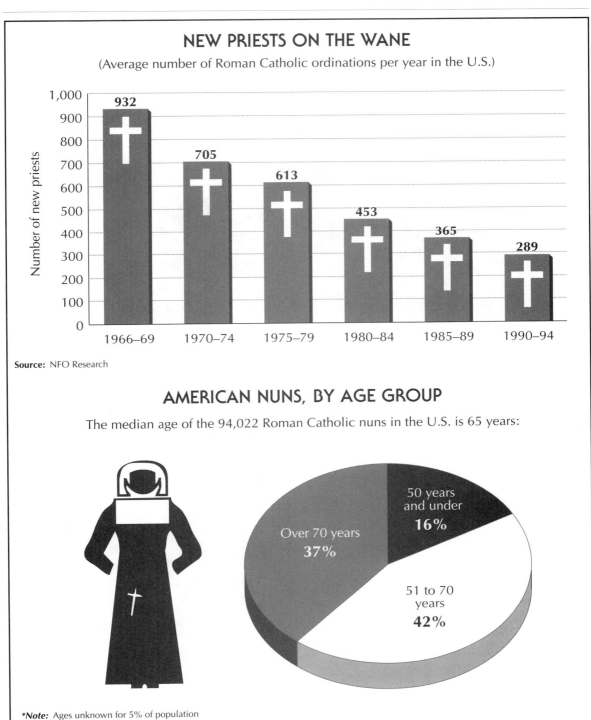

NEW PRIESTS ON THE WANE

(Average number of Roman Catholic ordinations per year in the U.S.)

Number of new priests

932 — 1966–69
705 — 1970–74
613 — 1975–79
453 — 1980–84
365 — 1985–89
289 — 1990–94

Source: NFO Research

AMERICAN NUNS, BY AGE GROUP

The median age of the 94,022 Roman Catholic nuns in the U.S. is 65 years:

Over 70 years **37%**

50 years and under **16%**

51 to 70 years **42%**

Note: Ages unknown for 5% of population
Source: *The Los Angeles Times*

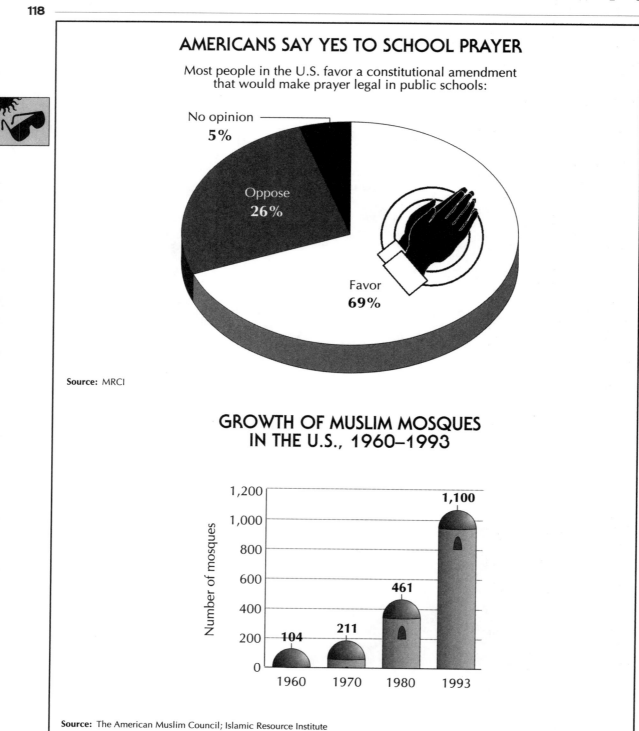

AMERICANS SAY YES TO SCHOOL PRAYER

Most people in the U.S. favor a constitutional amendment
that would make prayer legal in public schools:

No opinion
5%

Oppose
26%

Favor
69%

Source: MRCI

GROWTH OF MUSLIM MOSQUES
IN THE U.S., 1960–1993

Number of mosques

1,200

1,000

800

600

400

200

0

104 — 1960

211 — 1970

461 — 1980

1,100 — 1993

Source: The American Muslim Council; Islamic Resource Institute

TOP 10 U.S. STATES WITH HIGHEST MUSLIM POPULATION
(With rankings)

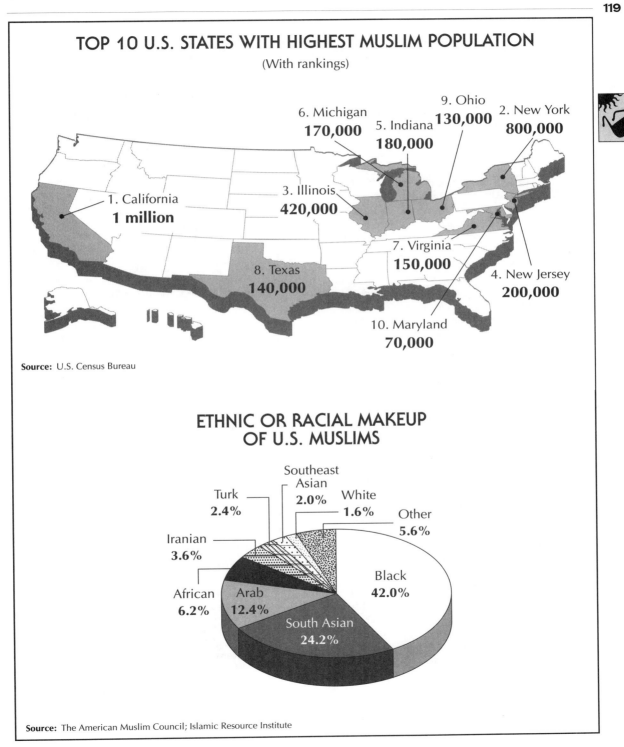

6. Michigan
170,000

5. Indiana
180,000

9. Ohio
130,000

2. New York
800,000

1. California
1 million

3. Illinois
420,000

7. Virginia
150,000

8. Texas
140,000

4. New Jersey
200,000

10. Maryland
70,000

Source: U.S. Census Bureau

ETHNIC OR RACIAL MAKEUP OF U.S. MUSLIMS

Southeast Asian
2.0%

White
1.6%

Turk
2.4%

Other
5.6%

Iranian
3.6%

African
6.2%

Arab
12.4%

South Asian
24.2%

Black
42.0%

Source: The American Muslim Council; Islamic Resource Institute

DAILY LIFE

Not too long ago, nuclear families were the norm in America; mom spent the day at home cooking and cleaning, shopping was done in small neighborhood stores, and everyone gathered around the dinner table at night. Today, many families are headed by single parents; mothers often work outside the home, shopping is done in malls and megastores, or via phone, computer, or mail; and only 22% of American families say they eat together every night.

Fathers are now taking a more active role in caring for their children, but the majority of young American children are cared for outside their own homes during at least part of the day, either in another home, at a day care center, or at a parent's workplace. Only 35% of children today are cared for primarily in their own home. School-age children, however, still find their parents peeking over their shoulders; 44% of parents say they spend 5 hours or more each week helping children with schoolwork.

Economic status affects people's daily lives enormously. Insufficient income limits the choices people can make about where they live and how they live. Poverty was defined in 1993 as an income of $14,763 for a family of 4. By this standard, poverty afflicted some 39.3 million Americans in that year. Blacks had the highest poverty rate, and poverty was higher in rural areas than urban areas. Many of the nation's poor are children. In 1992, the number of U.S. children under age 6 who were living in poverty reached a record high of 6 million, or 26% of that age group.

FINGERTIP FACTS

- Only 31% of Americans get an average of 8 or more hours of sleep each night; 38% get 6 hours or less.

- The percentage of fathers who look after their children, ages 5 and under, increased from 14.4% in 1977 to 20.0% in 1991.

- People are getting more mail. In 1983, the U.S. Postal Service handled 119.4 billion pieces of mail; by 1993, the figure had risen to 171.1 billion.

- Some 13.5 billion merchandise catalogs were mailed to American consumers in 1992—that's 54 catalogs for every man, woman, and child in America.

- Saturday is America's favorite shopping day; Friday ranks a close second.

- Cable shopping channels and "cybermalls" (on-line computer shopping services) are beginning to compete with stores and mail-order catalogs. More than 60 million Americans had access to cable shopping networks at the beginning of 1995; about 25 million had access to on-line services.

- American women outrank men more than two to one as the primary buyers of men's clothes.

- In 1987, there were 1.2 million subscribers to cellular telephone systems; by 1993, there were 16.0 million.

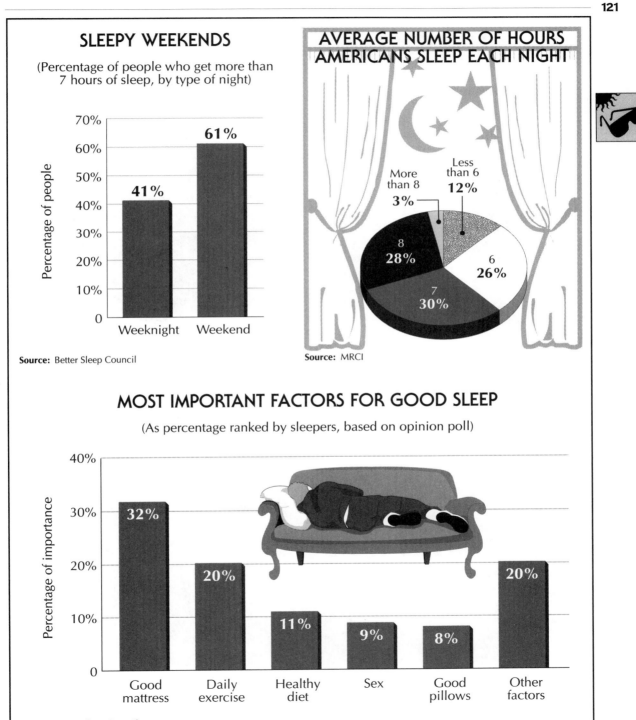

SLEEPY WEEKENDS

(Percentage of people who get more than
7 hours of sleep, by type of night)

Source: Better Sleep Council

AVERAGE NUMBER OF HOURS AMERICANS SLEEP EACH NIGHT

Source: MRCI

MOST IMPORTANT FACTORS FOR GOOD SLEEP

(As percentage ranked by sleepers, based on opinion poll)

Source: Better Sleep Council

U.S. MEN TAKE INCREASED ROLE IN CHILD CARE

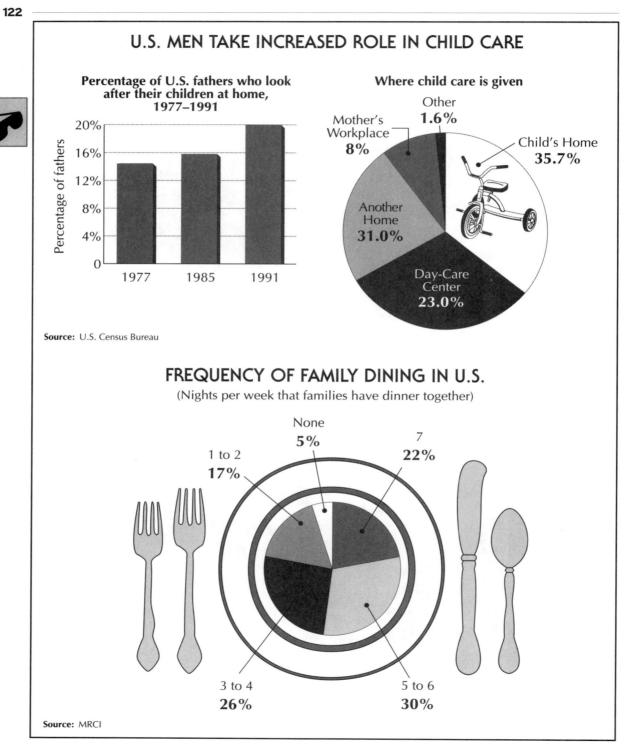

Percentage of U.S. fathers who look after their children at home, 1977–1991

Percentage of fathers

20%
16%
12%
8%
4%
0

1977 1985 1991

Where child care is given

Other **1.6%**

Mother's Workplace **8%**

Child's Home **35.7%**

Another Home **31.0%**

Day-Care Center **23.0%**

Source: U.S. Census Bureau

FREQUENCY OF FAMILY DINING IN U.S.

(Nights per week that families have dinner together)

None **5%**

1 to 2 **17%**

7 **22%**

3 to 4 **26%**

5 to 6 **30%**

Source: MRCI

WHO TAKES CARE OF U.S. CHILDREN?

(Living arrangements, by primary caregiver, of the 66 million children in the U.S.)

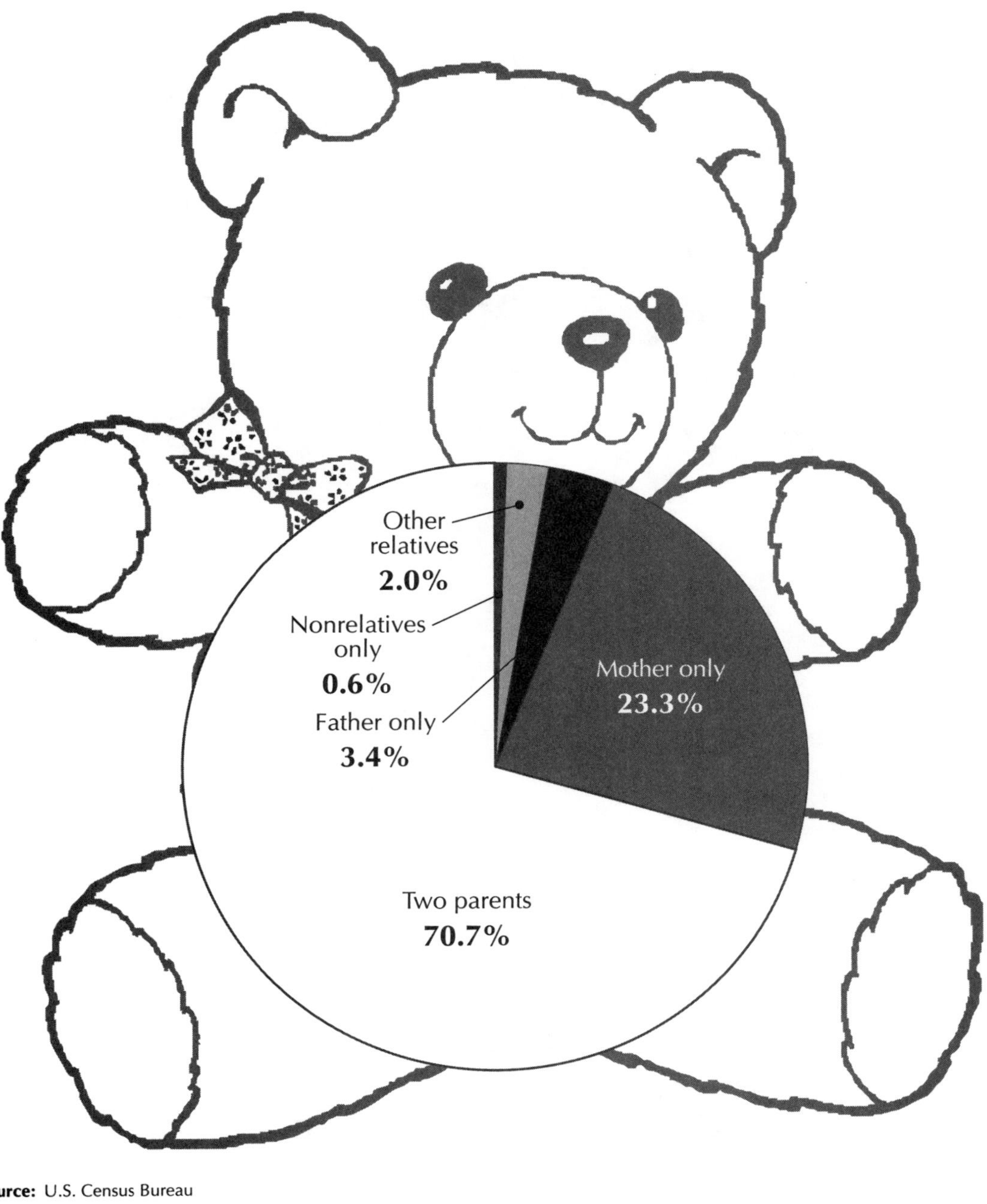

Other relatives
2.0%

Nonrelatives only
0.6%

Father only
3.4%

Mother only
23.3%

Two parents
70.7%

Source: U.S. Census Bureau

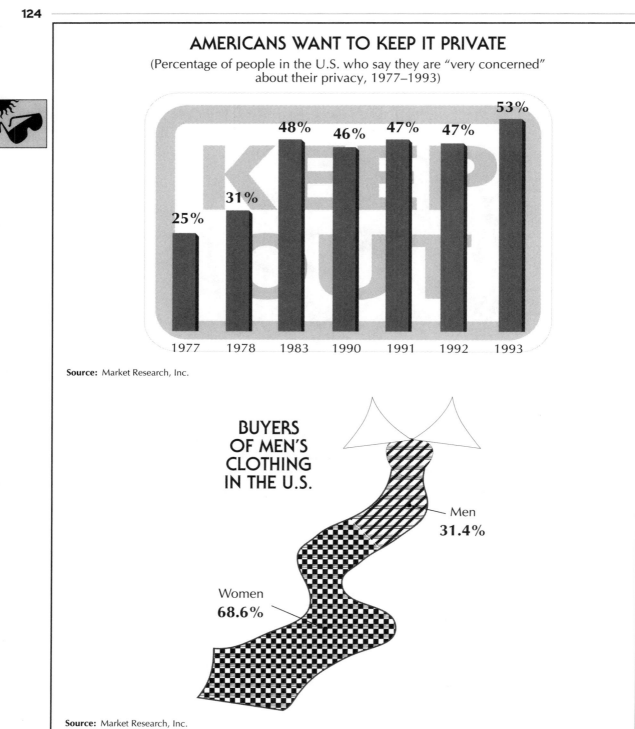

AMERICANS WANT TO KEEP IT PRIVATE

(Percentage of people in the U.S. who say they are "very concerned"
about their privacy, 1977–1993)

25% 1977
31% 1978
48% 1983
46% 1990
47% 1991
47% 1992
53% 1993

Source: Market Research, Inc.

BUYERS OF MEN'S CLOTHING IN THE U.S.

Men
31.4%

Women
68.6%

Source: Market Research, Inc.

U.S. MAIL STORM

Mailings in the U.S. have increased by more than 40% over the past decade.
Pieces of mail, in billions:

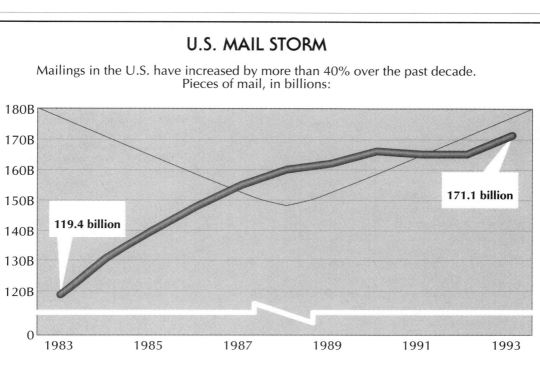

119.4 billion

171.1 billion

MUCH MORE MAIL

(Number of merchandise catalogs mailed to U.S. consumers, in billions)

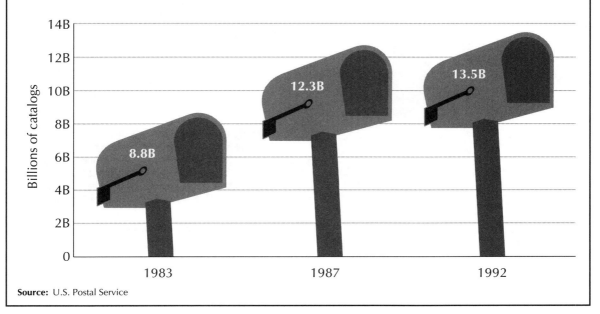

Source: U.S. Postal Service

HOME LIFE

There were some 96.4 million households in the U.S. in 1993. The typical occupants of those households, however, are constantly changing. The number of homes occupied by people living alone has increased, for instance, but most home-buyers are married.

Most households today are equipped with high-tech appliances that were unheard of only a few decades ago. As recently as 1960, for example, 16.8% of all housing units lacked complete plumbing facilities, and 21.5% did not have a telephone. By 1990, only 1.1% lacked complete plumbing facilities, and only 5.2% were without telephones. Nearly all of today's homes have refrigerators (97.2%), and most have clothes washers (76.3%), dishwashers (45.4%), microwave ovens (78.8%), freezers (32.4%), and many other conveniences.

Types of homes vary with income levels. People with limited incomes can apply to live in low-income public housing; 1,199,400 such units were occupied in 1992, an increase from 893,500 in 1970. Sadly, there also is a significant and growing homeless population in America; families with young children make up the fastest-growing component of that troubling problem.

In 1993, there were 68.1 million families in the U.S.; 33.0 million had children under age 18. The percentage of married-couple families has declined over the years, from 86.9% of all family households in 1970 to 78.0% in 1993. Meanwhile, the family households headed by women has increased, from 10.7% of all family households in 1970 to 17.5%—a total of 11.9 million—in 1993. Among black families, 46.7% were headed by women.

FINGERTIP FACTS

- Most American households in 1993 were occupied by couples: 26% with children younger than age 18 and 30% without children under 18.

- People living alone comprised 25.1% of households; single mothers with children younger than 18 made up 7.4%.

- The percentage of people living alone has increased—from 17.1% of households in 1970 to 25.1% in 1992.

- Renters move more frequently than homeowners; 34.3% of renters change residence during a year, as contrasted with 8.9% of homeowners.

- Most of America's 66 million children—some 70.7%—live with both parents; 23.3% live only with their mother and 3.3% live only with their father.

- Family homelessness has sharply increased. A 1993 survey of 26 cities indicated that 43% of the urban homeless were families, up from 32% in 1988. Of the homeless, 30% were children in 1993, up from 25% in 1988.

- In 1970, the median sales price of a new single-family house was $23,400. In 1993, it was more than 5 times higher, at $126,500. In both years, prices were highest in the Northeast and lowest in the South.

PROFILE: U.S. HOUSEHOLDS

Composition of U.S. households, 1970 vs. 1993

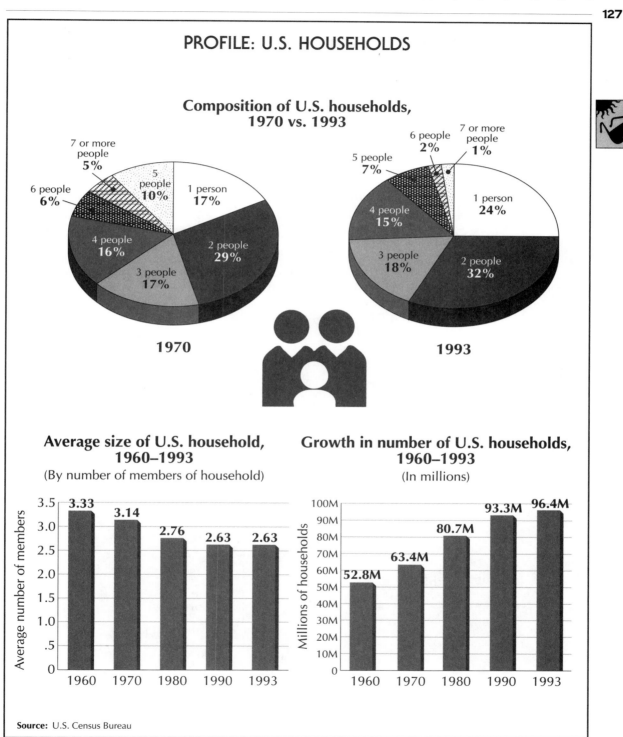

1970

7 or more people **5%**
6 people **6%**
5 people **10%**
4 people **16%**
3 people **17%**
2 people **29%**
1 person **17%**

1993

6 people **2%**
7 or more people **1%**
5 people **7%**
4 people **15%**
3 people **18%**
2 people **32%**
1 person **24%**

Average size of U.S. household, 1960–1993

(By number of members of household)

Average number of members

- 1960: 3.33
- 1970: 3.14
- 1980: 2.76
- 1990: 2.63
- 1993: 2.63

Growth in number of U.S. households, 1960–1993

(In millions)

Millions of households

- 1960: 52.8M
- 1970: 63.4M
- 1980: 80.7M
- 1990: 93.3M
- 1993: 96.4M

Source: U.S. Census Bureau

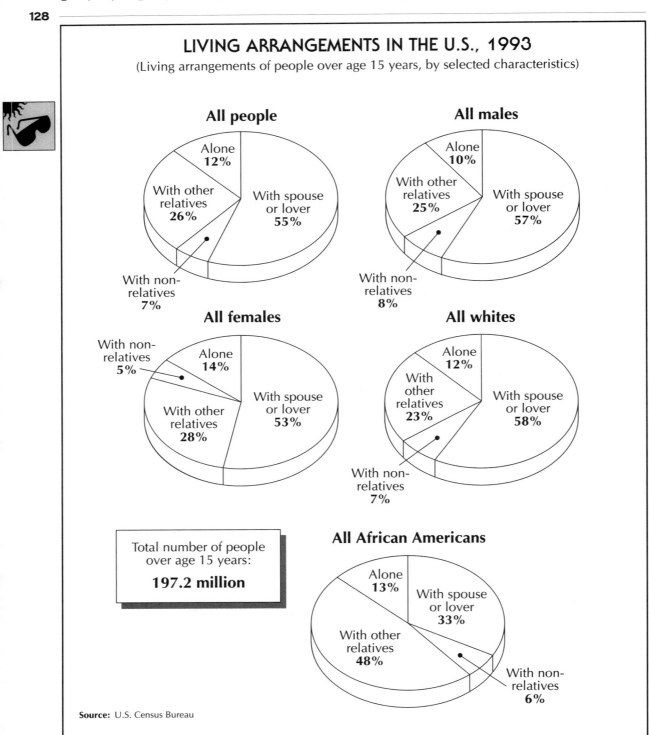

LIVING ARRANGEMENTS IN THE U.S., 1993
(Living arrangements of people over age 15 years, by selected characteristics)

All people
- Alone 12%
- With other relatives 26%
- With spouse or lover 55%
- With non-relatives 7%

All males
- Alone 10%
- With other relatives 25%
- With spouse or lover 57%
- With non-relatives 8%

All females
- With non-relatives 5%
- Alone 14%
- With other relatives 28%
- With spouse or lover 53%

All whites
- Alone 12%
- With other relatives 23%
- With spouse or lover 58%
- With non-relatives 7%

Total number of people over age 15 years: **197.2 million**

All African Americans
- Alone 13%
- With spouse or lover 33%
- With other relatives 48%
- With non-relatives 6%

Source: U.S. Census Bureau

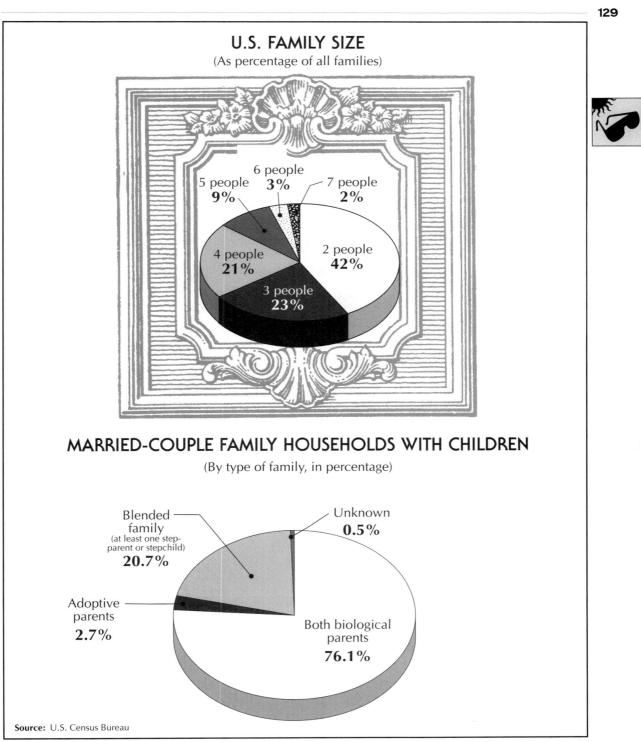

U.S. FAMILY SIZE
(As percentage of all families)

6 people **3%**

5 people **9%**

7 people **2%**

4 people **21%**

2 people **42%**

3 people **23%**

MARRIED-COUPLE FAMILY HOUSEHOLDS WITH CHILDREN
(By type of family, in percentage)

Blended family
(at least one step-parent or stepchild)
20.7%

Unknown **0.5%**

Adoptive parents **2.7%**

Both biological parents **76.1%**

Source: U.S. Census Bureau

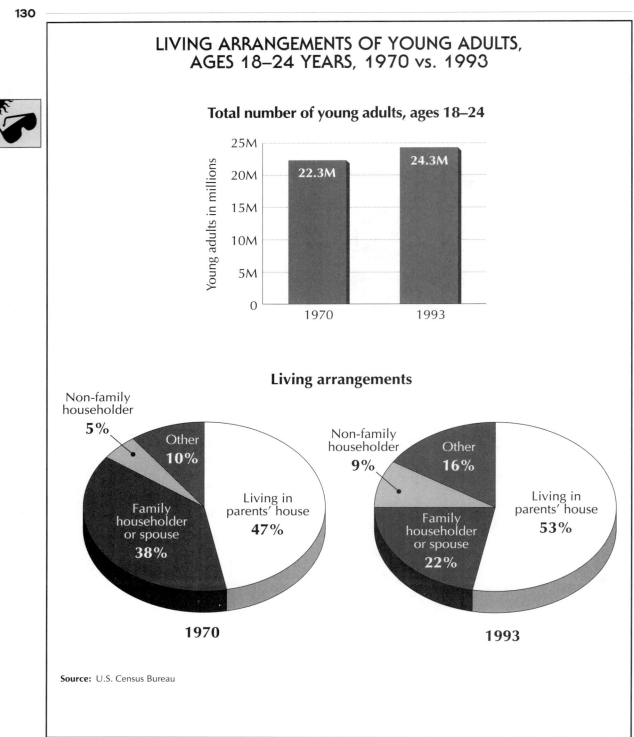

LIVING ARRANGEMENTS OF YOUNG ADULTS, AGES 18–24 YEARS, 1970 vs. 1993

Total number of young adults, ages 18–24

Young adults in millions

22.3M   24.3M

1970   1993

Living arrangements

1970

Non-family householder 5%

Other 10%

Family householder or spouse 38%

Living in parents' house 47%

1993

Non-family householder 9%

Other 16%

Family householder or spouse 22%

Living in parents' house 53%

Source: U.S. Census Bureau

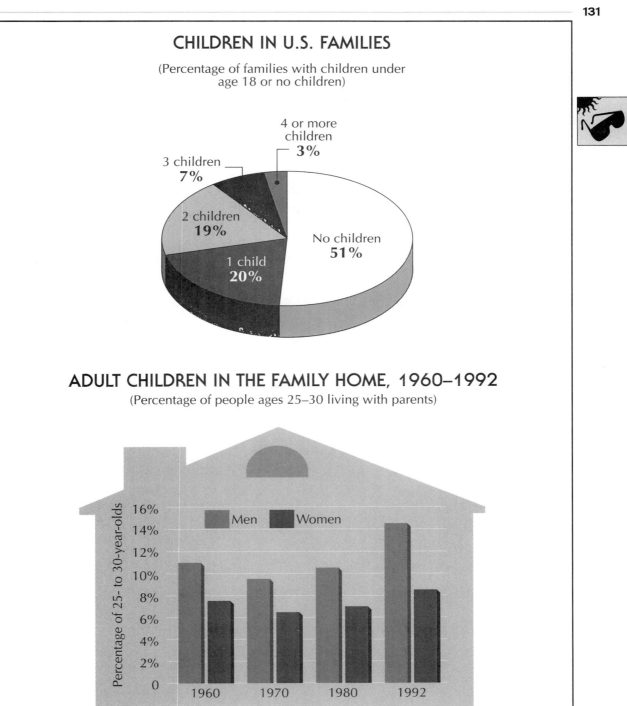

CHILDREN IN U.S. FAMILIES

(Percentage of families with children under
age 18 or no children)

4 or more
children
3%

3 children
7%

2 children
19%

1 child
20%

No children
51%

ADULT CHILDREN IN THE FAMILY HOME, 1960–1992

(Percentage of people ages 25–30 living with parents)

Percentage of 25- to 30-year-olds

16%
14%
12%
10%
8%
6%
4%
2%
0

Men   Women

1960   1970   1980   1992

Source: U.S. Census Bureau

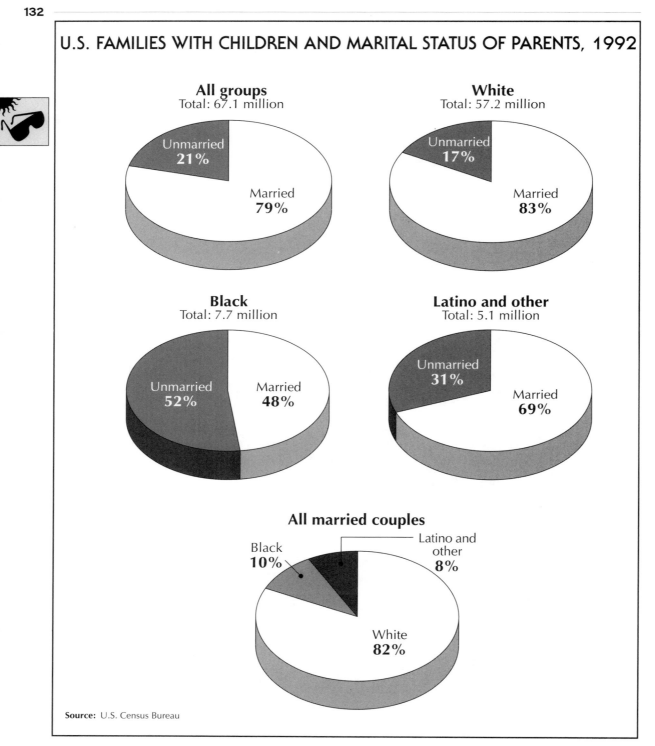

U.S. FAMILIES WITH CHILDREN AND MARITAL STATUS OF PARENTS, 1992

All groups
Total: 67.1 million

Unmarried
21%

Married
79%

White
Total: 57.2 million

Unmarried
17%

Married
83%

Black
Total: 7.7 million

Unmarried
52%

Married
48%

Latino and other
Total: 5.1 million

Unmarried
31%

Married
69%

All married couples

Black
10%

Latino and
other
8%

White
82%

Source: U.S. Census Bureau

U.S. CHILDREN IN BLENDED FAMILIES

(In millions)

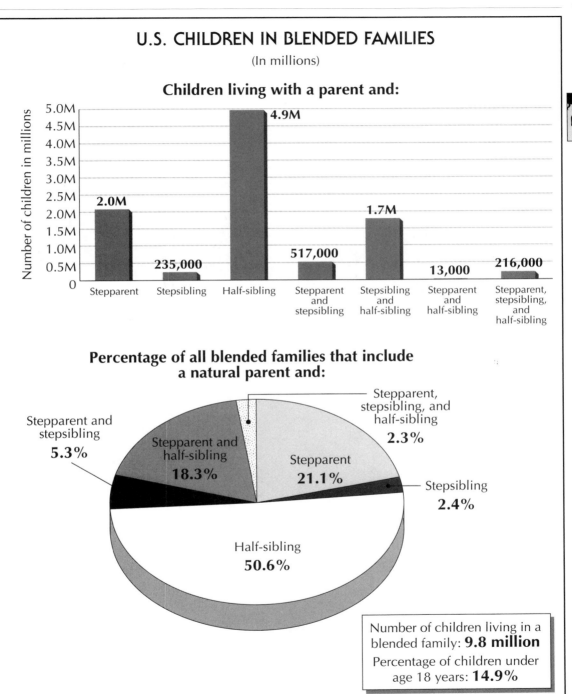

Children living with a parent and:

- Stepparent: **2.0M**
- Stepsibling: **235,000**
- Half-sibling: **4.9M**
- Stepparent and stepsibling: **517,000**
- Stepsibling and half-sibling: **1.7M**
- Stepparent and half-sibling: **13,000**
- Stepparent, stepsibling, and half-sibling: **216,000**

Percentage of all blended families that include a natural parent and:

- Stepparent and stepsibling **5.3%**
- Stepparent and half-sibling **18.3%**
- Stepparent, stepsibling, and half-sibling **2.3%**
- Stepparent **21.1%**
- Stepsibling **2.4%**
- Half-sibling **50.6%**

Number of children living in a blended family: **9.8 million**

Percentage of children under age 18 years: **14.9%**

Source: U.S. Census Bureau; U.S. Department of Commerce

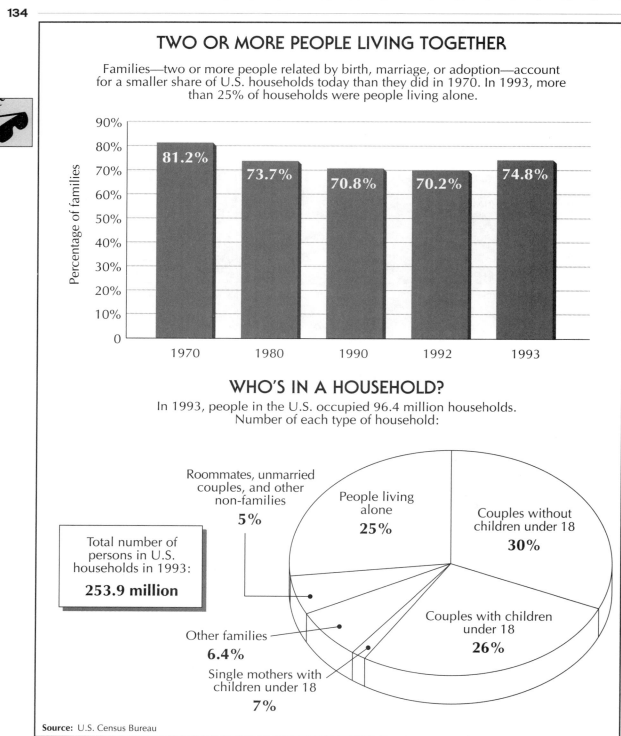

TWO OR MORE PEOPLE LIVING TOGETHER

Families—two or more people related by birth, marriage, or adoption—account for a smaller share of U.S. households today than they did in 1970. In 1993, more than 25% of households were people living alone.

Percentage of families

1970	1980	1990	1992	1993
81.2%	73.7%	70.8%	70.2%	74.8%

WHO'S IN A HOUSEHOLD?

In 1993, people in the U.S. occupied 96.4 million households.
Number of each type of household:

Roommates, unmarried couples, and other non-families
5%

People living alone
25%

Couples without children under 18
30%

Total number of persons in U.S. households in 1993:
253.9 million

Couples with children under 18
26%

Other families
6.4%

Single mothers with children under 18
7%

Source: U.S. Census Bureau

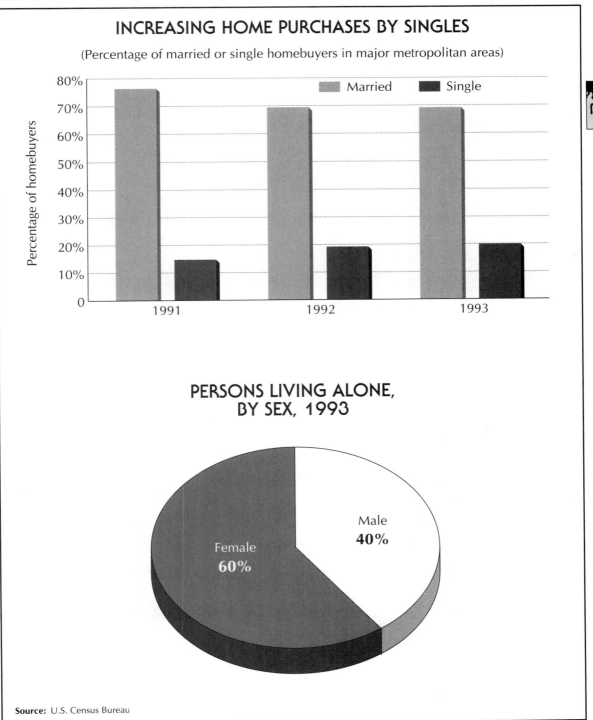

INCREASING HOME PURCHASES BY SINGLES

(Percentage of married or single homebuyers in major metropolitan areas)

Legend: Married, Single

Y-axis: Percentage of homebuyers (0, 10%, 20%, 30%, 40%, 50%, 60%, 70%, 80%)

X-axis: 1991, 1992, 1993

PERSONS LIVING ALONE,
BY SEX, 1993

Female 60%

Male 40%

Source: U.S. Census Bureau

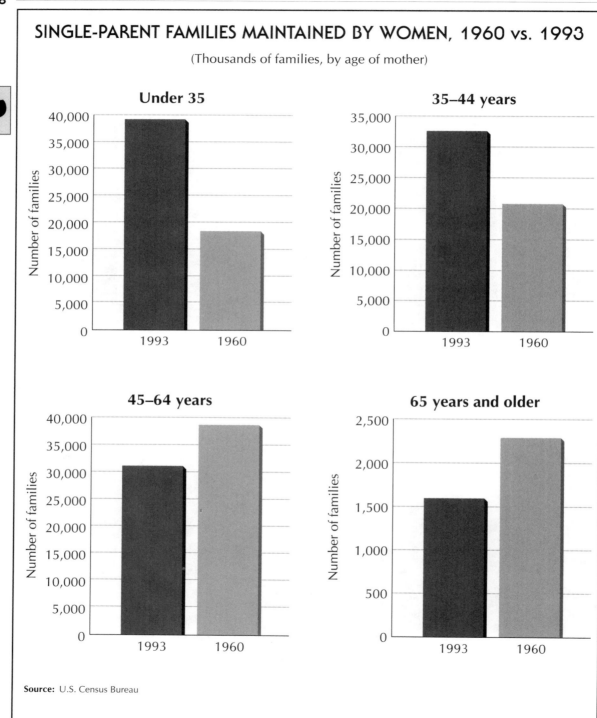

SINGLE-PARENT FAMILIES MAINTAINED BY WOMEN, 1960 vs. 1993

(Thousands of families, by age of mother)

Source: U.S. Census Bureau

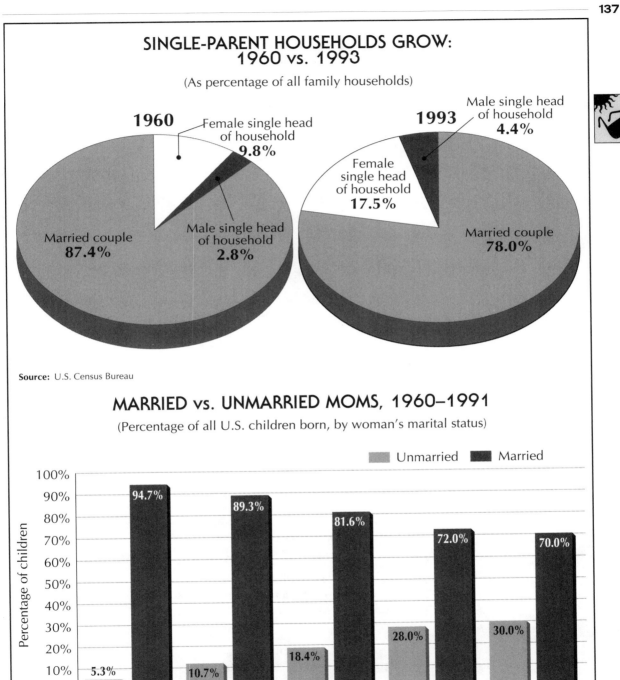

SINGLE-PARENT HOUSEHOLDS GROW:
1960 vs. 1993

(As percentage of all family households)

1960

Female single head of household
9.8%

Married couple
87.4%

Male single head of household
2.8%

1993

Male single head of household
4.4%

Female single head of household
17.5%

Married couple
78.0%

Source: U.S. Census Bureau

MARRIED vs. UNMARRIED MOMS, 1960–1991

(Percentage of all U.S. children born, by woman's marital status)

Unmarried   Married

Percentage of children

Year	Unmarried	Married
1960	5.3%	94.7%
1970	10.7%	89.3%
1980	18.4%	81.6%
1990	28.0%	72.0%
1991	30.0%	70.0%

Source: U.S. Census Bureau; U.S. Bureau of Labor Statistics

AT A GLANCE

Violence at home

More than **18%** of American women say they've been physically abused by a husband or boyfriend

For every 100 instances of violent victimization reported by men, the number reported by women: **132**

Days of hospitalization every year in the United States due to domestic violence: **100,000**

Visits to emergency rooms: **30,000**
Visits to a physician: **40,000**

Percentage of Americans who think women sometimes deserve to be hit by their husbands or boyfriends: **12%**

Percentage of Americans who believe men sometimes deserve to be hit by their wives or girlfriends: **39%**

An estimated **1.15 million** American women have been victims of one or more rapes by their husbands.

Male-on-female assaults with weapons: **25%** of all such assaults
Female-on-male assaults: **86%**

Source: Based on statistics from *U.S. News & World Report*

CHILD NEGLECT AND ABUSE CASES REPORTED IN U.S., 1980–1992

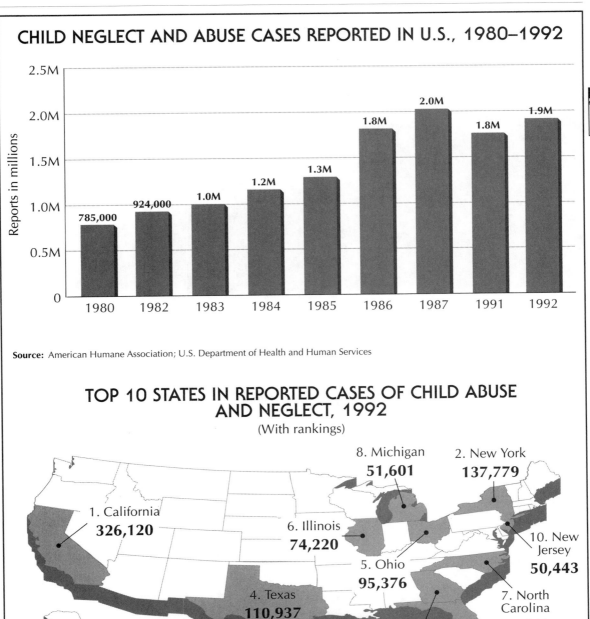

Reports in millions

- 1980: 785,000
- 1982: 924,000
- 1983: 1.0M
- 1984: 1.2M
- 1985: 1.3M
- 1986: 1.8M
- 1987: 2.0M
- 1991: 1.8M
- 1992: 1.9M

Source: American Humane Association; U.S. Department of Health and Human Services

TOP 10 STATES IN REPORTED CASES OF CHILD ABUSE AND NEGLECT, 1992
(With rankings)

8. Michigan **51,601**

2. New York **137,779**

1. California **326,120**

6. Illinois **74,220**

10. New Jersey **50,443**

5. Ohio **95,376**

7. North Carolina **55,411**

4. Texas **110,937**

9. Georgia **51,225**

3. Florida **116,403**

Total cases reported, 1992: 1.9 million

Source: U.S. Department of Health and Human Services, National Center on Child Abuse and Neglect, National Child Abuse and Neglect Data System

U.S. RENTERS ON THE MOVE

(Percentage of renters and homeowners
changing residence during the year)

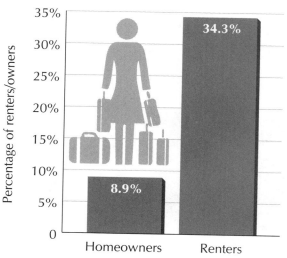

Percentage of renters/owners

- Homeowners: **8.9%**
- Renters: **34.3%**

Source: U.S. Census Bureau

U.S. HOUSES: CURRENT CLEANING HABITS

How often people in the U.S. say their
current house is cleaned, compared to
the house they grew up in:

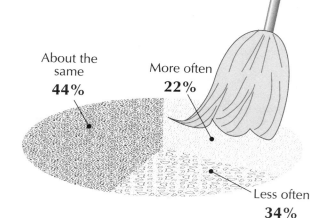

About the
same
44%

More often
22%

Less often
34%

Source: Market Research, Inc.

APPLIANCES FILL THE AMERICAN HOME

Percentage of American households:

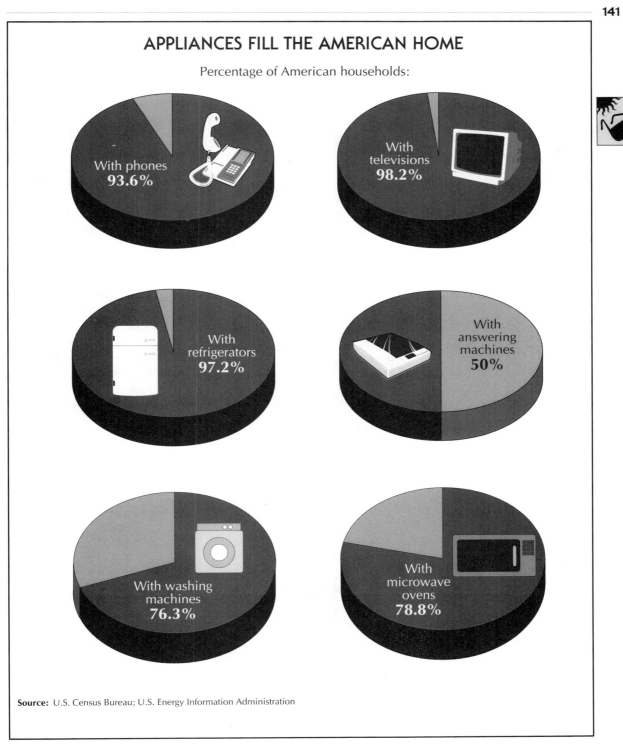

With phones
93.6%

With televisions
98.2%

With refrigerators
97.2%

With answering machines
50%

With washing machines
76.3%

With microwave ovens
78.8%

Source: U.S. Census Bureau; U.S. Energy Information Administration

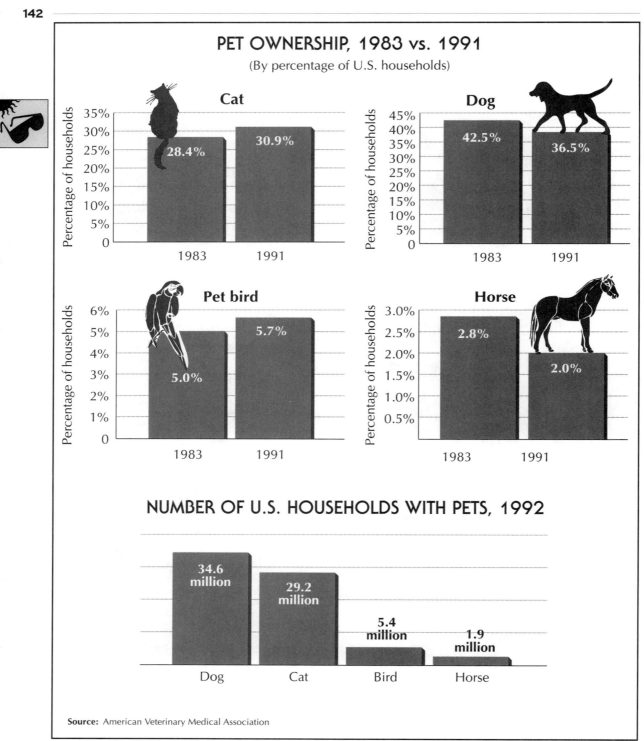

PET OWNERSHIP, 1983 vs. 1991

(By percentage of U.S. households)

Cat

Percentage of households

	1983	1991
	28.4%	30.9%

Dog

Percentage of households

	1983	1991
	42.5%	36.5%

Pet bird

Percentage of households

	1983	1991
	5.0%	5.7%

Horse

Percentage of households

	1983	1991
	2.8%	2.0%

NUMBER OF U.S. HOUSEHOLDS WITH PETS, 1992

Dog	Cat	Bird	Horse
34.6 million	29.2 million	5.4 million	1.9 million

Source: American Veterinary Medical Association

AMERICAN PET OWNERSHIP, 1993
(Millions of U.S. households)

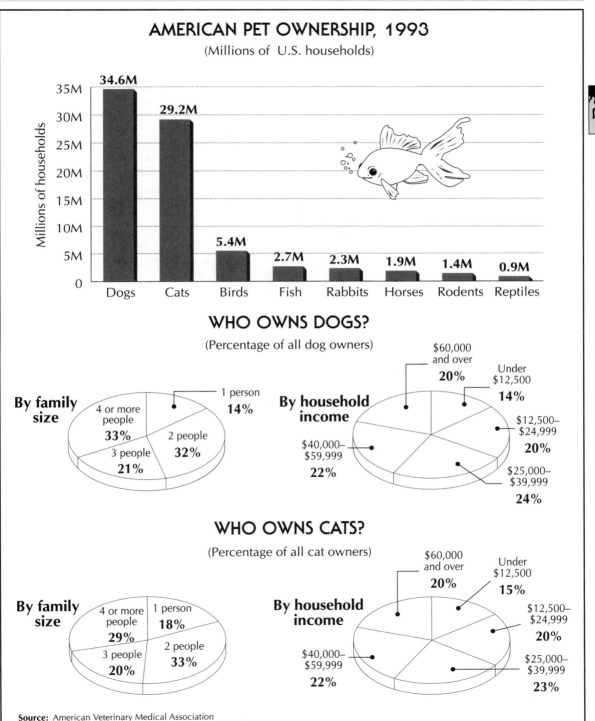

Millions of households

- Dogs: 34.6M
- Cats: 29.2M
- Birds: 5.4M
- Fish: 2.7M
- Rabbits: 2.3M
- Horses: 1.9M
- Rodents: 1.4M
- Reptiles: 0.9M

WHO OWNS DOGS?
(Percentage of all dog owners)

By family size
- 4 or more people: 33%
- 3 people: 21%
- 2 people: 32%
- 1 person: 14%

By household income
- $60,000 and over: 20%
- Under $12,500: 14%
- $12,500–$24,999: 20%
- $25,000–$39,999: 24%
- $40,000–$59,999: 22%

WHO OWNS CATS?
(Percentage of all cat owners)

By family size
- 4 or more people: 29%
- 3 people: 20%
- 2 people: 33%
- 1 person: 18%

By household income
- $60,000 and over: 20%
- Under $12,500: 15%
- $12,500–$24,999: 20%
- $25,000–$39,999: 23%
- $40,000–$59,999: 22%

Source: American Veterinary Medical Association

LEISURE AND RECREATION

Over the past few decades, time for leisure activities has increased for most Americans. The work week has gradually decreased; people have retired at earlier ages and in better health; and growing affluence has created more disposable income and made it easier to escape from work and other responsibilities. At the same time, the range of leisure-time activities has expanded greatly. Today, people can choose from an almost infinite variety of ways to relax, amuse themselves, or participate in active forms of recreation.

Watching television and other passive activities fill much leisure time for many people. Most U.S. households have 2 or more TVs, and every day, more than 75 million Americans tune in to watch prime-time programs. Videos and movies also are enormously popular diversions; in 1993, consumers spent $13.2 billion on videos and $5.2 billion on movies. Some $8.8 billion was spent on books, with self-improvement books making up 19% of the year's top-selling titles. As more and more people buy computers, playing computer games continues to grow in popularity; sales of entertainment software totaled $410 million in 1993.

More active pursuits and diversions include sports and hobbies such as gardening and photography. Tourism, camping, and exploring the great outdoors are also increasingly popular. Many of America's majestic national parks are overrun with vacationers, but the nation's most popular tourist attractions by far are Walt Disney World and Disneyland. A rapidly growing recreational activity in America is gambling. Americans wagered $33 billion in 1992, a sum likely to increase dramatically as the number of casinos in America continues to rise.

FINGERTIP FACTS

- Each day, more than 75 million Americans tune in to prime-time TV; Thursday is the biggest draw, averaging 94 million viewers.

- Americans have fallen in love with CDs. In 1975, music sales included 164 million singles, 257 million albums, and 16.2 million cassettes. In 1992, sales consisted of 20 million singles, 2 million albums, 336 million cassettes, and 408 million CDs.

- Americans spent $44.6 billion on sporting goods in 1993, up from $16.7 billion in 1980.

- New York is the most expensive U.S. city to visit; in 1993, the cost of 3 meals and a night in a hotel averaged $297. Washington, D.C., was second, at $248.

- More Americans are traveling to foreign countries—up from 34.7 million in 1985 to 45.5 million in 1993. Canada was the most popular destination in 1985, Mexico in 1993.

- National parks are growing increasingly crowded. Nearly 5 million people visited the Grand Canyon in 1993—twice as many as in 1983.

- The most popular national park in 1992 was the Great Smokey Mountains, with 8.9 million visitors.

- Legal gaming generated gross revenues of $29.9 billion in 1992—on a staggering total amount wagered of $33 billion. Revenues of various segments of the industry included casinos, $10.1 billion; Native-American-run gaming, $1.5 billion; and lotteries, $11.5 billion.

PERSONAL RECREATION SPENDING, BY TYPE OF RECREATION, 1970–1992

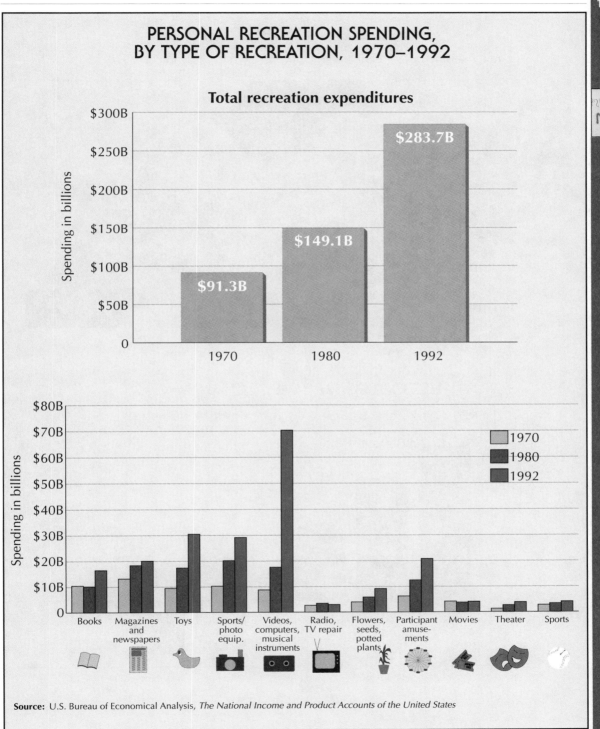

Total recreation expenditures

Spending in billions

$300B
$250B
$200B
$150B
$100B
$50B
0

$91.3B — 1970
$149.1B — 1980
$283.7B — 1992

Spending in billions

$80B
$70B
$60B
$50B
$40B
$30B
$20B
$10B
0

1970
1980
1992

Books · Magazines and newspapers · Toys · Sports/photo equip. · Videos, computers, musical instruments · Radio, TV repair · Flowers, seeds, potted plants · Participant amusements · Movies · Theater · Sports

Source: U.S. Bureau of Economical Analysis, *The National Income and Product Accounts of the United States*

MORE OR LESS FREE TIME?

(How much leisure time Americans feel they have today compared to 1990, by sex)

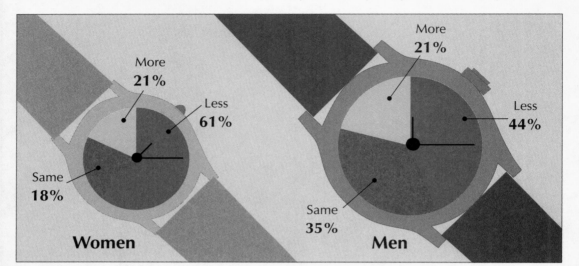

Women

More
21%

Less
61%

Same
18%

Men

More
21%

Less
44%

Same
35%

Source: Based on statistics from Market Directions

USE OF LEISURE TIME IS CHANGING

(Biggest changes in time spent on popular leisure activities, by percentages, 1991–1994)

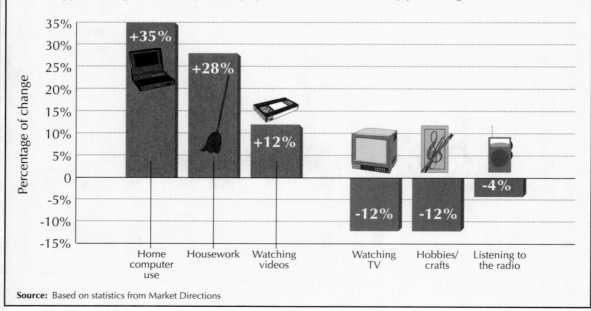

Percentage of change

+35% — Home computer use
+28% — Housework
+12% — Watching videos
-12% — Watching TV
-12% — Hobbies/crafts
-4% — Listening to the radio

Source: Based on statistics from Market Directions

LONG TRIPS INCREASE, 1984–1992

(Number of annual trips at least 100 miles from home taken by U.S. travelers)

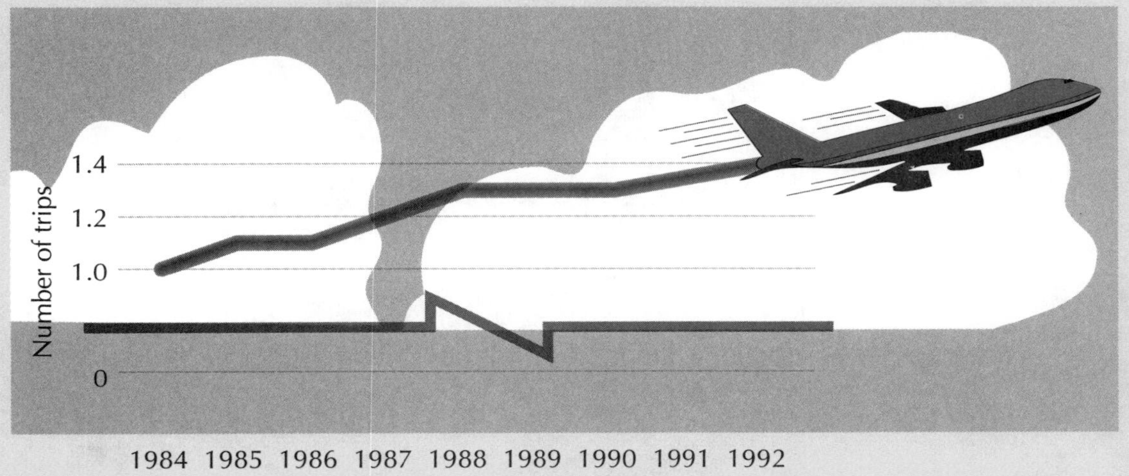

Number of trips

1.4
1.2
1.0
0

1984 1985 1986 1987 1988 1989 1990 1991 1992

PURPOSE FOR TRAVEL BY U.S. RESIDENTS, 1991

(Millions of of trips per year)

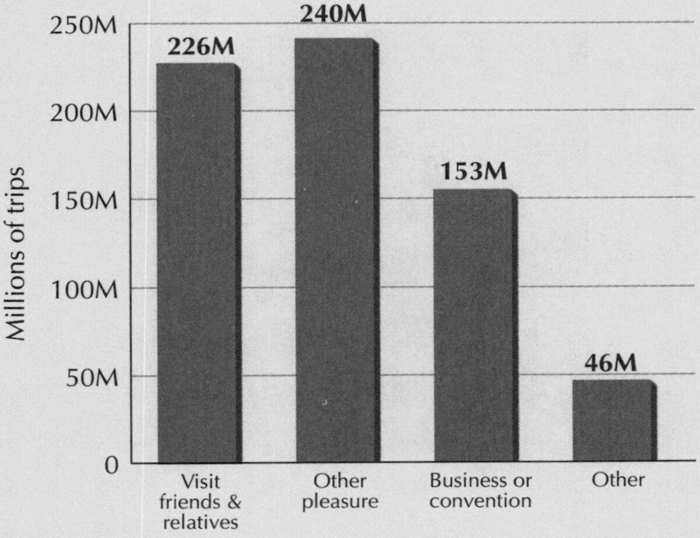

Millions of trips

250M
226M **240M**
200M
153M
150M
100M
50M
46M
0

Visit friends & relatives | Other pleasure | Business or convention | Other

Source: U.S. Travel Data Center

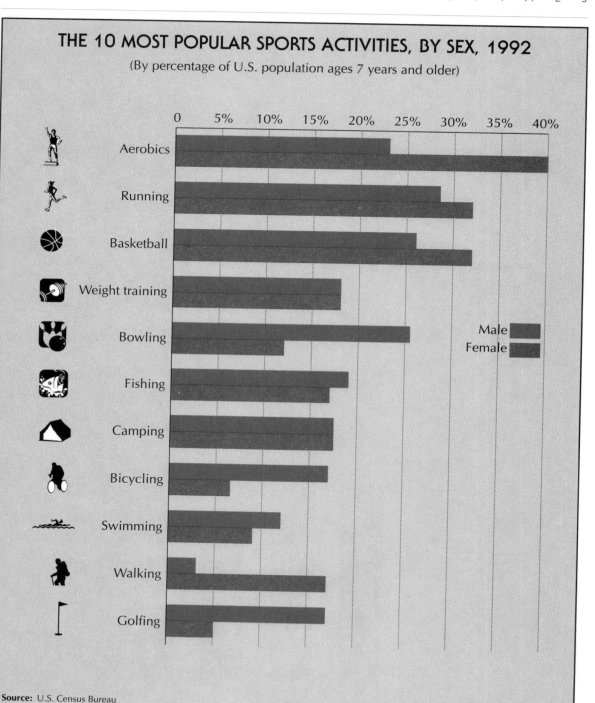

THE 10 MOST POPULAR SPORTS ACTIVITIES, BY SEX, 1992

(By percentage of U.S. population ages 7 years and older)

Aerobics
Running
Basketball
Weight training
Bowling
Fishing
Camping
Bicycling
Swimming
Walking
Golfing

Male
Female

Source: U.S. Census Bureau

ANNUAL AVERAGE ATTENDANCE AT SPECTATOR SPORTS, 1992

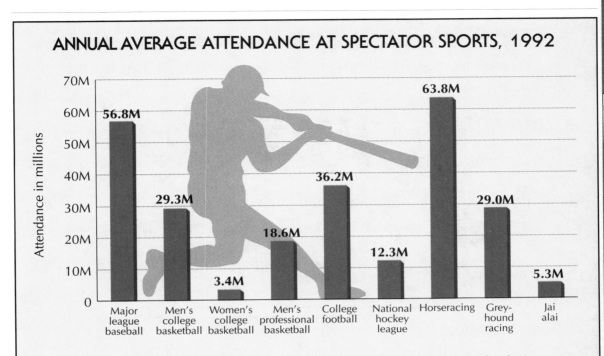

Sources: Based on statistics from National League of Professional Baseball Clubs; National Footbal League; National Hockey League; National Basketball Association; *The New York Times*

ATTENDANCE BY U.S. ADULTS FOR SELECTED LEISURE ACTIVITIES, 1992

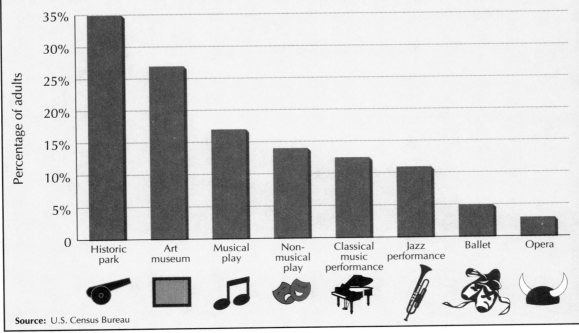

Source: U.S. Census Bureau

ATTENDANCE AT U.S. AMUSEMENT PARKS RISES, 1986–1992

(Annual attendance at the 40 busiest amusement/theme parks in North America)

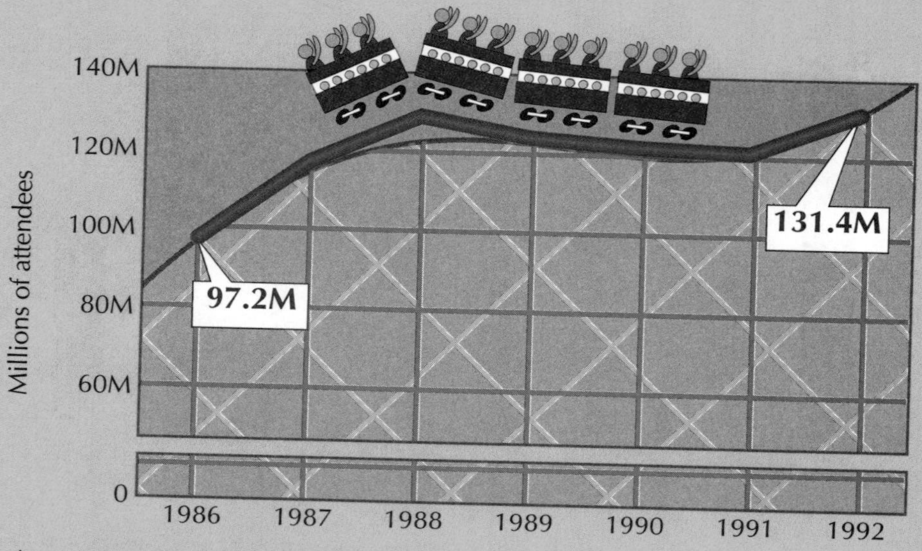

Millions of attendees

140M

120M

100M

97.2M

80M

60M

0

1986   1987   1988   1989   1990   1991   1992

131.4M

Source: Based on statistics from *Amusement Business* magazine

AMUSEMENT PARK ANNUAL RECEIPTS, 1986–1992

(In billions)

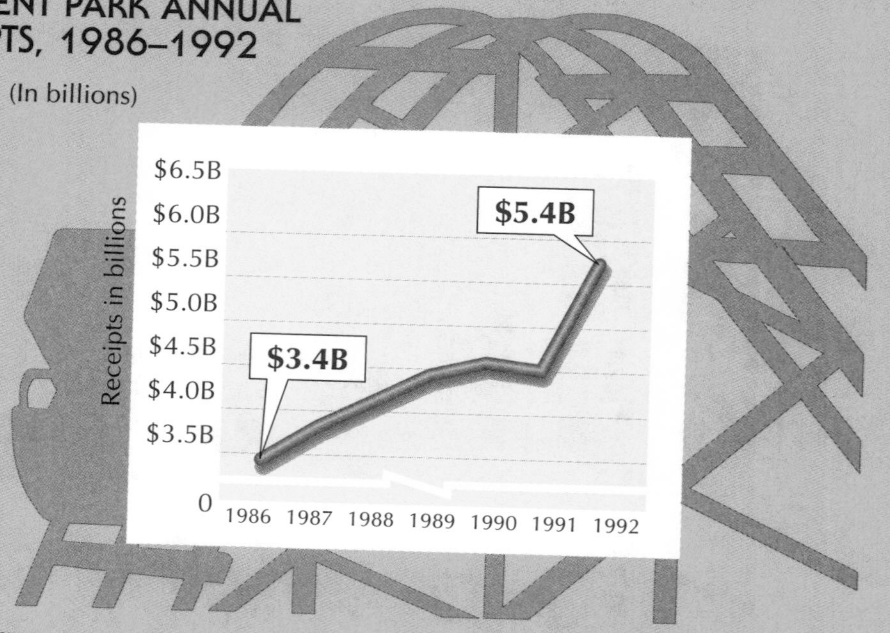

Receipts in billions

$6.5B

$6.0B

$5.5B

$5.0B

$4.5B

$4.0B

$3.5B

0

1986 1987 1988 1989 1990 1991 1992

$5.4B

$3.4B

Source: U.S. Census Bureau

MOST POPULAR TOURIST ATTRACTIONS, BY NUMBER OF VISITORS, 1992

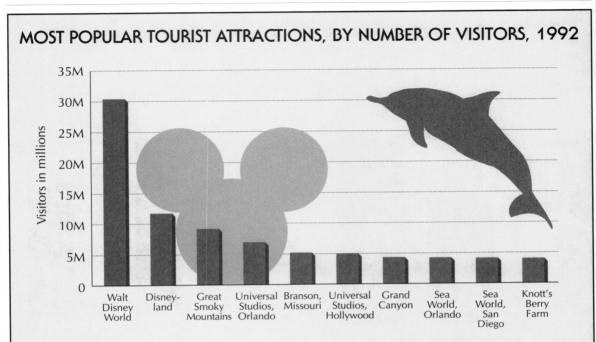

Visitors in millions

35M
30M
25M
20M
15M
10M
5M
0

Walt Disney World | Disney-land | Great Smoky Mountains | Universal Studios, Orlando | Branson, Missouri | Universal Studios, Hollywood | Grand Canyon | Sea World, Orlando | Sea World, San Diego | Knott's Berry Farm

Source: U.S. Tourism Board

U.S. THEME PARK ATTENDANCE, 1993

Attendance at North American theme parks reached an estimated 255 million in 1994. Walt Disney operates the top four most popular parks in America. Annual attendance, in millions:

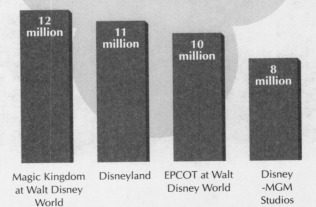

12 million — Magic Kingdom at Walt Disney World

11 million — Disneyland

10 million — EPCOT at Walt Disney World

8 million — Disney-MGM Studios

Source: Based on statistics from *Amusement Business* magazine

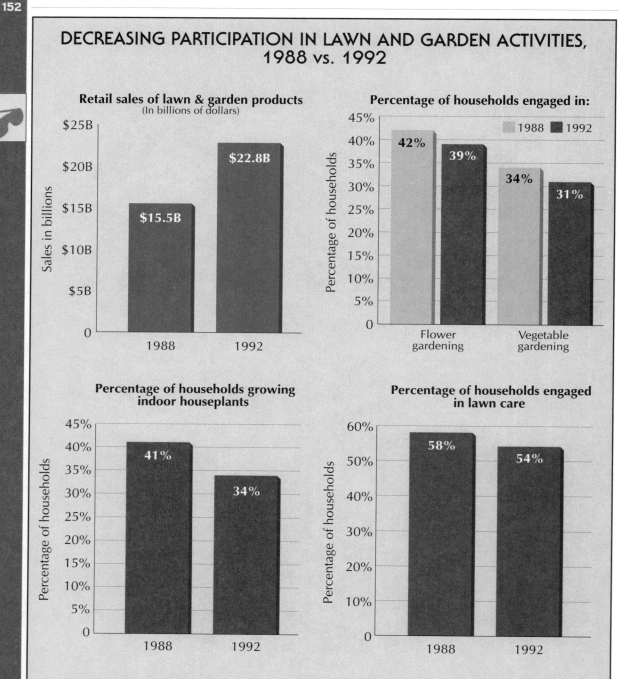

DECREASING PARTICIPATION IN LAWN AND GARDEN ACTIVITIES, 1988 vs. 1992

Retail sales of lawn & garden products
(In billions of dollars)

- $22.8B (1992)
- $15.5B (1988)

Sales in billions

Percentage of households engaged in:

1988 / 1992

- Flower gardening: 42% / 39%
- Vegetable gardening: 34% / 31%

Percentage of households

Percentage of households growing indoor houseplants

- 1988: 41%
- 1992: 34%

Percentage of households

Percentage of households engaged in lawn care

- 1988: 58%
- 1992: 54%

Percentage of households

Source: The National Gardening Association

AIR SHOW ATTENDANCE SOARS IN U.S.

(Annual attendance, in millions)

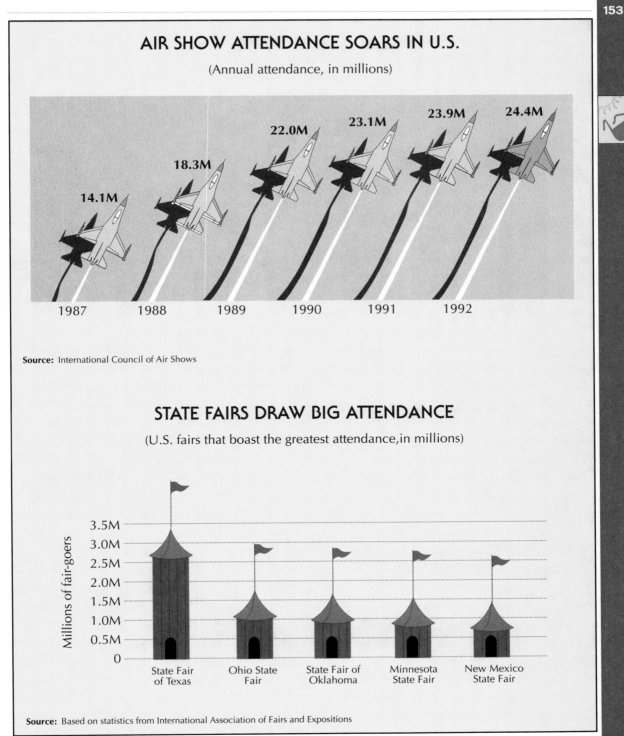

14.1M 18.3M 22.0M 23.1M 23.9M 24.4M

1987   1988   1989   1990   1991   1992

Source: International Council of Air Shows

STATE FAIRS DRAW BIG ATTENDANCE

(U.S. fairs that boast the greatest attendance, in millions)

Millions of fair-goers

3.5M
3.0M
2.5M
2.0M
1.5M
1.0M
0.5M
0

State Fair
of Texas

Ohio State
Fair

State Fair of
Oklahoma

Minnesota
State Fair

New Mexico
State Fair

Source: Based on statistics from International Association of Fairs and Expositions

MEGA-HIT MOVIE WEEKENDS

(Weekends with the highest gross at the box office for each year)

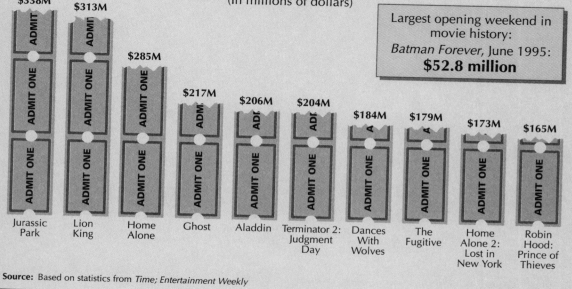

$98.6M	$97.3M	$99.2M	$86.3M	$90.8M	$80.8M	$96.7M
June 24, 1995	June 24, 1994	July 9, 1993	Dec. 25, 1992	Dec. 27, 1991	July 13, 1990	June 23, 1989

Source: Based on statistics from *Variety; Entertainment Weekly*

THE TOP 10 LARGEST-GROSSING FILMS, 1990–1995

(In millions of dollars)

Largest opening weekend in
movie history:
Batman Forever, June 1995:
$52.8 million

Film	Gross
Jurassic Park	$338M
Lion King	$313M
Home Alone	$285M
Ghost	$217M
Aladdin	$206M
Terminator 2: Judgment Day	$204M
Dances With Wolves	$184M
The Fugitive	$179M
Home Alone 2: Lost in New York	$173M
Robin Hood: Prince of Thieves	$165M

Source: Based on statistics from *Time; Entertainment Weekly*

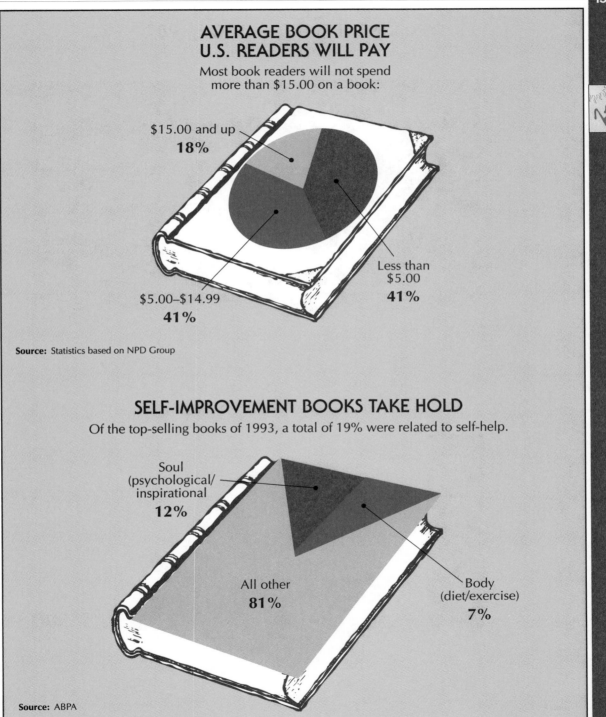

AVERAGE BOOK PRICE
U.S. READERS WILL PAY

Most book readers will not spend
more than $15.00 on a book:

$15.00 and up
18%

Less than
$5.00
41%

$5.00–$14.99
41%

Source: Statistics based on NPD Group

SELF-IMPROVEMENT BOOKS TAKE HOLD

Of the top-selling books of 1993, a total of 19% were related to self-help.

Soul
(psychological/
inspirational
12%

Body
(diet/exercise)
7%

All other
81%

Source: ABPA

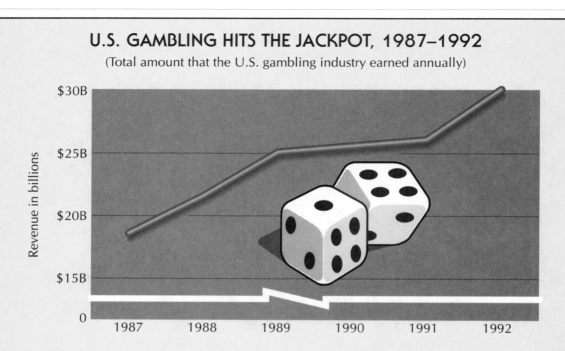

U.S. GAMBLING HITS THE JACKPOT, 1987–1992

(Total amount that the U.S. gambling industry earned annually)

Source: *The Wall Street Journal; The New York Times; The Washington Post*

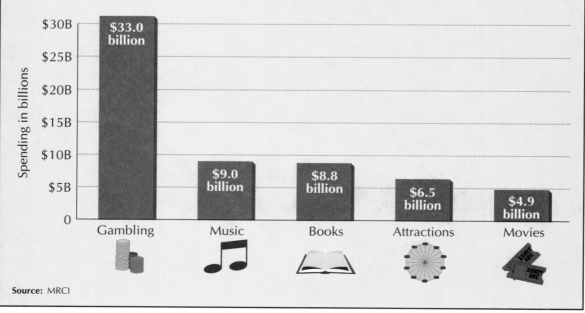

GAMBLING WINS BIG, 1992

(Amount that Americans spent on each form of entertainment)

Source: MRCI

BIG SPENDERS FOR GAMBLING, 1987–1992

(Average annual amount spent in the U.S.
on gambling, per capita)

BETTING BEATS BATTING

More people now go to casinos than attend
major league baseball games. Annual
attendance at U.S. casinos in 1994:

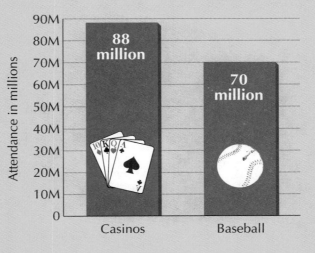

Source: MRCI

CITY SLICKERS LIKE LOTTERIES

(Percentage of population who bought lottery tickets in 1994, by area of residence)

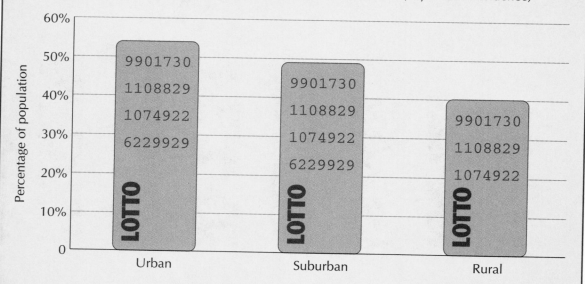

Percentage of population

60%

50%
9901730
1108829
1074922
6229929

40%

30%

20%

10%

0

Urban

9901730
1108829
1074922
6229929

Suburban

9901730
1108829
1074922

Rural

LOTTO   LOTTO   LOTTO

Source: Statistics based on *USA Today*

SHOPPING DAYS

(Percentage of U.S. shoppers who prefer specific days of the week for shopping)

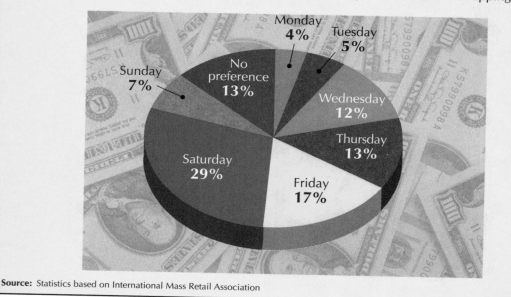

Monday **4%**
Tuesday **5%**
No preference **13%**
Sunday **7%**
Wednesday **12%**
Thursday **13%**
Saturday **29%**
Friday **17%**

Source: Statistics based on International Mass Retail Association

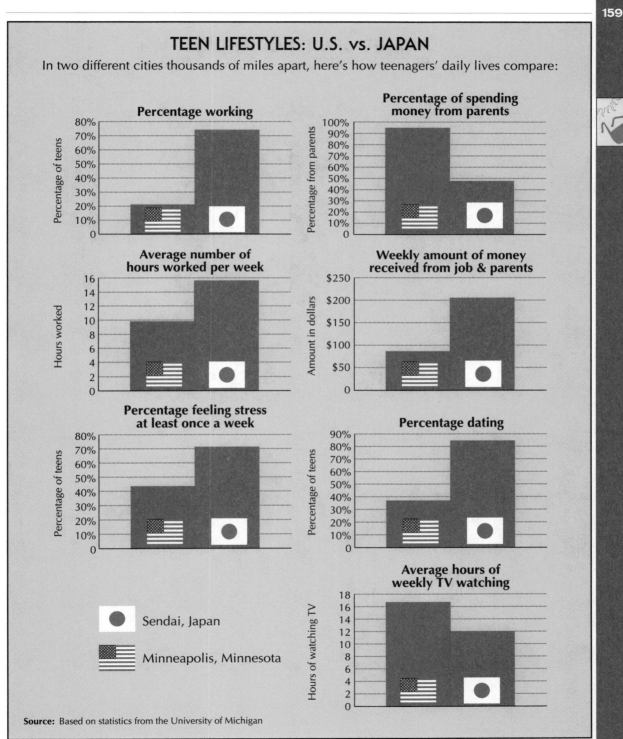

TEEN LIFESTYLES: U.S. vs. JAPAN

In two different cities thousands of miles apart, here's how teenagers' daily lives compare:

Percentage working

Percentage of spending money from parents

Average number of hours worked per week

Weekly amount of money received from job & parents

Percentage feeling stress at least once a week

Percentage dating

Sendai, Japan

Minneapolis, Minnesota

Average hours of weekly TV watching

Source: Based on statistics from the University of Michigan

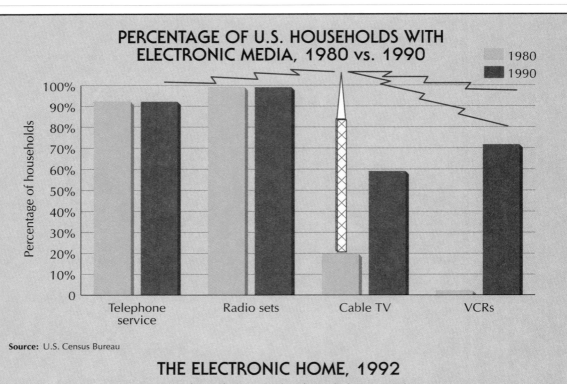

PERCENTAGE OF U.S. HOUSEHOLDS WITH ELECTRONIC MEDIA, 1980 vs. 1990

Source: U.S. Census Bureau

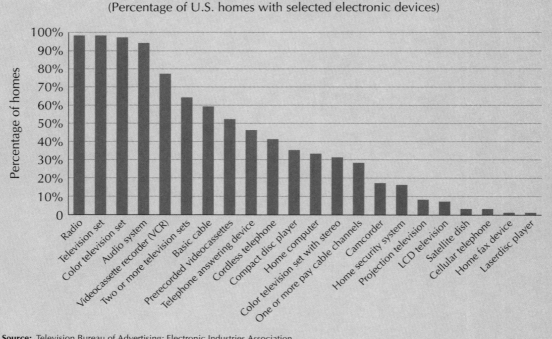

THE ELECTRONIC HOME, 1992

(Percentage of U.S. homes with selected electronic devices)

Source: Television Bureau of Advertising; Electronic Industries Association

SALES OF CELLULAR TELEPHONES BOOM, 1984–1993

(Millions of people with cellular telephone service)

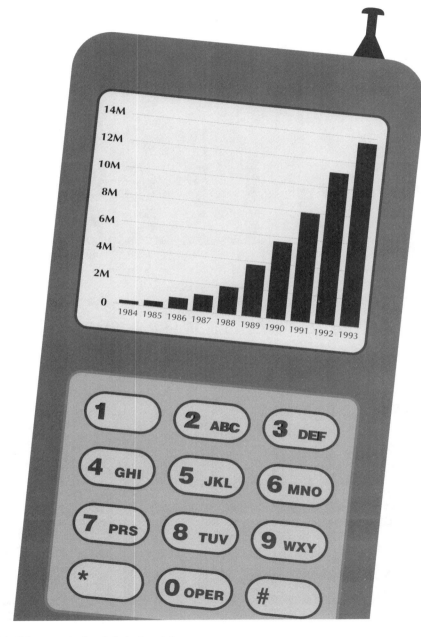

Source: Cellular Telecommunications Industry Association

SALES OF CELLULAR TELEPHONES, ANSWERING MACHINES, AND FAX MACHINES, 1983–1991

(Unit sales to dealer, in millions)

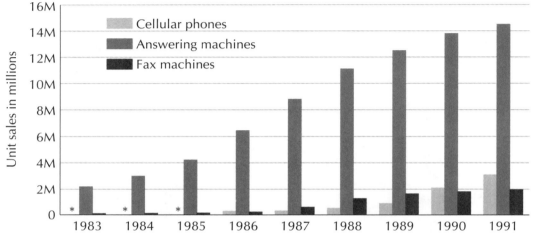

* **Note:** Data not available
Source: Electronic Industries Association; Computer and Business Equipment Manufacturers

THE BIGGEST NIGHTS FOR PRIME-TIME TV

(U.S. viewers per night, in millions)

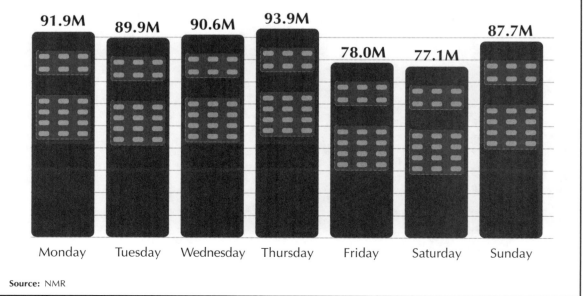

Monday	Tuesday	Wednesday	Thursday	Friday	Saturday	Sunday
91.9M	89.9M	90.6M	93.9M	78.0M	77.1M	87.7M

Source: NMR

MOST HOUSEHOLDS HAVE A VCR AND MULTIPLE TVs

Percentage of U.S. television households with:

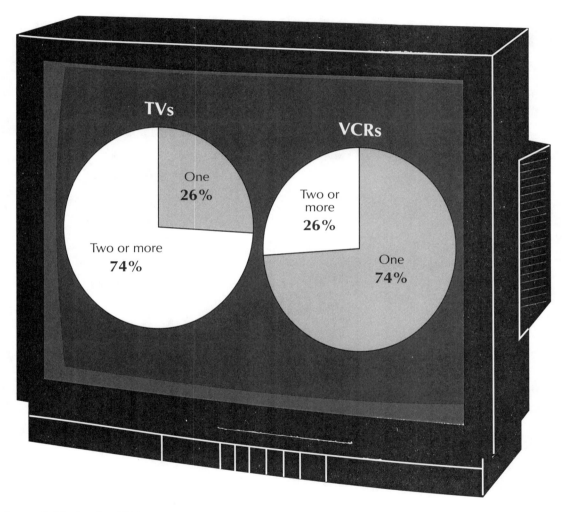

TVs

One
26%

Two or more
74%

VCRs

Two or more
26%

One
74%

Source: Statistics based on MRI, Inc.

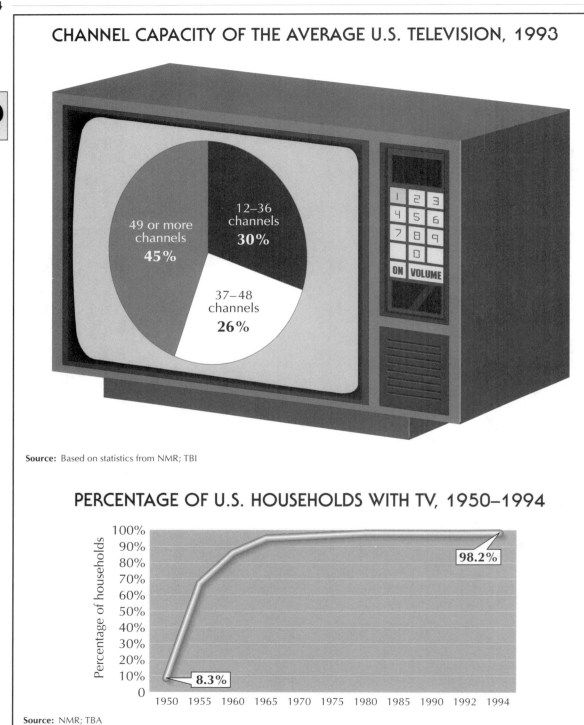

CHANNEL CAPACITY OF THE AVERAGE U.S. TELEVISION, 1993

49 or more channels
45%

12–36 channels
30%

37–48 channels
26%

Source: Based on statistics from NMR; TBI

PERCENTAGE OF U.S. HOUSEHOLDS WITH TV, 1950–1994

Percentage of households

100%
90%
80%
70%
60%
50%
40%
30%
20%
10%
0

98.2%

8.3%

1950 1955 1960 1965 1970 1975 1980 1985 1990 1992 1994

Source: NMR; TBA

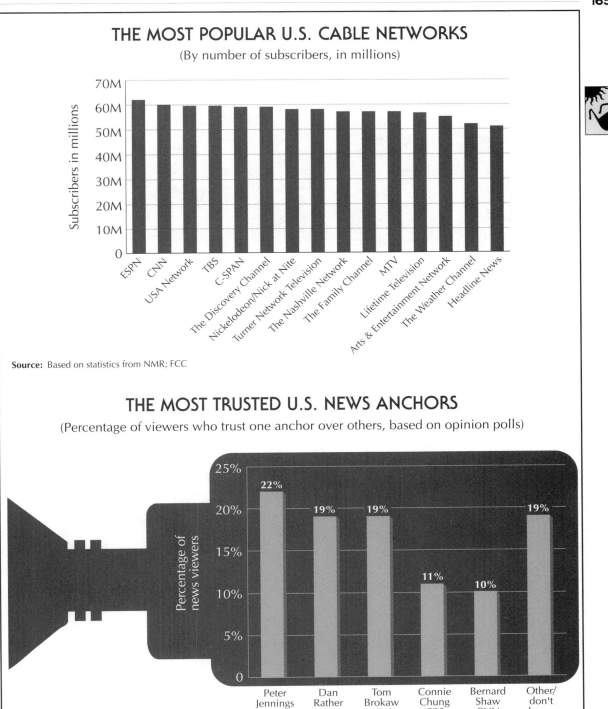

THE MOST POPULAR U.S. CABLE NETWORKS
(By number of subscribers, in millions)

Source: Based on statistics from NMR; FCC

THE MOST TRUSTED U.S. NEWS ANCHORS
(Percentage of viewers who trust one anchor over others, based on opinion polls)

Source: Based on statistics from NMR

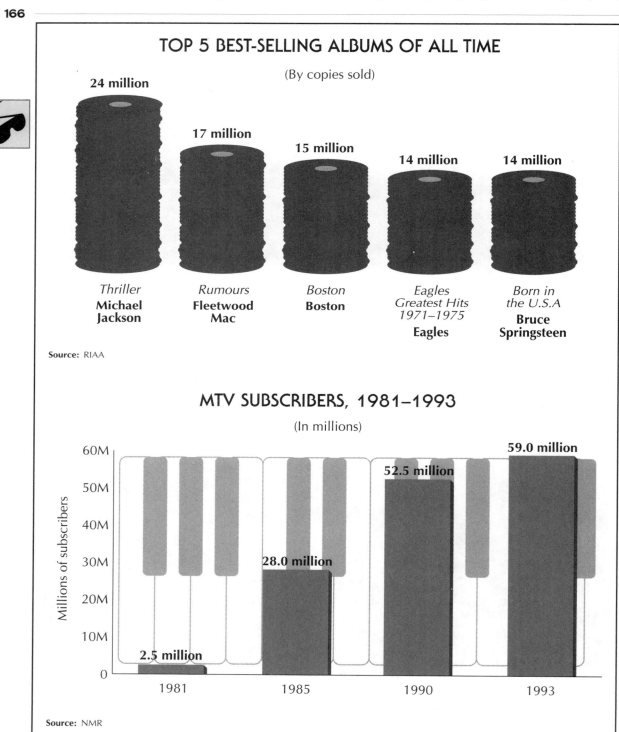

TOP 5 BEST-SELLING ALBUMS OF ALL TIME

(By copies sold)

24 million

17 million

15 million

14 million

14 million

Thriller
Michael Jackson

Rumours
Fleetwood Mac

Boston
Boston

Eagles Greatest Hits 1971–1975
Eagles

Born in the U.S.A
Bruce Springsteen

Source: RIAA

MTV SUBSCRIBERS, 1981–1993

(In millions)

Millions of subscribers

60M

50M

40M

30M

20M

10M

0

2.5 million

28.0 million

52.5 million

59.0 million

1981

1985

1990

1993

Source: NMR

CD SALES vs. CASSETTE SALES, 1992 vs. 1993

(In units sold)

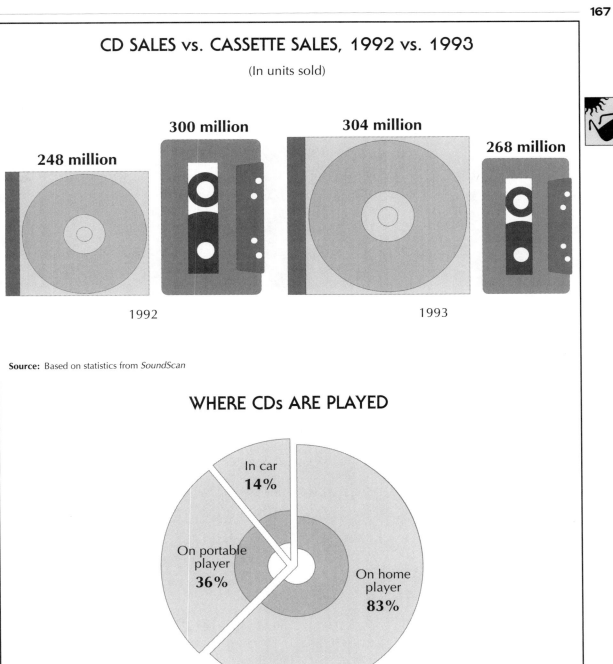

300 million

248 million

304 million

268 million

1992

1993

Source: Based on statistics from *SoundScan*

WHERE CDs ARE PLAYED

In car
14%

On portable
player
36%

On home
player
83%

Note: Some people use more than one player
Source: Based on statistics from NFO research

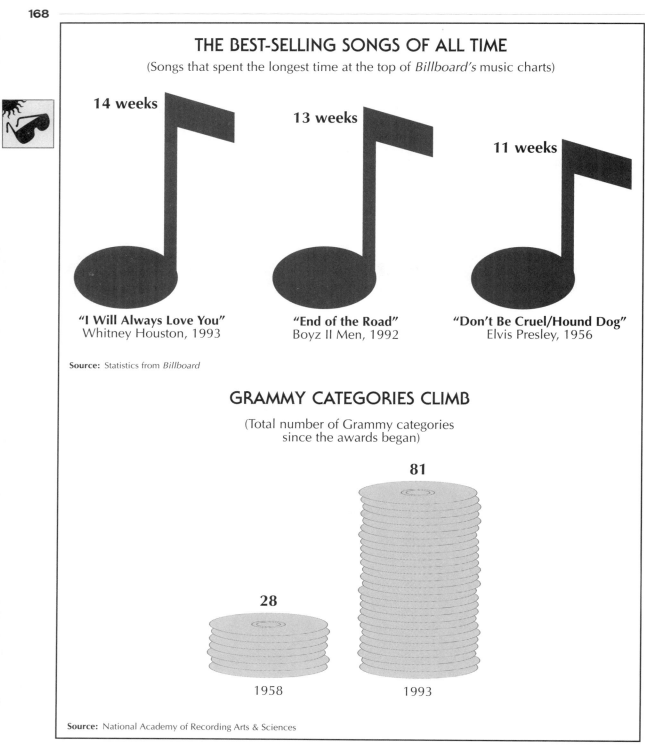

THE BEST-SELLING SONGS OF ALL TIME
(Songs that spent the longest time at the top of *Billboard's* music charts)

14 weeks

13 weeks

11 weeks

"I Will Always Love You"
Whitney Houston, 1993

"End of the Road"
Boyz II Men, 1992

"Don't Be Cruel/Hound Dog"
Elvis Presley, 1956

Source: Statistics from *Billboard*

GRAMMY CATEGORIES CLIMB
(Total number of Grammy categories
since the awards began)

81

28

1958

1993

Source: National Academy of Recording Arts & Sciences

THE TOP-GROSSING U.S. CONCERT TOURS, 1993

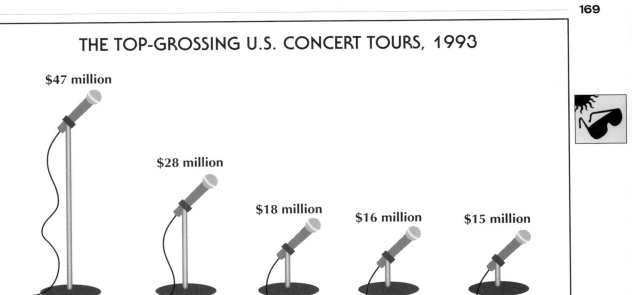

$47 million — Grateful Dead

$28 million — Paul McCartney

$18 million — Rod Stewart

$16 million — Jimmy Buffett

$15 million — Garth Brooks

Source: Based on statistics from *Amusement Business*

RHYTHM & BLUES PERFORMERS WITH THE MOST NO. 1 SINGLES

(Recording artists with the most number-one singles on the
Billboard Rhythm & Blues chart, since 1965)

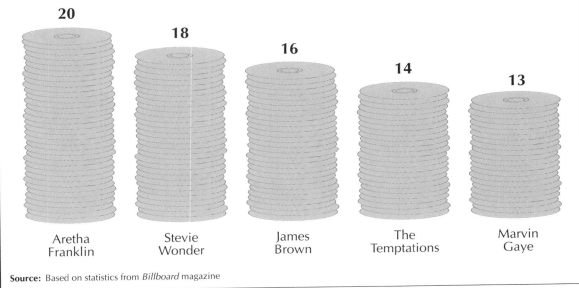

20 — Aretha Franklin

18 — Stevie Wonder

16 — James Brown

14 — The Temptations

13 — Marvin Gaye

Source: Based on statistics from *Billboard* magazine

3

POLITICS AND GOVERNMENT

THE GROWTH OF GOVERNMENT

Wherever they look, Americans see—or think they see—the growth of government. While it is true that local government employment has increased during the 1990s, the number of civilian federal employees has actually declined. Payrolls, however, have soared at all levels of government.

The public has demanded lower taxes and more fiscal prudence, forcing government officials to make major staff reductions. To further cut costs, obsolete programs, agencies, and departments have been consolidated or eliminated.

There has also been pressure to limit legislatures from mandating programs that provide funding without sufficient budgets. Mandated programs—covering education, Medicaid, welfare, and other areas—account for more than half of states' expenditures and for a large portion of local budgets. Since the 1970s, some 17 states have amended their constitutions or enacted statutes to limit their legislatures' ability to impose unfunded mandates on local governments. By the mid-1990s, many federal legislators were rallying to the cause, promising to limit Congress's ability to impose mandates on the states.

The "downsizing" of government promises to be a difficult and often explosive process. Decreasing government spending and size means not only a reduction in waste but also cutbacks in needed services and programs. It also means different groups in society will have to compete harder for fewer resources.

FINGERTIP FACTS

- In 1980, government employees—federal civilian plus state and local—totaled 16.2 million; state and local employees made up 82% of the total. In 1992, the number was 18.7 million, with state and local employees accounting for 84%.

- Total government revenues in 1992 were $3 trillion. Federal revenues accounted for 47.2% of this; the rest was state and local.

- Of the $3 trillion in revenues in 1992, a third—$1 trillion—came from taxes. The major portion of this came from individual income taxes ($592 billion), sales and gross receipts taxes ($260 billion), and corporate income taxes ($124 billion).

- Total government expenditures in 1992 were $2.4 trillion. Federal spending accounted for 61.4% of this total.

- In 1980, state and local debt totaled about $336 billion, or $1,482 per capita. By 1992, this debt had grown to $971 billion, or $3,807 per capita.

- In 1980, the federal debt was $908 billion. By 1993, it had quadrupled, to $3.4 trillion.

- The Internal Revenue Service processed approximately 115 million individual income tax forms in 1991.

GOVERNMENT GROWTH, 1972–1992

The number of local government units such as city governments, school districts, and special municipal authorities grew.

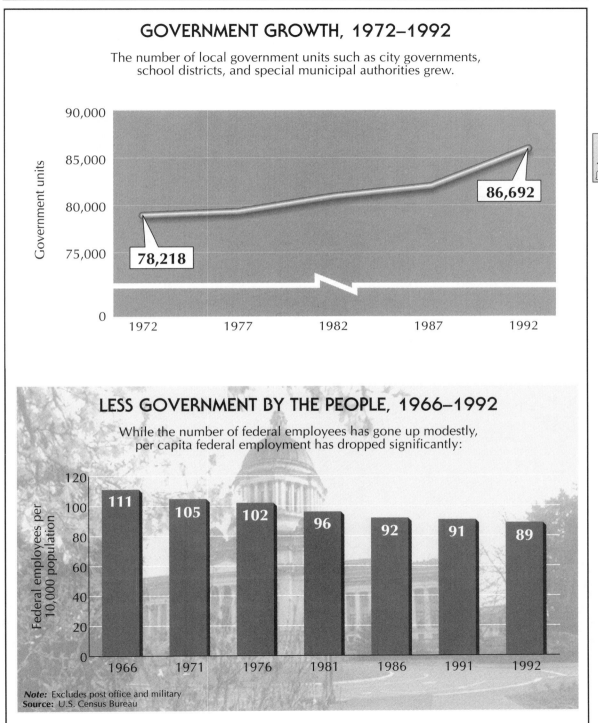

LESS GOVERNMENT BY THE PEOPLE, 1966–1992

While the number of federal employees has gone up modestly, per capita federal employment has dropped significantly:

Note: Excludes post office and military
Source: U.S. Census Bureau

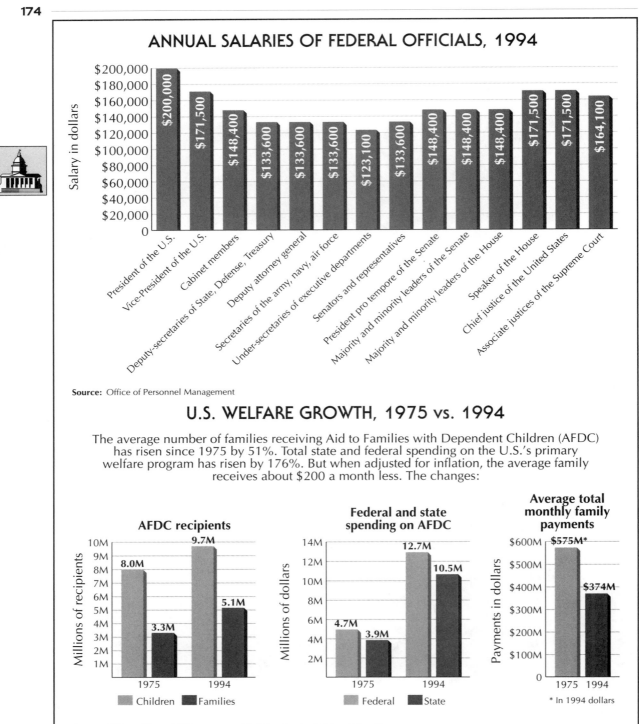

ANNUAL SALARIES OF FEDERAL OFFICIALS, 1994

Salary in dollars

Official	Salary
President of the U.S.	$200,000
Vice-President of the U.S.	$171,500
Cabinet members	$148,400
Deputy-secretaries of State, Defense, Treasury	$133,600
Deputy attorney general	$133,600
Secretaries of the army, navy, air force	$133,600
Under-secretaries of executive departments	$123,100
Senators and representatives	$133,600
President pro tempore of the Senate	$148,400
Majority and minority leaders of the Senate	$148,400
Majority and minority leaders of the House	$148,400
Speaker of the House	$171,500
Chief Justice of the United States	$171,500
Associate justices of the Supreme Court	$164,100

Source: Office of Personnel Management

U.S. WELFARE GROWTH, 1975 vs. 1994

The average number of families receiving Aid to Families with Dependent Children (AFDC) has risen since 1975 by 51%. Total state and federal spending on the U.S.'s primary welfare program has risen by 176%. But when adjusted for inflation, the average family receives about $200 a month less. The changes:

AFDC recipients

Millions of recipients

- Children 1975: 8.0M
- Families 1975: 3.3M
- Children 1994: 9.7M
- Families 1994: 5.1M

Children | Families

Federal and state spending on AFDC

Millions of dollars

- Federal 1975: 4.7M
- State 1975: 3.9M
- Federal 1994: 12.7M
- State 1994: 10.5M

Federal | State

Average total monthly family payments

Payments in dollars

- 1975: $575M*
- 1994: $374M

* In 1994 dollars

Source: Office of Financial Management; Administration for Children & Families

WHERE THE FEDERAL GOVERNMENT GETS ITS MONEY, 1980 vs. 1993

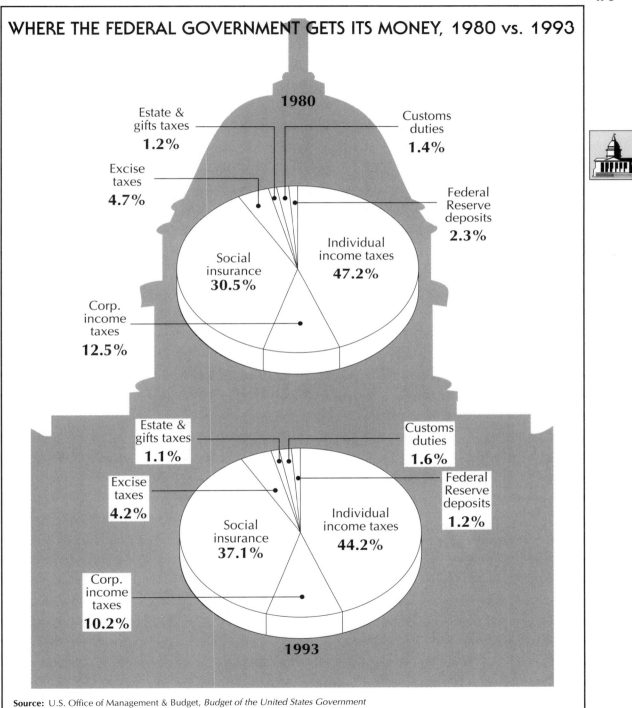

1980

Estate & gifts taxes **1.2%**

Customs duties **1.4%**

Excise taxes **4.7%**

Federal Reserve deposits **2.3%**

Individual income taxes **47.2%**

Social insurance **30.5%**

Corp. income taxes **12.5%**

Estate & gifts taxes **1.1%**

Customs duties **1.6%**

Excise taxes **4.2%**

Federal Reserve deposits **1.2%**

Individual income taxes **44.2%**

Social insurance **37.1%**

Corp. income taxes **10.2%**

1993

Source: U.S. Office of Management & Budget, *Budget of the United States Government*

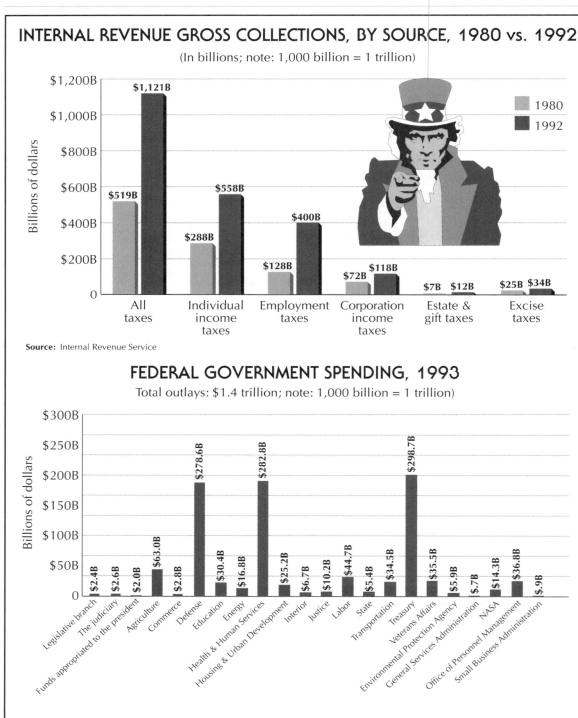

INTERNAL REVENUE GROSS COLLECTIONS, BY SOURCE, 1980 vs. 1992

(In billions; note: 1,000 billion = 1 trillion)

Billions of dollars

1980
1992

- All taxes: $519B (1980), $1,121B (1992)
- Individual income taxes: $288B (1980), $558B (1992)
- Employment taxes: $128B (1980), $400B (1992)
- Corporation income taxes: $72B (1980), $118B (1992)
- Estate & gift taxes: $7B (1980), $12B (1992)
- Excise taxes: $25B (1980), $34B (1992)

Source: Internal Revenue Service

FEDERAL GOVERNMENT SPENDING, 1993

Total outlays: $1.4 trillion; note: 1,000 billion = 1 trillion)

Billions of dollars

- Legislative branch: $2.4B
- The judiciary: $2.6B
- Funds appropriated to the president: $2.0B
- Agriculture: $63.0B
- Commerce: $2.8B
- Defense: $278.6B
- Education: $30.4B
- Energy: $16.8B
- Health & Human Services: $282.8B
- Housing & Urban Development: $25.2B
- Interior: $6.7B
- Justice: $10.2B
- Labor: $44.7B
- State: $5.4B
- Transportation: $34.5B
- Treasury: $298.7B
- Veterans Affairs: $35.5B
- Environmental Protection Agency: $5.9B
- General Services Administration: $.7B
- NASA: $14.3B
- Office of Personnel Management: $36.8B
- Small Business Administration: $.9B

Source: U.S. Office of Management and Budget, *Budget of the United States Government*

PROFILE: THE U.S. FEDERAL GOVERNMENT DOLLAR

(Note: 1,000 billion = 1 trillion)

Revenues: $1,165.0 billion

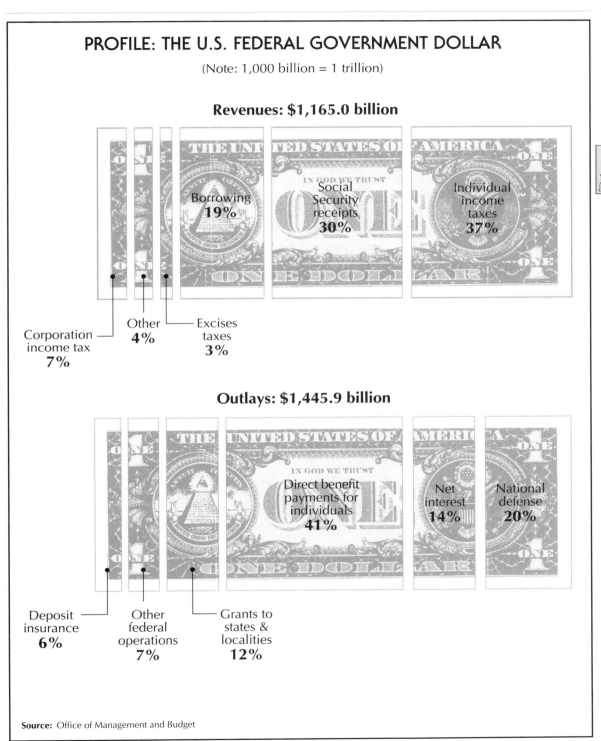

Borrowing
19%

Social
Security
receipts
30%

Individual
income
taxes
37%

Corporation
income tax
7%

Other
4%

Excises
taxes
3%

Outlays: $1,445.9 billion

Direct benefit
payments for
individuals
41%

Net
interest
14%

National
defense
20%

Deposit
insurance
6%

Other
federal
operations
7%

Grants to
states &
localities
12%

Source: Office of Management and Budget

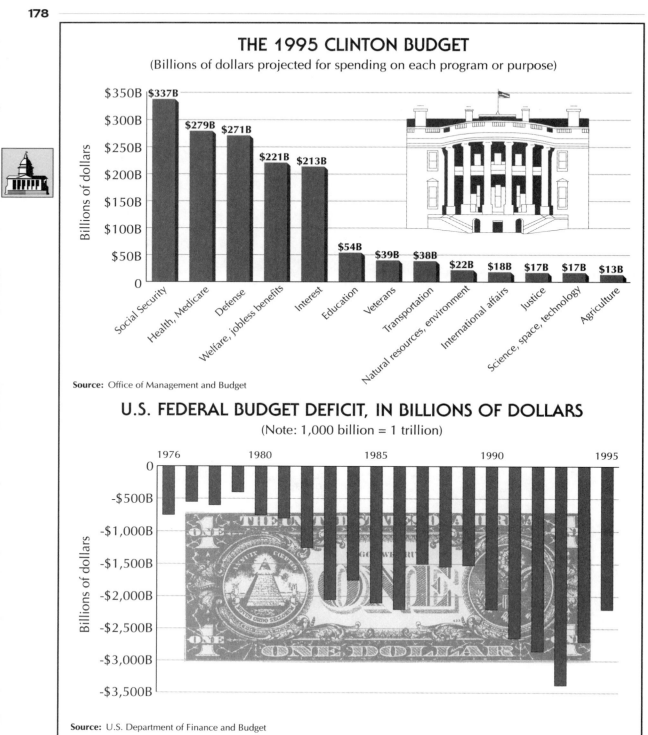

THE 1995 CLINTON BUDGET

(Billions of dollars projected for spending on each program or purpose)

Billions of dollars

- Social Security — $337B
- Health, Medicare — $279B
- Defense — $271B
- Welfare, jobless benefits — $221B
- Interest — $213B
- Education — $54B
- Veterans — $39B
- Transportation — $38B
- Natural resources, environment — $22B
- International affairs — $18B
- Justice — $17B
- Science, space, technology — $17B
- Agriculture — $13B

Source: Office of Management and Budget

U.S. FEDERAL BUDGET DEFICIT, IN BILLIONS OF DOLLARS

(Note: 1,000 billion = 1 trillion)

1976   1980   1985   1990   1995

Billions of dollars

Source: U.S. Department of Finance and Budget

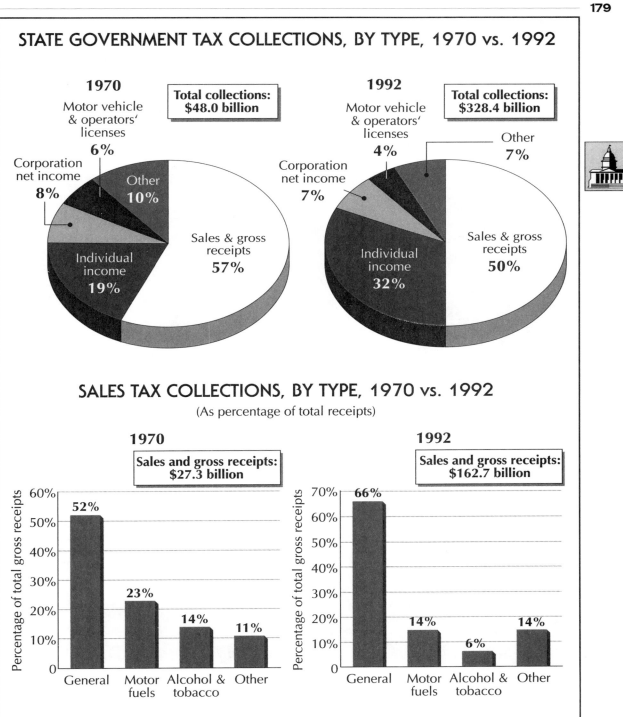

STATE GOVERNMENT TAX COLLECTIONS, BY TYPE, 1970 vs. 1992

1970

Total collections: $48.0 billion

Motor vehicle & operators' licenses **6%**

Corporation net income **8%**

Other **10%**

Individual income **19%**

Sales & gross receipts **57%**

1992

Total collections: $328.4 billion

Motor vehicle & operators' licenses **4%**

Corporation net income **7%**

Other **7%**

Individual income **32%**

Sales & gross receipts **50%**

SALES TAX COLLECTIONS, BY TYPE, 1970 vs. 1992

(As percentage of total receipts)

1970

Sales and gross receipts: $27.3 billion

Percentage of total gross receipts

- General **52%**
- Motor fuels **23%**
- Alcohol & tobacco **14%**
- Other **11%**

1992

Sales and gross receipts: $162.7 billion

Percentage of total gross receipts

- General **66%**
- Motor fuels **14%**
- Alcohol & tobacco **6%**
- Other **14%**

Source: U.S. Census Bureau

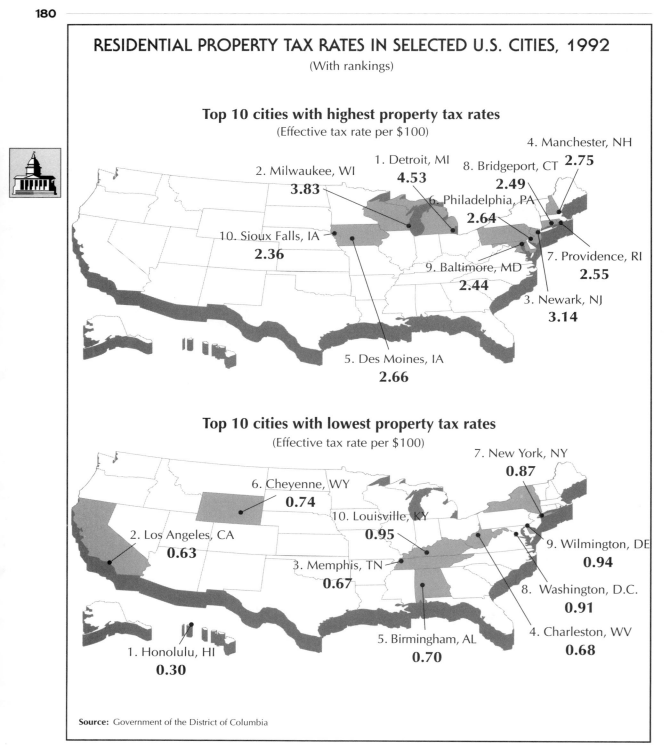

RESIDENTIAL PROPERTY TAX RATES IN SELECTED U.S. CITIES, 1992
(With rankings)

Top 10 cities with highest property tax rates
(Effective tax rate per $100)

4. Manchester, NH **2.75**

1. Detroit, MI
4.53

8. Bridgeport, CT
2.49

2. Milwaukee, WI
3.83

6. Philadelphia, PA
2.64

10. Sioux Falls, IA
2.36

9. Baltimore, MD
2.44

7. Providence, RI
2.55

3. Newark, NJ
3.14

5. Des Moines, IA
2.66

Top 10 cities with lowest property tax rates
(Effective tax rate per $100)

7. New York, NY
0.87

6. Cheyenne, WY
0.74

10. Louisville, KY
0.95

2. Los Angeles, CA
0.63

9. Wilmington, DE
0.94

3. Memphis, TN
0.67

8. Washington, D.C.
0.91

4. Charleston, WV
0.68

5. Birmingham, AL
0.70

1. Honolulu, HI
0.30

Source: Government of the District of Columbia

TOP 10 MOST EXPENSIVE CITIES, BY INCOME LEVEL, 1992

(As percentage of state and local taxes paid by a family of 4)

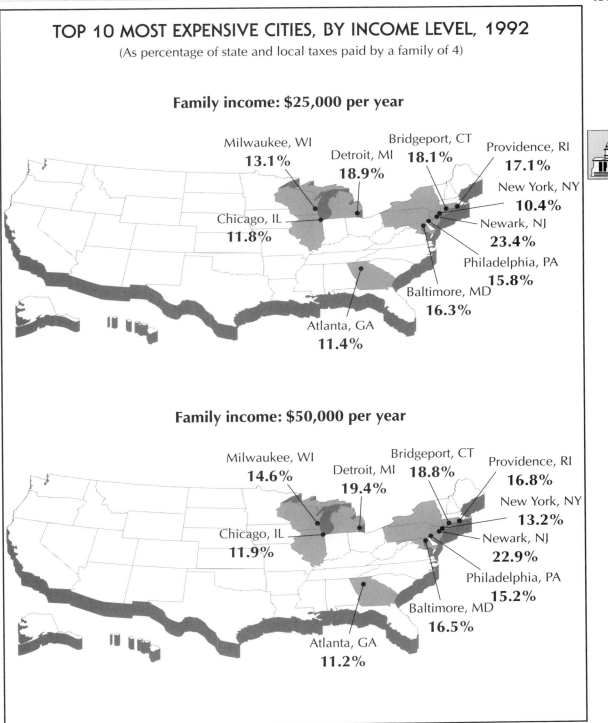

Family income: $25,000 per year

Milwaukee, WI **13.1%**

Detroit, MI **18.9%**

Bridgeport, CT **18.1%**

Providence, RI **17.1%**

New York, NY **10.4%**

Chicago, IL **11.8%**

Newark, NJ **23.4%**

Philadelphia, PA **15.8%**

Baltimore, MD **16.3%**

Atlanta, GA **11.4%**

Family income: $50,000 per year

Milwaukee, WI **14.6%**

Detroit, MI **19.4%**

Bridgeport, CT **18.8%**

Providence, RI **16.8%**

New York, NY **13.2%**

Chicago, IL **11.9%**

Newark, NJ **22.9%**

Philadelphia, PA **15.2%**

Baltimore, MD **16.5%**

Atlanta, GA **11.2%**

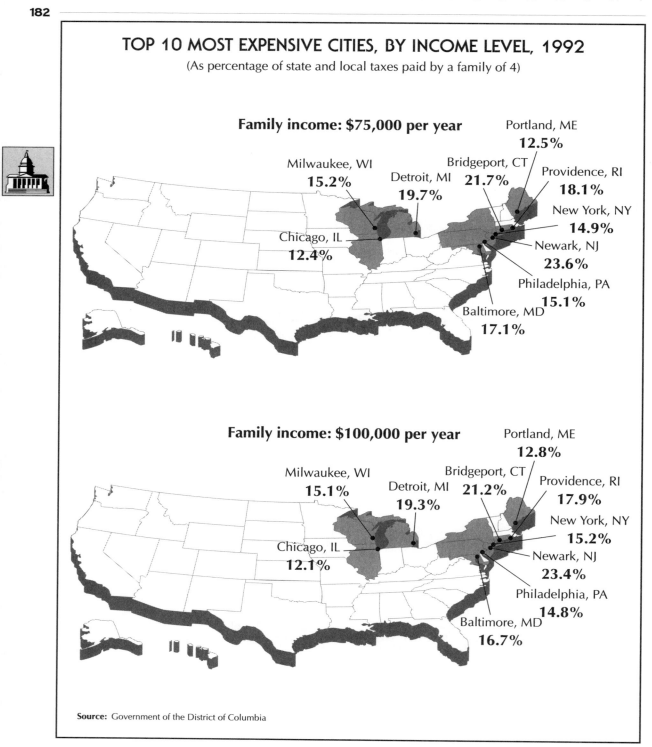

TOP 10 MOST EXPENSIVE CITIES, BY INCOME LEVEL, 1992

(As percentage of state and local taxes paid by a family of 4)

Family income: $75,000 per year

Portland, ME
12.5%

Milwaukee, WI
15.2%

Detroit, MI
19.7%

Bridgeport, CT
21.7%

Providence, RI
18.1%

New York, NY
14.9%

Chicago, IL
12.4%

Newark, NJ
23.6%

Philadelphia, PA
15.1%

Baltimore, MD
17.1%

Family income: $100,000 per year

Portland, ME
12.8%

Milwaukee, WI
15.1%

Detroit, MI
19.3%

Bridgeport, CT
21.2%

Providence, RI
17.9%

New York, NY
15.2%

Chicago, IL
12.1%

Newark, NJ
23.4%

Philadelphia, PA
14.8%

Baltimore, MD
16.7%

Source: Government of the District of Columbia

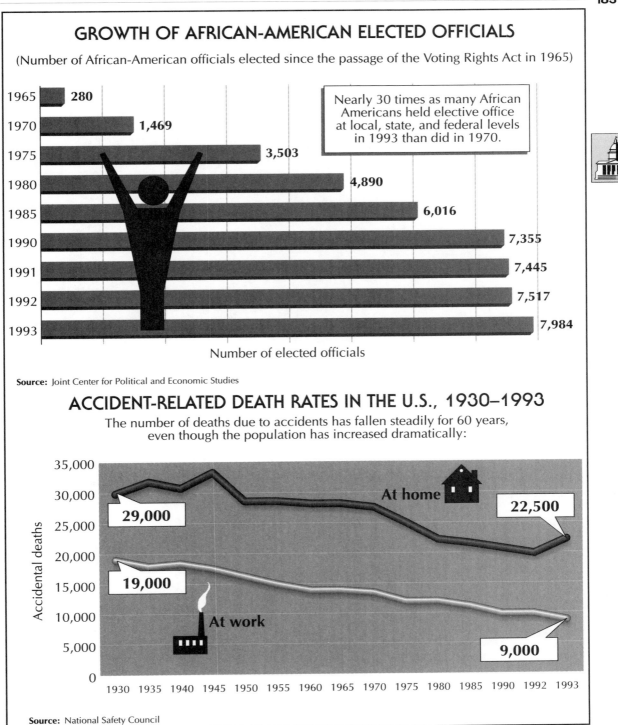

GROWTH OF AFRICAN-AMERICAN ELECTED OFFICIALS

(Number of African-American officials elected since the passage of the Voting Rights Act in 1965)

Year	Number
1965	280
1970	1,469
1975	3,503
1980	4,890
1985	6,016
1990	7,355
1991	7,445
1992	7,517
1993	7,984

Nearly 30 times as many African Americans held elective office at local, state, and federal levels in 1993 than did in 1970.

Number of elected officials

Source: Joint Center for Political and Economic Studies

ACCIDENT-RELATED DEATH RATES IN THE U.S., 1930–1993

The number of deaths due to accidents has fallen steadily for 60 years, even though the population has increased dramatically:

At home

29,000

22,500

Accidental deaths

19,000

At work

9,000

1930 1935 1940 1945 1950 1955 1960 1965 1970 1975 1980 1985 1990 1992 1993

Source: National Safety Council

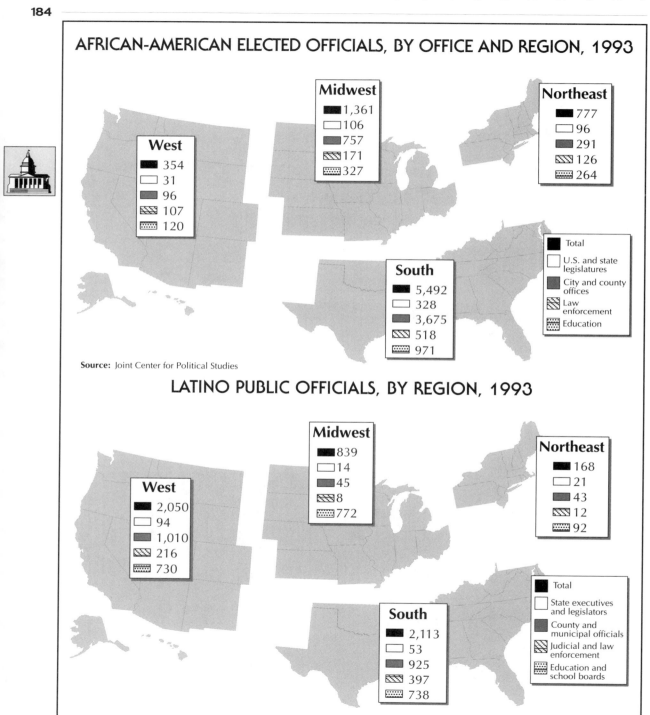

AFRICAN-AMERICAN ELECTED OFFICIALS, BY OFFICE AND REGION, 1993

Midwest
- 1,361
- 106
- 757
- 171
- 327

Northeast
- 777
- 96
- 291
- 126
- 264

West
- 354
- 31
- 96
- 107
- 120

South
- 5,492
- 328
- 3,675
- 518
- 971

- Total
- U.S. and state legislatures
- City and county offices
- Law enforcement
- Education

Source: Joint Center for Political Studies

LATINO PUBLIC OFFICIALS, BY REGION, 1993

Midwest
- 839
- 14
- 45
- 8
- 772

Northeast
- 168
- 21
- 43
- 12
- 92

West
- 2,050
- 94
- 1,010
- 216
- 730

South
- 2,113
- 53
- 925
- 397
- 738

- Total
- State executives and legislators
- County and municipal officials
- Judicial and law enforcement
- Education and school boards

Source: National Association of Latino Elected & Appointed Officials

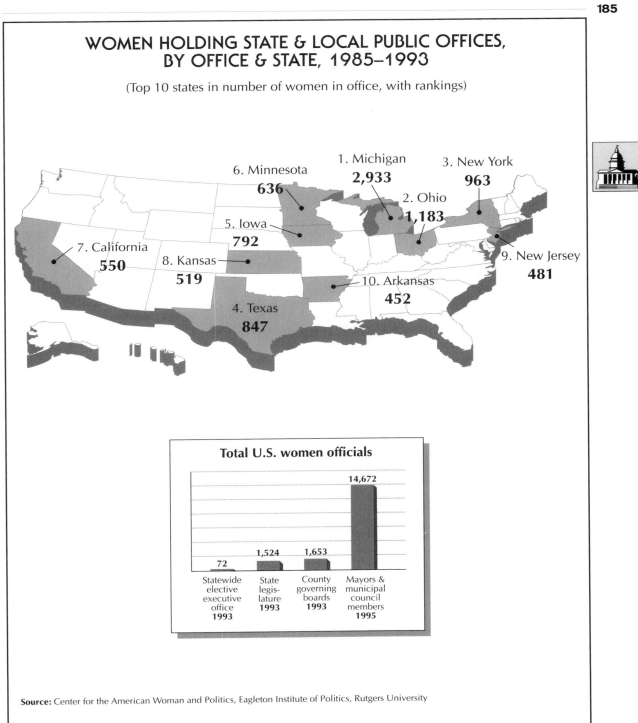

WOMEN HOLDING STATE & LOCAL PUBLIC OFFICES, BY OFFICE & STATE, 1985–1993

(Top 10 states in number of women in office, with rankings)

6. Minnesota
636

1. Michigan
2,933

3. New York
963

2. Ohio
1,183

5. Iowa
792

7. California
550

8. Kansas
519

9. New Jersey
481

10. Arkansas
452

4. Texas
847

Total U.S. women officials

			14,672
72	1,524	1,653	
Statewide elective executive office **1993**	State legis-lature **1993**	County governing boards **1993**	Mayors & municipal council members **1995**

Source: Center for the American Woman and Politics, Eagleton Institute of Politics, Rutgers University

VOTING AND ELECTIONS

In 1992, Democrat Bill Clinton defeated incumbent Republican George Bush to become the 42nd president of the United States. Despite his win, Clinton received only 43% of the popular vote, as compared to Bush's 38%. The strong showing of Independent third-party candidate H. Ross Perot (19% of the vote), coupled with the increasing inability of party leaders to maintain unity among their office holders, was proof of the growing independence of the U.S. voters. Americans have become more willing to cast their ballots for individuals rather than for parties. Among those who have profited from this trend, particularly at state and local levels, are the "single-issue candidates," whose political platforms tend to center around one issue, such as abortion or crime.

The Republicans may have lost the presidency in 1992, but they subsequently enjoyed a string of successes at other levels of government. In 1994, American voters gave Republican candidates a historic boost—in both houses of Congress as well as a majority of governorships. The results of these elections were perceived by the voting public as a mandate to reduce taxes and spending on social programs. The new office holders pledged sweeping tax cuts, reductions in welfare programs, balanced budgets, deficit reductions, stronger penalties for criminals, and fewer restrictions on businesses.

Results in the 1996 elections will depend greatly upon who actually turns out to vote. Seventy percent of eligible voters said they voted in the 1992 presidential election; but actions speak louder than words. In reality, only 68.2% of the voting-age population were even registered to vote, and only 61.3% actually cast ballots.

FINGERTIP FACTS

☛ More women (54% of voters) than men cast ballots in the 1992 elections.

☛ The percentage of registered voters in 1992 was highest in North Dakota (90.8%) and lowest in California (57.6%). The percentage of the voting-age population who actually voted was highest in Wisconsin (75.3%) and lowest in California (52.8%).

☛ The percentage of people who said they were political Independents grew in the period from 28% in 1988 to 33% in 1993.

☛ In 1992, the economy was the issue that voters said was most important to them; the deficit, health care, family values, and taxes followed in importance.

☛ From 1990 through 1994, voters in 21 states approved ballot measures to limit congressional terms to 12 years or less. Term limits for state legislators exist in 20 states and in about 240 cities and counties.

☛ At the end of 1993, there were 5,170 Latinos holding public office, including 17 U.S. representatives, 182 state executives and legislators, and 242 judges.

☛ In mid-1994, a total of 32 of the 435 congressional districts had a majority population of African Americans, and 20 had a majority of Latinos; two districts in Hawaii had Asian-majority populations.

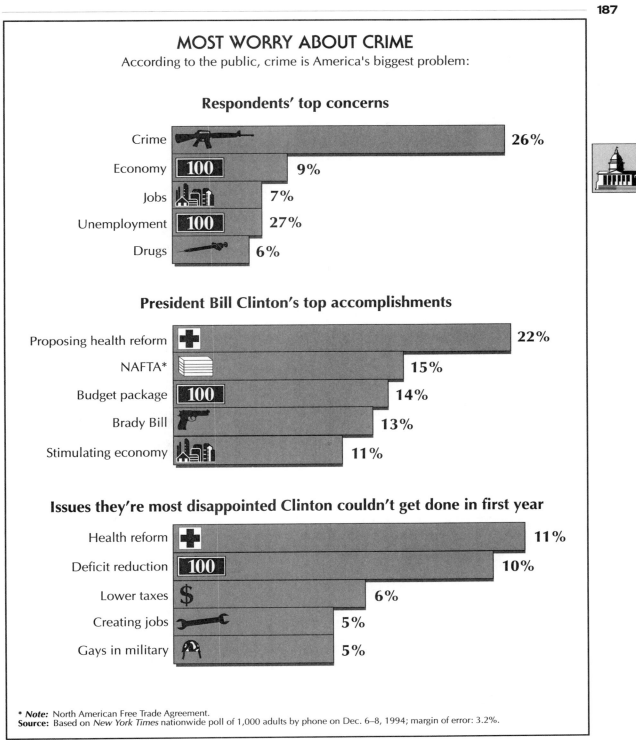

MOST WORRY ABOUT CRIME

According to the public, crime is America's biggest problem:

Respondents' top concerns

Crime	26%
Economy	9%
Jobs	7%
Unemployment	27%
Drugs	6%

President Bill Clinton's top accomplishments

Proposing health reform	22%
NAFTA*	15%
Budget package	14%
Brady Bill	13%
Stimulating economy	11%

Issues they're most disappointed Clinton couldn't get done in first year

Health reform	11%
Deficit reduction	10%
Lower taxes	6%
Creating jobs	5%
Gays in military	5%

Note: North American Free Trade Agreement.
Source: Based on *New York Times* nationwide poll of 1,000 adults by phone on Dec. 6–8, 1994; margin of error: 3.2%.

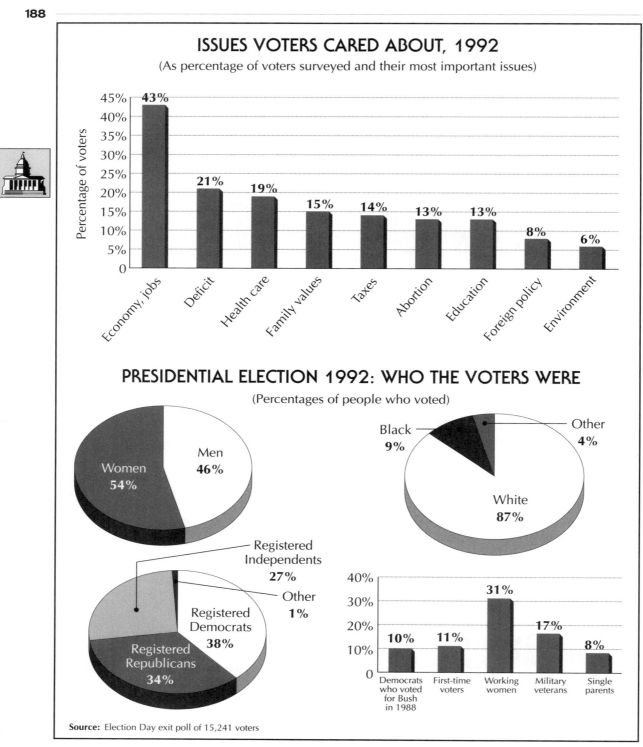

ISSUES VOTERS CARED ABOUT, 1992

(As percentage of voters surveyed and their most important issues)

- Economy, jobs: 43%
- Deficit: 21%
- Health care: 19%
- Family values: 15%
- Taxes: 14%
- Abortion: 13%
- Education: 13%
- Foreign policy: 8%
- Environment: 6%

PRESIDENTIAL ELECTION 1992: WHO THE VOTERS WERE

(Percentages of people who voted)

Women 54%
Men 46%

Black 9%
Other 4%
White 87%

Registered Independents 27%
Other 1%
Registered Democrats 38%
Registered Republicans 34%

- Democrats who voted for Bush in 1988: 10%
- First-time voters: 11%
- Working women: 31%
- Military veterans: 17%
- Single parents: 8%

Source: Election Day exit poll of 15,241 voters

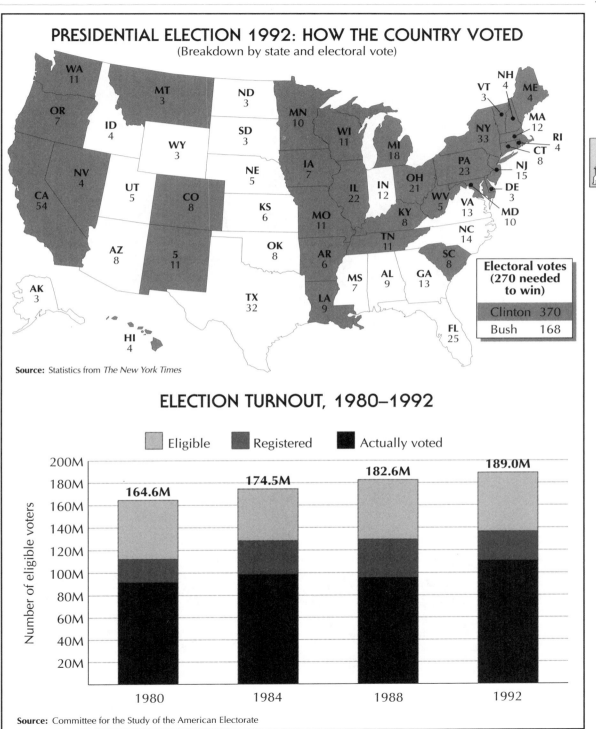

PRESIDENTIAL ELECTION 1992: HOW THE COUNTRY VOTED
(Breakdown by state and electoral vote)

WA 11
OR 7
MT 3
ND 3
MN 10
NH 4
VT 3
ME 4
NY 33
MA 12
RI 4
CT 8
NJ 15
DE 3
MD 10
ID 4
WY 3
SD 3
WI 11
MI 18
PA 23
OH 21
WV 5
VA 13
NV 4
CA 54
UT 5
CO 8
NE 5
IA 7
IL 22
IN 12
KY 8
NC 14
KS 6
MO 11
TN 11
SC 8
AZ 8
5 11
OK 8
AR 6
MS 7
AL 9
GA 13
AK 3
TX 32
LA 9
HI 4
FL 25

Electoral votes (270 needed to win)

Clinton 370
Bush 168

Source: Statistics from *The New York Times*

ELECTION TURNOUT, 1980–1992

Eligible   Registered   Actually voted

Number of eligible voters

200M
180M
160M
140M
120M
100M
80M
60M
40M
20M

164.6M — 1980
174.5M — 1984
182.6M — 1988
189.0M — 1992

Source: Committee for the Study of the American Electorate

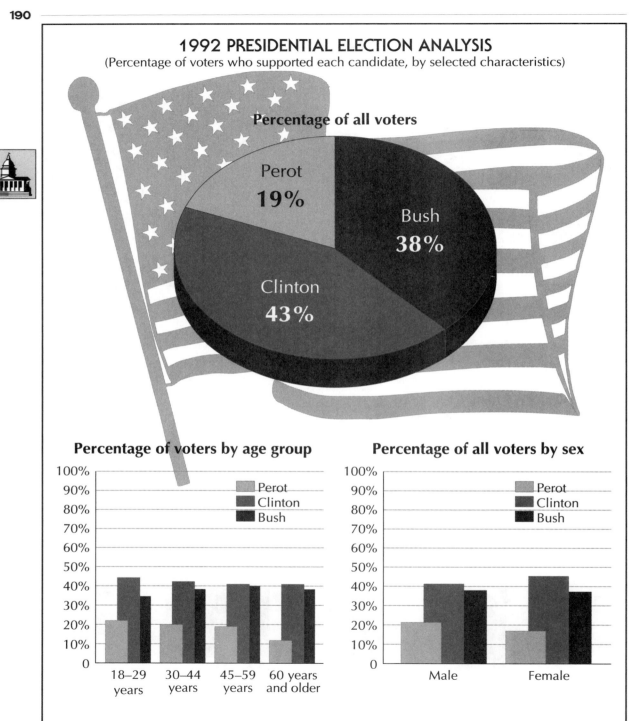

1992 PRESIDENTIAL ELECTION ANALYSIS
(Percentage of voters who supported each candidate, by selected characteristics)

Percentage of all voters

Perot 19%

Bush 38%

Clinton 43%

Percentage of voters by age group

Perot
Clinton
Bush

18–29 years | 30–44 years | 45–59 years | 60 years and older

Percentage of all voters by sex

Perot
Clinton
Bush

Male | Female

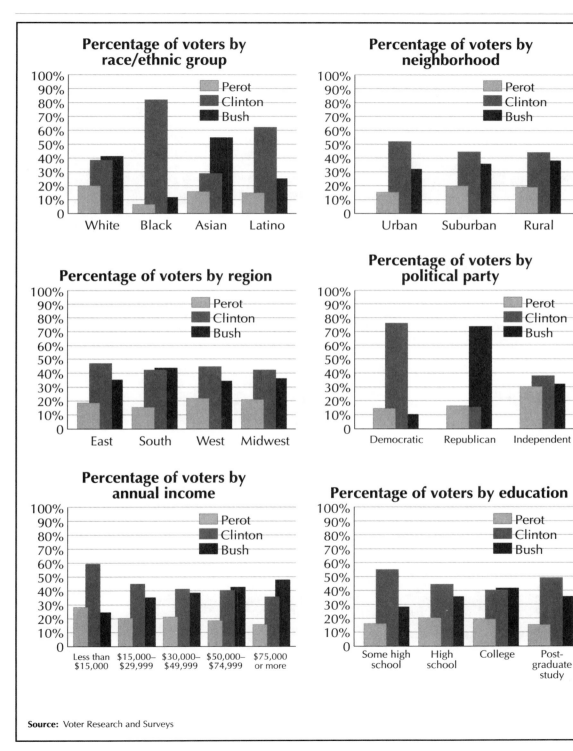

Percentage of voters by race/ethnic group

Legend: Perot, Clinton, Bush

(White, Black, Asian, Latino)

Percentage of voters by neighborhood

Legend: Perot, Clinton, Bush

(Urban, Suburban, Rural)

Percentage of voters by region

Legend: Perot, Clinton, Bush

(East, South, West, Midwest)

Percentage of voters by political party

Legend: Perot, Clinton, Bush

(Democratic, Republican, Independent)

Percentage of voters by annual income

Legend: Perot, Clinton, Bush

(Less than $15,000; $15,000–$29,999; $30,000–$49,999; $50,000–$74,999; $75,000 or more)

Percentage of voters by education

Legend: Perot, Clinton, Bush

(Some high school, High school, College, Post-graduate study)

Source: Voter Research and Surveys

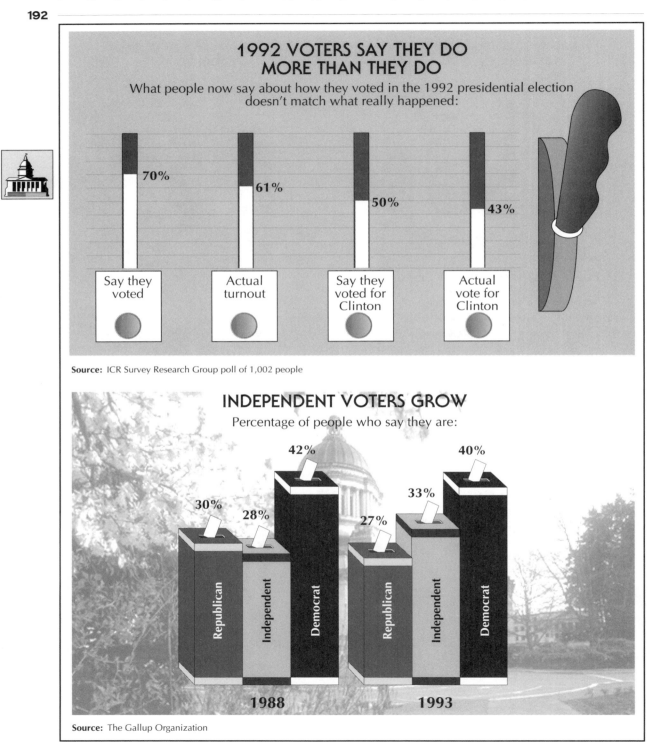

1992 VOTERS SAY THEY DO MORE THAN THEY DO

What people now say about how they voted in the 1992 presidential election doesn't match what really happened:

70% — Say they voted

61% — Actual turnout

50% — Say they voted for Clinton

43% — Actual vote for Clinton

Source: ICR Survey Research Group poll of 1,002 people

INDEPENDENT VOTERS GROW

Percentage of people who say they are:

1988
- 30% Republican
- 28% Independent
- 42% Democrat

1993
- 27% Republican
- 33% Independent
- 40% Democrat

Source: The Gallup Organization

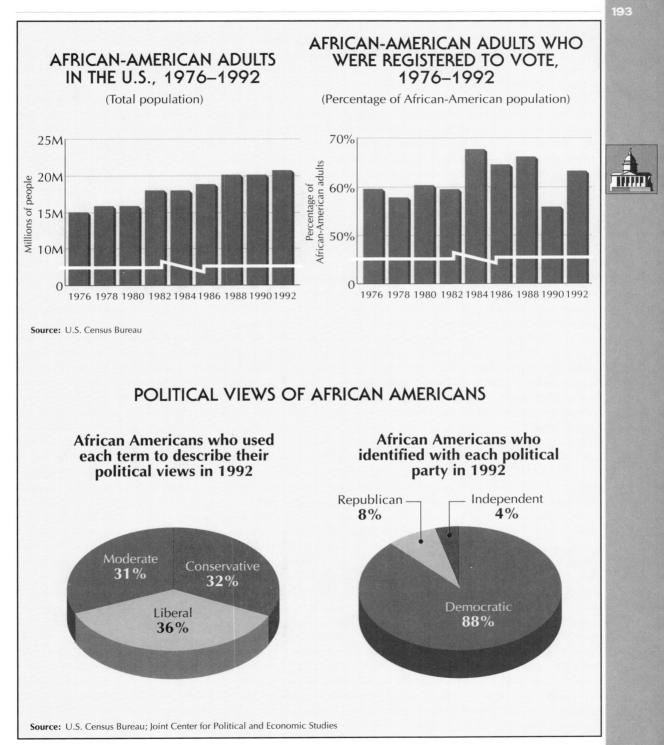

AFRICAN-AMERICAN ADULTS IN THE U.S., 1976–1992

(Total population)

AFRICAN-AMERICAN ADULTS WHO WERE REGISTERED TO VOTE, 1976–1992

(Percentage of African-American population)

Source: U.S. Census Bureau

POLITICAL VIEWS OF AFRICAN AMERICANS

African Americans who used each term to describe their political views in 1992

Moderate 31%
Conservative 32%
Liberal 36%

African Americans who identified with each political party in 1992

Republican 8%
Independent 4%
Democratic 88%

Source: U.S. Census Bureau; Joint Center for Political and Economic Studies

LOBBY GROUPS

Even though lobbies—special-interest groups—have been part of the American political process since the nation's beginnings, citizens have always viewed them with ambivalence. While these organizations exist primarily to influence the opinions of legislators and other public officials, they can also serve the public interest, supplying valuable, practical information to busy legislators.

Today, a broad range of interests are represented by lobbies. Some of the major ones are corporations, labor, agriculture, educational and health organizations, environmental groups, foreign political and economic concerns, consumers, senior citizens, the poor, and religious groups. In addition, there are single-issue groups—such as the National Rifle Association—that lobby public officials on specific concerns, such as gun control.

The number of lobby groups in the U.S. has soared. One segment that has shown particularly strong growth is political action committees (PACs), which raise money and make contributions to candidates running for political office. PAC contributions to congressional candidates—especially incumbents—now account for a significant portion of every candidate's campaign chest. There is much evidence that money flows the fastest and most generously to candidates who share the views of well-financed PACs and influential other lobby groups. There is also much suspicion that, when it comes time to vote in Congress, these groups expect favors from elected officials in return for their contributions. During 1991 and 1992, PACs contributed $188.9 million to candidates, with the most going to incumbents.

FINGERTIP FACTS

- Lobbyists must register with Congress and file quarterly reports disclosing their clients, their objectives, and the amount of money they receive and spend. The reports are published in the Congressional Record.

- Corporate PAC contributions are higher than those of opposing PACs. The Sierra Club, an environmental group, contributed $680,000 to congressional campaigns in the 1991-1992 session. In contrast, energy and other natural resource companies contributed $21.3 million during the same period.

- In 1991, the National Health Council found 741 health groups represented in Washington, D.C. —up from 117 in 1979.

- PACs are a growth industry. In 1980, there were 2,551 PACs, of which 1,206 were corporate. By 1993, the number of PACs had reached 4,025, of which 1,715 were corporate.

- Some members of Congress have created their own PACs. Among the many fund-raising organizations created by Newt Gingrich (R-GA) is GOPAC, which raised $7.8 million from 1991 to 1994. Thirty-three of the 73 new Republicans in the 104th Congress were recruited and trained by GOPAC.

- Ralph Nader's group Public Citizen found that of 300 former members of the U.S. House of Representatives, 177 of them (59%) had taken lucrative lobbying-related jobs.

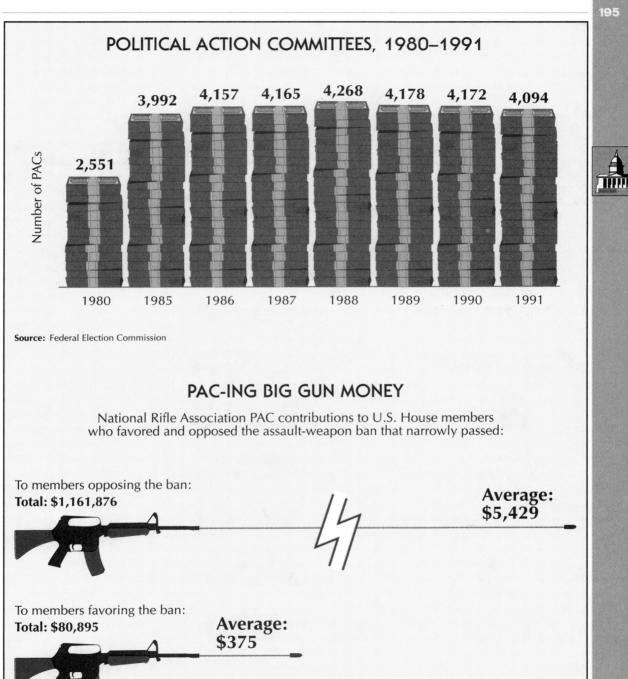

POLITICAL ACTION COMMITTEES, 1980–1991

Number of PACs

2,551 — 1980
3,992 — 1985
4,157 — 1986
4,165 — 1987
4,268 — 1988
4,178 — 1989
4,172 — 1990
4,094 — 1991

Source: Federal Election Commission

PAC-ING BIG GUN MONEY

National Rifle Association PAC contributions to U.S. House members
who favored and opposed the assault-weapon ban that narrowly passed:

To members opposing the ban:
Total: $1,161,876

**Average:
$5,429**

To members favoring the ban:
Total: $80,895

**Average:
$375**

Source: *Capital Eye: A Close Look at Money in Politics*

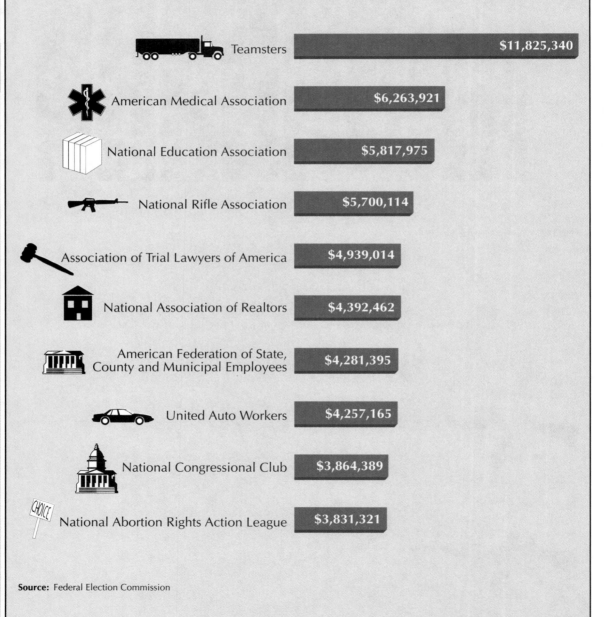

TOP 10 U.S. PAC SPENDERS, 1992

Political action committees dished out $205 million in special-interest contributions to favored legislators and political parties in 1991–1992. Nearly $189 million went to congressional candidates, up 19% over the previous period, with three-fourths of the money going to incumbents:

Teamsters	$11,825,340
American Medical Association	$6,263,921
National Education Association	$5,817,975
National Rifle Association	$5,700,114
Association of Trial Lawyers of America	$4,939,014
National Association of Realtors	$4,392,462
American Federation of State, County and Municipal Employees	$4,281,395
United Auto Workers	$4,257,165
National Congressional Club	$3,864,389
National Abortion Rights Action League	$3,831,321

Source: Federal Election Commission

HEALTHY PAC CONTRIBUTIONS: SOURCES AND RECIPIENTS

Political action committees (PACs) that represent health and insurance industries upped their contributions to congressional members in 1993—just as debate heated up over President Clinton's health care reforms.

Top givers: political action committees, 1991 vs. 1993

Millions of dollars

- 1991
- 1993

Health industry: $4.2M (1991), $5.6M (1993)
Insurance industry: $2.6M (1991), $2.7M (1993)

Top PAC recipients

Senate

- Kay Bailey Hutchison, R–TX **$377,069**
- Daniel Patrick Moynihan, D–NY **$140,370**
- Joseph Lieberman, D–CT **$139,600**
- Orrin Hatch, R–UT **$130,700**
- John Chafee, R–RI **$124,125**
- Edward Kennedy, D–MA **$123,150**
- Connie Mack, R–FL **$123,041**
- Frank Lautenberg, D–NJ **$115,991**
- Kent Conrad, D–ND **$95,333**
- Jim Sasser, D–TN **$88,900**

House

- Jim Cooper, D–TN **$163,486**
- Fortney "Pete" Stark, D–CA **$100,770**
- Richard Gephart, D–MO **$90,401**
- Dan Rostenkowski, D–IL **$77,000**
- Jon Kyl, R–AZ **$64,000**
- Robert Matsui, D–CA **$54,500**
- Newt Gingrich, R–GA **$54,050**
- Fred Grandy, R–IA **$51,572**
- Sam Farr, D–CA **$50,493**
- Rob Portman, R–OH **$50,150**

Source: CAC

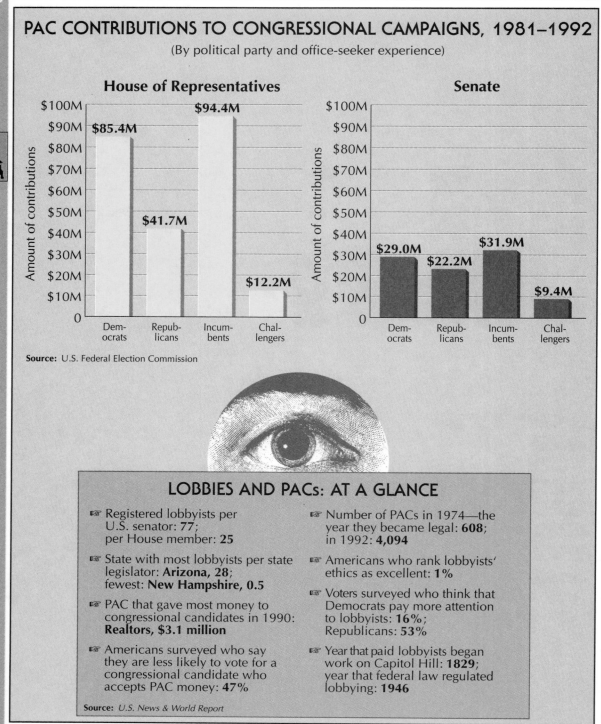

PAC CONTRIBUTIONS TO CONGRESSIONAL CAMPAIGNS, 1981–1992

(By political party and office-seeker experience)

House of Representatives

Amount of contributions

Democrats	$85.4M
Republicans	$41.7M
Incumbents	$94.4M
Challengers	$12.2M

Senate

Amount of contributions

Democrats	$29.0M
Republicans	$22.2M
Incumbents	$31.9M
Challengers	$9.4M

Source: U.S. Federal Election Commission

LOBBIES AND PACs: AT A GLANCE

☞ Registered lobbyists per U.S. senator: **77**; per House member: **25**

☞ State with most lobbyists per state legislator: **Arizona, 28**; fewest: **New Hampshire, 0.5**

☞ PAC that gave most money to congressional candidates in 1990: **Realtors, $3.1 million**

☞ Americans surveyed who say they are less likely to vote for a congressional candidate who accepts PAC money: **47%**

☞ Number of PACs in 1974—the year they became legal: **608**; in 1992: **4,094**

☞ Americans who rank lobbyists' ethics as excellent: **1%**

☞ Voters surveyed who think that Democrats pay more attention to lobbyists: **16%**; Republicans: **53%**

☞ Year that paid lobbyists began work on Capitol Hill: **1829**; year that federal law regulated lobbying: **1946**

Source: *U.S. News & World Report*

NAFTA VOTE, BY PARTY

The North American Free Trade Agreement
took effect on January 1, 1994.
This is how Congress voted:

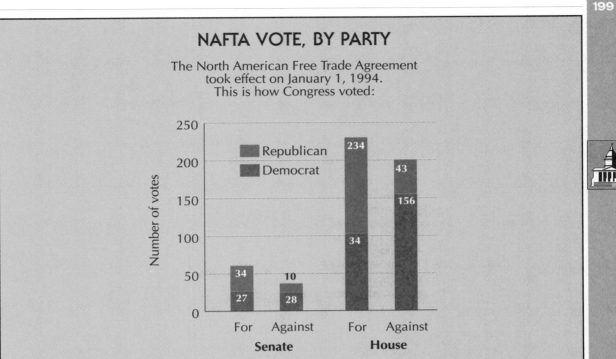

Source: Congressional Record

HOW SUPPORT FOR NAFTA WAS DIVIDED

An analysis of announced votes on NAFTA shows deep divisions within the parties, and among congressional coalitions. Even new members, expected to tilt heavily against NAFTA, were split:

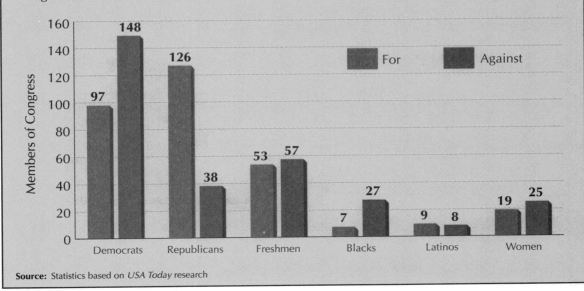

Source: Statistics based on *USA Today* research

THE FACE OF CONGRESS

As a result of the 1994 midterm elections, Congress had a dramatically new look: For the first time since 1954, Republicans were in the majority in both houses. They controlled the Senate by 53 to 47, and the House of Representatives by 230 to 205 (204 Democrats and one Independent).

From a historical perspective, however, the most striking changes of 1994 were found in the race, gender, and class makeup of America's representatives. The 104th Congress looked more like the nation's real population than did the First Congress, which met in 1789-1790 and which contained only white males.

From an economic and social class standpoint, however, the Congress in 1994 looked quite similar to that of 1789. Most members—then as well as now—are quite wealthy. The percentage of millionaires in Congress far exceeds that in the U.S. population as a whole (and, historically, always has). Many nominees are also wealthy, perhaps reflecting the skyrocketing cost of running for office.

The 104th Congress included 86 first-term members in the House, 73 of them Republicans, and 11 new Republicans in the Senate. Eight women—a record—were seated, up from 6 in the previous Congress. Four senators belonged to minority groups: one African American, and 2 Asian Americans. In the House, there were 47 women, 38 blacks, 17 Latinos, and 4 Asian Americans.

FINGERTIP FACTS

- African Americans constitute 12.5% of the U.S. population. Black membership of the 104th Congress was 8.7% of the House, 1.0% of the Senate.

- Women, who constitute more than 50% of the U.S. population, made up 8.0% of the Senate and 10.8% of the House in the 104th Congress, 1995-1996.

- In 1994, Republican contender Michael Huffington spent more than $25 million in his unsuccessful bid to unseat California senator Dianne Feinstein, who spent $14 million. It was the most expensive congressional race in U.S. history.

- Once in office, the financial rewards are great. Most members of Congress earn $133,600 a year. The Senate's president pro tempore and the majority and minority leaders each earn $148,400, as do the majority and minority leaders of the House. The speaker of the House earns $171,500. All members of Congress are given generous allowances for expenses and staff.

- The personal staff of congressional members began to shrink in 1987. In 1991, the personal staff of House members totaled 7,278 (an average of 16.7 per representative). Staff for Senate members totaled 4,294 (42.9 per senator).

PERCENTAGE OF MILLIONAIRES IN CONGRESS

(As percentage of each group)

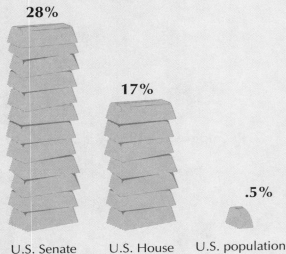

28%

17%

.5%

U.S. Senate   U.S. House   U.S. population

Source: Internal Revenue Service, Congress

MINORITY REPRESENTATION IN CONGRESS

Since the Voting Rights Act was passed in 1965, minority membership in Congress has never matched the minority population of the U.S. Here's how the makeup of Congress compared with the U.S. population in 1990:

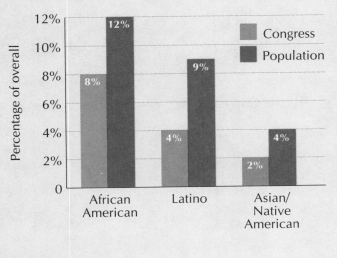

Percentage of overall

- Congress
- Population

	African American	Latino	Asian/ Native American
Congress	8%	4%	2%
Population	12%	9%	4%

Source: Congressional Quarterly; U.S. Census Bureau

WHO MAKES UP CONGRESS? SELECTED CHARACTERISTICS, 1977–1994

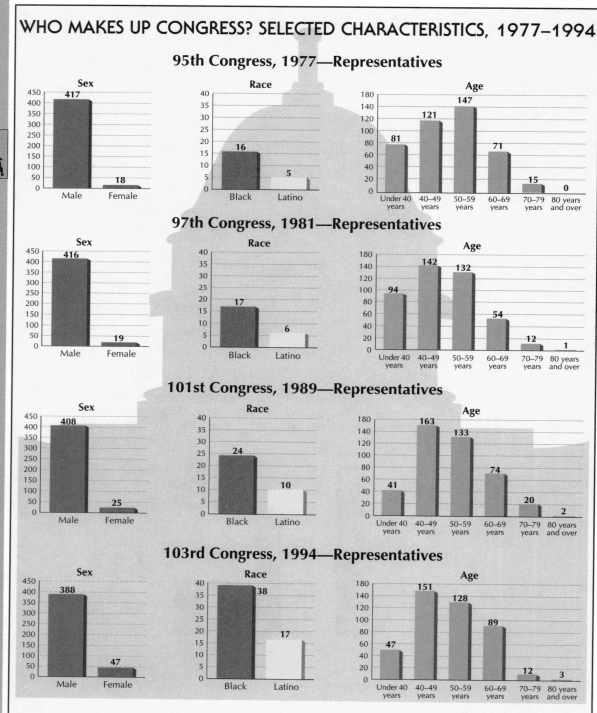

95th Congress, 1977—Representatives

Sex
- Male: 417
- Female: 18

Race
- Black: 16
- Latino: 5

Age
- Under 40 years: 81
- 40–49 years: 121
- 50–59 years: 147
- 60–69 years: 71
- 70–79 years: 15
- 80 years and over: 0

97th Congress, 1981—Representatives

Sex
- Male: 416
- Female: 19

Race
- Black: 17
- Latino: 6

Age
- Under 40 years: 94
- 40–49 years: 142
- 50–59 years: 132
- 60–69 years: 54
- 70–79 years: 12
- 80 years and over: 1

101st Congress, 1989—Representatives

Sex
- Male: 408
- Female: 25

Race
- Black: 24
- Latino: 10

Age
- Under 40 years: 41
- 40–49 years: 163
- 50–59 years: 133
- 60–69 years: 74
- 70–79 years: 20
- 80 years and over: 2

103rd Congress, 1994—Representatives

Sex
- Male: 388
- Female: 47

Race
- Black: 38
- Latino: 17

Age
- Under 40 years: 47
- 40–49 years: 151
- 50–59 years: 128
- 60–69 years: 89
- 70–79 years: 12
- 80 years and over: 3

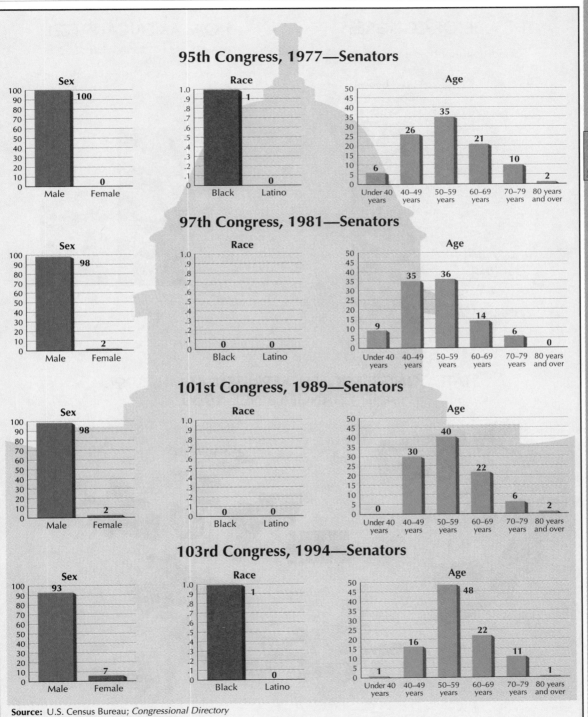

95th Congress, 1977—Senators

Sex

Male	Female
100	0

Race

Black	Latino
1	0

Age

Under 40 years	40–49 years	50–59 years	60–69 years	70–79 years	80 years and over
6	26	35	21	10	2

97th Congress, 1981—Senators

Sex

Male	Female
98	2

Race

Black	Latino
0	0

Age

Under 40 years	40–49 years	50–59 years	60–69 years	70–79 years	80 years and over
9	35	36	14	6	0

101st Congress, 1989—Senators

Sex

Male	Female
98	2

Race

Black	Latino
0	0

Age

Under 40 years	40–49 years	50–59 years	60–69 years	70–79 years	80 years and over
0	30	40	22	6	2

103rd Congress, 1994—Senators

Sex

Male	Female
93	7

Race

Black	Latino
1	0

Age

Under 40 years	40–49 years	50–59 years	60–69 years	70–79 years	80 years and over
1	16	48	22	11	1

Source: U.S. Census Bureau; *Congressional Directory*

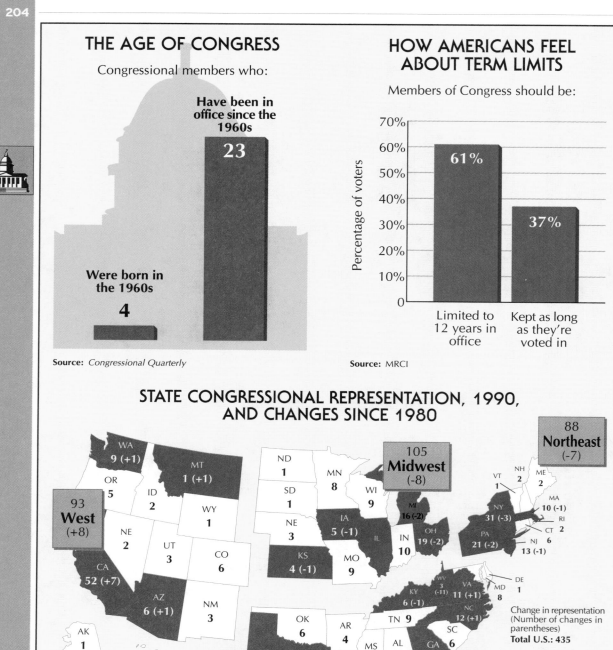

THE AGE OF CONGRESS

Congressional members who:

Have been in office since the 1960s

23

Were born in the 1960s

4

Source: *Congressional Quarterly*

HOW AMERICANS FEEL ABOUT TERM LIMITS

Members of Congress should be:

Percentage of voters

- Limited to 12 years in office — **61%**
- Kept as long as they're voted in — **37%**

Source: MRCI

STATE CONGRESSIONAL REPRESENTATION, 1990, AND CHANGES SINCE 1980

Northeast 88 (-7)
Midwest 105 (-8)
West 93 (+8)
South 149 (+7)

WA 9 (+1)
MT 1 (+1)
OR 5
ID 2
WY 1
ND 1
MN 8
SD 1
WI 9
MI 16 (-2)
NE 2
UT 3
CO 6
IA 5 (-1)
IL
IN 10
OH 19 (-2)
CA 52 (+7)
AZ 6 (+1)
NM 3
KS 4 (-1)
MO 9
AK 1
HI 2
OK 6
AR 4
TX 30 (+3)
LA 7 (-1)
MS 5
AL 7
TN 9
KY 6 (-1)
WV 3 (-11)
VA 11 (+1)
NC 12 (+1)
SC 6
GA 11 (+1)
FL 23 (+4)
MD 8
DE 1
PA 21 (-2)
NY 31 (-3)
VT 1
NH 2
ME 2
MA 10 (-1)
RI 2
CT 2
NJ 13 (-1)
NJ 6

Change in representation (Number of changes in parentheses)
Total U.S.: 435

- ■ Loss (13)
- □ No change (29)
- ■ Gain (8)

Source: U.S. Census Bureau

COMPOSITION OF U.S. CONGRESS: REPRESENTATIVES, 1987–1994
(By political party)

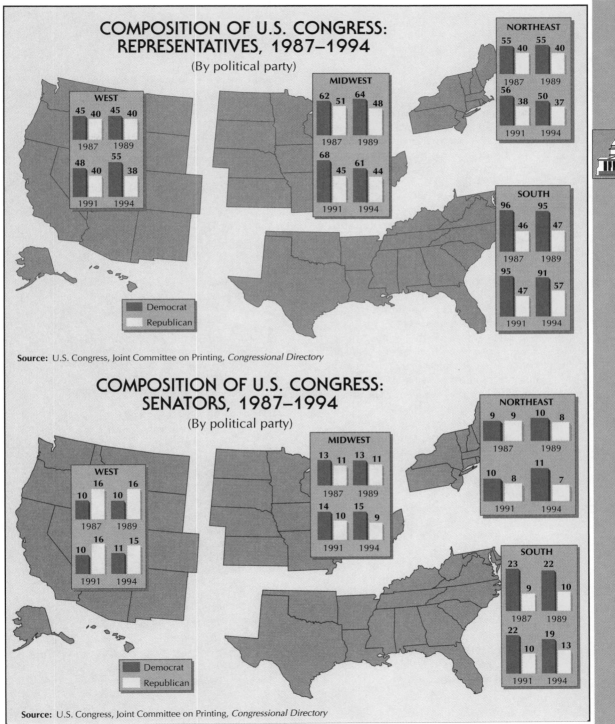

WEST
45	40	45	40
1987		1989	
48	40	55	38
1991		1994	

MIDWEST
62	51	64	48
1987		1989	
68	45	61	44
1991		1994	

NORTHEAST
55	40	55	40
1987		1989	
56	38	50	37
1991		1994	

SOUTH
96	46	95	47
1987		1989	
95	47	91	57
1991		1994	

■ Democrat
□ Republican

Source: U.S. Congress, Joint Committee on Printing, *Congressional Directory*

COMPOSITION OF U.S. CONGRESS: SENATORS, 1987–1994
(By political party)

WEST
10	16	10	16
1987		1989	
10	16	11	15
1991		1994	

MIDWEST
13	11	13	11
1987		1989	
14	10	15	9
1991		1994	

NORTHEAST
9	9	10	8
1987		1989	
10	8	11	7
1991		1994	

SOUTH
23	9	22	10
1987		1989	
22	10	19	13
1991		1994	

■ Democrat
□ Republican

Source: U.S. Congress, Joint Committee on Printing, *Congressional Directory*

J U S T I C E

Most civil and criminal litigation is begun and determined in state courts. Only when the U.S. Constitution and Acts of Congress specifically confer jurisdiction upon the federal courts may civil litigation be heard and decided by the federal courts.

The 94 federal courts that have the authority to try a case initially and pass judgment are the U.S. district courts. One or more of these courts is established in every state as well as in Washington, D.C. and the U.S. territories. Appeals from the district courts are taken to courts of appeals, of which there are 13. The final and highest appellate court in the federal system is the U.S. Supreme Court.

Over the years, the number of cases begun by U.S. district courts and courts of appeals has grown. A growing number of cases is being filed before the U.S. Supreme Court, too, but the number argued annually there has declined. Most cases filed before the Supreme Court are denied, dismissed, or withdrawn.

The composition and political leanings of the courts have become issues of intense interest in the U.S. The Supreme Court has been the focus of much of this interest. Appointments by recent Republican administrations gave the Supreme Court, as well as the other federal courts, their most conservative ideology in decades. In 1993, President Bill Clinton became the first Democratic president in more than a quarter century to appoint new Supreme Court justices. He named Ruth Bader Ginsberg and Stephen G. Breyer to the Court, giving the body a more centrist outlook.

FINGERTIP FACTS

☞ Almost all of the 107 members of the Supreme Courts have been white Christian males. The first Jew to sit on the court, Louis Brandeis, was appointed in 1916. The first black, Thurgood Marshall, joined the Court in 1967. The first woman, Sandra Day O'Connor, was appointed in 1981.

☞ In 1980, there were 5,144 cases on the Supreme Court docket, of which 154 (2.9%) were argued. In 1992, there were 7,245 on the docket and 116 (1.6%) were argued.

☞ In 1992, a full 2,618 of the 2,919 offenders convicted of violent offenses before U.S. district courts were sentenced to prison, with sentences averaging 88.5 months; 16,401 of the 18,698 people convicted of drug offenses were jailed, with sentences averaging 82.2 months.

☞ The U.S. Department of Justice was established in 1870. It is the world's largest law firm, with 96,927 employees in 1992.

☞ In 1992, nearly 12 million people were arrested in the U.S. Of these, 2.5 million were arrested for serious crimes (such as murder, rape, robbery, larceny, and arson; 9.4 million were arrested for other crimes (including fraud, forgery, vandalism, drug abuse, drunkenness, and gambling).

☞ In 1991, a total of 665 federal, 77 state, and 180 local officials were convicted of corruption.

SEX AND RACE OF U.S. FEDERAL JUDGES

There are 837 federal judgeships, including the Supreme Court; 88 of those are vacant:

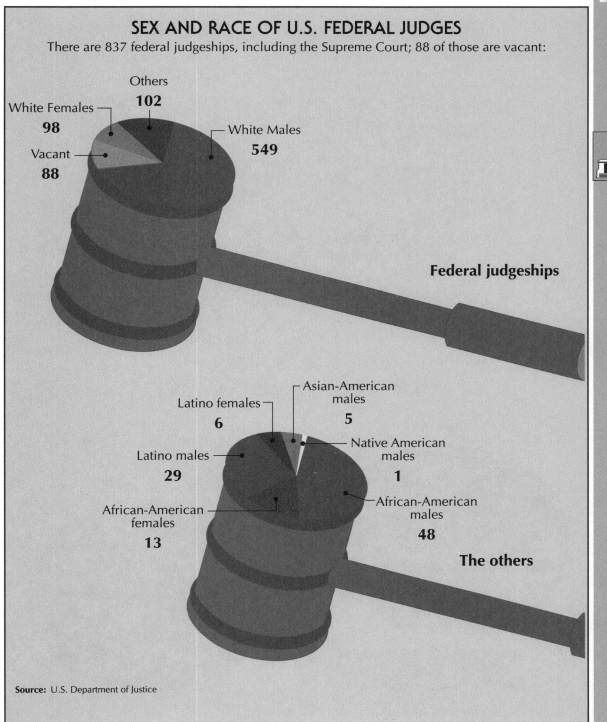

Others
102

White Females
98

Vacant
88

White Males
549

Federal judgeships

Latino females
6

Asian-American males
5

Latino males
29

Native American males
1

African-American females
13

African-American males
48

The others

Source: U.S. Department of Justice

U.S. SUPREME COURT CASES DECLINE, 1982–1993

In 1992–1993, the Supreme Court decided 107 cases, compared with 151 in 1982–1983. The total cases argued each year also has dropped sharply:

Number of cases

181

Cases argued

151

Decisions

118

107

1982– 1983– 1984– 1985– 1986– 1987– 1988– 1989– 1990– 1991– 1992–
1983 1984 1985 1986 1987 1988 1989 1990 1991 1992 1993

Source: The Supreme Court

WHO ARE AMERICA'S LAWYERS?

By sex (1991)

Female
20%
(159,377)

Male
80%
(646,495)

Total number of lawyers in
U.S., 1991: **805,872**

Kind of practice (1991)

Salaried/staff
11.6%

Government
8.3%

Inactive/
retired
4.5%

Judicial
2.8%

Private
practice
72.8%

Source: Statistics based on data from the American Bar Association

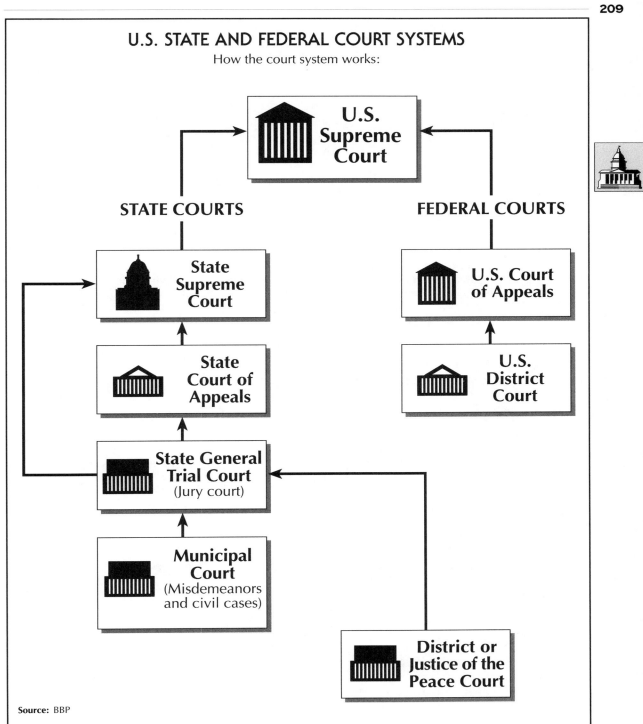

U.S. STATE AND FEDERAL COURT SYSTEMS

How the court system works:

U.S. Supreme Court

STATE COURTS

FEDERAL COURTS

State Supreme Court

U.S. Court of Appeals

State Court of Appeals

U.S. District Court

State General Trial Court
(Jury court)

Municipal Court
(Misdemeanors and civil cases)

District or Justice of the Peace Court

Source: BBP

THE U.S. MILITARY

The U.S. ranks Number One in the world in its total amount of military expenditures, military technology, nuclear warheads and bombs, combat aircraft, naval fleet, military bases worldwide, military aid to foreign countries, and amount of military training of foreign forces.

The U.S. military budget grew rapidly during the 1980s, helping to create a massive federal budget deficit. During the first half of the 1990s, the military budget declined—from $304 billion in 1989 to an estimated $280 billion in 1994. Among the casualties of this downsizing were military bases—many of which were consolidated, closed, or subjected to cutbacks. Troops levels and budgets for new equipment were also cut. Such steps were mirrored by other developed nations, including Russia and North Atlantic Treaty Organization (NATO) members.

The end of the Cold War and the breakup of the Soviet Union in 1991 were important factors in justifying decreases in the U.S. military budget, as were growing concerns on the funding of domestic programs. However, today there is considerable pressure from conservative politicians, military leaders, and the defense industry to increase military spending once again.

Political threats to national security in the coming years are expected to be radically different from the perceived threats of the past. Two major concerns today are the epidemic of ethnic and national conflicts raging during this post-Cold War period and the possibility that nuclear materials may find their way into the hands of terrorists. Military authorities and strategists must find ways to address these and other un-certainties in a rapidly changing world.

FINGERTIP FACTS

- In 1993, global spending was more than $600 billion on military programs. The U.S. military budget accounted for 41% of the world's military expenditures.

- The U.S. ranks third on per capita military expenditures, spending about $1,097 per person. Qatar leads ($1,656); Israel is second ($1,121).

- The U.S. is the major supplier of military weapons to developing world buyers. Its share of the world's arms exports in 1994 was 70%.

- In 1983, the 5 acknowledged nuclear powers (U.S., Soviet Union, Great Britain, France, and China) held 64,360 nuclear weapons. By 1993, the total had declined to 26,700.

- Currently, more nuclear weapons are being retired and dismantled than are being produced. By 2003, arsenals in the U.S. and Russia are expected to be at their lowest levels since the nuclear arms race began in the late 1950s.

- The U.S. communities receiving the most defense dollars in 1993 were San Diego, California ($6.4 billion); St. Louis, Missouri ($5.4 billion); and Norfolk, Virginia ($3.3 billion).

- The largest defense contractor during the fiscal year 1993 was McDonnell Douglas, which was awarded contracts totaling $7.5 billion. Second was Lockheed, $6.9 billion; third was Martin Marietta, $4.7 billion.

ACTIVE-DUTY PERSONNEL, 1987 vs. 1992

(Number of people on active duty in each branch of the armed forces)

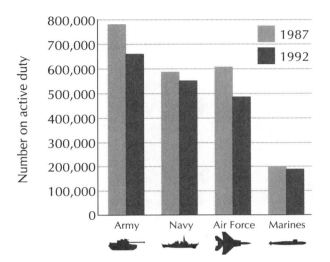

CIVILIAN STAFF IN THE MILITARY, 1985–1993

(Number of civilians who worked for the armed forces in each year)

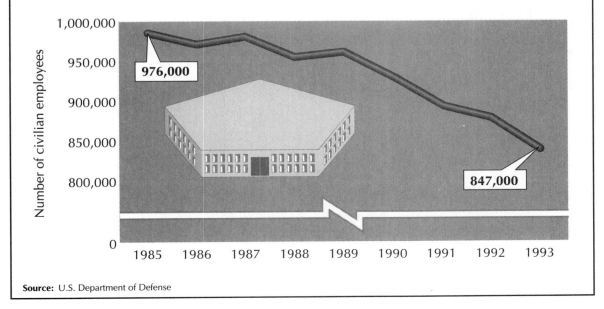

Source: U.S. Department of Defense

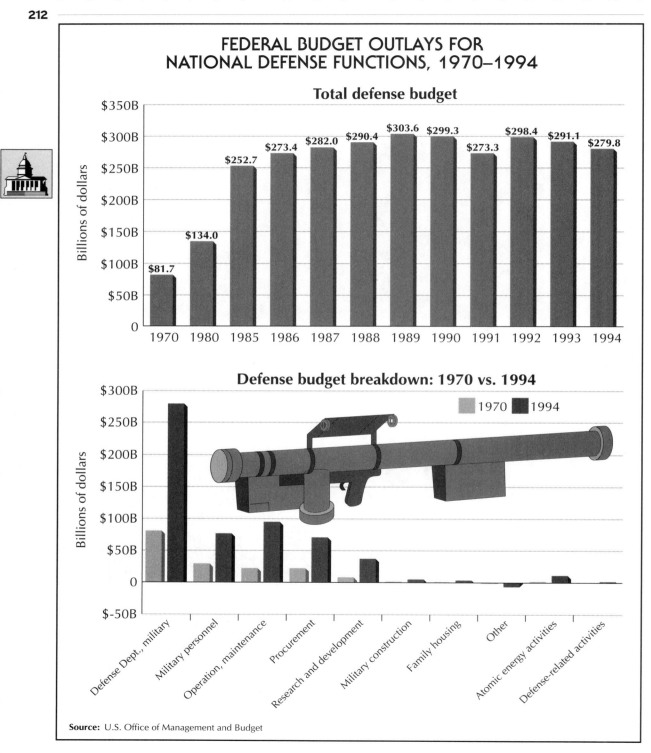

FEDERAL BUDGET OUTLAYS FOR
NATIONAL DEFENSE FUNCTIONS, 1970–1994

Total defense budget

Billions of dollars

1970	$81.7
1980	$134.0
1985	$252.7
1986	$273.4
1987	$282.0
1988	$290.4
1989	$303.6
1990	$299.3
1991	$273.3
1992	$298.4
1993	$291.1
1994	$279.8

Defense budget breakdown: 1970 vs. 1994

1970   1994

Billions of dollars

Defense Dept., military; Military personnel; Operation, maintenance; Procurement; Research and development; Military construction; Family housing; Other; Atomic energy activities; Defense-related activities

Source: U.S. Office of Management and Budget

MONEY FOR MILITARY EQUIPMENT, 1991–1993

(Equipment budget of each branch of the armed forces)

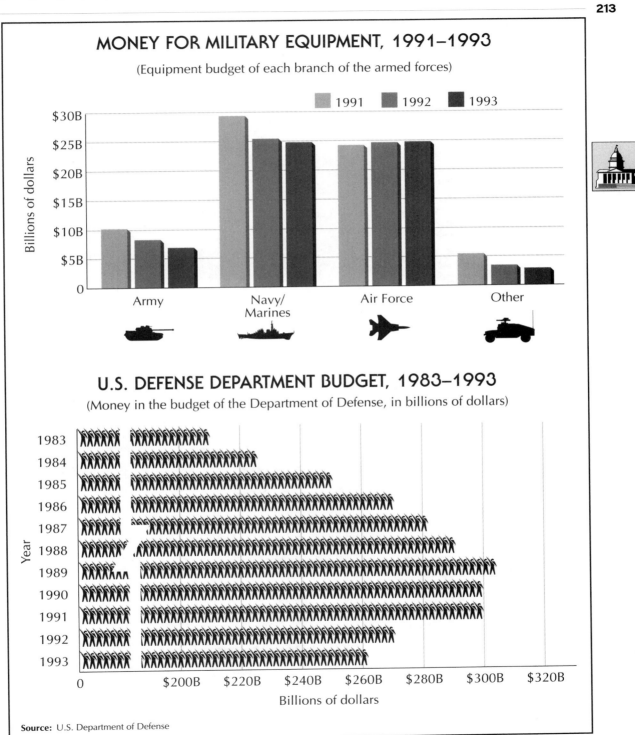

U.S. DEFENSE DEPARTMENT BUDGET, 1983–1993

(Money in the budget of the Department of Defense, in billions of dollars)

Source: U.S. Department of Defense

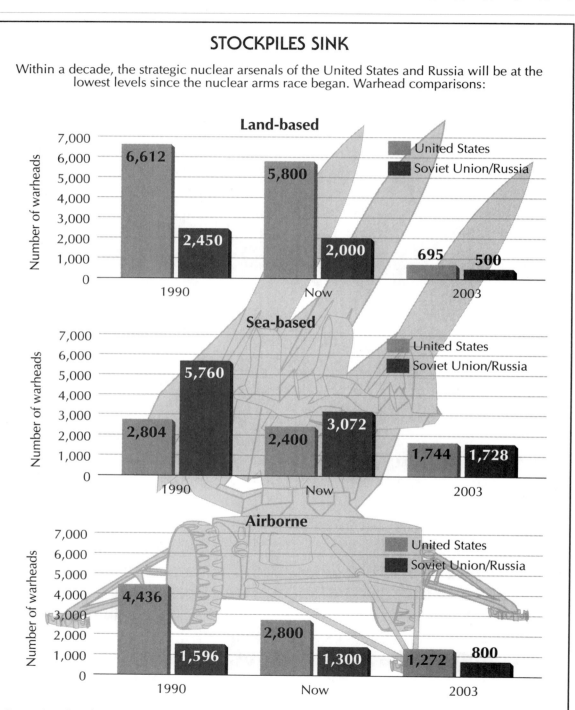

STOCKPILES SINK

Within a decade, the strategic nuclear arsenals of the United States and Russia will be at the lowest levels since the nuclear arms race began. Warhead comparisons:

Land-based

United States
Soviet Union/Russia

Number of warheads

6,612
2,450
5,800
2,000
695
500

1990   Now   2003

Sea-based

United States
Soviet Union/Russia

Number of warheads

2,804
5,760
2,400
3,072
1,744
1,728

1990   Now   2003

Airborne

United States
Soviet Union/Russia

Number of warheads

4,436
1,596
2,800
1,300
1,272
800

1990   Now   2003

Source: Arms Control Association; Bulletin of Atomic Scientists

NUMBER OF INTERCONTINENTAL BALLISTIC MISSILES (ICBMs), 1980–1989

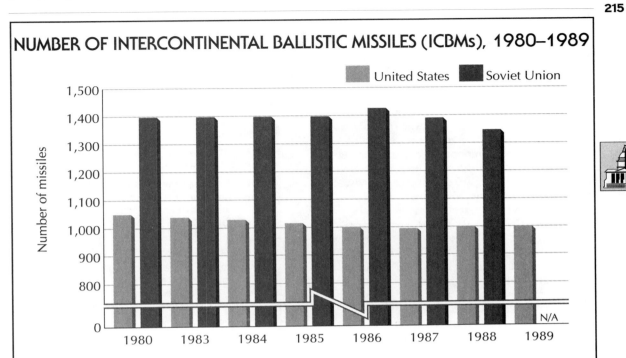

Source: Library of Congress

THE COSTS OF MAJOR AMERICAN WARS

(Estimates of total dollar costs, in descending order)

	Original costs in current dollars	Current cost to 1990
World War II	$360.0B	$466.0B
Vietnam Conflict	$140.6B	$179.0B
Korean Conflict	$50.0B	$72.0B
Persian Gulf War	$36.4B	$47.3B
World War I	$32.7B	$62.5B
Civil War: Union	$2.3B	$6.8B
Civil War: Confederacy	$1.0B	N/A
Spanish-American War	$270.0M	$2.5B
American Revolution	$100.0–$140.0M	$170.0M
War of 1812	$89.0M	$120.0M
Mexican War	$82.0M	$120.0M

Source: Congress, Joint Economic Committee

THE FACE OF THE MILITARY

On September 30, 1993, some 1.7 million Americans were on active military duty. These individuals, however, represented a somewhat skewed cross-section of the American population; males far outnumbered females; blacks made up a disproportionate percentage of enlisted personnel; and whites were disproportionately represented among officers.

Over the years, as American society has changed, so has the U.S. military. Although African Americans have fought for their country since the Revolutionary War, they long had to serve in their own units. It wasn't until 1948 that President Harry S. Truman issued an order to desegregate the armed forces. U.S. history is also filled with women willing to risk their lives for their country, but it wasn't until the all-volunteer military was launched in 1973 that large numbers of brave women began to be integrated into the services.

Many homosexual men and women have also served with great distinction in all of America's wars, but these soldiers have historically been required to conceal their sexual orientation. During his 1992 presidential campaign, Bill Clinton indicated that he wanted to lift the longstanding ban against homosexuals in the military, although he said he would first consider the views of military leaders.

Stiff opposition resulted in a compromise policy termed "Don't ask, don't tell." Gays may now serve if they do not engage in homosexual acts, and commanders may not investigate individuals for homosexual behavior solely on the basis of suspicion or hearsay. This policy is controversial and has been challenged by people on both sides of the issue.

FINGERTIP FACTS

- The U.S. has the world's third-largest armed forces. China leads; Russia is #2.

- In 1970, there were 3.1 million military personnel on active duty; in 1993, that number was 1.7 million.

- Most U.S. military personnel are based in the U.S. In 1993, some 1.4 million were based in the U.S. and its territories; 0.3 million were based in foreign countries, most in Western Europe.

- In 1993, a total of 86% of the recruits were males, 14% were females; 78% were white, 17% black, and 5% other races.

- African Americans make up 12.5% of the U.S. population. In 1993, they accounted for 22% of enlisted personnel and 7.3% of officers. The army had the largest number and percentage of blacks.

- In 1993, there were 1,057,676 people in the reserves; 78.5% were white, 16.4% black, 1.3% Asian, and 0.4% Native American.

- In 1993, there were 26.8 million veterans living in the U.S. and Puerto Rico, including 20.7 million wartime veterans and 6.1 million peacetime veterans.

- From 1970 to 1993, veterans benefits more than tripled, going from $10.2 billion to $33.9 billion. The fastest growing component was medical costs, which rose from $1.8 billion to $13.8 billion.

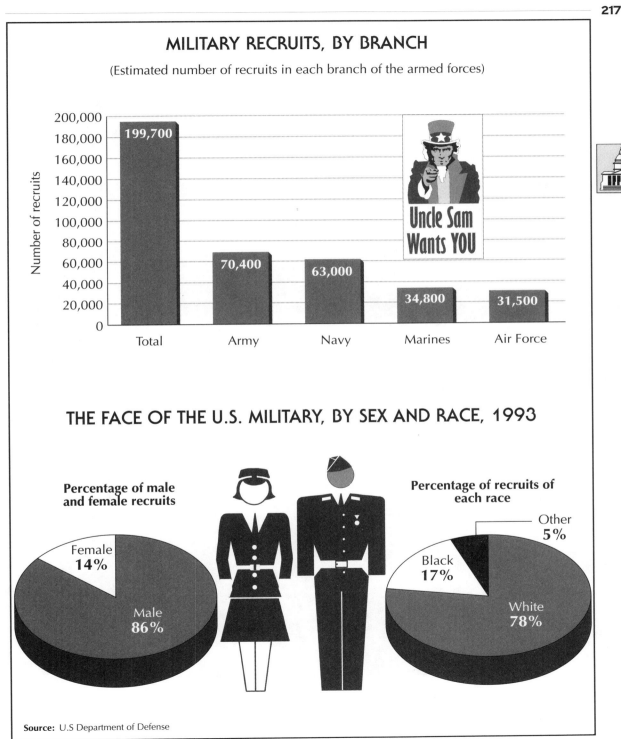

MILITARY RECRUITS, BY BRANCH

(Estimated number of recruits in each branch of the armed forces)

Number of recruits

Total	Army	Navy	Marines	Air Force
199,700	70,400	63,000	34,800	31,500

Uncle Sam Wants YOU

THE FACE OF THE U.S. MILITARY, BY SEX AND RACE, 1993

Percentage of male and female recruits

Female 14%

Male 86%

Percentage of recruits of each race

Other 5%

Black 17%

White 78%

Source: U.S Department of Defense

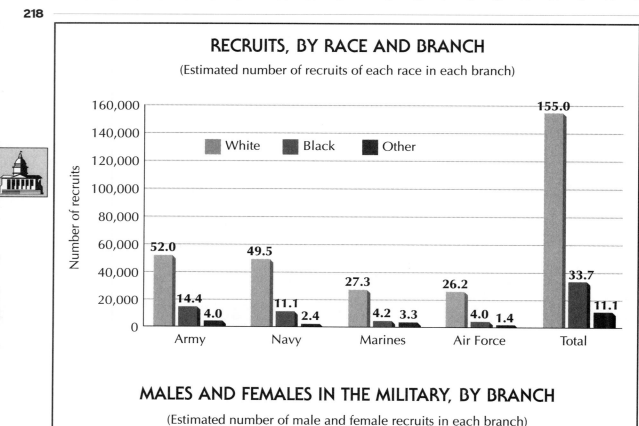

RECRUITS, BY RACE AND BRANCH

(Estimated number of recruits of each race in each branch)

White   Black   Other

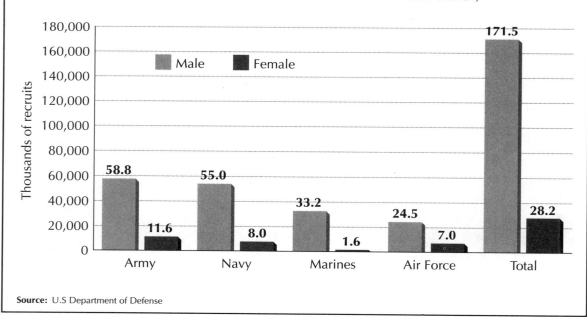

MALES AND FEMALES IN THE MILITARY, BY BRANCH

(Estimated number of male and female recruits in each branch)

Male   Female

Source: U.S Department of Defense

HONORABLE DISCHARGES FOR GAY SOLDIERS, 1982–1994

(Acknowledged homosexuals honorably discharged since
the military policy barring gays started in 1982)

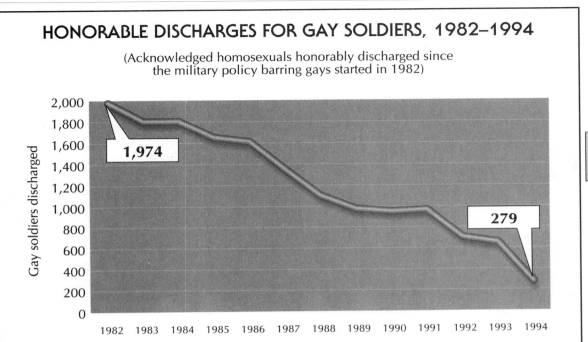

READY MILITARY RESERVE PERSONNEL, BY RACE AND SEX, 1993

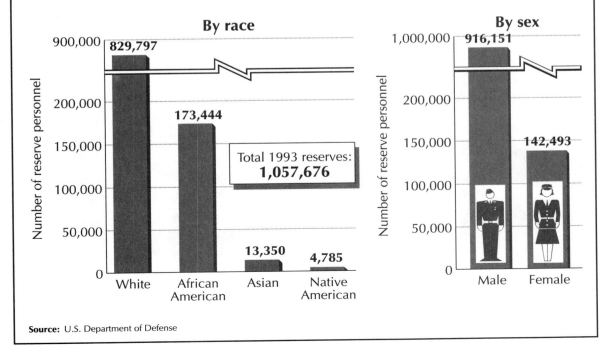

Source: U.S. Department of Defense

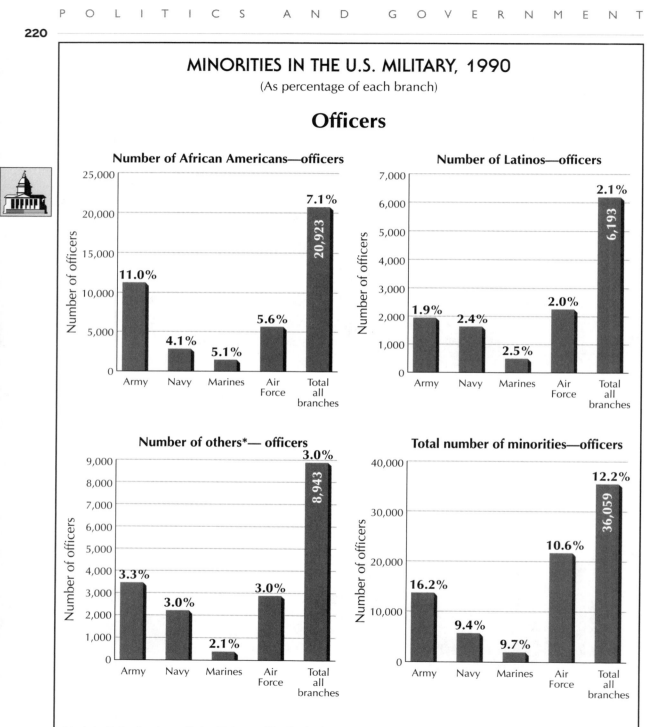

MINORITIES IN THE U.S. MILITARY, 1990
(As percentage of each branch)

Officers

Number of African Americans—officers

- Army: 11.0%
- Navy: 4.1%
- Marines: 5.1%
- Air Force: 5.6%
- Total all branches: 7.1% (20,923)

Number of Latinos—officers

- Army: 1.9%
- Navy: 2.4%
- Marines: 2.5%
- Air Force: 2.0%
- Total all branches: 2.1% (6,193)

Number of others*— officers

- Army: 3.3%
- Navy: 3.0%
- Marines: 2.1%
- Air Force: 3.0%
- Total all branches: 3.0% (8,943)

Total number of minorities—officers

- Army: 16.2%
- Navy: 9.4%
- Marines: 9.7%
- Air Force: 10.6%
- Total all branches: 12.2% (36,059)

* Includes Native Americans, Alaskan Natives, and Pacific Islanders
Source: U.S. Department of Defense

MINORITIES IN THE U.S. MILITARY, 1990

(As percentage of each branch)

Enlisted

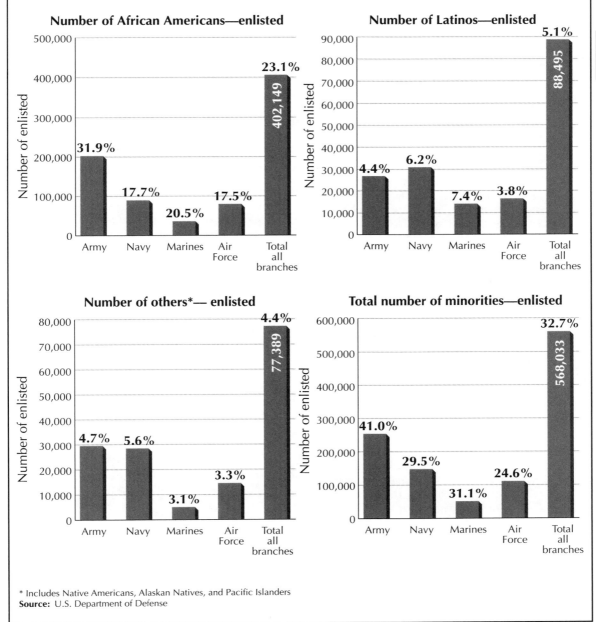

Number of African Americans—enlisted

Number of enlisted

Army	Navy	Marines	Air Force	Total all branches
31.9%	17.7%	20.5%	17.5%	23.1% / 402,149

Number of Latinos—enlisted

Number of enlisted

Army	Navy	Marines	Air Force	Total all branches
4.4%	6.2%	7.4%	3.8%	5.1% / 88,495

Number of others*— enlisted

Number of enlisted

Army	Navy	Marines	Air Force	Total all branches
4.7%	5.6%	3.1%	3.3%	4.4% / 77,389

Total number of minorities—enlisted

Number of enlisted

Army	Navy	Marines	Air Force	Total all branches
41.0%	29.5%	31.1%	24.6%	32.7% / 568,033

* Includes Native Americans, Alaskan Natives, and Pacific Islanders
Source: U.S. Department of Defense

WOMEN IN THE MILITARY

Officially, women have been allowed to join the U.S. armed forces since 1901. It was not until 1973, however, when the all-volunteer military was launched (while under pressure from the women's movement), that the services actively began to recruit women. In 1976, the U.S. military academies were opened to women. Today, 12% of the 1.7 million active duty personnel are female. The Air Force is the branch of the armed forces with the largest percentage of women, while the Marine Corps has the lowest.

One of the most serious problems faced by military women has been sexual harassment. The issue received widespread attention following the 1991 annual convention of the Tail Hook Association, an organization for Navy and Marine Corps pilots. During that convention, more than 2 dozen women, half of them officers, accused male aviators of mauling them and other acts of sexual misconduct. Coupled with disclosures of other incidents, including assaults of female soldiers by army men during the Persian Gulf War, this scandal finally led to serious efforts by the armed forces to enforce policies designed to prevent abuse.

Another substantial obstacle faced by military women has been exclusion from combat situations. Without combat experience, a person's chances of being promoted into the military's top ranks are slim. Following the Persian Gulf War, in which more than 40,000 women participated (5% of deployed U.S. forces; 15 were killed), a movement began to repeal laws that bar women from participating equally with men in combat roles. In 1993, women were allowed to serve aboard warships and to fly combat aircraft, though they still may not serve in ground combat units.

FINGERTIP FACTS

- The Air Force has the highest percentage of women in any branch of the armed forces (14.7% of all officers and enlisted personnel); the Marine Corps has the lowest (4.5%).

- Women are underrepresented in higher military ranks. In 1992, of a total of 1,021 generals and admirals, only 11 were women.

- African-American women are disproportionately represented in the military. Some 31.0% of military women are black, versus approximately 12.5% of all U.S. women.

- According to the Pentagon, 9% of military women and 2% of military men were unable to ship out during the Persian Gulf War, a difference due mainly to pregnancy. However, studies have shown that military men lose more time because of drug and alcohol abuse than women do for drug and alcohol abuse and pregnancy combined.

- In 1993, President Bill Clinton appointed Sheila Widnall as secretary of the Air Force—the first woman to head a branch of the U.S. armed forces.

- The first major study of sexual harassment in the military, completed in 1990, found that nearly two-thirds of the 20,000 women surveyed experienced some type of sexual harassment while on the job. The most common category of unwanted behavior—experienced by a total of 52% of women surveyed—was teasing and jokes.

WOMEN IN THE MILITARY, 1994

(Active duty personnel)

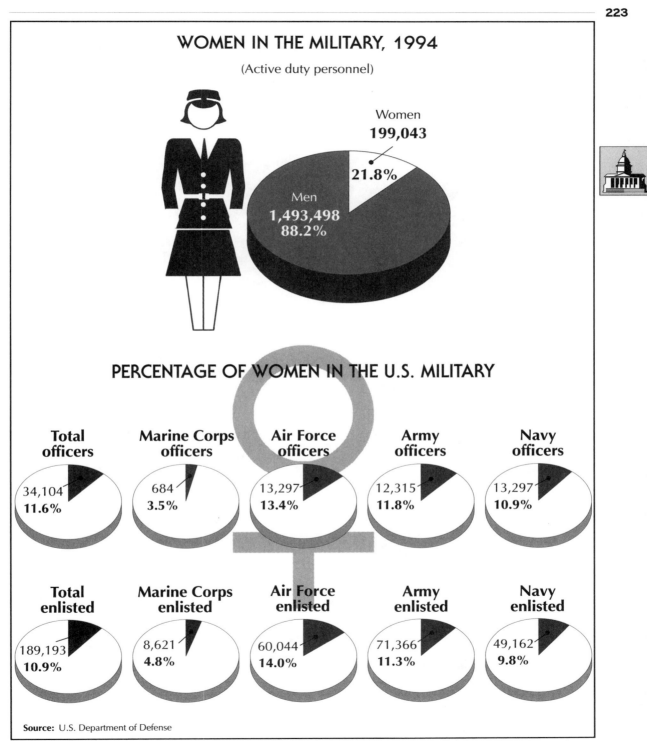

Women
199,043
21.8%

Men
1,493,498
88.2%

PERCENTAGE OF WOMEN IN THE U.S. MILITARY

Total officers
34,104
11.6%

Marine Corps officers
684
3.5%

Air Force officers
13,297
13.4%

Army officers
12,315
11.8%

Navy officers
13,297
10.9%

Total enlisted
189,193
10.9%

Marine Corps enlisted
8,621
4.8%

Air Force enlisted
60,044
14.0%

Army enlisted
71,366
11.3%

Navy enlisted
49,162
9.8%

Source: U.S. Department of Defense

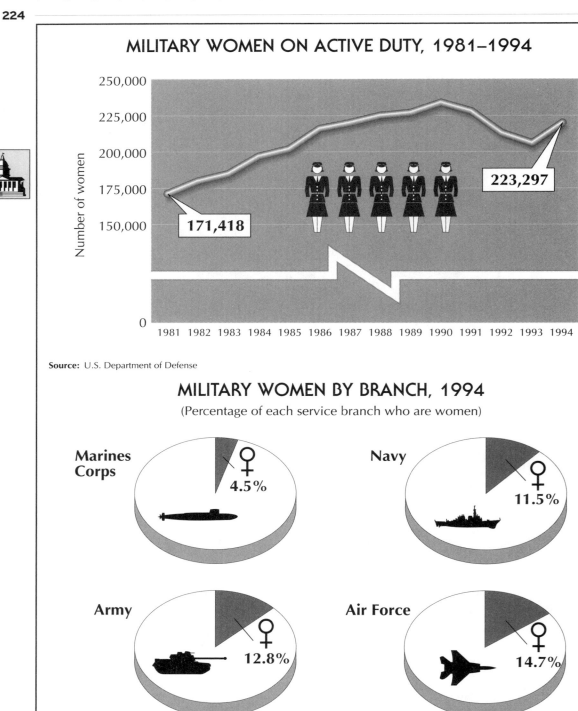

MILITARY WOMEN ON ACTIVE DUTY, 1981–1994

Number of women

250,000
225,000
200,000
175,000
150,000
0

171,418

223,297

1981 1982 1983 1984 1985 1986 1987 1988 1989 1990 1991 1992 1993 1994

Source: U.S. Department of Defense

MILITARY WOMEN BY BRANCH, 1994

(Percentage of each service branch who are women)

Marines Corps ♀ 4.5%

Navy ♀ 11.5%

Army ♀ 12.8%

Air Force ♀ 14.7%

Source: U.S. Department of Defense

PROFILE: RACE OR ETHNICITY OF WOMEN IN THE MILITARY

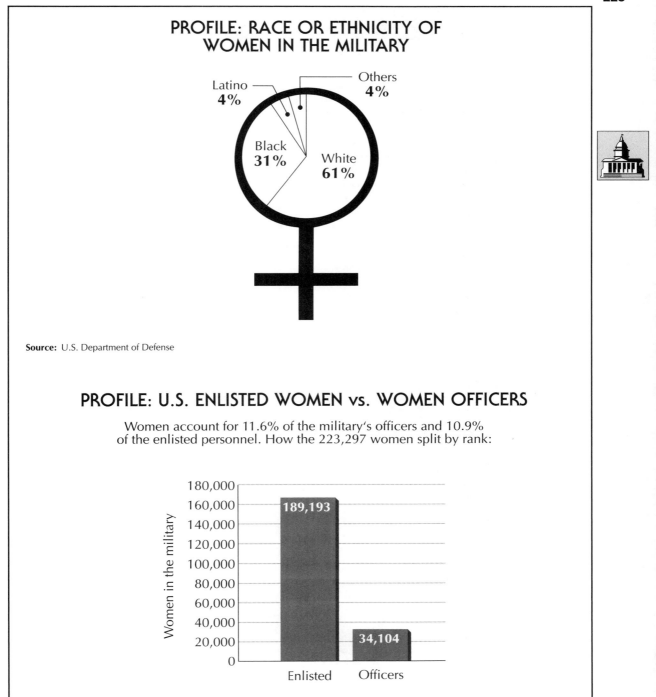

Latino
4%

Others
4%

Black
31%

White
61%

Source: U.S. Department of Defense

PROFILE: U.S. ENLISTED WOMEN vs. WOMEN OFFICERS

Women account for 11.6% of the military's officers and 10.9% of the enlisted personnel. How the 223,297 women split by rank:

Women in the military

- 180,000
- 160,000
- 140,000
- 120,000
- 100,000
- 80,000
- 60,000
- 40,000
- 20,000
- 0

189,193 — Enlisted

34,104 — Officers

Source: U.S. Department of Defense

PUERTO RICO

Puerto Rico, today a bustling island of 3.6 million people, has been a U.S. commonwealth since July 25, 1952. It is governed under the Constitution of the Commonwealth of Puerto Rico and the Federal Relations Statutes; the latter defines the relationship between Puerto Rico and the federal U.S. government. Residents of Puerto Rico have no voting representation in the U.S. Congress, do not vote in U.S. presidential elections, and do not pay federal taxes. The economy, however, is closely geared to that of the U.S., with a common currency and unrestricted free trade.

Puerto Rico's political status has been a matter of continuing debate among the island's residents. Some support independence, while others desire statehood, and still others favor continued commonwealth status but with greater autonomy. The most recent referendum occurred on November 14, 1993, when 48.9% of the voters opted to maintain commonwealth status; 46.7% favored statehood, and only 4.4% voted for independence.

The everyday problems that plague residents of Puerto Rico mirror those on the U.S. mainland. People are concerned about such issues as the economy, crime, drugs, health care, and education. In 1993, in response to a record-breaking homicide rate, a program to use the U.S. National Guard in the occupation of public housing projects known to be drug distribution spots marked the first time in the island's history that police and National Guard troops had together taken over public housing units. It also signaled a growing sense of cooperation between the two governments.

FINGERTIP FACTS

- The majority of Puerto Ricans are racially defined as white. Most are Christian, primarily Roman Catholic.

- Puerto Rican residents' median age has increased dramatically, from 18.5 years in 1960 to 28.4 years in 1990. During that period, the population of the island increased by nearly 50%.

- In 1960, Puerto Rico had a birth rate of 32.5 per 1,000 population. By 1990, the rate was only 18.9.

- Before 1955, Puerto Rico's economy was dominated by agriculture, with sugar the dominant agricultural product. Today, manufacturing and services (including tourism) prevail.

- In 1950, agriculture employed 246,000 people—36% of the labor force—and dominated the economy. Sugar was the primary agricultural product. In 1975, the industry employed only 61,000, or 7%.

- In 1980, Puerto Rico's net income was $9 billion, of which $0.7 billion came from manufacturing and $0.4 billion from agriculture. By 1993, net income had grown to $21.0 billion, with $13.0 billion from manufacturing and $0.4 billion for agriculture.

- In 1970, Puerto Rico had 1.2 million visitors and a net income of $89.8 million from tourism. By 1993, the number of visitors had grown to 3.9 million, with net income of $464.7 million.

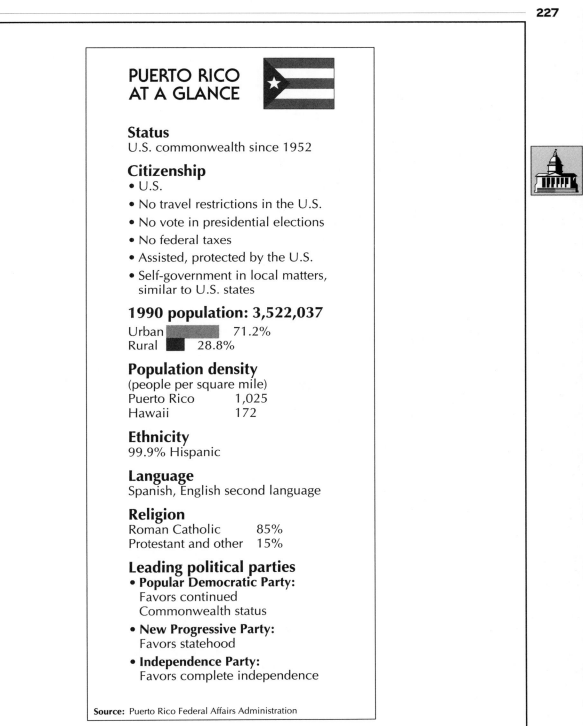

PUERTO RICO AT A GLANCE

Status
U.S. commonwealth since 1952

Citizenship
- U.S.
- No travel restrictions in the U.S.
- No vote in presidential elections
- No federal taxes
- Assisted, protected by the U.S.
- Self-government in local matters, similar to U.S. states

1990 population: 3,522,037
Urban   71.2%
Rural   28.8%

Population density
(people per square mile)
Puerto Rico   1,025
Hawaii   172

Ethnicity
99.9% Hispanic

Language
Spanish, English second language

Religion
Roman Catholic   85%
Protestant and other   15%

Leading political parties
- **Popular Democratic Party:**
  Favors continued Commonwealth status
- **New Progressive Party:**
  Favors statehood
- **Independence Party:**
  Favors complete independence

Source: Puerto Rico Federal Affairs Administration

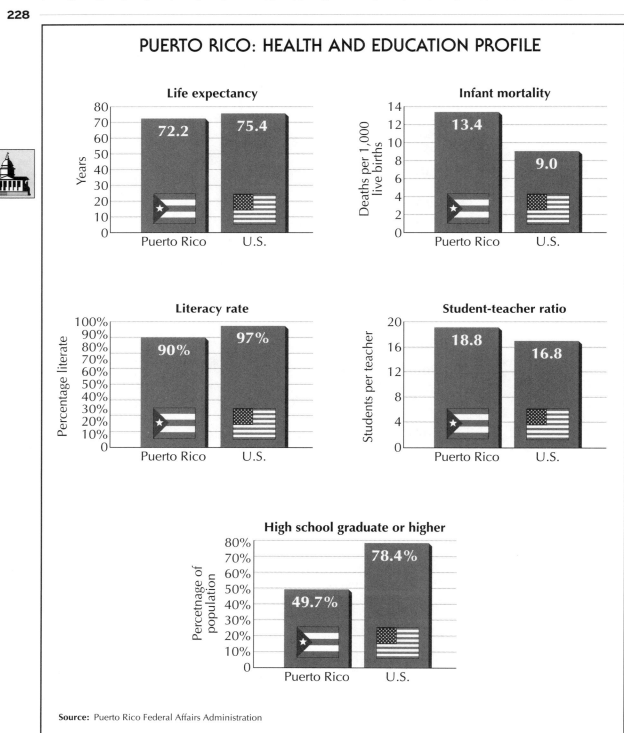

PUERTO RICO: HEALTH AND EDUCATION PROFILE

Life expectancy
- Puerto Rico: 72.2
- U.S.: 75.4
(Years)

Infant mortality
- Puerto Rico: 13.4
- U.S.: 9.0
(Deaths per 1,000 live births)

Literacy rate
- Puerto Rico: 90%
- U.S.: 97%
(Percentage literate)

Student-teacher ratio
- Puerto Rico: 18.8
- U.S.: 16.8
(Students per teacher)

High school graduate or higher
- Puerto Rico: 49.7%
- U.S.: 78.4%
(Percetnage of population)

Source: Puerto Rico Federal Affairs Administration

PROFILE: THE ECONOMY OF PUERTO RICO

(Currency: U.S. dollar)

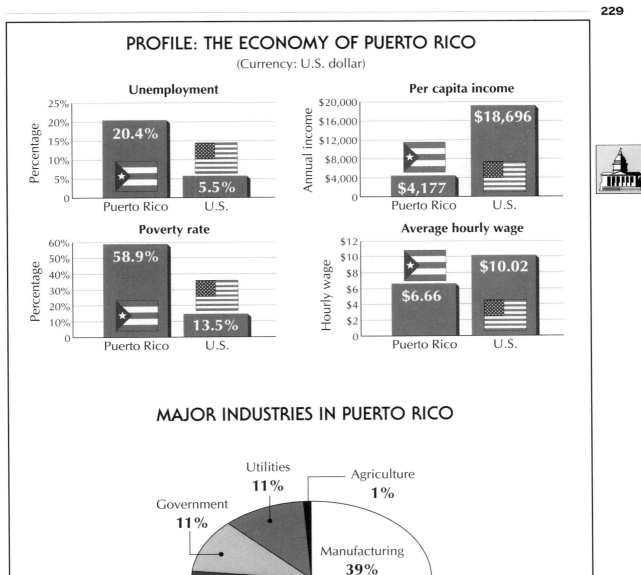

Unemployment

Puerto Rico: 20.4%
U.S.: 5.5%

Per capita income

Puerto Rico: $4,177
U.S.: $18,696

Poverty rate

Puerto Rico: 58.9%
U.S.: 13.5%

Average hourly wage

Puerto Rico: $6.66
U.S.: $10.02

MAJOR INDUSTRIES IN PUERTO RICO

Utilities 11%
Agriculture 1%
Government 11%
Manufacturing 39%
Services 38%

Source: Puerto Rico Federal Affairs Administration

4

POPULATION
AND
VITAL STATISTICS

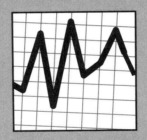

MARRIAGE AND DIVORCE

Each year in the United States, wedding bells ring for well over 2 million happy couples. Marriage is a popular convention in America. More than 60% of Americans over age 18 are married. Yet, since the 1970s, the number of marriages and the marriage rate have declined; the 2,334,000 marriages in 1993 accounted for the lowest number since 1979. One explanation is that many baby-boomers are past the ages (15 to 44) at which marriage is most likely to occur. Also, studies suggest that fewer Americans will marry during their lifetimes today than in the past.

Many marriages are successful—but many others are not. Divorce and separation are now commonplace events. Each year, more than a million marriages are legally dissolved in a court of law. Indeed, statistics suggest that the United States has the highest divorce rate in the world. Its divorce rate soared during the mid-1960s and through most of the 1970s, but has declined somewhat in more recent years. The divorce rate per 1,000 people ages 15 and older in 1993 was 4.6—which was the lowest rate since 1975.

Approximately half the couples who divorce have children under age 18. In most cases, custody of the children is given to the mother, but fathers have pressed for more rights and more access to their children. Men are now increasingly being awarded custody or granted shared custody of the children. A study of divorce in 19 states released in 1995 indicated that custody went to mothers in 71.0% of the cases, to fathers in 8.5%, and was shared in 15.5%. Friends or relatives were awarded custody in the remaining cases.

FINGERTIP FACTS

- Research presented in 1995 indicates that marriage provides health, emotional, and financial benefits. For example, divorced men have higher rates of depression and drug and alcohol abuse than do married men.

- In 1992, Americans spent $32 billion on marriage-related purchases, including $4.4 billion for engagement and wedding rings.

- In 1993, just 9% of women ages 15 to 44 got married, compared with 14% in 1973.

- More marriages take place in Nevada than in any other state.

- More than half of all marriages occur after a couple has lived together. In 1993, unmarried couples headed 3.5 million households, including 1.2 million with children under age 15.

- Approximately one in 4 Americans over age 18 has never married, compared with one in 6 in 1970. Only 4.4% of Americans age 65 and older have never married.

- In the U.S., 1,187,000 divorces were granted in 1993; the divorce rate of 4.6 per 1,000 population was the lowest since 1974.

- Divorce is most common among the young. Approximately half the people who divorce are under age 25.

- Most divorced people remarry; men are more likely to remarry than women.

Note: Before comparing statistics, consider that different rates apply to different population ratios—for example some rates are figured per 1,000 people, other rates are figured per 100,000 people.

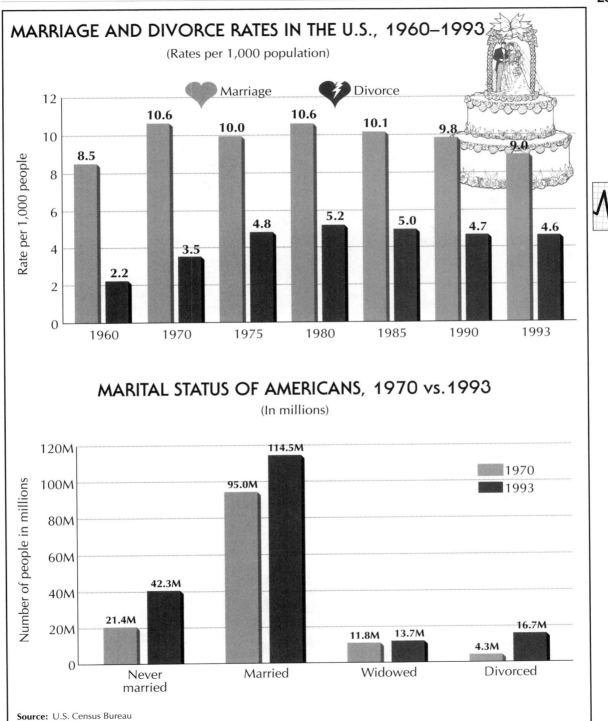

MARRIAGE AND DIVORCE RATES IN THE U.S., 1960–1993

(Rates per 1,000 population)

Marriage   Divorce

Rate per 1,000 people

	1960	1970	1975	1980	1985	1990	1993
Marriage	8.5	10.6	10.0	10.6	10.1	9.8	9.0
Divorce	2.2	3.5	4.8	5.2	5.0	4.7	4.6

MARITAL STATUS OF AMERICANS, 1970 vs. 1993

(In millions)

Number of people in millions

	Never married	Married	Widowed	Divorced
1970	21.4M	95.0M	11.8M	4.3M
1993	42.3M	114.5M	13.7M	16.7M

Source: U.S. Census Bureau

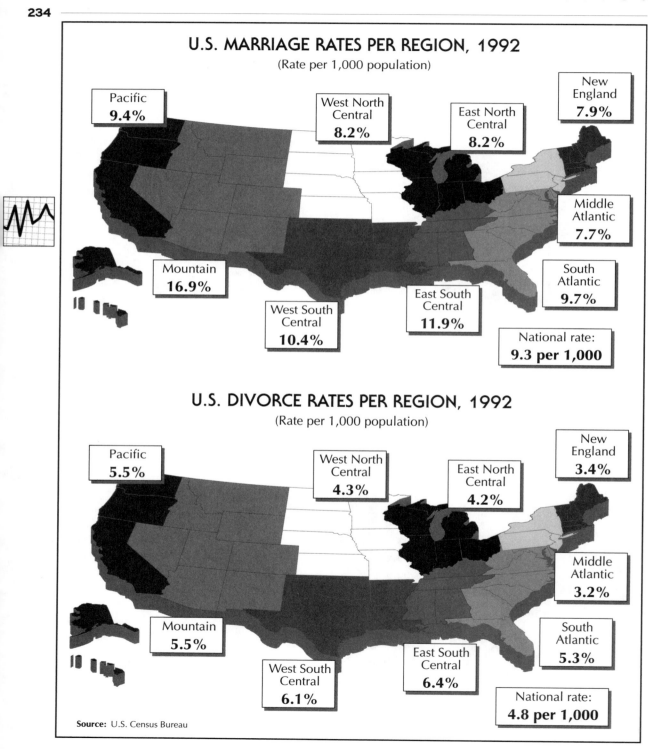

U.S. MARRIAGE RATES PER REGION, 1992
(Rate per 1,000 population)

Pacific
9.4%

West North Central
8.2%

East North Central
8.2%

New England
7.9%

Middle Atlantic
7.7%

Mountain
16.9%

South Atlantic
9.7%

West South Central
10.4%

East South Central
11.9%

National rate:
9.3 per 1,000

U.S. DIVORCE RATES PER REGION, 1992
(Rate per 1,000 population)

Pacific
5.5%

West North Central
4.3%

East North Central
4.2%

New England
3.4%

Middle Atlantic
3.2%

Mountain
5.5%

South Atlantic
5.3%

West South Central
6.1%

East South Central
6.4%

National rate:
4.8 per 1,000

Source: U.S. Census Bureau

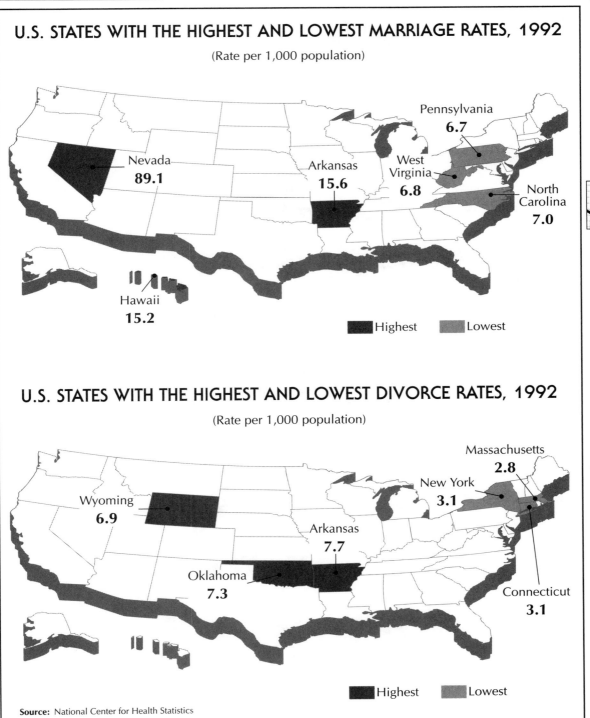

U.S. STATES WITH THE HIGHEST AND LOWEST MARRIAGE RATES, 1992

(Rate per 1,000 population)

Nevada
89.1

Arkansas
15.6

Pennsylvania
6.7

West Virginia
6.8

North Carolina
7.0

Hawaii
15.2

■ Highest   ■ Lowest

U.S. STATES WITH THE HIGHEST AND LOWEST DIVORCE RATES, 1992

(Rate per 1,000 population)

Wyoming
6.9

Arkansas
7.7

Oklahoma
7.3

Massachusetts
2.8

New York
3.1

Connecticut
3.1

■ Highest   ■ Lowest

Source: National Center for Health Statistics

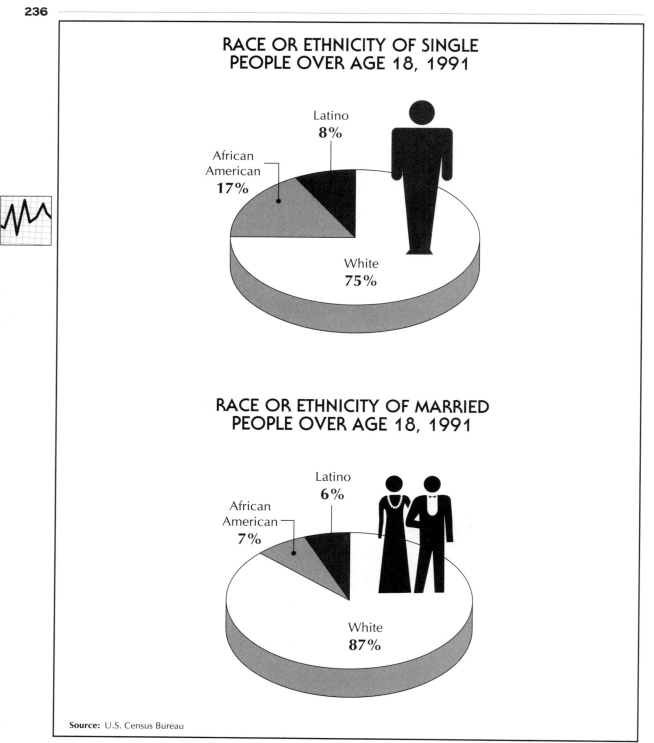

RACE OR ETHNICITY OF SINGLE PEOPLE OVER AGE 18, 1991

Latino
8%

African American
17%

White
75%

RACE OR ETHNICITY OF MARRIED PEOPLE OVER AGE 18, 1991

Latino
6%

African American
7%

White
87%

Source: U.S. Census Bureau

RACE OR ETHNICITY OF DIVORCED PEOPLE OVER AGE 18, 1991

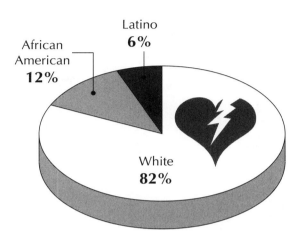

Latino
6%

African American
12%

White
82%

RACE OR ETHNICITY OF WIDOWED PEOPLE OVER AGE 18, 1991

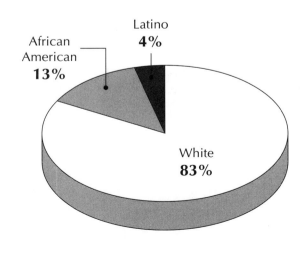

Latino
4%

African American
13%

White
83%

Source: U.S. Census Bureau

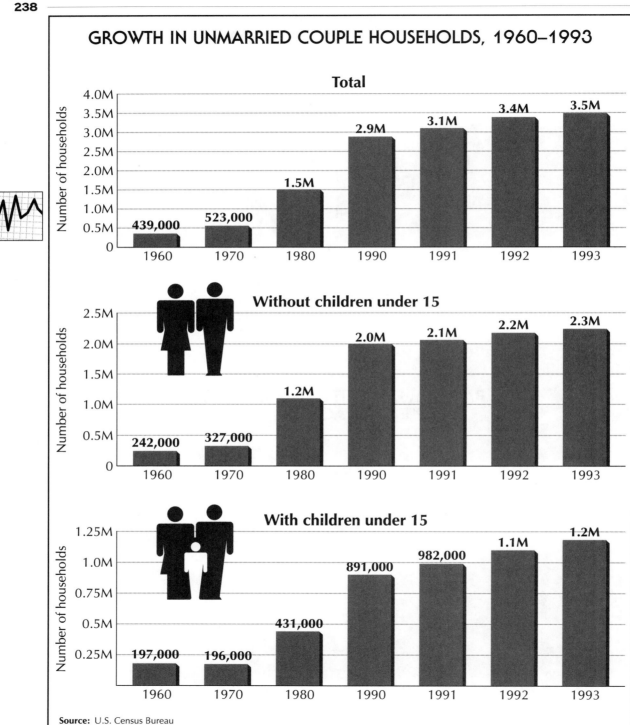

GROWTH IN UNMARRIED COUPLE HOUSEHOLDS, 1960–1993

Total

Number of households

| 1960 | 1970 | 1980 | 1990 | 1991 | 1992 | 1993 |
| 439,000 | 523,000 | 1.5M | 2.9M | 3.1M | 3.4M | 3.5M |

Without children under 15

Number of households

| 1960 | 1970 | 1980 | 1990 | 1991 | 1992 | 1993 |
| 242,000 | 327,000 | 1.2M | 2.0M | 2.1M | 2.2M | 2.3M |

With children under 15

Number of households

| 1960 | 1970 | 1980 | 1990 | 1991 | 1992 | 1993 |
| 197,000 | 196,000 | 431,000 | 891,000 | 982,000 | 1.1M | 1.2M |

Source: U.S. Census Bureau

MEDIAN AGE IN U.S. AT FIRST MARRIAGE, BY SEX, 1900–1993

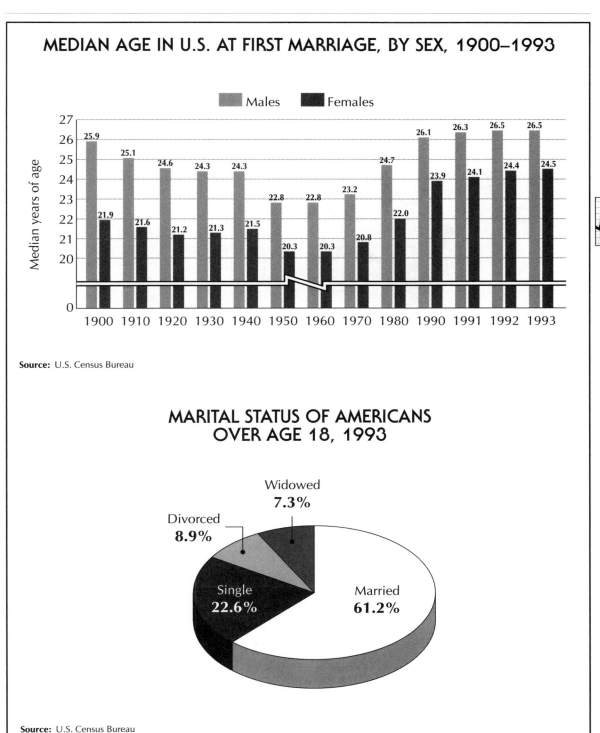

Males   Females

Median years of age

	1900	1910	1920	1930	1940	1950	1960	1970	1980	1990	1991	1992	1993
Males	25.9	25.1	24.6	24.3	24.3	22.8	22.8	23.2	24.7	26.1	26.3	26.5	26.5
Females	21.9	21.6	21.2	21.3	21.5	20.3	20.3	20.8	22.0	23.9	24.1	24.4	24.5

Source: U.S. Census Bureau

MARITAL STATUS OF AMERICANS
OVER AGE 18, 1993

Widowed
7.3%

Divorced
8.9%

Single
22.6%

Married
61.2%

Source: U.S. Census Bureau

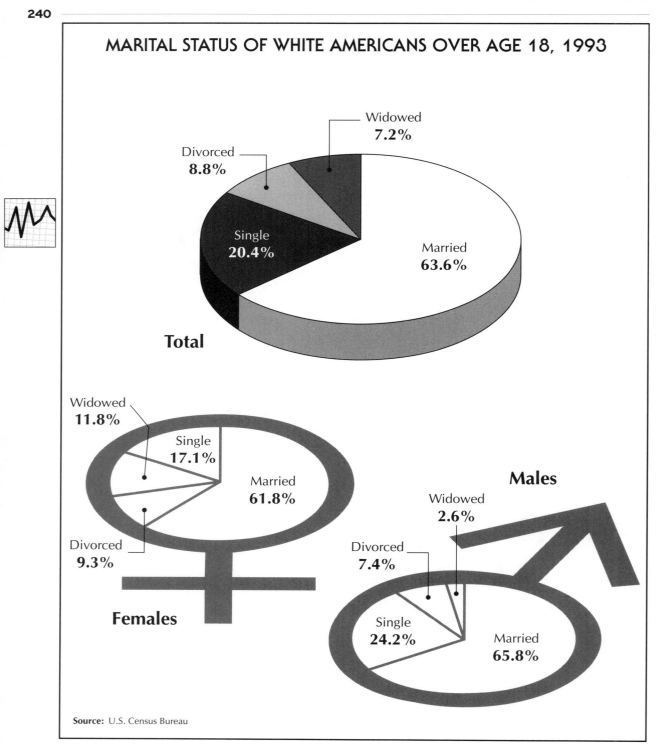

MARITAL STATUS OF WHITE AMERICANS OVER AGE 18, 1993

Widowed
7.2%

Divorced
8.8%

Single
20.4%

Married
63.6%

Total

Widowed
11.8%

Single
17.1%

Married
61.8%

Divorced
9.3%

Females

Males

Widowed
2.6%

Divorced
7.4%

Single
24.2%

Married
65.8%

Source: U.S. Census Bureau

MARITAL STATUS OF AFRICAN AMERICANS OVER AGE 18, 1993

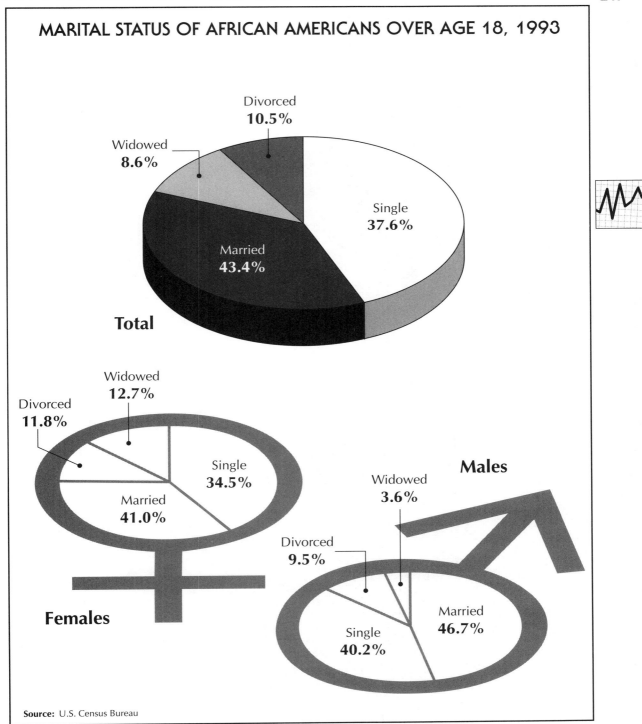

Divorced
10.5%

Widowed
8.6%

Single
37.6%

Married
43.4%

Total

Widowed
12.7%

Divorced
11.8%

Single
34.5%

Married
41.0%

Females

Males

Widowed
3.6%

Divorced
9.5%

Married
46.7%

Single
40.2%

Source: U.S. Census Bureau

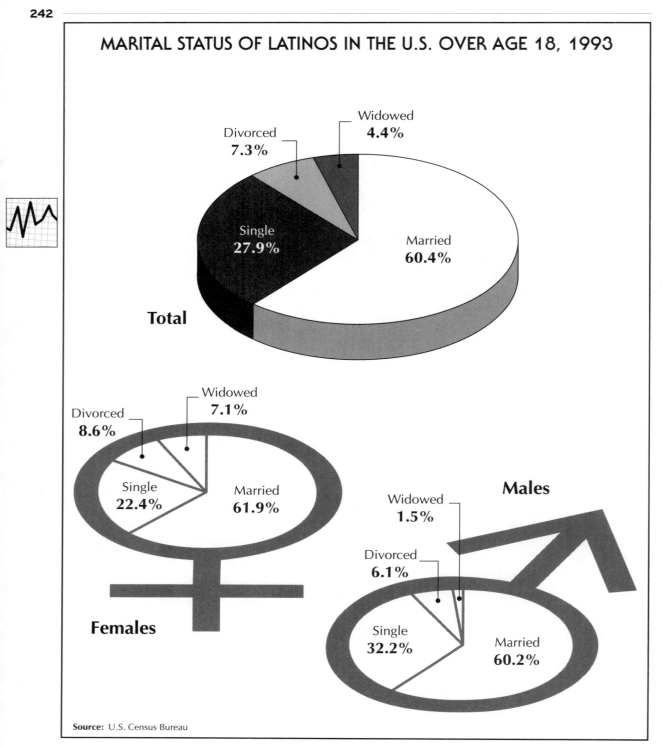

MARITAL STATUS OF LATINOS IN THE U.S. OVER AGE 18, 1993

Total

Widowed
4.4%

Divorced
7.3%

Single
27.9%

Married
60.4%

Widowed
7.1%

Divorced
8.6%

Single
22.4%

Married
61.9%

Females

Males

Widowed
1.5%

Divorced
6.1%

Single
32.2%

Married
60.2%

Source: U.S. Census Bureau

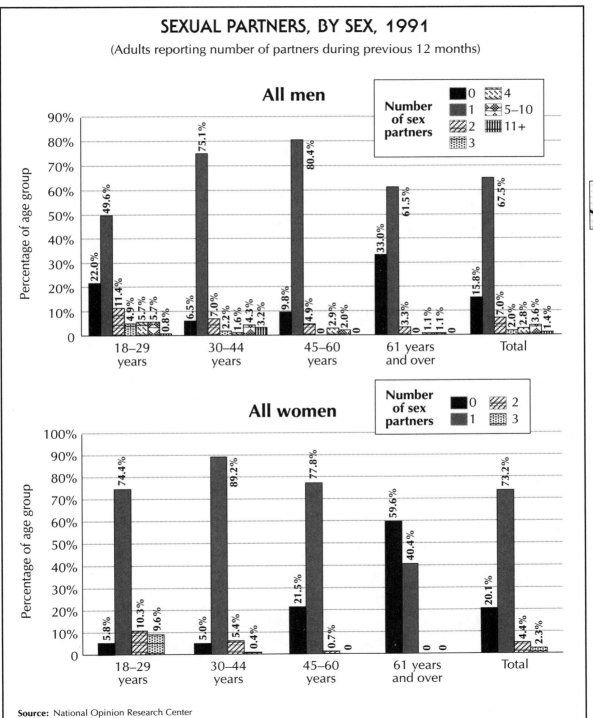

SEXUAL PARTNERS, BY SEX, 1991

(Adults reporting number of partners during previous 12 months)

All men

Number of sex partners

0	4
1	5–10
2	11+
3	

All women

Number of sex partners

| 0 | 2 |
| 1 | 3 |

Source: National Opinion Research Center

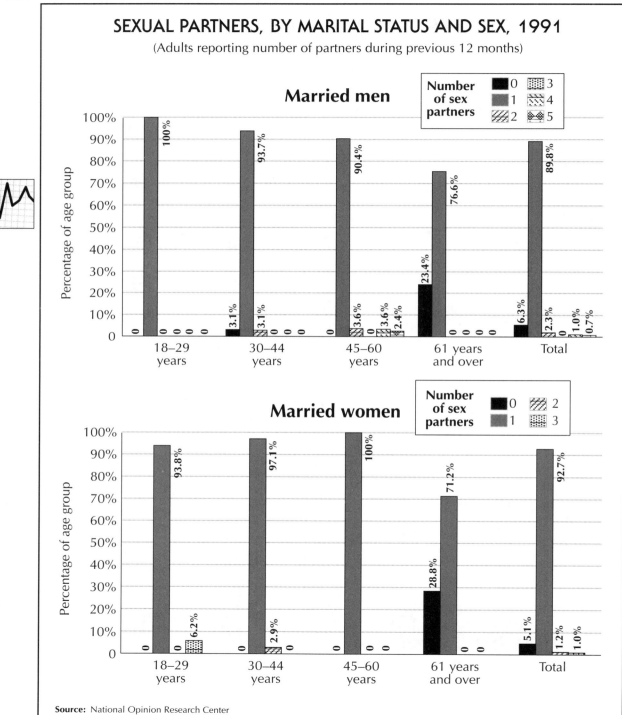

SEXUAL PARTNERS, BY MARITAL STATUS AND SEX, 1991

(Adults reporting number of partners during previous 12 months)

Married men

Number of sex partners: 0, 1, 2, 3, 4, 5

	18–29 years	30–44 years	45–60 years	61 years and over	Total
0	0	3.1%	0	23.4%	6.3%
1	100%	93.7%	90.4%	76.6%	89.8%
2	0	3.1%	3.6%	0	2.3%
3	0	0	3.6%	0	0
4	0	0	2.4%	0	1.0%
5	0	0		0	0.7%

Married women

Number of sex partners: 0, 1, 2, 3

	18–29 years	30–44 years	45–60 years	61 years and over	Total
0	0	0	0	28.8%	5.1%
1	93.8%	97.1%	100%	71.2%	92.7%
2	0	2.9%	0	0	1.2%
3	6.2%	0	0	0	1.0%

Source: National Opinion Research Center

TOP WEDDING MONTHS: RATE OF MARRIAGE, BY MONTH, 1991

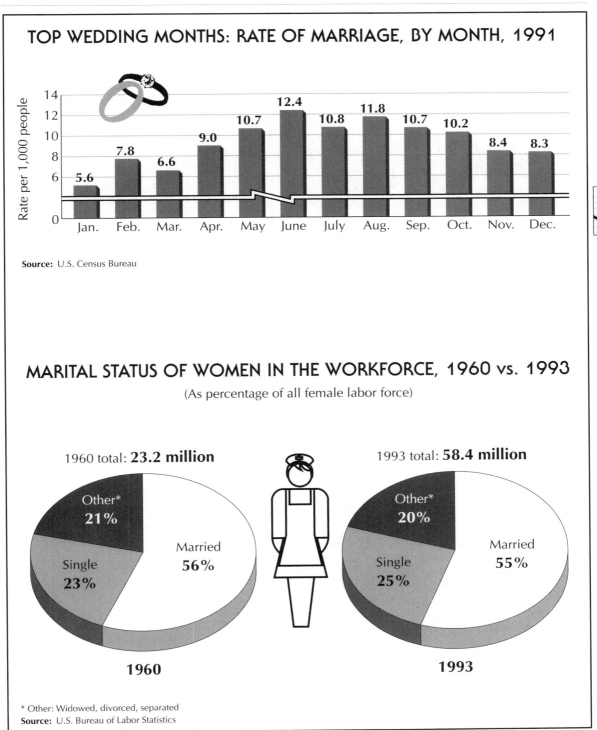

Rate per 1,000 people

Jan.	Feb.	Mar.	Apr.	May	June	July	Aug.	Sep.	Oct.	Nov.	Dec.
5.6	7.8	6.6	9.0	10.7	12.4	10.8	11.8	10.7	10.2	8.4	8.3

Source: U.S. Census Bureau

MARITAL STATUS OF WOMEN IN THE WORKFORCE, 1960 vs. 1993

(As percentage of all female labor force)

1960 total: **23.2 million**

Other*
21%

Single
23%

Married
56%

1960

1993 total: **58.4 million**

Other*
20%

Single
25%

Married
55%

1993

* Other: Widowed, divorced, separated
Source: U.S. Bureau of Labor Statistics

B I R T H S   A N D   D E A T H S

The numbers of births and deaths in the United States are among the basic statistics tracked by the National Center for Health Statistics (NCHS), a division of the Department of Health and Human Services. Birth rates—the number of live births per 1,000 population—increased dramatically during the 1940s and 1950s, then rapidly declined in the 1960s and early 1970s. Since then, the number of live births per 1,000 women ages 15 to 44 has followed a generally downward pattern. The NCHS estimates that 4,039,000 babies were born in the U.S. in 1993, a 1% decline from 1992. However, this does not necessarily mean that there will be a consistently downward trend for the future. Some experts expect another baby boom to take place early in the 21st century, with annual births reaching or exceeding an estimated 4.3 million.

An estimated 2,268,000 deaths occurred in the United States during 1993, the highest number ever reported, and 4% higher than in 1992. Influenza epidemics were believed to be partly responsible for the increase.

The NCHS reports two kinds of death rates: the crude death rate and the age-adjusted death rate. The latter is considered a more accurate indicator of risk of death over time and of differences among racial and sexual groups. The age-adjusted death rate reached a record low of 504.5 per 100,000 population in 1992; it rose to 514 in 1993. Death rates were lower for females than males, and lower for whites than blacks ages one through 54. The estimated 1993 in-fant death rate of 8.5 per 1,000 live births was the lowest ever recorded for the U.S.

FINGERTIP FACTS

- In 1992, the birth rate was highest in Utah (21.6) and Alaska (20.7) and lowest in Maine (13.1) and West Virginia (12.6).

- Birth rates are highest for Latinos (especially Mexican) and black women, followed by Native American, Asian American, and white women.

- In 1993, August saw the most births (367,000), February the fewest (308,000).

- More males are born each year than females. In 1992, about 1,050 male babies were born for every 1,000 female babies. However, infant death rates are higher for males.

- The fertility rate declined from 106.2 in 1950 to 68.3 in 1993.

- The fertility rate is significantly higher for black women (83.2 in 1992) than Asian American (67.2) and white (66.5) women.

- The 15 leading causes of death—headed by heart disease and cancer —accounted for 86% of all U.S. deaths in 1993.

- The U.S. death rate in 1993 was highest in March (10.0 per 1,000), lowest in August and September (8.2 per 1,000).

- Death rates for infants under a year old are higher than those for people ages 1 through 54.

- Death rates (per 1,000) in 1993 for infants less than a year old were highest in Washington, D.C. (18.5) and Mississippi (11.9) and lowest in New Hampshire (4.8) and Vermont (4.9).

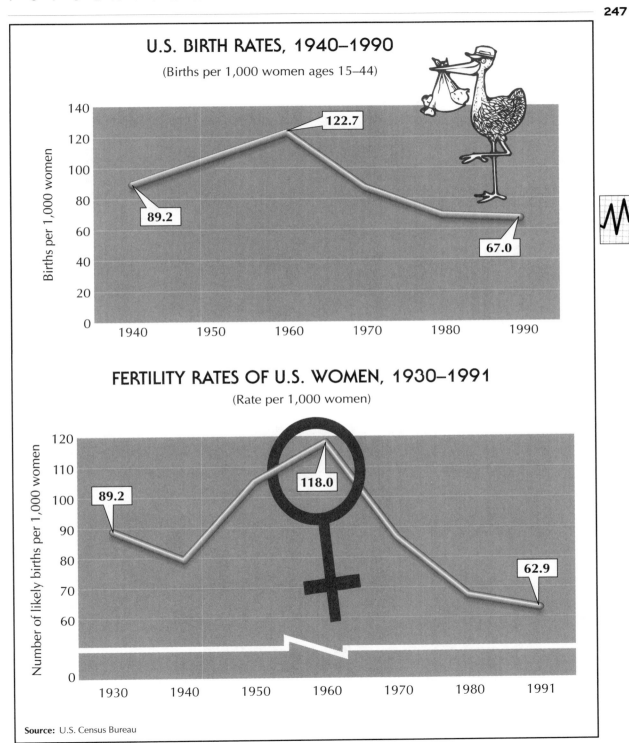

U.S. BIRTH RATES, 1940–1990

(Births per 1,000 women ages 15–44)

122.7

89.2

67.0

Births per 1,000 women

1940   1950   1960   1970   1980   1990

FERTILITY RATES OF U.S. WOMEN, 1930–1991

(Rate per 1,000 women)

118.0

89.2

62.9

Number of likely births per 1,000 women

1930   1940   1950   1960   1970   1980   1991

Source: U.S. Census Bureau

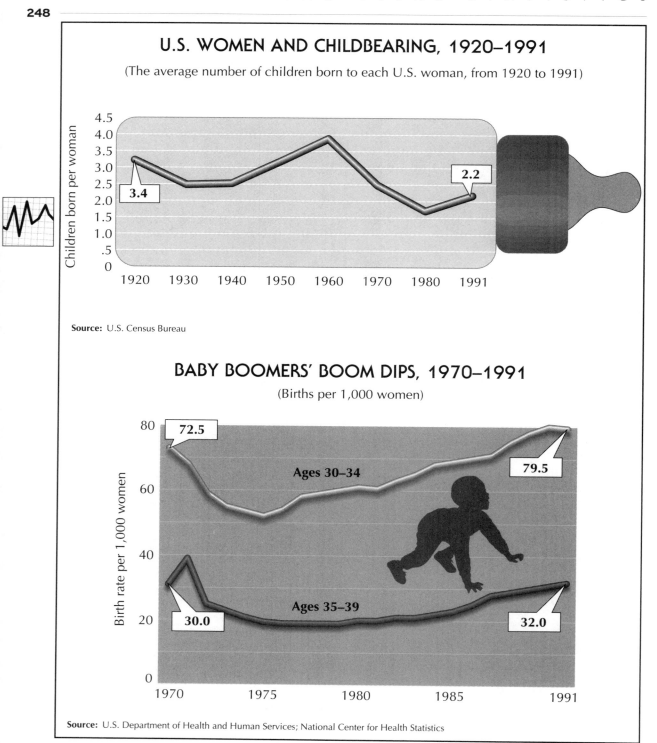

U.S. WOMEN AND CHILDBEARING, 1920–1991

(The average number of children born to each U.S. woman, from 1920 to 1991)

Children born per woman

3.4

2.2

1920 1930 1940 1950 1960 1970 1980 1991

Source: U.S. Census Bureau

BABY BOOMERS' BOOM DIPS, 1970–1991

(Births per 1,000 women)

Birth rate per 1,000 women

72.5

Ages 30–34

79.5

Ages 35–39

30.0

32.0

1970 1975 1980 1985 1991

Source: U.S. Department of Health and Human Services; National Center for Health Statistics

RATE OF LIVE BIRTHS AND DEATHS BY MONTH IN U.S., 1991

(Rate per 1,000 population)

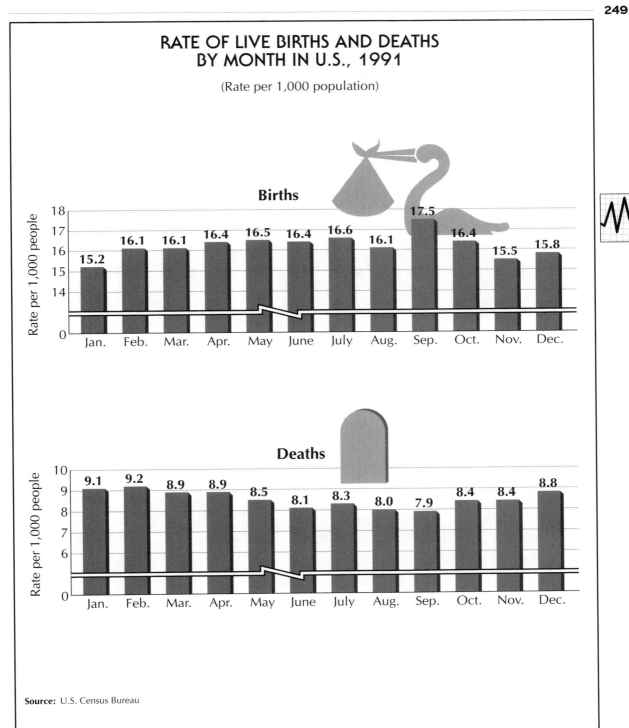

Births

Month	Rate
Jan.	15.2
Feb.	16.1
Mar.	16.1
Apr.	16.4
May	16.5
June	16.4
July	16.6
Aug.	16.1
Sep.	17.5
Oct.	16.4
Nov.	15.5
Dec.	15.8

Deaths

Month	Rate
Jan.	9.1
Feb.	9.2
Mar.	8.9
Apr.	8.9
May	8.5
June	8.1
July	8.3
Aug.	8.0
Sep.	7.9
Oct.	8.4
Nov.	8.4
Dec.	8.8

Rate per 1,000 people

Source: U.S. Census Bureau

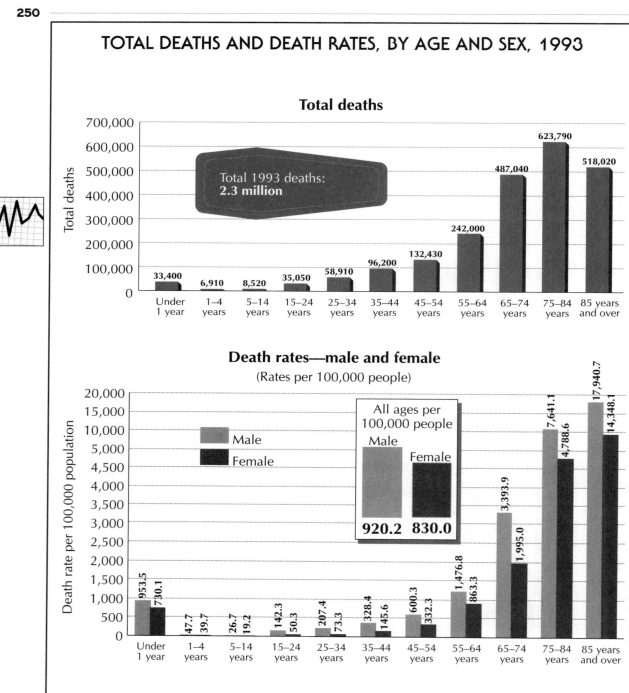

TOTAL DEATHS AND DEATH RATES, BY AGE AND SEX, 1993

Total deaths

Total 1993 deaths: **2.3 million**

Age group	Total deaths
Under 1 year	33,400
1–4 years	6,910
5–14 years	8,520
15–24 years	35,050
25–34 years	58,910
35–44 years	96,200
45–54 years	132,430
55–64 years	242,000
65–74 years	487,040
75–84 years	623,790
85 years and over	518,020

Death rates—male and female
(Rates per 100,000 people)

All ages per 100,000 people
Male 920.2   Female 830.0

Age group	Male	Female
Under 1 year	953.5	730.1
1–4 years	47.7	39.7
5–14 years	26.7	19.2
15–24 years	142.3	50.3
25–34 years	207.4	73.3
35–44 years	328.4	145.6
45–54 years	600.3	332.3
55–64 years	1,476.8	863.3
65–74 years	3,393.9	1,995.0
75–84 years	7,641.1	4,788.6
85 years and over	17,940.7	14,348.1

Source: U.S. Department of Health and Human Services; National Center for Health Statistics

CHANGES IN THE LEADING CAUSES OF DEATH, 1900–1992

(Rates per 100,000 population)

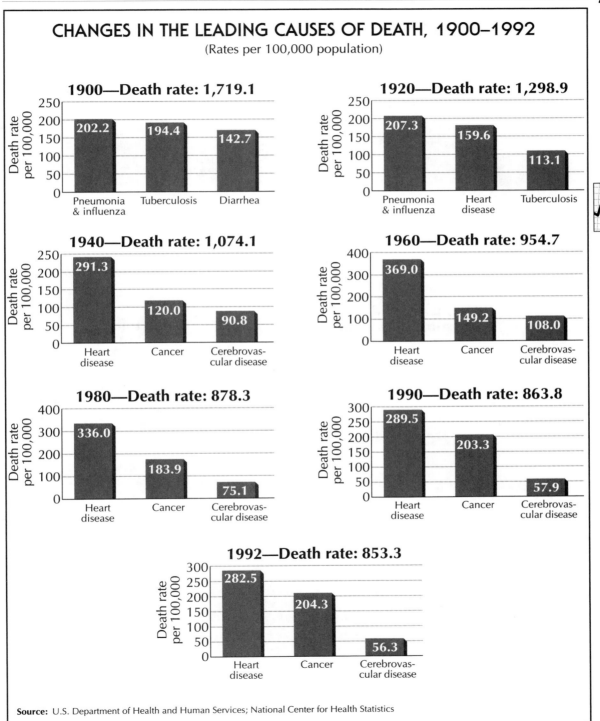

1900—Death rate: 1,719.1

	Death rate per 100,000
Pneumonia & influenza	202.2
Tuberculosis	194.4
Diarrhea	142.7

1920—Death rate: 1,298.9

	Death rate per 100,000
Pneumonia & influenza	207.3
Heart disease	159.6
Tuberculosis	113.1

1940—Death rate: 1,074.1

	Death rate per 100,000
Heart disease	291.3
Cancer	120.0
Cerebrovascular disease	90.8

1960—Death rate: 954.7

	Death rate per 100,000
Heart disease	369.0
Cancer	149.2
Cerebrovascular disease	108.0

1980—Death rate: 878.3

	Death rate per 100,000
Heart disease	336.0
Cancer	183.9
Cerebrovascular disease	75.1

1990—Death rate: 863.8

	Death rate per 100,000
Heart disease	289.5
Cancer	203.3
Cerebrovascular disease	57.9

1992—Death rate: 853.3

	Death rate per 100,000
Heart disease	282.5
Cancer	204.3
Cerebrovascular disease	56.3

Source: U.S. Department of Health and Human Services; National Center for Health Statistics

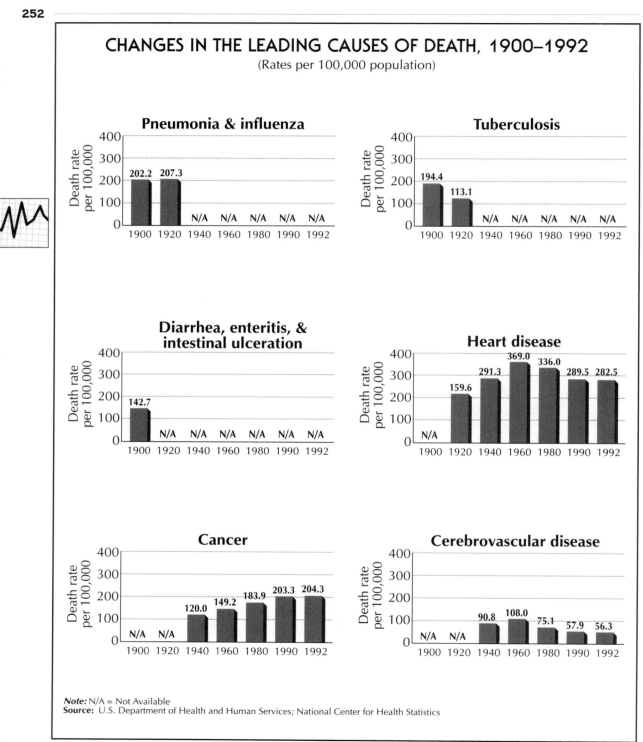

CHANGES IN THE LEADING CAUSES OF DEATH, 1900–1992
(Rates per 100,000 population)

Pneumonia & influenza

Death rate per 100,000

1900	1920	1940	1960	1980	1990	1992
202.2	207.3	N/A	N/A	N/A	N/A	N/A

Tuberculosis

Death rate per 100,000

1900	1920	1940	1960	1980	1990	1992
194.4	113.1	N/A	N/A	N/A	N/A	N/A

Diarrhea, enteritis, & intestinal ulceration

Death rate per 100,000

1900	1920	1940	1960	1980	1990	1992
142.7	N/A	N/A	N/A	N/A	N/A	N/A

Heart disease

Death rate per 100,000

1900	1920	1940	1960	1980	1990	1992
N/A	159.6	291.3	369.0	336.0	289.5	282.5

Cancer

Death rate per 100,000

1900	1920	1940	1960	1980	1990	1992
N/A	N/A	120.0	149.2	183.9	203.3	204.3

Cerebrovascular disease

Death rate per 100,000

1900	1920	1940	1960	1980	1990	1992
N/A	N/A	90.8	108.0	75.1	57.9	56.3

Note: N/A = Not Available
Source: U.S. Department of Health and Human Services; National Center for Health Statistics

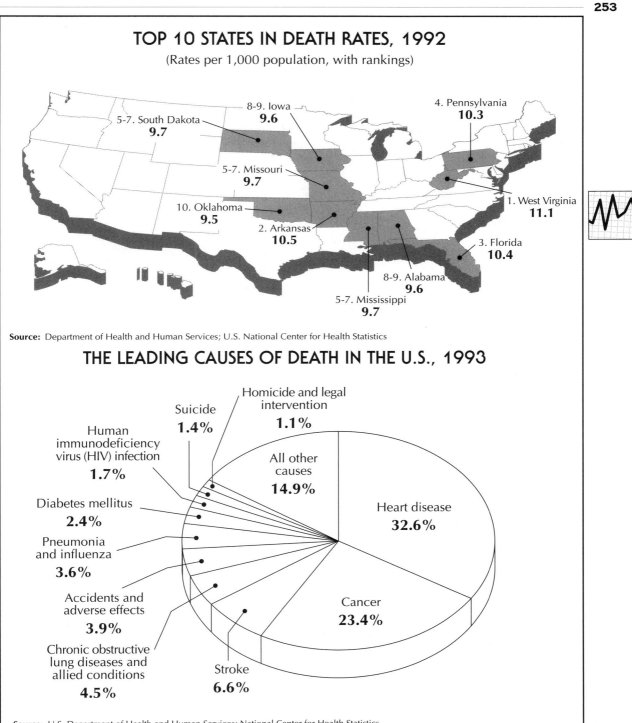

TOP 10 STATES IN DEATH RATES, 1992

(Rates per 1,000 population, with rankings)

8-9. Iowa
9.6

5-7. South Dakota
9.7

4. Pennsylvania
10.3

5-7. Missouri
9.7

10. Oklahoma
9.5

1. West Virginia
11.1

2. Arkansas
10.5

3. Florida
10.4

8-9. Alabama
9.6

5-7. Mississippi
9.7

Source: Department of Health and Human Services; U.S. National Center for Health Statistics

THE LEADING CAUSES OF DEATH IN THE U.S., 1993

Suicide
1.4%

Homicide and legal
intervention
1.1%

Human
immunodeficiency
virus (HIV) infection
1.7%

All other
causes
14.9%

Heart disease
32.6%

Diabetes mellitus
2.4%

Pneumonia
and influenza
3.6%

Accidents and
adverse effects
3.9%

Cancer
23.4%

Chronic obstructive
lung diseases and
allied conditions
4.5%

Stroke
6.6%

Source: U.S. Department of Health and Human Services; National Center for Health Statistics

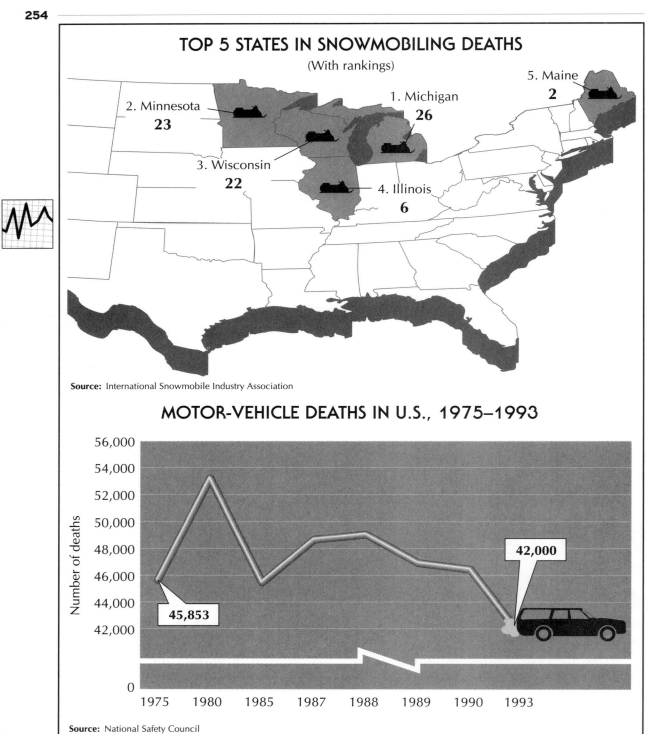

TOP 5 STATES IN SNOWMOBILING DEATHS
(With rankings)

5. Maine
2

2. Minnesota
23

1. Michigan
26

3. Wisconsin
22

4. Illinois
6

Source: International Snowmobile Industry Association

MOTOR-VEHICLE DEATHS IN U.S., 1975–1993

Number of deaths

56,000
54,000
52,000
50,000
48,000
46,000
44,000
42,000
0

42,000

45,853

1975   1980   1985   1987   1988   1989   1990   1993

Source: National Safety Council

U.S. DEATH RATES BY RACE, 1970–1992

(Deaths per 100,000 population)

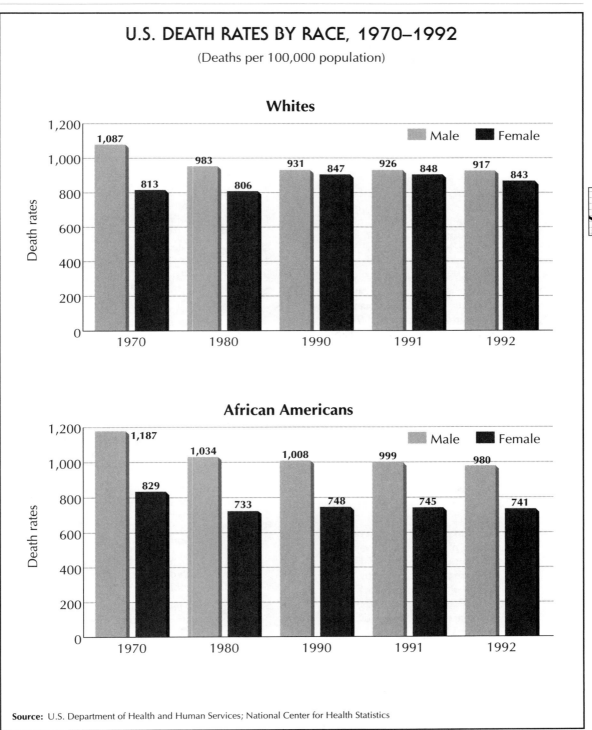

Whites

	1970	1980	1990	1991	1992
Male	1,087	983	931	926	917
Female	813	806	847	848	843

African Americans

	1970	1980	1990	1991	1992
Male	1,187	1,034	1,008	999	980
Female	829	733	748	745	741

Source: U.S. Department of Health and Human Services; National Center for Health Statistics

P O P U L A T I O N

The population of the United States is currently increasing at a rate of about 1% a year. In 1790, when the first federal census was conducted, about 4 million people lived in the new nation. By 1995, the population had grown by almost 66 times, to 263 million.

Two factors have caused the country's population growth: natural increase (the difference between the number of births and deaths), and migration increase (the difference between the number of immigrants and emigrants). Approximately two-thirds of current U.S. growth is due to natural increase, and one-third to immigration. In 1992, for example, there was a natural increase of 1.9 million and a migration increase of 1.1 million. If current fertility and immigration trends continue, the U.S. population will double by about the year 2050.

Various factors influence the actual distribution of population. For example, since the beginning of the Industrial Age in the late 18th century, people have migrated from rural areas to cities for jobs. Today, the vast majority of Americans live in urban environments. In recent years, mild climates coupled with booming economies have attracted many people to the South.

Population growth affects communities and the nation in many ways. It dramatically alters both the quality of life for each citizen and it directly affects the environment. For example, a 1994 report commissioned by the non-profit Carrying Capacity Network indicated that if current U.S. population growth and related trends continue, some 15 million acres of farmland will be lost to urbanization, highways, erosion, and pollution by the year 2000.

FINGERTIP FACTS

- The United States had a population in 1995 of approximately 263 million—the third most populous nation, after China and India.

- Nevada has been the fastest-growing state Its population increased 50.1% during the 1980s and 15.6% from 1990 to 1993.

- California is the most populous state, with 31.2 million people in 1993. Wyoming has the fewest people—about 470,000 in 1993.

- In 1993, state population per square mile of land area ranged from one person in Alaska to 1,062 in New Jersey.

- Of the U.S. population in 1960, 69.6% lived in urban areas; by 1990, the figure had grown to 75.2%.

- New York City is the largest U.S. city, with a population of 7.3 million in 1990. Los Angeles, California is second (3.5 million).

- Five cities had populations of 1 million or more in 1960; by 1990, there were 8 cities in this category, accounting for 13.0% of the nation's population.

- Since 1960, most urban growth has occurred in cities of under 250,000 people.

- Between 1980 and 1990, some 29 cities increased their populations to 100,000 or more. Of these, 18 were in California.

- Projections of the U.S. population by the year 2050 range from 392 million to 522 million.

NATIONAL CENSUSES

(Resident U.S. population reported by census)

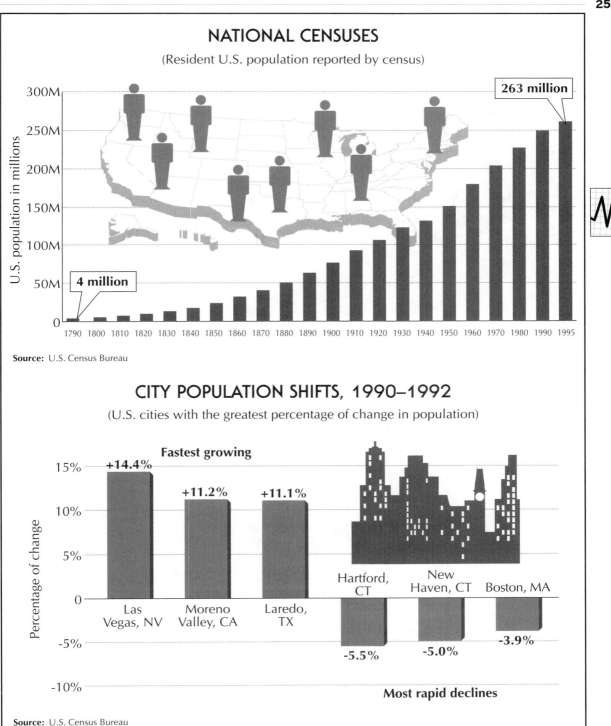

263 million

4 million

Source: U.S. Census Bureau

CITY POPULATION SHIFTS, 1990–1992

(U.S. cities with the greatest percentage of change in population)

Fastest growing

- +14.4% Las Vegas, NV
- +11.2% Moreno Valley, CA
- +11.1% Laredo, TX

- -5.5% Hartford, CT
- -5.0% New Haven, CT
- -3.9% Boston, MA

Most rapid declines

Source: U.S. Census Bureau

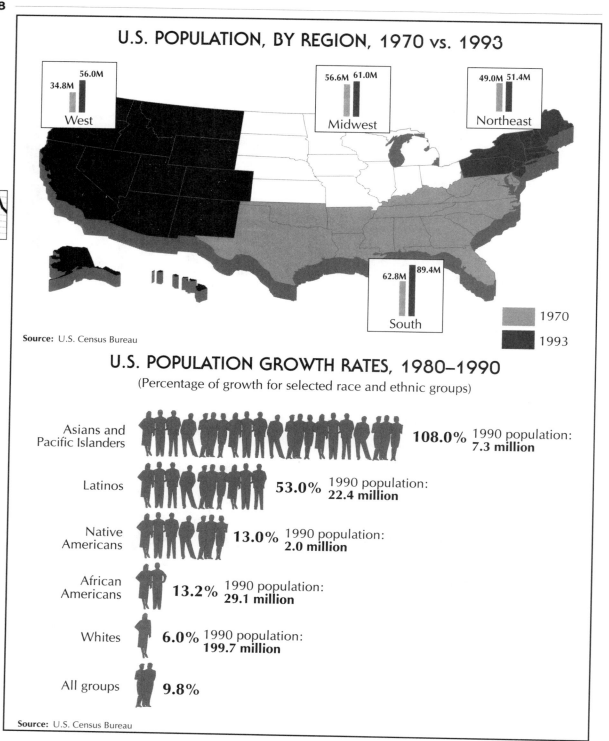

U.S. POPULATION, BY REGION, 1970 vs. 1993

West
34.8M 56.0M

Midwest
56.6M 61.0M

Northeast
49.0M 51.4M

South
62.8M 89.4M

1970
1993

Source: U.S. Census Bureau

U.S. POPULATION GROWTH RATES, 1980–1990
(Percentage of growth for selected race and ethnic groups)

Asians and Pacific Islanders **108.0%** 1990 population: **7.3 million**

Latinos **53.0%** 1990 population: **22.4 million**

Native Americans **13.0%** 1990 population: **2.0 million**

African Americans **13.2%** 1990 population: **29.1 million**

Whites **6.0%** 1990 population: **199.7 million**

All groups **9.8%**

Source: U.S. Census Bureau

U.S. POPULATION BY STATE: THE TOP 20, 1993
(With rankings)

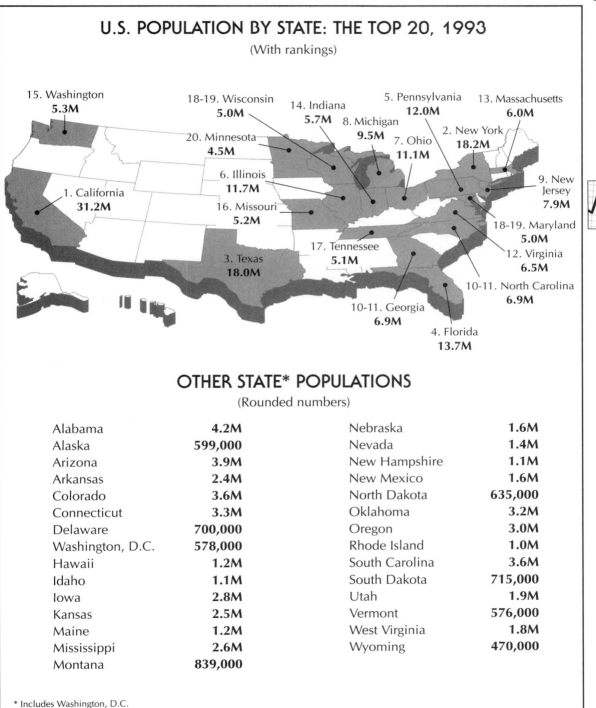

15. Washington
5.3M

18-19. Wisconsin
5.0M

14. Indiana
5.7M

8. Michigan
9.5M

5. Pennsylvania
12.0M

13. Massachusetts
6.0M

20. Minnesota
4.5M

7. Ohio
11.1M

2. New York
18.2M

6. Illinois
11.7M

9. New Jersey
7.9M

1. California
31.2M

16. Missouri
5.2M

18-19. Maryland
5.0M

17. Tennessee
5.1M

12. Virginia
6.5M

3. Texas
18.0M

10-11. North Carolina
6.9M

10-11. Georgia
6.9M

4. Florida
13.7M

OTHER STATE* POPULATIONS
(Rounded numbers)

Alabama	**4.2M**	Nebraska	**1.6M**
Alaska	**599,000**	Nevada	**1.4M**
Arizona	**3.9M**	New Hampshire	**1.1M**
Arkansas	**2.4M**	New Mexico	**1.6M**
Colorado	**3.6M**	North Dakota	**635,000**
Connecticut	**3.3M**	Oklahoma	**3.2M**
Delaware	**700,000**	Oregon	**3.0M**
Washington, D.C.	**578,000**	Rhode Island	**1.0M**
Hawaii	**1.2M**	South Carolina	**3.6M**
Idaho	**1.1M**	South Dakota	**715,000**
Iowa	**2.8M**	Utah	**1.9M**
Kansas	**2.5M**	Vermont	**576,000**
Maine	**1.2M**	West Virginia	**1.8M**
Mississippi	**2.6M**	Wyoming	**470,000**
Montana	**839,000**		

* Includes Washington, D.C.
Source: U.S. Census Bureau

TOP 20 U.S. METROPOLITAN AREAS, BY POPULATION, 1990

(With rankings)

1.	NY, Northern NJ, CT	**18.0M**	
2.	Los Angeles-Anaheim-Riverside, CA	**14.5M**	
3.	Chicago-Gary-Lake City, IL, IN, WI	**8.0M**	
4.	San Francisco-Oakland-San Jose, CA	**6.2M**	
5.	Philadelphia-Wilmington-Trenton, PA, DE, NJ	**5.9M**	
6.	Detroit-Ann Arbor, MI	**4.7M**	
7.	Boston-Lawrence-Salem, MA, NH	**4.2M**	
8.	Washington, D.C., MD, VA	**3.9M**	
9.	Dallas-Ft. Worth, TX	**3.9M**	
10.	Houston-Galveston-Brazoria, TX	**3.7M**	
11.	Miami-Ft. Lauderdale, FL	**3.2M**	
12.	Atlanta, GA	**2.8M**	
13.	Cleveland-Akron-Lorain, OH	**2.8M**	
14.	Seattle-Tacoma, WA	**2.6M**	
15.	San Diego, CA	**2.5M**	
16.	Minneapolis-St. Paul, MN	**2.5M**	
17.	St. Louis, MO	**2.4M**	
18.	Baltimore, MD	**2.4M**	
19.	Pittsburgh-Beaver Valley, PA	**2.2M**	
20.	Phoenix, AZ	**2.1M**	

Source: U.S. Census Bureau

TOP 10 FASTEST-GROWING MAJOR U.S. CITIES, 1980–1990

(With rankings)

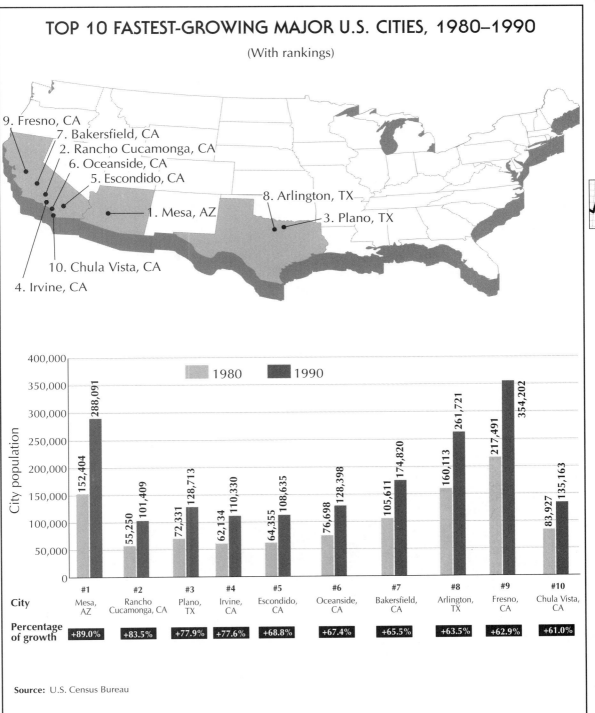

9. Fresno, CA

7. Bakersfield, CA

2. Rancho Cucamonga, CA

6. Oceanside, CA

5. Escondido, CA

8. Arlington, TX

1. Mesa, AZ

3. Plano, TX

10. Chula Vista, CA

4. Irvine, CA

	1980	1990
	☐	■

City population — 400,000 / 350,000 / 300,000 / 250,000 / 200,000 / 150,000 / 100,000 / 50,000 / 0

City	#1 Mesa, AZ	#2 Rancho Cucamonga, CA	#3 Plano, TX	#4 Irvine, CA	#5 Escondido, CA	#6 Oceanside, CA	#7 Bakersfield, CA	#8 Arlington, TX	#9 Fresno, CA	#10 Chula Vista, CA
1980	152,404	55,250	72,331	62,134	64,355	76,698	105,611	160,113	217,491	83,927
1990	288,091	101,409	128,713	110,330	108,635	128,398	174,820	261,721	354,202	135,163
Percentage of growth	+89.0%	+83.5%	+77.9%	+77.6%	+68.8%	+67.4%	+65.5%	+63.5%	+62.9%	+61.0%

Source: U.S. Census Bureau

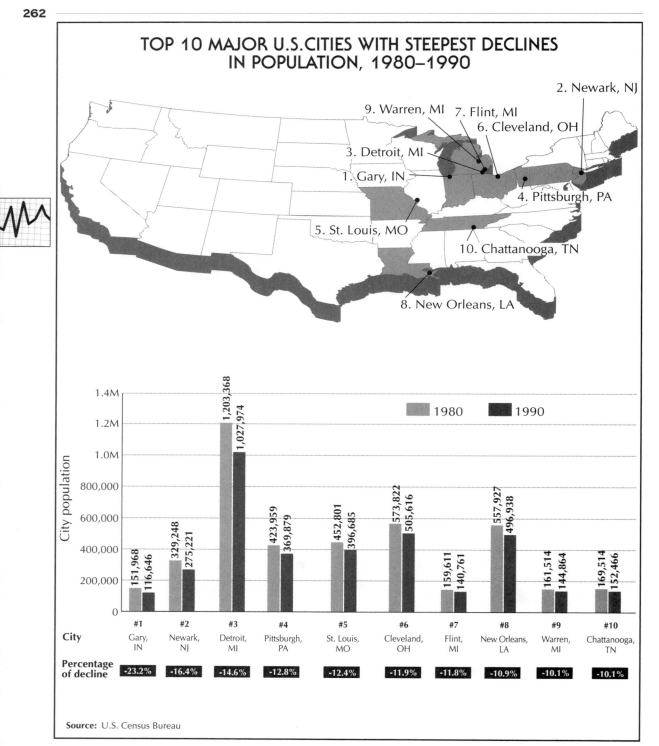

TOP 10 MAJOR U.S. CITIES WITH STEEPEST DECLINES IN POPULATION, 1980–1990

9. Warren, MI   7. Flint, MI

2. Newark, NJ

6. Cleveland, OH

3. Detroit, MI

1. Gary, IN

4. Pittsburgh, PA

5. St. Louis, MO

10. Chattanooga, TN

8. New Orleans, LA

City population

1980   1990

	#1 Gary, IN	#2 Newark, NJ	#3 Detroit, MI	#4 Pittsburgh, PA	#5 St. Louis, MO	#6 Cleveland, OH	#7 Flint, MI	#8 New Orleans, LA	#9 Warren, MI	#10 Chattanooga, TN
1980	151,968	329,248	1,203,368	423,959	452,801	573,822	159,611	557,927	161,514	169,514
1990	116,646	275,221	1,027,974	369,879	396,685	505,616	140,761	496,938	144,864	152,466

City	#1 Gary, IN	#2 Newark, NJ	#3 Detroit, MI	#4 Pittsburgh, PA	#5 St. Louis, MO	#6 Cleveland, OH	#7 Flint, MI	#8 New Orleans, LA	#9 Warren, MI	#10 Chattanooga, TN
Percentage of decline	-23.2%	-16.4%	-14.6%	-12.8%	-12.4%	-11.9%	-11.8%	-10.9%	-10.1%	-10.1%

Source: U.S. Census Bureau

U.S. ASIAN POPULATION BOOMS, 1980–1990

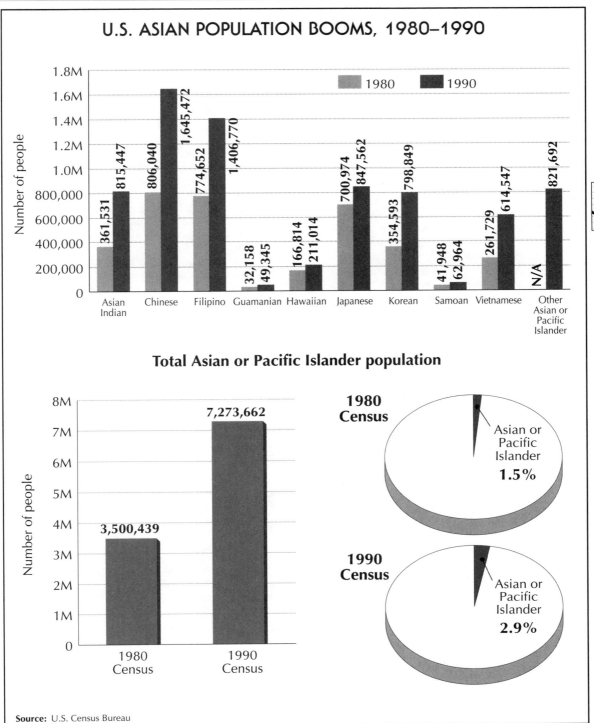

Number of people

■ 1980   ■ 1990

	1980	1990
Asian Indian	361,531	815,447
Chinese	806,040	1,645,472
Filipino	774,652	1,406,770
Guamanian	32,158	49,345
Hawaiian	166,814	211,014
Japanese	700,974	847,562
Korean	354,593	798,849
Samoan	41,948	62,964
Vietnamese	261,729	614,547
Other Asian or Pacific Islander	N/A	821,692

Total Asian or Pacific Islander population

Number of people

3,500,439 — 1980 Census
7,273,662 — 1990 Census

1980 Census — Asian or Pacific Islander **1.5%**

1990 Census — Asian or Pacific Islander **2.9%**

Source: U.S. Census Bureau

P O V E R T Y

Being poor, or living in poverty, has different meanings in different countries, in different regions of a single country, and even in different times in history. In the United States today, a primary measurement of poverty is income. The Census Bureau reported that in 1993, some 39.3 million Americans—about 15.1% of the total population—lived below the poverty line. This was the highest number of poor people since 39.6 million were defined as living under the poverty line in 1961.

Poverty rates vary by race, age, sex, family composition, and other factors. For example, rates are higher among blacks than whites, higher in rural areas than in metropolitan areas, higher in the South than in other regions of the U.S., and higher among immigrant families than among native-born families.

Particularly distressing is the increasing number of children who are living in poverty. In 1992, more than one of every 4 American children under age 6—a record 6 million youngsters—lived in families with incomes below the poverty line. The Food Research and Action Center, a nonprofit organization that works to alleviate hunger, reported that more than 5 million children under age 12 go hungry each month.

FINGERTIP FACTS

- According to the Children's Defense Fund (CDF), one U.S. infant is born into poverty every 35 seconds.

- Every 31 seconds, an infant is born to an unmarried mother, according to the CDF.

- The poverty line is adjusted periodically and varies according to family size. In 1992, for example, it was $9,137 for a family of 2; $14,335 for a family of 4; and $19,137 for a family of 6.

- In 1993, blacks were the group with the highest poverty rate in the U.S. (33.1%), as compared to Latinos (30.6%), Asians and Pacific Islanders (15.3%), and whites (12.2%).

- In 1992, the South was home to the most poor people (40% of the nation's total); the Northeast had the fewest (17%). The South also had the highest percentage of poor residents (17% of its total population), while the Northeast had the smallest percentage (12%).

- The Community Childhood Hunger Identification Program, which documents hunger in America, reported in 1991 that poor households spend a much larger portion of their income on housing (54%) than do typical families (20%). This leaves less money for food and other necessities.

- The poverty rate is higher than average in families headed by females (with no spouse present). In 1992, a total of 38.5% of these families were below the poverty level.

- The higher the education of the householder, the less likely that the family lives below the poverty level. In 1992, only 2.2% of families headed by someone with a college degree lived in poverty, as compared to 24.1% of those headed by someone without a high school diploma.

TOP 10 RICHEST AND POOREST STATES, BY MEDIAN INCOME

Census reports show more Americans in poverty, which reflects a population increase.
The reports track state numbers on 1992 median incomes and poverty rates.
The results, with rankings:

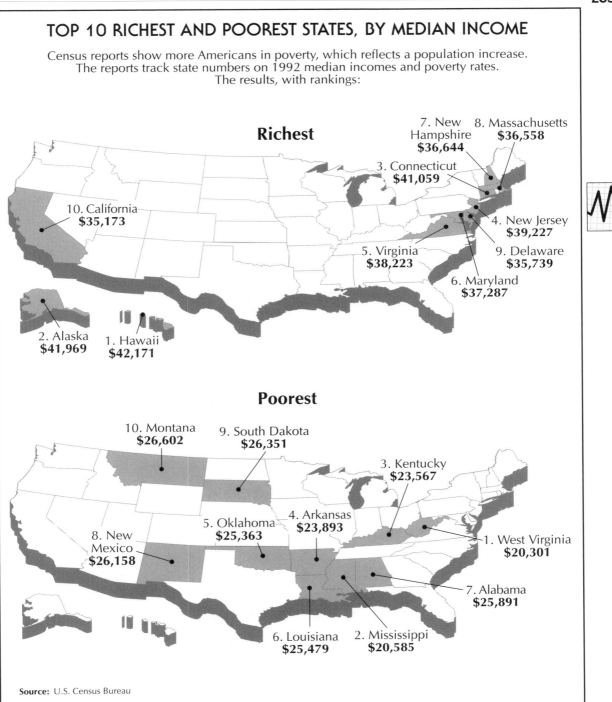

Richest

7. New Hampshire **$36,644**

8. Massachusetts **$36,558**

3. Connecticut **$41,059**

10. California **$35,173**

4. New Jersey **$39,227**

5. Virginia **$38,223**

9. Delaware **$35,739**

6. Maryland **$37,287**

2. Alaska **$41,969**

1. Hawaii **$42,171**

Poorest

10. Montana **$26,602**

9. South Dakota **$26,351**

3. Kentucky **$23,567**

4. Arkansas **$23,893**

5. Oklahoma **$25,363**

8. New Mexico **$26,158**

1. West Virginia **$20,301**

7. Alabama **$25,891**

6. Louisiana **$25,479**

2. Mississippi **$20,585**

Source: U.S. Census Bureau

AMERICA'S POOR AT A GLANCE, 1992

There were **36,880,000** poor people in the U.S., which was **14.5%** of the population.

27,372,000 of the poor lived in urban areas, which was **13.9%** of urban dwellers.

24,523,000 people, or **11.6%** of the poor, were whites (including Latinos).

18,308,000 people, or **9.6%** of the poor, were whites (non-Latinos).

Of the people ages 18 to 64, **11.7%**, or **18,281,000,** were poor.

14,763,000, or **16.9%** of the people in the Southern states, were poor.

40% of the poor—**14,763,000**—lived in the South.

14,617,000 people, or **21.9%** people under 18, were poor.

33.3% of African Americans, **10,613,000** people, were poor.

Outside urban areas, **9,509,000,** or **16.8%,** of the people were poor.

8,955,000 white children under 18, or **16.9%,** were poor.

In the Midwest states, **7,983,000** people—**13.1%**—were poor.

7,983,000 people, or **21.6%** of the poor, lived in the Midwest.

7,960,000 people in the U.S. were poor, which was **11.7%** of all families.

In the Western states, **7,907,000** of the people, or **14.4%,** were poor.

7,906,000 people, or **21.4%** of the poor, lived in the West.

6,655,000 Latinos—**29.3%**—were poor.

6,277,000, or **12.3%** of the people in the Northwest states, were poor.

16.9%, or **6,277,000,** of the poor lived in the Northeast.

8.9% of white families (including Latinos), **5,160,000** people, were poor.

4,938,000 African-American children under 18, or **46.6%,** were poor.

4,171,000 people, or **34.9%** of female-led households, were poor.

3,983,000 people over 64, or **12.9%,** were poor.

7.3% of white families (non-Latino), or **3,860,000,** were poor.

3,318,000 people—**6.2%** of all married-couple families— were poor.

Of Latino children under 18, **39.9%,** or **3,116,000,** were poor.

30.9% of African-American families, or **2,435,000** people, were poor.

49.8% of African-American female-led households, or **1,835,000** people, were poor.

26.2% of Latino families, or **1,395,000** people, were poor.

912,000 Asian/Pacific Islanders, or **12.5%** of their population, were poor.

13% of African-American married-couple families—**486,000** people—were poor.

199,000 people, or **12%** of Asian/Pacific Islander families, were poor.

Source: *Newsweek;* U.S. Census Bureau

U.S. CITIES WHERE POVERTY INCREASED, 1980–1990

In the 1980s, the percentage of African Americans living in ghettos
rose the most in these U.S. cities:

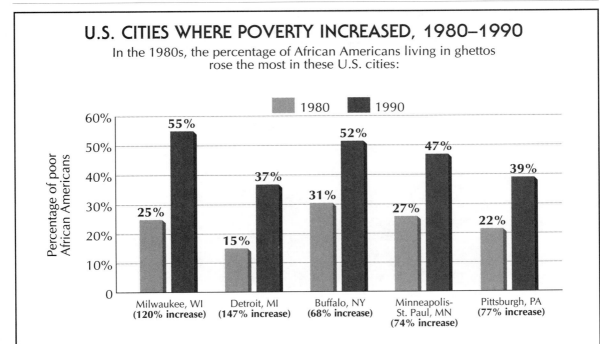

U.S. CITIES WHERE POVERTY DECREASED, 1980–1990

In the 1980s, poverty among African Americans with access to strong job markets generally
decreased. The percentage of blacks living in ghettos fell the most in these U.S. cities:

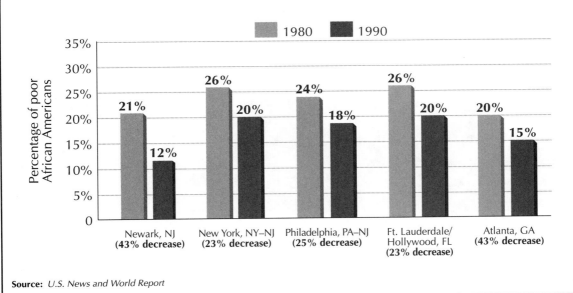

Source: *U.S. News and World Report*

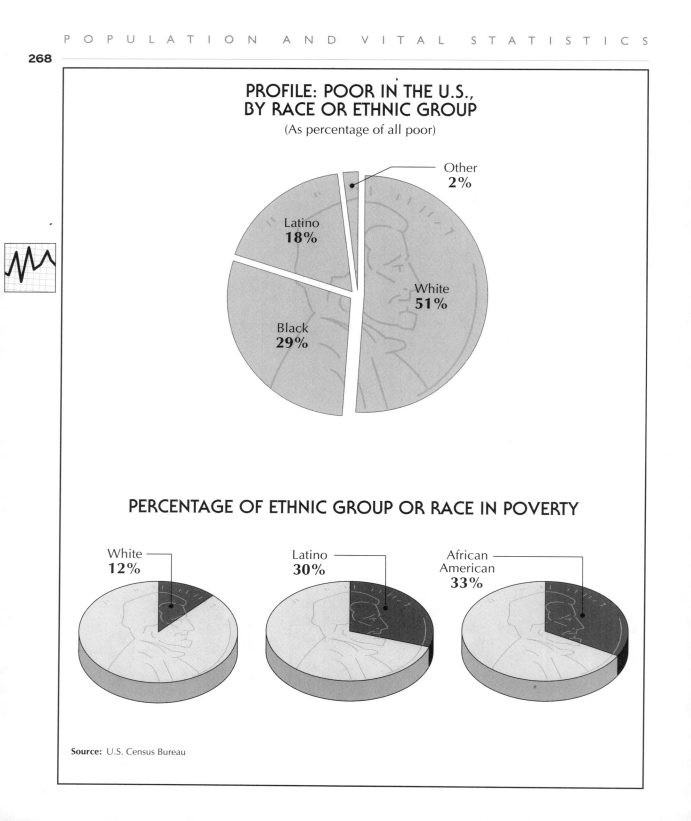

PROFILE: POOR IN THE U.S., BY RACE OR ETHNIC GROUP

(As percentage of all poor)

Other
2%

Latino
18%

White
51%

Black
29%

PERCENTAGE OF ETHNIC GROUP OR RACE IN POVERTY

White
12%

Latino
30%

African
American
33%

Source: U.S. Census Bureau

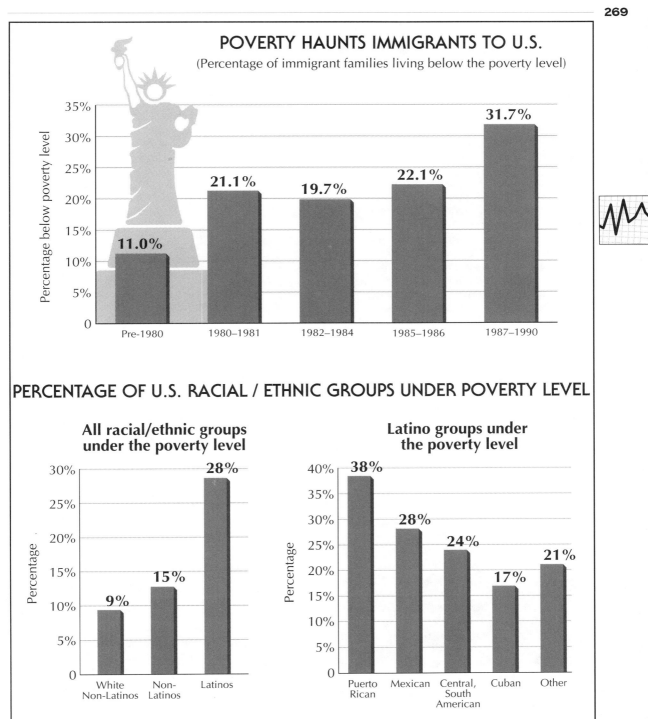

POVERTY HAUNTS IMMIGRANTS TO U.S.
(Percentage of immigrant families living below the poverty level)

Percentage below poverty level

- Pre-1980: 11.0%
- 1980–1981: 21.1%
- 1982–1984: 19.7%
- 1985–1986: 22.1%
- 1987–1990: 31.7%

PERCENTAGE OF U.S. RACIAL / ETHNIC GROUPS UNDER POVERTY LEVEL

All racial/ethnic groups under the poverty level

Percentage

- White Non-Latinos: 9%
- Non-Latinos: 15%
- Latinos: 28%

Latino groups under the poverty level

Percentage

- Puerto Rican: 38%
- Mexican: 28%
- Central, South American: 24%
- Cuban: 17%
- Other: 21%

Source: U.S. Census Bureau

H O M E L E S S N E S S

One of the most troubling and tragic social problems in the U.S. is the country's large population of homeless people. Determining how many people are without permanent homes is difficult, because of the transient and often hidden nature of the population. For these reasons, estimates on the number of homeless vary widely. In 1994, U.S. Secretary of Housing and Urban Development Henry Cisneros cited "reasonable estimates" that some 600,000 Americans were homeless, and that as many as 7 million had been homeless at some point during the previous 5 years. The Interagency Council on the Homeless concluded that "the crisis of homelessness is greater than commonly known or previously acknowledged."

At one time, most U.S. homeless people were middle-age men. Today, single men account for only about 43% of the homeless population. The fastest-growing homeless group consists of families with young children. Indeed, about 30% of the homeless are children. Many of them are in families, but a substantial number are runaways or "throwaways" —children rejected by their parents.

A primary reason for homelessness is a lack of low-cost housing. Other causes include poverty, unemployment, mental illness, substance abuse, and domestic violence. Government agencies, churches, and community groups help many homeless people, but public financing and other assistance—such as job training and drug treatment programs—are being restricted as elected officials continue to slash budgets. Many cities have cracked down on homeless people, arresting them for loitering, panhandling, public drunkenness, blocking traffic, and other disruptive behaviors.

FINGERTIP FACTS

☛ The homeless problem is most apparent in big cities. New York City has the largest homeless population in the U.S., followed by Los Angeles, Chicago, and San Francisco.

☛ About 27% of the homeless have severe mental illnesses, such as chronic schizophrenia and personality disorders.

☛ A U.S. Conference of Mayors study found that 21% of the homeless in 1993 were war veterans; 18% were employed, either full- or part-time.

☛ About 72% of homeless families are headed by a single parent, usually a mother.

☛ In 1993, some 67% of those who sought emergency food assistance were families with children.

☛ In many cities, "food banks" and other food-assistance programs are unable to keep up with the demand. In 72% of cities surveyed in 1993, such programs had to turn people away.

☛ Approximately 25 million young Americans—about half of them under age 17—used food banks, soup kitchens, or other kinds of food-distribution programs in 1994.

☛ Federal programs to help the homeless are grouped under the Steward B. McKinney Homeless Assistance Act, which began in 1987. Most funding for homeless programs, however, comes from state and city budgets.

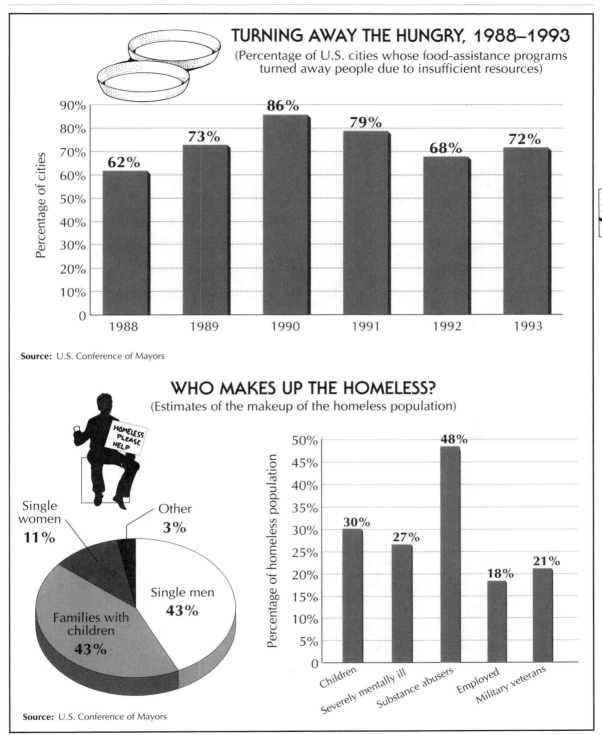

TURNING AWAY THE HUNGRY, 1988–1993
(Percentage of U.S. cities whose food-assistance programs turned away people due to insufficient resources)

Percentage of cities

- 1988: 62%
- 1989: 73%
- 1990: 86%
- 1991: 79%
- 1992: 68%
- 1993: 72%

Source: U.S. Conference of Mayors

WHO MAKES UP THE HOMELESS?
(Estimates of the makeup of the homeless population)

HOMELESS PLEASE HELP

Pie chart:
- Single women 11%
- Other 3%
- Single men 43%
- Families with children 43%

Bar chart — Percentage of homeless population:
- Children: 30%
- Severely mentally ill: 27%
- Substance abusers: 48%
- Employed: 18%
- Military veterans: 21%

Source: U.S. Conference of Mayors

TOP 10 U.S. CITIES IN HOMELESS POPULATION

(Estimated numbers of homeless people, with rankings)

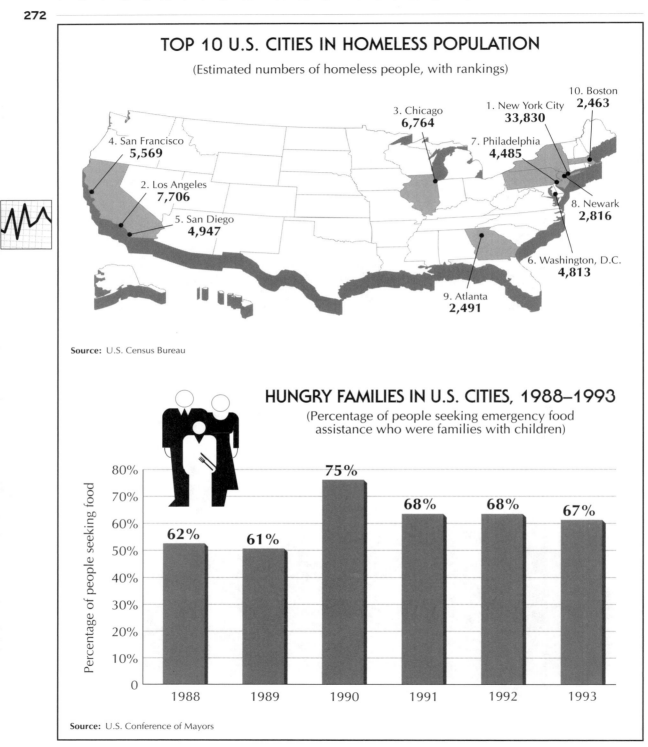

10. Boston
2,463

3. Chicago
6,764

1. New York City
33,830

4. San Francisco
5,569

7. Philadelphia
4,485

2. Los Angeles
7,706

5. San Diego
4,947

8. Newark
2,816

6. Washington, D.C.
4,813

9. Atlanta
2,491

Source: U.S. Census Bureau

HUNGRY FAMILIES IN U.S. CITIES, 1988–1993

(Percentage of people seeking emergency food
assistance who were families with children)

Percentage of people seeking food

Year	Percentage
1988	62%
1989	61%
1990	75%
1991	68%
1992	68%
1993	67%

Source: U.S. Conference of Mayors

HOMELESSNESS RISES FOR SOME, FALLS FOR OTHERS, 1988 vs. 1993

In 1993, a 26-city survey of homeless in the U.S. revealed changes in the makeup of the urban homeless since 1988. Fewer are single men; more are substance abusers or families with children:

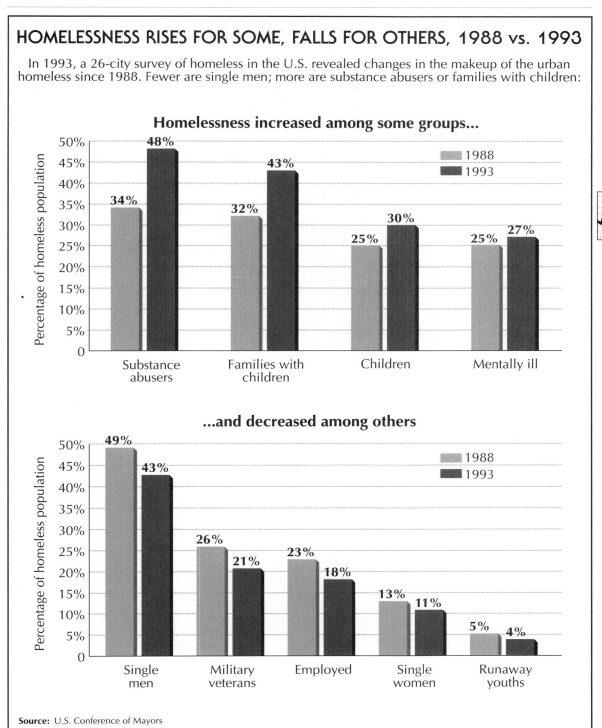

Homelessness increased among some groups...

Percentage of homeless population

- Substance abusers: 34% (1988), 48% (1993)
- Families with children: 32% (1988), 43% (1993)
- Children: 25% (1988), 30% (1993)
- Mentally ill: 25% (1988), 27% (1993)

...and decreased among others

Percentage of homeless population

- Single men: 49% (1988), 43% (1993)
- Military veterans: 26% (1988), 21% (1993)
- Employed: 23% (1988), 18% (1993)
- Single women: 13% (1988), 11% (1993)
- Runaway youths: 5% (1988), 4% (1993)

Source: U.S. Conference of Mayors

PUBLIC ASSISTANCE

During the 20th century, the U.S. government has passed a broad range of programs designed to provide financial help and social services to its citizens. The first federal U.S. program for the needy was created during the Great Depression of the 1930s. Today, programs include unemployment insurance, Social Security for retired people, health insurance plans, funds for education and training, subsidized day care for children, public housing, low-interest loans, veterans' benefits, food stamps, school lunch programs, and so on. At some time in their lives, almost all U.S. citizens will benefit from some type of public assistance.

But public attention and debate have focused largely on those programs known as "welfare"—programs that provide money, food, housing, medical care, and other assistance to low-income people. According to the Social Security Administration, approximately 14.1 million people, including 9.5 million children, were beneficiaries of Aid to Families with Dependent Children (AFDC) in 1993. AFDC provides monthly cash benefits to families; in 1993, the average monthly benefit was $373. Food stamps were distributed to 27.0 million people, with each participant receiving an average of $68 in monthly coupons. Five million households received rental subsidies, and 33.4 million people received medical care and services under Medicaid. Most people benefited from a combination of some or all of these programs.

Many voters feel that welfare is too generous. Public debate on the issue heated up following the 1994 elections, when Republicans gained control of both houses of Congress. Numerous proposals were advanced, both in Congress and at state levels, for overhauling welfare and redefining needs in hopes of cutting costs and weaning people from a continued reliance on the programs.

FINGERTIP FACTS

- Social insurance programs make up an average of 67% of federal social welfare spending. The same programs make up only 23% of such spending for states and local governments.

- Federal and state spending for Aid to Families with Dependent Children totaled $25.2 billion in 1993. The average cost for each taxpayer was about $156. The average monthly AFDC benefit per family in 1993 was $373.

- Half the families on AFDC leave in 4 years or less; 30% stay on for 8 years or longer. The main reasons why families leave AFDC are marriage (35%) and increased earnings of the single working mother (21%).

- Divorce or separation is the main reason why families go on welfare (45%); an unmarried woman having a child is second (30%).

- In 1993, some 10.4% of all U.S. families received food stamps. The average monthly food stamp allotment for a family of 3 was $68; the maximum was $295.

- In 1993, there were 24.8 million pupils who participated in the national School Lunch Program, at a cost of almost $4 billion to U.S. taxpayers.

- Between 1970 and 1992, Social Security payments to beneficiaries increased by about 800%, from $31.9 billion to $285.9 billion per year.

PUBLIC AID PAYMENTS IN THE U.S., 1980–1992

(In billions of dollars)

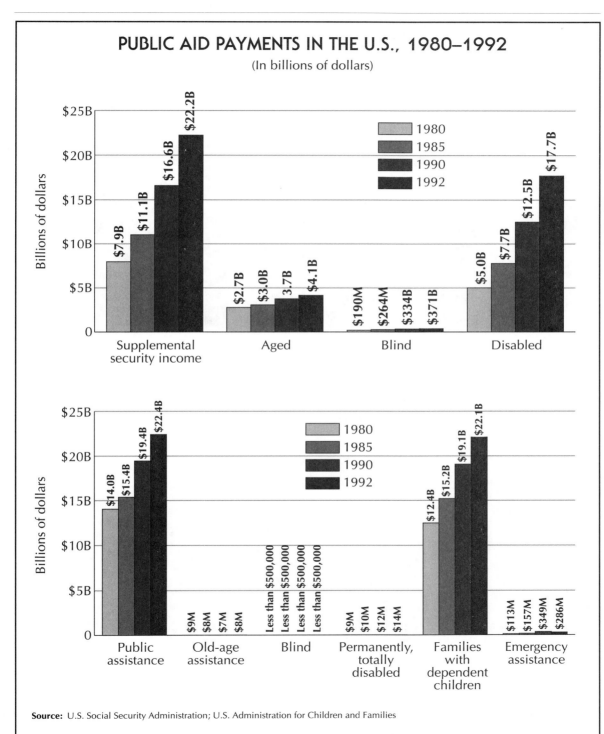

Source: U.S. Social Security Administration; U.S. Administration for Children and Families

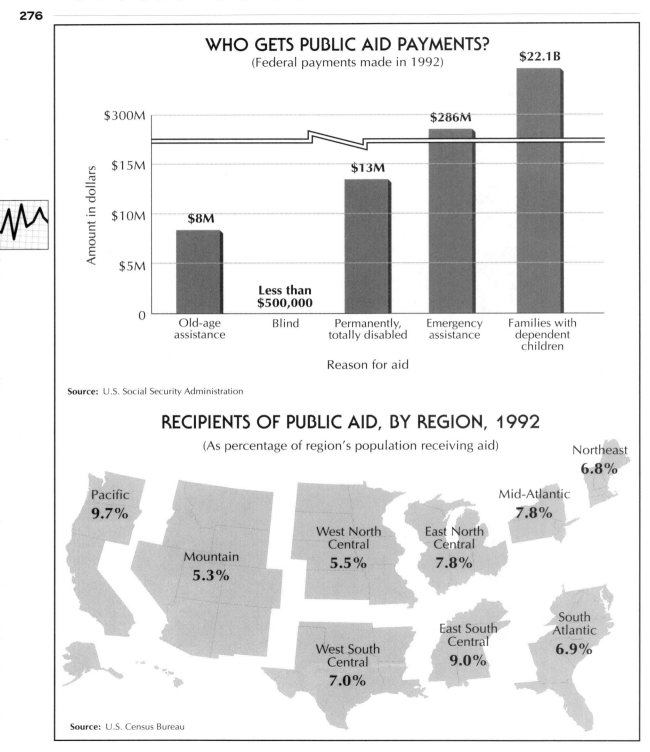

WHO GETS PUBLIC AID PAYMENTS?
(Federal payments made in 1992)

Amount in dollars / Reason for aid

- Old-age assistance: **$8M**
- Blind: **Less than $500,000**
- Permanently, totally disabled: **$13M**
- Emergency assistance: **$286M**
- Families with dependent children: **$22.1B**

Source: U.S. Social Security Administration

RECIPIENTS OF PUBLIC AID, BY REGION, 1992
(As percentage of region's population receiving aid)

- Northeast **6.8%**
- Mid-Atlantic **7.8%**
- Pacific **9.7%**
- West North Central **5.5%**
- East North Central **7.8%**
- Mountain **5.3%**
- West South Central **7.0%**
- East South Central **9.0%**
- South Atlantic **6.9%**

Source: U.S. Census Bureau

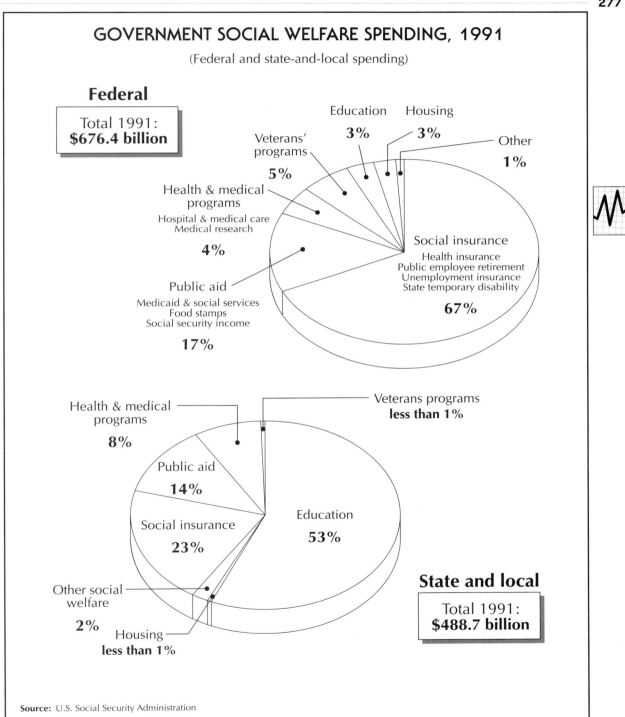

GOVERNMENT SOCIAL WELFARE SPENDING, 1991

(Federal and state-and-local spending)

Federal

Total 1991:
$676.4 billion

Education
3%

Housing
3%

Other
1%

Veterans'
programs
5%

Health & medical
programs
Hospital & medical care
Medical research
4%

Social insurance
Health insurance
Public employee retirement
Unemployment insurance
State temporary disability
67%

Public aid
Medicaid & social services
Food stamps
Social security income
17%

Health & medical
programs
8%

Veterans programs
less than 1%

Public aid
14%

Education
53%

Social insurance
23%

State and local

Total 1991:
$488.7 billion

Other social
welfare
2%

Housing
less than 1%

Source: U.S. Social Security Administration

WELFARE PAYMENTS BY ETHNIC GROUP, 1971–1991

The percentage of recipients of Aid to Families with Dependent Children who are African American has decreased. Other race or ethnic groups have stayed the same or increased:

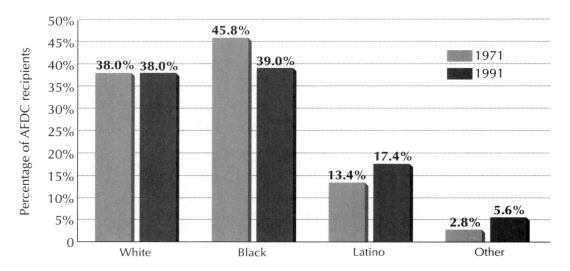

Source: University analysis of U.S. Census Bureau data; U.S. Department of Health and Human Services; *USA Today*

SOCIAL SECURITY PAYS OFF: THE NUMBER OF TOTAL PAYMENTS BY YEAR, 1970–1992

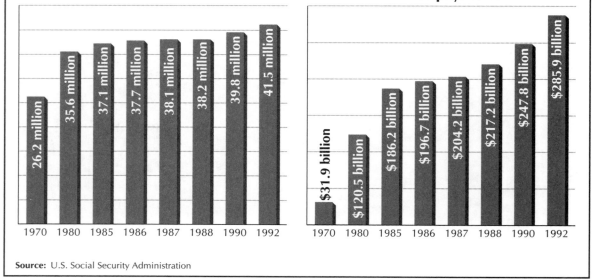

Source: U.S. Social Security Administration

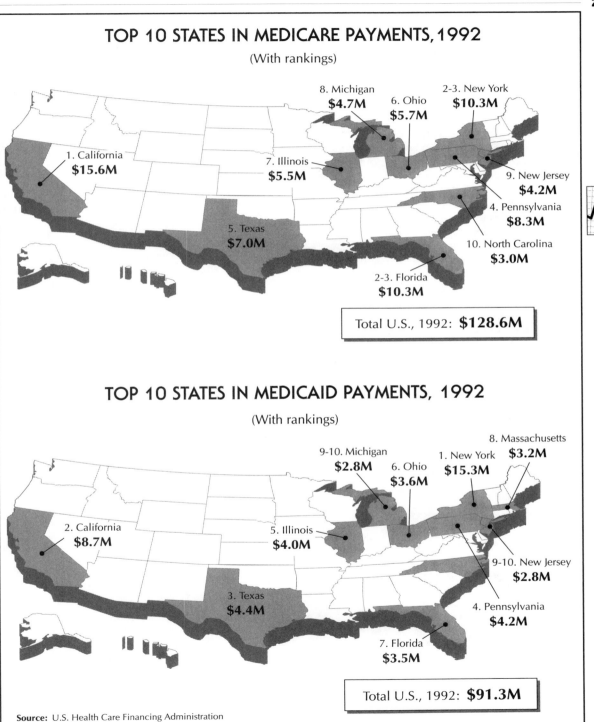

TOP 10 STATES IN MEDICARE PAYMENTS, 1992

(With rankings)

8. Michigan **$4.7M**

6. Ohio **$5.7M**

2-3. New York **$10.3M**

1. California **$15.6M**

7. Illinois **$5.5M**

9. New Jersey **$4.2M**

4. Pennsylvania **$8.3M**

5. Texas **$7.0M**

10. North Carolina **$3.0M**

2-3. Florida **$10.3M**

Total U.S., 1992: **$128.6M**

TOP 10 STATES IN MEDICAID PAYMENTS, 1992

(With rankings)

9-10. Michigan **$2.8M**

6. Ohio **$3.6M**

1. New York **$15.3M**

8. Massachusetts **$3.2M**

2. California **$8.7M**

5. Illinois **$4.0M**

9-10. New Jersey **$2.8M**

3. Texas **$4.4M**

4. Pennsylvania **$4.2M**

7. Florida **$3.5M**

Total U.S., 1992: **$91.3M**

Source: U.S. Health Care Financing Administration

STANDARD OF LIVING

The term "standard of living" usually refers to the economic well-being enjoyed by a person, family, community, or nation. A standard of living is considered high when it includes not only necessities but also certain comforts and luxuries; it is considered low when food, clean water, housing, and other necessities are limited or lacking.

Economists use various methods to measure standard of living. One measurement is the percentage of income that citizens spend on certain necessities; the higher this percentage, the lower the standard of living. Another measurement is based on consumption expenditures—the amount of money spent on basic goods and services. Still another measurement calculates average disposable income—the amount left over after taxes that is available for spending or saving.

The U.S. has one of the world's highest standards of living. But income is not distributed evenly throughout the population. The nation is one of extremes. Some people enjoy great wealth, while others are trapped in extreme poverty. Major differences exist along racial, educational, and geographic lines. Household composition and family size, of course, are also factors in determining overall standards of living.

FINGERTIP FACTS

- Switzerland is the world's wealthiest nation in terms of economic output per person—$36,410 in 1993. The U.S. ranks 7th, with $24,750.

- In terms of buying power, which measures how much people get for their money, the U.S. is rated #2, behind only Luxembourg.

- In 1993, personal income per capita in the U.S. was $20,817, up from $20,105 in 1992 and $9,940 in 1980.

- In 1993, disposable personal income per capita in the U.S. was $18,177. It was highest in the Northeast ($20,753), lowest in the South ($16,939).

- In 1993, the poorest one-fifth of the U.S. population received 3.6% of all household income; the top one-fifth accounted for a record 48.2%.

- Connecticut ranked #1 in 1993 in disposable personal income per capita with ($23,776); Mississippi ranked #50, with $13,631.

- According to the U.S. Census Bureau, the nation's median household income in 1993—when adjusted for inflation—fell for the fourth consecutive year, to $31,241.

- In 1993, white men employed full-time had a median income of $31,090; for black men, it was $23,020. For white women, it was $22,020; for black women, it was $19,820.

- College graduates earn more than workers with only a high school degree. In 1993, white male college graduates ages 25 and older earned an average of $43,690; high school graduates earned $26,790.

- Between 1973 and 1990, median income of families with children fell 6.7%, while that of families without children rose 11.2%.

- Median household income in 1992 was higher among whites ($32,368) than among Latinos ($22,848) and blacks ($18,660).

PER CAPITA DISPOSABLE PERSONAL INCOME, BY REGION, 1993

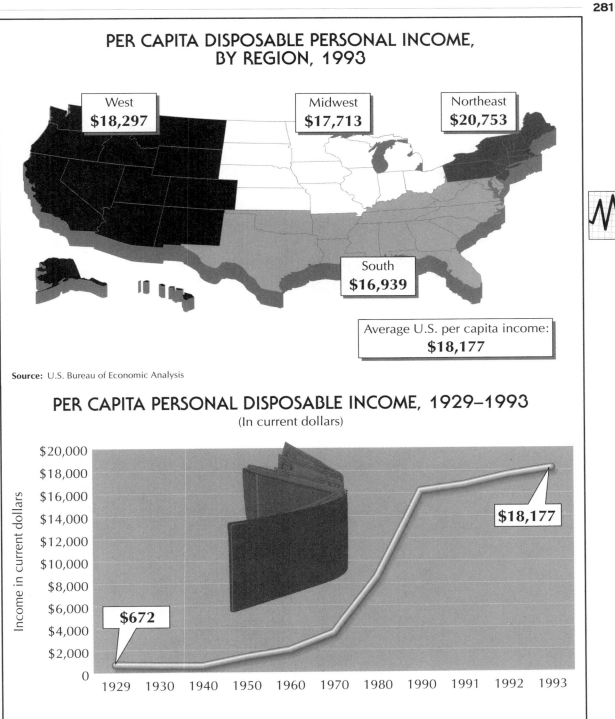

West
$18,297

Midwest
$17,713

Northeast
$20,753

South
$16,939

Average U.S. per capita income:
$18,177

Source: U.S. Bureau of Economic Analysis

PER CAPITA PERSONAL DISPOSABLE INCOME, 1929–1993
(In current dollars)

$18,177

$672

Source: U.S. Bureau of Economic Analysis
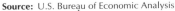

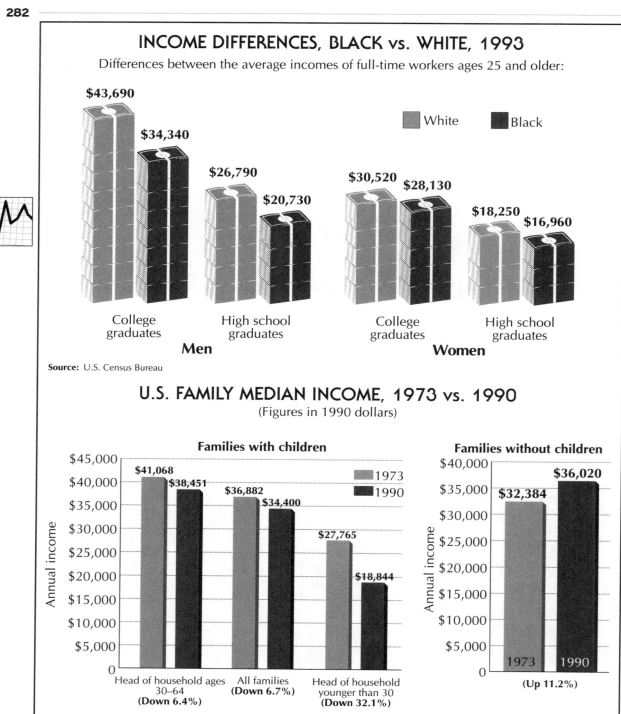

INCOME DIFFERENCES, BLACK vs. WHITE, 1993

Differences between the average incomes of full-time workers ages 25 and older:

White **Black**

Men

College graduates: $43,690 / $34,340
High school graduates: $26,790 / $20,730

Women

College graduates: $30,520 / $28,130
High school graduates: $18,250 / $16,960

Source: U.S. Census Bureau

U.S. FAMILY MEDIAN INCOME, 1973 vs. 1990
(Figures in 1990 dollars)

Families with children

1973 / 1990

Head of household ages 30–64: $41,068 / $38,451 **(Down 6.4%)**
All families: $36,882 / $34,400 **(Down 6.7%)**
Head of household younger than 30: $27,765 / $18,844 **(Down 32.1%)**

Families without children

1973: $32,384 / 1990: $36,020 **(Up 11.2%)**

Annual income

Source: *U.S. News & World Report;* Children's Defense Fund data

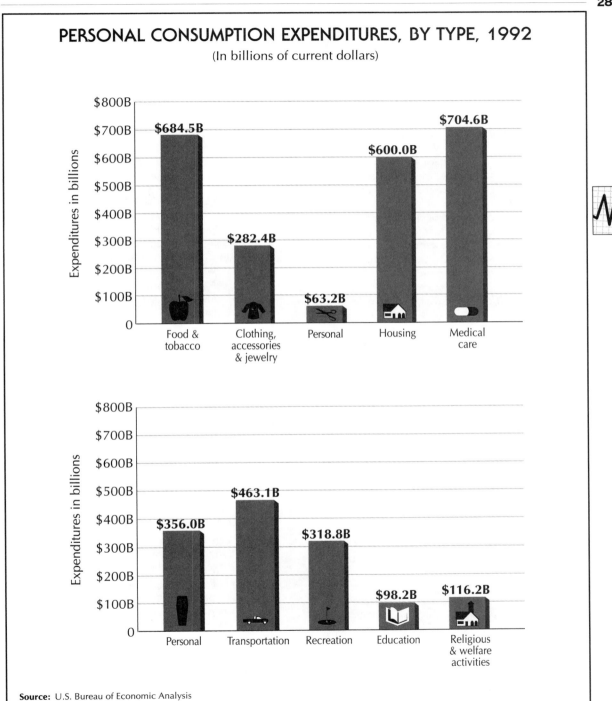

PERSONAL CONSUMPTION EXPENDITURES, BY TYPE, 1992

(In billions of current dollars)

Chart 1 (Expenditures in billions)

Category	Expenditure
Food & tobacco	$684.5B
Clothing, accessories & jewelry	$282.4B
Personal	$63.2B
Housing	$600.0B
Medical care	$704.6B

Chart 2 (Expenditures in billions)

Category	Expenditure
Personal	$356.0B
Transportation	$463.1B
Recreation	$318.8B
Education	$98.2B
Religious & welfare activities	$116.2B

Source: U.S. Bureau of Economic Analysis

ACCIDENTS AND DEATH

Accidents are the fourth leading cause of death in the U.S., after heart disease, cancer, and strokes. In general, accident victims are much younger than people who die from the three leading causes of death. Accidents are the #1 cause of death among Americans ages one to 38. They are the #7 cause among people ages 65 and older.

Motor-vehicle accidents are the main cause of accidental death in the U.S. Accidents in the home—mainly falls, fires, poisoning, suffocation, and drowning—are second.

The leading causes of death have changed during recent years. In 1900, a number of respiratory diseases—particularly pneumonia and influenza—were the main causes of death in the U.S. By 1990, these problems had decreased to #6. During the same period, however, cardiovascular diseases (diseases of the heart and blood vessels) and cancer grew significantly in frequency and have taken the lead.

Over the years, death rates per capita have fallen. In 1990, the U.S. death rate was 1,719 per 100,000 population. In 1950, the death rate was 963.8 per 100,000. By 1992, it had fallen to 853.3 per 100,000, but by 1993, had risen 3%, to 880.3 per 100,000.

Death rates vary by age, sex, race, cause, geographical location, and other factors. Death rates are rather high during the first year of life, then they drop sharply. They gradually increase again as people get older. Of course, death rates are highest among the elderly. Throughout life, however, males have higher death rates than females and black males have higher death rates than white males.

FINGERTIP FACTS

- Every 10 minutes, 2 people die in accidents in the U.S.

- Each year in the U.S., accidents cause almost half of all deaths among people ages 1 to 24. Motor-vehicle accidents are the main cause of accidental death in this age group.

- Among Americans ages 80 and older, falls are the main cause of accidental death.

- In 1992, accidental death rates ranged from 18.0 per 100,000 population in New York to 81.1 in Alaska.

- In 1993, medical expenses for accidents in the U.S. totaled about $75 billion. Damage to motor vehicles cost about $38 billion.

- Automobile travel is more risky than other kinds of travel. People are much more likely to be injured or killed in auto accidents than in train, bus, or airplane accidents.

- Deaths from motor-vehicle accidents are more common in rural areas than in cities.

- About 60% of Americans who die in motor-vehicle accidents are ages 15 to 44.

- About 300,000 people in the U.S. commit suicide each year. Males commit about 4 times as many suicides as do females.

- Each year, about 90 Americans are killed by lightning. More than two-thirds of all lightning deaths occur during the summer.

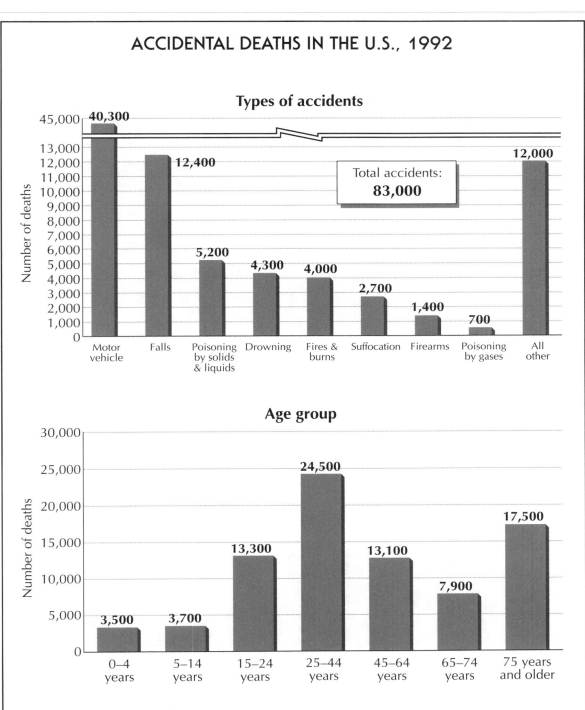

ACCIDENTAL DEATHS IN THE U.S., 1992

Types of accidents

Total accidents: 83,000

Type	Number of deaths
Motor vehicle	40,300
Falls	12,400
Poisoning by solids & liquids	5,200
Drowning	4,300
Fires & burns	4,000
Suffocation	2,700
Firearms	1,400
Poisoning by gases	700
All other	12,000

Age group

Age group	Number of deaths
0–4 years	3,500
5–14 years	3,700
15–24 years	13,300
25–44 years	24,500
45–64 years	13,100
65–74 years	7,900
75 years and older	17,500

Source: National Safety Council, *Accident Facts* (1993)

ACCIDENT-RELATED DEATH RATES IN THE U.S., 1930–1993

The number of deaths due to accidents has fallen steadily for 60 years,
even though the population has increased dramatically:

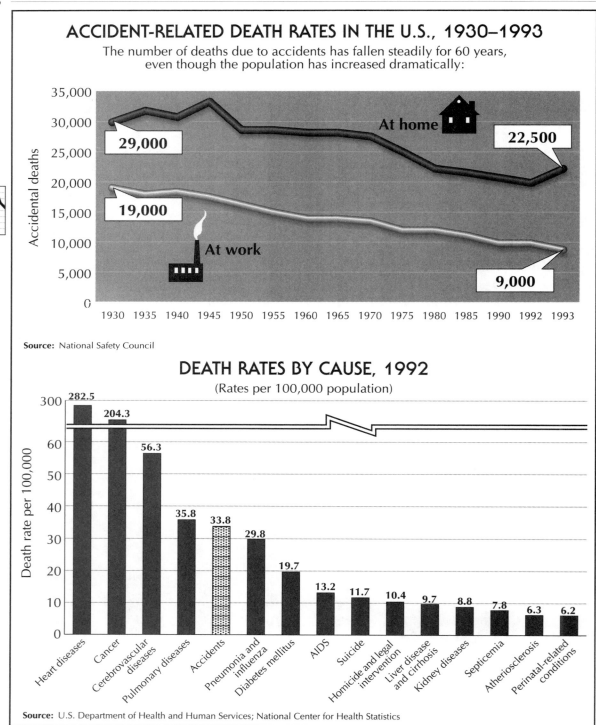

29,000

At home

22,500

19,000

At work

9,000

Accidental deaths

35,000 — 30,000 — 25,000 — 20,000 — 15,000 — 10,000 — 5,000 — 0

1930 1935 1940 1945 1950 1955 1960 1965 1970 1975 1980 1985 1990 1992 1993

Source: National Safety Council

DEATH RATES BY CAUSE, 1992

(Rates per 100,000 population)

Death rate per 100,000

300 — 60 — 50 — 40 — 30 — 20 — 10 — 0

- Heart diseases — 282.5
- Cancer — 204.3
- Cerebrovascular diseases — 56.3
- Pulmonary diseases — 35.8
- Accidents — 33.8
- Pneumonia and influenza — 29.8
- Diabetes mellitus — 19.7
- AIDS — 13.2
- Suicide — 11.7
- Homicide and legal intervention — 10.4
- Liver disease and cirrhosis — 9.7
- Kidney diseases — 8.8
- Septicemia — 7.8
- Atheriosclerosis — 6.3
- Perinatal-related conditions — 6.2

Source: U.S. Department of Health and Human Services; National Center for Health Statistics

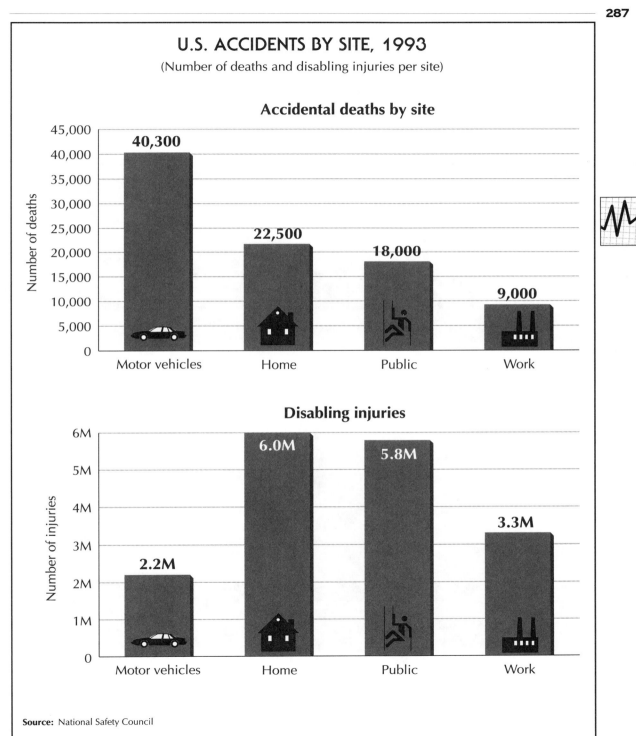

U.S. ACCIDENTS BY SITE, 1993
(Number of deaths and disabling injuries per site)

Accidental deaths by site

Number of deaths

45,000
40,000
35,000
30,000
25,000
20,000
15,000
10,000
5,000
0

40,300 — Motor vehicles
22,500 — Home
18,000 — Public
9,000 — Work

Disabling injuries

Number of injuries

6M
5M
4M
3M
2M
1M
0

2.2M — Motor vehicles
6.0M — Home
5.8M — Public
3.3M — Work

Source: National Safety Council

PROFILE: INJURIES ASSOCIATED WITH CONSUMER PRODUCTS

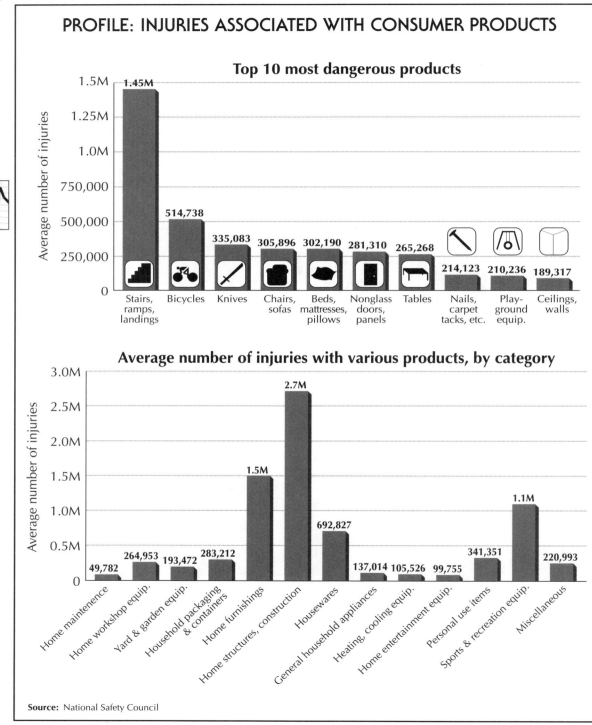

Top 10 most dangerous products

Average number of injuries

- Stairs, ramps, landings: 1.45M
- Bicycles: 514,738
- Knives: 335,083
- Chairs, sofas: 305,896
- Beds, mattresses, pillows: 302,190
- Nonglass doors, panels: 281,310
- Tables: 265,268
- Nails, carpet tacks, etc.: 214,123
- Play-ground equip.: 210,236
- Ceilings, walls: 189,317

Average number of injuries with various products, by category

Average number of injuries

- Home maintenence: 49,782
- Home workshop equip.: 264,953
- Yard & garden equip.: 193,472
- Household packaging & containers: 283,212
- Home furnishings: 1.5M
- Home structures, construction: 2.7M
- Housewares: 692,827
- General household appliances: 137,014
- Heating, cooling equip.: 105,526
- Home entertainment equip.: 99,755
- Personal use items: 341,351
- Sports & recreation equip.: 1.1M
- Miscellaneous: 220,993

Source: National Safety Council

ESTIMATED NUMBER OF INJURIES IN U.S. FROM SELECTED PRODUCTS, 1994

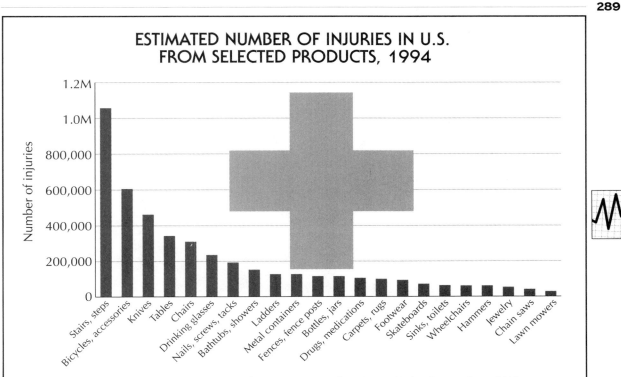

Number of injuries

1.2M
1.0M
800,000
600,000
400,000
200,000
0

Stairs, steps / Bicycles, accessories / Knives / Tables / Chairs / Drinking glasses / Nails, screws, tacks / Bathtubs, showers / Ladders / Metal containers / Fences, fence posts / Bottles, jars / Drugs, medications / Carpets, rugs / Footwear / Skateboards / Sinks, toilets / Wheelchairs / Hammers / Jewelry / Chain saws / Lawn mowers

Source: Consumer Product Safety Commission, National Electronic Injury Surveillance System, *Product Summary Report* (1994)

PLANE DEATHS ON THE WANE, 1988–1993

The number of deaths and the fatal accident rate for major U.S. airlines operating scheduled flights fell drastically from 1988 to 1993:

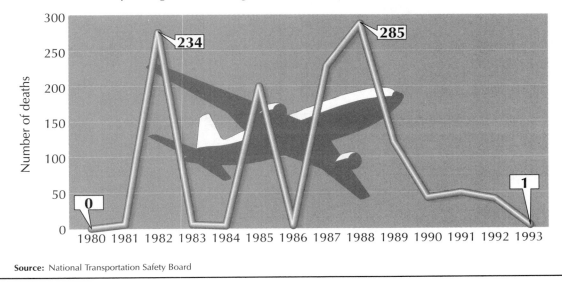

Number of deaths

300
250
200
150
100
50
0

234 · 285 · 0 · 1

1980 1981 1982 1983 1984 1985 1986 1987 1988 1989 1990 1991 1992 1993

Source: National Transportation Safety Board

UP IN FLAMES: FIRE DEATHS IN THE HOME, 1983–1994

Children playing with matches or lighters caused 12.6% of home-fire deaths in 1991, the fourth-biggest cause after smoking, arson, and heating accidents. The number of fire fatalities caused by children:

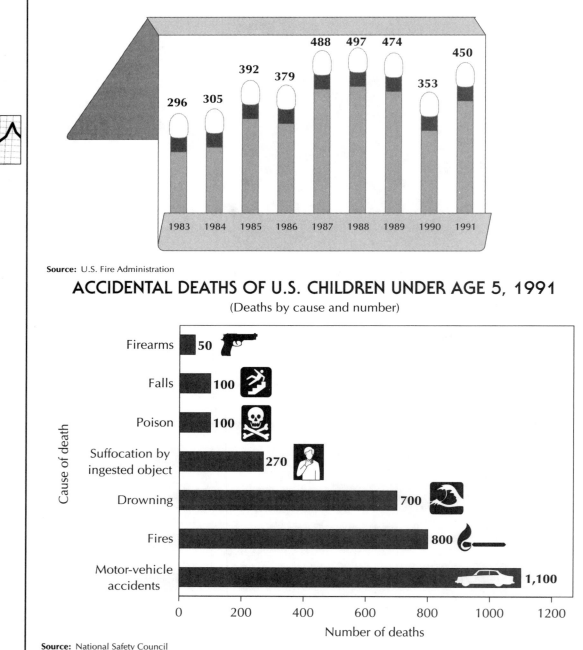

Source: U.S. Fire Administration

ACCIDENTAL DEATHS OF U.S. CHILDREN UNDER AGE 5, 1991
(Deaths by cause and number)

Source: National Safety Council

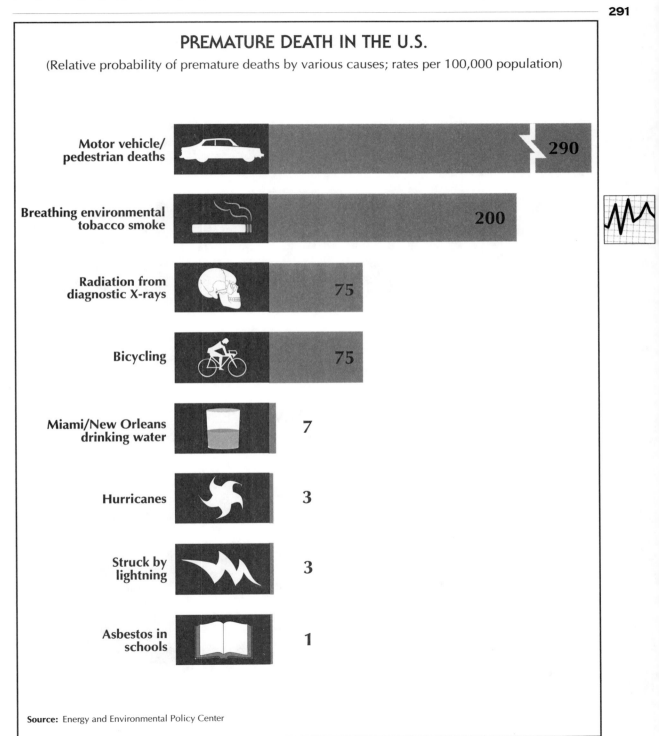

PREMATURE DEATH IN THE U.S.

(Relative probability of premature deaths by various causes; rates per 100,000 population)

Motor vehicle/ pedestrian deaths	290
Breathing environmental tobacco smoke	200
Radiation from diagnostic X-rays	75
Bicycling	75
Miami/New Orleans drinking water	7
Hurricanes	3
Struck by lightning	3
Asbestos in schools	1

Source: Energy and Environmental Policy Center

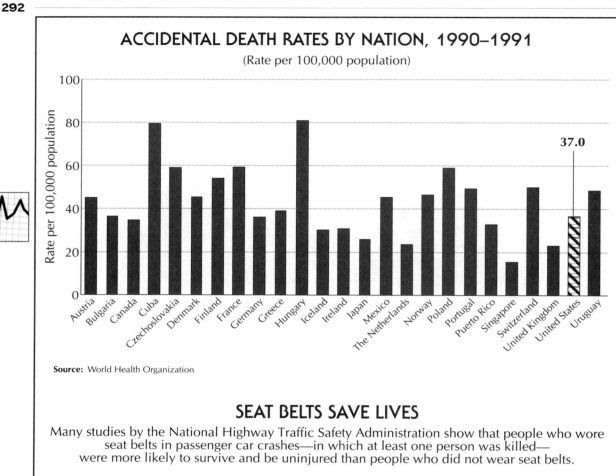

ACCIDENTAL DEATH RATES BY NATION, 1990–1991

(Rate per 100,000 population)

Source: World Health Organization

SEAT BELTS SAVE LIVES

Many studies by the National Highway Traffic Safety Administration show that people who wore seat belts in passenger car crashes—in which at least one person was killed—were more likely to survive and be uninjured than people who did not wear seat belts.

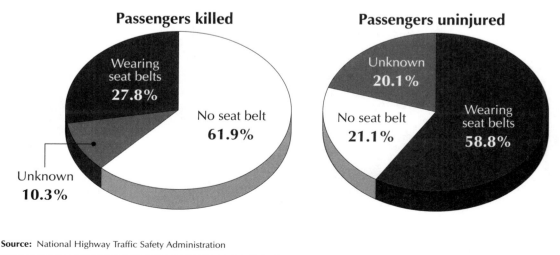

Passengers killed

- Wearing seat belts **27.8%**
- No seat belt **61.9%**
- Unknown **10.3%**

Passengers uninjured

- Unknown **20.1%**
- No seat belt **21.1%**
- Wearing seat belts **58.8%**

Source: National Highway Traffic Safety Administration

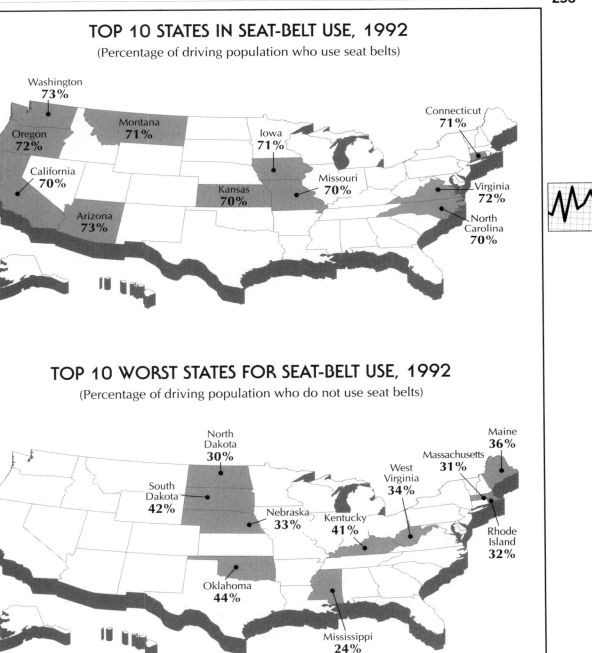

TOP 10 STATES IN SEAT-BELT USE, 1992
(Percentage of driving population who use seat belts)

Washington **73%**

Montana **71%**

Oregon **72%**

Iowa **71%**

California **70%**

Kansas **70%**

Missouri **70%**

Connecticut **71%**

Virginia **72%**

Arizona **73%**

North Carolina **70%**

TOP 10 WORST STATES FOR SEAT-BELT USE, 1992
(Percentage of driving population who do not use seat belts)

North Dakota **30%**

Maine **36%**

Massachusetts **31%**

West Virginia **34%**

South Dakota **42%**

Nebraska **33%**

Kentucky **41%**

Rhode Island **32%**

Oklahoma **44%**

Mississippi **24%**

Source: National Highway Traffic Safety Administration

ALCOHOL-RELATED MOTOR-VEHICLE DEATHS DECLINE, 1982–1993

In 1982, out of 43,945 traffic deaths, 25,170 were alcohol-related. By 1993, only 17,461 of 40,115 traffic deaths were alcohol-related. How the percentage of alcohol-related deaths has declined:

57%

44%

Percentage of deaths

58% 56% 54% 52% 50% 48% 46% 44% 0

1982 1984 1986 1988 1990 1992 1993

Source: National Highway Traffic Safety Administration

SAFETY ON THE ROAD, BY STATE

(Average traffic deaths per 1 million miles traveled)

2.5 and more   2.0–2.4   1.5–1.9   Fewer than 1.5

WA 1.5
OR 1.8
MT 2.4
ND 1.6
MN 1.4
VT 1.9
NH 1.5
ME 1.7
ID 2.6
WY 2.0
SD 2.1
WI 1.8
MI 1.7
NY 1.9
MA 1.2
NE 2.9
UT 1.8
NE 1.9
IO 2.1
IL 1.7
IN 1.9
OH 1.9
PA 1.9
RI 1.3
CT 1.2
CA 1.8
CO 2.0
KS 1.8
MO 2.0
KY 2.4
WV 2.7
VA 1.5
NJ 1.3
DE 1.5
AZ 2.2
NM 2.8
OK 1.9
AR 2.8
TN 2.4
NC 2.2
SC 2.6
MD 1.7
DC 2.0
AK 2.5
TX 1.9
MS 2.8
AL 2.6
LA 2.2
GA 1.9
FL 2.2
HI 1.7

Source: National Highway Traffic Safety Administration

ROAD HAZARDS: ACCIDENTS AND DEATH, 1992

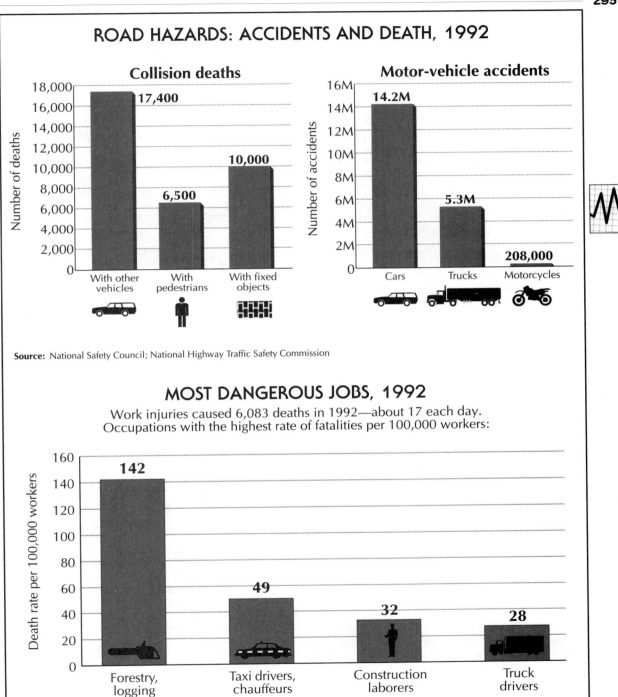

Collision deaths

Number of deaths

- With other vehicles: 17,400
- With pedestrians: 6,500
- With fixed objects: 10,000

Motor-vehicle accidents

Number of accidents

- Cars: 14.2M
- Trucks: 5.3M
- Motorcycles: 208,000

Source: National Safety Council; National Highway Traffic Safety Commission

MOST DANGEROUS JOBS, 1992

Work injuries caused 6,083 deaths in 1992—about 17 each day.
Occupations with the highest rate of fatalities per 100,000 workers:

Death rate per 100,000 workers

- Forestry, logging: 142
- Taxi drivers, chauffeurs: 49
- Construction laborers: 32
- Truck drivers: 28

Source: Bureau of Labor Statistics

IMMIGRATION

Since the first colonists settled on these shores, the United States has been a land of immigrants. More people have immigrated to this nation than to any other. Immigrants have included scientists and doctors, artists and musicians, farmers and teachers, and untold millions of hard-working laborers. They've made America their home, adopted its values, and made innumerable contributions to its economy and culture.

More than 8% of the current U.S. population were born elsewhere. In 1993, some 1.3 million people entered the country—1.0 million of them legally, the rest illegally. Many of the legal immigrants were refugees escaping war, ethnic or religious persecution, or other disasters in their homelands.

A sagging economy, rising unemployment, and overpopulation problems have made immigration a hotly debated topic. Some argue that the "nation of immigrants" has a moral obligation to accept an unrestricted flow of people from other lands. Others argue for a closing of U.S. borders.

In recent years, anti-immigrant sentiment has been rising in the U.S.— as it has in other wealthy industrialized nations of the world. Many want the government to step up efforts to apprehend illegal aliens, to cut immigration quotas, and to eliminate—or at least limit—benefits and services for both legal and illegal immigrants. In 1994, in their so-called Contract With America, Republicans running for the House of Representatives included a proposal to ban welfare benefits for legal immigrants. California voters also passed the hotly debated Proposition 187, which would deny illegal aliens access to public schools, non-emergency care at public health clinics, and other social services. This result reflected the sentiments toward illegal immigrants expressed by a majority of Americans. Judicial orders at least temporarily blocked implementation of the proposition.

FINGERTIP FACTS

- Since 1970, some 20.7 million immigrants have settled in the U.S.; 1,536,500 people legally immigrated to the U.S. in 1990, which was an all-time record.

- Between 1820 and 1991, the largest percentage of U.S. immigrants came from Germany, followed by Great Britain, Italy, Mexico, Vietnam, the Philippines, and countries of the former Soviet Union.

- The states with the highest percentage of foreign-born residents are California (21.7%), New York (15.8%), and Hawaii (14.7%).

- Worldwide, 18 million people fled their homeland in 1992. Of these refugees, 132,173 were admitted to the U.S.

- The Immigration and Naturalization Service (INS) estimated in 1993 that about 300,000 people illegally enter the U.S. each year. In recent years, the greatest percentage of illegal immigrants to the U.S. have come from Mexico.

- California has the highest number of illegal immigrants. In 1994, there were an estimated 1.5 million to 2.0 million illegal aliens living in California.

NUMBER OF IMMIGRANTS TO U.S., BY DECADE, 1820–1990

(In millions)

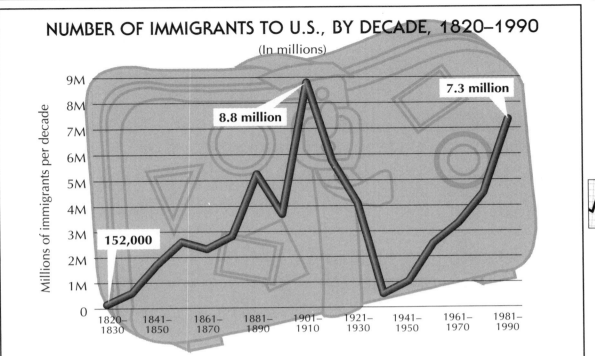

Source: U.S. Immigration and Naturalization Service

IMMIGRANTS SHORE UP U.S. POPULATION, 1901–1990

(Percentage of U.S. population growth created by immigration in the 20th century)

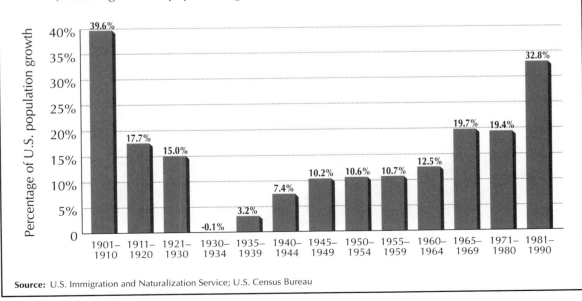

Source: U.S. Immigration and Naturalization Service; U.S. Census Bureau

U.S. IMMIGRANTS: TOP 10 COUNTRIES OF ORIGIN, 1992
(As percentage of all legal immigrants)

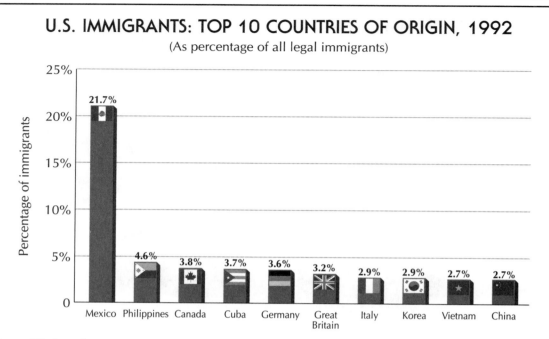

Source: U.S. Census Bureau

TOP 20 IMMIGRANT GROUPS IN U.S. LARGER THAN 100,000, 1994

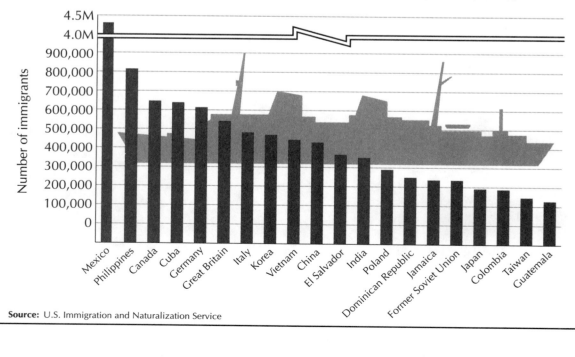

Source: U.S. Immigration and Naturalization Service

TOP 5 STATES WITH HIGHEST PERCENTAGE OF FOREIGN-BORN POPULATION, 1990
(With rankings)

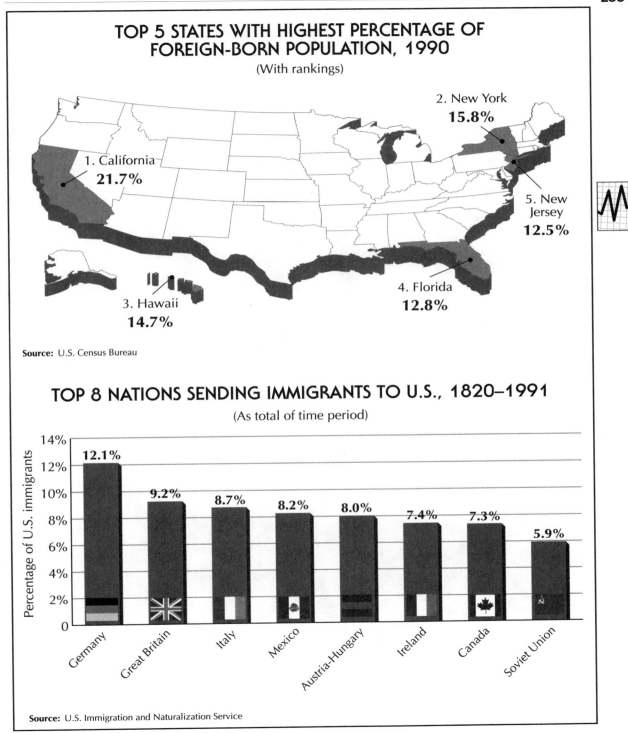

2. New York
15.8%

1. California
21.7%

5. New Jersey
12.5%

3. Hawaii
14.7%

4. Florida
12.8%

Source: U.S. Census Bureau

TOP 8 NATIONS SENDING IMMIGRANTS TO U.S., 1820–1991
(As total of time period)

Percentage of U.S. immigrants

Nation	Percentage
Germany	12.1%
Great Britain	9.2%
Italy	8.7%
Mexico	8.2%
Austria-Hungary	8.0%
Ireland	7.4%
Canada	7.3%
Soviet Union	5.9%

Source: U.S. Immigration and Naturalization Service

COMPARATIVE PERCENTAGES OF FOREIGN-BORN PEOPLE IN U.S., 1960–1993

Percentage of total U.S. population

- 1960: 5.4%
- 1970: 4.7%
- 1980: 6.2%
- 1990: 7.9%
- 1993: 8.6%

Source: U.S. State Department

PROFILE: BIRTHPLACES OF FOREIGN-BORN U.S. POPULATION

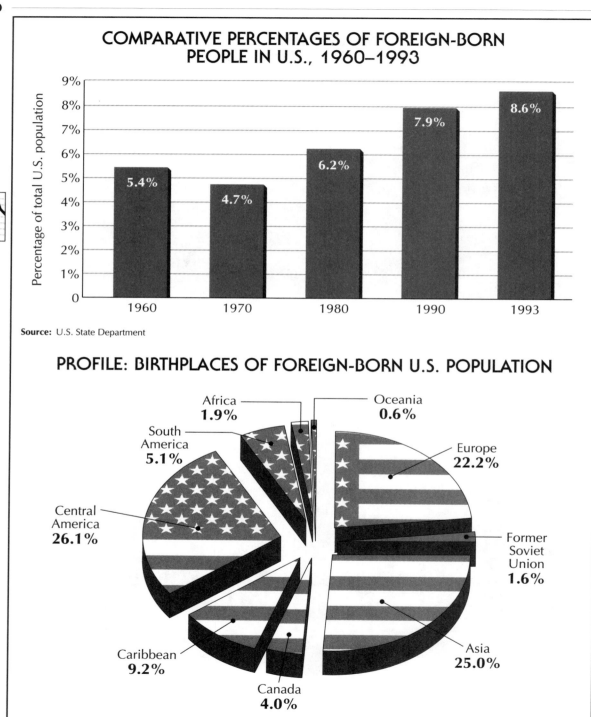

- Africa 1.9%
- Oceania 0.6%
- South America 5.1%
- Europe 22.2%
- Central America 26.1%
- Former Soviet Union 1.6%
- Caribbean 9.2%
- Canada 4.0%
- Asia 25.0%

PROFILE: SELECTED ANCESTRY GROUPS OF U.S. POPULATION

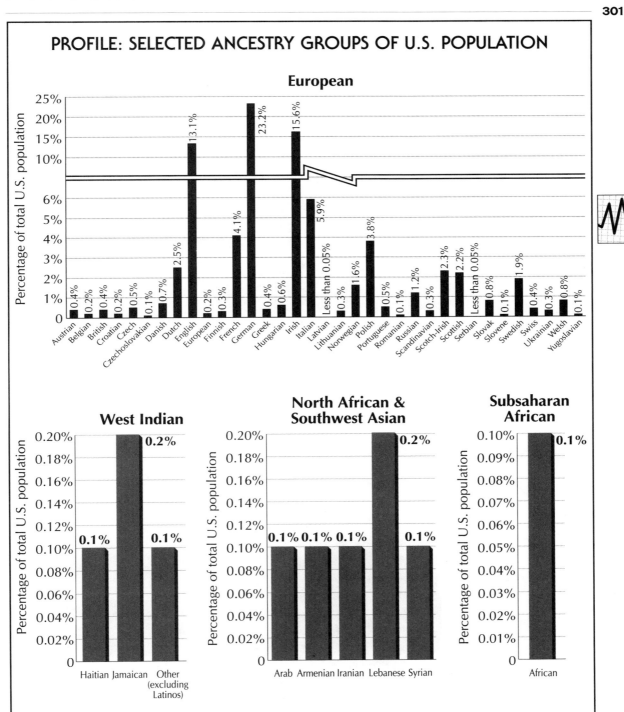

European

Percentage of total U.S. population

- Austrian: 0.4%
- Belgian: 0.2%
- British: 0.4%
- Croatian: 0.2%
- Czech: 0.5%
- Czechoslovakian: 0.1%
- Danish: 0.7%
- Dutch: 2.5%
- English: 13.1%
- European: 0.2%
- Finnish: 0.3%
- French: 4.1%
- German: 23.2%
- Greek: 0.4%
- Hungarian: 0.6%
- Irish: 15.6%
- Italian: 5.9%
- Latvian: Less than 0.05%
- Lithuanian: 0.3%
- Norwegian: 1.6%
- Polish: 3.8%
- Portuguese: 0.5%
- Romanian: 0.1%
- Russian: 1.2%
- Scandinavian: 0.3%
- Scotch-Irish: 2.3%
- Scottish: 2.2%
- Serbian: Less than 0.05%
- Slovak: 0.8%
- Slovene: 0.1%
- Swedish: 1.9%
- Swiss: 0.4%
- Ukrainian: 0.3%
- Welsh: 0.8%
- Yugoslavian: 0.1%

West Indian

Percentage of total U.S. population

- Haitian: 0.1%
- Jamaican: 0.2%
- Other (excluding Latinos): 0.1%

North African & Southwest Asian

Percentage of total U.S. population

- Arab: 0.1%
- Armenian: 0.1%
- Iranian: 0.1%
- Lebanese: 0.2%
- Syrian: 0.1%

Subsaharan African

Percentage of total U.S. population

- African: 0.1%

Source: U.S. Census Bureau

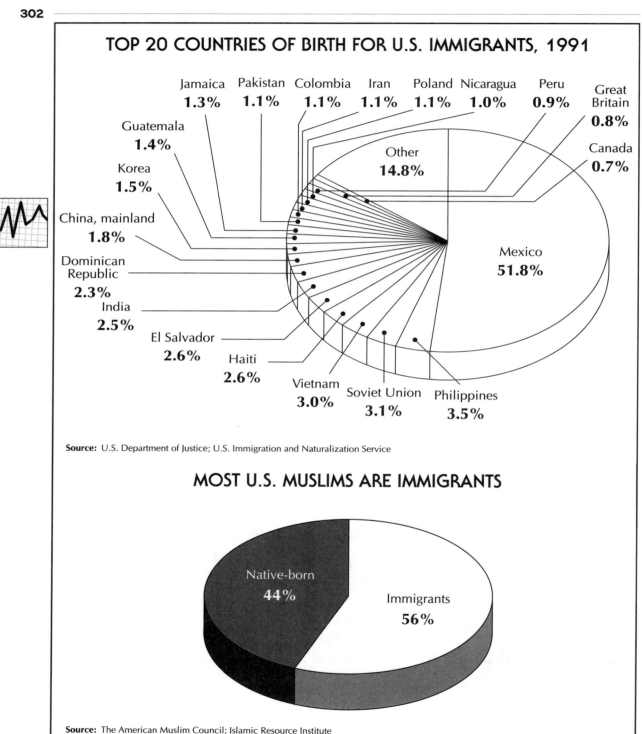

TOP 20 COUNTRIES OF BIRTH FOR U.S. IMMIGRANTS, 1991

Jamaica 1.3%
Pakistan 1.1%
Colombia 1.1%
Iran 1.1%
Poland 1.1%
Nicaragua 1.0%
Peru 0.9%
Great Britain 0.8%
Guatemala 1.4%
Korea 1.5%
China, mainland 1.8%
Dominican Republic 2.3%
India 2.5%
El Salvador 2.6%
Haiti 2.6%
Vietnam 3.0%
Soviet Union 3.1%
Philippines 3.5%
Other 14.8%
Canada 0.7%
Mexico 51.8%

Source: U.S. Department of Justice; U.S. Immigration and Naturalization Service

MOST U.S. MUSLIMS ARE IMMIGRANTS

Native-born 44%
Immigrants 56%

Source: The American Muslim Council; Islamic Resource Institute

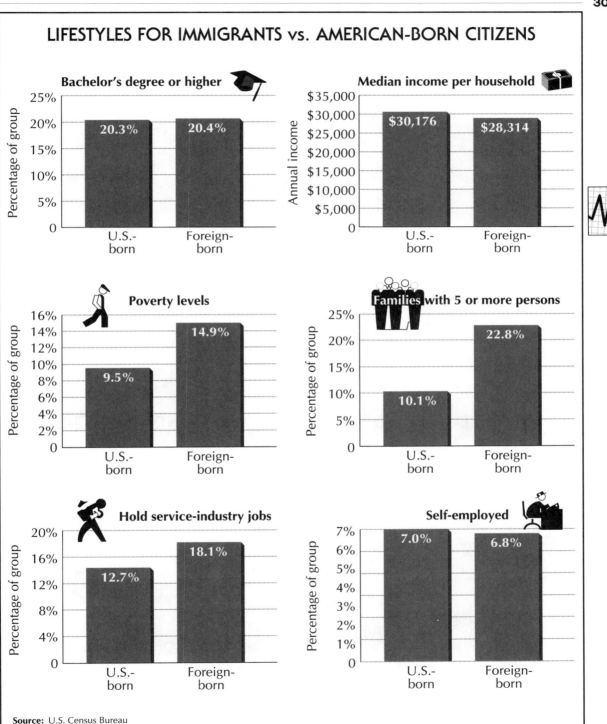

LIFESTYLES FOR IMMIGRANTS vs. AMERICAN-BORN CITIZENS

Bachelor's degree or higher

U.S.-born: 20.3%
Foreign-born: 20.4%

Median income per household

U.S.-born: $30,176
Foreign-born: $28,314

Poverty levels

U.S.-born: 9.5%
Foreign-born: 14.9%

Families with 5 or more persons

U.S.-born: 10.1%
Foreign-born: 22.8%

Hold service-industry jobs

U.S.-born: 12.7%
Foreign-born: 18.1%

Self-employed

U.S.-born: 7.0%
Foreign-born: 6.8%

Source: U.S. Census Bureau

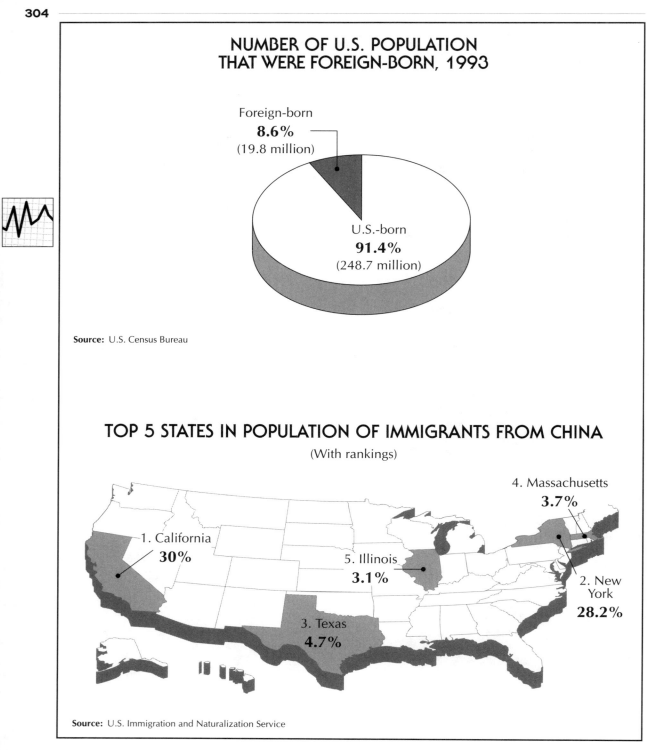

NUMBER OF U.S. POPULATION THAT WERE FOREIGN-BORN, 1993

Foreign-born
8.6%
(19.8 million)

U.S.-born
91.4%
(248.7 million)

Source: U.S. Census Bureau

TOP 5 STATES IN POPULATION OF IMMIGRANTS FROM CHINA
(With rankings)

4. Massachusetts
3.7%

1. California
30%

5. Illinois
3.1%

2. New York
28.2%

3. Texas
4.7%

Source: U.S. Immigration and Naturalization Service

TOP 10 STATES WITH HIGHEST NUMBER OF ILLEGAL IMMIGRANTS

(With rankings)

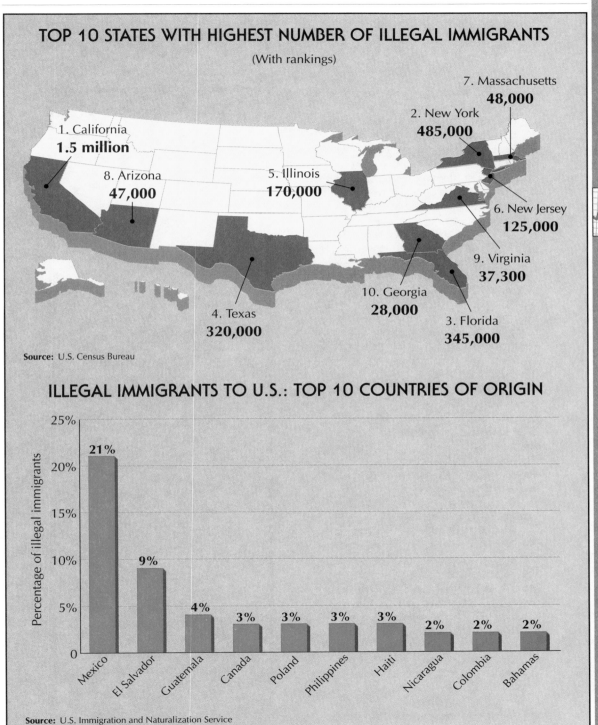

7. Massachusetts
48,000

2. New York
485,000

1. California
1.5 million

8. Arizona
47,000

5. Illinois
170,000

6. New Jersey
125,000

9. Virginia
37,300

10. Georgia
28,000

4. Texas
320,000

3. Florida
345,000

Source: U.S. Census Bureau

ILLEGAL IMMIGRANTS TO U.S.: TOP 10 COUNTRIES OF ORIGIN

Percentage of illegal immigrants

Country	Percentage
Mexico	21%
El Salvador	9%
Guatemala	4%
Canada	3%
Poland	3%
Philippines	3%
Haiti	3%
Nicaragua	2%
Colombia	2%
Bahamas	2%

Source: U.S. Immigration and Naturalization Service

POPULATION PROFILE

The United States is a pluralistic nation—it is composed of numerous cultures and ethnic groups. Less than 1% of its population are descended of Aleuts, Eskimos, and other groups who lived on the North American continent prior to its settlement by Europeans. The other main groups are whites who are not Latinos (an estimated 73.6% of the 1995 population), blacks who are not Latinos (12.0%), Latinos (10.2%), and Asians and Pacific Islanders (3.5%).

The nation's ethnic profile has changed over the years and is expected to continue changing in the near future. Current trends suggest that by the year 2050, non-Latino whites will make up 52.5% of the population; Latino 22.5%; blacks, 14.4%; Asians and Pacific Islanders, 9.7%; and Aleuts, Eskimos, and American Indians, 0.9%.

Many other aspects of the U.S. population profile have also changed over the years. Prior to 1950, for example, males outnumbered females; since then, the reverse has been true. The median age has also increased, more Americans are living in urban areas, more profess to having no religious preference, more are attending college, and a good deal more have interracial marriages.

Members of ethnic groups are not distributed evenly across the nation. For example, in New York, German is the leading ancestry group, while in Hawaii, it's Japanese. In El Paso, Texas, 69.6% of the residents are Latino; in Knoxville, Tennessee, only 0.5% are. The South has the highest percentage of blacks, and a majority of Asians live in the West. Florida has the highest percentage of people ages 65 and older, Alaska the lowest. In Alabama, 70.7% of residents are members of Christian churches; in Maine, only 35.8% are.

FINGERTIP FACTS

- The 1993 Latino population in the U.S. totaled 22.8 million. Mexicans made up the largest number (14.6 million), followed by Puerto Ricans (2.4 million) and Cubans (1.1 million).

- Of the 75 largest metropolitan areas in the U.S. in 1990, Memphis, Tennessee, had the highest percentage of blacks (40.7%); the Scranton-Wilkes Barre, Pennsylvania, area had the lowest (0.9%). El Paso, Texas, had the largest percentage of Latinos (69.6%); and Birmingham, Alabama, had the lowest percentage (0.4%).

- In 1992, there were 130.6 million females and 124.5 million males in the U.S.—100 females for every 95.3 males.

- In 1970, residents ages 65 and older made up 9.8% of the U.S. population; in 1992, they made up 12.6%. Projections suggest that they will equal 20.4% of the 2050 population.

- German is the #1 ancestry group in the U.S. Some 57.9 million people reported German ancestry in 1990. The largest percentage of them (39%) lived in the Midwest.

- Chinese is the leading Asian ancestry group in the U.S., more than 1.5 million people reported Chinese ancestry in 1990.

- The percentage of foreign-born residents in the U.S. declined during the period from 1920 (13.2%) to 1970 (4.8%), and then rose by 1990 (7.9%).

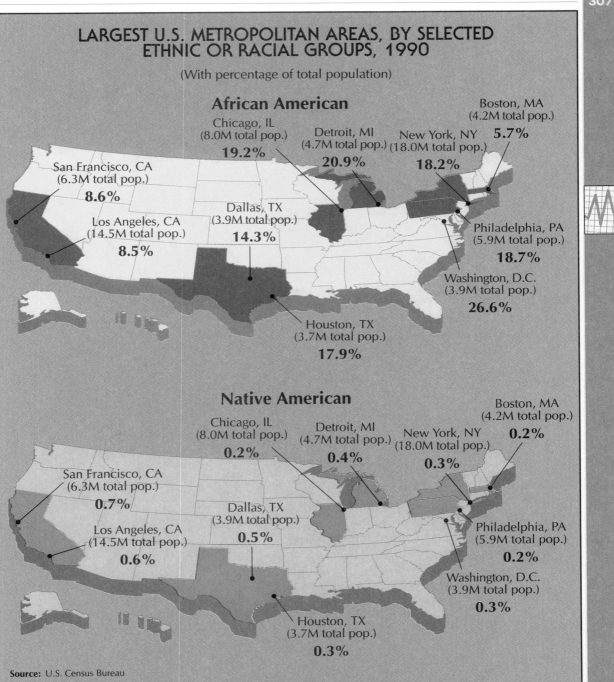

LARGEST U.S. METROPOLITAN AREAS, BY SELECTED ETHNIC OR RACIAL GROUPS, 1990

(With percentage of total population)

African American

Boston, MA
(4.2M total pop.)
5.7%

Chicago, IL
(8.0M total pop.)
19.2%

Detroit, MI
(4.7M total pop.)
20.9%

New York, NY
(18.0M total pop.)
18.2%

San Francisco, CA
(6.3M total pop.)
8.6%

Dallas, TX
(3.9M total pop.)
14.3%

Los Angeles, CA
(14.5M total pop.)
8.5%

Philadelphia, PA
(5.9M total pop.)
18.7%

Washington, D.C.
(3.9M total pop.)
26.6%

Houston, TX
(3.7M total pop.)
17.9%

Native American

Boston, MA
(4.2M total pop.)
0.2%

Chicago, IL
(8.0M total pop.)
0.2%

Detroit, MI
(4.7M total pop.)
0.4%

New York, NY
(18.0M total pop.)
0.3%

San Francisco, CA
(6.3M total pop.)
0.7%

Dallas, TX
(3.9M total pop.)
0.5%

Los Angeles, CA
(14.5M total pop.)
0.6%

Philadelphia, PA
(5.9M total pop.)
0.2%

Washington, D.C.
(3.9M total pop.)
0.3%

Houston, TX
(3.7M total pop.)
0.3%

Source: U.S. Census Bureau

LARGEST U.S. METROPOLITAN AREAS, BY SELECTED ETHNIC OR RACIAL GROUPS, 1990

(With percentage of total population)

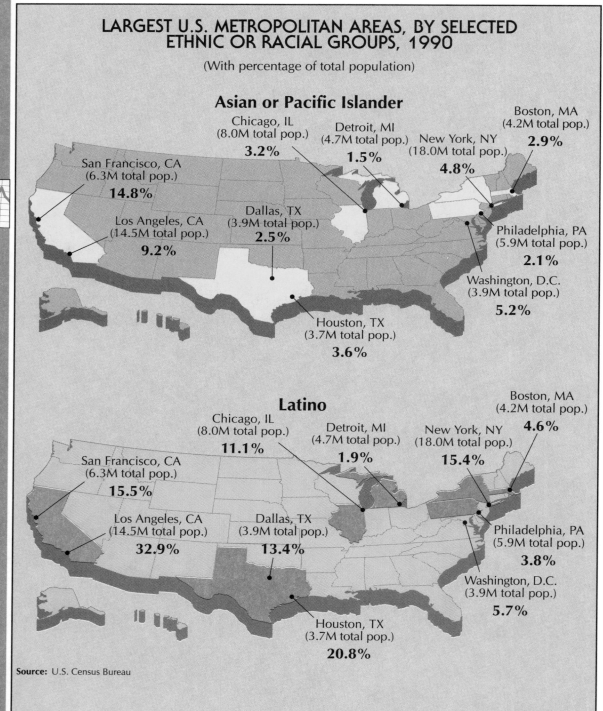

Asian or Pacific Islander

Chicago, IL
(8.0M total pop.)
3.2%

Detroit, MI
(4.7M total pop.)
1.5%

New York, NY
(18.0M total pop.)
4.8%

Boston, MA
(4.2M total pop.)
2.9%

San Francisco, CA
(6.3M total pop.)
14.8%

Los Angeles, CA
(14.5M total pop.)
9.2%

Dallas, TX
(3.9M total pop.)
2.5%

Philadelphia, PA
(5.9M total pop.)
2.1%

Washington, D.C.
(3.9M total pop.)
5.2%

Houston, TX
(3.7M total pop.)
3.6%

Latino

Chicago, IL
(8.0M total pop.)
11.1%

Detroit, MI
(4.7M total pop.)
1.9%

New York, NY
(18.0M total pop.)
15.4%

Boston, MA
(4.2M total pop.)
4.6%

San Francisco, CA
(6.3M total pop.)
15.5%

Los Angeles, CA
(14.5M total pop.)
32.9%

Dallas, TX
(3.9M total pop.)
13.4%

Philadelphia, PA
(5.9M total pop.)
3.8%

Washington, D.C.
(3.9M total pop.)
5.7%

Houston, TX
(3.7M total pop.)
20.8%

Source: U.S. Census Bureau

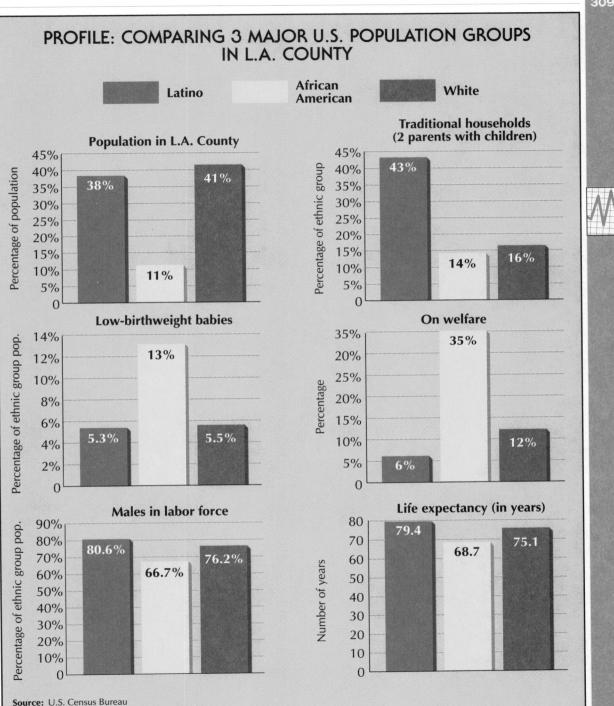

PROFILE: COMPARING 3 MAJOR U.S. POPULATION GROUPS IN L.A. COUNTY

Latino   African American   White

Population in L.A. County
- Latino: 38%
- African American: 11%
- White: 41%

Traditional households (2 parents with children)
- Latino: 43%
- African American: 14%
- White: 16%

Low-birthweight babies
- Latino: 5.3%
- African American: 13%
- White: 5.5%

On welfare
- Latino: 6%
- African American: 35%
- White: 12%

Males in labor force
- Latino: 80.6%
- African American: 66.7%
- White: 76.2%

Life expectancy (in years)
- Latino: 79.4
- African American: 68.7
- White: 75.1

Source: U.S. Census Bureau

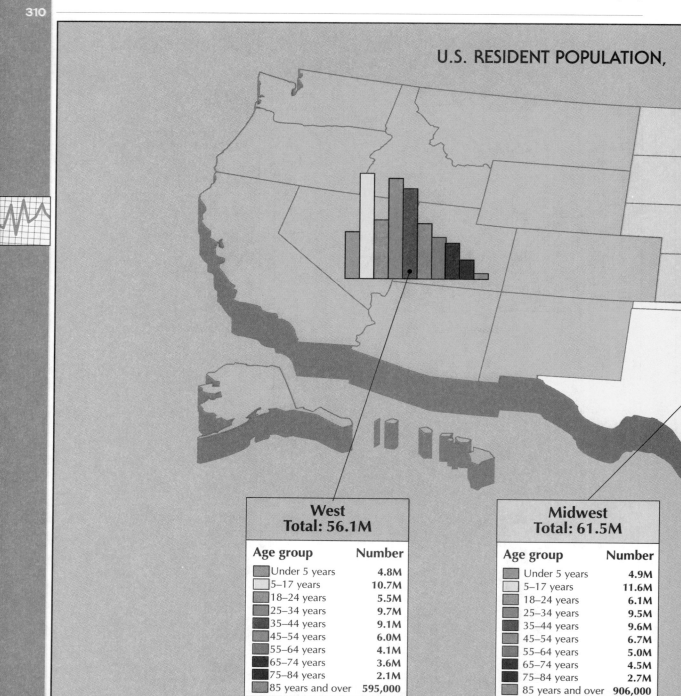

U.S. RESIDENT POPULATION,

West
Total: 56.1M

Age group	Number
Under 5 years	4.8M
5–17 years	10.7M
18–24 years	5.5M
25–34 years	9.7M
35–44 years	9.1M
45–54 years	6.0M
55–64 years	4.1M
65–74 years	3.6M
75–84 years	2.1M
85 years and over	595,000

Midwest
Total: 61.5M

Age group	Number
Under 5 years	4.9M
5–17 years	11.6M
18–24 years	6.1M
25–34 years	9.5M
35–44 years	9.6M
45–54 years	6.7M
55–64 years	5.0M
65–74 years	4.5M
75–84 years	2.7M
85 years and over	906,000

Source: U.S. Census Bureau

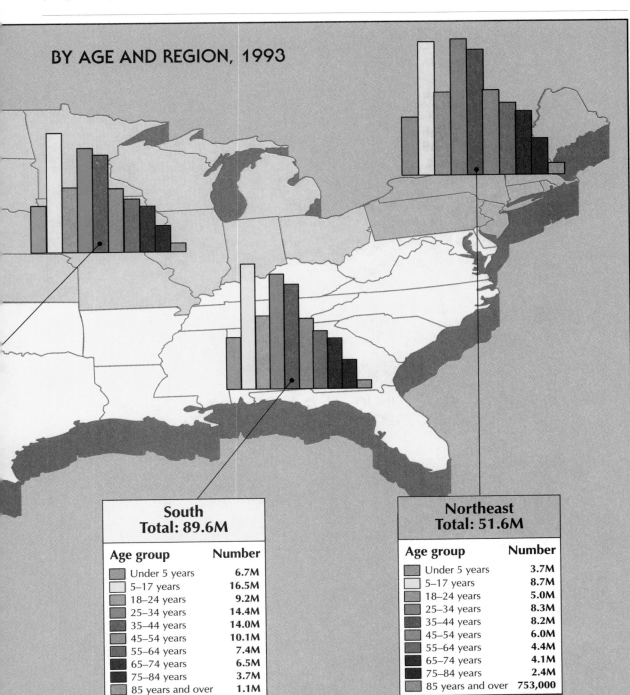

BY AGE AND REGION, 1993

South
Total: 89.6M

Age group	Number
Under 5 years	6.7M
5–17 years	16.5M
18–24 years	9.2M
25–34 years	14.4M
35–44 years	14.0M
45–54 years	10.1M
55–64 years	7.4M
65–74 years	6.5M
75–84 years	3.7M
85 years and over	1.1M

Northeast
Total: 51.6M

Age group	Number
Under 5 years	3.7M
5–17 years	8.7M
18–24 years	5.0M
25–34 years	8.3M
35–44 years	8.2M
45–54 years	6.0M
55–64 years	4.4M
65–74 years	4.1M
75–84 years	2.4M
85 years and over	753,000

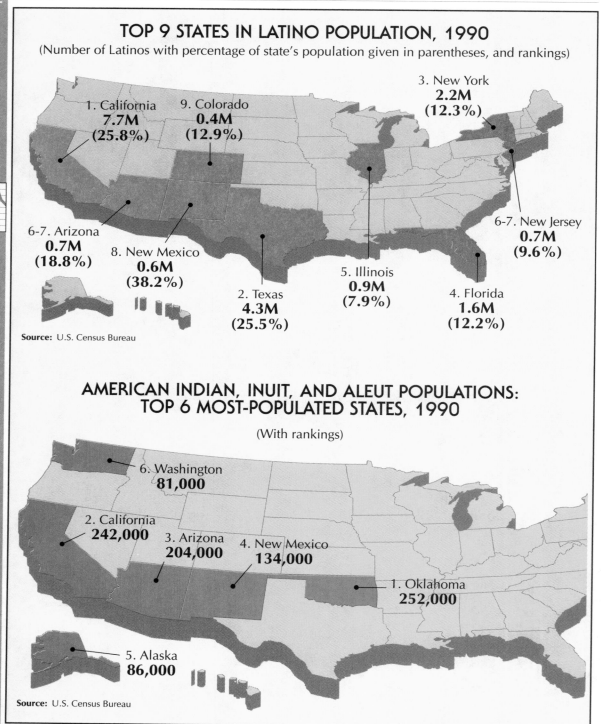

TOP 9 STATES IN LATINO POPULATION, 1990
(Number of Latinos with percentage of state's population given in parentheses, and rankings)

3. New York
2.2M
(12.3%)

1. California
7.7M
(25.8%)

9. Colorado
0.4M
(12.9%)

6-7. Arizona
0.7M
(18.8%)

8. New Mexico
0.6M
(38.2%)

6-7. New Jersey
0.7M
(9.6%)

5. Illinois
0.9M
(7.9%)

2. Texas
4.3M
(25.5%)

4. Florida
1.6M
(12.2%)

Source: U.S. Census Bureau

AMERICAN INDIAN, INUIT, AND ALEUT POPULATIONS:
TOP 6 MOST-POPULATED STATES, 1990

(With rankings)

6. Washington
81,000

2. California
242,000

3. Arizona
204,000

4. New Mexico
134,000

1. Oklahoma
252,000

5. Alaska
86,000

Source: U.S. Census Bureau

TOP 10 STATES IN AMERICAN INDIAN POPULATION, 1990

(Population defined by U.S. Census Bureau as American Indian,
not including Inuits and Aleuts, with rankings)

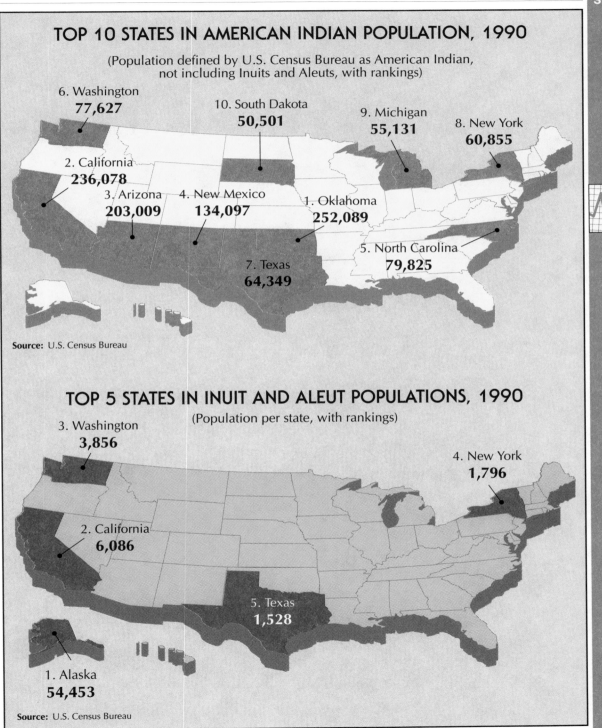

6. Washington
77,627

10. South Dakota
50,501

9. Michigan
55,131

8. New York
60,855

2. California
236,078

3. Arizona
203,009

4. New Mexico
134,097

1. Oklahoma
252,089

5. North Carolina
79,825

7. Texas
64,349

Source: U.S. Census Bureau

TOP 5 STATES IN INUIT AND ALEUT POPULATIONS, 1990

(Population per state, with rankings)

3. Washington
3,856

4. New York
1,796

2. California
6,086

5. Texas
1,528

1. Alaska
54,453

Source: U.S. Census Bureau

TOP 10 STATES IN POPULATION OF AFRICAN AMERICANS, 1990
(With rankings)

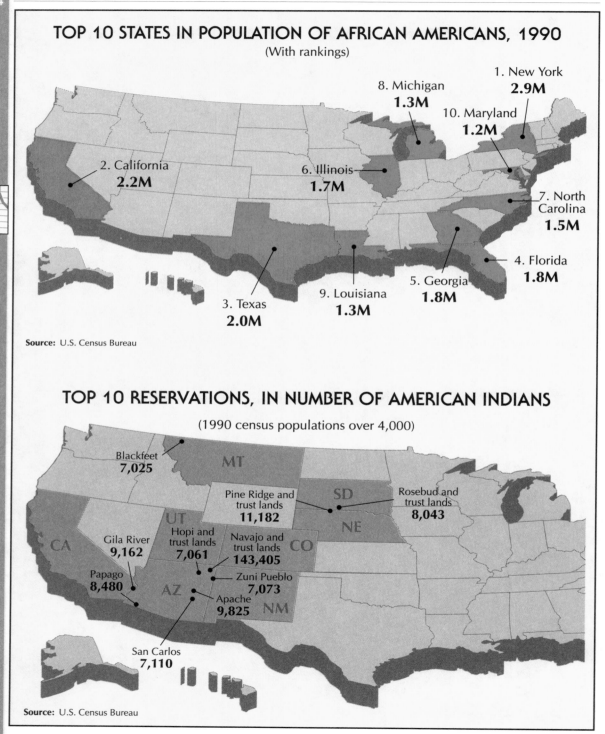

8. Michigan
1.3M

1. New York
2.9M

10. Maryland
1.2M

2. California
2.2M

6. Illinois
1.7M

7. North Carolina
1.5M

4. Florida
1.8M

5. Georgia
1.8M

9. Louisiana
1.3M

3. Texas
2.0M

Source: U.S. Census Bureau

TOP 10 RESERVATIONS, IN NUMBER OF AMERICAN INDIANS

(1990 census populations over 4,000)

Blackfeet
7,025

MT

Pine Ridge and trust lands
11,182

SD

Rosebud and trust lands
8,043

NE

UT

Gila River
9,162

Hopi and trust lands
7,061

Navajo and trust lands
143,405

CO

CA

Papago
8,480

AZ

Zuni Pueblo
7,073

Apache
9,825

NM

San Carlos
7,110

Source: U.S. Census Bureau

TOP 10 STATES IN PERCENTAGE OF
AFRICAN-AMERICAN POPULATION, 1990

(As percentage of state population, with rankings)

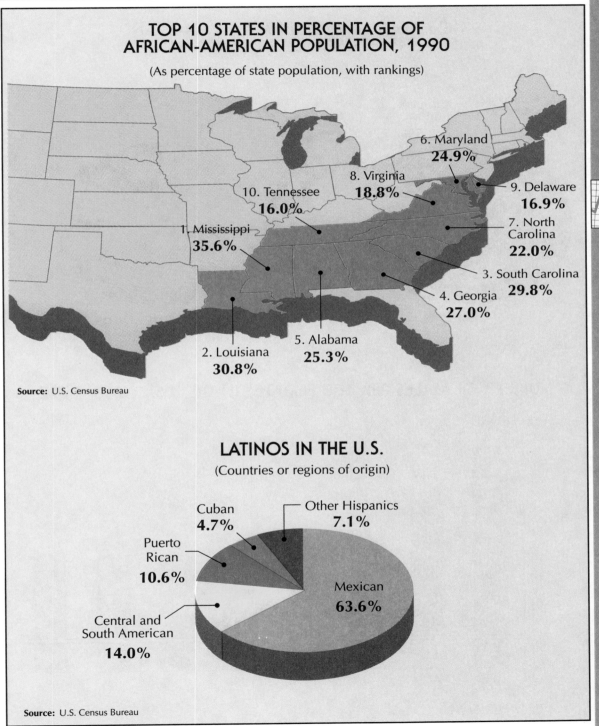

6. Maryland **24.9%**

8. Virginia **18.8%**

9. Delaware **16.9%**

10. Tennessee **16.0%**

7. North Carolina **22.0%**

1. Mississippi **35.6%**

3. South Carolina **29.8%**

4. Georgia **27.0%**

2. Louisiana **30.8%**

5. Alabama **25.3%**

Source: U.S. Census Bureau

LATINOS IN THE U.S.

(Countries or regions of origin)

Cuban **4.7%**

Other Hispanics **7.1%**

Puerto Rican **10.6%**

Mexican **63.6%**

Central and South American **14.0%**

Source: U.S. Census Bureau

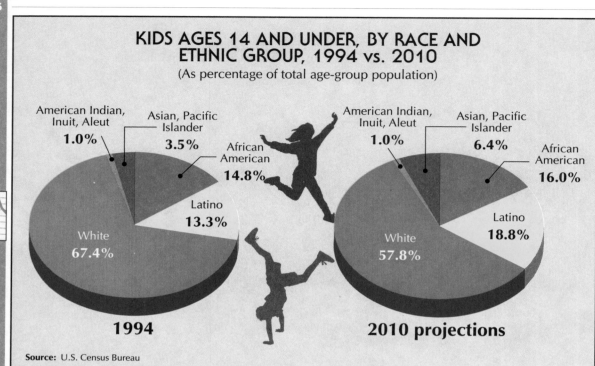

KIDS AGES 14 AND UNDER, BY RACE AND ETHNIC GROUP, 1994 vs. 2010
(As percentage of total age-group population)

1994

American Indian, Inuit, Aleut **1.0%**
Asian, Pacific Islander **3.5%**
African American **14.8%**
Latino **13.3%**
White **67.4%**

2010 projections

American Indian, Inuit, Aleut **1.0%**
Asian, Pacific Islander **6.4%**
African American **16.0%**
Latino **18.8%**
White **57.8%**

Source: U.S. Census Bureau

NUMBER OF MALES PER 100 FEMALES IN THE U.S., 1940–1992

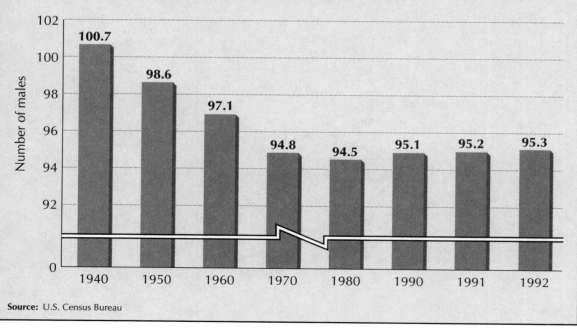

Number of males

Year	Value
1940	100.7
1950	98.6
1960	97.1
1970	94.8
1980	94.5
1990	95.1
1991	95.2
1992	95.3

Source: U.S. Census Bureau

THE AMERICAN POPULATION,

(In millions, by age group)

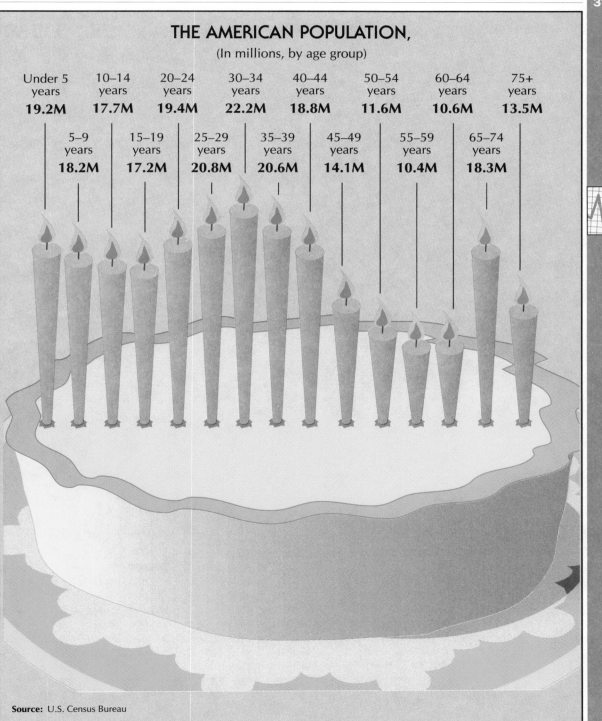

Under 5 years	10–14 years	20–24 years	30–34 years	40–44 years	50–54 years	60–64 years	75+ years
19.2M	**17.7M**	**19.4M**	**22.2M**	**18.8M**	**11.6M**	**10.6M**	**13.5M**

5–9 years	15–19 years	25–29 years	35–39 years	45–49 years	55–59 years	65–74 years
18.2M	**17.2M**	**20.8M**	**20.6M**	**14.1M**	**10.4M**	**18.3M**

Source: U.S. Census Bureau

WHO LIVES WHERE?

(U.S. regions by ethnic populations)

Pacific: 12.1 million

American Indian	387,000	Vietnamese	314,000
Inuit	49,000	Hawaiian	182,000
Aleut	16,000	Samoan	52,000
Chinese	823,000	Guamanian	32,000
Filipino	960,000	Mexican	6.4 million
Japanese	609,000	Puerto Rican	166,000
Asian Indian	173,000	Cuban	76,000
Korean	327,000	Other Latino	1.5 million

West: 14.7 million

American Indian	866,000	Vietnamese	334,000
Inuit	51,000	Hawaiian	189,000
Aleut	17,000	Samoan	55,000
Chinese	863,000	Guamanian	34,000
Filipino	991,000	Mexican	7.8 million
Japanese	643,000	Puerto Rican	192,000
Asian Indian	189,000	Cuban	88,000
Korean	355,000	Other Latino	2.0 million

Source: U.S. Census Bureau

Northeast: 5.1 million

American Indian	122,000	Vietnamese	61,000
Inuit	2,000	Hawaiian	4,000
Aleut	2,000	Samoan	2,000
Chinese	445,000	Guamanian	4,000
Filipino	143,000	Mexican	175,000
Japanese	74,000	Puerto Rican	1.9 million
Asian Indian	285,000	Cuban	184,000
Korean	182,000	Other Latino	1.5 million

Midwest: 2.7 million

American Indian	334,000	Vietnamese	52,000
Inuit	2,000	Hawaiian	6,000
Aleut	2,000	Samoan	2,000
Chinese	133,000	Guamanian	3,000
Filipino	113,000	Mexican	1.2 million
Japanese	63,000	Puerto Rican	258,000
Asian Indian	146,000	Cuban	37,000
Korean	109,000	Other Latino	279,000

South: 8.3 million

American Indian	557,000	Vietnamese	169,000
Inuit	3,000	Hawaiian	12,000
Aleut	3,000	Samoan	4,000
Chinese	204,000	Guamanian	8,000
Filipino	159,000	Mexican	4.3 million
Japanese	67,000	Puerto Rican	406,000
Asian Indian	196,000	Cuban	735,000
Korean	153,000	Other Latino	1.3 million

TEEN PREGNANCY

Beginning in the mid-1980s, the number of births to teenage girls increased. By 1991, there were 62.1 births for every 1,000 females ages 15 to 19. This trend is disturbing, because teenagers are not usually ready to handle the complex responsibilities of parenthood.

There are many stereotypes about teenage mothers. Sadly, the stereotypes often are true. Teenage mothers are more likely to drop out of school than mothers whose first child is born later. Teens with children are also more likely to live in poverty. One study showed that about 50% of all teenage mothers are on welfare within one year of their first child's birth. Teenagers also have a higher-than-average risk of giving birth to low-weight, premature babies. These babies often face serious health problems.

The majority of teenage births are to unmarried mothers. Often, the males who fathered the children abandon the mothers. It then becomes the mothers' responsibility—emotionally and financially—to raise the children.

Experts disagree about the causes for the increase in teenage pregnancy. Many point to the fact that American teenagers are sexually active at increasingly younger ages. More than half of America's teenagers report having had intercourse before leaving high school.

Experts agree that it is important to prevent teenage pregnancy. How to do this, however, is a matter of much controversy. Many communities have programs that counsel teenagers to abstain from sex until adulthood and marriage. They counsel those who do have sex to use contraceptives (birth control devices) consistently. They also encourage young people to consider—ahead of time—the responsibilities of parenthood.

Communities often offer help to teenage mothers. In some communities, day care centers accommodate infants and toddlers while their mothers are at school. Parenting classes teach mothers about infant health, diet, and development. There are programs for teenage fathers, too, which teach them how to help raise and be responsible for their children.

FINGERTIP FACTS

- There was a 27% increase in births to girls ages 15 to 17 from 1986 to 1991, then a 2% decline in 1992.

- Some 67% of the births to teens in 1990 were to unmarried mothers. In 1960, only 15% were to unmarried mothers.

- Black babies have twice the risk of low birthweight as white babies. This is a reason why black babies are twice as likely as white babies to die before their first birthday.

- It costs taxpayers more than $25 billion a year in welfare payments, food stamps, and Medicaid to support families that began with a teenage birth.

- At least 56% of girls and 73% of boys in the U.S. reportedly have had intercourse before their 18th birthday.

- Fewer than 20% of U.S. school-based health clinics supply teens with contraceptives. About 28% provide teenagers with prescriptions for contraceptives.

- Unlike the U.S., most developed countries have declining birth rates among teenagers.

PROFILE: OUT-OF-WEDLOCK BIRTHS IN THE U.S.

Out-of-wedlock births have soared in recent years:

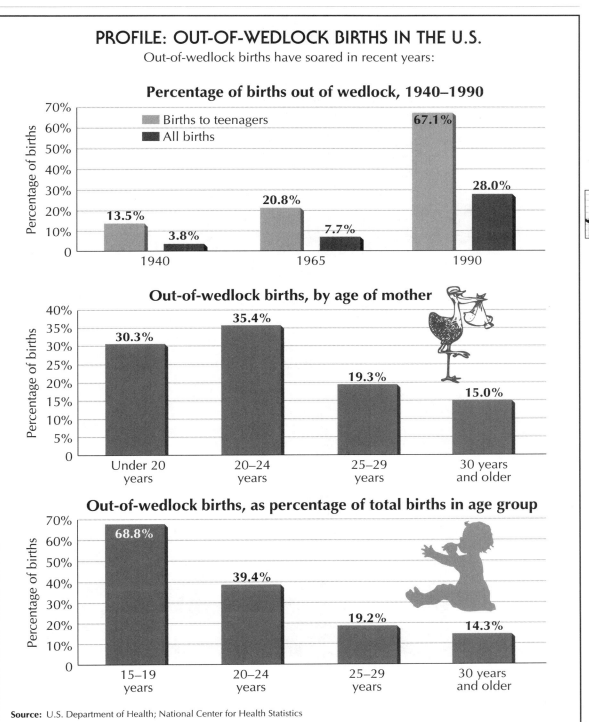

Percentage of births out of wedlock, 1940–1990

Births to teenagers
All births

1940: 13.5%, 3.8%
1965: 20.8%, 7.7%
1990: 67.1%, 28.0%

Out-of-wedlock births, by age of mother

Under 20 years: 30.3%
20–24 years: 35.4%
25–29 years: 19.3%
30 years and older: 15.0%

Out-of-wedlock births, as percentage of total births in age group

15–19 years: 68.8%
20–24 years: 39.4%
25–29 years: 19.2%
30 years and older: 14.3%

Source: U.S. Department of Health; National Center for Health Statistics

PROFILE: BIRTH RATES FOR UNWED MOTHERS

(Rates of births to unmarried women ages 15–44, per 1,000 unmarried women, 1970–1991)

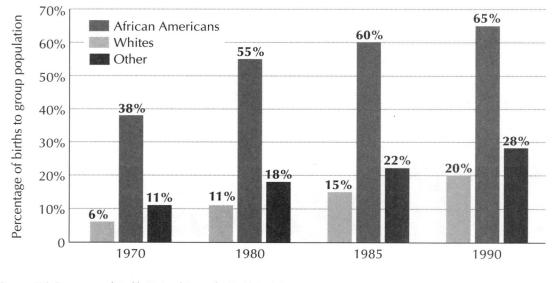

(Percentages of all births to unmarried women, by race or ethnic group, 1970–1991)

Source: U.S. Department of Health; National Center for Health Statistics

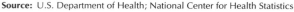

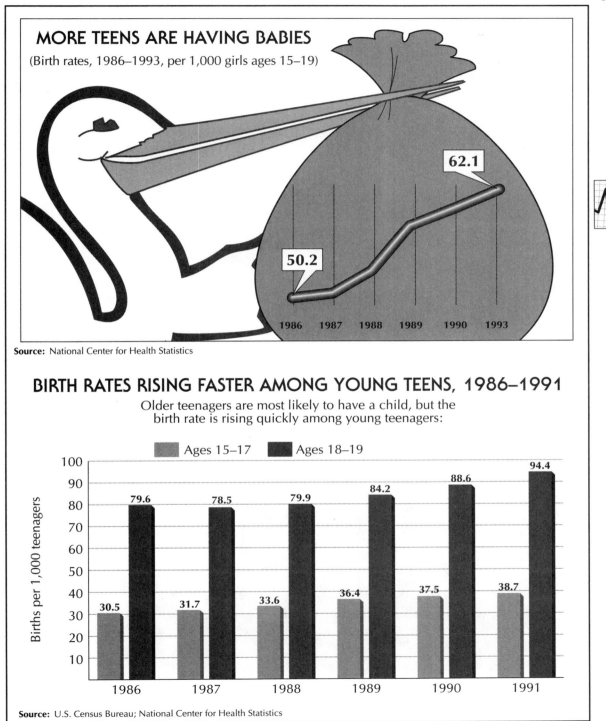

MORE TEENS ARE HAVING BABIES

(Birth rates, 1986–1993, per 1,000 girls ages 15–19)

62.1

50.2

1986   1987   1988   1989   1990   1993

Source: National Center for Health Statistics

BIRTH RATES RISING FASTER AMONG YOUNG TEENS, 1986–1991

Older teenagers are most likely to have a child, but the
birth rate is rising quickly among young teenagers:

Ages 15–17   Ages 18–19

Births per 1,000 teenagers

Year	Ages 15–17	Ages 18–19
1986	30.5	79.6
1987	31.7	78.5
1988	33.6	79.9
1989	36.4	84.2
1990	37.5	88.6
1991	38.7	94.4

Source: U.S. Census Bureau; National Center for Health Statistics

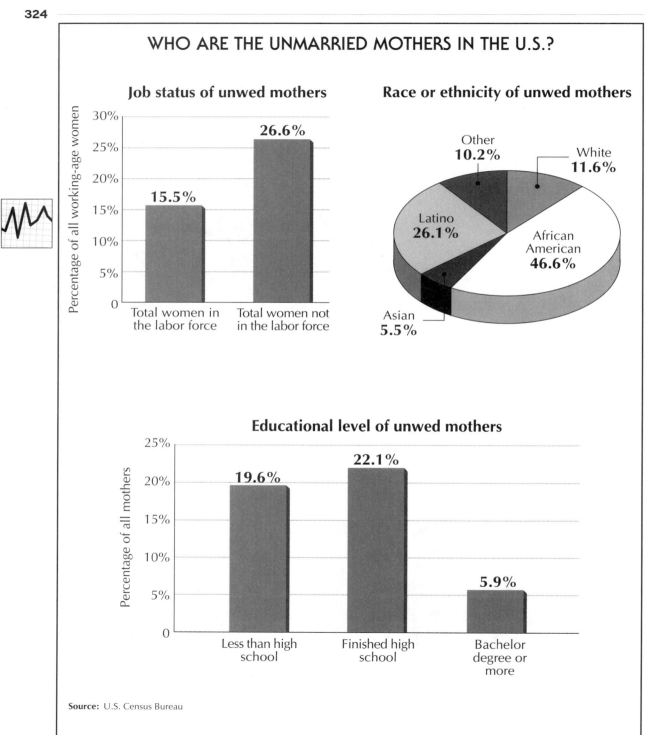

WHO ARE THE UNMARRIED MOTHERS IN THE U.S.?

Job status of unwed mothers

Percentage of all working-age women

- 26.6% — Total women not in the labor force
- 15.5% — Total women in the labor force

Race or ethnicity of unwed mothers

- Other 10.2%
- White 11.6%
- Latino 26.1%
- African American 46.6%
- Asian 5.5%

Educational level of unwed mothers

Percentage of all mothers

- Less than high school — 19.6%
- Finished high school — 22.1%
- Bachelor degree or more — 5.9%

Source: U.S. Census Bureau

TOP 10 STATES* FOR LOW BIRTHWEIGHT BABIES, 1991

(As percentage of all births, with rankings)

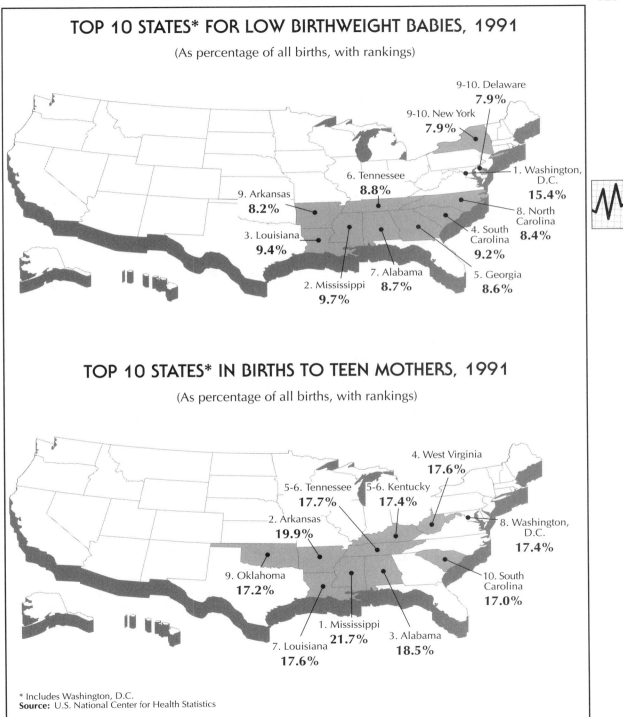

9-10. Delaware
7.9%

9-10. New York
7.9%

6. Tennessee
8.8%

1. Washington, D.C.
15.4%

9. Arkansas
8.2%

8. North Carolina
8.4%

3. Louisiana
9.4%

4. South Carolina
9.2%

7. Alabama
8.7%

5. Georgia
8.6%

2. Mississippi
9.7%

TOP 10 STATES* IN BIRTHS TO TEEN MOTHERS, 1991

(As percentage of all births, with rankings)

4. West Virginia
17.6%

5-6. Tennessee
17.7%

5-6. Kentucky
17.4%

2. Arkansas
19.9%

8. Washington, D.C.
17.4%

9. Oklahoma
17.2%

10. South Carolina
17.0%

1. Mississippi
21.7%

3. Alabama
18.5%

7. Louisiana
17.6%

* Includes Washington, D.C.
Source: U.S. National Center for Health Statistics

SUICIDE AND TEEN SUICIDE

Each year, there are 30,000 Americans—more than 80 a day—who intentionally kill themselves. There are also an estimated 400,000 unsuccessful suicide attempts annually. Many mental health experts, however, believe that these figures are highly inaccurate—mostly because of the profound social stigma that is associated with suicide. They believe that many suicides are actually reported as accidental deaths.

The U.S. death rate from suicide has gradually increased, from an average of 11.4 suicide deaths per 100,000 population in 1950 to 12.2 deaths per 100,000 in 1991. Although women are more likely to attempt suicide, men more often succeed at it. Firearms, especially handguns, are the primary method used to commit suicide by both sexes. Among men, hangings are the second leading method; among women, poisonings (including overdoses of barbituates and other drugs) rank #2.

The greatest recent increase in suicide rates has occurred among America's young people; during the period between 1950 and 1991, the rate among people ages 15 to 24 nearly tripled, from 4.5 to 13.1 deaths per 100,000. The great majority of these deaths were white males. Why so many teenagers take their lives is unclear. Possible factors include an increasing number of mental health problems, abuse of alcohol and illicit drugs, disruptive or abusive home lives, and other new or evolving pressures in school or in life with peers.

FINGERTIP FACTS

☞ Suicide is among the top 10 causes of death in the United States. It resulted in 29,760 deaths in 1992.

☞ Older men have the highest rates of suicide. In 1991, the suicide rate among men ages 75 to 84 was 53.0; among men 85 years and over, it was 69.7.

☞ For women, suicide rates are highest among those ages 45 to 54 (7.6 per 100,000).

☞ Suicide rates are higher among whites than blacks. In 1991, the rate for white males was 21.7 per 100,000 population; for black males, it was 12.1. The rate for white females was 5.2; for black females, it was 1.9.

☞ Firearms and explosives were used by 65% of the men and 40% of the women who committed suicide in 1991.

☞ Suicide rates vary widely from state to state. In 1991, the highest rate was reported in Nevada (24.8 per 100,000), the lowest rate in New Jersey (6.6).

☞ Worldwide, suicide rates vary considerably. For example, in 1991, the male suicide rate in the U.S. was 20.1 deaths per 100,000 population; in Austria, it was 34.6; in Poland, 23.9; in Japan, 20.6; and in England and Wales, 12.1.

TEENAGE DEATHS BY SUICIDE, 1960–1992

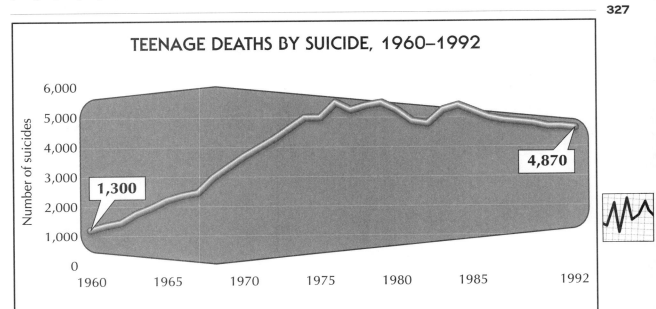

Source: Division of Vital Statistics; National Center for Health Statistics

TEENAGE SUICIDE IN 1991, COMPARED TO OTHER AGE GROUPS

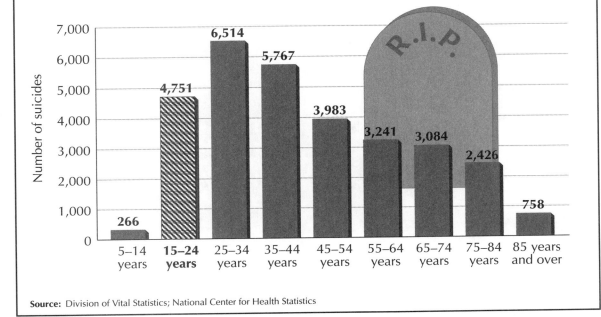

Source: Division of Vital Statistics; National Center for Health Statistics

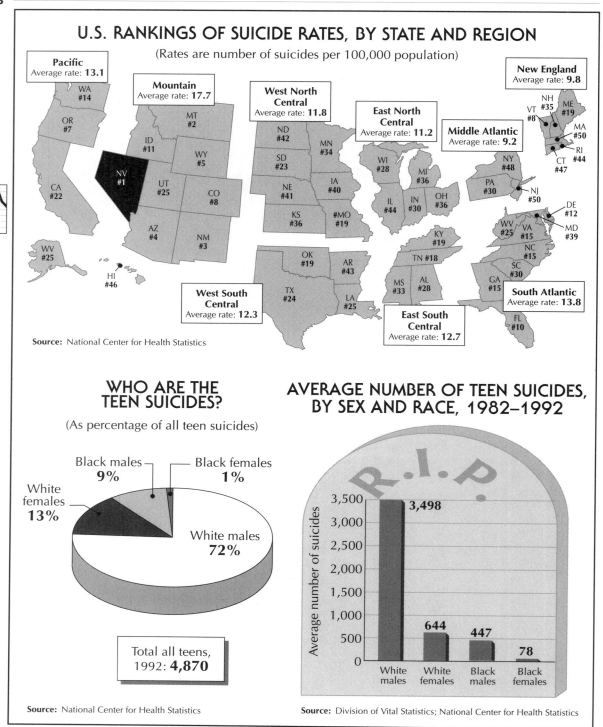

U.S. RANKINGS OF SUICIDE RATES, BY STATE AND REGION
(Rates are number of suicides per 100,000 population)

Pacific
Average rate: **13.1**

Mountain
Average rate: **17.7**

West North Central
Average rate: **11.8**

East North Central
Average rate: **11.2**

Middle Atlantic
Average rate: **9.2**

New England
Average rate: **9.8**

South Atlantic
Average rate: **13.8**

West South Central
Average rate: **12.3**

East South Central
Average rate: **12.7**

WA #14 · OR #7 · CA #22 · HI #46 · WV #25 · MT #2 · ID #11 · WY #5 · NV #1 · UT #25 · CO #8 · AZ #4 · NM #3 · ND #42 · SD #23 · NE #41 · KS #36 · MN #34 · IA #40 · #MO #19 · WI #28 · MI #36 · IL #44 · IN #30 · OH #36 · KY #19 · TN #18 · OK #19 · AR #43 · TX #24 · LA #25 · MS #33 · AL #28 · GA #15 · FL #10 · NY #48 · PA #30 · NJ #50 · DE #12 · MD #39 · WV #25 · VA #15 · NC #15 · SC #30 · NH #35 · VT #8 · ME #19 · MA #50 · RI #44 · CT #47

Source: National Center for Health Statistics

WHO ARE THE TEEN SUICIDES?
(As percentage of all teen suicides)

Black males
9%

Black females
1%

White females
13%

White males
72%

Total all teens, 1992: **4,870**

Source: National Center for Health Statistics

AVERAGE NUMBER OF TEEN SUICIDES, BY SEX AND RACE, 1982–1992

R.I.P.

Average number of suicides

White males	**3,498**
White females	**644**
Black males	**447**
Black females	**78**

Source: Division of Vital Statistics; National Center for Health Statistics

SUICIDE IN THE U.S., BY AGE GROUP, 1991

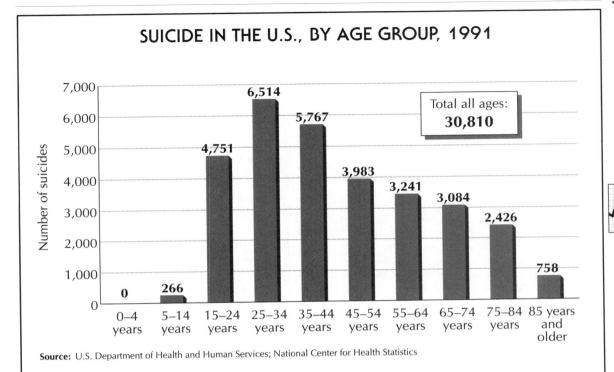

Total all ages:
30,810

Source: U.S. Department of Health and Human Services; National Center for Health Statistics

SUICIDE RATES, BY AGE GROUP, 1950 vs. 1991

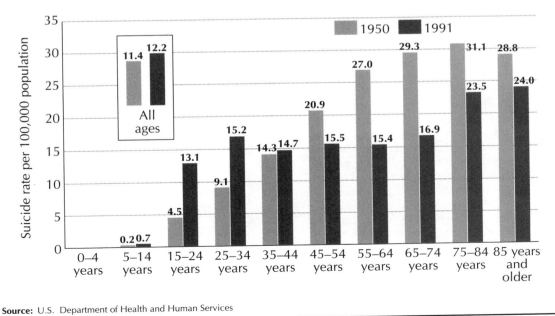

Source: U.S. Department of Health and Human Services

UNEMPLOYMENT

On any particular day, millions of American workers are unemployed. Some may be temporarily out of work because of the seasonal nature of their jobs. Some may be looking for new jobs because they moved, or because the firms for which they worked have downsized or gone out of business. Government statistics indicate that unemployment in America lasts an average of about 18 weeks, though many people remain without work for so long that they become discouraged and drop out of the labor force entirely. (The "labor force" is defined as all people, ages 16 and older, who are working or who are looking for work.)

The U.S. unemployment rate, which is tabulated monthly, indicates the percentage of the U.S. labor force that is currently unemployed. The rate does not consider non-workers who are not seeking jobs; nor does it consider people who are underemployed, such as part-time workers who want full-time jobs. In 1993, there were 129.5 million people in the U.S. labor force; the U.S. Department of Labor estimated that 8.7 million of these—6.7% of the total—were unemployed.

The great majority of U.S. workers are eligible for unemployment insurance if they lose their jobs. Unemployment insurance was introduced into the U.S. in 1935 as part of the Social Security Act. This insurance is designed to provide them with income for a limited period of time while they look for new jobs. The insurance is financed by a payroll tax on employers; the program is administered by the states in cooperation with the U.S. Department of Labor in Washington, D.C.

FINGERTIP FACTS

- U.S. unemployment decreased during 1994—from 6.7% early in of the year to 5.4% in December, when 7.3 million workers were without jobs. In mid-1995, the rate was 5.7%.

- In 1993, some 7.1 million unemployed workers were looking for full-time work, 1.6 million for part-time work.

- In 1993, unemployment lasted an average of 18.1 weeks; 36.2% of the unemployed were without work for 27 weeks or more.

- Some 400,000 U.S. workers had left the labor market by the end of 1994, discouraged about their prospects of finding work.

- More education means less likelihood of unemployment. In 1993, unemployment rates among workers ages 25 and older ranged from 10.7% for workers with less than 4 years of high school to 2.9% for college graduates.

- Unemployment is greater among teenagers than among adults. In late 1994, teenage unemployment was 15.3%, adult female 5.0%, and adult male 4.9%.

- Unemployment rates are lowest among whites—4.8% in late 1994, as compared to 8.6% for Latinos and 10.5% for blacks.

- Unemployment rates vary across the nation. In 1993, rates ranged from 2.6% in Nebraska to 10.8% in West Virginia.

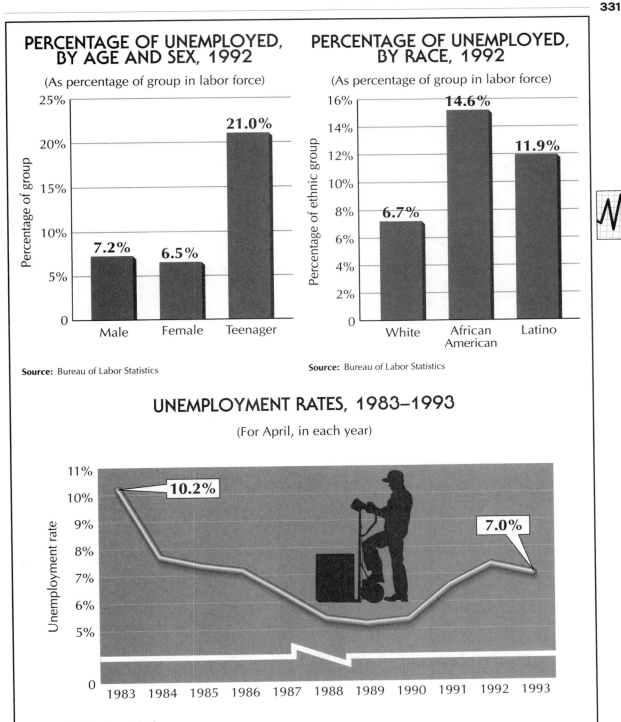

PERCENTAGE OF UNEMPLOYED, BY AGE AND SEX, 1992

(As percentage of group in labor force)

Source: Bureau of Labor Statistics

PERCENTAGE OF UNEMPLOYED, BY RACE, 1992

(As percentage of group in labor force)

Source: Bureau of Labor Statistics

UNEMPLOYMENT RATES, 1983–1993

(For April, in each year)

Source: U.S. Department of Labor

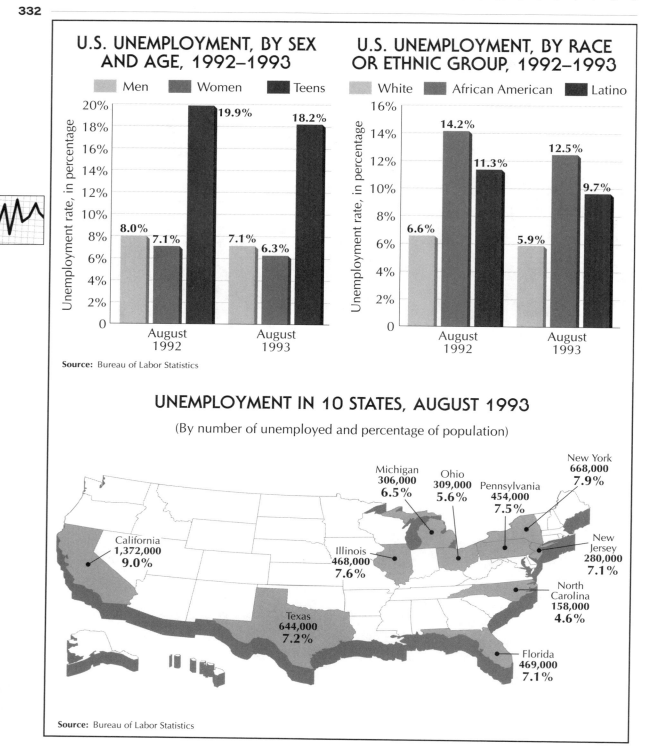

U.S. UNEMPLOYMENT, BY SEX AND AGE, 1992–1993

Men Women Teens

Unemployment rate, in percentage

8.0% 7.1% 19.9%
7.1% 6.3% 18.2%

August 1992   August 1993

Source: Bureau of Labor Statistics

U.S. UNEMPLOYMENT, BY RACE OR ETHNIC GROUP, 1992–1993

White African American Latino

Unemployment rate, in percentage

6.6% 14.2% 11.3%
5.9% 12.5% 9.7%

August 1992   August 1993

UNEMPLOYMENT IN 10 STATES, AUGUST 1993

(By number of unemployed and percentage of population)

Michigan
306,000
6.5%

Ohio
309,000
5.6%

Pennsylvania
454,000
7.5%

New York
668,000
7.9%

California
1,372,000
9.0%

Illinois
468,000
7.6%

New Jersey
280,000
7.1%

North Carolina
158,000
4.6%

Texas
644,000
7.2%

Florida
469,000
7.1%

Source: Bureau of Labor Statistics

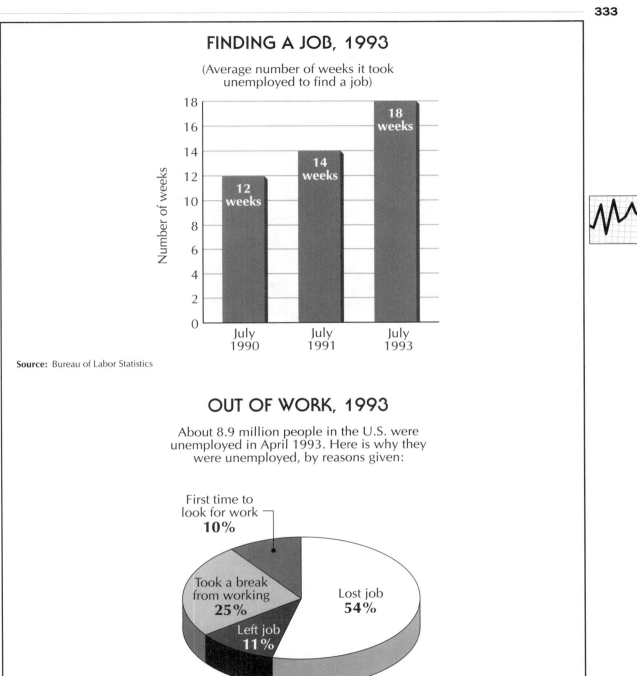

FINDING A JOB, 1993

(Average number of weeks it took
unemployed to find a job)

Source: Bureau of Labor Statistics

OUT OF WORK, 1993

About 8.9 million people in the U.S. were
unemployed in April 1993. Here is why they
were unemployed, by reasons given:

First time to
look for work
10%

Took a break
from working
25%

Left job
11%

Lost job
54%

Source: U.S. Department of Labor

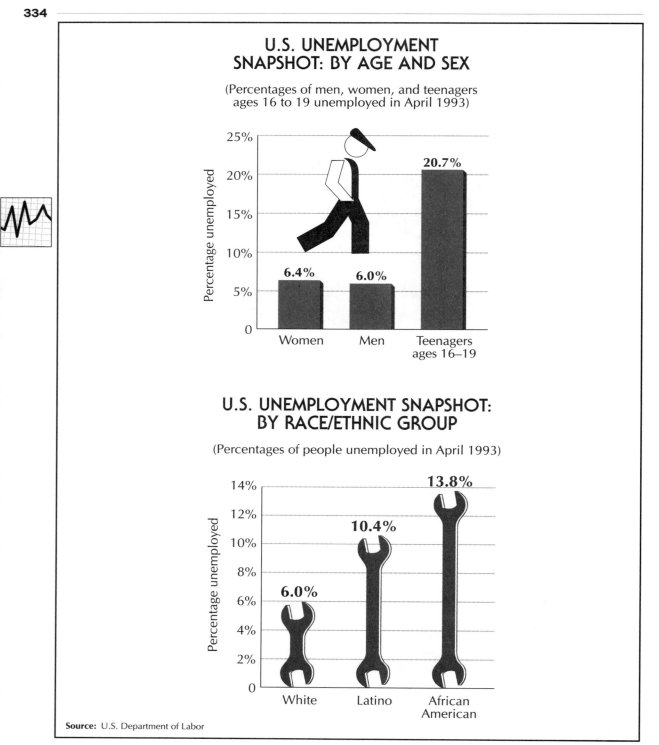

U.S. UNEMPLOYMENT SNAPSHOT: BY AGE AND SEX

(Percentages of men, women, and teenagers
ages 16 to 19 unemployed in April 1993)

Women 6.4%
Men 6.0%
Teenagers ages 16–19 20.7%

Percentage unemployed

U.S. UNEMPLOYMENT SNAPSHOT: BY RACE/ETHNIC GROUP

(Percentages of people unemployed in April 1993)

White 6.0%
Latino 10.4%
African American 13.8%

Percentage unemployed

Source: U.S. Department of Labor

TOP 10 STATES IN UNEMPLOYMENT, 1993

(With rankings)

9-10. Massachusetts
6.5%

5-6. Michigan
6.7%

7-8. Pennsylvania
6.6%

4. New York
7.0%

2. California
8.6%

3. Illinois
8.1%

1. New Jersey
9.1%

9-10. Ohio
6.5%

5-6. Texas
6.7%

7-8. Florida
6.6%

Source: U.S. Department of Labor

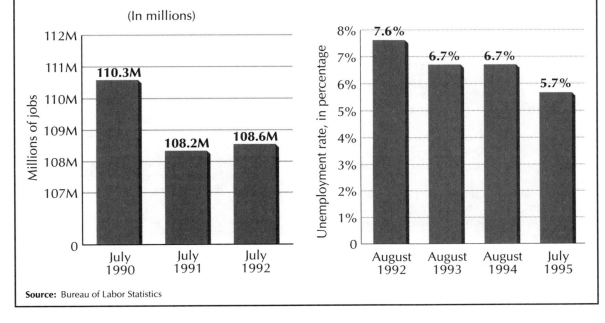

NUMBER OF JOBS IN THE U.S., 1990–1992

(In millions)

Millions of jobs

	July 1990	July 1991	July 1992
	110.3M	108.2M	108.6M

UNEMPLOYMENT RATES DROP, 1992–1995

Unemployment rate, in percentage

August 1992	August 1993	August 1994	July 1995
7.6%	6.7%	6.7%	5.7%

Source: Bureau of Labor Statistics

POPULATION GROWTH AMONG OLDER AMERICANS

Healthier lifestyles and medical advances are enabling Americans to enjoy longer, more active lives than ever before. Coupled with declining birth rates and fertility rates, this means that the percentage of people ages 65 and older is growing rapidly. This age group currently makes up about 13% of the U.S. population—up from 9.2% in 1960, and more than a 1,000% increase since 1900. The percentage is expected to increase dramatically as the baby boomers reach retirement age.

The economic quality of life has also improved for older Americans. Poverty has declined dramatically, due in large part to government programs that provide payments to retired or disabled workers, their dependents, and their survivors. Such programs also defray some of the medical expenses of retirees and their spouses. People have come to rely on Social Security and other government programs in increasing numbers. For example, in 1970, there were 26.2 million beneficiaries of Social Security; they received payments totaling $31.9 million. By 1991, there were 40.6 million beneficiaries receiving $268.1 billion.

Public debate is growing over how these massive programs are to be funded and distributed in coming years. Of particular concern is the high cost of health care for this age group. People ages 65 and over account for more than one-third of the nation's health care expenditures, fill 40% of all hospital beds, and use twice as much prescription medicine as all other age groups combined. Many Americans fear that Medicare, which pays hospital bills for older people, will run out of money within the next decade.

FINGERTIP FACTS

- In 1970, the median age of Americans was 28.0 years; by 1992, the median age was 33.4.

- Each day, about 6,000 Americans turn age 65.

- In 1992, some 32.3 million Americans were ages 65 or older. By the year 2040, the U.S. Census Bureau expects that this population will reach 76.0 million.

- In 1900, only 0.1% of Americans were age 85 or older. By 1990, the figure had grown to 3.0%—and by 2040, it is expected to reach 12.3%.

- In 1992, there were an estimated 45,000 Americans age 100 years or older—more than three-fourths of them women.

- Florida has the highest percentage of residents ages 65 and older (18.3%); Alaska has the lowest (4.1%).

- More than 47 million people—including some 18 million ages 65 and older—are grandparents of children under age 18.

- Thanks largely to Social Security, poverty among the elderly declined from 35.0% in 1959 to 12.2% in 1990. It then increased to 12.9% by 1992.

- In 1990, some 6.1% of people ages 75 to 84 and 33.1% of those ages 90 to 94 lived in nursing homes.

- People enrolled for Medicare coverage increased from 19.5 million in 1967 to an estimated 36.9 million in 1994—an 89% increase.

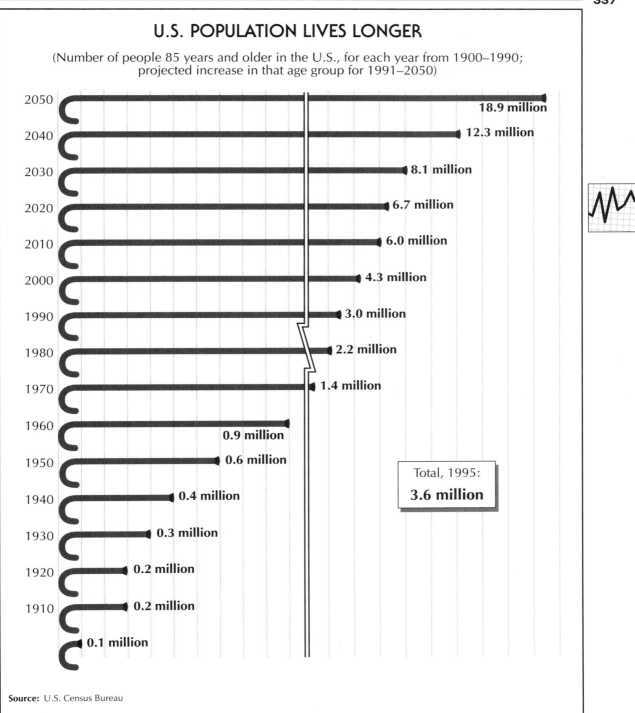

U.S. POPULATION LIVES LONGER

(Number of people 85 years and older in the U.S., for each year from 1900–1990;
projected increase in that age group for 1991–2050)

2050	18.9 million
2040	12.3 million
2030	8.1 million
2020	6.7 million
2010	6.0 million
2000	4.3 million
1990	3.0 million
1980	2.2 million
1970	1.4 million
1960	0.9 million
1950	0.6 million
1940	0.4 million
1930	0.3 million
1920	0.2 million
1910	0.2 million
1900	0.1 million

Total, 1995:
3.6 million

Source: U.S. Census Bureau

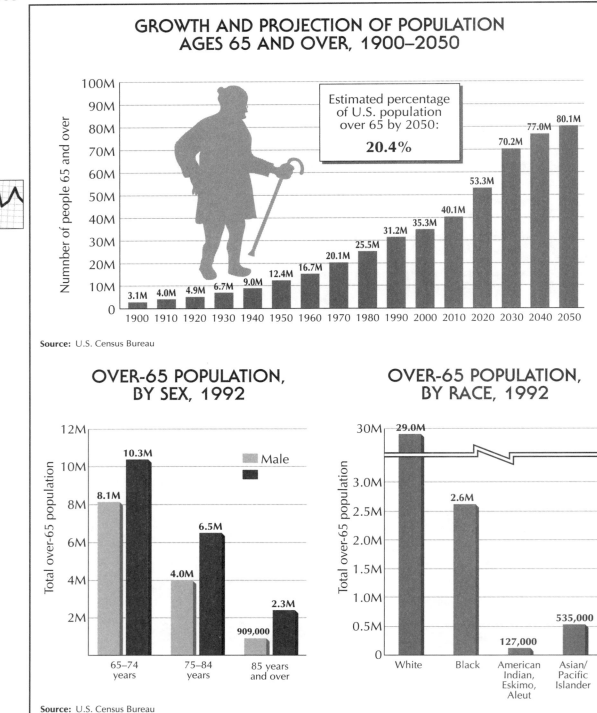

GROWTH AND PROJECTION OF POPULATION AGES 65 AND OVER, 1900–2050

Nummber of people 65 and over

Estimated percentage of U.S. population over 65 by 2050:

20.4%

3.1M 4.0M 4.9M 6.7M 9.0M 12.4M 16.7M 20.1M 25.5M 31.2M 35.3M 40.1M 53.3M 70.2M 77.0M 80.1M

1900 1910 1920 1930 1940 1950 1960 1970 1980 1990 2000 2010 2020 2030 2040 2050

Source: U.S. Census Bureau

OVER-65 POPULATION, BY SEX, 1992

Total over-65 population

Male

8.1M 10.3M 4.0M 6.5M 909,000 2.3M

65–74 years · 75–84 years · 85 years and over

OVER-65 POPULATION, BY RACE, 1992

Total over-65 population

29.0M 2.6M 127,000 535,000

White · Black · American Indian, Eskimo, Aleut · Asian/ Pacific Islander

Source: U.S. Census Bureau

A NATION OF GRANDPARENTS

More than 47 million people in the U.S.
have at least one grandchild under age 18.
Here is how they add up, by age:

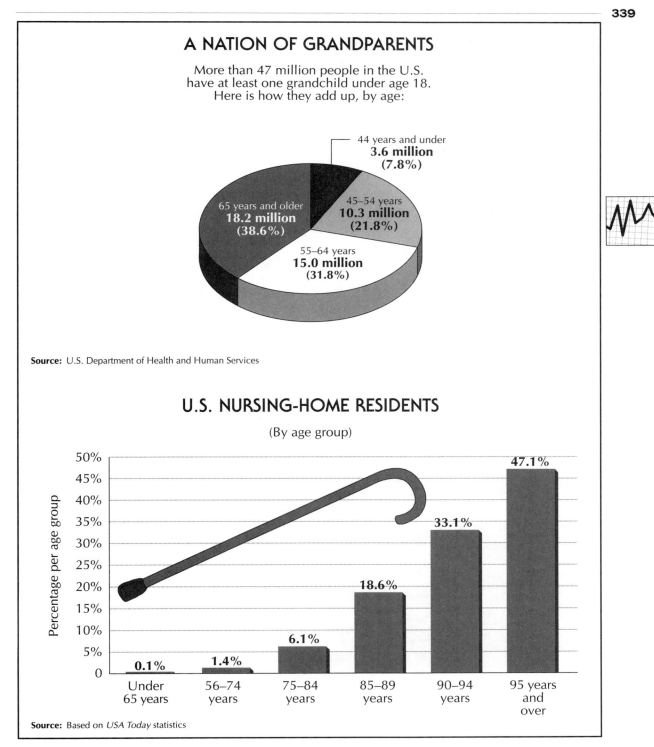

44 years and under
3.6 million
(7.8%)

45–54 years
10.3 million
(21.8%)

65 years and older
18.2 million
(38.6%)

55–64 years
15.0 million
(31.8%)

Source: U.S. Department of Health and Human Services

U.S. NURSING-HOME RESIDENTS

(By age group)

Percentage per age group

- Under 65 years: **0.1%**
- 56–74 years: **1.4%**
- 75–84 years: **6.1%**
- 85–89 years: **18.6%**
- 90–94 years: **33.1%**
- 95 years and over: **47.1%**

Source: Based on *USA Today* statistics

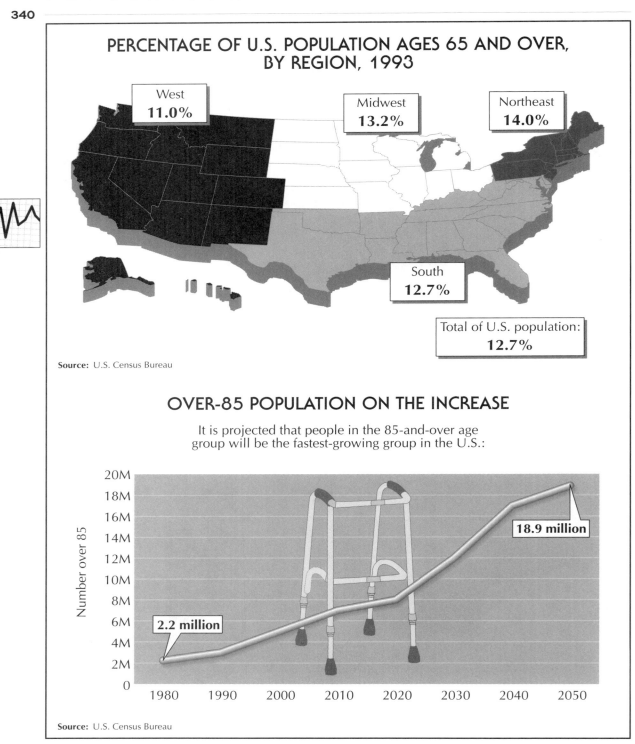

PERCENTAGE OF U.S. POPULATION AGES 65 AND OVER, BY REGION, 1993

West
11.0%

Midwest
13.2%

Northeast
14.0%

South
12.7%

Total of U.S. population:
12.7%

Source: U.S. Census Bureau

OVER-85 POPULATION ON THE INCREASE

It is projected that people in the 85-and-over age group will be the fastest-growing group in the U.S.:

2.2 million

18.9 million

Number over 85

20M
18M
16M
14M
12M
10M
8M
6M
4M
2M
0

1980   1990   2000   2010   2020   2030   2040   2050

Source: U.S. Census Bureau

U.S. STATES WITH THE HIGHEST PERCENTAGES OF RESIDENTS OVER AGE 65, 1993

(With rankings)

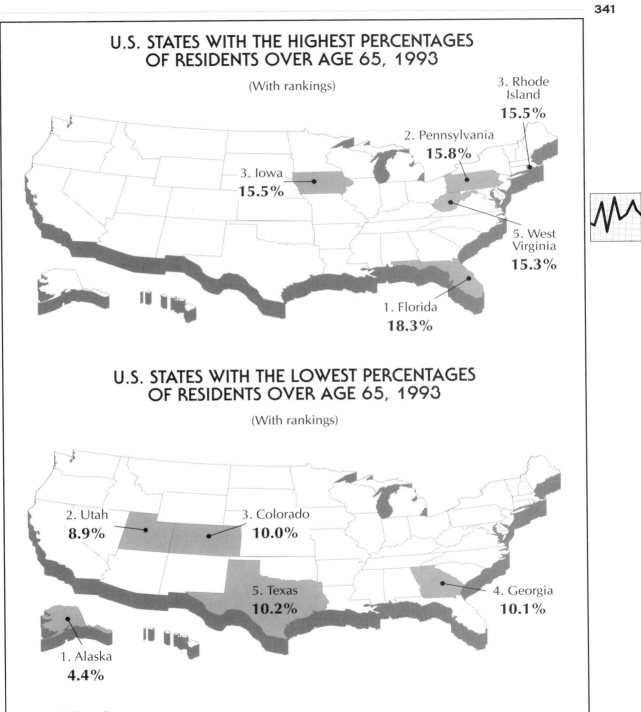

3. Rhode Island
15.5%

2. Pennsylvania
15.8%

3. Iowa
15.5%

5. West Virginia
15.3%

1. Florida
18.3%

U.S. STATES WITH THE LOWEST PERCENTAGES OF RESIDENTS OVER AGE 65, 1993

(With rankings)

2. Utah
8.9%

3. Colorado
10.0%

4. Georgia
10.1%

5. Texas
10.2%

1. Alaska
4.4%

Source: U.S. Census Bureau

5

DRUGS AND CRIME

ILLEGAL DRUGS

Much crime in the U.S. is associated with illegal drugs. Arrest rates for traffickers and users increased from 256 arrests per 100,000 population in 1980 to 431 in 1992.

There has also been a large increase in arrests of drug users for non-drug-related crimes. A Bureau of Justice Statistics study found that about 33% of convicted robbers and burglars had committed their crimes to obtain money for drugs. Urinalysis samples show that more than 50% of the people arrested in big cities for serious non-drug crimes test positive for drugs. For example, 66% of such males and 78% of such females arrested in Los Angeles, California, during the second quarter of 1993 tested positive.

The federal "war on drugs" has grown dramatically since it was begun in the early 1970s, but U.S. demand for drugs remains high, and it is difficult to determine the impact of law enforcement efforts. Surveys indicate that drug use declined in the early 1990s—at least among the affluent and middle class—but drug-related crime grew. And although law enforcement agencies have confiscated unprecedented amounts of illegal drugs, there is no shortage of these substances in America.

A large portion of federal anti-drug money has been spent on fighting drugs overseas, particularly in Asia and Latin America, where most opium (heroin's main ingredient) and cocaine are produced. Nonetheless, worldwide drug production has increased significantly. Under the Clinton administration, anti-drug operations on foreign soil were scaled down, and greater emphasis was placed on drug treatment and prevention.

FINGERTIP FACTS

- In the second quarter of 1993, 82% of the men and 86% of the women arrested in New York City for non-drug crimes were drug users.

- Approximately 920,000 people were arrested in 1992 for violating drug laws. Of these, 59% were white and 40% were black.

- In 1970, there were 71,517 juvenile (ages 10 to 17) arrests for drug-law violations. The number rose to 86,757 in 1987, then declined to 73,220 in 1992.

- America's "war on drugs" was first declared in 1971. Since then, the federal government has spent about $100 billion on anti-drug efforts.

- Domestic drug seizures by the Drug Enforcement Agency (DEA) in 1993 included 1,200 pounds of heroin, 123,700 pounds of cocaine, and 357,000 pounds of marijuana.

- The federal government spent $3.4 billion in 1992 on drug-abuse prevention and treatment.

- In 1992, a total of $22.5 million was spent on drug-abuse treatment in federal prisons, a jump from $4.1 million in 1989.

- The 1992 federal anti-drug effort had a budget of approximately $12 billion; about 68% was spent on law enforcement, including international interdiction and control programs. The 1995 budget was $12 billion, with about 59% for law enforcement.

Note: Before comparing statistics, consider that different rates apply to different population ratios—for example, some rates are figured per 1,000 people, other rates are figured per 100,000 people.

PERCENTAGE OF ILLEGAL DRUG USE, BY TYPE AND AGE GROUP, 1974 vs. 1992

(People who have ever used selected drug)

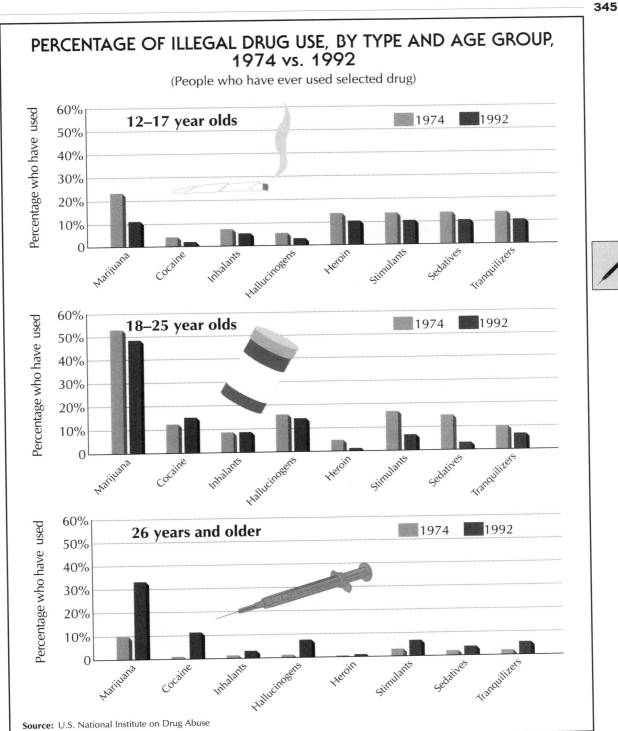

Source: U.S. National Institute on Drug Abuse

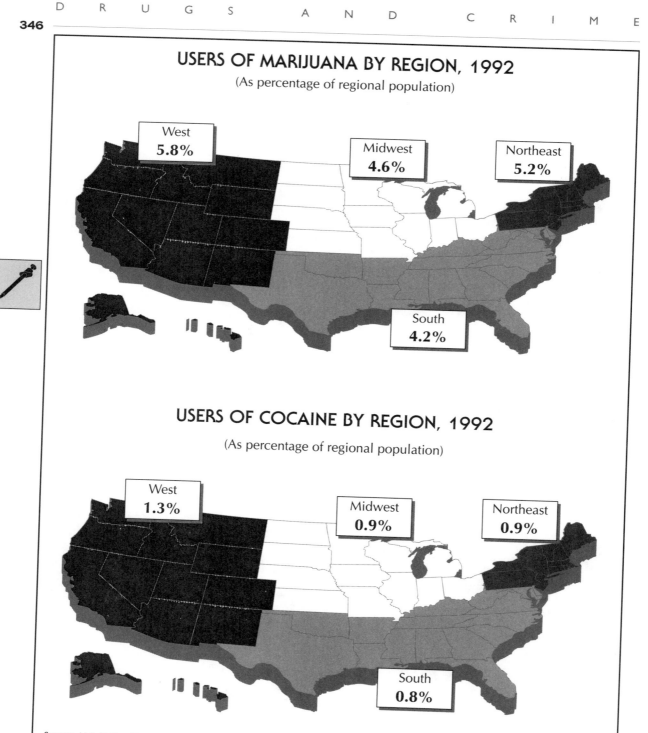

USERS OF MARIJUANA BY REGION, 1992
(As percentage of regional population)

West
5.8%

Midwest
4.6%

Northeast
5.2%

South
4.2%

USERS OF COCAINE BY REGION, 1992
(As percentage of regional population)

West
1.3%

Midwest
0.9%

Northeast
0.9%

South
0.8%

Source: U.S. National Institute on Drug Abuse

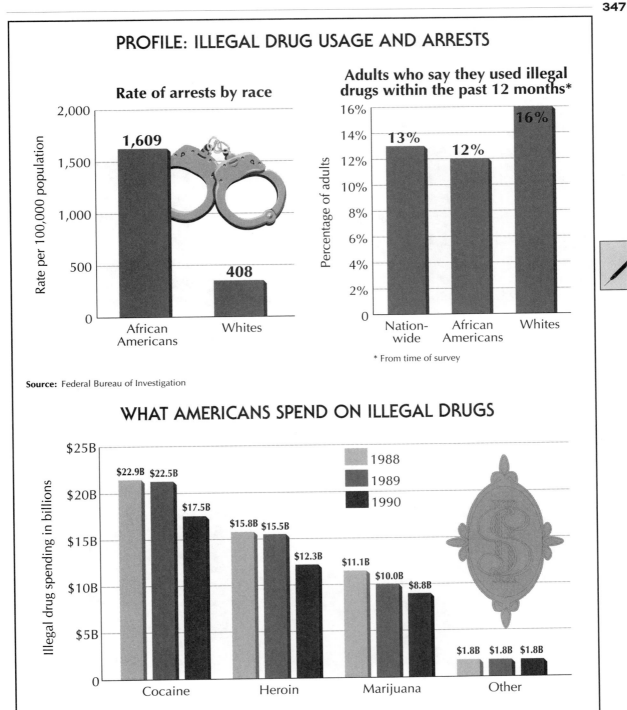

PROFILE: ILLEGAL DRUG USAGE AND ARRESTS

Rate of arrests by race

Rate per 100,000 population

- 1,609 — African Americans
- 408 — Whites

Adults who say they used illegal drugs within the past 12 months*

Percentage of adults

- 13% — Nation-wide
- 12% — African Americans
- 16% — Whites

* From time of survey

Source: Federal Bureau of Investigation

WHAT AMERICANS SPEND ON ILLEGAL DRUGS

Illegal drug spending in billions

Legend: 1988, 1989, 1990

	1988	1989	1990
Cocaine	$22.9B	$22.5B	$17.5B
Heroin	$15.8B	$15.5B	$12.3B
Marijuana	$11.1B	$10.0B	$8.8B
Other	$1.8B	$1.8B	$1.8B

Source: Office of National Drug Control Policy

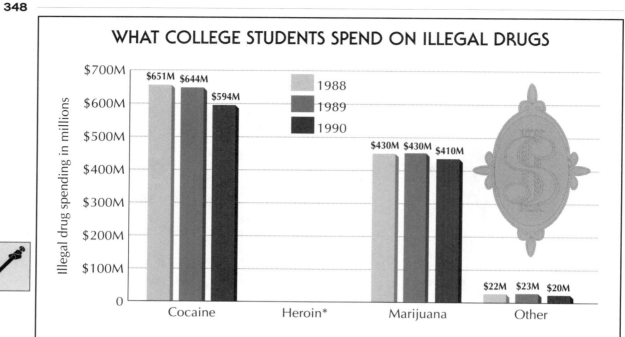

WHAT COLLEGE STUDENTS SPEND ON ILLEGAL DRUGS

Illegal drug spending in millions

1988
1989
1990

Cocaine: $651M, $644M, $594M

Heroin*

Marijuana: $430M, $430M, $410M

Other: $22M, $23M, $20M

* Amount spent on heroin is insignificant

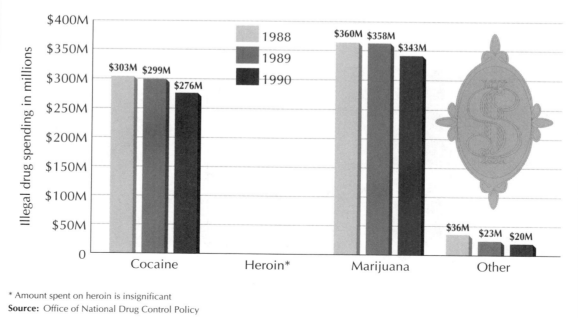

WHAT HIGH SCHOOL STUDENTS SPEND ON ILLEGAL DRUGS

Illegal drug spending in millions

1988
1989
1990

Cocaine: $303M, $299M, $276M

Heroin*

Marijuana: $360M, $358M, $343M

Other: $36M, $23M, $20M

* Amount spent on heroin is insignificant
Source: Office of National Drug Control Policy

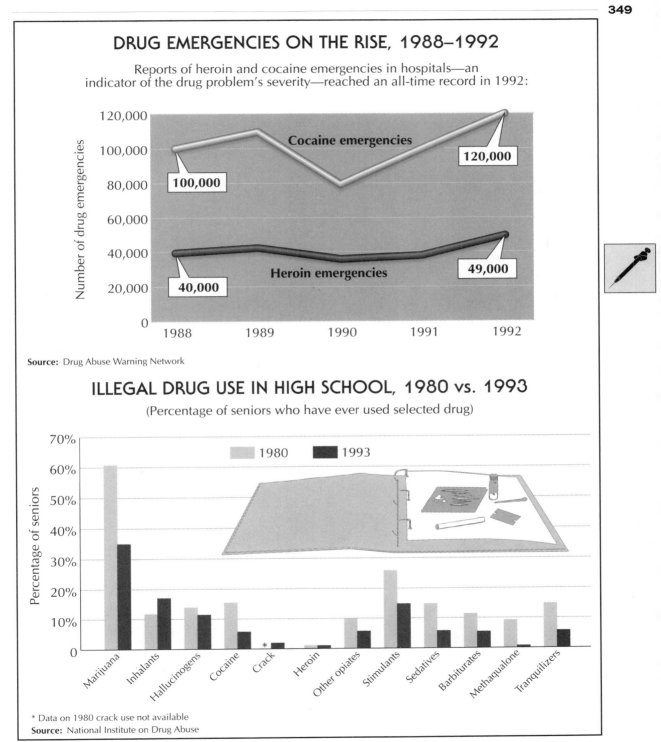

DRUG EMERGENCIES ON THE RISE, 1988–1992

Reports of heroin and cocaine emergencies in hospitals—an
indicator of the drug problem's severity—reached an all-time record in 1992:

Number of drug emergencies

120,000
100,000
80,000
60,000
40,000
20,000
0

Cocaine emergencies

120,000
100,000

Heroin emergencies

49,000
40,000

1988   1989   1990   1991   1992

Source: Drug Abuse Warning Network

ILLEGAL DRUG USE IN HIGH SCHOOL, 1980 vs. 1993

(Percentage of seniors who have ever used selected drug)

Percentage of seniors

70%
60%
50%
40%
30%
20%
10%
0

1980   1993

Marijuana, Inhalants, Hallucinogens, Cocaine, Crack, Heroin, Other opiates, Stimulants, Sedatives, Barbiturates, Methaqualone, Tranquilizers

* Data on 1980 crack use not available
Source: National Institute on Drug Abuse

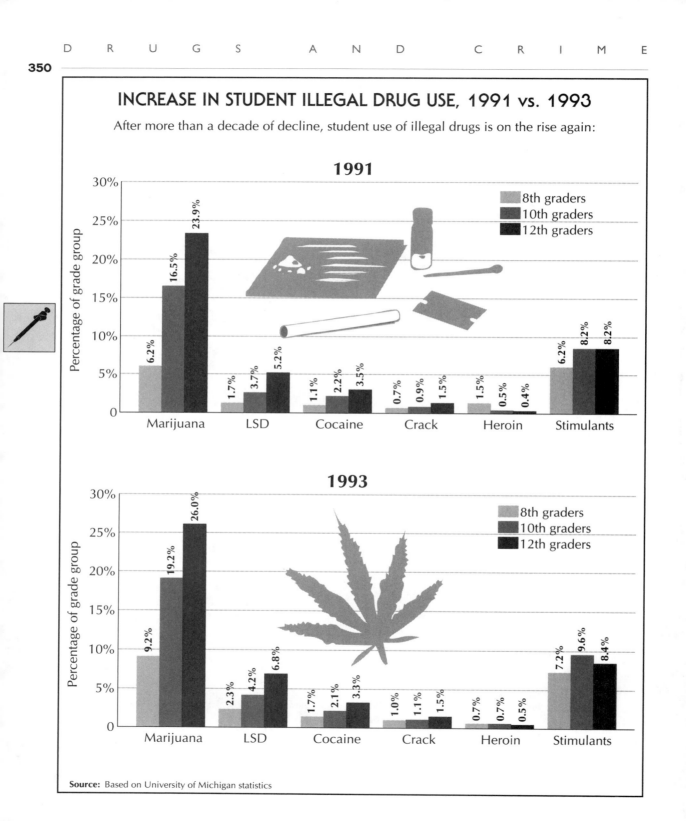

INCREASE IN STUDENT ILLEGAL DRUG USE, 1991 vs. 1993

After more than a decade of decline, student use of illegal drugs is on the rise again:

1991

Percentage of grade group

Legend:
- 8th graders
- 10th graders
- 12th graders

Drug	8th graders	10th graders	12th graders
Marijuana	6.2%	16.5%	23.9%
LSD	1.7%	3.7%	5.2%
Cocaine	1.1%	2.2%	3.5%
Crack	0.7%	0.9%	1.5%
Heroin	1.5%	0.5%	0.4%
Stimulants	6.2%	8.2%	8.2%

1993

Percentage of grade group

Legend:
- 8th graders
- 10th graders
- 12th graders

Drug	8th graders	10th graders	12th graders
Marijuana	9.2%	19.2%	26.0%
LSD	2.3%	4.2%	6.8%
Cocaine	1.7%	2.1%	3.3%
Crack	1.0%	1.1%	1.5%
Heroin	0.7%	0.7%	0.5%
Stimulants	7.2%	9.6%	8.4%

Source: Based on University of Michigan statistics

SPENDING ON DRUG-CONTROL SKYROCKETING, 1981–1994

(Government spending on drug interceptions and
seizures as part of the total federal drug-control budget)

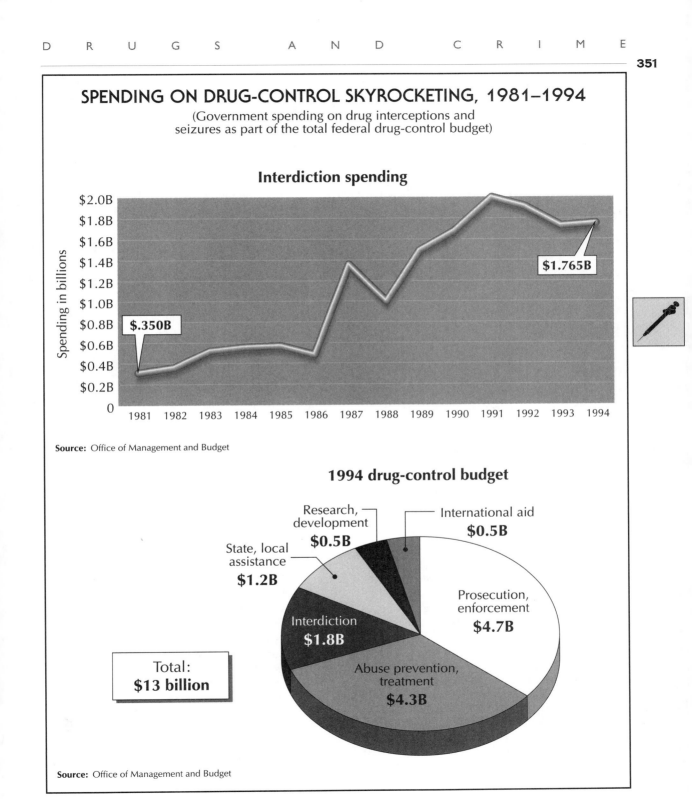

Interdiction spending

$.350B

$1.765B

Source: Office of Management and Budget

1994 drug-control budget

Research, development **$0.5B**

International aid **$0.5B**

State, local assistance **$1.2B**

Prosecution, enforcement **$4.7B**

Interdiction **$1.8B**

Abuse prevention, treatment **$4.3B**

Total: **$13 billion**

Source: Office of Management and Budget

C R I M E

Fear of violent crime is a major concern of Americans, and for good reason: A U.S. Justice Department study found that 8 out of 10 Americans will be victims of violent crimes in their lifetimes. The U.S. has some of the highest crime rates in the world.

In 1992, there were 1.9 million violent crimes, an increase of 53.6% since 1983, and 12.5 million property crimes, an increase of 15.3% from 1983. Violent crime rates per 100,000 inhabitants rose from 537.7 in 1983 to 757.5 in 1992, an increase of 40.9%. And these figures may not tell the whole story. Not all crimes are reported. National crime statistics are based on reports from police departments and other law enforcement agencies. According to federal officials, some crimes, such as rape and domestic violence, are vastly underreported as compared to other crimes.

Security at homes, schools, hospitals, shopping malls, and other buildings has increased exponentially. Police forces have grown, prison sentences have become more severe, and the number of prison inmates has soared. Attempts to fund drug-rehabilitation programs and other crime-prevention efforts have often been criticized as too expensive. Supporters, however, cite costs of more than $20,000 a year to keep a person in prison.

Another contentious issue is the glorification of violence in the media. By the time most children complete elementary school, it is estimated that each has seen some 8,000 murders and 100,000 other acts of violence on television. Many studies have found a correlation between television violence and aggressive behavior. The data, however, are not conclusive, and so the debate over cause-and-effect rages on.

FINGERTIP FACTS

- Forcible rape rates per 100,000 females increased from 30.4 in 1970 to 83.5 in 1992. There were 109,060 reported forcible rapes in 1992.

- According to the U.S. Justice Department, 7,684 crimes in 1993, including 20 murders, were hate crimes motivated by prejudice based on race, ethnicity, religion, or sexual orientation.

- Juvenile crime has increased. Between 1988 and 1992, juvenile court cases increased 26%, to almost 1.5 million. Cases involving murder, aggravated assault, and other serious crimes increased 68%, to 118,700.

- The most common crime committed by juveniles is theft, followed by burglary.

- Most victims of violent crimes are teens. In 1992, 1.6 million violent crimes were committed against juveniles ages 12 to 17, a 23% increase from 1988. One of every 13 juveniles was a violent-crime victim.

- Blacks are more likely to be crime victims than are other racial and ethnic groups.

- In 1992, there were 14.8 million burglaries, larcenies, and motor-vehicle thefts, the lowest total in at least 20 years.

- In 1992, there were 2.3 full-time law enforcement officers for every 1,000 Americans.

- In 1982, there were 597 bombings in the U.S. In 1992, there were 1,911.

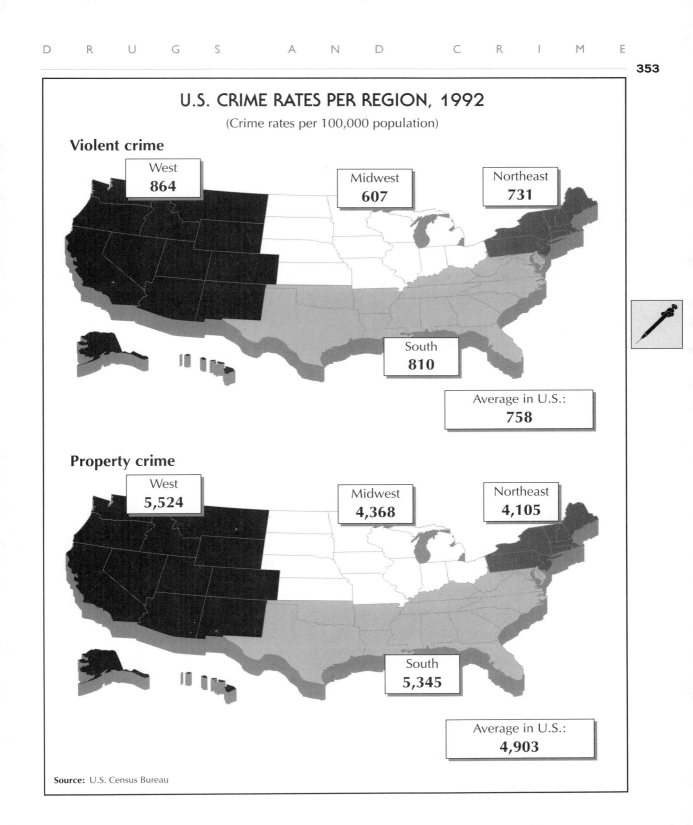

U.S. CRIME RATES PER REGION, 1992

(Crime rates per 100,000 population)

Violent crime

West
864

Midwest
607

Northeast
731

South
810

Average in U.S.:
758

Property crime

West
5,524

Midwest
4,368

Northeast
4,105

South
5,345

Average in U.S.:
4,903

Source: U.S. Census Bureau

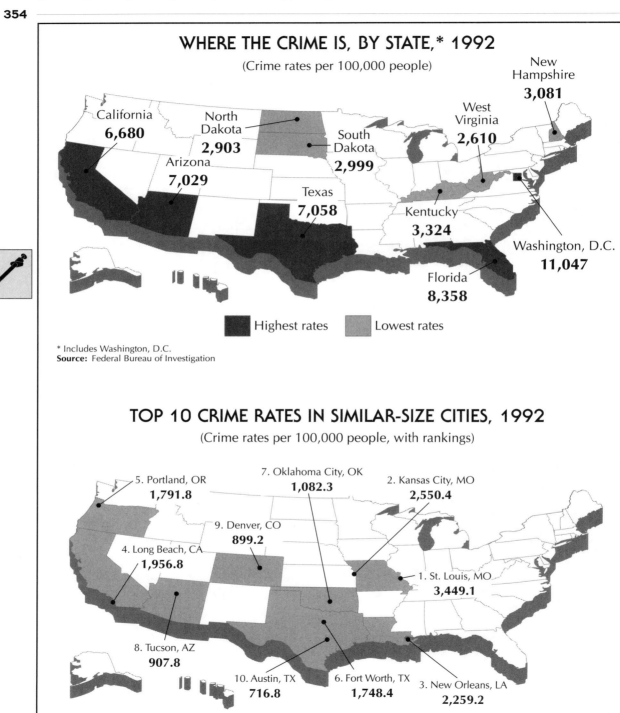

WHERE THE CRIME IS, BY STATE,* 1992

(Crime rates per 100,000 people)

New Hampshire
3,081

West Virginia
2,610

California
6,680

North Dakota
2,903

South Dakota
2,999

Arizona
7,029

Texas
7,058

Kentucky
3,324

Washington, D.C.
11,047

Florida
8,358

Highest rates   Lowest rates

* Includes Washington, D.C.
Source: Federal Bureau of Investigation

TOP 10 CRIME RATES IN SIMILAR-SIZE CITIES, 1992

(Crime rates per 100,000 people, with rankings)

5. Portland, OR
1,791.8

7. Oklahoma City, OK
1,082.3

2. Kansas City, MO
2,550.4

9. Denver, CO
899.2

4. Long Beach, CA
1,956.8

1. St. Louis, MO
3,449.1

8. Tucson, AZ
907.8

10. Austin, TX
716.8

6. Fort Worth, TX
1,748.4

3. New Orleans, LA
2,259.2

Source: Bureau of Justice Statistics

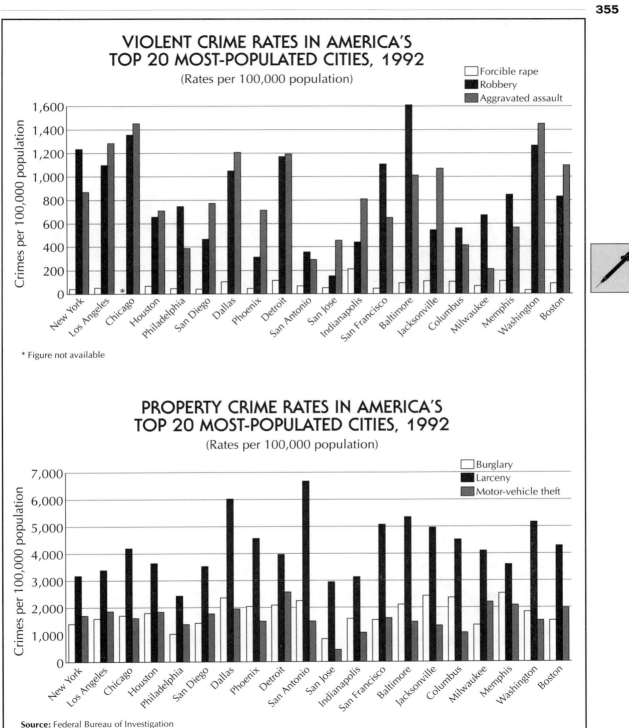

VIOLENT CRIME RATES IN AMERICA'S TOP 20 MOST-POPULATED CITIES, 1992
(Rates per 100,000 population)

Legend: Forcible rape, Robbery, Aggravated assault

* Figure not available

PROPERTY CRIME RATES IN AMERICA'S TOP 20 MOST-POPULATED CITIES, 1992
(Rates per 100,000 population)

Legend: Burglary, Larceny, Motor-vehicle theft

Source: Federal Bureau of Investigation

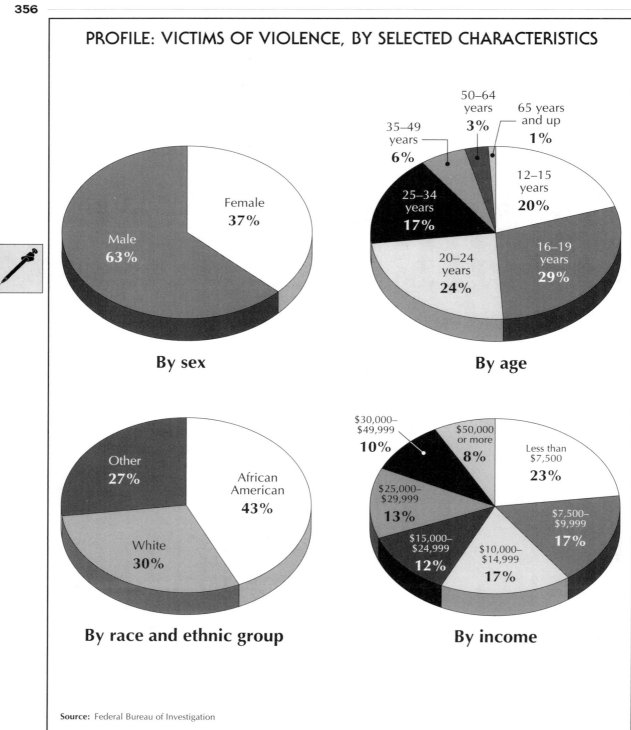

PROFILE: VICTIMS OF VIOLENCE, BY SELECTED CHARACTERISTICS

By sex

Female **37%**

Male **63%**

By age

50–64 years **3%**

65 years and up **1%**

35–49 years **6%**

25–34 years **17%**

20–24 years **24%**

16–19 years **29%**

12–15 years **20%**

By race and ethnic group

Other **27%**

African American **43%**

White **30%**

By income

$30,000–$49,999 **10%**

$50,000 or more **8%**

Less than $7,500 **23%**

$25,000–$29,999 **13%**

$7,500–$9,999 **17%**

$15,000–$24,999 **12%**

$10,000–$14,999 **17%**

Source: Federal Bureau of Investigation

VIOLENCE: WHO ATTACKS WHOM?

A new Justice Department survey shows that more than 2.5 million women are victimized each year in the U.S. Most are attacked by single offenders, usually men, and most offenders are friends or relatives. Most men, on the other hand, are attacked by acquaintances or strangers:

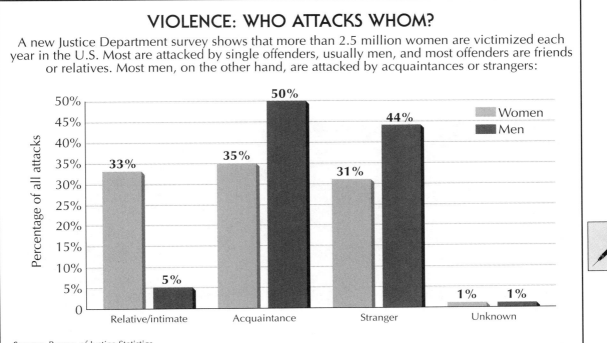

Source: Bureau of Justice Statistics

BLACK MALE TEENS ARE MOST COMMON VIOLENT CRIME TARGETS

(Violent crime victimization rates, per 1,000 persons ages 12–19)

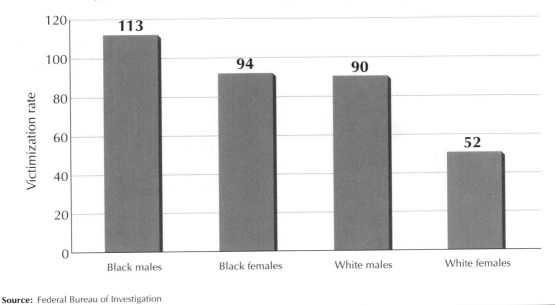

Source: Federal Bureau of Investigation

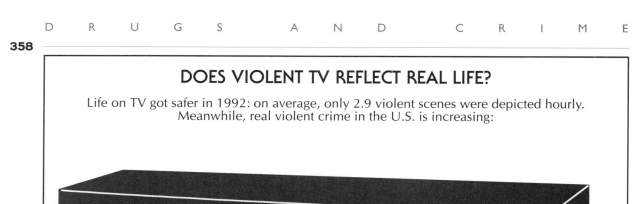

DOES VIOLENT TV REFLECT REAL LIFE?

Life on TV got safer in 1992: on average, only 2.9 violent scenes were depicted hourly.
Meanwhile, real violent crime in the U.S. is increasing:

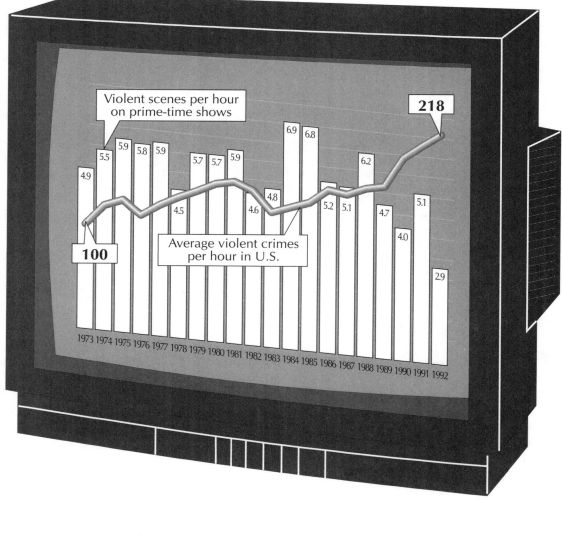

Violent scenes per hour on prime-time shows

Average violent crimes per hour in U.S.

218

100

4.9 5.5 5.9 5.8 5.9 4.5 5.7 5.7 5.9 4.6 4.8 6.9 6.8 5.2 5.1 6.2 4.7 4.0 5.1 2.9

1973 1974 1975 1976 1977 1978 1979 1980 1981 1982 1983 1984 1985 1986 1987 1988 1989 1990 1991 1992

Source: University of Pennsylvania; Federal Bureau of Investigation

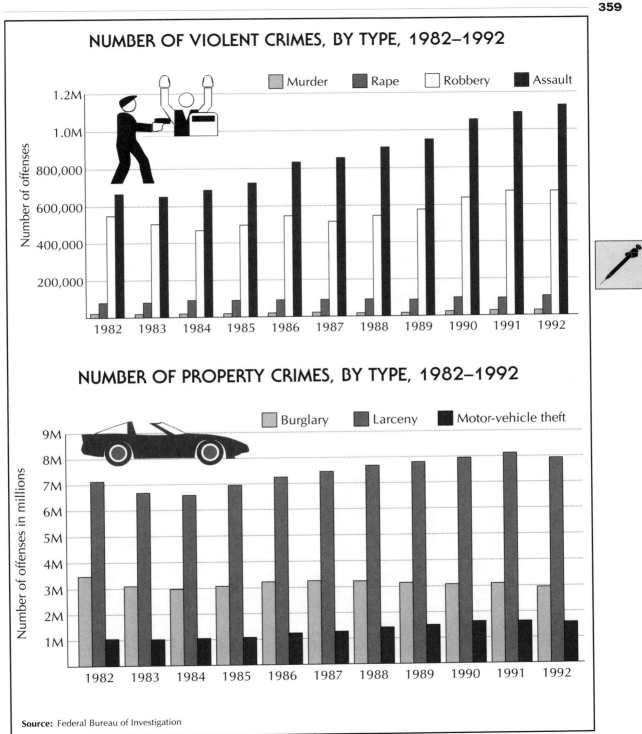

NUMBER OF VIOLENT CRIMES, BY TYPE, 1982–1992

Murder ▫ Rape ▪ Robbery □ Assault ■

NUMBER OF PROPERTY CRIMES, BY TYPE, 1982–1992

Burglary ▫ Larceny ▪ Motor-vehicle theft ■

Source: Federal Bureau of Investigation

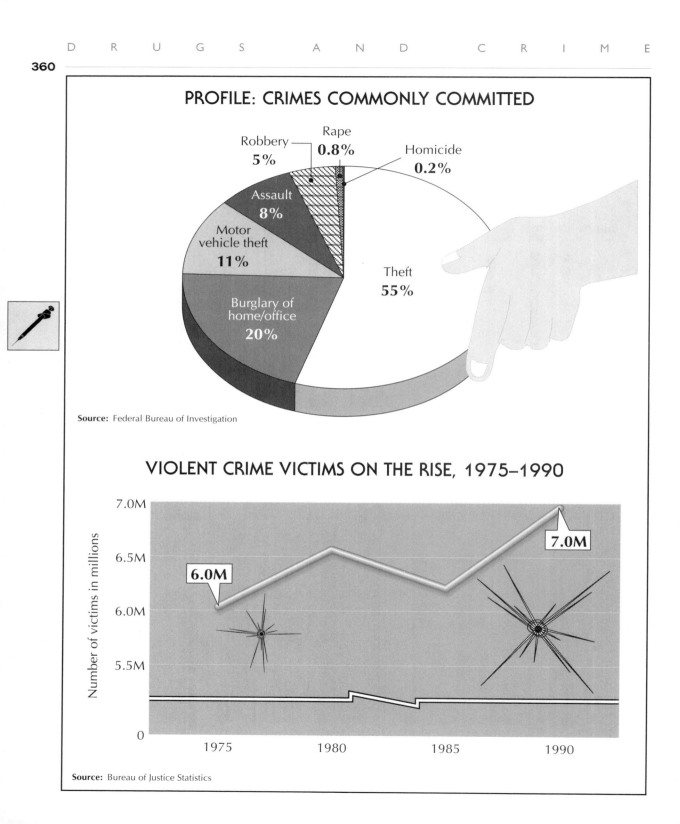

PROFILE: CRIMES COMMONLY COMMITTED

Robbery
5%

Rape
0.8%

Homicide
0.2%

Assault
8%

Motor
vehicle theft
11%

Burglary of
home/office
20%

Theft
55%

Source: Federal Bureau of Investigation

VIOLENT CRIME VICTIMS ON THE RISE, 1975–1990

Number of victims in millions

7.0M

6.5M

6.0M

5.5M

0

6.0M

7.0M

1975   1980   1985   1990

Source: Bureau of Justice Statistics

PROFILE: CRIME VICTIMS, BY TYPES OF CRIME

(Rates per 1,000 persons or households)

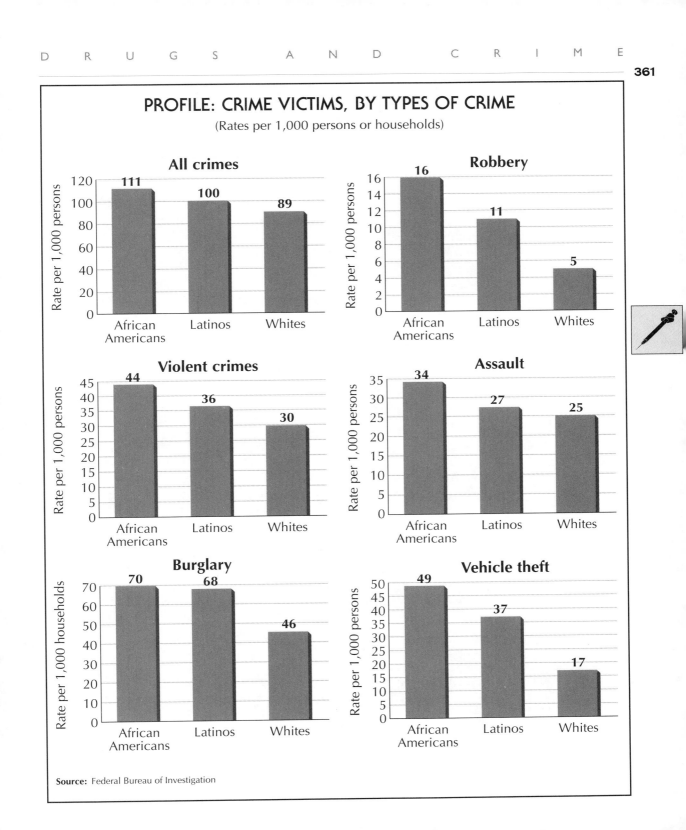

All crimes

- African Americans: 111
- Latinos: 100
- Whites: 89

(Rate per 1,000 persons)

Robbery

- African Americans: 16
- Latinos: 11
- Whites: 5

(Rate per 1,000 persons)

Violent crimes

- African Americans: 44
- Latinos: 36
- Whites: 30

(Rate per 1,000 persons)

Assault

- African Americans: 34
- Latinos: 27
- Whites: 25

(Rate per 1,000 persons)

Burglary

- African Americans: 70
- Latinos: 68
- Whites: 46

(Rate per 1,000 households)

Vehicle theft

- African Americans: 49
- Latinos: 37
- Whites: 17

(Rate per 1,000 persons)

Source: Federal Bureau of Investigation

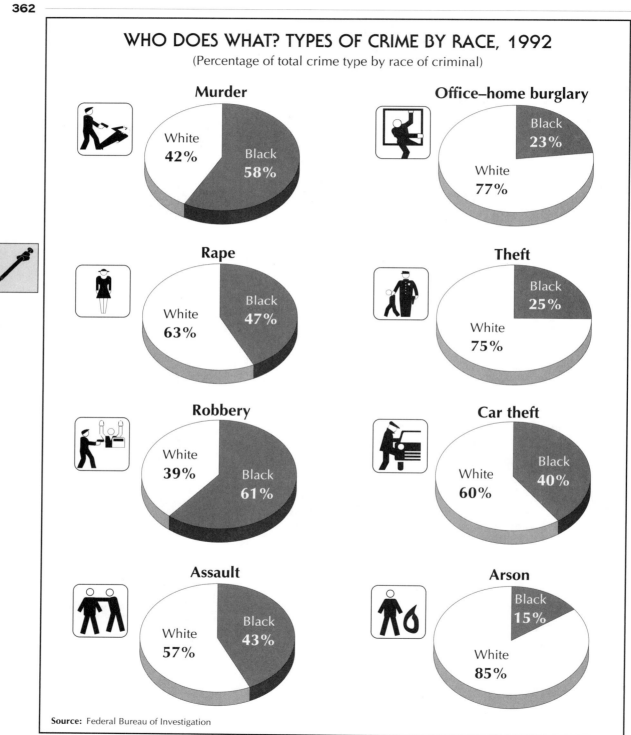

WHO DOES WHAT? TYPES OF CRIME BY RACE, 1992
(Percentage of total crime type by race of criminal)

Murder
White 42%
Black 58%

Office–home burglary
Black 23%
White 77%

Rape
White 63%
Black 47%

Theft
Black 25%
White 75%

Robbery
White 39%
Black 61%

Car theft
White 60%
Black 40%

Assault
White 57%
Black 43%

Arson
Black 15%
White 85%

Source: Federal Bureau of Investigation

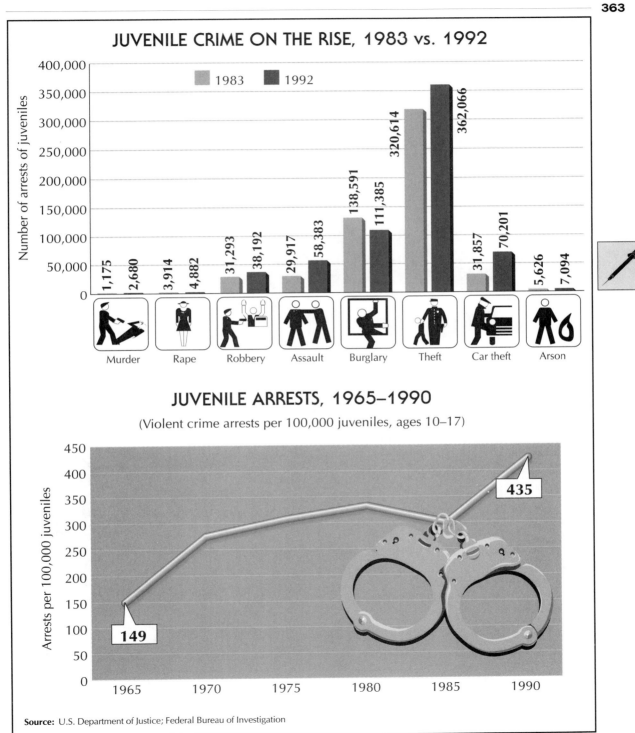

JUVENILE CRIME ON THE RISE, 1983 vs. 1992

Legend: 1983 (light), 1992 (dark)

Number of arrests of juveniles (y-axis: 0 to 400,000)

Crime	1983	1992
Murder	1,175	2,680
Rape	3,914	4,882
Robbery	31,293	38,192
Assault	29,917	58,383
Burglary	138,591	111,385
Theft	320,614	362,066
Car theft	31,857	70,201
Arson	5,626	7,094

JUVENILE ARRESTS, 1965–1990

(Violent crime arrests per 100,000 juveniles, ages 10–17)

Arrests per 100,000 juveniles (y-axis: 0 to 450)

x-axis: 1965, 1970, 1975, 1980, 1985, 1990

149 (1965) ... 435 (1990)

Source: U.S. Department of Justice; Federal Bureau of Investigation

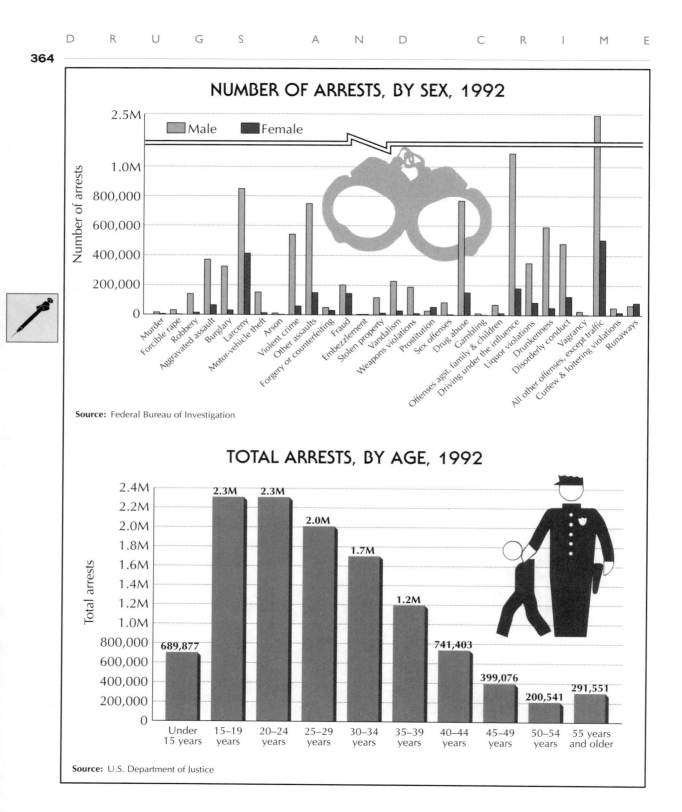

NUMBER OF ARRESTS, BY SEX, 1992

Male   Female

Number of arrests

2.5M
1.0M
800,000
600,000
400,000
200,000
0

Murder, Forcible rape, Robbery, Aggravated assault, Burglary, Larceny, Motor-vehicle theft, Arson, Violent crime, Other assaults, Forgery or counterfeiting, Fraud, Embezzlement, Stolen property, Vandalism, Weapons violations, Prostitution, Sex offenses, Drug abuse, Gambling, Offenses agst. family & children, Driving under the influence, Liquor violations, Drunkenness, Disorderly conduct, Vagrancy, All other offenses, except traffic, Curfew & loitering violations, Runaways

Source: Federal Bureau of Investigation

TOTAL ARRESTS, BY AGE, 1992

Total arrests

2.4M
2.2M
2.0M
1.8M
1.6M
1.4M
1.2M
1.0M
800,000
600,000
400,000
200,000
0

Under 15 years	15–19 years	20–24 years	25–29 years	30–34 years	35–39 years	40–44 years	45–49 years	50–54 years	55 years and older
689,877	2.3M	2.3M	2.0M	1.7M	1.2M	741,403	399,076	200,541	291,551

Source: U.S. Department of Justice

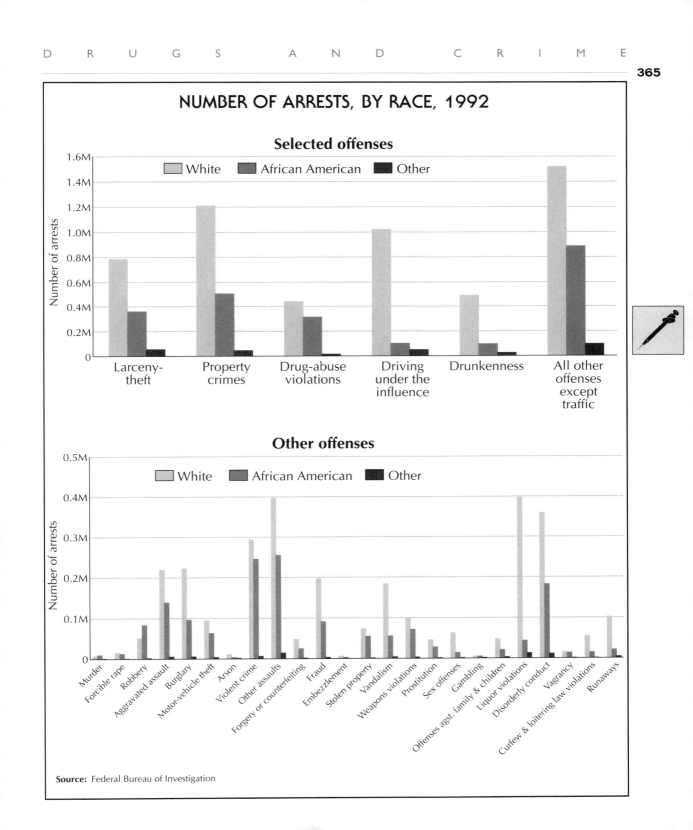

NUMBER OF ARRESTS, BY RACE, 1992

Selected offenses

Number of arrests

□ White   ■ African American   ■ Other

Categories: Larceny-theft | Property crimes | Drug-abuse violations | Driving under the influence | Drunkenness | All other offenses except traffic

Other offenses

Number of arrests

□ White   ■ African American   ■ Other

Categories: Murder | Forcible rape | Robbery | Aggravated assault | Burglary | Motor-vehicle theft | Arson | Violent crime | Other assaults | Forgery or counterfeiting | Fraud | Embezzlement | Stolen property | Vandalism | Weapons violations | Prostitution | Sex offenses | Gambling | Offenses agst. family & children | Liquor violations | Disorderly conduct | Vagrancy | Curfew & loitering law violations | Runaways

Source: Federal Bureau of Investigation

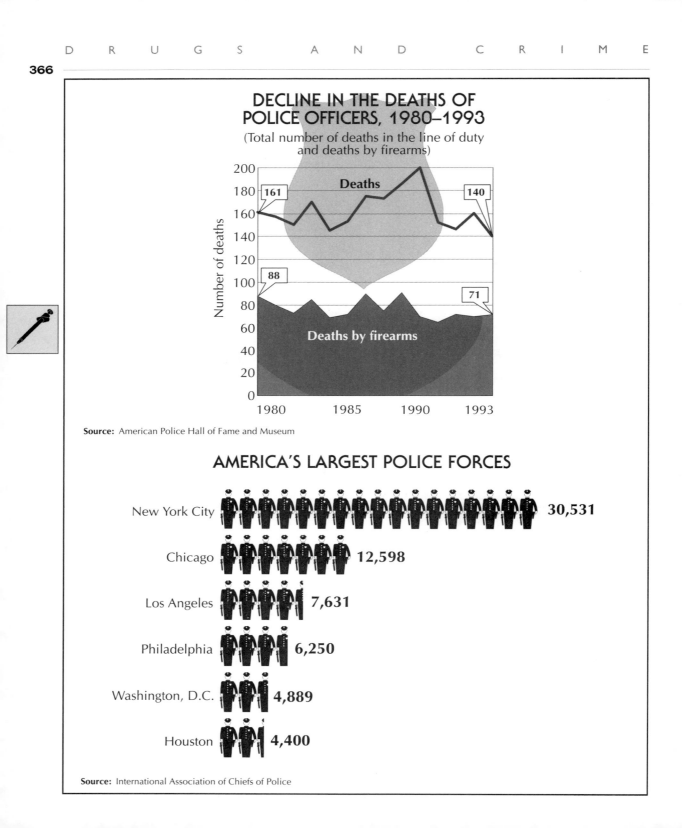

DECLINE IN THE DEATHS OF POLICE OFFICERS, 1980–1993
(Total number of deaths in the line of duty and deaths by firearms)

Source: American Police Hall of Fame and Museum

AMERICA'S LARGEST POLICE FORCES

New York City — **30,531**

Chicago — **12,598**

Los Angeles — **7,631**

Philadelphia — **6,250**

Washington, D.C. — **4,889**

Houston — **4,400**

Source: International Association of Chiefs of Police

TEACHERS AS VICTIMS OF CRIMES

Percentage of teachers in U.S. who say they have been:

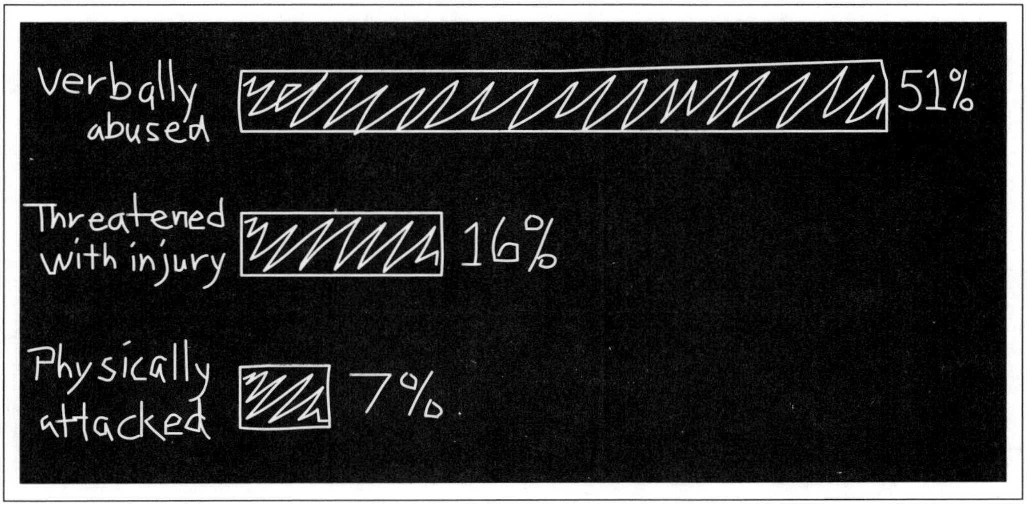

verbally abused — 51%

Threatened with injury — 16%

Physically attacked — 7%

Source: Carnegie Foundation

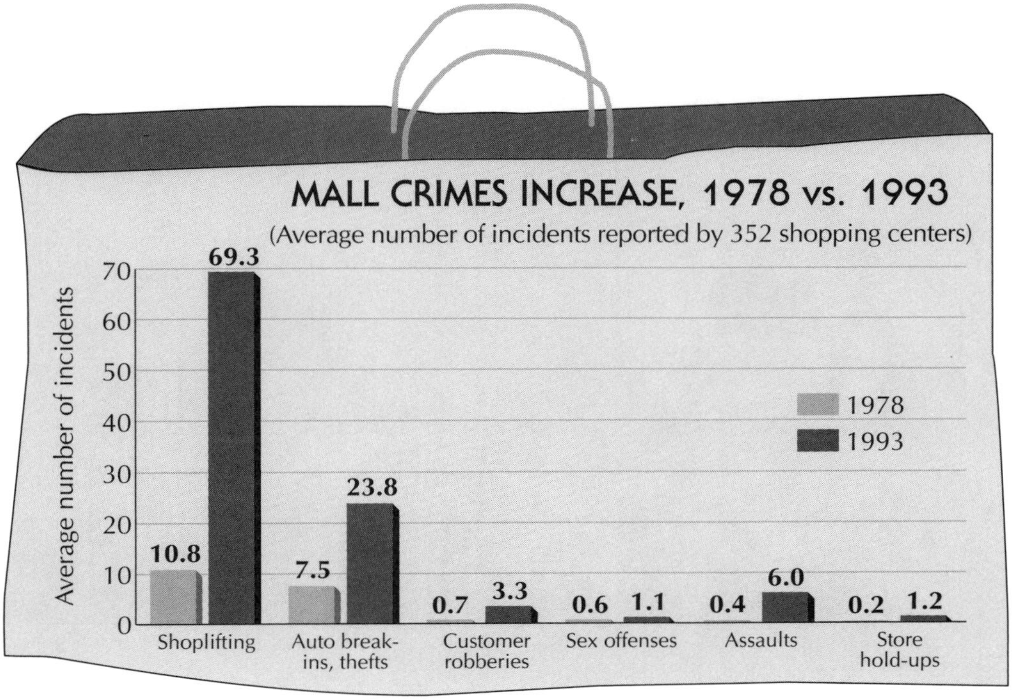

MALL CRIMES INCREASE, 1978 vs. 1993

(Average number of incidents reported by 352 shopping centers)

	1978	1993
Shoplifting	10.8	69.3
Auto break-ins, thefts	7.5	23.8
Customer robberies	0.7	3.3
Sex offenses	0.6	1.1
Assaults	0.4	6.0
Store hold-ups	0.2	1.2

Average number of incidents

Source: Statistics based on Burns Security Institute survey

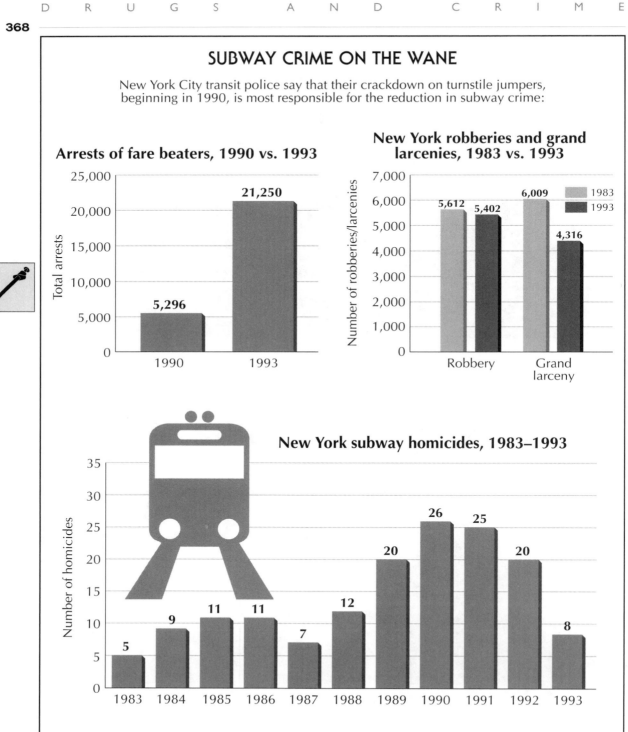

SUBWAY CRIME ON THE WANE

New York City transit police say that their crackdown on turnstile jumpers, beginning in 1990, is most responsible for the reduction in subway crime:

Arrests of fare beaters, 1990 vs. 1993

Total arrests

- 1990: 5,296
- 1993: 21,250

New York robberies and grand larcenies, 1983 vs. 1993

Number of robberies/larcenies

	1983	1993
Robbery	5,612	5,402
Grand larceny	6,009	4,316

New York subway homicides, 1983–1993

Number of homicides

1983	1984	1985	1986	1987	1988	1989	1990	1991	1992	1993
5	9	11	11	7	12	20	26	25	20	8

Source: New York Transit Police

STATE POLICIES ON TV CAMERAS IN COURT

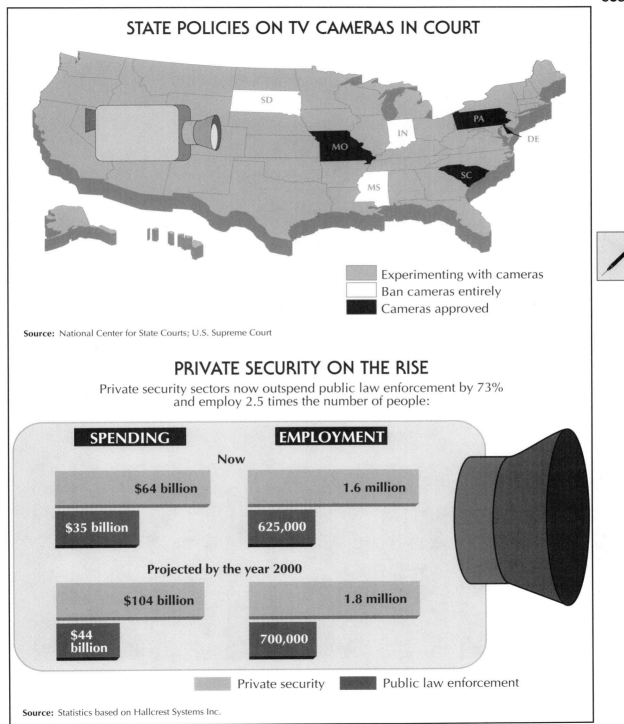

SD

IN

PA

DE

MO

SC

MS

Experimenting with cameras
Ban cameras entirely
Cameras approved

Source: National Center for State Courts; U.S. Supreme Court

PRIVATE SECURITY ON THE RISE

Private security sectors now outspend public law enforcement by 73%
and employ 2.5 times the number of people:

SPENDING	EMPLOYMENT

Now

$64 billion — 1.6 million

$35 billion — 625,000

Projected by the year 2000

$104 billion — 1.8 million

$44 billion — 700,000

Private security   Public law enforcement

Source: Statistics based on Hallcrest Systems Inc.

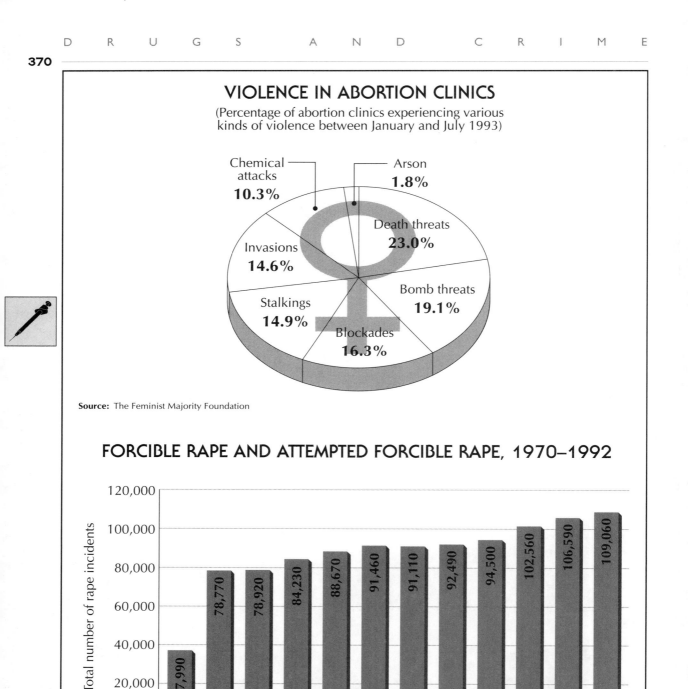

VIOLENCE IN ABORTION CLINICS
(Percentage of abortion clinics experiencing various
kinds of violence between January and July 1993)

Chemical attacks
10.3%

Arson
1.8%

Death threats
23.0%

Invasions
14.6%

Bomb threats
19.1%

Stalkings
14.9%

Blockades
16.3%

Source: The Feminist Majority Foundation

FORCIBLE RAPE AND ATTEMPTED FORCIBLE RAPE, 1970–1992

Total number of rape incidents

Year	Incidents
1970	37,990
1982	78,770
1983	78,920
1984	84,230
1985	88,670
1986	91,460
1987	91,110
1988	92,490
1989	94,500
1990	102,560
1991	106,590
1992	109,060

Source: Federal Bureau of Investigation

SEXUAL HARASSMENT COMPLAINTS BY EMPLOYEES ON THE RISE, 1989–1993

- 1989: 5,603
- 1990: 6,128
- 1991: 6,892
- 1992: 10,578
- 1993: 12,537

Source: Equal Employment Opportunity Commission

MALE SEXUAL HARASSMENT COMPLAINTS GROW, 1991–1993
(Number of sexual harassment cases filed by men against women)

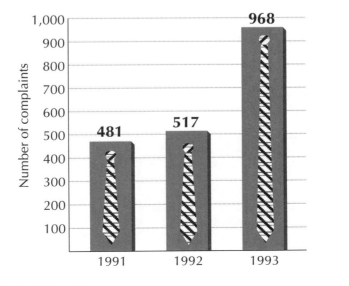

- 1991: 481
- 1992: 517
- 1993: 968

Source: Equal Employment Opportunity Commission

HOMICIDE

Homicide—the killing of one person by another—is one of the top 10 causes of death in the United States. It is an event that always grabs headlines and inspires fascination on the part of the American public.

Homicide is not necessarily a crime. Killing in self-defense, to protect family members from grave bodily harm, or to prevent a felony is considered justifiable homicide. Killing someone accidentally, without gross negligence, is considered excusable homicide. There are two types of criminal homicide: murder and manslaughter. A charge of murder generally requires concrete proof of malice, or deliberate intent to kill. Manslaughter is unplanned homicide, done without malice or intent to kill.

The number of criminal homicides in the U.S. increased from approximately 19,000 in 1985 to 23,800 in 1992. Males were the victims in more than 75% of the cases, and more blacks were killed than whites. Guns were the overwhelming weapon of choice, used in the great majority of homicide incidents.

A detailed government study of 8,063 homicides found that only 20% of the victims were killed by strangers; 64% were killed by acquaintances, and 16% were related to their killers. In family murder cases, wives were the most frequent victims. One-fifth of family murders, however, involved parents killing their children. About half the defendants in family killings had been arrested previously, as compared to three-quarters of the defendants in non-family killings.

FINGERTIP FACTS

☛ In 1985, there were about 19,000 criminal homicides in the U.S., or 7.9 per 100,000 population; in 1992, there were 23,800, or 9.3 per 100,000 population.

☛ In 1992, the states with the highest criminal homicide rates were Louisiana (17.4 per 100,000 population), New York (13.2), California (12.7), and Texas (12.7). South Dakota (0.6), New Hampshire (1.6), and Iowa (1.6) had the lowest rates.

☛ Most homicide victims are under age 30.

☛ African Americans were victims in almost 50% of criminal homicides in 1992, even though they made up only 12.5% of the U.S. population.

☛ Black males ages 15 to 19 are more than 10 times as likely to be shot to death as are white males of that age group.

☛ Juvenile arrests for criminal homicide increased by almost 150% between 1970 and 1992.

☛ Mothers are more likely than fathers to murder their children; 64% of mothers' victims are sons, as compared to 48% of fathers' victims.

☛ Almost one-third of all murders committed in the U.S. are the result of an argument.

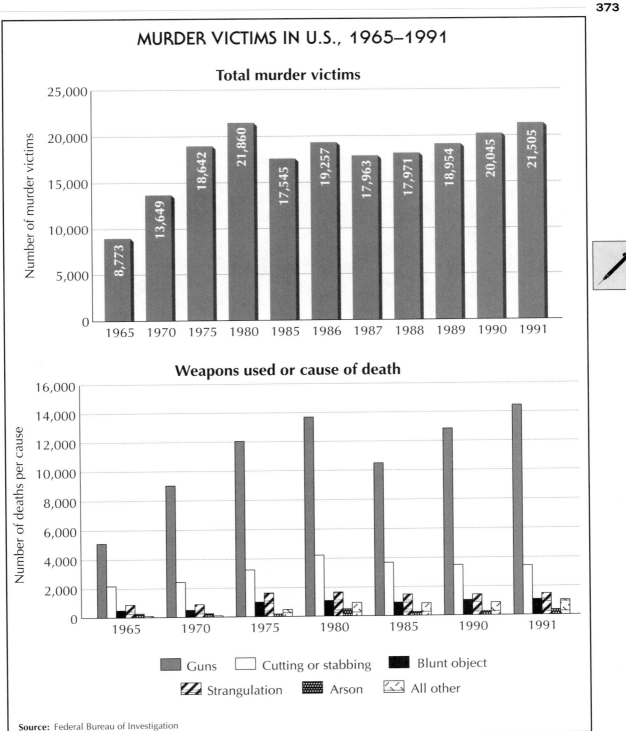

MURDER VICTIMS IN U.S., 1965–1991

Total murder victims

Number of murder victims

Year	Victims
1965	8,773
1970	13,649
1975	18,642
1980	21,860
1985	17,545
1986	19,257
1987	17,963
1988	17,971
1989	18,954
1990	20,045
1991	21,505

Weapons used or cause of death

Number of deaths per cause

Guns   Cutting or stabbing   Blunt object   Strangulation   Arson   All other

Source: Federal Bureau of Investigation

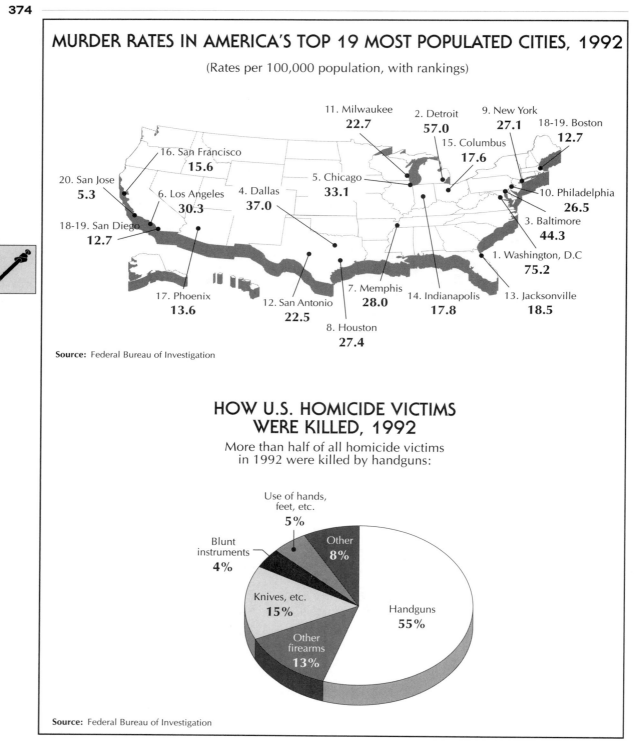

MURDER RATES IN AMERICA'S TOP 19 MOST POPULATED CITIES, 1992

(Rates per 100,000 population, with rankings)

11. Milwaukee **22.7**

2. Detroit **57.0**

9. New York **27.1**

18-19. Boston **12.7**

15. Columbus **17.6**

16. San Francisco **15.6**

5. Chicago **33.1**

10. Philadelphia **26.5**

20. San Jose **5.3**

6. Los Angeles **30.3**

4. Dallas **37.0**

3. Baltimore **44.3**

18-19. San Diego **12.7**

1. Washington, D.C **75.2**

17. Phoenix **13.6**

12. San Antonio **22.5**

7. Memphis **28.0**

14. Indianapolis **17.8**

13. Jacksonville **18.5**

8. Houston **27.4**

Source: Federal Bureau of Investigation

HOW U.S. HOMICIDE VICTIMS WERE KILLED, 1992

More than half of all homicide victims in 1992 were killed by handguns:

Use of hands, feet, etc. **5%**

Other **8%**

Blunt instruments **4%**

Knives, etc. **15%**

Other firearms **13%**

Handguns **55%**

Source: Federal Bureau of Investigation

HOMICIDE IS IN THE TOP 10 KILLERS

(Number of deaths in 1991 per 100,000 people)

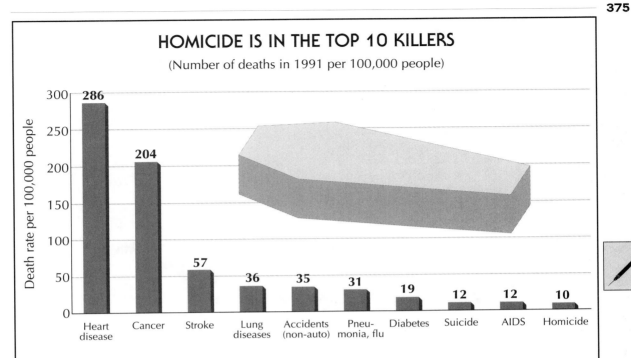

Death rate per 100,000 people

Heart disease	286
Cancer	204
Stroke	57
Lung diseases	36
Accidents (non-auto)	35
Pneumonia, flu	31
Diabetes	19
Suicide	12
AIDS	12
Homicide	10

Source: National Center for Health Statistics

MOST HOMICIDE VICTIMS ARE YOUNG

(The ages of 22,231 homicide victims
for whom ages were known in 1992)

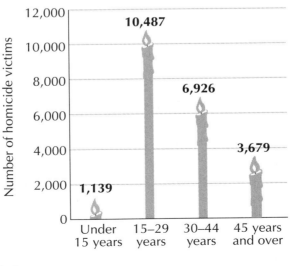

Number of homicide victims

Under 15 years	1,139
15–29 years	10,487
30–44 years	6,926
45 years and over	3,679

Source: Federal Bureau of Investigation

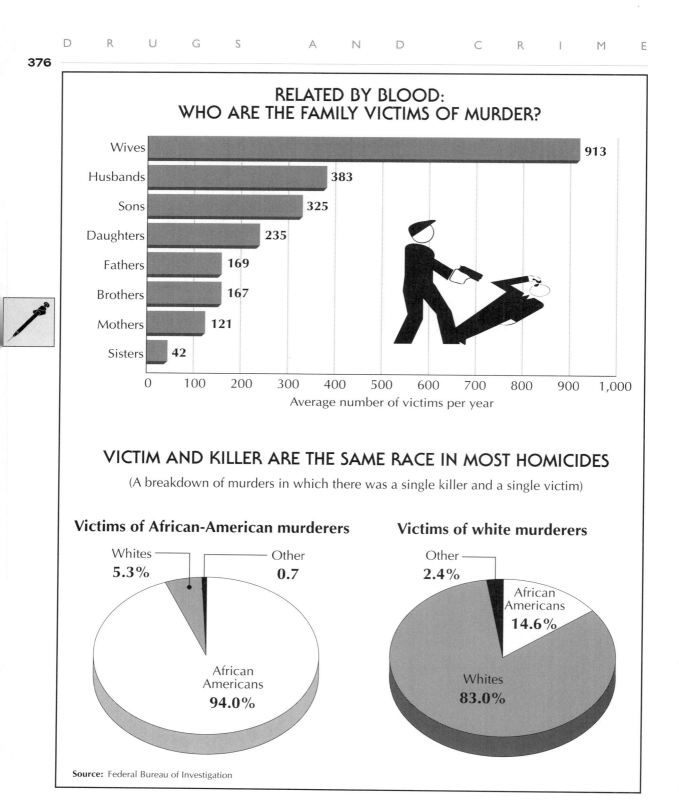

RELATED BY BLOOD:
WHO ARE THE FAMILY VICTIMS OF MURDER?

Wives	913
Husbands	383
Sons	325
Daughters	235
Fathers	169
Brothers	167
Mothers	121
Sisters	42

0   100   200   300   400   500   600   700   800   900   1,000

Average number of victims per year

VICTIM AND KILLER ARE THE SAME RACE IN MOST HOMICIDES

(A breakdown of murders in which there was a single killer and a single victim)

Victims of African-American murderers

Whites 5.3%
Other 0.7
African Americans 94.0%

Victims of white murderers

Other 2.4%
African Americans 14.6%
Whites 83.0%

Source: Federal Bureau of Investigation

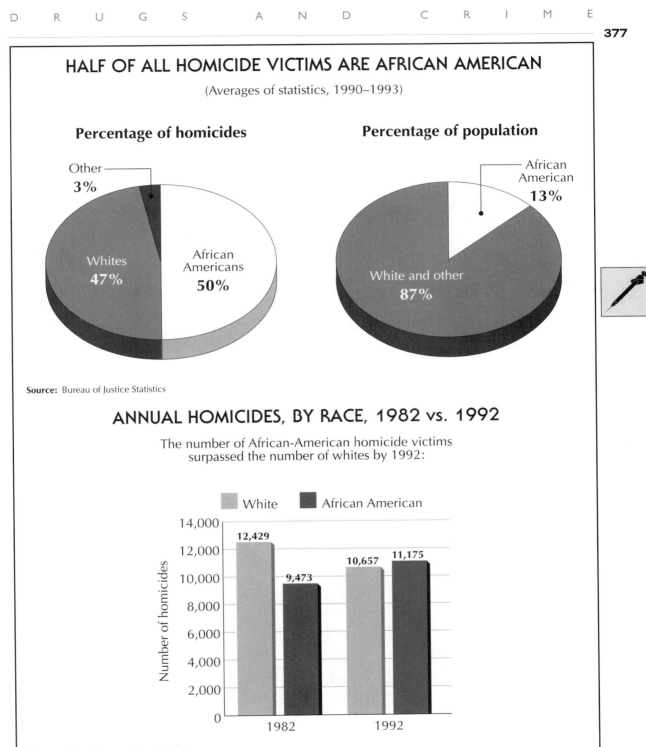

HALF OF ALL HOMICIDE VICTIMS ARE AFRICAN AMERICAN

(Averages of statistics, 1990–1993)

Percentage of homicides

Other
3%

Whites
47%

African
Americans
50%

Percentage of population

African
American
13%

White and other
87%

Source: Bureau of Justice Statistics

ANNUAL HOMICIDES, BY RACE, 1982 vs. 1992

The number of African-American homicide victims
surpassed the number of whites by 1992:

White   African American

Number of homicides

	1982		1992	
White	12,429		10,657	
African American		9,473		11,175

Source: Federal Bureau of Investigation

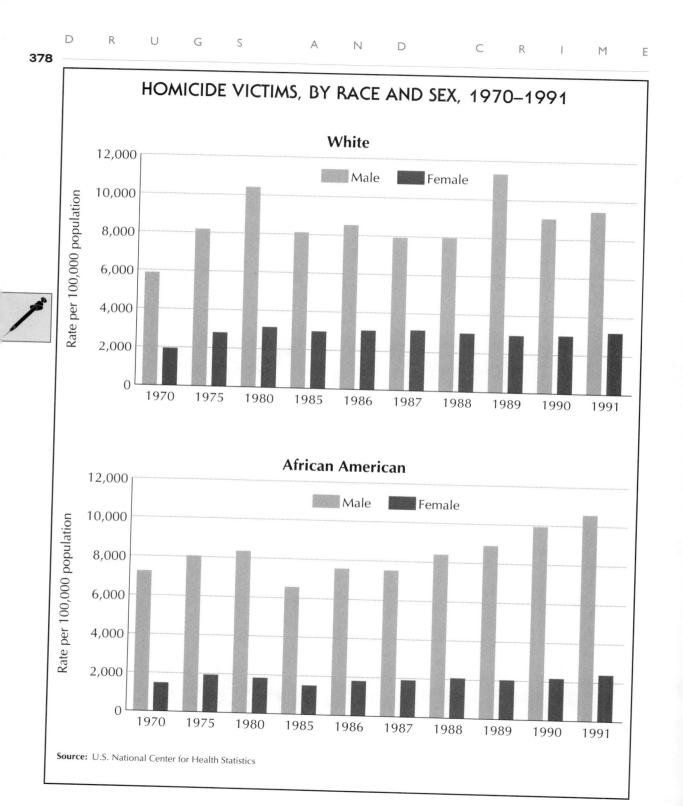

HOMICIDE VICTIMS, BY RACE AND SEX, 1970–1991

White

Rate per 100,000 population

■ Male ■ Female

1970, 1975, 1980, 1985, 1986, 1987, 1988, 1989, 1990, 1991

African American

Rate per 100,000 population

■ Male ■ Female

1970, 1975, 1980, 1985, 1986, 1987, 1988, 1989, 1990, 1991

Source: U.S. National Center for Health Statistics

GUNS ARE MOST USED WEAPONS IN HOMICIDE, 1976–1991

(Weapons used in homicides by juveniles under age 18)

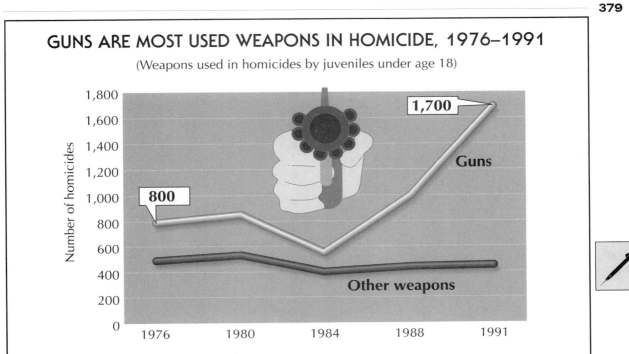

Source: U.S. Department of Justice; Federal Bureau of Investigation

HOMICIDE ARRESTS: YOUNG MEN, BY AGE GROUP, 1970–1991

(Rates per 100,000 population)

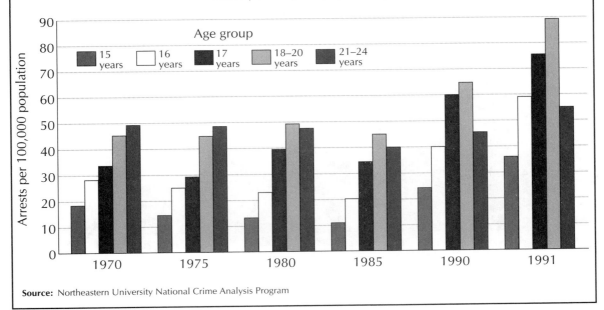

Source: Northeastern University National Crime Analysis Program

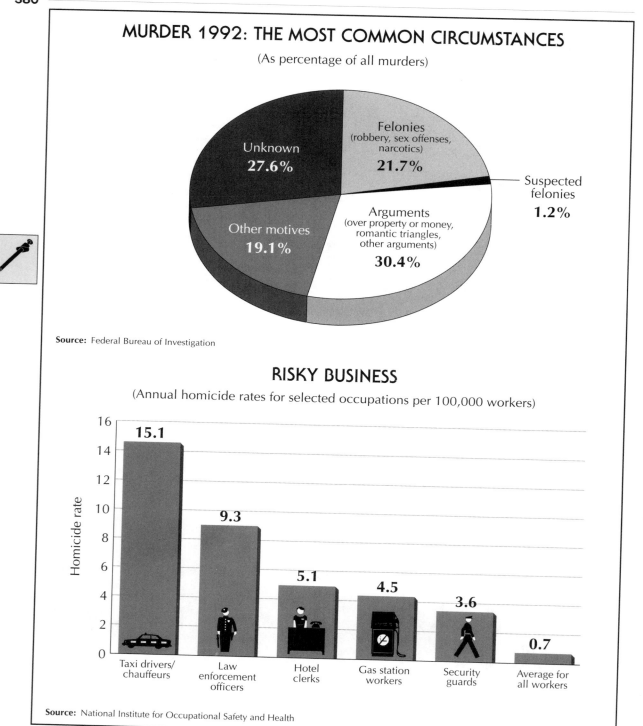

MURDER 1992: THE MOST COMMON CIRCUMSTANCES

(As percentage of all murders)

- Unknown **27.6%**
- Felonies (robbery, sex offenses, narcotics) **21.7%**
- Suspected felonies **1.2%**
- Arguments (over property or money, romantic triangles, other arguments) **30.4%**
- Other motives **19.1%**

Source: Federal Bureau of Investigation

RISKY BUSINESS

(Annual homicide rates for selected occupations per 100,000 workers)

Occupation	Homicide rate
Taxi drivers/chauffeurs	15.1
Law enforcement officers	9.3
Hotel clerks	5.1
Gas station workers	4.5
Security guards	3.6
Average for all workers	0.7

Source: National Institute for Occupational Safety and Health

MURDER VICTIMS BY SEX, 1992

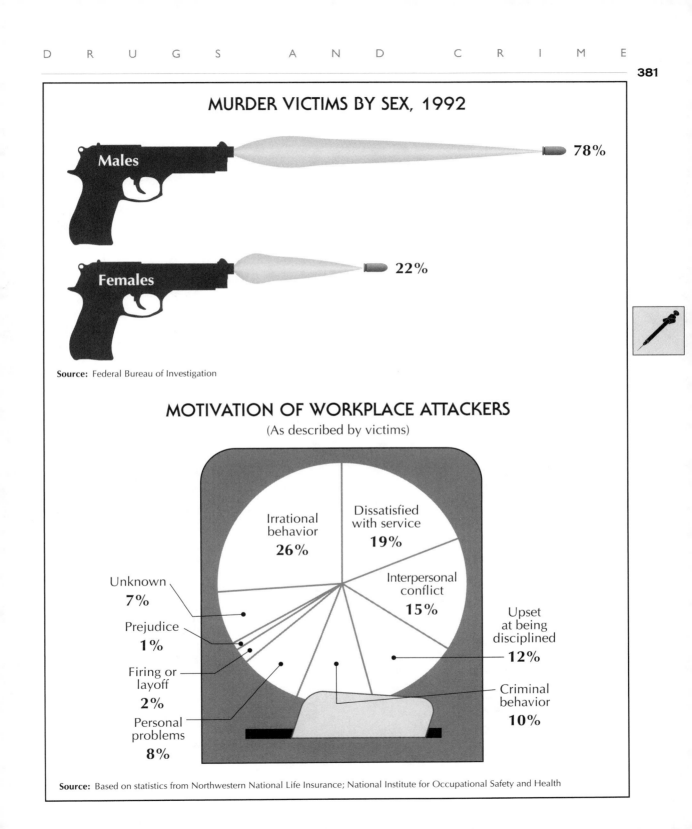

Males **78%**

Females **22%**

Source: Federal Bureau of Investigation

MOTIVATION OF WORKPLACE ATTACKERS
(As described by victims)

Irrational behavior **26%**

Dissatisfied with service **19%**

Interpersonal conflict **15%**

Upset at being disciplined **12%**

Criminal behavior **10%**

Unknown **7%**

Prejudice **1%**

Firing or layoff **2%**

Personal problems **8%**

Source: Based on statistics from Northwestern National Life Insurance; National Institute for Occupational Safety and Health

G U N S

Guns play a central role in many of the crimes committed in the U.S. In 1992, for example, handguns were used in 931,000 murders, rapes, robberies, and assaults. A growing amount of this violence is committed by teenagers, for whom firearms are the weapon of choice. Between 1984 and 1994, the number of gun homicides committed by teens nearly quadrupled. Other youths frequently are the targets. Every 2 hours, a U.S. child dies of a gunshot wound.

The widespread availability of guns is one of the nation's most controversial issues. Public opinion polls have repeatedly shown that a large majority of Americans favor stricter gun controls, believing that stricter regulation will help reduce gun-related crimes. A sizable minority, however, are strongly opposed to controls of any kind. For example, leaders of the National Rifle Association (NRA) —a tremendously powerful pro-gun organization that, in 1995, had 3.5 million members and revenues of $148 million—claim that any effort to control guns is an effort "to eliminate private firearms ownership completely and forever."

Despite strong NRA opposition in 1993, Congress passed the Brady Bill, which requires a 5-day waiting period for handgun purchases and background checks of people who buy guns. It also provided for a Crime Bill that bans 19 types of assault weapons. Both laws were applauded by police organizations nationwide. States and local communities also have enacted gun-control laws. The debate, however, continues. When Republicans won control of both houses of Congress in 1994, they vowed to repeal the assault weapons ban.

FINGERTIP FACTS

- In 1987, handguns were used in 666,000 U.S. crimes; in 1992, they were used in 931,000 crimes.

- In 1991, there were 38,317 firearm deaths in the U.S. Of these, suicide accounted for 18,526 deaths, homicide for 17,746.

- Handguns were used in 55.4% of U.S. homicides in 1992, up from 43.5% in 1982.

- Every 14 minutes during 1993, someone in the U.S. died of a gunshot wound, nearly half in homicides. In that same year, there were about 1,600 accidental firearm deaths, an increase of 7% from 1992.

- The U.S. firearms industry is booming. U.S. gun and ammunition production nearly doubled from 1987 to 1992.

- According to a December 1993 CNN/Gallup poll, 87% of Americans favored the Brady Bill and 77% favored the ban on assault weapons.

- According to the National School Safety Center, some 135,000 children carry guns into school every day. About 25% of the nation's major urban school districts have installed metal detectors.

- In 1992, handguns were used in the murders of 13 people in Australia, 36 in Sweden, 128 in Canada ... and 13,220 in the United States.

HANDGUNS AND HOMICIDES, 1982 vs. 1992

Handguns were used in 55.4% of all homicides in 1992, up from 43.5% in 1982:

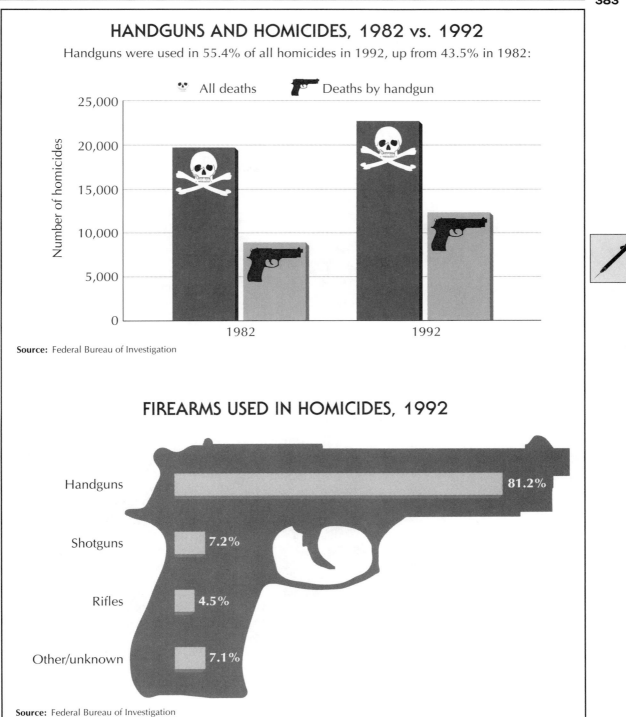

Source: Federal Bureau of Investigation

FIREARMS USED IN HOMICIDES, 1992

Handguns — 81.2%

Shotguns — 7.2%

Rifles — 4.5%

Other/unknown — 7.1%

Source: Federal Bureau of Investigation

TOP 5 STATES WITH THE HIGHEST PERCENTAGE OF HOMICIDES BY FIREARM, 1991

Authorities say there are more than 200 million firearms in circulation in the U.S. Firearms were used in most homicides in 1991, particularly in the 5 states with the highest number of slayings:

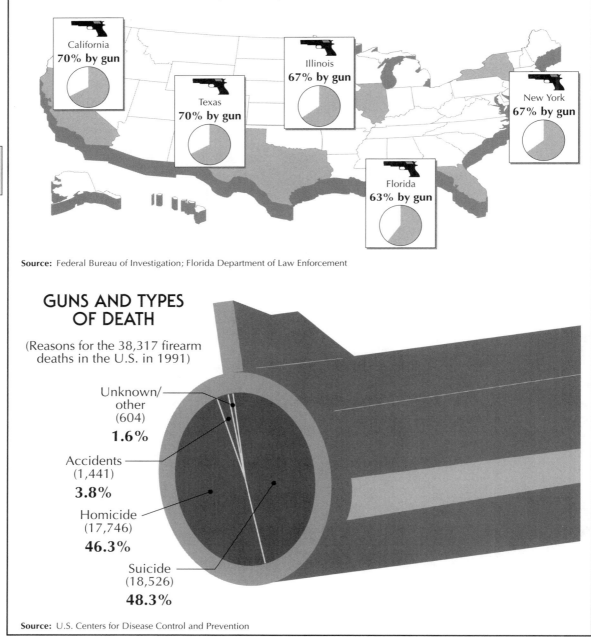

Source: Federal Bureau of Investigation; Florida Department of Law Enforcement

GUNS AND TYPES OF DEATH

(Reasons for the 38,317 firearm deaths in the U.S. in 1991)

Unknown/
other
(604)
1.6%

Accidents
(1,441)
3.8%

Homicide
(17,746)
46.3%

Suicide
(18,526)
48.3%

Source: U.S. Centers for Disease Control and Prevention

WHO'S KILLING WHOM?

Firearms were used in 7 of 10 U.S. homicides in 1992; usually that firearm was a handgun:

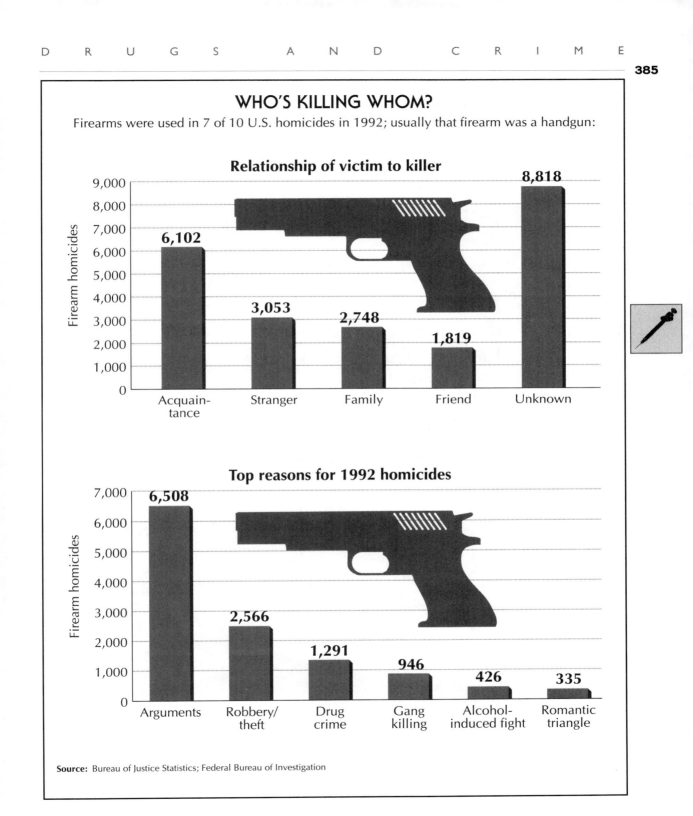

Relationship of victim to killer

Category	Firearm homicides
Acquaintance	6,102
Stranger	3,053
Family	2,748
Friend	1,819
Unknown	8,818

Top reasons for 1992 homicides

Category	Firearm homicides
Arguments	6,508
Robbery/theft	2,566
Drug crime	1,291
Gang killing	946
Alcohol-induced fight	426
Romantic triangle	335

Source: Bureau of Justice Statistics; Federal Bureau of Investigation

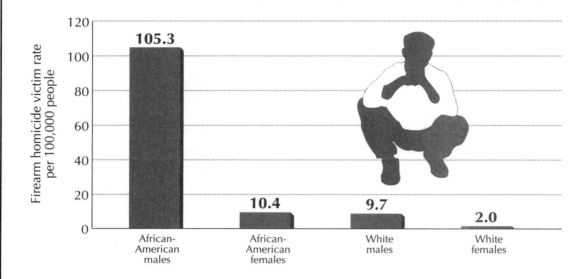

MORE YOUNG AFRICAN-AMERICAN MALES SHOT TO DEATH

Young black males are 10 times more likely than white males to be firearm homicide victims. Firearm homicides per 100,000 people in the 15–19 years age group:

- African-American males: **105.3**
- African-American females: **10.4**
- White males: **9.7**
- White females: **2.0**

Firearm homicide victim rate per 100,000 people

Source: U.S. Centers for Disease Control and Prevention

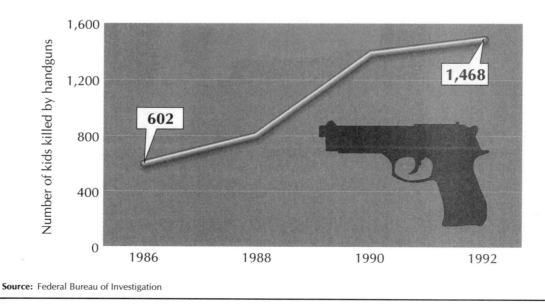

KIDS KILLED IN HANDGUN HOMICIDES, 1982–1992

Number of kids killed by handguns

602 ... **1,468**

1986 1988 1990 1992

Source: Federal Bureau of Investigation

WHICH GUNS DO KIDS HAVE?

A survey of 758 male students at 10 inner-city high schools found that 22% had possessed one or more firearms at some time. Types of guns that the 22% possessed:

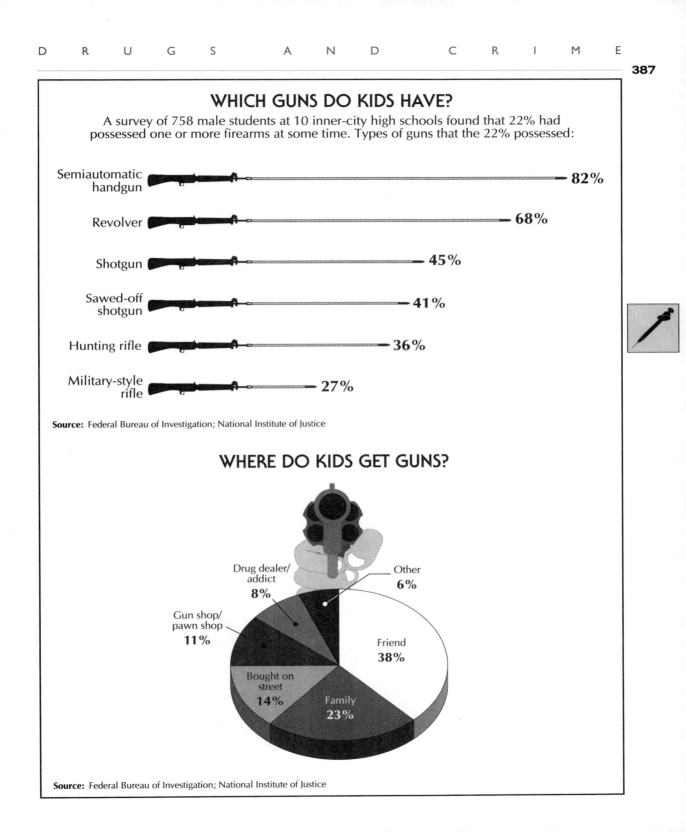

Semiautomatic handgun	**82%**
Revolver	**68%**
Shotgun	**45%**
Sawed-off shotgun	**41%**
Hunting rifle	**36%**
Military-style rifle	**27%**

Source: Federal Bureau of Investigation; National Institute of Justice

WHERE DO KIDS GET GUNS?

Drug dealer/addict
8%

Other
6%

Gun shop/pawn shop
11%

Friend
38%

Bought on street
14%

Family
23%

Source: Federal Bureau of Investigation; National Institute of Justice

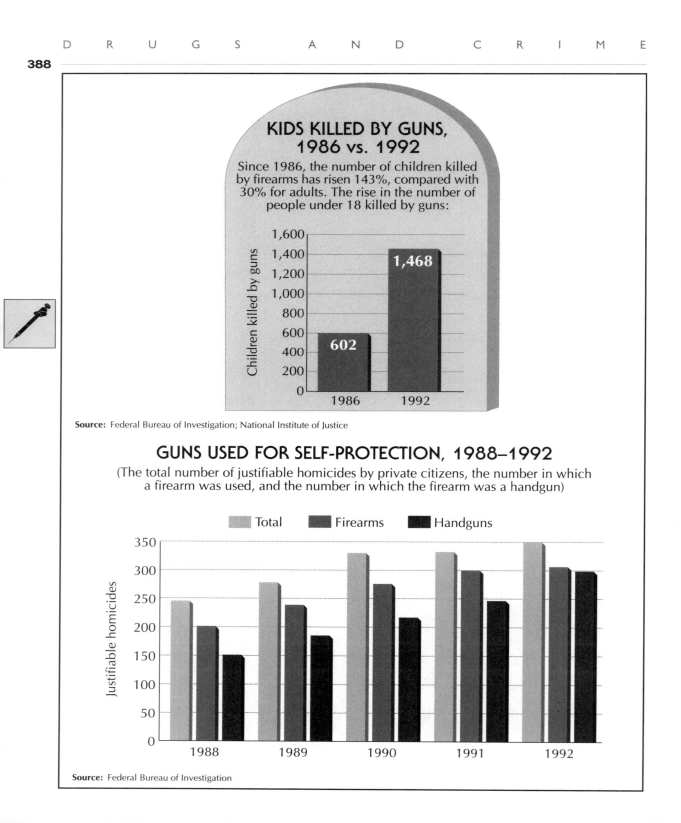

KIDS KILLED BY GUNS, 1986 vs. 1992

Since 1986, the number of children killed by firearms has risen 143%, compared with 30% for adults. The rise in the number of people under 18 killed by guns:

Source: Federal Bureau of Investigation; National Institute of Justice

GUNS USED FOR SELF-PROTECTION, 1988–1992

(The total number of justifiable homicides by private citizens, the number in which a firearm was used, and the number in which the firearm was a handgun)

Source: Federal Bureau of Investigation

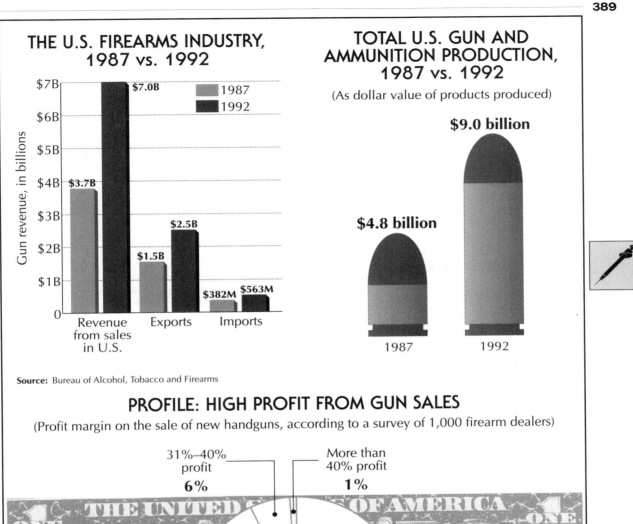

THE U.S. FIREARMS INDUSTRY, 1987 vs. 1992

1987
1992

Gun revenue, in billions

$7B — $7.0B
$6B
$5B
$4B — $3.7B
$3B
$2B — $2.5B
$1B — $1.5B
0 — $382M $563M

Revenue from sales in U.S.   Exports   Imports

Source: Bureau of Alcohol, Tobacco and Firearms

TOTAL U.S. GUN AND AMMUNITION PRODUCTION, 1987 vs. 1992

(As dollar value of products produced)

$9.0 billion

$4.8 billion

1987   1992

PROFILE: HIGH PROFIT FROM GUN SALES

(Profit margin on the sale of new handguns, according to a survey of 1,000 firearm dealers)

31%–40% profit
6%

More than 40% profit
1%

21%–30% profit
41%

10%–20% profit
52%

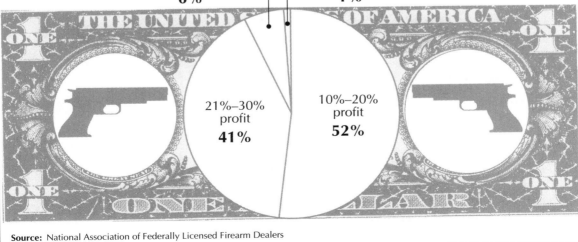

Source: National Association of Federally Licensed Firearm Dealers

JAIL

The U.S. has more people in jail and prison per capita than any other nation. In mid-1992, the U.S. had 444,584 jail inmates; it also had 847,271 inmates sentenced to terms of more than one year in federal and state prisons. Many U.S. jails and prisons are overcrowded, which has led to the early release of some convicts and a growing number who are placed instead under house arrest, where their movements may be electronically monitored.

Although the vast majority of people in U.S. jails and prisons are males, females make up a growing percentage of inmates. More and more juveniles are also spending time behind bars. Generally, juveniles are placed in special facilities apart from adult prisoners. There is a trend, however, to try and sentence some juveniles in adult court; for example, the 1994 federal crime bill permits juveniles ages 13 and older to be tried as adults in federal courts for such crimes as murder, rape, assault, and robbery.

Penalties for crimes vary widely from case to case and from one jurisdiction to another. Throughout the nation, it has been customary to fix minimum and maximum limitations on punishments for specific crimes; more recently, states have moved toward mandated sentences for certain crimes.

Capital punishment was suspended in the U.S. from 1967 to 1977, but was then resumed. There is strong support among Americans across the country for the death penalty, and, predictably, the number of executions has increased in recent years. Capital punishment is permitted in 38 states; in addition, some 60 crimes are subject to the federal death penalty. About 3,000 U.S. prisoners are currently on death row.

FINGERTIP FACTS

- In 1992, there were 847,271 prisoners in the U.S., an increase of 7% from 1991—and a whopping 168% increase from 1980. At the same time, the violent crime rate rose 27%.

- In the 10-year period between 1982 and 1992, the number of people in state and federal prisons more than doubled.

- In 1992, U.S. prisons held 847,271 inmates sentenced to more than one year, a rate of 330.2 per 100,000 population. This was an increase from 196,429 such prisoners in 1970, a rate of 96.7 per 100,000.

- Males in jail outnumber females by about 10 to 1.

- Federal, state, and local governments spent a total of about $25 billion on corrections in 1990. The equivalent of 556,000 full-time employees worked in corrections—a figure expected to increase more than 60% by the year 2005.

- A 1994 Gallup Poll indicated that 80% of Americans favor the death penalty for convicted murderers; their primary objective is revenge against the murderers, not any expectations that the death penalty will deter other criminals.

- Electrocution is the most frequently used method of execution in the U.S., followed closely by lethal injection. From 1977 to 1992, these methods combined were used in 96% of all executions.

PROFILE: U.S. JAILS AND PRISONS

The number of criminals in prisons in the U.S. in 1992 had increased by 168% since 1980, and the number in local jails more than doubled. The number of full-time law enforcement officers rose by 40%, yet the violent crime rate rose by 27%:

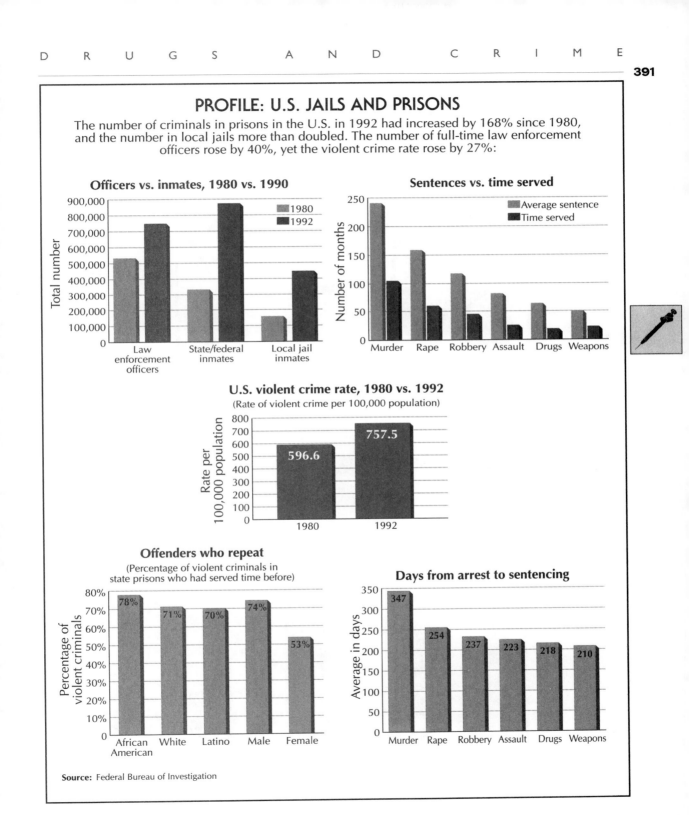

Officers vs. inmates, 1980 vs. 1990

Sentences vs. time served

U.S. violent crime rate, 1980 vs. 1992
(Rate of violent crime per 100,000 population)

Offenders who repeat
(Percentage of violent criminals in state prisons who had served time before)

Days from arrest to sentencing

Source: Federal Bureau of Investigation

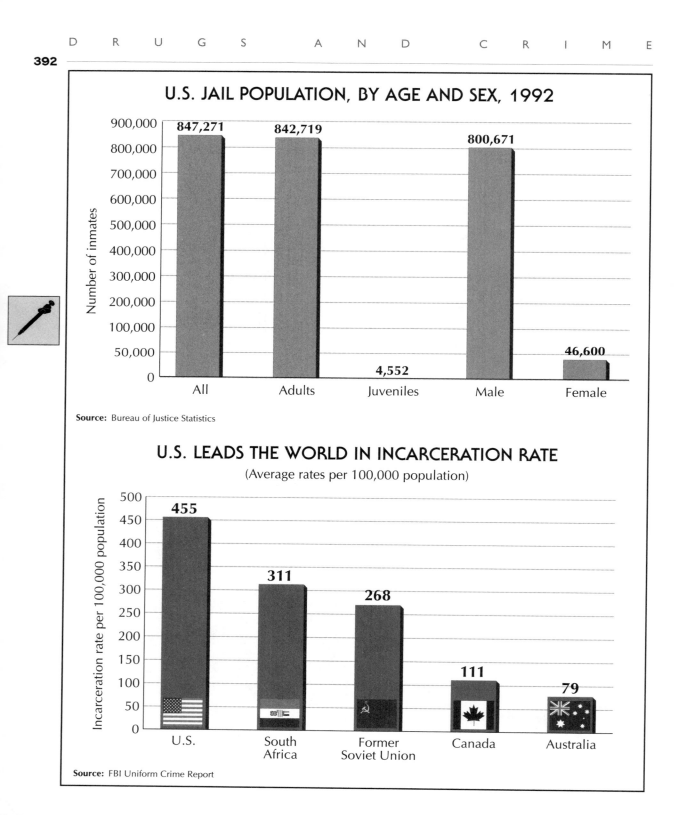

U.S. JAIL POPULATION, BY AGE AND SEX, 1992

Number of inmates

All	847,271
Adults	842,719
Juveniles	4,552
Male	800,671
Female	46,600

Source: Bureau of Justice Statistics

U.S. LEADS THE WORLD IN INCARCERATION RATE
(Average rates per 100,000 population)

Incarceration rate per 100,000 population

U.S.	455
South Africa	311
Former Soviet Union	268
Canada	111
Australia	79

Source: FBI Uniform Crime Report

PRISON POPULATION BOOMS AS THE CRIME RATE SOARS

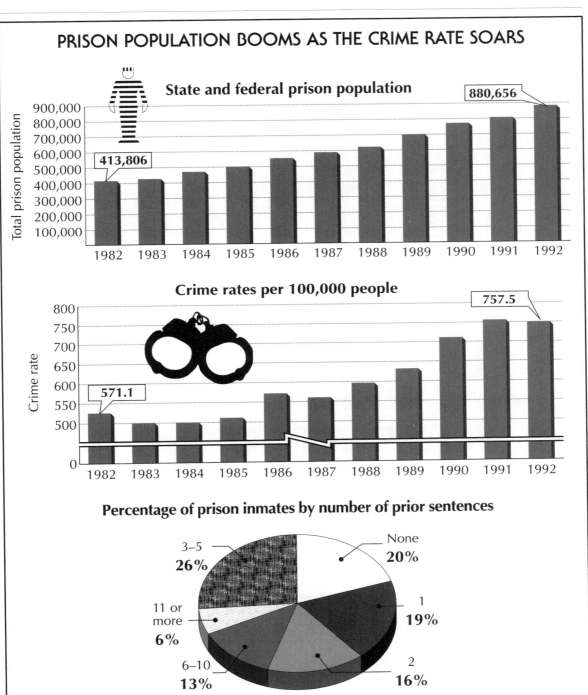

State and federal prison population

880,656

413,806

Total prison population

900,000
800,000
700,000
600,000
500,000
400,000
300,000
200,000
100,000

1982 1983 1984 1985 1986 1987 1988 1989 1990 1991 1992

Crime rates per 100,000 people

757.5

571.1

Crime rate

800
750
700
650
600
550
500

0

1982 1983 1984 1985 1986 1987 1988 1989 1990 1991 1992

Percentage of prison inmates by number of prior sentences

3–5
26%

None
20%

11 or more
6%

1
19%

6–10
13%

2
16%

Source: Bureau of Justice Statistics

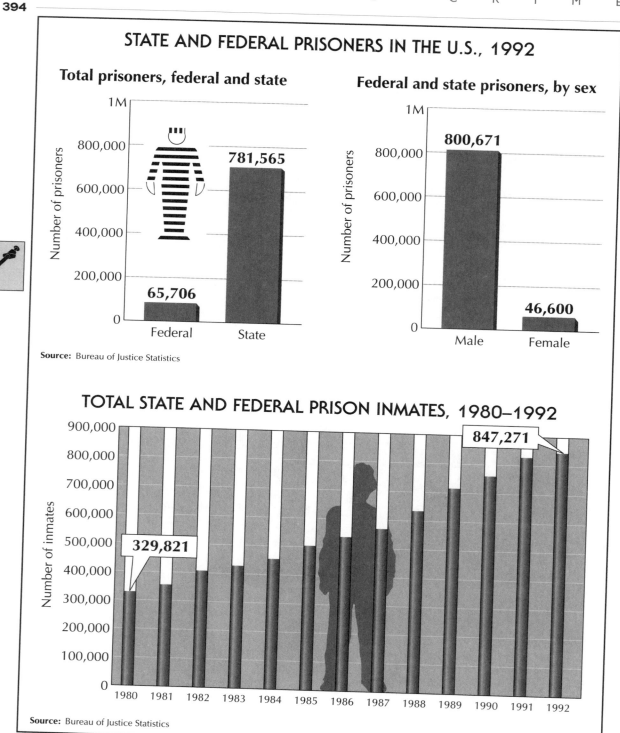

STATE AND FEDERAL PRISONERS IN THE U.S., 1992

Total prisoners, federal and state

- 781,565 (State)
- 65,706 (Federal)

Federal and state prisoners, by sex

- 800,671 (Male)
- 46,600 (Female)

Source: Bureau of Justice Statistics

TOTAL STATE AND FEDERAL PRISON INMATES, 1980–1992

- 329,821
- 847,271

Source: Bureau of Justice Statistics

DOING TIME FOR CRIME

Non-violent drug offenders account for 21.1% of the federal prison population.
Punishments for first-time drug offenses in months served, compared with other offenses:

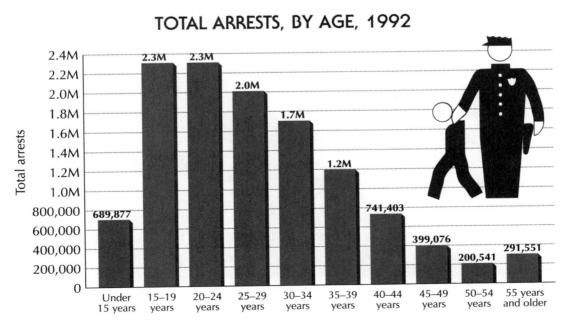

Number of months served

Drugs	Kidnapping	Robbery	Arson	Extortion	Sex abuse	Assault	Firearms	Man-slaughter
60	57	51	36	36	27	24	15	12

Source: U.S. Sentencing Commission; U.S. Justice Department

TOTAL ARRESTS, BY AGE, 1992

Total arrests

Under 15 years	15–19 years	20–24 years	25–29 years	30–34 years	35–39 years	40–44 years	45–49 years	50–54 years	55 years and older
689,877	2.3M	2.3M	2.0M	1.7M	1.2M	741,403	399,076	200,541	291,551

Source: U.S. Department of Justice

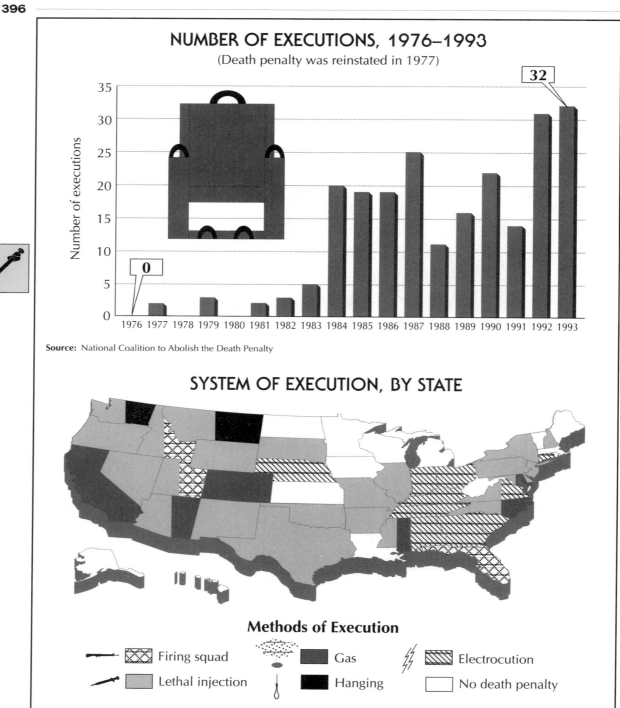

NUMBER OF EXECUTIONS, 1976–1993
(Death penalty was reinstated in 1977)

Source: National Coalition to Abolish the Death Penalty

SYSTEM OF EXECUTION, BY STATE

Methods of Execution

Firing squad

Lethal injection

Gas

Hanging

Electrocution

No death penalty

* Some states use more than one method of execution
Source: Bureau of Justice Statistics

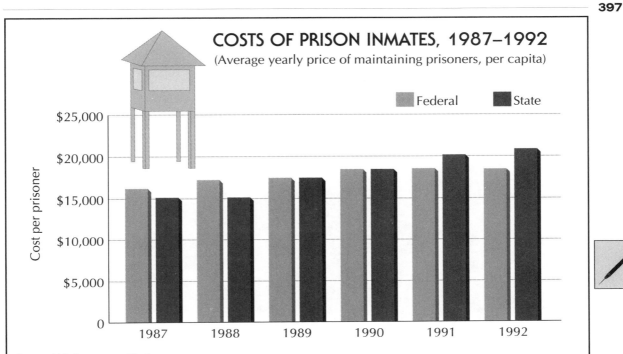

COSTS OF PRISON INMATES, 1987–1992
(Average yearly price of maintaining prisoners, per capita)

Federal   State

Cost per prisoner

$25,000
$20,000
$15,000
$10,000
$5,000
0

1987   1988   1989   1990   1991   1992

Source: U.S. Department of Justice

ELECTRONIC HOUSE ARRESTS GROW, 1986 vs. 1993

Because prison populations continue to climb rapidly, electronic monitoring programs are becoming more commonplace. Number of convicts under electronic house arrest:

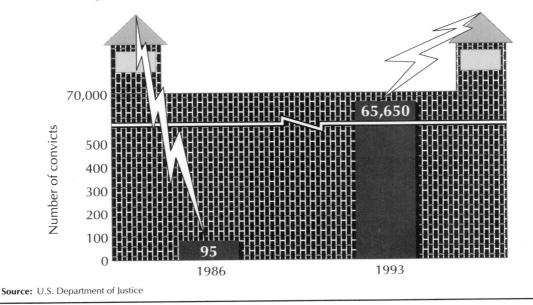

Number of convicts

70,000

65,650

500
400
300
200
100
0

95

1986   1993

Source: U.S. Department of Justice

6

ENVIRONMENT AND GEOGRAPHY

GEOGRAPHY AND CLIMATE

The United States covers a total area of 3,732,396 square miles—3,536,338 square miles of land plus 196,058 square miles of inland and coastal waters. Of its 50 states, 49 lie on the North American continent; the 50th, Hawaii, consists of a group of islands in the Pacific Ocean. The nation's capital city, Washington, D.C., is not part of any state—it is situated on the Potomac River between Maryland and Virginia. The nation also administers several overseas territories and possessions, including the U.S. Virgin Islands, Puerto Rico, Guam, American Samoa, and the Northern Mariana Islands.

America's topography varies tremendously across the nation. In the continental U.S., there are highlands in the East and mountains in the West, with wide plains in between. Each of these three broad regions includes many smaller landforms, including vast deserts and dramatic seashores, deep-green plateaus and windswept sandhills, crystal lakes and deep canyons.

Because of the nation's great size and its varied topography, the U.S. experiences widely ranging weather. A region's climate—the average weather over a long period of time—is a factor of many elements, including latitude, prevailing winds, elevation, and distance from oceans. Earth's three major climatic zones—polar, temperate, and tropical —are all represented within the boundaries of the U.S.

FINGERTIP FACTS

- The major U.S. inland waterway is the Mississippi River, which is esti-mated at 2,340 miles long. It emp-ties 593,000 cubic feet of water into the Gulf of Mexico every second.

- The U.S. Geological Survey reports that, at 2,540 miles, the Missouri River is the longest in the U.S.

- For all its great size, the U.S. shares borders with only two other nations: Canada to the north and Mexico to the south.

- Alaska is the largest state (615,230 square miles); Rhode Island is the smallest (1,231 square miles).

- The U.S. is the world's fourth-largest country; only Russia, Canada, and China are bigger.

- The largest inland bodies of water in the U.S. are the Great Lakes. Lake Michigan covers about 22,342 square miles.

- The highest point in the U.S. is atop Alaska's Mount McKinley, which has an elevation of 20,400 feet. The lowest point is in Death Valley, California—282 feet below sea level.

- The U.S. National Oceanic and Atmospheric Administration (NOAA) maintains about 11,600 weather stations.

- The city of Phoenix, Arizona, lies in a desert; it receives average yearly precipitation of 7.66 inches. In con-trast, Mobile, Alabama, receives an average of 63.96 inches a year.

- The wettest spot in the U.S. is Mount Waialeale, on the Hawaiian island of Kauai; it receives about 480 inches of rainfall every year. In contrast, Death Valley, California, receives only 1.5 inches annually.

- Juneau, Alaska, is one of the snowiest places in the United States, averaging about 99 inches of snow every year.

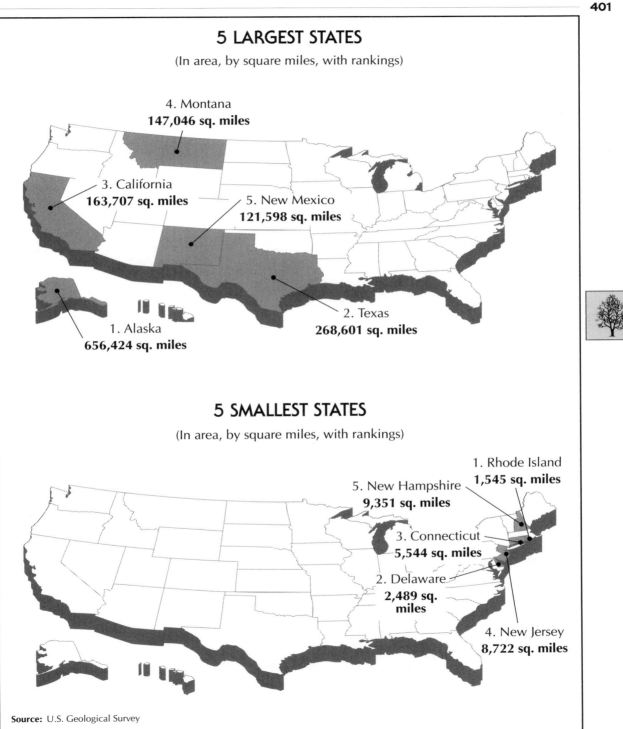

5 LARGEST STATES
(In area, by square miles, with rankings)

4. Montana
147,046 sq. miles

3. California
163,707 sq. miles

5. New Mexico
121,598 sq. miles

1. Alaska
656,424 sq. miles

2. Texas
268,601 sq. miles

5 SMALLEST STATES
(In area, by square miles, with rankings)

1. Rhode Island
1,545 sq. miles

5. New Hampshire
9,351 sq. miles

3. Connecticut
5,544 sq. miles

2. Delaware
2,489 sq. miles

4. New Jersey
8,722 sq. miles

Source: U.S. Geological Survey

TOP 10 LONGEST U.S. RIVERS
(In miles)

Length in miles

River	Length
Missouri	2,540
Mississippi	2,340
Yukon	1,980
St. Lawrence	1,900
Arkansas	1,460
Atchasalaya	1,420
Ohio	1,310
Red	1,290
Columbia	1,240
Snake	1,040

Source: U.S. Geological Survey

TOP 10 STATES WITH LARGEST STATE PARKS AND RECREATION AREAS*
(In acreage, with rankings)

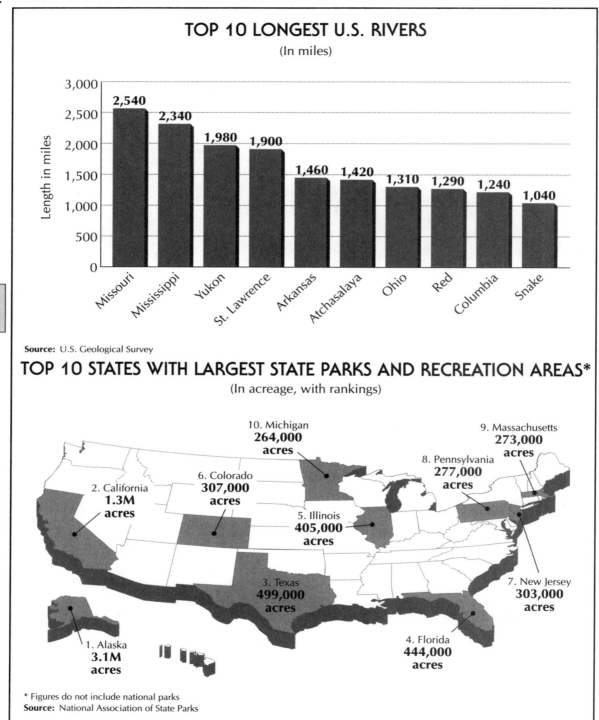

10. Michigan
264,000 acres

9. Massachusetts
273,000 acres

8. Pennsylvania
277,000 acres

2. California
1.3M acres

6. Colorado
307,000 acres

5. Illinois
405,000 acres

7. New Jersey
303,000 acres

3. Texas
499,000 acres

1. Alaska
3.1M acres

4. Florida
444,000 acres

* Figures do not include national parks
Source: National Association of State Parks

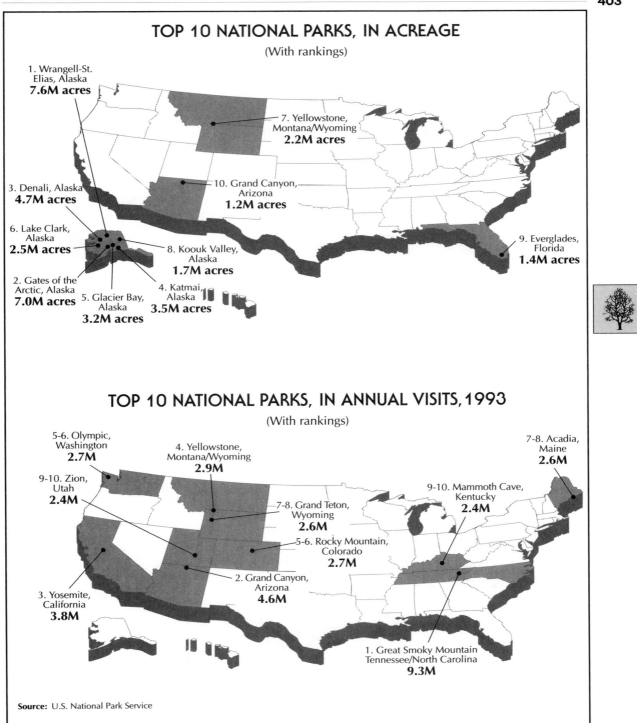

TOP 10 NATIONAL PARKS, IN ACREAGE
(With rankings)

1. Wrangell-St. Elias, Alaska **7.6M acres**

7. Yellowstone, Montana/Wyoming **2.2M acres**

3. Denali, Alaska **4.7M acres**

10. Grand Canyon, Arizona **1.2M acres**

6. Lake Clark, Alaska **2.5M acres**

8. Koouk Valley, Alaska **1.7M acres**

9. Everglades, Florida **1.4M acres**

2. Gates of the Arctic, Alaska **7.0M acres**

5. Glacier Bay, Alaska **3.2M acres**

4. Katmai, Alaska **3.5M acres**

TOP 10 NATIONAL PARKS, IN ANNUAL VISITS, 1993
(With rankings)

5-6. Olympic, Washington **2.7M**

4. Yellowstone, Montana/Wyoming **2.9M**

7-8. Acadia, Maine **2.6M**

9-10. Zion, Utah **2.4M**

9-10. Mammoth Cave, Kentucky **2.4M**

7-8. Grand Teton, Wyoming **2.6M**

5-6. Rocky Mountain, Colorado **2.7M**

3. Yosemite, California **3.8M**

2. Grand Canyon, Arizona **4.6M**

1. Great Smoky Mountain Tennessee/North Carolina **9.3M**

Source: U.S. National Park Service

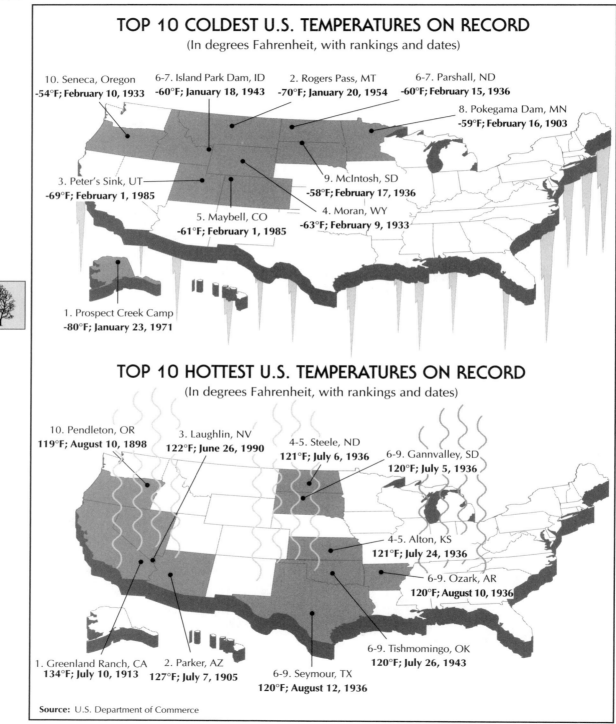

TOP 10 COLDEST U.S. TEMPERATURES ON RECORD
(In degrees Fahrenheit, with rankings and dates)

10. Seneca, Oregon
-54°F; February 10, 1933

6-7. Island Park Dam, ID
-60°F; January 18, 1943

2. Rogers Pass, MT
-70°F; January 20, 1954

6-7. Parshall, ND
-60°F; February 15, 1936

8. Pokegama Dam, MN
-59°F; February 16, 1903

3. Peter's Sink, UT
-69°F; February 1, 1985

9. McIntosh, SD
-58°F; February 17, 1936

5. Maybell, CO
-61°F; February 1, 1985

4. Moran, WY
-63°F; February 9, 1933

1. Prospect Creek Camp
-80°F; January 23, 1971

TOP 10 HOTTEST U.S. TEMPERATURES ON RECORD
(In degrees Fahrenheit, with rankings and dates)

10. Pendleton, OR
119°F; August 10, 1898

3. Laughlin, NV
122°F; June 26, 1990

4-5. Steele, ND
121°F; July 6, 1936

6-9. Gannvalley, SD
120°F; July 5, 1936

4-5. Alton, KS
121°F; July 24, 1936

6-9. Ozark, AR
120°F; August 10, 1936

1. Greenland Ranch, CA
134°F; July 10, 1913

2. Parker, AZ
127°F; July 7, 1905

6-9. Seymour, TX
120°F; August 12, 1936

6-9. Tishmomingo, OK
120°F; July 26, 1943

Source: U.S. Department of Commerce

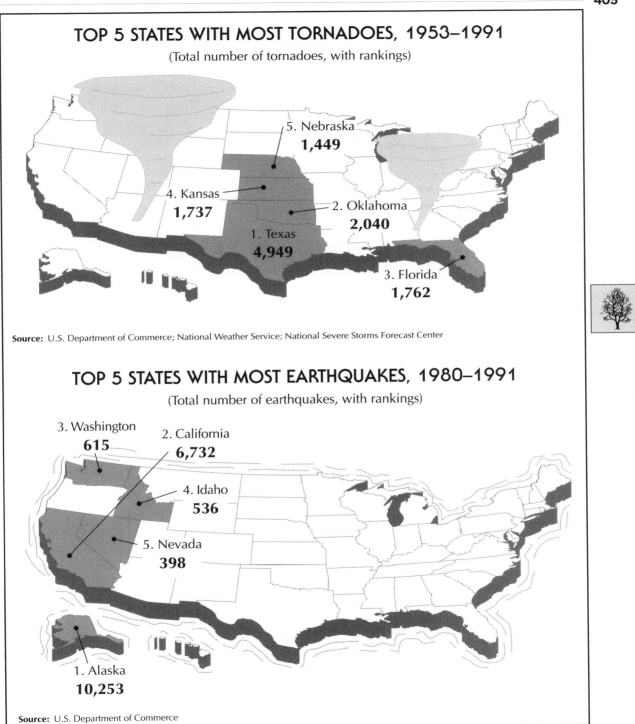

TOP 5 STATES WITH MOST TORNADOES, 1953–1991

(Total number of tornadoes, with rankings)

5. Nebraska
1,449

4. Kansas
1,737

2. Oklahoma
2,040

1. Texas
4,949

3. Florida
1,762

Source: U.S. Department of Commerce; National Weather Service; National Severe Storms Forecast Center

TOP 5 STATES WITH MOST EARTHQUAKES, 1980–1991

(Total number of earthquakes, with rankings)

3. Washington
615

2. California
6,732

4. Idaho
536

5. Nevada
398

1. Alaska
10,253

Source: U.S. Department of Commerce

WATER

Water is one of the world's most precious resources. It is also one that is vastly underappreciated. People often don't value it until it becomes hard to come by. And as both population and pollution increase, so do conflicts over water rights. Communities located downstream object to water pollution created by industries upstream; cities compete with farms for scarce supplies; and taxpayers howl over increased water and sewer rates.

Water pollution that stems from emissions from factories, utilities, and municipal sewage plants is relatively easy to identify, and has been significantly controlled since passage of the Clean Water Act in 1972. Much more difficult to identify and combat is "non-point pollution," which is contamination that cannot be traced to a specific source. Dumping of used motor oil, and runoff of pesticides and fertilizer from farmland, are common examples of non-point pollution.

An important part of the water-quality equation is wetlands—swamps, marshes, estuaries, and other lands regularly saturated by water. These are essential areas for water birds. The U.S. has lost more than 50% of its wetlands, most of which has been drained for farmland. Yet, despite this serious threat to our water supply and quality, some individuals and companies have made concerted efforts to weaken the government's safeguards over wetlands, because they fear higher costs for pollution controls. Also coming under attack are the Clean Water Act and Safe Drinking Water Act, two major U.S. anti-pollution measures.

FINGERTIP FACTS

- Groundwater is the source of more than half the drinking water in the U.S. In many parts of the country, groundwater supplies are being depleted faster than they are being replaced.

- Daily water consumption in the U.S. rose steadily from 1960, reaching 100 billion gallons in 1980. It declined to 92 billion gallons in 1985, then rose again to almost 94 billion gallons in 1990.

- The states that consumed the most water in 1990 were California (20.9 billion gallons per day), Texas (9.0 billion), and Idaho (6.1 billion).

- Traditional toilets used in the U.S. use 3 to 7 gallons of water per flush. Newer water-efficient toilets use less than 2 gallons per flush.

- About 13.5% of all water consumed in New York City is used to flush toilets in people's homes. Replacing traditional toilets with water-efficient toilets would save the city about 250 million gallons every day.

- Data from 1991–1992 indicate that 40% of U.S. waters are not suitable for swimming and fishing.

- Wetlands are nurseries and spawning grounds for shrimp, crabs, oysters, bluefish, flounder, sea trout, striped bass, and other species of commercial importance. Since its birth, the U.S. has lost more than 50% of its wetlands. It continues to lose almost 300,000 acres each year.

- Historically, drainage for agriculture has been responsible for about 80% of all freshwater wetlands losses.

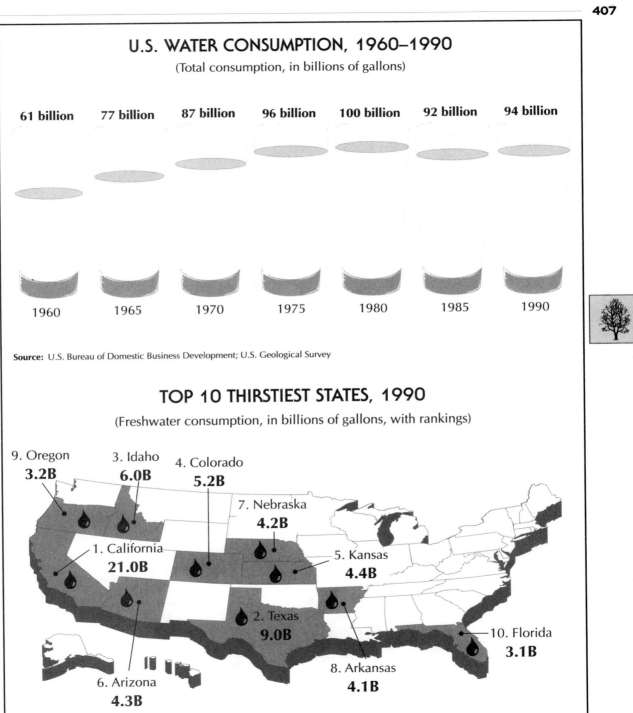

U.S. WATER CONSUMPTION, 1960–1990
(Total consumption, in billions of gallons)

| 61 billion | 77 billion | 87 billion | 96 billion | 100 billion | 92 billion | 94 billion |
| 1960 | 1965 | 1970 | 1975 | 1980 | 1985 | 1990 |

Source: U.S. Bureau of Domestic Business Development; U.S. Geological Survey

TOP 10 THIRSTIEST STATES, 1990
(Freshwater consumption, in billions of gallons, with rankings)

9. Oregon **3.2B**

3. Idaho **6.0B**

4. Colorado **5.2B**

7. Nebraska **4.2B**

1. California **21.0B**

5. Kansas **4.4B**

2. Texas **9.0B**

6. Arizona **4.3B**

8. Arkansas **4.1B**

10. Florida **3.1B**

Source: U.S. Geological Survey

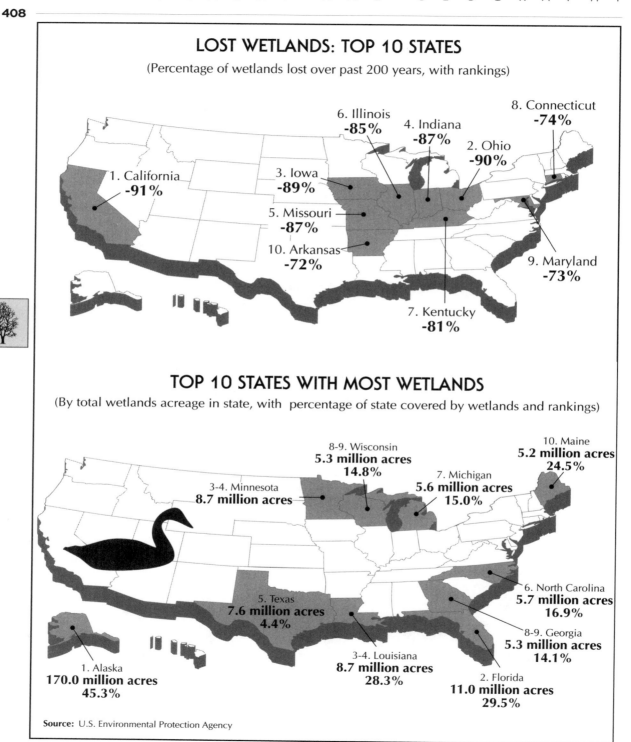

LOST WETLANDS: TOP 10 STATES
(Percentage of wetlands lost over past 200 years, with rankings)

6. Illinois **-85%**

4. Indiana **-87%**

8. Connecticut **-74%**

2. Ohio **-90%**

1. California **-91%**

3. Iowa **-89%**

5. Missouri **-87%**

10. Arkansas **-72%**

9. Maryland **-73%**

7. Kentucky **-81%**

TOP 10 STATES WITH MOST WETLANDS
(By total wetlands acreage in state, with percentage of state covered by wetlands and rankings)

8-9. Wisconsin **5.3 million acres** **14.8%**

10. Maine **5.2 million acres** **24.5%**

3-4. Minnesota **8.7 million acres**

7. Michigan **5.6 million acres** **15.0%**

6. North Carolina **5.7 million acres** **16.9%**

5. Texas **7.6 million acres** **4.4%**

8-9. Georgia **5.3 million acres** **14.1%**

1. Alaska **170.0 million acres** **45.3%**

3-4. Louisiana **8.7 million acres** **28.3%**

2. Florida **11.0 million acres** **29.5%**

Source: U.S. Environmental Protection Agency

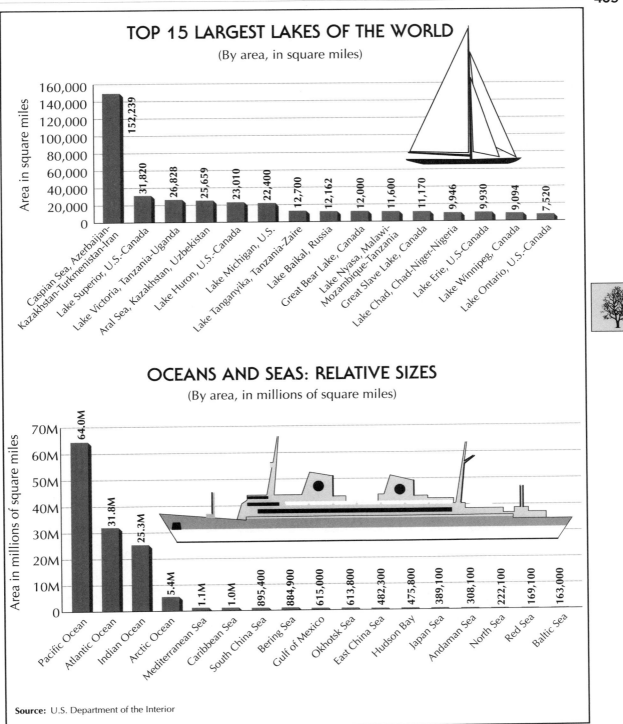

TOP 15 LARGEST LAKES OF THE WORLD
(By area, in square miles)

Area in square miles

- Caspian Sea, Azerbaijan-Kazakhstan-Turkmenistan-Iran: 152,239
- Lake Superior, U.S.-Canada: 31,820
- Lake Victoria, Tanzania-Uganda: 26,828
- Aral Sea, Kazakhstan, Uzbekistan: 25,659
- Lake Huron, U.S.-Canada: 23,010
- Lake Michigan, U.S.: 22,400
- Lake Tanganyika, Tanzania-Zaire: 12,700
- Lake Baikal, Russia: 12,162
- Great Bear Lake, Canada: 12,000
- Lake Nyasa, Malawi-Mozambique-Tanzania: 11,600
- Great Slave Lake, Canada: 11,170
- Lake Chad, Chad-Niger-Nigeria: 9,946
- Lake Erie, U.S.-Canada: 9,930
- Lake Winnipeg, Canada: 9,094
- Lake Ontario, U.S.-Canada: 7,520

OCEANS AND SEAS: RELATIVE SIZES
(By area, in millions of square miles)

Area in millions of square miles

- Pacific Ocean: 64.0M
- Atlantic Ocean: 31.8M
- Indian Ocean: 25.3M
- Arctic Ocean: 5.4M
- Mediterranean Sea: 1.1M
- Caribbean Sea: 1.0M
- South China Sea: 895,400
- Bering Sea: 884,900
- Gulf of Mexico: 615,000
- Okhotsk Sea: 613,800
- East China Sea: 482,300
- Hudson Bay: 475,800
- Japan Sea: 389,100
- Andaman Sea: 308,100
- North Sea: 222,100
- Red Sea: 169,100
- Baltic Sea: 163,000

Source: U.S. Department of the Interior

E N D A N G E R E D   S P E C I E S

Thousands of the world's plant and animal species are currently in danger of becoming extinct—not from the effects of natural forces, but from the harmful actions of humans—their destruction of natural habitats, pollution, hunting, overfishing, introduction of alien species into various environments, and so on.

In 1973, the U.S. Congress enacted the Endangered Species Act, which was intended to protect and restore endangered and threatened populations of plants and animals, whose survival was in jeopardy. The bald eagle, peregrine falcon, California sea otter, and black-footed ferret are among the species that the law has helped to save from extinction. Yet, despite strong public support for this tighter control, loggers and other businesses that are threatened by its provisions continue to try to weaken its protections.

As of October 1994, the U.S. Fish and Wildlife Service had listed 637 plant and animal species in the country as endangered and 194 other species as threatened. There were a total of 1,190 species endangered throughout the world in 1994. Many additional species, including numerous migratory birds, are in serious decline.

The U.S. National Wildlife Refuge System was established to help conserve the nation's wildlife resources. A significant portion of the current U.S. habitat of 94 species listed as endangered is located on 66 wildlife refuges. Many other listed species use refuge lands temporarily, for breeding or during migration.

FINGERTIP FACTS

☛ Scientists estimate that at least 500 plant and animal species have become extinct in the U.S. since the 1500s.

☛ The Wilderness Society reported in 1995 that if current trends continue, up to 20% of the world's plant and animal species could become extinct by the year 2000.

☛ Thirteen species have been removed from the endangered list—7 of them because they are now extinct.

☛ The states with the greatest number of endangered species are California (64), Hawaii (51), and Florida (45).

☛ Of all the known endangered species of plants, 97% can be found somewhere in the U.S.

☛ The U.S. National Wildlife Refuge System, which in 1994 included 499 refuges covering more than 91 million acres, comprises the only federal lands managed primarily for the benefit of wildlife.

☛ A 1994 poll commissioned by the National Wildlife Federation found that 57% of U.S. voters wanted strong requirements to be maintained in the Endangered Species Act.

☛ The U.S. is home to all of the known endangered species of crustaceans and arachnids and almost all endangered species of snails and clams.

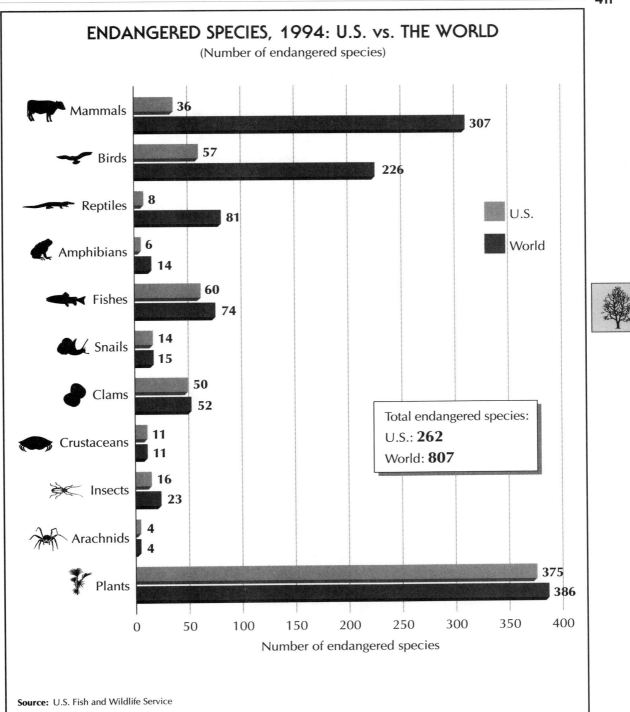

ENDANGERED SPECIES, 1994: U.S. vs. THE WORLD
(Number of endangered species)

	U.S.	World
Mammals	36	307
Birds	57	226
Reptiles	8	81
Amphibians	6	14
Fishes	60	74
Snails	14	15
Clams	50	52
Crustaceans	11	11
Insects	16	23
Arachnids	4	4
Plants	375	386

Total endangered species:
U.S.: **262**
World: **807**

Number of endangered species

Source: U.S. Fish and Wildlife Service

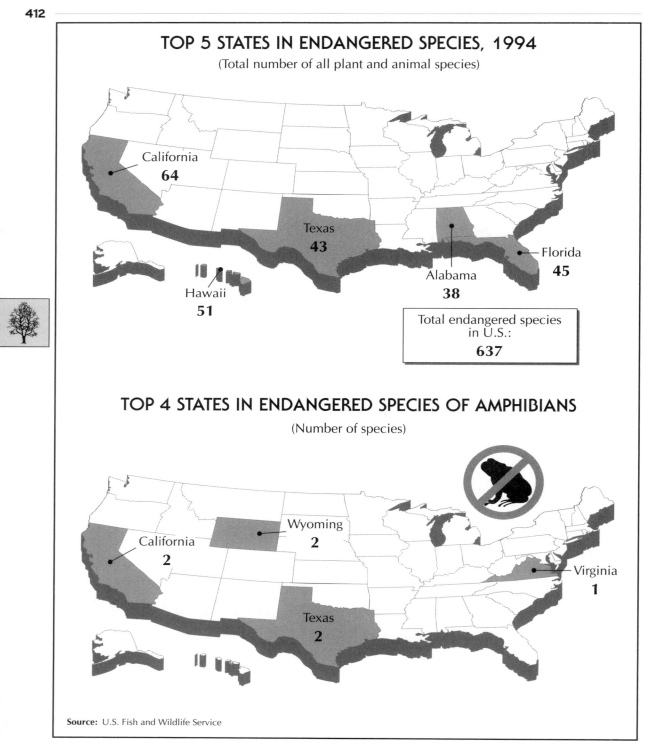

TOP 5 STATES IN ENDANGERED SPECIES, 1994

(Total number of all plant and animal species)

California
64

Texas
43

Hawaii
51

Alabama
38

Florida
45

Total endangered species
in U.S.:
637

TOP 4 STATES IN ENDANGERED SPECIES OF AMPHIBIANS

(Number of species)

Wyoming
2

California
2

Texas
2

Virginia
1

Source: U.S. Fish and Wildlife Service

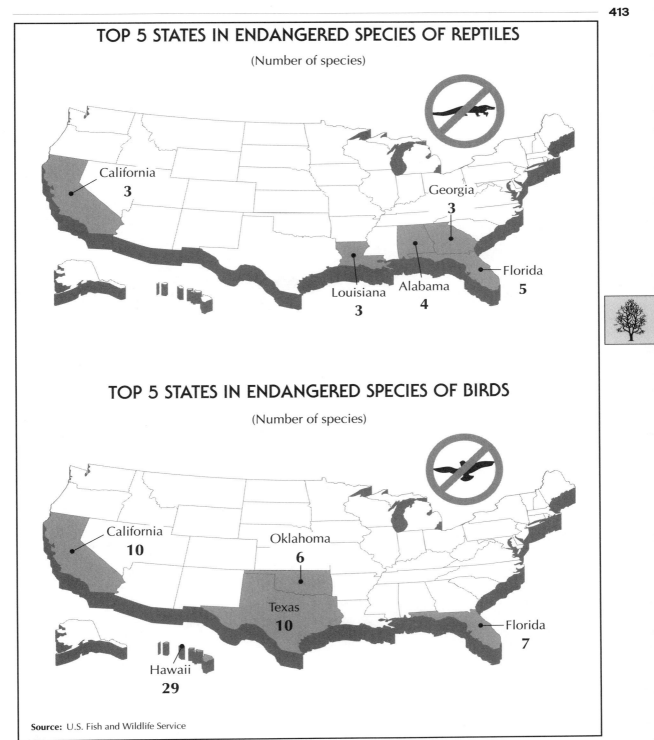

TOP 5 STATES IN ENDANGERED SPECIES OF REPTILES

(Number of species)

California
3

Georgia
3

Louisiana
3

Alabama
4

Florida
5

TOP 5 STATES IN ENDANGERED SPECIES OF BIRDS

(Number of species)

California
10

Oklahoma
6

Texas
10

Florida
7

Hawaii
29

Source: U.S. Fish and Wildlife Service

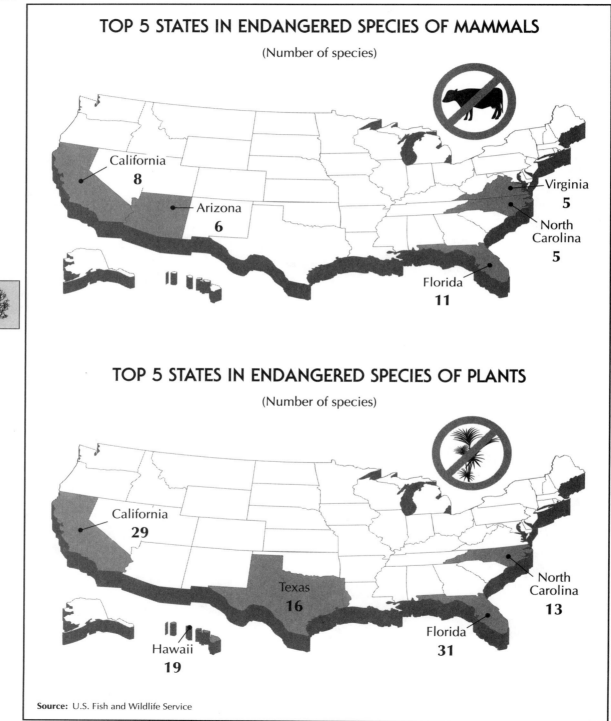

TOP 5 STATES IN ENDANGERED SPECIES OF MAMMALS

(Number of species)

California **8**

Arizona **6**

Virginia **5**

North Carolina **5**

Florida **11**

TOP 5 STATES IN ENDANGERED SPECIES OF PLANTS

(Number of species)

California **29**

Texas **16**

Hawaii **19**

North Carolina **13**

Florida **31**

Source: U.S. Fish and Wildlife Service

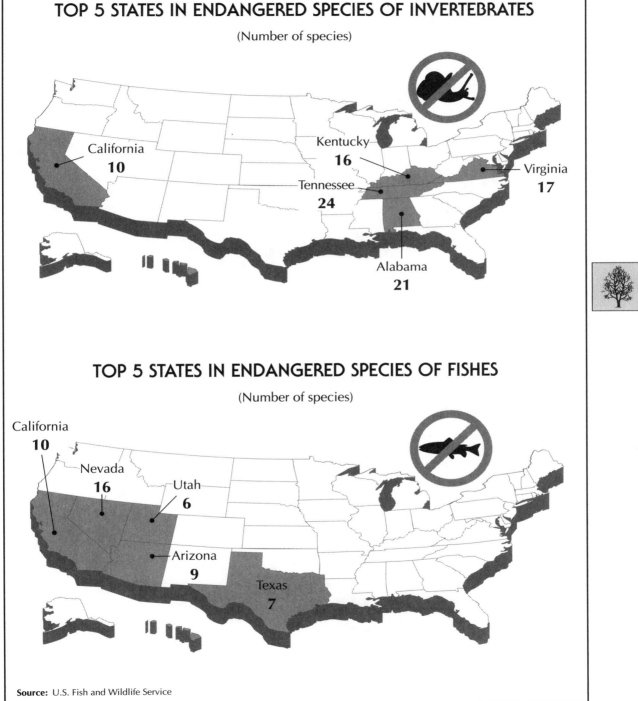

TOP 5 STATES IN ENDANGERED SPECIES OF INVERTEBRATES

(Number of species)

California
10

Kentucky
16

Tennessee
24

Virginia
17

Alabama
21

TOP 5 STATES IN ENDANGERED SPECIES OF FISHES

(Number of species)

California
10

Nevada
16

Utah
6

Arizona
9

Texas
7

Source: U.S. Fish and Wildlife Service

POLLUTION

Pollution is contamination caused by the release of wastes into the environment. Today, there are multitudes of pollutants; they include everything that can harm natural surroundings; sulfur gases from smokestacks, poisonous pesticides that run off land into nearby waters, used bandages from hospitals, radioactive materials from nuclear power plants, construction debris from building sites, manure from farms, human food-and-household wastes, and so on.

Pollution occurs indoors as well as outdoors. Sick-building syndrome—characterized by occupants having burning eyes, skin irritations, and various respiratory symptoms—has been on the increase in the U.S. Inefficient ventilation systems, chemicals from office equipment and carpeting, and tobacco smoke contribute to this problem.

The effects of pollution are many. Pollution may cause or worsen a variety of illnesses among humans and animals, including cancers and respiratory ailments. It can also poison wildlife, destroy the habitats of wild creatures, and raise atmospheric temperatures (the "greenhouse effect") and destroy high altitude ozone (causing ozone "holes").

The federal government has enacted a variety of legislation directed at preventing pollution in the U.S. These measures include the Clean Water Act and the Clean Air Act.

FINGERTIP FACTS

- The U.S. is home to only 5% of the world's population, but it releases 20% of the world's greenhouse gases—more than any other nation.

- The U.S. spent $15.8 billion in 1972 for pollution abatement; by 1991, the figure had grown to $86.4 billion.

- The U.S. generates more garbage than any other nation—even China, which has 4 times as many people.

- Americans generated an average of 4.4 pounds of wastes per person per day in 1993—up from 2.7 pounds in 1960 and 3.3 pounds in 1970.

- The U.S. generated nearly 207 million tons of municipal solid wastes in 1993—up from about 88 million tons in 1960, 151 million tons in 1980, and 196 million tons in 1990.

- Paper and paperboard products are the heaviest component of U.S. municipal solid wastes.

- Americans throw away more than 242 million automotive tires each year; 77.7% are dumped illegally or in a landfill.

- Paper is the most recycled material in the U.S. More than one-third of all paper products generated were recycled in 1993. Metals are the second-most-recycled material.

- The U.S. recycled 38.5 million tons of municipal solid wastes in 1993 and composted an additional 6.5 million tons.

- In the U.S., an estimated 200 million gallons of used motor oil are improperly disposed of each year. One gallon of used oil has the potential to contaminate up to a million gallons of drinking water.

- About 68% of all aluminum beverage cans and 46% of all steel cans used in the U.S. are recycled.

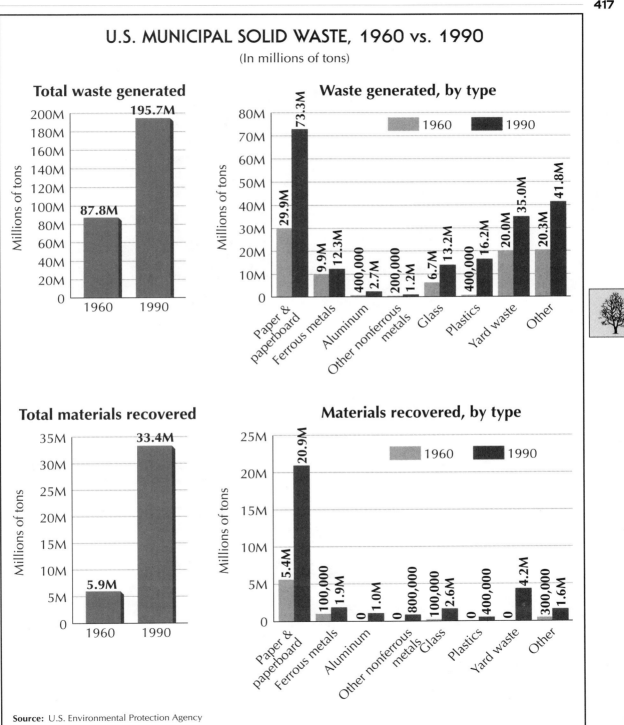

U.S. MUNICIPAL SOLID WASTE, 1960 vs. 1990
(In millions of tons)

Total waste generated

Waste generated, by type

Total materials recovered

Materials recovered, by type

Source: U.S. Environmental Protection Agency

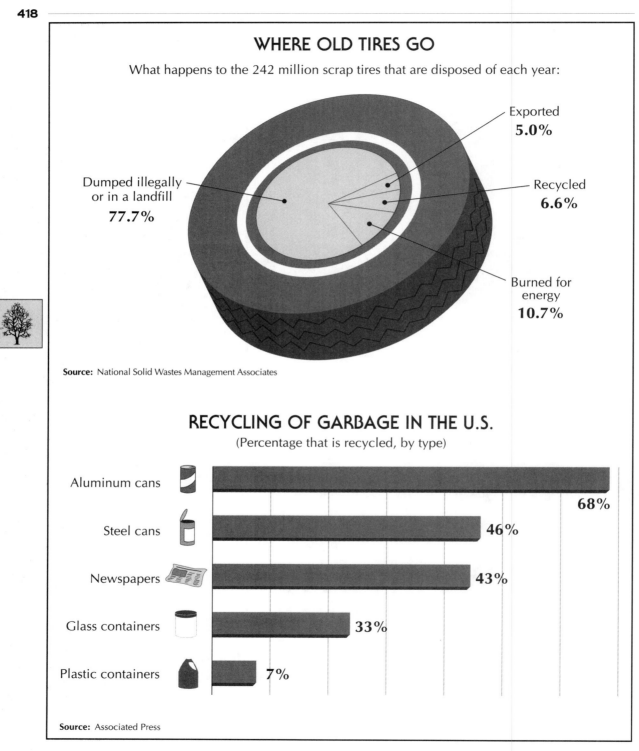

WHERE OLD TIRES GO

What happens to the 242 million scrap tires that are disposed of each year:

Exported
5.0%

Dumped illegally
or in a landfill
77.7%

Recycled
6.6%

Burned for
energy
10.7%

Source: National Solid Wastes Management Associates

RECYCLING OF GARBAGE IN THE U.S.

(Percentage that is recycled, by type)

Aluminum cans — **68%**

Steel cans — **46%**

Newspapers — **43%**

Glass containers — **33%**

Plastic containers — **7%**

Source: Associated Press

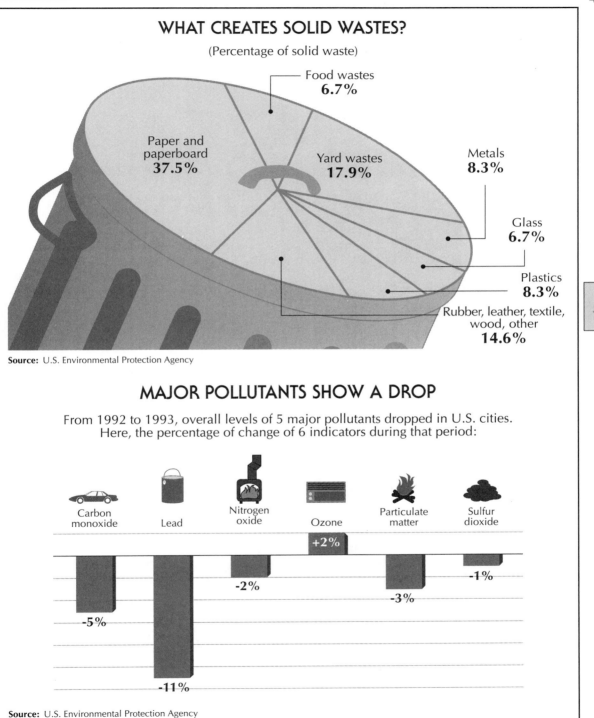

WHAT CREATES SOLID WASTES?

(Percentage of solid waste)

Food wastes
6.7%

Paper and
paperboard
37.5%

Yard wastes
17.9%

Metals
8.3%

Glass
6.7%

Plastics
8.3%

Rubber, leather, textile,
wood, other
14.6%

Source: U.S. Environmental Protection Agency

MAJOR POLLUTANTS SHOW A DROP

From 1992 to 1993, overall levels of 5 major pollutants dropped in U.S. cities.
Here, the percentage of change of 6 indicators during that period:

Carbon monoxide	Lead	Nitrogen oxide	Ozone	Particulate matter	Sulfur dioxide
-5%	-11%	-2%	+2%	-3%	-1%

Source: U.S. Environmental Protection Agency

CFC PRODUCTION, 1971–1992

Chlorofluorocarbons (CFCs), which are used in air conditioners, refrigerators, and other products, are known to damage Earth's protective ozone layer. In the U.S., CFC production is mandated to end in 1996. Here, decline in CFC production from 1971 to 1992:

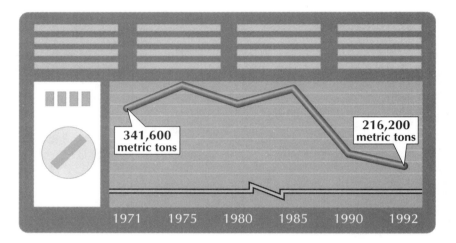

341,600 metric tons

216,200 metric tons

1971 1975 1980 1985 1990 1992

Source: U.S. Environmental Protection Agency

EMISSIONS OF AIR POLLUTANTS, 1970–1991

(Emission by pollutant and source, in millions of metric tons)

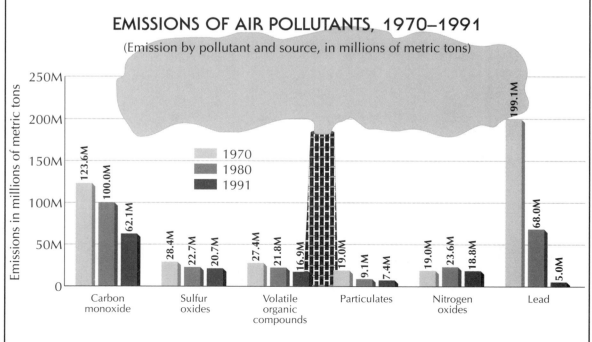

Emissions in millions of metric tons

1970
1980
1991

Carbon monoxide: 123.6M, 100.0M, 62.1M
Sulfur oxides: 28.4M, 22.7M, 20.7M
Volatile organic compounds: 27.4M, 21.8M, 16.9M
Particulates: 19.0M, 9.1M, 7.4M
Nitrogen oxides: 19.0M, 23.6M, 18.8M
Lead: 199.1M, 68.0M, 5.0M

Source: U.S. Environmental Protection Agency

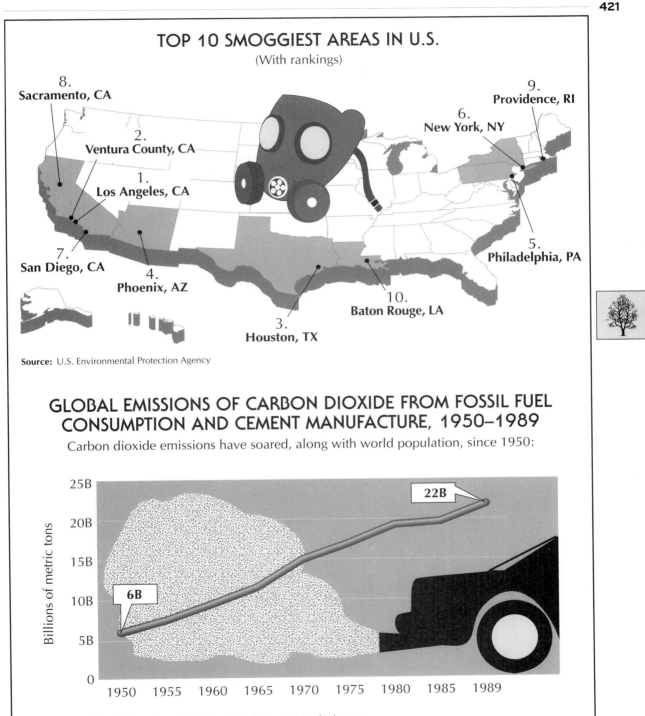

TOP 10 SMOGGIEST AREAS IN U.S.
(With rankings)

8. Sacramento, CA

9. Providence, RI

2. Ventura County, CA

6. New York, NY

1. Los Angeles, CA

7. San Diego, CA

5. Philadelphia, PA

4. Phoenix, AZ

10. Baton Rouge, LA

3. Houston, TX

Source: U.S. Environmental Protection Agency

GLOBAL EMISSIONS OF CARBON DIOXIDE FROM FOSSIL FUEL CONSUMPTION AND CEMENT MANUFACTURE, 1950–1989

Carbon dioxide emissions have soared, along with world population, since 1950:

22B

6B

Billions of metric tons

25B
20B
15B
10B
5B
0

1950 1955 1960 1965 1970 1975 1980 1985 1989

Source: Carbon Dioxide Information Analysis Center, Oak Ridge National Laboratory

TOP 10 MOST UNHEALTHY U.S. CITIES, BY AIR QUALITY, 1991

(By number of days in year with poor air quality, as measured by
emissions of 5 major pollutants, with rankings)

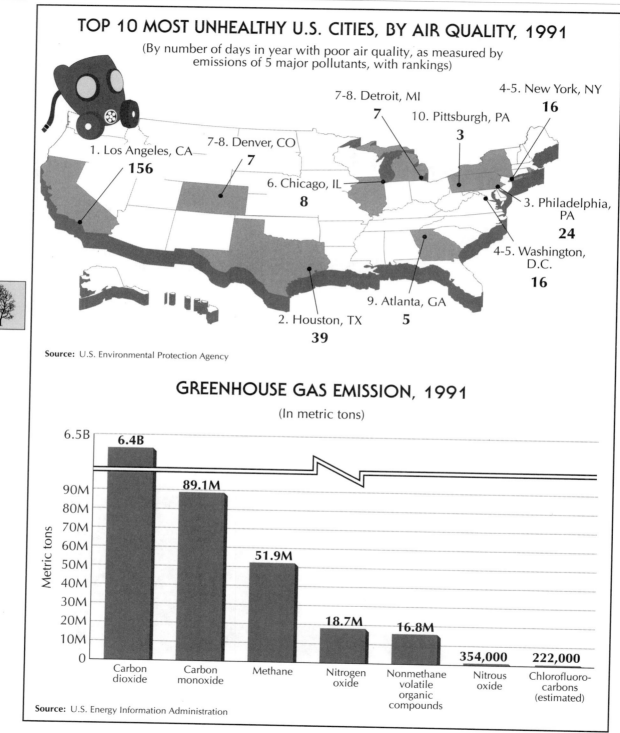

7-8. Detroit, MI
7

10. Pittsburgh, PA
3

4-5. New York, NY
16

7-8. Denver, CO
7

1. Los Angeles, CA
156

6. Chicago, IL
8

3. Philadelphia, PA
24

4-5. Washington, D.C.
16

9. Atlanta, GA
5

2. Houston, TX
39

Source: U.S. Environmental Protection Agency

GREENHOUSE GAS EMISSION, 1991

(In metric tons)

Metric tons

Gas	Emission
Carbon dioxide	6.4B
Carbon monoxide	89.1M
Methane	51.9M
Nitrogen oxide	18.7M
Nonmethane volatile organic compounds	16.8M
Nitrous oxide	354,000
Chlorofluoro-carbons (estimated)	222,000

Source: U.S. Energy Information Administration

TOP 10 U.S. CITIES WITH LEAD PROBLEMS IN WATER SUPPLY

In 1992, the EPA found that 130 of the 660 major public water systems in the U.S. exceed safe levels of lead in drinking water. Safe levels are 15 parts per billion (ppb). Here, with rankings, the cities with the highest lead content:

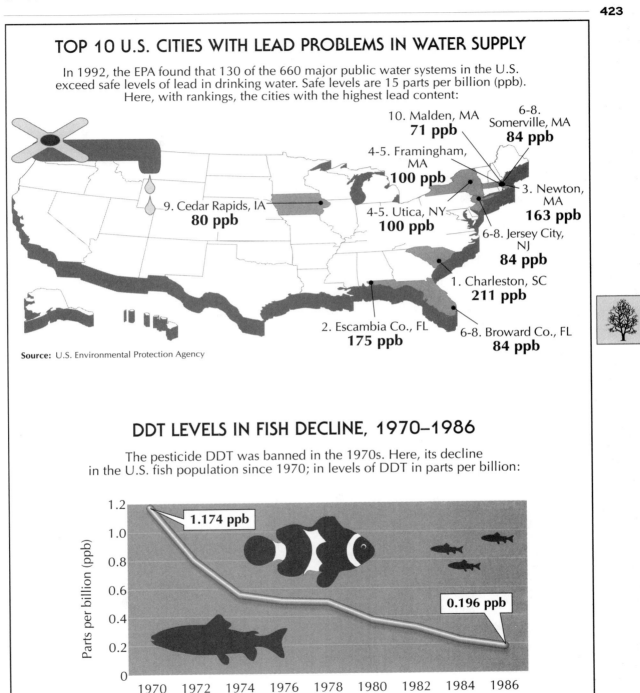

10. Malden, MA
71 ppb

6-8. Somerville, MA
84 ppb

4-5. Framingham, MA
100 ppb

3. Newton, MA
163 ppb

9. Cedar Rapids, IA
80 ppb

4-5. Utica, NY
100 ppb

6-8. Jersey City, NJ
84 ppb

1. Charleston, SC
211 ppb

2. Escambia Co., FL
175 ppb

6-8. Broward Co., FL
84 ppb

Source: U.S. Environmental Protection Agency

DDT LEVELS IN FISH DECLINE, 1970–1986

The pesticide DDT was banned in the 1970s. Here, its decline in the U.S. fish population since 1970; in levels of DDT in parts per billion:

1.174 ppb

0.196 ppb

Parts per billion (ppb)

1.2
1.0
0.8
0.6
0.4
0.2
0

1970 1972 1974 1976 1978 1980 1982 1984 1986

Source: U.S. Environmental Protection Agency; U.S. Geological Survey

H A Z A R D O U S   W A S T E

Substances known as hazardous wastes pose serious threats to all life. To avoid such threats, it is necessary to eliminate or reduce the production of hazardous wastes or to properly store, transport, and dispose of them.

The U.S. Emergency Planning and Community Right-to-Know Act of 1986 requires certain public and private facilities to prepare annual reports on their releases of toxic chemicals into the environment. The reports are to be made available to local communities. In 1993, President Bill Clinton signed an Executive Order requiring federal agencies to comply with this law. There are now 654 chemicals in the Toxic Release Inventory, a database maintained by the Environmental Protection Agency (EPA) under the act.

Since the first reports were made under the 1986 law, the amount of toxic chemicals released into the nation's environment by manufacturing facilities (not including power plants and mining facilities) has decreased. The 3.2 billion pounds released in 1992 appear to represent an encouraging downward trend with a decline of some 35% since 1988.

Since many producers of hazardous wastes were not required to prepare reports, however, and since many toxic substances were not part of the inventory, these figures are deceptive. A 1994 report from the General Accounting Office noted that an estimated 275 million tons (550 billion pounds) of hazardous waste are treated, stored, and disposed of annually in the U.S. — and the volume is growing.

Hazardous waste cleanup is both a costly and time-consuming process. The major federal cleanup effort is called the Superfund program, which by 1994 had constructed toxic waste cleanup systems in 278 communities. As of mid-1994, a total of 1,286 hazardous waste sites were targeted for cleanup. By early 1995, the federal government had spent more than $13 billion on the Superfund program. Through Superfund, polluters had, by late 1994, committed nearly $10 billion to clean up the most seriously contaminated sites.

FINGERTIP FACTS

☛ The Environmental Protection Agency estimates that it costs an average of $25 million to $30 million to clean up a single Superfund hazardous waste site.

☛ In 1994, the most hazardous waste sites on the National Priorities List were located in New Jersey (109), Pennsylvania (101), and California (96). Those figures dropped slightly by 1994.

☛ In 1994, according to the EPA, 1 out of 4 Americans lived within 4 miles of a toxic dumpsite.

☛ In 1990, lead-acid automotive batteries were recovered at a rate of more than 96%, thus keeping an impressive amount of lead out of U.S. landfills.

☛ Nuclear power plants lack places for waste disposal. Some 86,000 tons of high-level radioactive wastes and spent fuel from nuclear power plants are in temporary storage while the government determines what to do with them. The wastes will be dangerous for more than 10,000 years.

☛ In 1994, the U.S. and 63 other nations signed the Basel Convention, banning the export of hazardous wastes from industrialized to developing countries.

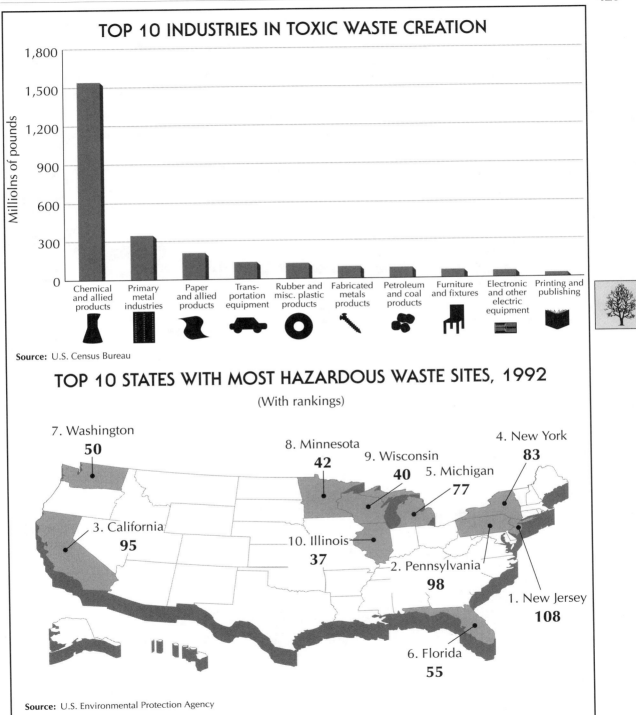

TOP 10 INDUSTRIES IN TOXIC WASTE CREATION

Milliolns of pounds

Chemical and allied products | Primary metal industries | Paper and allied products | Trans-portation equipment | Rubber and misc. plastic products | Fabricated metals products | Petroleum and coal products | Furniture and fixtures | Electronic and other electric equipment | Printing and publishing

Source: U.S. Census Bureau

TOP 10 STATES WITH MOST HAZARDOUS WASTE SITES, 1992

(With rankings)

7. Washington
50

8. Minnesota
42

9. Wisconsin
40

4. New York
83

5. Michigan
77

3. California
95

10. Illinois
37

2. Pennsylvania
98

1. New Jersey
108

6. Florida
55

Source: U.S. Environmental Protection Agency

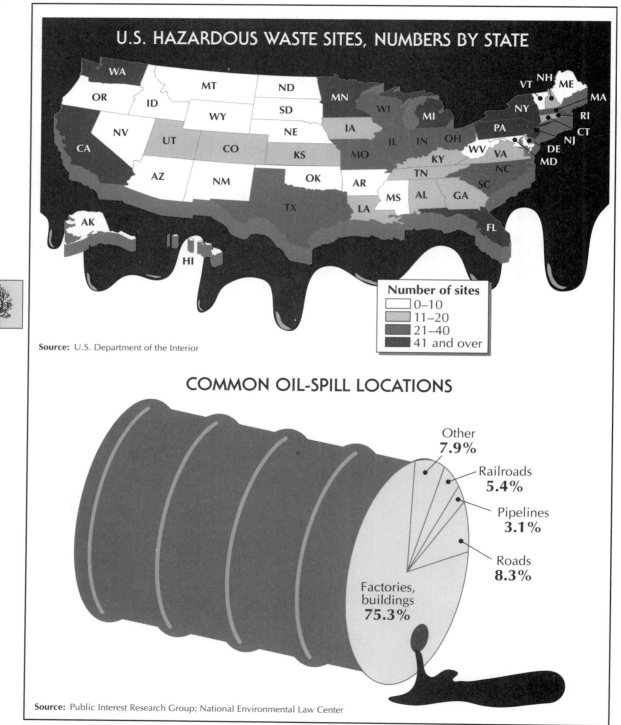

U.S. HAZARDOUS WASTE SITES, NUMBERS BY STATE

Number of sites
- 0–10
- 11–20
- 21–40
- 41 and over

Source: U.S. Department of the Interior

COMMON OIL-SPILL LOCATIONS

Other
7.9%

Railroads
5.4%

Pipelines
3.1%

Roads
8.3%

Factories,
buildings
75.3%

Source: Public Interest Research Group; National Environmental Law Center

TOP 10 STATES FOR TOXIC CHEMICAL SPILLS, 1988–1992

(By number of accidents, with rankings)

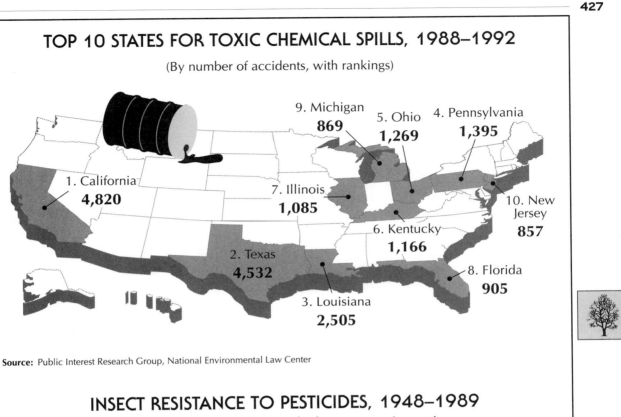

9. Michigan
869

5. Ohio
1,269

4. Pennsylvania
1,395

1. California
4,820

7. Illinois
1,085

10. New Jersey
857

6. Kentucky
1,166

2. Texas
4,532

8. Florida
905

3. Louisiana
2,505

Source: Public Interest Research Group, National Environmental Law Center

INSECT RESISTANCE TO PESTICIDES, 1948–1989

With the soaring use of pesticides has come an increasing
number of insect species resistant to these poisons:

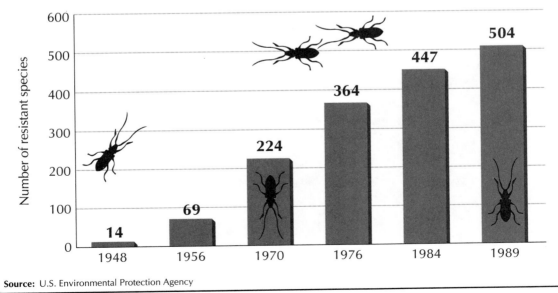

Number of resistant species

600
500
400
300
200
100
0

1948	1956	1970	1976	1984	1989
14	**69**	**224**	**364**	**447**	**504**

Source: U.S. Environmental Protection Agency

7

AGRICULTURE AND NATURAL RESOURCES

FARMS AND FARMING

Thanks to the efficiency of U.S. farms, most Americans enjoy an abundance of inexpensive food. But as the nation's population has soared, the land devoted to growing food has declined. Between 1987 and 1992, almost 20 million acres of productive cropland were lost due to such factors as erosion and housing developments. Currently, there are about 1.8 acres of cropland to grow food for each American. But if the current trends in population growth and farmland loss continue, there will be only 0.6 acre per American in the year 2050. (That is the rate that currently exists worldwide.)

The number of farms has steadily declined in recent decades—from about 6.0 million covering more than 1 billion acres in 1975, to 2.1 million farms with a total acreage of 978 million acres in 1993. Today's farms are significantly larger than farms of the past. In 1940, the average farm had 174 acres. By 1993, the average size was 473 acres.

A broad range of programs and services is designed to support the nation's agricultural sector. The U.S. Department of Agriculture, one of the largest departments of the federal government, provides aid in the way of farm price supports, crop insurance, loans to farmers, and funds for soil conservation and wetlands protection. Some of these programs have come under attack, partly from various special interest groups, partly because of their cost to consumers, and partly because they tend to enrich wealthy farmers more than help small farmers.

FINGERTIP FACTS

- Americans spend about 15% of their incomes on food. In most developing countries, food costs eat up 50% to 60% of people's incomes.

- The number of U.S. farms fell from 2.5 million in 1975 to 1.9 million in 1994—the lowest since 1850.

- In 1993, the three states with the most acreage devoted to farming were Texas (130 million acres), Montana (60 million acres), and Kansas (48 million acres).

- Nebraska has the highest percentage of land used as farmland (96.1%); Alaska has the least (0.3%).

- The total value of farms in the 48 contiguous U.S. states in 1993 was $684.6 billion, with an average value of $700 per acre.

- Total farm income in 1992 was $171.2 billion, up from $139.7 billion in 1980. Crops accounted for $84.8 billion, livestock and products for $86.4 billion.

- The state with the highest 1992 farm income was California ($18.2 billion), followed by Texas ($11.6 billion), Iowa ($10.3 billion), and Nebraska ($8.8 billion).

- Government payments to farmers totaled $13 billion in 1993. Texas farmers received the biggest chunk ($1.4 billion), followed by Iowa ($1.2 billion), Illinois ($851 million), Minnesota ($823 million), and Nebraska ($806 million).

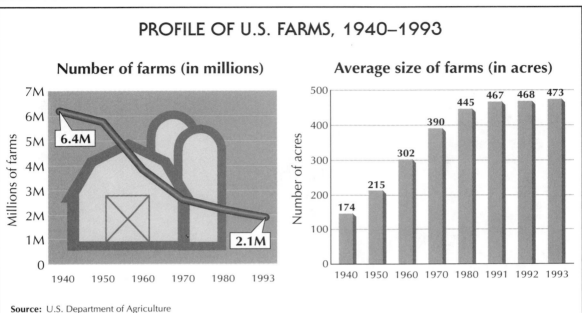

PROFILE OF U.S. FARMS, 1940–1993

Number of farms (in millions)

6.4M

2.1M

Average size of farms (in acres)

174, 215, 302, 390, 445, 467, 468, 473

1940 1950 1960 1970 1980 1991 1992 1993

Source: U.S. Department of Agriculture

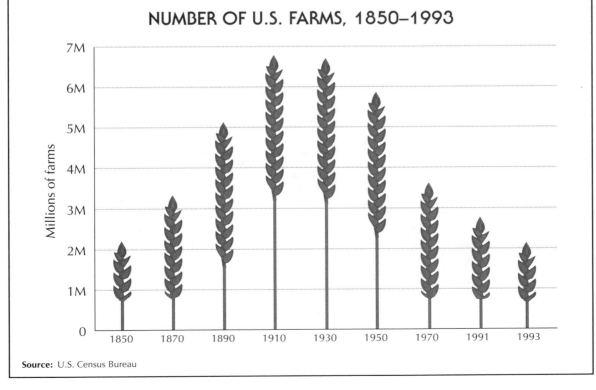

NUMBER OF U.S. FARMS, 1850–1993

1850 1870 1890 1910 1930 1950 1970 1991 1993

Source: U.S. Census Bureau

STATES WITH MOST AND LEAST AMOUNT OF LAND USED AS FARMLAND

(As percentage of total land)

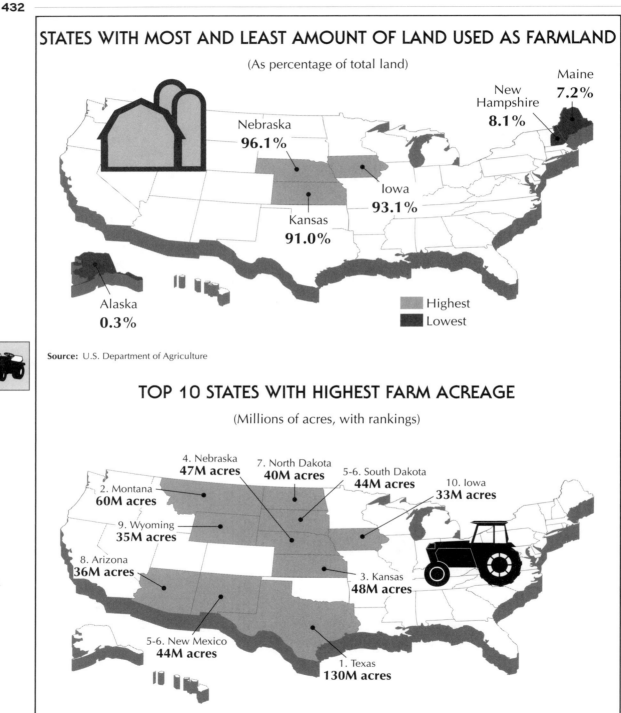

Maine
7.2%

New Hampshire
8.1%

Nebraska
96.1%

Iowa
93.1%

Kansas
91.0%

Alaska
0.3%

Highest
Lowest

Source: U.S. Department of Agriculture

TOP 10 STATES WITH HIGHEST FARM ACREAGE

(Millions of acres, with rankings)

4. Nebraska
47M acres

7. North Dakota
40M acres

5-6. South Dakota
44M acres

10. Iowa
33M acres

2. Montana
60M acres

9. Wyoming
35M acres

8. Arizona
36M acres

3. Kansas
48M acres

5-6. New Mexico
44M acres

1. Texas
130M acres

Source: U.S. Department of Agriculture

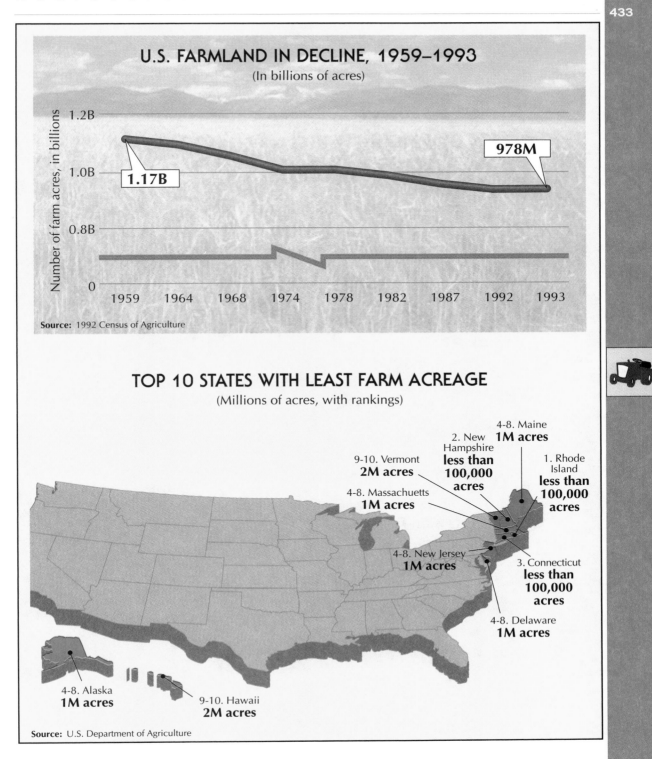

U.S. FARMLAND IN DECLINE, 1959–1993
(In billions of acres)

Number of farm acres, in billions

1.2B

1.17B

978M

1.0B

0.8B

0

1959   1964   1968   1974   1978   1982   1987   1992   1993

Source: 1992 Census of Agriculture

TOP 10 STATES WITH LEAST FARM ACREAGE
(Millions of acres, with rankings)

4-8. Maine **1M acres**

2. New Hampshire **less than 100,000 acres**

9-10. Vermont **2M acres**

1. Rhode Island **less than 100,000 acres**

4-8. Massachuetts **1M acres**

4-8. New Jersey **1M acres**

3. Connecticut **less than 100,000 acres**

4-8. Delaware **1M acres**

4-8. Alaska **1M acres**

9-10. Hawaii **2M acres**

Source: U.S. Department of Agriculture

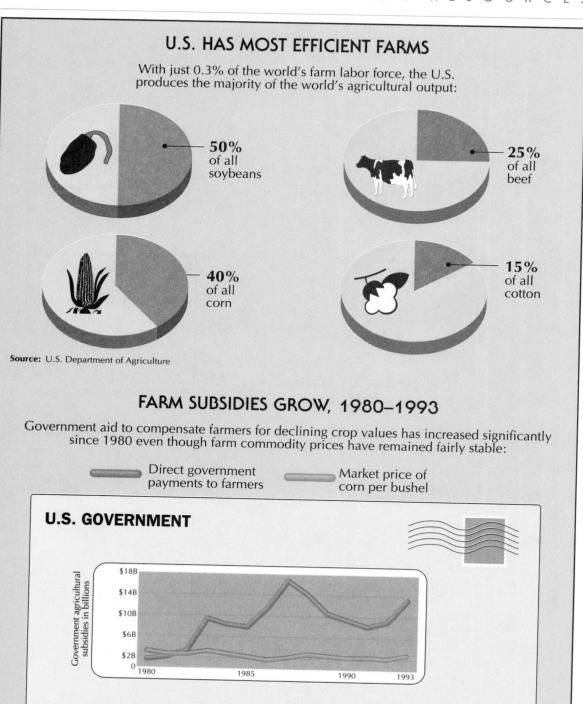

U.S. HAS MOST EFFICIENT FARMS

With just 0.3% of the world's farm labor force, the U.S. produces the majority of the world's agricultural output:

50% of all soybeans

25% of all beef

40% of all corn

15% of all cotton

Source: U.S. Department of Agriculture

FARM SUBSIDIES GROW, 1980–1993

Government aid to compensate farmers for declining crop values has increased significantly since 1980 even though farm commodity prices have remained fairly stable:

Direct government payments to farmers

Market price of corn per bushel

U.S. GOVERNMENT

Government agricultural subsidies in billions

$18B
$14B
$10B
$6B
$2B
0

1980   1985   1990   1993

Source: U.S. Department of Agriculture

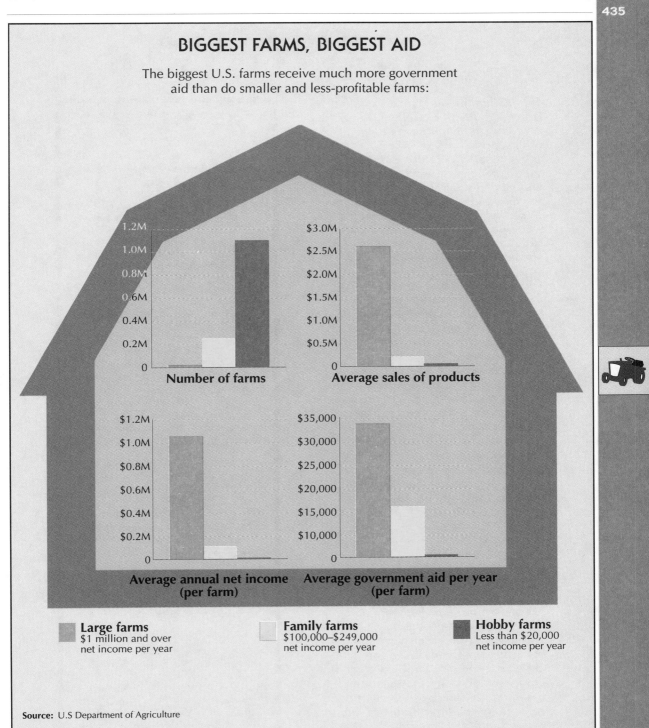

BIGGEST FARMS, BIGGEST AID

The biggest U.S. farms receive much more government
aid than do smaller and less-profitable farms:

Number of farms

Average sales of products

Average annual net income (per farm)

Average government aid per year (per farm)

Large farms
$1 million and over
net income per year

Family farms
$100,000–$249,000
net income per year

Hobby farms
Less than $20,000
net income per year

Source: U.S Department of Agriculture

FARMERS AND PRODUCTIVITY

The U.S. has the world's most efficient farms. It has only 0.3% of the world's farm workers, but produces about 50% of all soybeans, 40% of all corn, 25% of all beef, and 15% of all cotton. Large-scale irrigation projects, artificial fertilizers and pesticides, genetic technology, and mechanization have been major factors in increasing the amount of food that can be produced per acre. The largest farms are highly specialized and account for the bulk of farm production; small family farms have declined. For example, in 1940, some 12% of the nation's farms produced 50% of farms sales; in 1992, only 3% of the farms produced 50% of sales.

Today's farmers are much better educated than farmers of the past. They have access to specially trained agricultural agents and up-to-the-minute weather forecasts. Many also use computers to track crop yields and other data. But the average age of farmers has increased, and a growing number of farm households rely on non-farming activities for a large part of their income. Interestingly, the number of female farmers—though small— has grown from 129,189 in 1987 to 145,156 in 1992—but the total number of farmworkers has steadily declined. This is primarily because the use of grain harvesters and other sophisticated machines has reduced the need for labor.

Farms are the main employers of migrant laborers—people who move from one place to another to take advantage of seasonal employment opportunities. These laborers are often denied safe and sanitary working conditions, decent housing, and adequate health care. Unions and government agencies, however, have had some success in improving these conditions.

FINGERTIP FACTS

☞ The U.S. had 1,037,000 farmers in 1991. They had a median age of 48 years and had been farmers for an average of 21.8 years.

☞ In 1880, nearly 44% of U.S. residents lived on farms. In 1991, about 2% did.

☞ In 1982, 84.1% of farmers were age 35 or older; by 1992, the percentage had risen to 89.3%.

☞ Black farmers are older than white farmers. The percentage age 35 or older rose from 90.2% in 1982 to 92.5% in 1992.

☞ Some 848,000 people were employed as farmworkers in 1992. The majority (57%) did not have high school diplomas. Average weekly earnings were highest for white farm workers ($225), followed by Latinos ($200) and blacks and other groups ($190).

☞ In 1993, about 801,000 people were employed as farmworkers—down from 1.1 million in 1983.

☞ In 1993, some 28.5% of the nation's farmworkers were Latinos, up from 15.9% in 1983. The percentage of black farmworkers declined to 7.0% in 1993, from 11.6% in 1983.

☞ In 1990 in the U.S., one farmworker supplied agricultural products for an average of 96 people.

☞ Employment in the U.S. fishing industry grew from 227,000 people in 1970 to 364,000 in 1988.

☞ The U.S. Department of Agriculture had about 115,000 employees working in more than 15,000 offices in 1994. Its annual budget was about $70 billion.

FARM EMPLOYMENT AND WORKER PRODUCTIVITY, 1950–1990

By 1990, U.S. farms had become so productive that each worker supplied agricultural products for an average of 96 people. Farm employment, however, is down more than two-thirds from 1950:

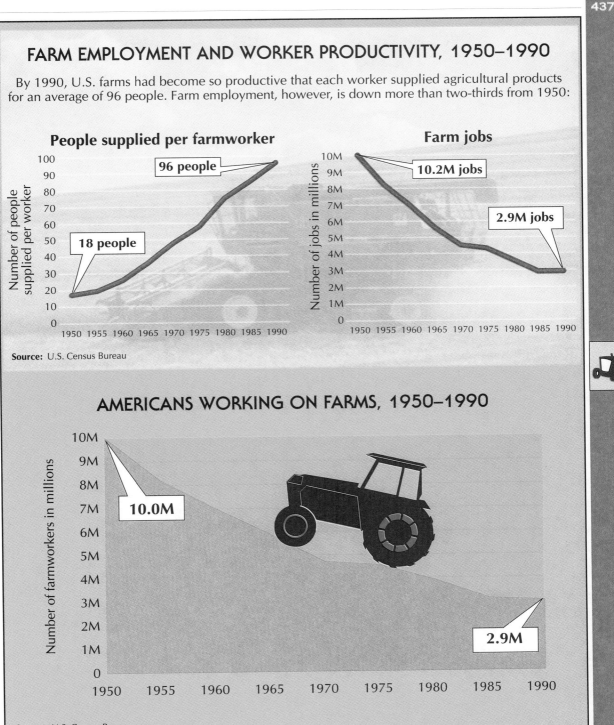

People supplied per farmworker

96 people

18 people

Number of people supplied per worker

1950 1955 1960 1965 1970 1975 1980 1985 1990

Farm jobs

10.2M jobs

2.9M jobs

Number of jobs in millions

1950 1955 1960 1965 1970 1975 1980 1985 1990

Source: U.S. Census Bureau

AMERICANS WORKING ON FARMS, 1950–1990

Number of farmworkers in millions

10.0M

2.9M

1950 1955 1960 1965 1970 1975 1980 1985 1990

Source: U.S. Census Bureau

DECLINING FARM POPULATION, 1880–1991

The percentage of farmers in the U.S. population
has dropped dramatically since 1880:

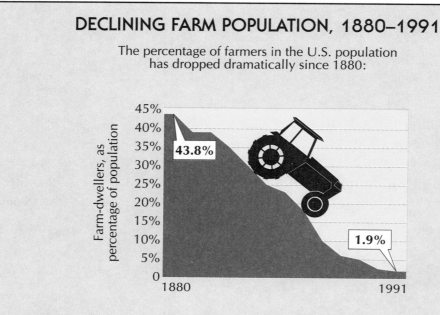

Source: U.S. Agriculture Census

FEMALE FARMERS, 1987 vs. 1992

The number of farmers overall in the U.S. is decreasing, but
the number of women farmers has climbed:

129,189

145,156

1987

1992

Source: U.S. Census Bureau

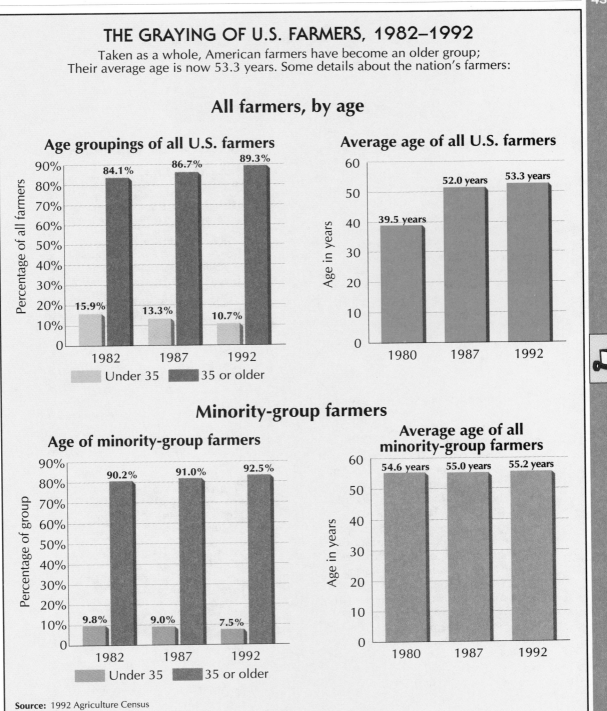

THE GRAYING OF U.S. FARMERS, 1982–1992

Taken as a whole, American farmers have become an older group;
Their average age is now 53.3 years. Some details about the nation's farmers:

All farmers, by age

Age groupings of all U.S. farmers

Percentage of all farmers

- 1982: Under 35 15.9%, 35 or older 84.1%
- 1987: Under 35 13.3%, 35 or older 86.7%
- 1992: Under 35 10.7%, 35 or older 89.3%

Under 35   35 or older

Average age of all U.S. farmers

Age in years

- 1980: 39.5 years
- 1987: 52.0 years
- 1992: 53.3 years

Minority-group farmers

Age of minority-group farmers

Percentage of group

- 1982: Under 35 9.8%, 35 or older 90.2%
- 1987: Under 35 9.0%, 35 or older 91.0%
- 1992: Under 35 7.5%, 35 or older 92.5%

Under 35   35 or older

Average age of all minority-group farmers

Age in years

- 1980: 54.6 years
- 1987: 55.0 years
- 1992: 55.2 years

Source: 1992 Agriculture Census

CROP PRODUCTION

Grains such as corn, wheat, and rice, and pulses—the seed parts of legumes such as beans, soybeans, and peanuts—are the major crops in the U.S. Over the years, production of these and other crops has risen steadily, as have yields per acre. In individual years, however, dramatic production declines have resulted from drought, flooding, and other bad weather.

There are farms in every state. California is the nation's top agricultural producer, thanks to its climate and widespread irrigation. More than 200 different crops are grown in the state. It is a major source of "truck crops" (tomatoes, lettuce, celery, etc.). With Florida, California produces the bulk of the nation's citrus. Together with Texas, it accounts for more than half of all U.S. cotton production.

Midwestern states produce most of the nation's corn and soybeans; North Dakota leads in barley production; and North Carolina and Kentucky lead in tobacco production.

Farmers often switch to new crop varieties that promise higher yields and increased income. In recent years, many such varieties have been created in the laboratory using genetic-engineering techniques. "Improved crops" include potatoes that are resistant to blight disease and tomatoes that yield thicker ketchup with less processing.

Farmers also experiment with new, untried crops. For example, many farmers have added oil-seed rape to their crop-rotation schemes, hoping to meet market demands for low-saturated canola fat and to combat disease cycles in the other crops they grow. Quinoa (an Andean grain), cherimoya (an Andean fruit), and kiwi (a fruit native to China) are other crops that have enjoyed increased production in the U.S. in recent years.

FINGERTIP FACTS

- Corn is the nation's biggest cash crop, with $16.6 billion worth of production in 1993.

- Soybeans, introduced into the U.S. from China in 1765, are the nation's second most valuable crop, at $11.7 billion worth of production in 1993.

- Average yield per acre for cotton rose from 614 pounds in 1989 to 699 pounds in 1992.

- Illinois and Iowa are the leading corn-growing states, producing 1,300 billion and 880 million bushels respectively in 1993.

- Tobacco is the nation's sixth-largest cash crop. It is grown in 51 of the 435 congressional districts. Two-thirds of annual production comes from North Carolina and Kentucky.

- Tobacco is the most lucrative U.S. crop, bringing growers $3,862 an acre. Peanuts ($691) and cotton ($380) are next.

- The U.S. produced 3.3 million tons of lettuce in 1992; California, Arizona, and Florida are the leading lettuce-growing states.

- The U.S. produces nearly 11 billion pounds of apples each year.

- Almonds are the nation's leading tree-nut crop, with production totaling 545 million pounds in 1992. California is the leading almond-growing state.

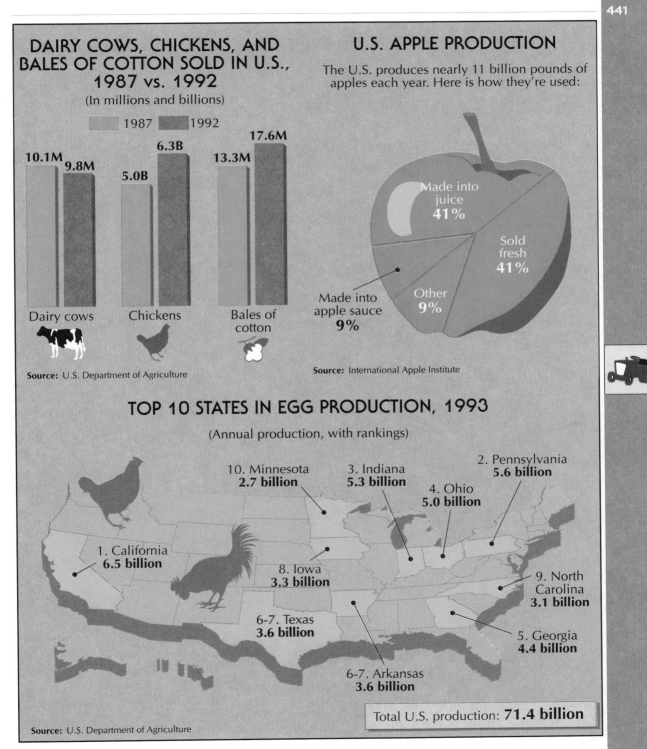

DAIRY COWS, CHICKENS, AND BALES OF COTTON SOLD IN U.S., 1987 vs. 1992

(In millions and billions)

▢ 1987 ▢ 1992

- Dairy cows: 10.1M (1987), 9.8M (1992)
- Chickens: 5.0B (1987), 6.3B (1992)
- Bales of cotton: 13.3M (1987), 17.6M (1992)

Source: U.S. Department of Agriculture

U.S. APPLE PRODUCTION

The U.S. produces nearly 11 billion pounds of apples each year. Here is how they're used:

- Made into juice 41%
- Sold fresh 41%
- Made into apple sauce 9%
- Other 9%

Source: International Apple Institute

TOP 10 STATES IN EGG PRODUCTION, 1993

(Annual production, with rankings)

- 10. Minnesota 2.7 billion
- 3. Indiana 5.3 billion
- 2. Pennsylvania 5.6 billion
- 4. Ohio 5.0 billion
- 1. California 6.5 billion
- 8. Iowa 3.3 billion
- 9. North Carolina 3.1 billion
- 6-7. Texas 3.6 billion
- 5. Georgia 4.4 billion
- 6-7. Arkansas 3.6 billion

Total U.S. production: **71.4 billion**

Source: U.S. Department of Agriculture

1994 BROKE RECORDS FOR CORN, SOYBEAN, AND COTTON HARVESTS

U.S. soybean, corn, and cotton crops have reached record levels.
Yields per acre are also at record levels:

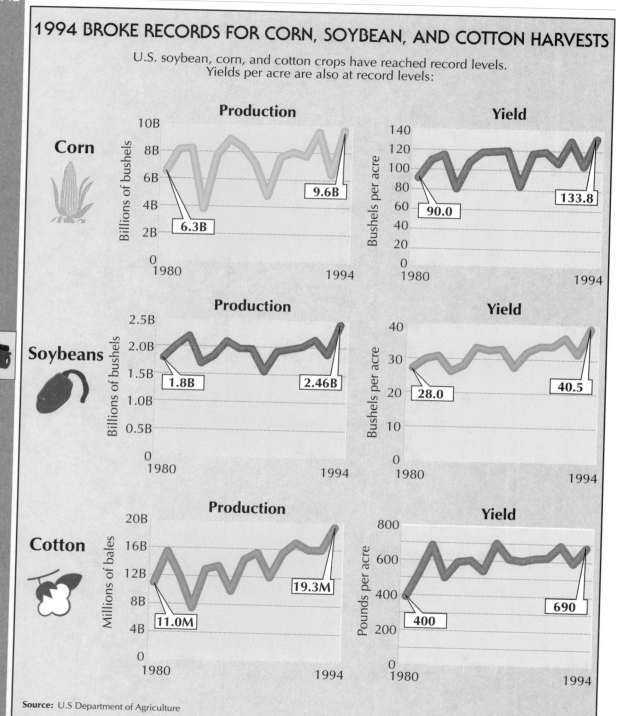

Source: U.S Department of Agriculture

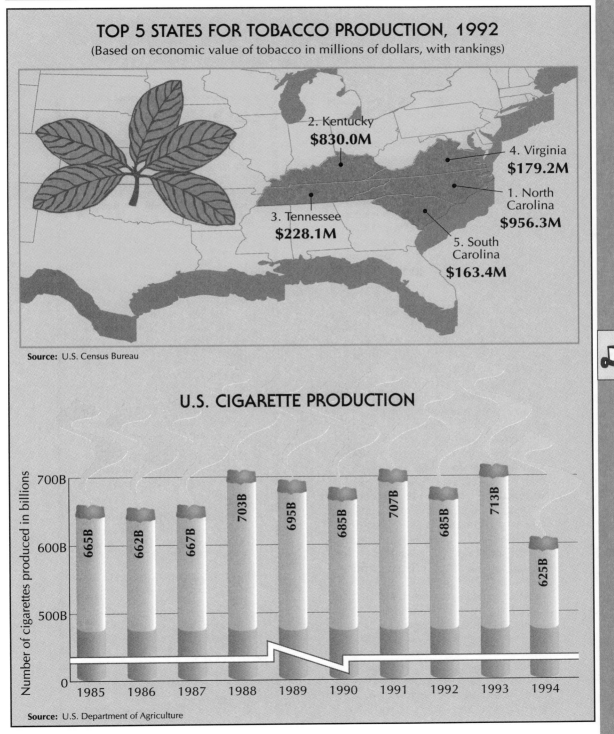

TOP 5 STATES FOR TOBACCO PRODUCTION, 1992

(Based on economic value of tobacco in millions of dollars, with rankings)

2. Kentucky
$830.0M

4. Virginia
$179.2M

1. North
Carolina
$956.3M

3. Tennessee
$228.1M

5. South
Carolina
$163.4M

Source: U.S. Census Bureau

U.S. CIGARETTE PRODUCTION

Number of cigarettes produced in billions

1985	1986	1987	1988	1989	1990	1991	1992	1993	1994
665B	662B	667B	703B	695B	685B	707B	685B	713B	625B

Source: U.S. Department of Agriculture

LIVESTOCK FARMING AND PRODUCTION

Approximately 50% of U.S. farm income is derived from livestock—cattle, hogs, chickens, turkeys, and other domesticated animals. Cattle and calves bred for beef are the primary source of farm income, earning $37.9 billion in 1992 (22.1% of total farm income). Dairy products are second, at $19.8 billion (11.6%). The leading 1992 plant crop, corn, brought in $14.7 billion (8.6%).

Most livestock in the U.S. is now raised by large, specialized operations, which has resulted in greater productivity and lower prices for consumers. Some farms, for example, specifically raise and market broiler chickens (about 5.8 billion annually). One study found that the retail price of broilers fell from $1.62 a pound in 1960 to $0.72 a pound in 1993.

Automation and other technologies are used in livestock farming to keep down labor costs and improve agricultural productivity. Automated feeders are programmed to give livestock a proper mix of food and water. Milking machines milk cows and keep track of how much milk each cow produces. Automatic sorters sort eggs according to weight and color and electrically powered cleaners sweep out barns.

Selective breeding and genetic engineering create new breeds of livestock as well as new drugs to boost production of existing breeds. One of the most controversial products of genetic engineering is recombinant bovine somatotropin (rBST), a growth hormone that significantly boosts milk production in dairy cows. Approved by the U.S. Food and Drug Administration (FDA) in 1993, it has been opposed by some consumer and environmental groups, who question its safety.

FINGERTIP FACTS

- In 1992, some 50.5% of U.S. farm income came from livestock, including cattle and calves (22.1%), dairy products (11.6%), hogs (5.9%), broiler chickens (5.3%), eggs (2.0%), turkeys (1.4%), sheep and lambs (0.3%), and other commodities.

- The number of U.S. farms with milk cows declined from 334,000 in 1980 to 172,000 in 1992. But over the same periods, total milk production increased, from 128 billion pounds to 152 billion pounds. Milk production per cow also increased, from 11,900 pounds to 15,400 pounds.

- The leading milk-producing states in 1992 were Wisconsin (24.1 billion pounds), California (22.1 billion), and New York (11.6 billion).

- In 1992, more than 135 million cattle, hogs and pigs, and lambs and sheep were slaughtered in the U.S.

- There were 100.1 million head of cattle on U.S. farms at the start of 1993. Texas led the states, with 14.3 million head.

- At the start of 1993, there were more than 59 million hogs and pigs on America's farms. Iowa led the states, with 15.8 million.

- In 1993, U.S. farmers produced 30.6 billion pounds of poultry.

- Arkansas is the leading chicken-producing state, with 4.5 billion pounds in 1992.

- Some 457.4 million pounds of catfish and 55.2 million pounds of trout were sold by aquaculture operations in 1992. Aquaculture accounted for 0.3% of total farm income in 1992.

U.S. HOG FARMS INCREASE IN SIZE, 1983–1993

Small hog farms are declining in number in the U.S.,
but the number of larger operations is growing dramatically:

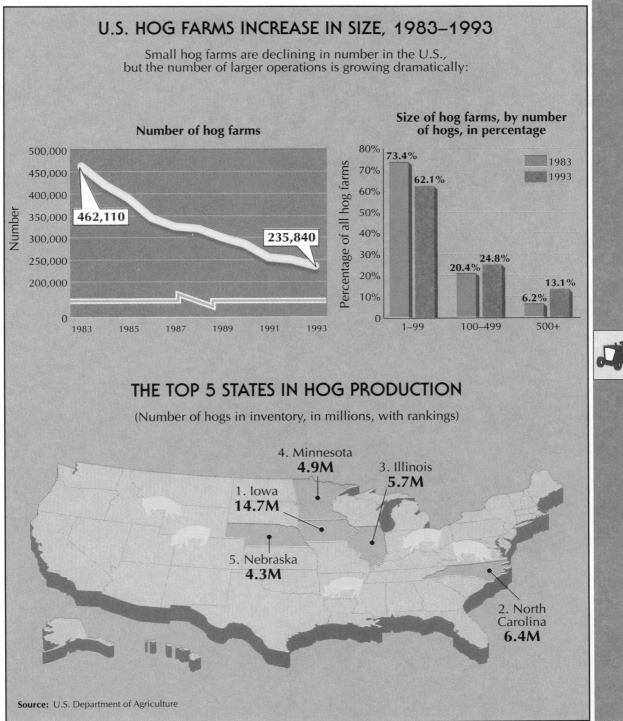

Number of hog farms

462,110

235,840

Size of hog farms, by number of hogs, in percentage

1983
1993

73.4%
62.1%
20.4%
24.8%
6.2%
13.1%

1–99   100–499   500+

THE TOP 5 STATES IN HOG PRODUCTION

(Number of hogs in inventory, in millions, with rankings)

4. Minnesota
4.9M

3. Illinois
5.7M

1. Iowa
14.7M

5. Nebraska
4.3M

2. North
Carolina
6.4M

Source: U.S. Department of Agriculture

U.S. PORK PRODUCTION CLIMBS, 1980–1994

(In billions of pounds)

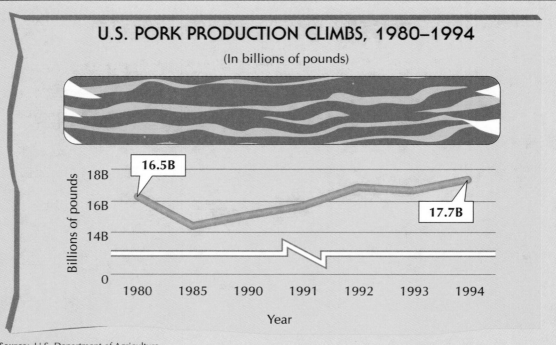

16.5B

17.7B

Billions of pounds: 18B, 16B, 14B, 0

Year: 1980 1985 1990 1991 1992 1993 1994

Source: U.S. Department of Agriculture

WHOLESALE HOG PRICES FALL, 1982–1994

It costs U.S. farmers as much as $0.40 a pound to raise hogs.
The average price that farmers receive compared to the average retail price, per pound:

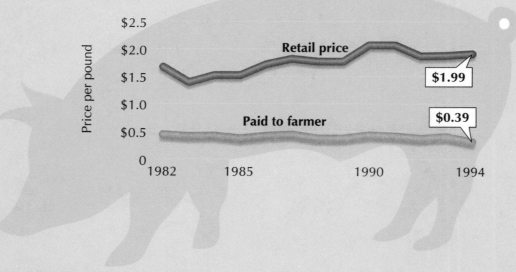

Price per pound: $2.5, $2.0, $1.5, $1.0, $0.5, 0

Retail price — **$1.99**

Paid to farmer — **$0.39**

1982 1985 1990 1994

Source: U.S. Department of Agriculture

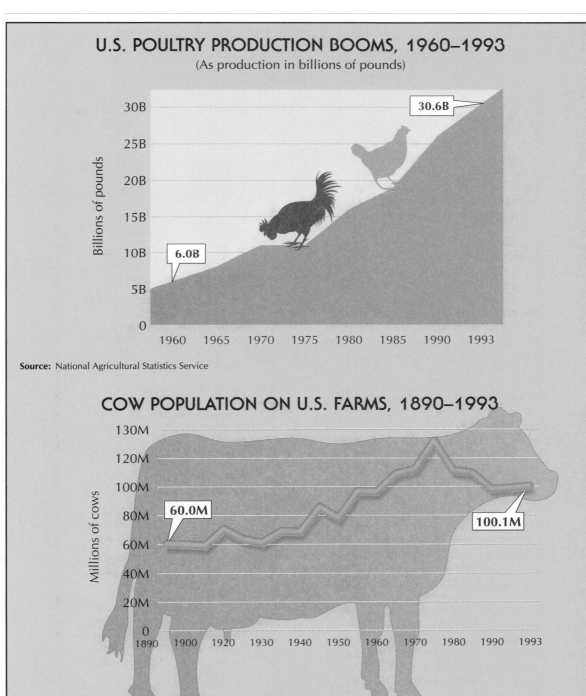

U.S. POULTRY PRODUCTION BOOMS, 1960–1993
(As production in billions of pounds)

30.6B

6.0B

Source: National Agricultural Statistics Service

COW POPULATION ON U.S. FARMS, 1890–1993

60.0M

100.1M

Source: U.S. Department of Agriculture

AGRICULTURE EXPORTS AND IMPORTS

U.S. farmers produce crops in excess of the country's domestic needs. While some of the excess is stockpiled, most of it is sold in foreign markets. America is the world's top food exporter, with exports in 1992 valued at $42.9 billion. Grains and feeds are the major U.S. exports, followed by oilseeds, animals and animal products, cotton, fruits, and vegetables. Asian countries, led by Japan, are the top U.S. food importers.

Government policies and trade agreements affect exports and imports in various ways. For example, if U.S. government subsidies for sugar growers were dropped, the percentage of imported sugar consumed in the U.S. —currently about 13%—would probably increase.

Political unrest, bad weather, and other calamities in foreign countries also create markets for U.S. farmers. For example, a severe drought in Australia in 1994 reduced that nation's wheat crop by more than 50%; wheat buyers who usually purchase Australian wheat had to turn to U.S., Canadian, and European sources.

Of course, the reverse can also occur. In 1994, the U.S. imported millions of tons of grain—mainly wheat, oats, and barley—in part because U.S. production was severely reduced by the 1993 floods in the Midwest. Food imports to the U.S. totaled $24.6 billion in 1992. Canada, Mexico, and Brazil were the leading countries of origin. Fruits, vegetables, beef and veal, coffee, and grains and feed were the leading imports. Yet from 1980 to 1992, the percentage of imports to the U.S. made up of agricultural products declined from 7% to 5%.

FINGERTIP FACTS

☛ The U.S. is the world's leading exporter and importer of tobacco.

☛ The U.S. exported 6.1 million tons of fruits, nuts, and vegetables in 1992, and imported 8.0 million tons— including 3.5 million tons of bananas.

☛ More than 41% of all agricultural exports are bought by Asia, with Japan taking the largest share.

☛ The Western European market for U.S. agricultural products fell from 31.4% of total U.S. agricultural exports in 1980 to 18.2% in 1992.

☛ The approval in 1993 of the North American Free Trade Agreement, NAFTA, plus strong growth in the Mexican economy led to a substantial increase in U.S. corn and soybean exports to Mexico during 1994.

☛ The U.S. imported $2.2 billion worth of fruits in 1992. Chile, Mexico, and Brazil were the leading countries of origin.

☛ In 1992, some 38.3% of the fruit consumed by Americans was imported, as was 6.7% of the vegetables.

☛ The U.S. imported $2.2 billion worth of vegetables in 1992, with Mexico, Canada, and Spain the main countries of origin.

☛ The U.S. imported 498 million pounds of spices in 1992, led by mustard seed (122.8 million pounds), pepper (102.8 million pounds), and sesame seed (77.1 million pounds).

EXPORT AND IMPORT VALUE OF SELECTED COMMODITIES, 1980 vs. 1992

(Exports and imports from and to the U.S.)

Exports

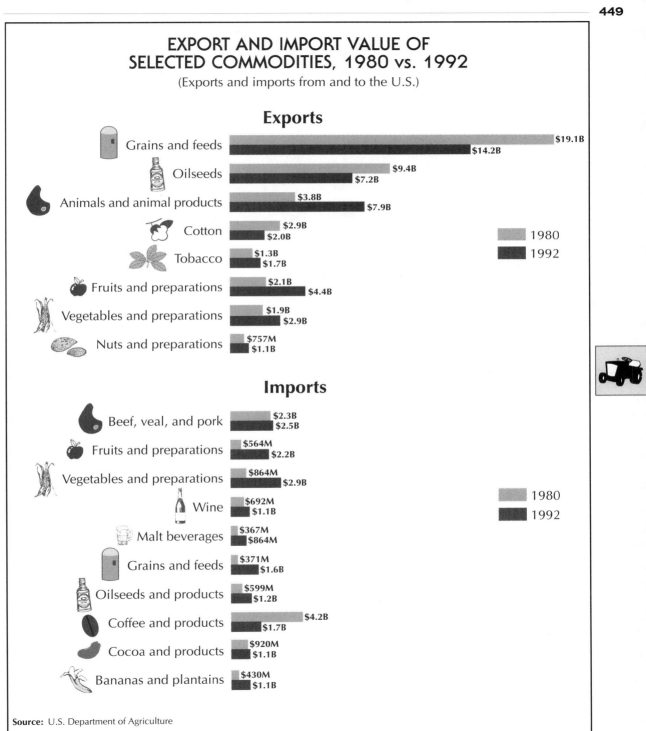

Commodity	1980	1992
Grains and feeds	$19.1B	$14.2B
Oilseeds	$9.4B	$7.2B
Animals and animal products	$3.8B	$7.9B
Cotton	$2.9B	$2.0B
Tobacco	$1.3B	$1.7B
Fruits and preparations	$2.1B	$4.4B
Vegetables and preparations	$1.9B	$2.9B
Nuts and preparations	$757M	$1.1B

1980
1992

Imports

Commodity	1980	1992
Beef, veal, and pork	$2.3B	$2.5B
Fruits and preparations	$564M	$2.2B
Vegetables and preparations	$864M	$2.9B
Wine	$692M	$1.1B
Malt beverages	$367M	$864M
Grains and feeds	$371M	$1.6B
Oilseeds and products	$599M	$1.2B
Coffee and products	$4.2B	$1.7B
Cocoa and products	$920M	$1.1B
Bananas and plantains	$430M	$1.1B

1980
1992

Source: U.S. Department of Agriculture

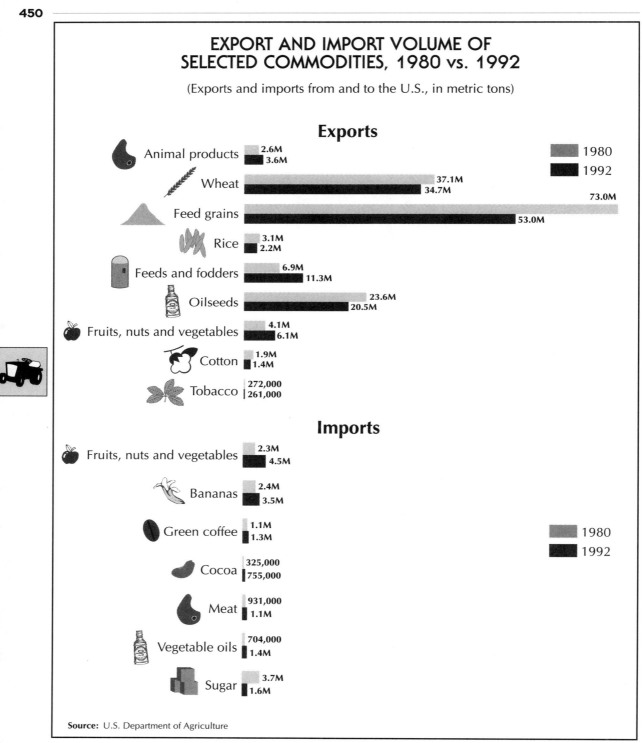

EXPORT AND IMPORT VOLUME OF SELECTED COMMODITIES, 1980 vs. 1992

(Exports and imports from and to the U.S., in metric tons)

Exports

Commodity	1980	1992
Animal products	2.6M	3.6M
Wheat	37.1M	34.7M
Feed grains	73.0M	53.0M
Rice	3.1M	2.2M
Feeds and fodders	6.9M	11.3M
Oilseeds	23.6M	20.5M
Fruits, nuts and vegetables	4.1M	6.1M
Cotton	1.9M	1.4M
Tobacco	272,000	261,000

Imports

Commodity	1980	1992
Fruits, nuts and vegetables	2.3M	4.5M
Bananas	2.4M	3.5M
Green coffee	1.1M	1.3M
Cocoa	325,000	755,000
Meat	931,000	1.1M
Vegetable oils	704,000	1.4M
Sugar	3.7M	1.6M

Source: U.S. Department of Agriculture

WHO EXPORTS THE MOST WHEAT, RICE, CORN?

(By dollar value in millions and billions, 1991)

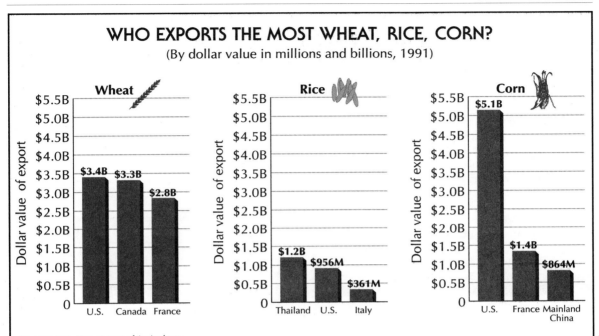

Wheat

Dollar value of export

- U.S. $3.4B
- Canada $3.3B
- France $2.8B

Rice

Dollar value of export

- Thailand $1.2B
- U.S. $956M
- Italy $361M

Corn

Dollar value of export

- U.S. $5.1B
- France $1.4B
- Mainland China $864M

Source: U.S. Department of Agriculture

WHO IMPORTS THE MOST WHEAT, RICE, CORN?

(By dollar value in millions and billions, 1991)

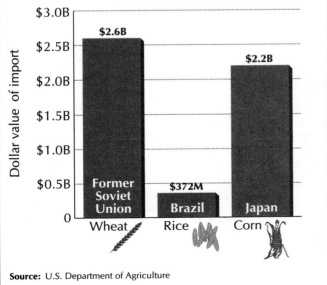

Dollar value of import

- Wheat — Former Soviet Union $2.6B
- Rice — Brazil $372M
- Corn — Japan $2.2B

Source: U.S. Department of Agriculture

WHO BUYS THE MOST FOOD FROM THE U.S.?

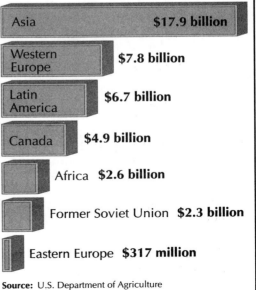

- Asia $17.9 billion
- Western Europe $7.8 billion
- Latin America $6.7 billion
- Canada $4.9 billion
- Africa $2.6 billion
- Former Soviet Union $2.3 billion
- Eastern Europe $317 million

Source: U.S. Department of Agriculture

A G R I C U L T U R E   A N D
T H E   E N V I R O N M E N T

While technological advancements have substantially increased agricultural productivity and the competitiveness of U.S. farmers, some of these practices have had undesirable effects. For example, large expanses of single crops (called monocultures) and the removal of "belts" of sheltering trees and shrubs between fields have contributed to soil erosion. The U.S. loses an estimated 4 billion tons of topsoil annually, making farmland less fertile and causing ecological damage. Overgrazing of rangelands also causes extensive erosion.

Damming rivers for irrigation destroys natural habitats. For example, California's Central Valley Project—which includes 5 major dams and thousands of miles of aqueducts—has contributed to the destruction of 92% of the valley's waterfowl wetlands habitat. Fertilizer- and pesticide-laden runoff from farms also causes terrible damage to wildlife habitats. In addition, pesticides create health risks to farmworkers and to the general public, as people ingest pesticide residues in food and water.

Agriculture, especially rice growing and cattle raising, is also a major source of atmospheric methane, a gas that is a prime contributor to "greenhouse warming."

During the past decade, however, significant progress has been made in combating the harmful environmental effects of agriculture. Scientists have been able to engineer crops to be resistant to diseases that once had to be controlled with pesticides. Farmers are cutting their per-acre use of chemicals,

partly by switching to biological pest controls; manure is being used instead of fossil-based fertilizers to improve soil; and federal programs such as the Conservation Reserve Program and Swampbuster protect wildlife and natural habitats.

FINGERTIP FACTS

☞ Each year, the U.S. loses more than 2 million acres of prime cropland to erosion, salinization, and waterlogging. Another 1 million acres are lost to urbanization, industry, road construction, and other development.

☞ U.S. topsoil is being lost 17 times faster than it is being replaced. It takes nature more than 200 years to form one inch of topsoil.

☞ In 1776, when the U.S. declared its independence, the average topsoil was 9 inches deep. Today, it's 5.9 inches deep.

☞ More than 500 million tons of livestock wastes—manure, feathers, and so on—are produced in the U.S. each year.

☞ More than 20,000 different pesticide products, containing more than 600 different active ingredients, are sold in the U.S.

☞ The U.S. Environmental Protection Agency found 98 different pesticides, including DDT, in groundwater in 40 states in 1991—contaminating the drinking water of more than 10 million people.

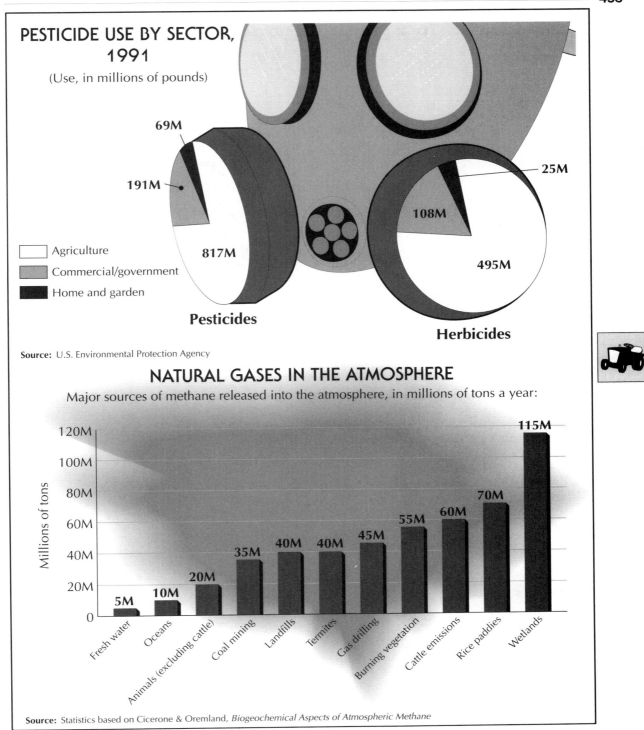

PESTICIDE USE BY SECTOR, 1991

(Use, in millions of pounds)

69M

191M

25M

108M

817M

495M

◻ Agriculture
▨ Commercial/government
◼ Home and garden

Pesticides

Herbicides

Source: U.S. Environmental Protection Agency

NATURAL GASES IN THE ATMOSPHERE

Major sources of methane released into the atmosphere, in millions of tons a year:

Millions of tons

120M
100M
80M
60M
40M
20M
0

Fresh water	5M
Oceans	10M
Animals (excluding cattle)	20M
Coal mining	35M
Landfills	40M
Termites	40M
Gas drilling	45M
Burning vegetation	55M
Cattle emissions	60M
Rice paddies	70M
Wetlands	115M

Source: Statistics based on Cicerone & Oremland, *Biogeochemical Aspects of Atmospheric Methane*

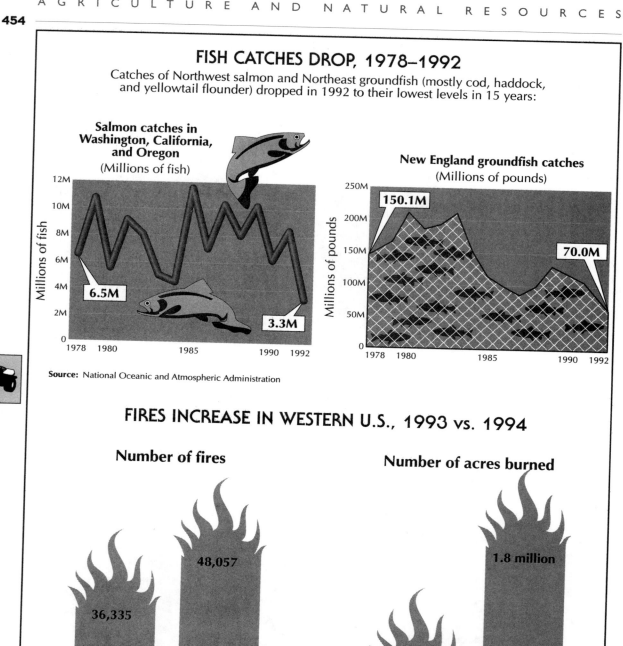

FISH CATCHES DROP, 1978–1992

Catches of Northwest salmon and Northeast groundfish (mostly cod, haddock, and yellowtail flounder) dropped in 1992 to their lowest levels in 15 years:

Salmon catches in Washington, California, and Oregon
(Millions of fish)

6.5M
3.3M

New England groundfish catches
(Millions of pounds)

150.1M
70.0M

Source: National Oceanic and Atmospheric Administration

FIRES INCREASE IN WESTERN U.S., 1993 vs. 1994

Number of fires

36,335 — 1993
48,057 — 1994

Number of acres burned

1.3 million — 1993
1.8 million — 1994

Source: National Interagency Fire Agency

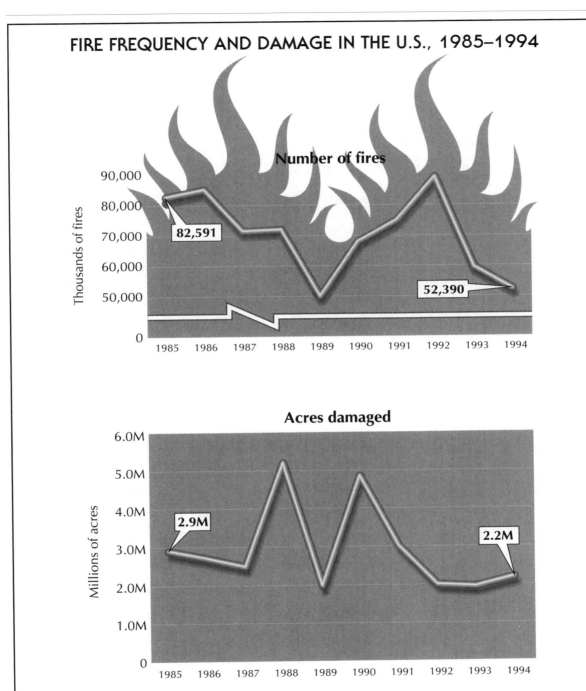

FIRE FREQUENCY AND DAMAGE IN THE U.S., 1985–1994

Number of fires

82,591

52,390

Acres damaged

2.9M

2.2M

Source: National Interagency Fire Center, National Oceanic and Atmospheric Administration

USING NATURAL RESOURCES

Today's farmers depend on 3 major groups of natural resources: fertile soil rich in nitrogen, phosphorus, and other nutrients; water from rivers and other surface supplies plus water pumped from groundwater supplies; and energy, derived primarily from oil and other non-renewable fossil fuels. About 400 gallons of oil equivalents are used annually to produce the food used by each American—to operate tractors and other equipment, and to produce fertilizers and pesticides.

Raising livestock uses far more resources than does growing fruits and vegetables. An estimated 20,000 pounds of potatoes can be grown on one acre—only 165 pounds of beef can be grown on the same land.

Farming methods also are a factor in the efficiency of resource use. No-till farming—where new seeds are planted directly into the previous crop's stubble—reduces soil erosion. Surge irrigation regulates water delivery rather than let water flow into all furrows at once, saving water, energy, and labor costs. Crop rotation cuts the need for nitrogen fertilizer. Organic farming uses cover crops instead of fertilizers to enrich the soil, and beneficial insects instead of pesticides to fight harmful pests.

Like other natural resources on which modern society depends, supplies of many of the natural resources needed by farmers are dwindling. Major efforts are being made to develop alternate sources. For example, scientists are developing environmentally sound processes to convert manure and other animal wastes into methane gas for fuel, liquid nutrients for aquaculture, and high-nutrient feed additives for livestock.

FINGERTIP FACTS

- About 14% of U.S. farms are irrigated. In 1960, the U.S. used 52 billion gallons of water each day for irrigation. By 1990, that figure had jumped to 76 billion gallons a day.

- Irrigation is wasteful. Worldwide, 70% of the water used for irrigation never reaches the crops.

- More than 2,000 gallons of water are used to produce one pound of butter or beef; fewer than 250 gallons of water are needed to produce one pound of grain crops such as oats and corn.

- About 9 pounds of feed are needed to produce one pound of beef; about 2 pounds of feed are needed to produce one pound of chicken.

- In commercial pork-farming operations, about one pound of meat can be produced from 3 pounds of feed.

- Timber harvested in national forests jumped from 3.5 billion board feet in 1950 to more than 10.5 billion board feet in 1990.

- Alaska's rainforests are dwindling rapidly. From 1930 to 1939, only 27.2 million board feet of timber were harvested in southeastern Alaska. From 1990 to 1993, there were 884.8 million board feet cut.

- Fertile soil contains up to 1,000 pounds of earthworms per square acre.

- Certain techniques, such as no-till farming, can reduce erosion.

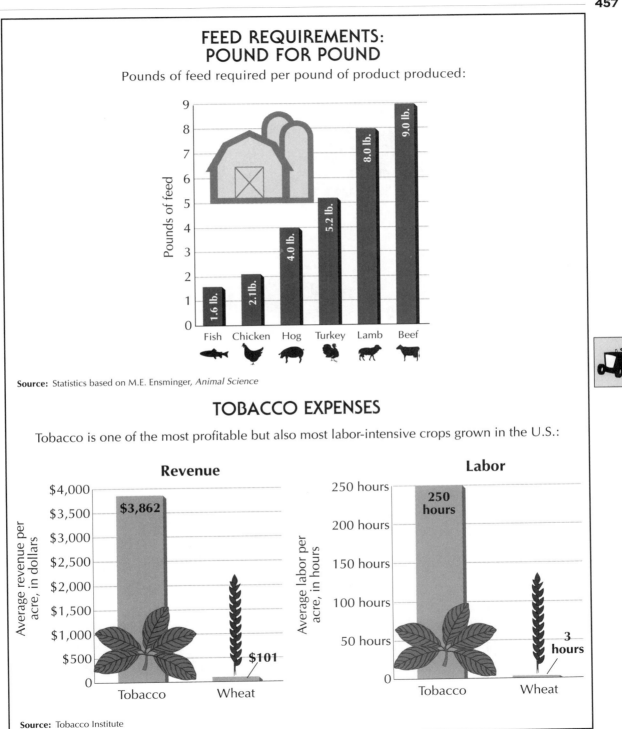

FEED REQUIREMENTS: POUND FOR POUND

Pounds of feed required per pound of product produced:

Pounds of feed

Fish — 1.6 lb.
Chicken — 2.1 lb.
Hog — 4.0 lb.
Turkey — 5.2 lb.
Lamb — 8.0 lb.
Beef — 9.0 lb.

Source: Statistics based on M.E. Ensminger, *Animal Science*

TOBACCO EXPENSES

Tobacco is one of the most profitable but also most labor-intensive crops grown in the U.S.:

Revenue

Average revenue per acre, in dollars

Tobacco — $3,862
Wheat — $101

Labor

Average labor per acre, in hours

Tobacco — 250 hours
Wheat — 3 hours

Source: Tobacco Institute

WATER REQUIREMENTS: OUNCE FOR OUNCE
(Gallons of water used per pound of food produced)

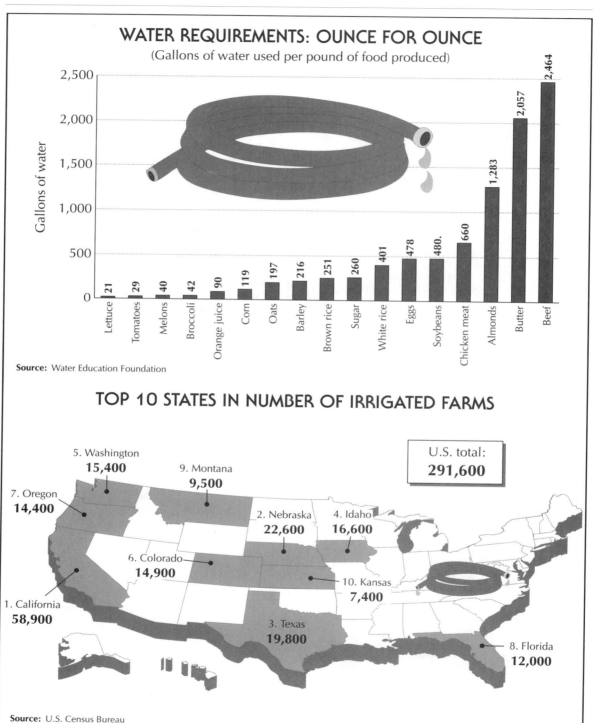

Gallons of water

Food	Gallons
Lettuce	21
Tomatoes	29
Melons	40
Broccoli	42
Orange juice	90
Corn	119
Oats	197
Barley	216
Brown rice	251
Sugar	260
White rice	401
Eggs	478
Soybeans	480.
Chicken meat	660
Almonds	1,283
Butter	2,057
Beef	2,464

Source: Water Education Foundation

TOP 10 STATES IN NUMBER OF IRRIGATED FARMS

U.S. total:
291,600

5. Washington
15,400

9. Montana
9,500

7. Oregon
14,400

2. Nebraska
22,600

4. Idaho
16,600

6. Colorado
14,900

10. Kansas
7,400

1. California
58,900

3. Texas
19,800

8. Florida
12,000

Source: U.S. Census Bureau

TAKING TIMBER FROM ALASKA, 1930–1993

The rainforests of Alaska's 17-million acre Tongass National Forest are dwindling rapidly, as more and more timber is cut. Mean average timber harvest each decade in southeastern Alaska, in millions of board feet:

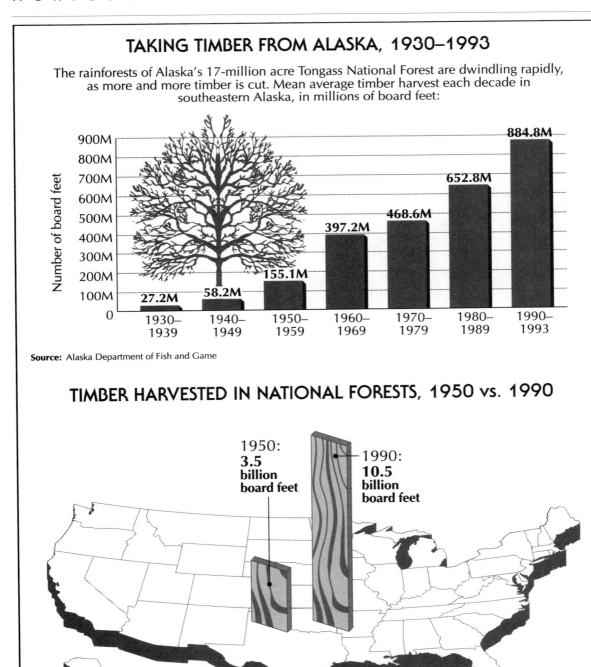

Source: Alaska Department of Fish and Game

TIMBER HARVESTED IN NATIONAL FORESTS, 1950 vs. 1990

1950:
**3.5
billion
board feet**

1990:
**10.5
billion
board feet**

Source: U.S. Forest Service

8

TRANSPORTATION AND ENERGY

GETTING AROUND

Whether it is for business or pleasure, most Americans depend on their cars to get around—or, at least, to try to get around. Growth in traffic has led to increasing congestion, especially during "rush hours," when people travel to and from work. Despite these problems, the U.S. transportation program remains focused on highway travel, with a much greater percentage of federal transportation funds going to highway programs than to mass transit.

Airplanes, railroads, and buses are the primary alternatives to automobiles for long-distance travel. For short distances, there are various mass transit options. Buses are the primary mass transit vehicles for "commuter services" between cities and the suburbs. About 950 U.S. cities have mass transit systems; almost all of these consist solely of bus service. Most of the largest cities, however, are also equipped with subway or surface rail systems or combinations of the two. New York City has the longest and most developed rail system in the country, with 492.9 miles of route in its famed subway system.

- In 1992, private automobiles carried 80.5% of all intercity passenger traffic, followed by airlines (17.7%), buses (1.1%), and railroads (0.7%).

- Between 1980 and 1992, the percentage of intercity passenger traffic carried by cars declined from 86.9% to 80.5%. Meanwhile, the airlines' share of this traffic rose from 10.1% to 17.7%—in part because airfares have risen much more slowly than fares for other transportation.

- In 1992, the U.S. had 3.9 million miles of public roads—785,000 in urban areas and more than 3.1 million in rural areas.

- As of 1992, there were 42,493 miles of road in the U.S. interstate system. The longest interstate was I-90, with 3,081 miles; the shortest was I-878 in New York City—only 0.7 mile.

- Texas leads the states in miles of interstate highway (3,230 miles in 1992). Delaware has the least (41 miles).

- Most American workers—86.5%—commute via car, truck, or van.

- Driving is by far the most common method of commuting in 9 of the nation's 10 largest cities; only in New York City is public transportation the favored mode.

- According to 1993 data, Los Angeles, California, is the nation's most traffic-congested metropolitan area.

- In Michigan, 81.5% of commuters drive alone, compared to 54.3% in New York.

- "Carpooling" is practiced by 20.5% of Hawaiian commuters, but only 10.1% of South Dakotans.

- New Yorkers spend an average of 27.8 minutes traveling to work; North Dakotans spend an average of only 11.9 minutes.

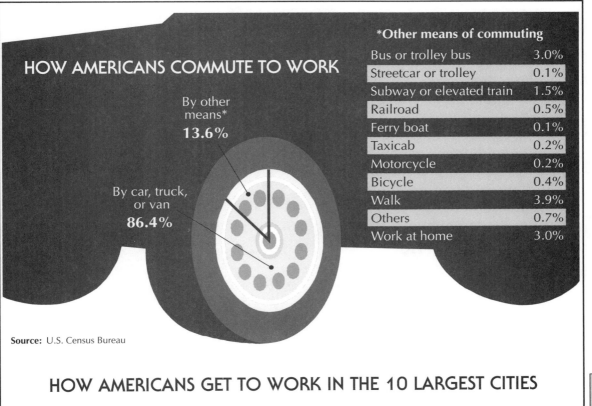

HOW AMERICANS COMMUTE TO WORK

By other means*
13.6%

By car, truck, or van
86.4%

*Other means of commuting	
Bus or trolley bus	3.0%
Streetcar or trolley	0.1%
Subway or elevated train	1.5%
Railroad	0.5%
Ferry boat	0.1%
Taxicab	0.2%
Motorcycle	0.2%
Bicycle	0.4%
Walk	3.9%
Others	0.7%
Work at home	3.0%

Source: U.S. Census Bureau

HOW AMERICANS GET TO WORK IN THE 10 LARGEST CITIES

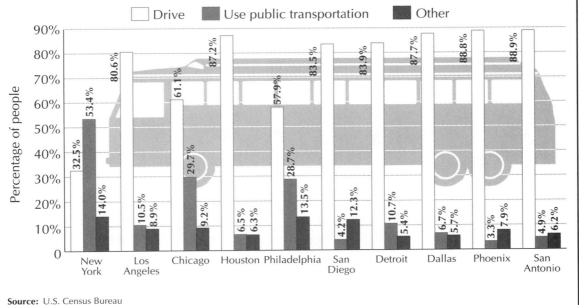

Drive   Use public transportation   Other

Percentage of people

City	Drive	Use public transportation	Other
New York	32.5%	53.4%	14.0%
Los Angeles	80.6%	10.5%	8.9%
Chicago	61.1%	29.7%	9.2%
Houston	87.2%	6.5%	6.3%
Philadelphia	57.9%	28.7%	13.5%
San Diego	83.5%	4.2%	12.3%
Detroit	83.9%	10.7%	5.4%
Dallas	87.7%	6.7%	5.7%
Phoenix	88.8%	3.3%	7.9%
San Antonio	88.9%	4.9%	6.2%

Source: U.S. Census Bureau

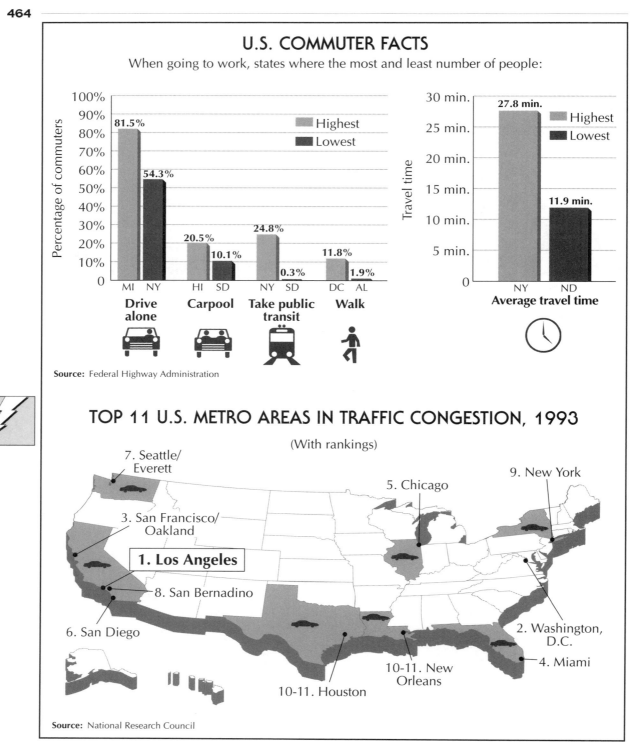

U.S. COMMUTER FACTS

When going to work, states where the most and least number of people:

Drive alone — MI 81.5% (Highest), NY 54.3% (Lowest)
Carpool — HI 20.5% (Highest), SD 10.1% (Lowest)
Take public transit — NY 24.8% (Highest), SD 0.3% (Lowest)
Walk — DC 11.8% (Highest), AL 1.9% (Lowest)

Average travel time — NY 27.8 min. (Highest), ND 11.9 min. (Lowest)

Source: Federal Highway Administration

TOP 11 U.S. METRO AREAS IN TRAFFIC CONGESTION, 1993

(With rankings)

7. Seattle/Everett
5. Chicago
9. New York
3. San Francisco/Oakland
1. Los Angeles
8. San Bernadino
6. San Diego
2. Washington, D.C.
4. Miami
10-11. New Orleans
10-11. Houston

Source: National Research Council

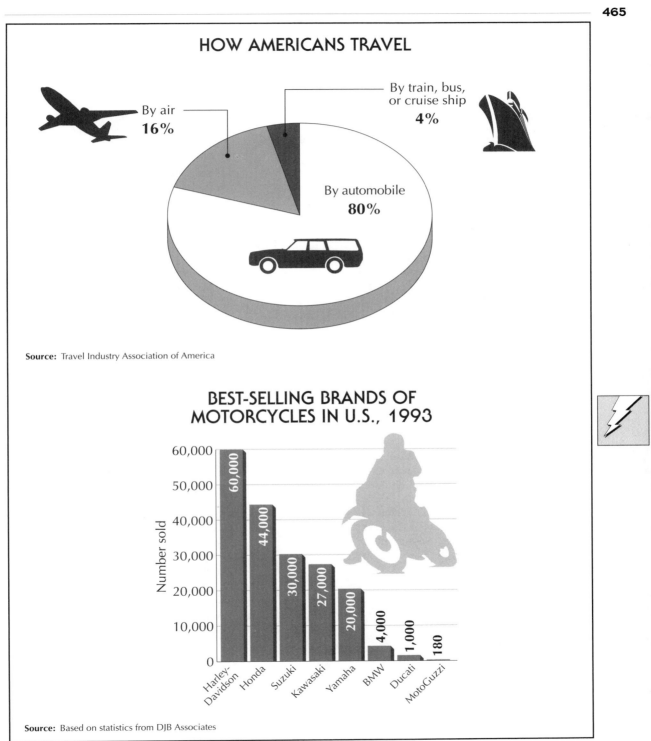

HOW AMERICANS TRAVEL

By air
16%

By train, bus,
or cruise ship
4%

By automobile
80%

Source: Travel Industry Association of America

BEST-SELLING BRANDS OF MOTORCYCLES IN U.S., 1993

Number sold

Brand	Number sold
Harley-Davidson	60,000
Honda	44,000
Suzuki	30,000
Kawasaki	27,000
Yamaha	20,000
BMW	4,000
Ducati	1,000
MotoGuzzi	180

Source: Based on statistics from DJB Associates

AMERICA'S LOVE AFFAIR WITH AUTOMOBILES

Americans drove their cars 1.6 trillion miles in 1992—more than 11,000 miles per vehicle—as they traveled to malls and mountains, farms and factories, homes and hospitals—indeed, to every conceivable destination.

All this freedom of movement, however, has a price. It cost 45.77 cents per mile to own and operate an automobile in 1992, up from 27.95 cents in 1980. Some costs are fixed. For example, car insurance averaged $747 in 1992, while depreciation averaged $2,780. Other costs—gasoline and oil, tires, and maintenance—are variable, depending on mileage. Society pays, too, especially as it deals with the air pollutants emitted by cars. But there is good news on this front. Engine modifications, such as the addition of catalytic converters, have helped reduce harmful emissions like carbon monoxide and nitrogen oxides.

Accidents are another problem. There were some 11.9 million motor-vehicle accidents and 42,000 deaths in 1993. These cost the nation an estimated $167.3 billion in damages, medical expenses, wage losses, and so on.

People over age 65 drive less than younger drivers do—but they are at greater risk when they get behind the wheel. For example, drivers ages 70 to 74 have more than twice as many fatal crashes—based on number of miles traveled—than do drivers ages 40 to 49.

FINGERTIP FACTS

- Motor-vehicle registrations in the U.S. reached 197 million in 1993.

- Males made up just over half (51%) of the 175.9 million licensed drivers in 1993, but they drove about 65% of the miles driven that year.

- Americans drove their cars a total of 1.6 trillion miles in 1992, up from 1.1 trillion in 1980.

- People in the Los Angeles, California, area drive 266 million miles a day.

- Gasoline is much cheaper in the U.S. than in other industrialized countries. U.S. prices averaged $1.22 a gallon in 1992, compared to $3.55 in Japan, $3.65 in Germany, and a whopping $4.74 in Italy.

- A car must be driven 800 miles to cause as much pollution as an outboard motor does in one hour.

- Based on miles driven, females are more likely to be involved in accidents, but males are more likely to be in fatal accidents.

- In 1993, there were 11.9 million motor-vehicle accidents. Safety belts were effective in preventing about 50% of fatalities and severe injuries.

- In 1993, there were 42,000 motor-vehicle fatalities, 65.2% occurred in rural areas; 51.9% occurred at night.

- In 1992, the use of safety belts saved an estimated 5,226 lives. An estimated 268 toddlers and infants were saved by child-restraint systems.

- From 1975 to 1995, the number of U.S. drivers ages 65 and older more than doubled, reaching 13 million. By the year 2020, there will be 30 million drivers in this age group.

- Each year, almost 1 million older drivers attend "refresher" driving courses.

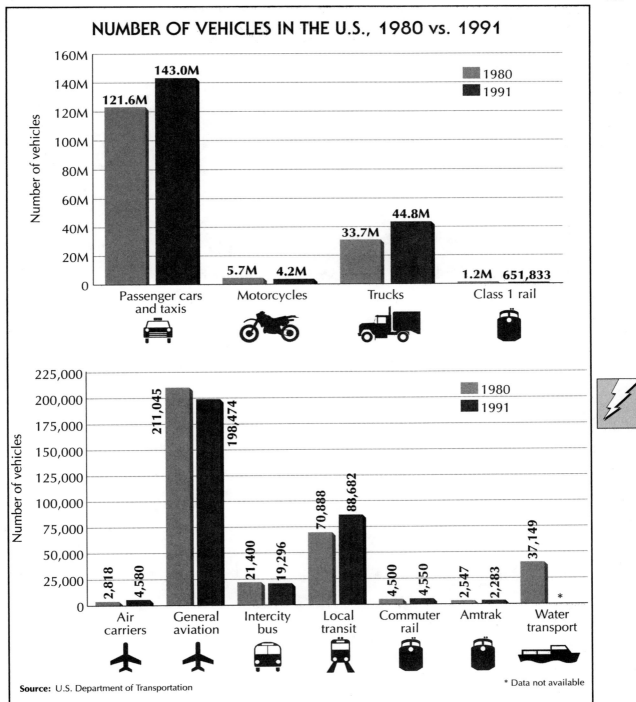

NUMBER OF VEHICLES IN THE U.S., 1980 vs. 1991

Number of vehicles

Legend: 1980, 1991

- Passenger cars and taxis: 121.6M (1980), 143.0M (1991)
- Motorcycles: 5.7M (1980), 4.2M (1991)
- Trucks: 33.7M (1980), 44.8M (1991)
- Class 1 rail: 1.2M (1980), 651,833 (1991)

Number of vehicles

Legend: 1980, 1991

- Air carriers: 2,818 (1980), 4,580 (1991)
- General aviation: 211,045 (1980), 198,474 (1991)
- Intercity bus: 21,400 (1980), 19,296 (1991)
- Local transit: 70,888 (1980), 88,682 (1991)
- Commuter rail: 4,500 (1980), 4,550 (1991)
- Amtrak: 2,547 (1980), 2,283 (1991)
- Water transport: 37,149 (1980), * (1991)

Source: U.S. Department of Transportation

* Data not available

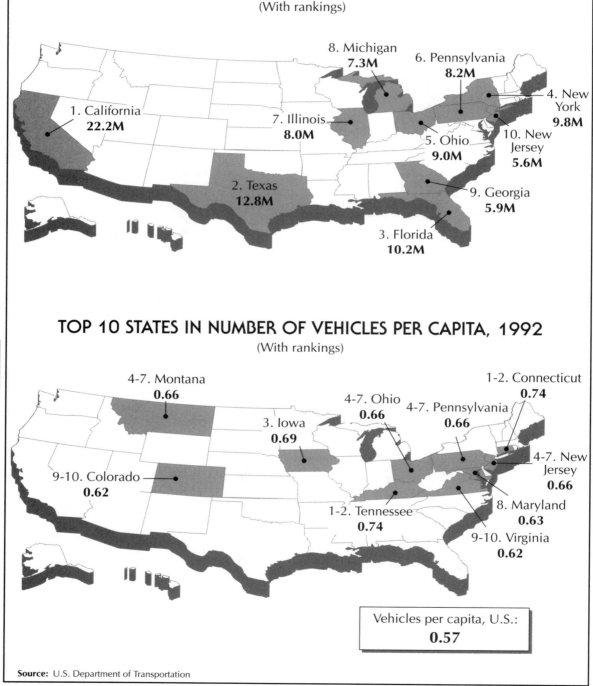

TOP 10 STATES IN TOTAL NUMBER OF VEHICLES, 1992
(With rankings)

8. Michigan **7.3M**
6. Pennsylvania **8.2M**
4. New York **9.8M**
1. California **22.2M**
7. Illinois **8.0M**
5. Ohio **9.0M**
10. New Jersey **5.6M**
2. Texas **12.8M**
9. Georgia **5.9M**
3. Florida **10.2M**

TOP 10 STATES IN NUMBER OF VEHICLES PER CAPITA, 1992
(With rankings)

4-7. Montana **0.66**
4-7. Ohio **0.66**
4-7. Pennsylvania **0.66**
1-2. Connecticut **0.74**
3. Iowa **0.69**
4-7. New Jersey **0.66**
9-10. Colorado **0.62**
1-2. Tennessee **0.74**
8. Maryland **0.63**
9-10. Virginia **0.62**

Vehicles per capita, U.S.:
0.57

Source: U.S. Department of Transportation

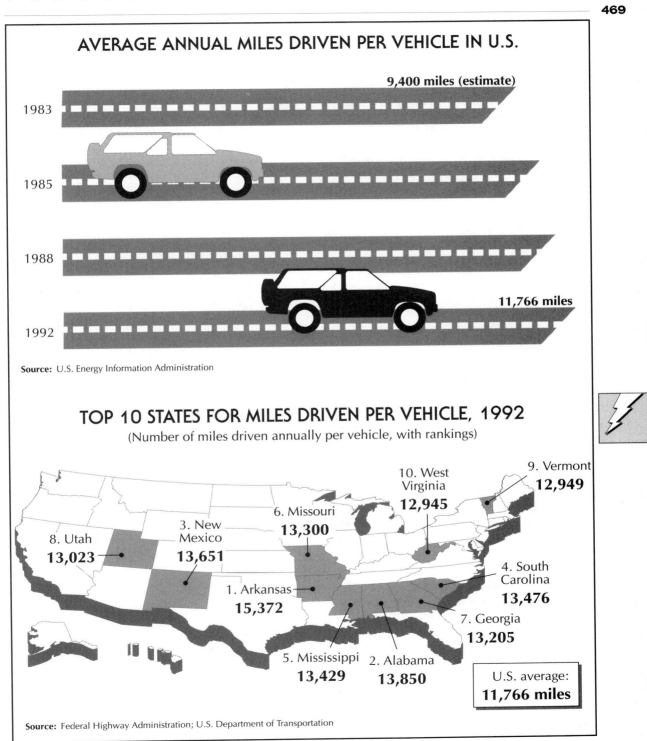

AVERAGE ANNUAL MILES DRIVEN PER VEHICLE IN U.S.

9,400 miles (estimate)

1983

1985

1988

11,766 miles

1992

Source: U.S. Energy Information Administration

TOP 10 STATES FOR MILES DRIVEN PER VEHICLE, 1992
(Number of miles driven annually per vehicle, with rankings)

10. West Virginia **12,945**

9. Vermont **12,949**

6. Missouri **13,300**

3. New Mexico **13,651**

8. Utah **13,023**

4. South Carolina **13,476**

1. Arkansas **15,372**

7. Georgia **13,205**

5. Mississippi **13,429**

2. Alabama **13,850**

U.S. average: **11,766 miles**

Source: Federal Highway Administration; U.S. Department of Transportation

THE U.S. AUTO INDUSTRY

U.S. automakers produced 5.7 million passenger cars in 1992. But the nation's auto industry is much broader, including importers (3.6 million cars in 1992); dealers; gasoline service stations; manufacturers and sellers of tires, batteries, and other parts; parking garages; and rental services.

Consumer demands have resulted in cars that are sleeker, faster, and more comfortable than ever before. They have better fuel efficiency, too. And today, the "family car" may not even be what has previously been considered a "car." Sales of light trucks and sport-utility vehicles (SUVs) for personal use have zoomed. Recreational-vehicle sales also are on the rise, after hitting a low in 1991.

People are holding onto vehicles longer than they did in the past. One reason may be "sticker shock." During the past 20 years, new car prices have risen at faster rates than most people's incomes have. By the end of 1994, the average cost of a new car exceeded $20,000, including taxes and other charges, as compared to $4,400 in 1974 (the equivalent of $12,800 after adjusting for inflation). As a result, used cars were outselling new cars 2 to 1 in 1994, accounting for one-third of all the dollars spent on vehicles.

FINGERTIP FACTS

☞ Americans spent more than $91 billion on new cars in 1993. Spending on used cars reached $43 billion in that same year.

☞ Business-related car sales increased significantly from 1983 to 1993, going from 33% of all sales to 45%.

☞ U.S. auto plants produced 5.9 million passenger cars in 1993, second only to Japan's 8.5 million.

☞ Production has declined since 1985, when 8.2 million cars were manufactured in the U.S. Importation of new cars also fell, from 4.4 million in 1985 to 3.6 million in 1992.

☞ Japan is the major source of imported cars in the U.S. (1.7 million in 1992), followed by Canada (1.2 million) and Germany (0.2 million).

☞ The U.S. exported 851,000 new cars to other countries in 1992, up from 617,000 in 1980.

☞ At General Motors, labor costs an average of $2,388 per vehicle; at Honda's U.S. plants, labor costs an average of $920 per vehicle.

☞ The fuel efficiency of new cars has improved over the years, from an average of 16.1 miles per gallon in 1955 to an average of 28.3 miles per gallon in 1993.

☞ The Ford Taurus was the best-selling car of 1993; Ford F-Pickups headed light-truck sales.

☞ Luxury cars and large cars accounted for only one-quarter of U.S. car sales in 1993; most Americans buy small and mid-size cars.

☞ Leasing is growing quickly in popularity—it has more than doubled in the past decade and is expected to continue as a major force in car sales.

☞ People are keeping their cars longer. The median age of U.S. cars rose from 4.9 years in 1970 to 7.0 years in 1992.

☞ In 1992, of the 120.3 million cars in use, 50.4 million were less than 5 years old while 26.4 million were at least 12 years old.

U.S. AUTOMOBILE SALES, BY SIZE AND TYPE, 1993

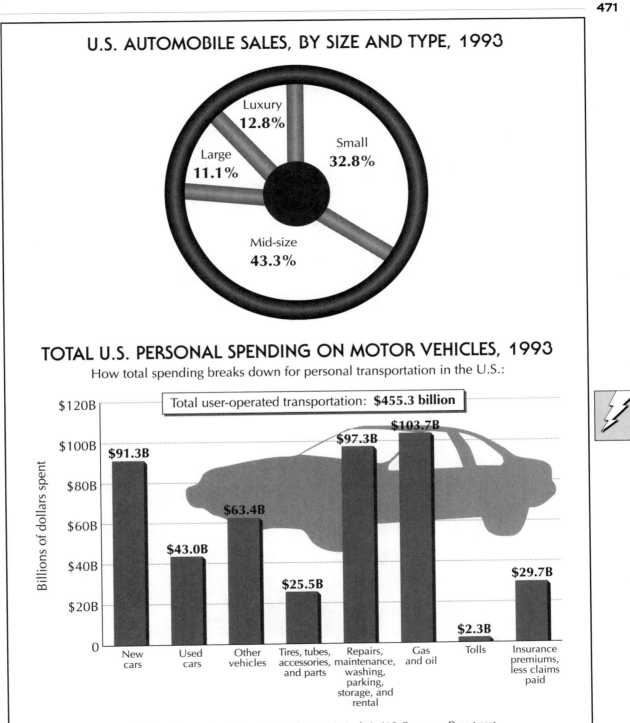

Luxury
12.8%

Small
32.8%

Large
11.1%

Mid-size
43.3%

TOTAL U.S. PERSONAL SPENDING ON MOTOR VEHICLES, 1993

How total spending breaks down for personal transportation in the U.S.:

Total user-operated transportation: **$455.3 billion**

Billions of dollars spent

$120B	
$100B	
$80B	
$60B	
$40B	
$20B	
0	

$91.3B — New cars
$43.0B — Used cars
$63.4B — Other vehicles
$25.5B — Tires, tubes, accessories, and parts
$97.3B — Repairs, maintenance, washing, parking, storage, and rental
$103.7B — Gas and oil
$2.3B — Tolls
$29.7B — Insurance premiums, less claims paid

Source: American Automobile Manufacturers Association; Bureau of Economic Analysis; U.S. Commerce Department

TOP 10 BEST-SELLING CARS AND LIGHT TRUCKS IN THE U.S., 1993

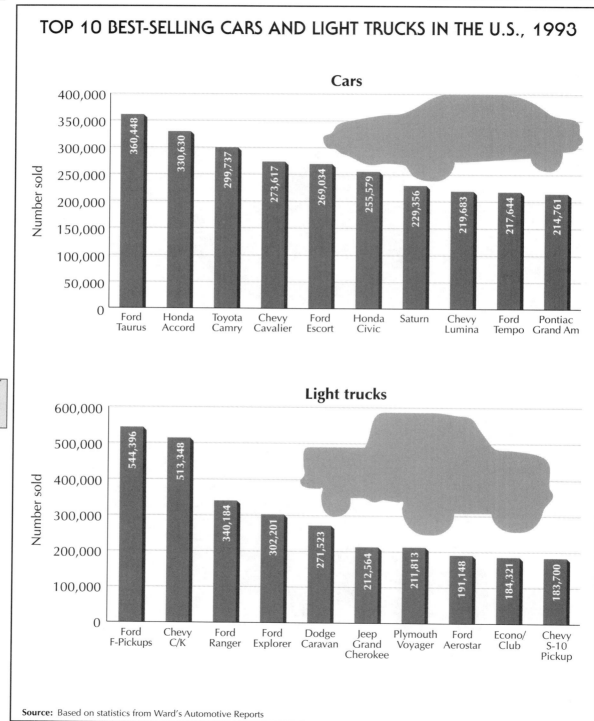

Cars

Number sold

	Number sold
Ford Taurus	360,448
Honda Accord	330,630
Toyota Camry	299,737
Chevy Cavalier	273,617
Ford Escort	269,034
Honda Civic	255,579
Saturn	229,356
Chevy Lumina	219,683
Ford Tempo	217,644
Pontiac Grand Am	214,761

Light trucks

	Number sold
Ford F-Pickups	544,396
Chevy C/K	513,348
Ford Ranger	340,184
Ford Explorer	302,201
Dodge Caravan	271,523
Jeep Grand Cherokee	212,564
Plymouth Voyager	211,813
Ford Aerostar	191,148
Econo/ Club	184,321
Chevy S-10 Pickup	183,700

Source: Based on statistics from Ward's Automotive Reports

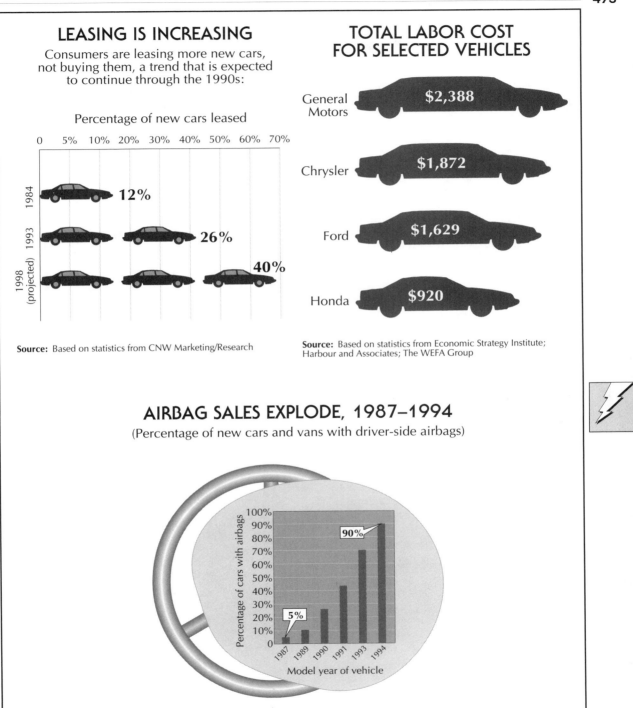

LEASING IS INCREASING

Consumers are leasing more new cars,
not buying them, a trend that is expected
to continue through the 1990s:

Percentage of new cars leased

| 0 | 5% | 10% | 20% | 30% | 40% | 50% | 60% | 70% |

1984 — **12%**

1993 — **26%**

1998 (projected) — **40%**

Source: Based on statistics from CNW Marketing/Research

TOTAL LABOR COST FOR SELECTED VEHICLES

General Motors — **$2,388**

Chrysler — **$1,872**

Ford — **$1,629**

Honda — **$920**

Source: Based on statistics from Economic Strategy Institute; Harbour and Associates; The WEFA Group

AIRBAG SALES EXPLODE, 1987–1994

(Percentage of new cars and vans with driver-side airbags)

Percentage of cars with airbags

100%
90%
80%
70%
60%
50%
40%
30%
20%
10%
0

90%

5%

1987 1989 1990 1991 1993 1994

Model year of vehicle

Source: Insurance Institute for Highway Safety; Highway Loss Data Institute

AIR TRAVEL

More people are taking to the skies than ever before, a trend that shows no signs of slowing. Indeed, U.S. air traffic is expected to double by the year 2010, with an estimated 1.0 billion passengers a year. Most passengers in the U.S. fly on major airlines, such as Delta, American, United, USAir, and Northwest. But the nation also has 125 scheduled commuter carriers, which fly short hauls and cover smaller cities no longer serviced by the major airlines. Commuter air traffic—about 58 million boardings annually—is growing steadily at the rate of 6% to 10% a year. Business travelers make up about 65% of these customers.

Safety concerns are always a big issue among air travelers, even though during the years 1990 to 1994, a person's chances of being killed on a flight with a major U.S. airline was 1 in 6.5 million. On international carriers, the risk was even less; 1 in 7.0 million.

The risk of death is higher on prop/turboprop planes, which are more likely to be used by commuter services. From 1985 to 1994, the risk was 1 in 2.0 million. In 1994, the Department of Transportation announced plans to improve commuter-airline safety standards to those of the major carriers, particularly in such areas as aircraft maintenance and pilot training.

FINGERTIP FACTS

- In 1992, personal spending on air travel in the U.S. totaled more than $25 billion, up from less than $15 billion in 1982.
- Delta carried the most passengers in 1993, followed closely by American; United was third but had the most revenue, followed by American and Delta.

- There were 6.6 million scheduled departures from U.S. airports in 1992. Chicago's O'Hare was the busiest airport, with 377,000 departures.

- The busiest domestic route in 1992 was between New York City and Los Angeles (2.9 million passengers).

- From 1985–1994, a U.S. traveler's chance of being killed on a domestic flight was 0 on American, Southwest, and TWA; it was 1 in 10 million on Continental; 1 in 8 million on Delta; and 1 in 2 million on USAir.

- Thunderstorm wind shear leads to more passenger deaths in U.S. domestic jet crashes (419 deaths from 1975 to 1994) than any other cause, including collisions (159 deaths) and ice buildup (122 deaths).

- The U.S. has 125 scheduled commuter carriers, which serve about 58 million travelers a year. The largest is American Eagle, which had 280 planes in mid-1995.

- In 1993, the 22 leading U.S. airports experienced more than 20,000 hours of flight delays, which cost the airlines a total of $1.6 million an hour.

- In 1992, U.S. airlines employed 540,000 people.

- Labor is the largest component of airline costs (34.2% in 1992), followed by fuel (13.5%) and commissions (10.9%). Passenger food ate up 4.0% of operating expenses.

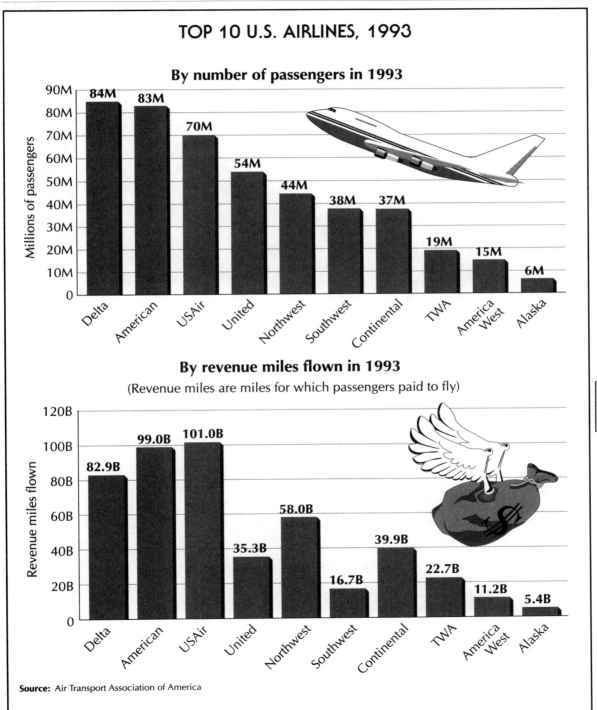

TOP 10 U.S. AIRLINES, 1993

By number of passengers in 1993

Millions of passengers

Airline	Passengers
Delta	84M
American	83M
USAir	70M
United	54M
Northwest	44M
Southwest	38M
Continental	37M
TWA	19M
America West	15M
Alaska	6M

By revenue miles flown in 1993

(Revenue miles are miles for which passengers paid to fly)

Revenue miles flown

Airline	Revenue miles flown
Delta	82.9B
American	99.0B
USAir	101.0B
United	35.3B
Northwest	58.0B
Southwest	16.7B
Continental	39.9B
TWA	22.7B
America West	11.2B
Alaska	5.4B

Source: Air Transport Association of America

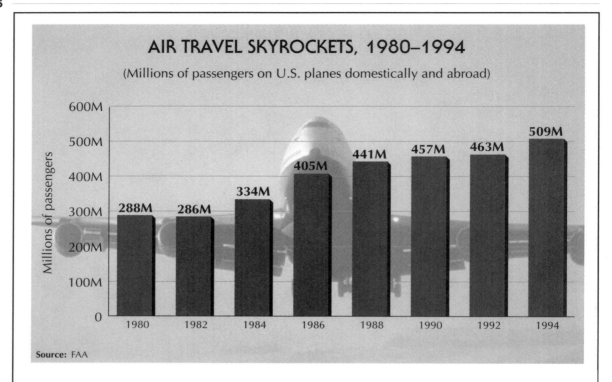

AIR TRAVEL SKYROCKETS, 1980–1994

(Millions of passengers on U.S. planes domestically and abroad)

Source: FAA

WORLD'S 10 BUSIEST AIRPORTS, 1993

The U.S. had 7 of the world's 10 busiest airports in 1993. The total number of passengers:

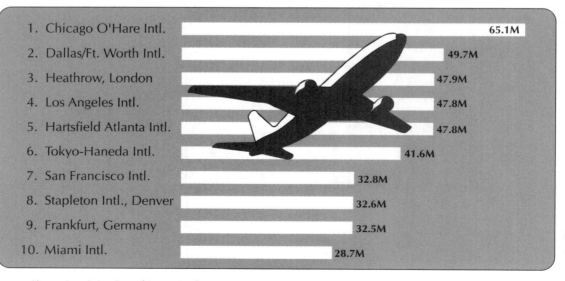

	Airport	Passengers
1.	Chicago O'Hare Intl.	65.1M
2.	Dallas/Ft. Worth Intl.	49.7M
3.	Heathrow, London	47.9M
4.	Los Angeles Intl.	47.8M
5.	Hartsfield Atlanta Intl.	47.8M
6.	Tokyo-Haneda Intl.	41.6M
7.	San Francisco Intl.	32.8M
8.	Stapleton Intl., Denver	32.6M
9.	Frankfurt, Germany	32.5M
10.	Miami Intl.	28.7M

Source: Airports Association Council International

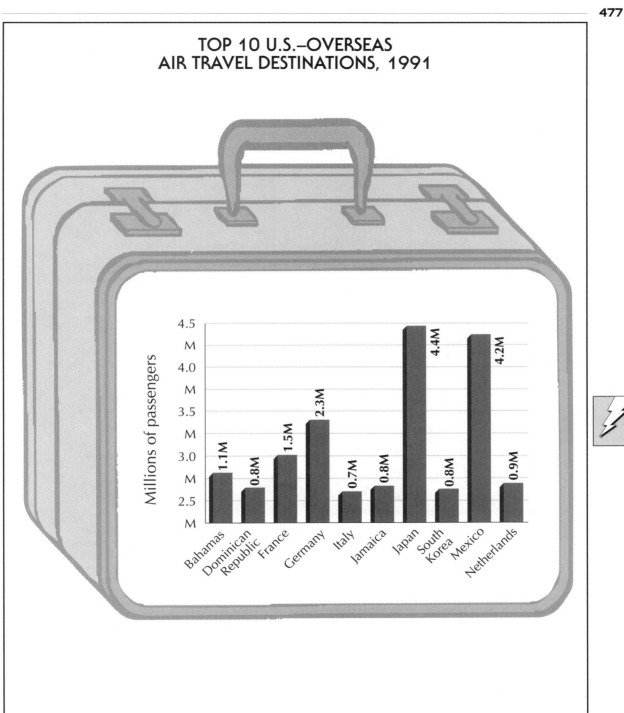

TOP 10 U.S.–OVERSEAS AIR TRAVEL DESTINATIONS, 1991

Source: U.S. Department of Transportation

RAILROADS

Railroads play a significant role in the transportation of both people and freight in America, even though competing modes of transport—particularly the various kinds of motor vehicles, but also airplanes—have been favored with more generous government subsidies and less strict regulation over the past 50 years.

Since 1971, almost all intercity train passenger service in the United States has been provided by the federally subsidized National Railroad Passenger Corporation, better known as Amtrak. Each year, more than 21 million passengers ride Amtrak trains, and the system takes in nearly $1 billion in revenues. However, reduced federal funding has forced deep cuts in Amtrak maintenance and service.

Amtrak and other railroads are classified by the Interstate Commerce Commission according to annual gross operating revenues. Currently, the revenue levels are: Class 1: $250 million or more; Class 2: more than $20 million but less than $250 million; and Class 3: $20 million or less.

Mergers and consolidations helped lead to a decline in the number of Class 1 freight lines. But freight traffic on railroads has increased in recent years, despite that downward trend. This is due in part to a shift to intermodal transport—the movement of freight by more than one method (for example, truck trailers transferred to freightcars for part of their journey, then transferred back to trucks for transport to the final destination).

FINGERTIP FACTS

- In 1993, passenger fares and other user revenues covered 80% of Amtrak's operating costs.

- Amtrak traffic declined from 22.4 million passengers in 1990 to 21.7 million in 1992.

- The average U.S. passenger rail trip covered 285.1 miles in 1992.

- According to 1994 timetables, the fastest scheduled passenger trains in the U.S. take 42 minutes, at average speeds of 97.7 miles per hour, to travel the 68.4 miles from Wilmington, Delaware, to Baltimore, Maryland.

- In 1980, U.S. railroads had 458,000 employees; by 1992, the number had fallen to 197,000.

- The cheapest way to move freight is by water. Using trains costs about 3 times as much.

- In 1940, railroads handled 61.3% of the nation's freight traffic; by 1980, the figure had dropped to 37.2%. Since then, there has been a slight increase, to an estimated total of 37.8% in 1993.

- Class 1 freight trains covered 390 million miles in 1992, up from lows of 347 million in 1985 and 1986, but below the 428 million miles traveled in 1980.

- In 1992, some 1,170 people were killed in train accidents in the U.S., including accidents at highway grade crossings.

AMTRAK OPERATING STATISTICS, 1985 vs. 1993

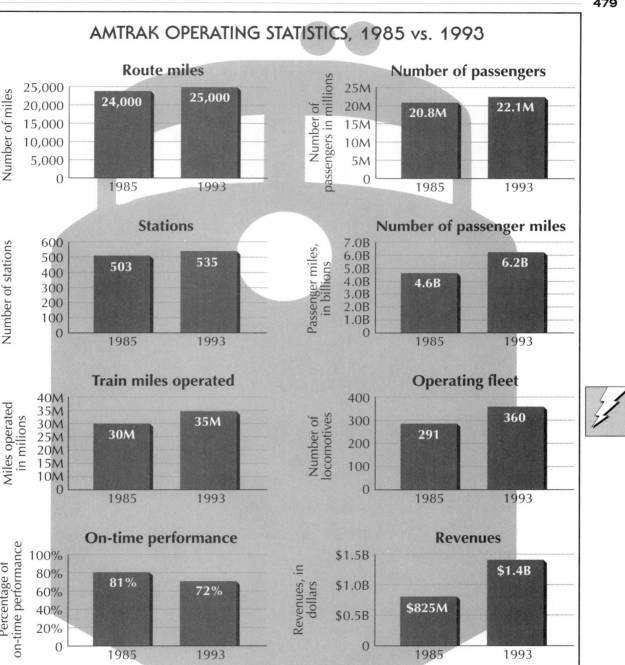

Route miles

Number of miles

	1985	1993
	24,000	25,000

Number of passengers

Number of passengers in millions

	1985	1993
	20.8M	22.1M

Stations

Number of stations

	1985	1993
	503	535

Number of passenger miles

Passenger miles, in billions

	1985	1993
	4.6B	6.2B

Train miles operated

Miles operated in millions

	1985	1993
	30M	35M

Operating fleet

Number of locomotives

	1985	1993
	291	360

On-time performance

Percentage of on-time performance

	1985	1993
	81%	72%

Revenues

Revenues, in dollars

	1985	1993
	$825M	$1.4B

Source: Amtrak

U.S. RAILROAD TRAFFIC RISES

Railroad traffic dropped in 1991 and recovered in 1992.
Container shipping, air freight, and trucking have also been rising:

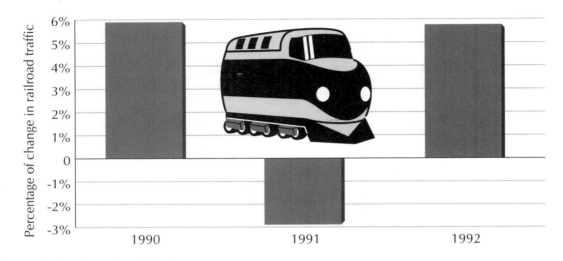

Source: American Association of Railroads

TOP 10 LARGEST RAPID OR HEAVY U.S. RAIL SYSTEMS, 1992

Route miles

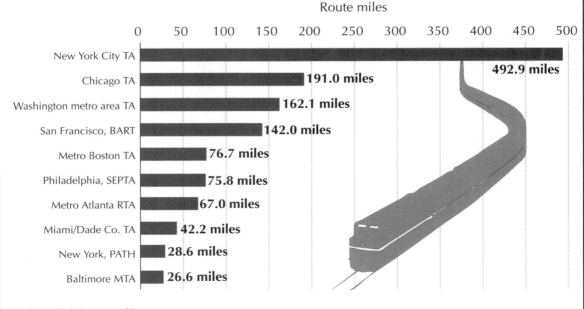

	Route miles
New York City TA	**492.9 miles**
Chicago TA	**191.0 miles**
Washington metro area TA	**162.1 miles**
San Francisco, BART	**142.0 miles**
Metro Boston TA	**76.7 miles**
Philadelphia, SEPTA	**75.8 miles**
Metro Atlanta RTA	**67.0 miles**
Miami/Dade Co. TA	**42.2 miles**
New York, PATH	**28.6 miles**
Baltimore MTA	**26.6 miles**

Source: U.S. Department of Transportation

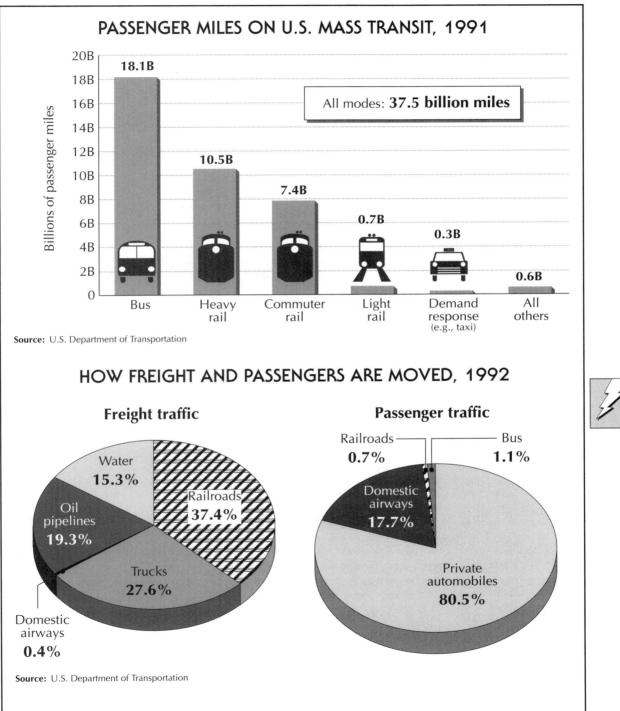

PASSENGER MILES ON U.S. MASS TRANSIT, 1991

All modes: **37.5 billion miles**

Billions of passenger miles

- Bus: 18.1B
- Heavy rail: 10.5B
- Commuter rail: 7.4B
- Light rail: 0.7B
- Demand response (e.g., taxi): 0.3B
- All others: 0.6B

Source: U.S. Department of Transportation

HOW FREIGHT AND PASSENGERS ARE MOVED, 1992

Freight traffic

- Water 15.3%
- Railroads 37.4%
- Oil pipelines 19.3%
- Trucks 27.6%
- Domestic airways 0.4%

Passenger traffic

- Railroads 0.7%
- Bus 1.1%
- Domestic airways 17.7%
- Private automobiles 80.5%

Source: U.S. Department of Transportation

ENERGY GENERATION AND PRODUCTION

Fossil fuels—which include coal, petroleum, and natural gas—provide almost 90% of the total energy used in the U.S. Other sources, primarily hydropower and nuclear power, supply the remaining 10%. Energy production from 1960 to 1993 increased more than 35%, from 41.5 quadrillion British thermal units (Btu's) to 65.8 quadrillion Btu's. Over that period, coal and nuclear power met growing percentages of the nation's energy needs, while petroleum's role declined significantly.

Fossil fuels are nonrenewable resources, so these fuels are limited in supply. They also are associated with environmental problems, including oil spills and air pollution. Many people oppose nuclear power generation because of the dangerous radioactive spent fuel that it creates. This relatively new form of extremely hazardous material is piling up quickly, but scientists still are not sure how—or if—such waste can be safely transported, disposed of, or stored.

A number of economic and technological problems have limited the development of safer and cleaner alternative energy sources, such as wind power and solar energy. Researchers continue to improve our access to these sources, but they are also searching for additional ones that are more practical on a large scale. For instance, hydrogen may become the fuel of the future if researchers can find an inexpensive and relatively speedy method of extracting it from water or natural gas.

FINGERTIP FACTS

- In 1990, the Soviet Union and the U.S. each produced more than 67 quadrillion Btu's of energy—more than twice that produced by China, the third-largest energy producer.

- In 1993, daily U.S. petroleum production was 6.8 million barrels.

- In 1994, for the first time, more new wells were drilled in the U.S. for natural gas than for petroleum.

- In 1950, 11.3% of homes used wood as their main heating fuel. In 1990, only 5.2% did.

- In 1980, the U.S. had 233 manufacturers of solar collectors, which convert sunlight to heat; they shipped 19,398 collectors. By 1992, there were only 45 manufacturers, who shipped 7,086 units.

- Most electricity generated in the U.S. comes from coal (56.9%). Nuclear energy (21.2%), hydroelectric power (9.3%), and gas (9.0%) are the other leading sources.

- In 1993, some 110 commercial nuclear power reactors were operating in the U.S., more than in any other nation.

- In 1992, the U.S. imported 16.88 quadrillion Btu's of petroleum, and exported 2.01 quadrillion Btu's.

- Producing electricity from natural gas costs about 3.0 cents per kilowatt-hour, less than from wind (5.0 cents), geothermal energy (5.5 cents), or solar energy (14.0 cents).

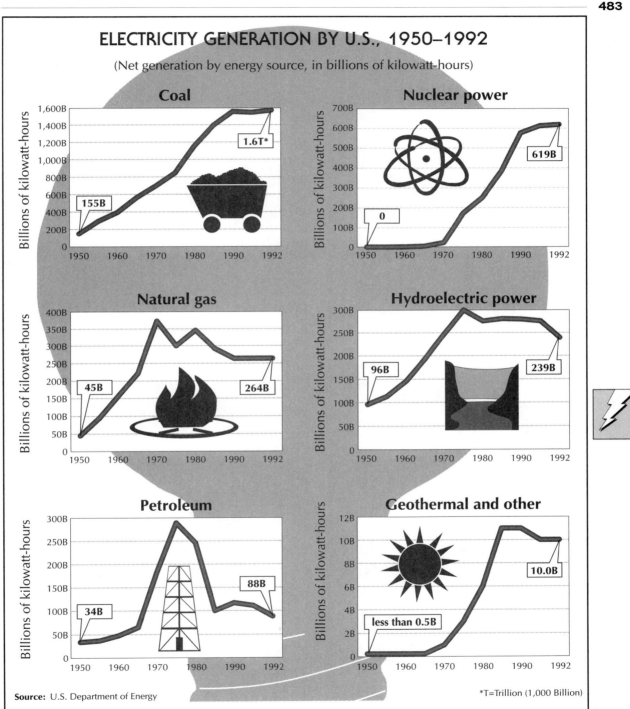

ELECTRICITY GENERATION BY U.S., 1950–1992

(Net generation by energy source, in billions of kilowatt-hours)

Coal

Nuclear power

Natural gas

Hydroelectric power

Petroleum

Geothermal and other

Source: U.S. Department of Energy

*T=Trillion (1,000 Billion)

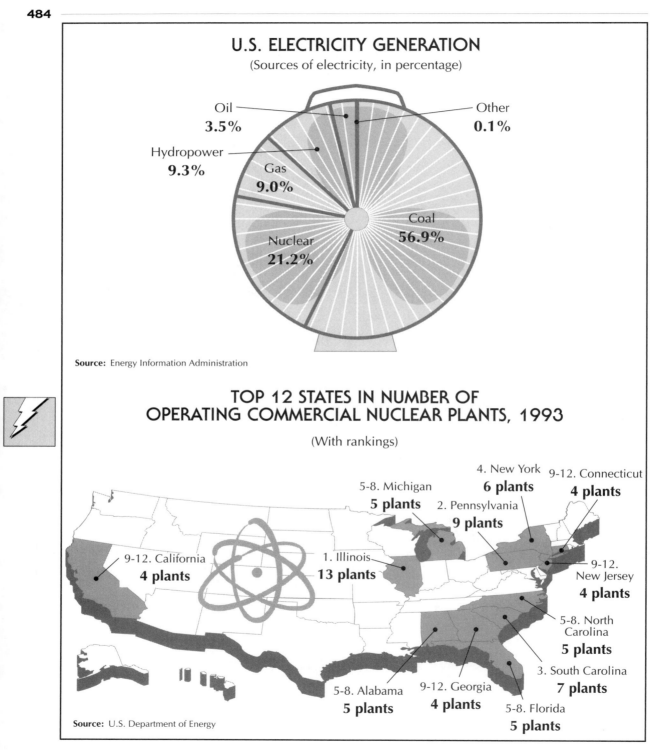

U.S. ELECTRICITY GENERATION
(Sources of electricity, in percentage)

Oil
3.5%

Other
0.1%

Hydropower
9.3%

Gas
9.0%

Coal
56.9%

Nuclear
21.2%

Source: Energy Information Administration

TOP 12 STATES IN NUMBER OF
OPERATING COMMERCIAL NUCLEAR PLANTS, 1993
(With rankings)

4. New York
6 plants

9-12. Connecticut
4 plants

5-8. Michigan
5 plants

2. Pennsylvania
9 plants

9-12. California
4 plants

1. Illinois
13 plants

9-12.
New Jersey
4 plants

5-8. North
Carolina
5 plants

3. South Carolina
7 plants

5-8. Alabama
5 plants

9-12. Georgia
4 plants

5-8. Florida
5 plants

Source: U.S. Department of Energy

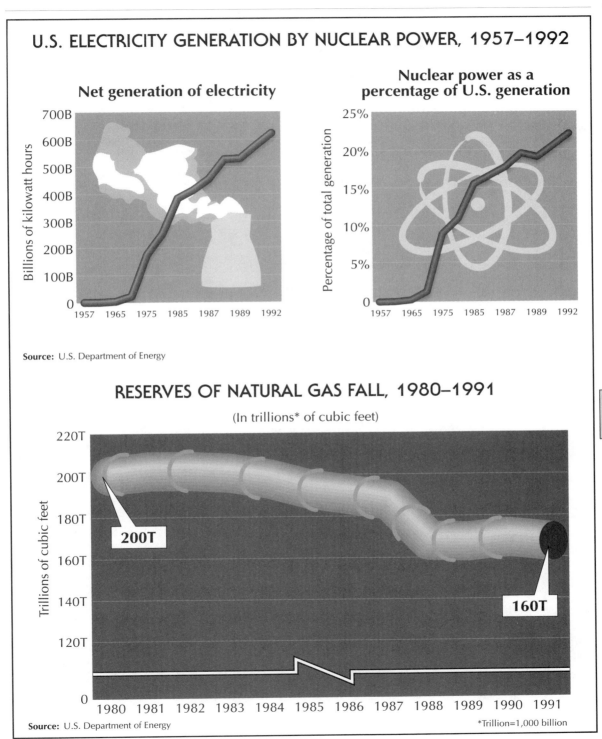

U.S. ELECTRICITY GENERATION BY NUCLEAR POWER, 1957–1992

Net generation of electricity

Billions of kilowatt hours

700B
600B
500B
400B
300B
200B
100B
0

1957 1965 1975 1985 1987 1989 1992

Nuclear power as a percentage of U.S. generation

Percentage of total generation

25%
20%
15%
10%
5%
0

1957 1965 1975 1985 1987 1989 1992

Source: U.S. Department of Energy

RESERVES OF NATURAL GAS FALL, 1980–1991

(In trillions* of cubic feet)

Trillions of cubic feet

220T
200T
180T
160T
140T
120T
0

200T

160T

1980 1981 1982 1983 1984 1985 1986 1987 1988 1989 1990 1991

Source: U.S. Department of Energy

*Trillion=1,000 billion

E N E R G Y   C O N S U M P T I O N

As the U.S. population has increased, so has its thirst for energy. The most dramatic increase has been in demand for electricity. The nation used 380 times more electricity in 1980 than it did in 1900. Furthermore, the U.S. uses more energy than any other nation in the world.

Growth in energy consumption has continued steadily in recent years. At the same time, however, people have become more energy-conscious, thanks to public education campaigns about environmental concerns and the growing realization that fossil fuel reserves are dwindling. This has led to energy-saving measures in industry, residences, and commercial establishments. Cars today travel farther on a gallon of gas, and new home appliances consume significantly less energy than their counterparts of 10 or 20 years ago. Economics also has spurred conservation efforts. The average price of electricity rose from 1.7 cents per kilowatt-hour in 1970 to 6.8 cents in 1992.

From 1980 to 1990, the average annual energy consumption per U.S. household dropped from 126 million Btu's to 98 million Btu's. Nonetheless, Americans continue to consume more energy per capita than residents of any other country.

FINGERTIP FACTS

- The U.S. produces less energy than it consumes. In 1993, it produced 65.8 quadrillion Btu's and consumed a record 84.0 quadrillion.

- In 1993, more than half of the oil used in the U.S. was imported.

- In per capita terms, the leading U.S. energy consumer is Alaska (1.0 billion Btu's per person in 1991).

- The U.S. spent $467.1 billion on energy in 1991, the equivalent of $1,853 per person.

- Residential energy consumption cost an average of $1,172 per household in 1990.

- The higher the family income, the greater the energy consumption. Households with family incomes under $20,000 in 1990 used an average of less than 84 million Btu's. Those with incomes of $50,000 or more consumed an average of 132 million Btu's.

- Of the 84 quadrillion Btu's consumed in the U.S. in 1993, electricity generation consumed the largest portion (36.3%).

- Energy consumption by the transportation sector rose from 10.6 quadrillion Btu's in 1960 to 22.8 quadrillion in 1993—but, in terms of percentage of total, it rose only slightly, from 24.2% to 27.1%. In contrast, electricity generation consumed 8.2 quadrillion Btu's in 1960 (18.7% of the total) and 30.4 quadrillion Btu's in 1993 (36.3%).

- Almost all (96%) U.S. commercial buildings use electricity; 55.5% use natural gas.

- Most U.S. homes are heated with natural gas (51.7%). Electricity heats 21.5% of U.S. homes.

- In 1992, gas utilities in the Midwest had the most customers—a total of 17.2 million, of which 15.7 million were residences.

- Households use energy mainly for heating (52% of energy consumed), followed by water heating (18%), cooking and refrigeration (11%), air conditioning (8%), and combined other uses (11%).

U.S. CONSUMPTION OF ENERGY, 1950–1992

(Total and per capita consumption of energy, in quadrillions* of British thermal units, or Btu's)

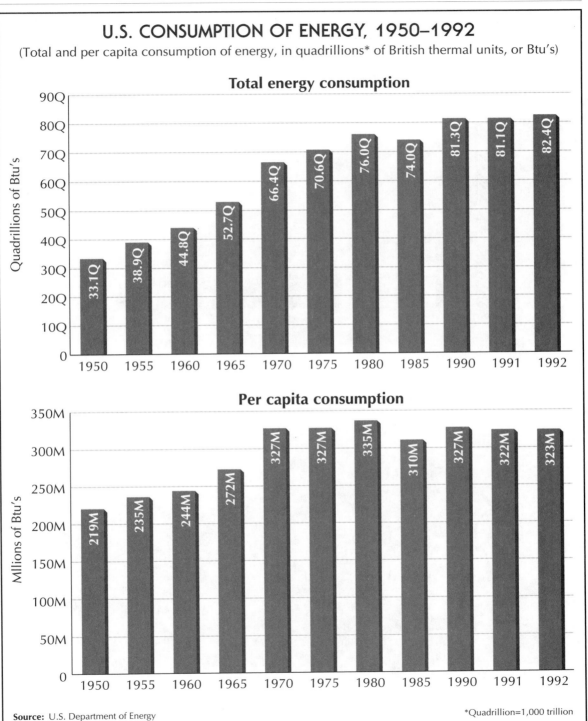

Total energy consumption

Year	Quadrillions of Btu's
1950	33.1Q
1955	38.9Q
1960	44.8Q
1965	52.7Q
1970	66.4Q
1975	70.6Q
1980	76.0Q
1985	74.0Q
1990	81.3Q
1991	81.1Q
1992	82.4Q

Per capita consumption

Year	Millions of Btu's
1950	219M
1955	235M
1960	244M
1965	272M
1970	327M
1975	327M
1980	335M
1985	310M
1990	327M
1991	322M
1992	323M

Source: U.S. Department of Energy

*Quadrillion=1,000 trillion

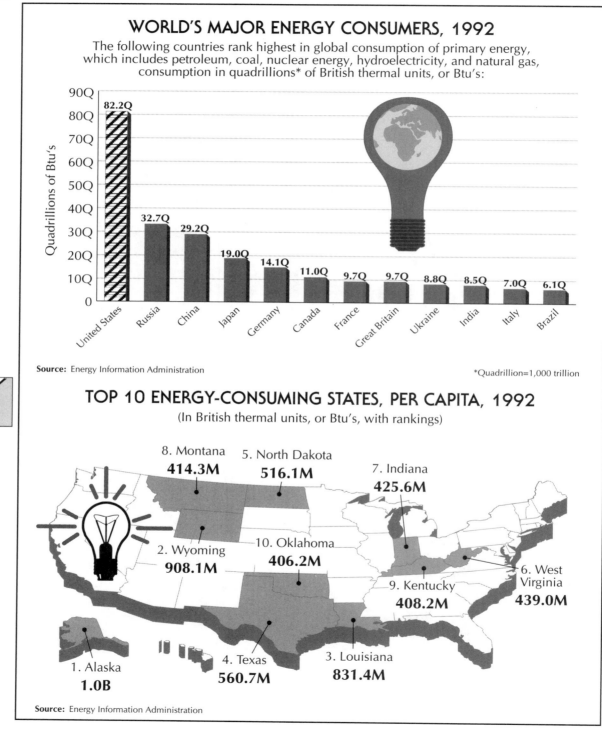

WORLD'S MAJOR ENERGY CONSUMERS, 1992

The following countries rank highest in global consumption of primary energy, which includes petroleum, coal, nuclear energy, hydroelectricity, and natural gas, consumption in quadrillions* of British thermal units, or Btu's:

Quadrillions of Btu's

United States	82.2Q
Russia	32.7Q
China	29.2Q
Japan	19.0Q
Germany	14.1Q
Canada	11.0Q
France	9.7Q
Great Britain	9.7Q
Ukraine	8.8Q
India	8.5Q
Italy	7.0Q
Brazil	6.1Q

Source: Energy Information Administration

*Quadrillion=1,000 trillion

TOP 10 ENERGY-CONSUMING STATES, PER CAPITA, 1992

(In British thermal units, or Btu's, with rankings)

8. Montana
414.3M

5. North Dakota
516.1M

7. Indiana
425.6M

2. Wyoming
908.1M

10. Oklahoma
406.2M

6. West Virginia
439.0M

9. Kentucky
408.2M

1. Alaska
1.0B

4. Texas
560.7M

3. Louisiana
831.4M

Source: Energy Information Administration

U.S. ENERGY OVERVIEW, 1960 vs. 1992
(In quadrillions* of British thermal units, or Btu's)

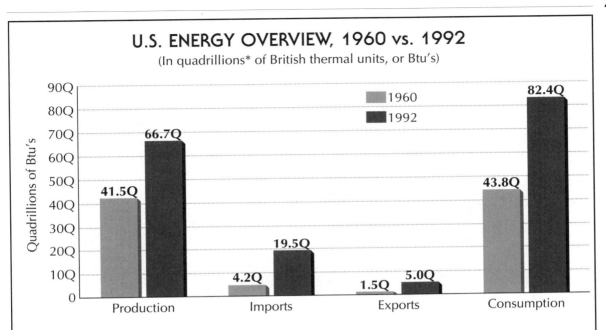

Production	1960	1992
Crude Oil	14.9Q	15.2Q
Natural gas and plant liquids	1.5Q	2.4Q
Natural gas	12.7Q	18.3Q
Coal	10.8Q	21.6Q
Nuclear electric power	0.01Q	6.7Q
Hydroelectric power	1.6Q	2.5Q
Others	Less than 0.005Q	0.2Q

Imports	1960	1992
Crude Oil	2.2Q	13.2Q
Petroleum products	1.8Q	3.7Q
Natural gas	0.2Q	2.1Q
Others	0.1Q	0.5Q

Exports	1960	1992
Coal	1.1Q	2.7Q
Crude oil and petroleum products	0.4Q	2.0Q
Others	0.1Q	0.3Q

Consumption	1960	1992
Petroleum products	19.9Q	33.5Q
Natural gas	12.4Q	20.3Q
Coal	9.8Q	18.9Q
Nuclear power	0.0Q	6.7Q
Hydroelectric power	1.7Q	2.8Q
Others	Less than 0.005Q	0.2Q

*Quadrillion=1,000 trillion

Source: U.S. Department of Energy

HOW AMERICAN HOMES ARE HEATED

(By source of heat, in percentage of homes)

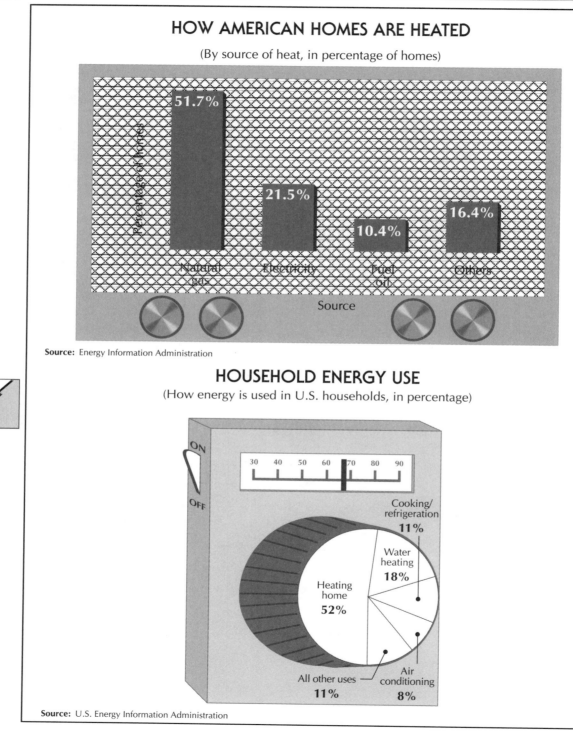

51.7% Natural gas

21.5% Electricity

10.4% Fuel oil

16.4% Others

Percentage of homes

Source

Source: Energy Information Administration

HOUSEHOLD ENERGY USE

(How energy is used in U.S. households, in percentage)

ON
OFF

30 40 50 60 70 80 90

Heating home
52%

Cooking/refrigeration
11%

Water heating
18%

Air conditioning
8%

All other uses
11%

Source: U.S. Energy Information Administration

PRODUCTION AND CONSUMPTION OF PETROLEUM PRODUCTS, 1970–1993

(In quadrillions* of British thermal units, or Btu's)

■ Production
■ Consumption

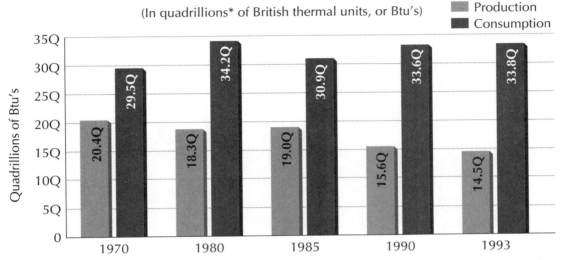

Quadrillions of Btu's

- 1970: 20.4Q / 29.5Q
- 1980: 18.3Q / 34.2Q
- 1985: 19.0Q / 30.9Q
- 1990: 15.6Q / 33.6Q
- 1993: 14.5Q / 33.8Q

Source: U.S. Energy Information Administration

*Quadrillion=1,000 trillion

PERCENTAGE OF IMPORTED OIL IN U.S., 1973 vs. 1993

In 1973, immediately after the Arab oil embargo, a much smaller percentage of foreign oil was used in the U.S. than in 1993:

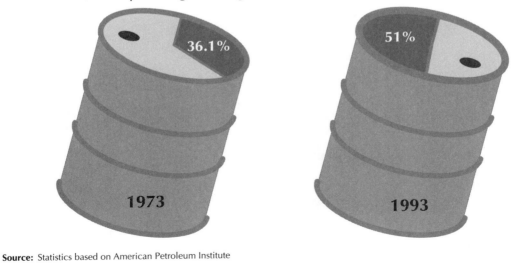

36.1% 1973

51% 1993

Source: Statistics based on American Petroleum Institute

9

MONEY
AND
BUSINESS

B I G   B U S I N E S S

The generally good health of big business during 1994 and the first half of 1995 was reflected in record profits and soaring stock market prices. General Motors, the largest corporation in the U.S., had 1994 sales of $155.6 billion and profits of $5.7 billion.

Even large corporations face stiff competition, both domestically and internationally. One response has been to "downsize" to make the company's operations "leaner and meaner." Another has been a movement toward mergers, alliances, and other agreements. This latter course has been particularly widespread in the health care and communications industries. In 1995, for example, United Healthcare, an operator of health maintenance organizations (HMOs), paid $1.65 billion to buy Metrahealth, a more traditional health insurance company. Two California HMOs merged to form a company with a stock market value exceeding $4 billion.

Even whole industries are merging. This is best seen among the communications, information, and entertainment industries, which have been dramatically changed by technological advances. One of the biggest match-ups of 1994 was made when Blockbuster Entertainment merged with Viacom, which then acquired Paramount. The new corporation encompassed TV networks, publishing, entertainment centers, music and film producers, retail stores, theme parks, and professional sports teams. And in 1995, the already massive Disney bought the television network ABC, while Westinghouse acquired ABC's rival, CBS. The impact of these moves will be felt throughout the entertainment industry and many other fields.

FINGERTIP FACTS

☞ In 1994, the U.S. companies with the highest sales were General Motors ($155.6 billion), Ford ($128.4 billion), and Exxon ($101.1 billion). The top-ranking companies in terms of profits were General Electric ($5.9 billion), General Motors ($5.6 billion), and Ford ($5.2 billion).

☞ The top U.S. companies, based on stock values on May 31, 1995, were General Electric ($98.2 billion), Exxon ($88.7 billion), AT&T ($80.3 billion), Coca-Cola ($78.6 billion), and Philip Morris ($61.6 billion).

☞ Wal-Mart is the world's largest retailer, with a market value of $57.1 billion in 1995 and 1993 sales of $67.3 billion. In second place is Sears—valued at $21.9 billion, with 1993 sales of $54.9 billion.

☞ IBM is the top-ranked corporation in the computer industry, with a market value of $54.0 billion, 1994 sales of $64.1 billion, and assets of $81.1 billion.

☞ In 1993, the companies with the most franchises were 7-Eleven (10,604), McDonald's (9,770), Subway (8,013), Burger King (5,903), and Century 21 Real Estate (5,891).

☞ The biggest deal in U.S. corporate history was the $26 billion takeover of RJR Nabisco by Kohlberg Kravis Roberts & Company, a Wall Street investment firm, in 1988.

☞ Major deals of 1994 included AT&T's $12.6 billion purchase of McCaw Cellular and the $8.4 billion merger of Blockbuster Entertainment and Viacom, which was followed by Viacom's $10.7 billion purchase of Paramount.

TOP 10 LARGEST U.S. INDUSTRIAL CORPORATIONS, 1993
(By sales, in billions)

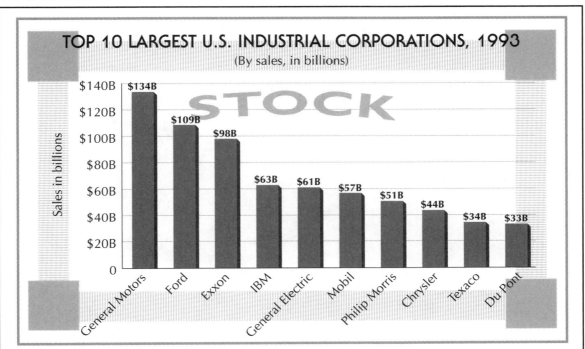

Sales in billions

- General Motors: $134B
- Ford: $109B
- Exxon: $98B
- IBM: $63B
- General Electric: $61B
- Mobil: $57B
- Philip Morris: $51B
- Chrysler: $44B
- Texaco: $34B
- Du Pont: $33B

Source: Statistics from *Fortune* magazine

TOP 6 U.S. BUSINESS BUYOUTS
Most expensive takeovers in U.S. history:

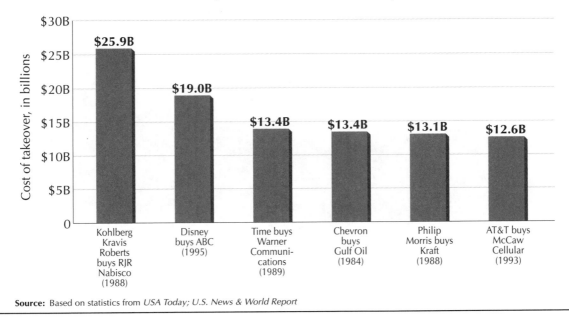

Cost of takeover, in billions

- Kohlberg Kravis Roberts buys RJR Nabisco (1988): $25.9B
- Disney buys ABC (1995): $19.0B
- Time buys Warner Communications (1989): $13.4B
- Chevron buys Gulf Oil (1984): $13.4B
- Philip Morris buys Kraft (1988): $13.1B
- AT&T buys McCaw Cellular (1993): $12.6B

Source: Based on statistics from *USA Today; U.S. News & World Report*

TOP 10 U.S RETAIL COMPANIES, 1993
(By sales in billions of dollars)

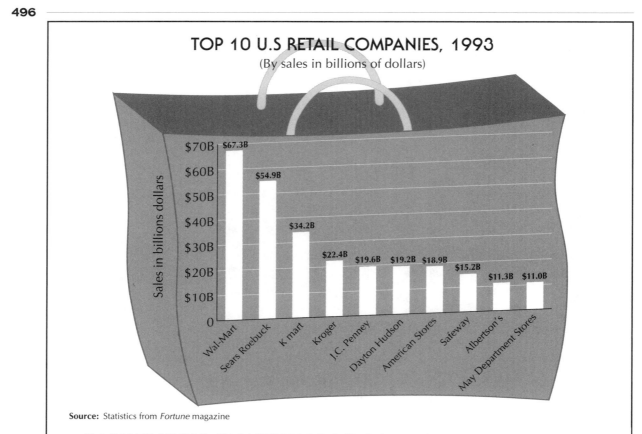

Sales in billions dollars

- $70B — $67.3B (Wal-Mart)
- $60B — $54.9B (Sears Roebuck)
- $50B
- $40B — $34.2B (K mart)
- $30B
- $20B — $22.4B (Kroger), $19.6B (J.C. Penney), $19.2B (Dayton Hudson), $18.9B (American Stores), $15.2B (Safeway), $11.3B (Albertson's), $11.0B (May Department Stores)
- $10B
- 0

Wal-Mart · Sears Roebuck · K mart · Kroger · J.C. Penney · Dayton Hudson · American Stores · Safeway · Albertson's · May Department Stores

Source: Statistics from *Fortune* magazine

DAILY TRADING ON NEW YORK STOCK EXCHANGE, 1900–1993
(Average number of shares traded daily)

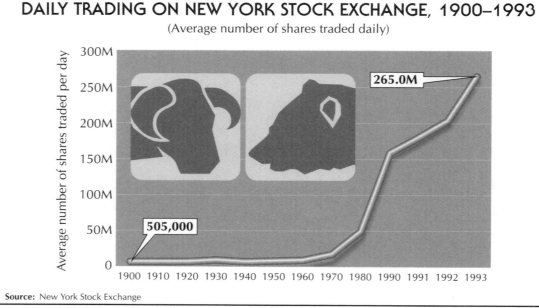

Average number of shares traded per day

300M
250M — **265.0M**
200M
150M
100M
50M
0 — **505,000**

1900 1910 1920 1930 1940 1950 1960 1970 1980 1990 1991 1992 1993

Source: New York Stock Exchange

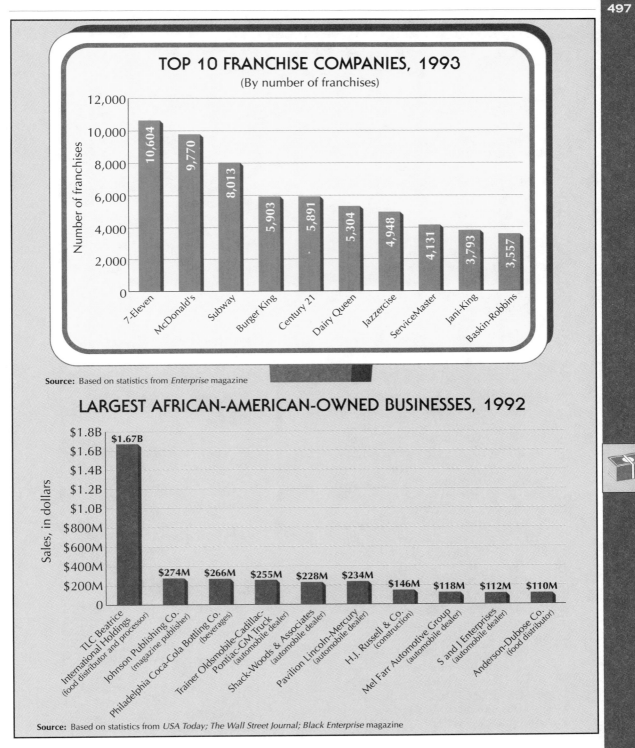

TOP 10 FRANCHISE COMPANIES, 1993
(By number of franchises)

Number of franchises

Company	Franchises
7-Eleven	10,604
McDonald's	9,770
Subway	8,013
Burger King	5,903
Century 21	5,891
Dairy Queen	5,304
Jazzercise	4,948
ServiceMaster	4,131
Jani-King	3,793
Baskin-Robbins	3,557

Source: Based on statistics from *Enterprise* magazine

LARGEST AFRICAN-AMERICAN-OWNED BUSINESSES, 1992

Sales, in dollars

Business	Sales
TLC Beatrice International Holdings (food distributor and processor)	$1.67B
Johnson Publishing Co. (magazine publisher)	$274M
Philadelphia Coca-Cola Bottling Co. (beverages)	$266M
Trainer Oldsmobile-Cadillac-Pontiac-GM Truck (automobile dealer)	$255M
Shack-Woods & Associates (automobile dealer)	$228M
Pavilion Lincoln-Mercury (automobile dealer)	$234M
H.J. Russell & Co. (construction)	$146M
Mel Farr Automotive Group (automobile dealer)	$118M
S and J Enterprises (automobile dealer)	$112M
Anderson-Dubose Co. (food distributor)	$110M

Source: Based on statistics from *USA Today; The Wall Street Journal; Black Enterprise* magazine

JOBS AND SMALL BUSINESS

The "civilian labor force" consists of all non-institutionalized civilians ages 16 and older who work or who are seeking work. In May 1995, some 124 million people were working in the U.S.—up from 119 million in 1993. Of the 1995 workers, 22 million worked part-time, and 8 million worked 2 or more jobs simultaneously.

The 1990s has been marked by the loss of job security for many U.S. workers. Large corporations have slashed thousands of jobs; Lockheed Martin, for example, cut its huge workforce by nearly 60%—from 32,000 employees in 1990 to 13,000 by 1995. Many of those lost jobs will never be replaced. In other cases, permanent employees have been replaced with temporary workers who work at lower wages and without health insurance and other fringe benefits. Between 1985 and 1995, the number of temporary workers in the American workforce tripled, to 2.1 million.

The corporate "downsizing" trend has contributed to the sharp decline in job stability. In the 1970s, employees had an average of only one or no job changes during that decade; in the 1980s, only 52% enjoyed such stability. The likelihood for the 1990s is that job instability will continue to worsen throughout the decade. Such instability hurts workers squarely in their wallets. In general, people who change jobs frequently, whether voluntarily or not, are more likely to experience wage declines; they will also have more difficulty accumulating pension benefits.

The good news is that there has been robust growth in new jobs—more than 3.5 million were created in 1994 alone. Small and start-up businesses were responsible for a significant portion of these jobs.

FINGERTIP FACTS

- The urban areas projected to gain the most new jobs in the U.S. between 1993 and 2015 are Atlanta, Georgia (1.46 million new jobs), Washington, D.C. (1.4 million), and Los Angeles-Long Beach, California (1.39 million).

- The number of self-employed workers increased from 7.0 million in 1970 to 10.3 million in 1993. The number in agriculture declined from 1.8 million to 1.3 million, while the self-employed in other industries rose from 5.2 million to 9.0 million.

- Women own 66% of businesses that are based in the home, but the percentage of men who are starting home-based businesses is growing.

- In 1992, the U.S. had 8.8 million incorporated businesses, 666,800 new incorporations, and 97,069 business failures.

- Florida led the states in new business incorporations in 1992 (86,037), followed by New York (67,503) and California (36,973). North Dakota (984), South Dakota (1,218), and Alaska (1,461) had the fewest.

- Most venture capital in 1993 went for expansion of companies (54.5%), while 7.0% was invested in company start-ups.

- In 1993, the Small Business Administration made a total of 28,100 loans worth $7.2 billion to small, independently owned and operated businesses in the U.S; 15% of the loans, valued at $932 million, were to minority-owned businesses.

- The fastest-growing occupation in the U.S. is expected to be home health aides, rising from 347,000 in 1992 to between 794,000 and 835,000 by 2005—an increase of up to 140.6%.

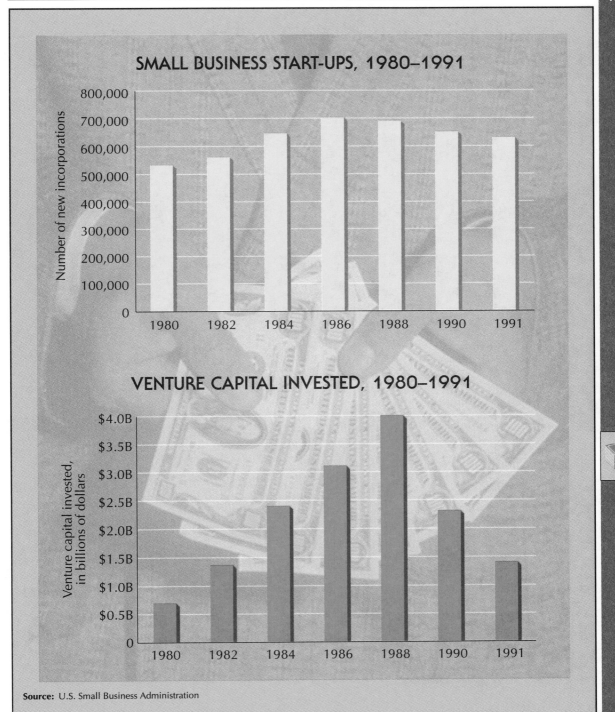

SMALL BUSINESS START-UPS, 1980–1991

Number of new incorporations

800,000
700,000
600,000
500,000
400,000
300,000
200,000
100,000
0

1980   1982   1984   1986   1988   1990   1991

VENTURE CAPITAL INVESTED, 1980–1991

Venture capital invested, in billions of dollars

$4.0B
$3.5B
$3.0B
$2.5B
$2.0B
$1.5B
$1.0B
$0.5B
0

1980   1982   1984   1986   1988   1990   1991

Source: U.S. Small Business Administration

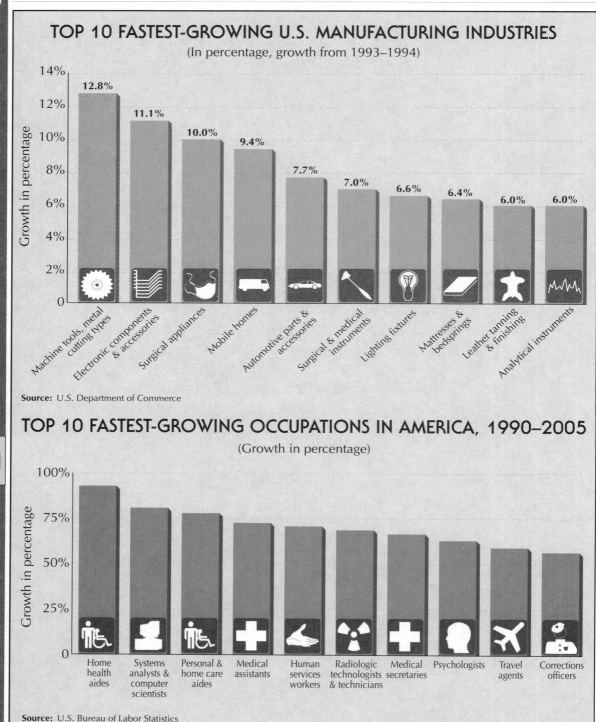

TOP 10 FASTEST-GROWING U.S. MANUFACTURING INDUSTRIES
(In percentage, growth from 1993–1994)

Growth in percentage

- Machine tools, metal cutting types — 12.8%
- Electronic components & accessories — 11.1%
- Surgical appliances — 10.0%
- Mobile homes — 9.4%
- Automotive parts & accessories — 7.7%
- Surgical & medical instruments — 7.0%
- Lighting fixtures — 6.6%
- Mattresses & bedsprings — 6.4%
- Leather tanning & finishing — 6.0%
- Analytical instruments — 6.0%

Source: U.S. Department of Commerce

TOP 10 FASTEST-GROWING OCCUPATIONS IN AMERICA, 1990–2005
(Growth in percentage)

Growth in percentage

- Home health aides
- Systems analysts & computer scientists
- Personal & home care aides
- Medical assistants
- Human services workers
- Radiologic technologists & technicians
- Medical secretaries
- Psychologists
- Travel agents
- Corrections officers

Source: U.S. Bureau of Labor Statistics

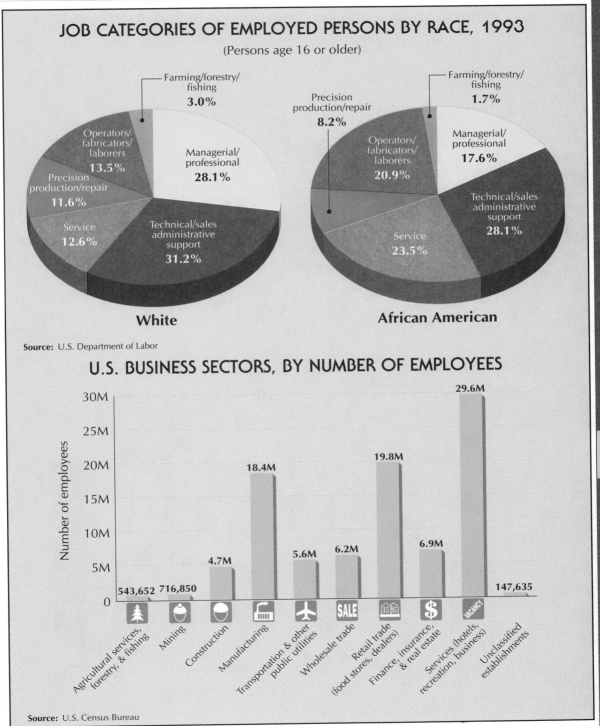

JOB CATEGORIES OF EMPLOYED PERSONS BY RACE, 1993

(Persons age 16 or older)

White

- Farming/forestry/fishing **3.0%**
- Operators/fabricators/laborers **13.5%**
- Precision production/repair **11.6%**
- Service **12.6%**
- Technical/sales administrative support **31.2%**
- Managerial/professional **28.1%**

African American

- Precision production/repair **8.2%**
- Farming/forestry/fishing **1.7%**
- Operators/fabricators/laborers **20.9%**
- Managerial/professional **17.6%**
- Technical/sales administrative support **28.1%**
- Service **23.5%**

Source: U.S. Department of Labor

U.S. BUSINESS SECTORS, BY NUMBER OF EMPLOYEES

Number of employees

Sector	Number of employees
Agricultural services, forestry, & fishing	543,652
Mining	716,850
Construction	4.7M
Manufacturing	18.4M
Transportation & other public utilities	5.6M
Wholesale trade	6.2M
Retail trade (food stores, dealers)	19.8M
Finance, insurance, & real estate	6.9M
Services (hotels, recreation, business)	29.6M
Unclassified establishments	147,635

Source: U.S. Census Bureau

RACE OR ETHNICITY OF PEOPLE IN THE U.S. WORKFORCE

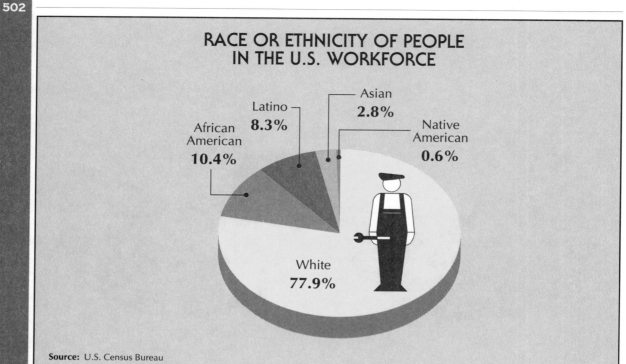

African American **10.4%**

Latino **8.3%**

Asian **2.8%**

Native American **0.6%**

White **77.9%**

Source: U.S. Census Bureau

PART-TIME WORKERS ON THE RISE, 1990–1993

More Americans are working part-time because they cannot get full-time jobs:

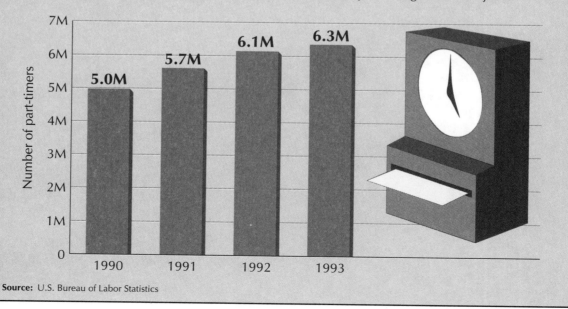

Number of part-timers

7M
6M
5M
4M
3M
2M
1M
0

5.0M — 1990
5.7M — 1991
6.1M — 1992
6.3M — 1993

Source: U.S. Bureau of Labor Statistics

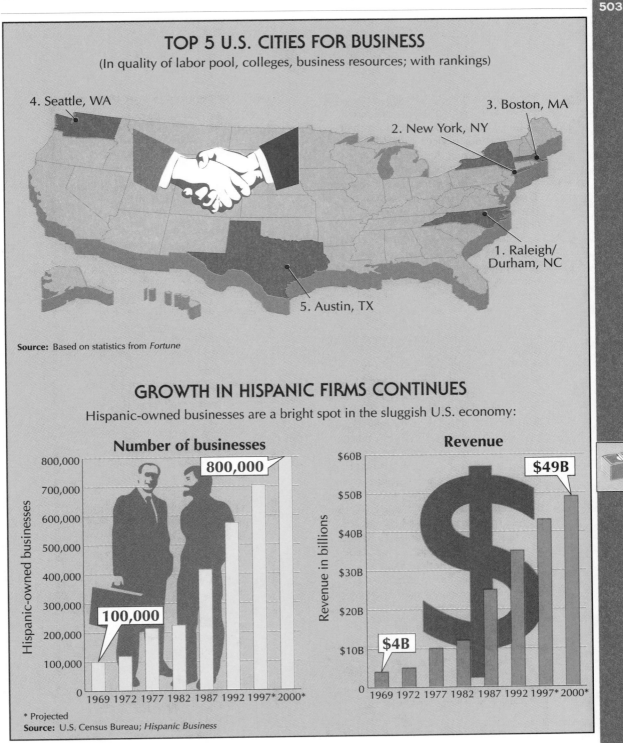

TOP 5 U.S. CITIES FOR BUSINESS

(In quality of labor pool, colleges, business resources; with rankings)

4. Seattle, WA

3. Boston, MA

2. New York, NY

1. Raleigh/Durham, NC

5. Austin, TX

Source: Based on statistics from *Fortune*

GROWTH IN HISPANIC FIRMS CONTINUES

Hispanic-owned businesses are a bright spot in the sluggish U.S. economy:

Number of businesses

Hispanic-owned businesses

800,000
700,000
600,000
500,000
400,000
300,000
200,000
100,000
0

800,000

100,000

1969 1972 1977 1982 1987 1992 1997* 2000*

Revenue

Revenue in billions

$60B
$50B
$40B
$30B
$20B
$10B
0

$49B

$4B

1969 1972 1977 1982 1987 1992 1997* 2000*

* Projected
Source: U.S. Census Bureau; *Hispanic Business*

ADVERTISING

Throughout the U.S. in 1994, national and local advertisers spent approximately $148 billion to promote their products and services—up 7.3% from 1993. Altogether, American companies spend more on advertising than their counterparts in other parts of the world. These expenditures include the costs of creating ads and then placing them in the media.

Newspapers, television, direct mail, magazines, and radio are the primary advertising media in the U.S. As greater numbers of consumers spend time "on-line" on various computer network services, however, advertisers are exploring that medium, too; in 1994, McDonald's aired what it called the first "on-line TV commercial."

The leading advertiser in 1993 was Procter & Gamble, which spent $1.3 billion for that year. Procter & Gamble was followed by Philip Morris ($1.0 billion), General Motors ($1.1 billion), and Ford ($723 million). Much of their advertising money was spent on national network and "spot" television (spot ads, which target local markets, appear on selected network stations). When viewed by product category, retailers were the biggest spenders, followed by automotive; business and consumer services; entertainment and amusements; foods; toiletries and cosmetics; drugs and remedies; travel, hotels, and resorts; direct response companies; and candy, snacks, and soft drinks.

FINGERTIP FACTS

- In 1993, the top 5 magazines in advertising pages sold more than 16,000 pages of ads combined.

- Ad spending to promote cigarettes totaled $340.2 million in 1993, with the bulk of it going to consumer magazines ($210.1 million) and outdoor advertising ($101.1 million).

- Issuers of credit cards upped their advertising to $250 million in 1993, from $161 million in 1992.

- Newspapers receive the largest market share of advertising revenues (23.2% in 1993), followed by television (22.1%), direct mail (19.8%), telephone "yellow pages" (6.9%), and radio (6.8%).

- Among magazine publishers, Time Warner receives the most advertising revenue, followed by Hearst, Condé Nast, and The New York Times.

- It cost an average of $222,000 to produce a TV commercial in 1994.

- It cost $300,000 to air a 30-second commercial during the 1994 Super Bowl.

- In 1995, it cost about $325,000 to place a single 30-second ad on the television sitcom "Home Improvement."

- 1993 advertising revenues for television totaled $10.6 billion.

- In 1991, the U.S. had 11,000 advertising agencies, which employed 132,000 people and had combined payrolls of $5.3 billion. Their receipts totaled $15.5 billion.

- Young & Rubicam topped U.S.-based ad agencies in 1993, with an income of approximately $407 million.

- Many advertisers use celebrities to promote their products. In the early 1990s, Michael Jordan earned an estimated $30 million annually from endorsing products for Nike, McDonald's, and other companies.

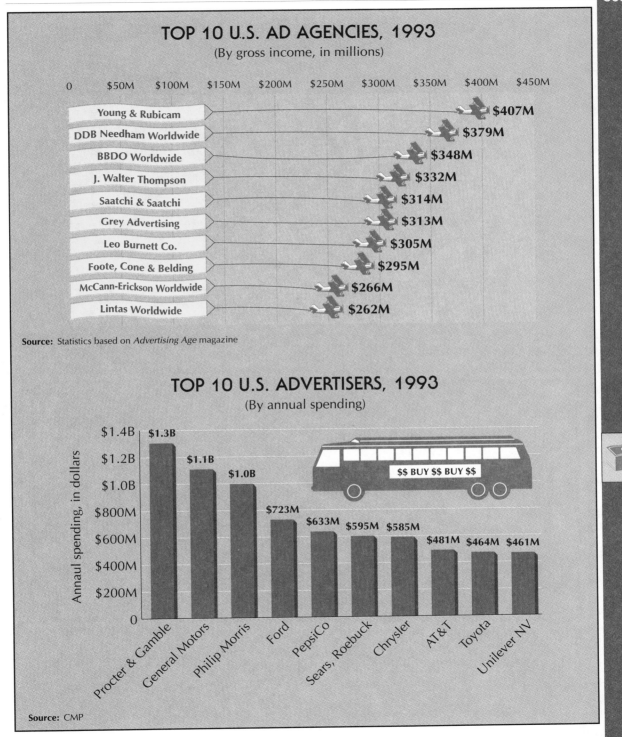

TOP 10 U.S. AD AGENCIES, 1993
(By gross income, in millions)

Agency	Gross income
Young & Rubicam	$407M
DDB Needham Worldwide	$379M
BBDO Worldwide	$348M
J. Walter Thompson	$332M
Saatchi & Saatchi	$314M
Grey Advertising	$313M
Leo Burnett Co.	$305M
Foote, Cone & Belding	$295M
McCann-Erickson Worldwide	$266M
Lintas Worldwide	$262M

Source: Statistics based on *Advertising Age* magazine

TOP 10 U.S. ADVERTISERS, 1993
(By annual spending)

Annaul spending, in dollars

$$ BUY $$ BUY $$

Advertiser	Annual spending
Procter & Gamble	$1.3B
General Motors	$1.1B
Philip Morris	$1.0B
Ford	$723M
PepsiCo	$633M
Sears, Roebuck	$595M
Chrysler	$585M
AT&T	$481M
Toyota	$464M
Unilever NV	$461M

Source: CMP

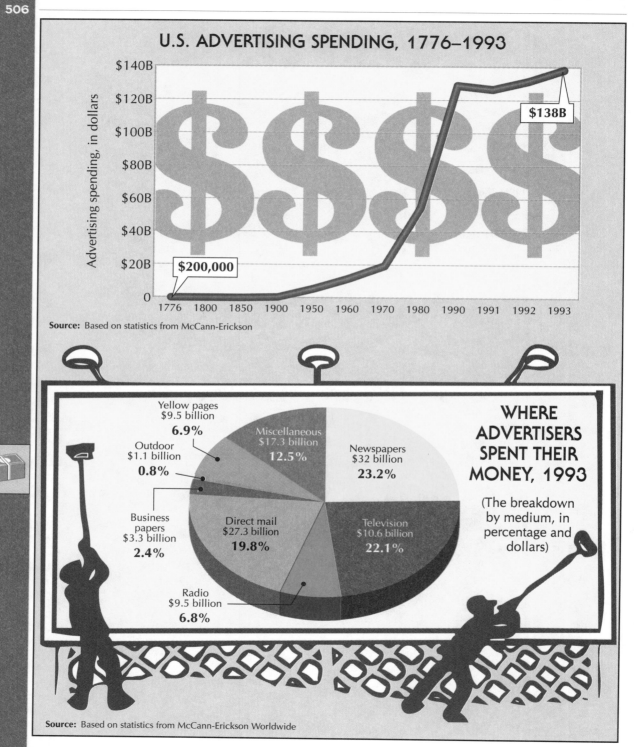

U.S. ADVERTISING SPENDING, 1776–1993

Advertising spending, in dollars

$140B
$120B
$100B
$80B
$60B
$40B
$20B
0

$138B

$200,000

1776 1800 1850 1900 1950 1960 1970 1980 1990 1991 1992 1993

Source: Based on statistics from McCann-Erickson

WHERE ADVERTISERS SPENT THEIR MONEY, 1993

(The breakdown by medium, in percentage and dollars)

Yellow pages
$9.5 billion
6.9%

Outdoor
$1.1 billion
0.8%

Business papers
$3.3 billion
2.4%

Radio
$9.5 billion
6.8%

Direct mail
$27.3 billion
19.8%

Miscellaneous
$17.3 billion
12.5%

Newspapers
$32 billion
23.2%

Television
$10.6 billion
22.1%

Source: Based on statistics from McCann-Erickson Worldwide

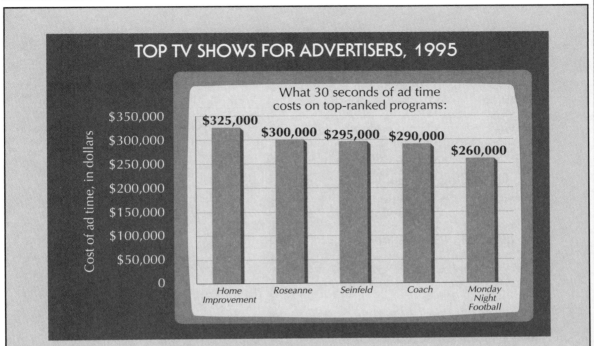

TOP TV SHOWS FOR ADVERTISERS, 1995

What 30 seconds of ad time costs on top-ranked programs:

Cost of ad time, in dollars

$350,000
$300,000
$250,000
$200,000
$150,000
$100,000
$50,000
0

$325,000 — Home Improvement
$300,000 — Roseanne
$295,000 — Seinfeld
$290,000 — Coach
$260,000 — Monday Night Football

Source: Based on statistics from *Advertising Age* magazine

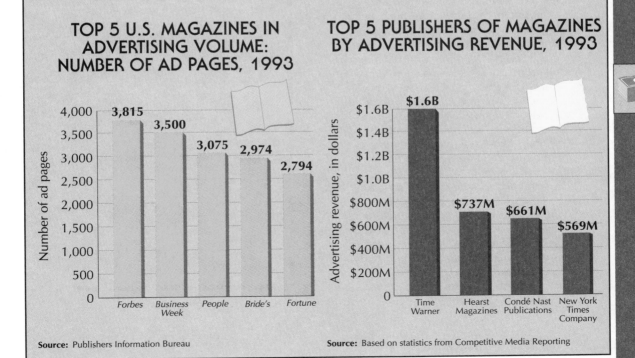

TOP 5 U.S. MAGAZINES IN ADVERTISING VOLUME: NUMBER OF AD PAGES, 1993

Number of ad pages

4,000
3,500
3,000
2,500
2,000
1,500
1,000
500
0

3,815 — Forbes
3,500 — Business Week
3,075 — People
2,974 — Bride's
2,794 — Fortune

Source: Publishers Information Bureau

TOP 5 PUBLISHERS OF MAGAZINES BY ADVERTISING REVENUE, 1993

Advertising revenue, in dollars

$1.6B
$1.4B
$1.2B
$1.0B
$800M
$600M
$400M
$200M
0

$1.6B — Time Warner
$737M — Hearst Magazines
$661M — Condé Nast Publications
$569M — New York Times Company

Source: Based on statistics from Competitive Media Reporting

THE COST OF LIVING

American consumers spent $4.4 trillion in 1993, up from $3.8 trillion in 1990, and $1.7 trillion in 1980. Increasingly, much of this money is not "cold cash," but, rather, hard plastic—outstanding balances on credit cards are growing much faster than the growth in consumer spending. At the end of 1994, balances outstanding on Visa and MasterCard credit cards were a record $256 billion, up 24% from 1993's $206 billion. And the number of credit cards has soared. At the end of 1993, there were 266.5 million Visa and MasterCard credit cards in circulation, up more than 25% from 208.3 million in 1990.

Everyone feels the pressure to "keep up"—whether it's a teenager who wants the latest footwear and CDs, parents who want their children to receive the best education and health care, or a company that needs high-tech equipment in order to meet customer demands. And few of us escape the costs of the unexpected—flood damage from a hurricane; hospital stays after an accident; losses from burglary, fraud, and other crimes. All these costs of living have continued to increase year by year.

The costs of some products and services have risen much faster than the consumer price index (which tracks the average change in prices over time); medical bills and the costs of attending college are examples of quick risers. Other products and services, however, have become bargains. Today, for example, personal computers far more powerful than the multi-million-dollar goliaths used to send men to the moon are affordable for millions of Americans.

FINGERTIP FACTS

- In 1992, some 98 million people owned a total of 500 million retail-store credit cards; they charged $77 billion on these cards.

- The average cost of a house in the U.S. in 1993 was $148,900; the average cost of a condo was $118,900.

- By the time American babies born in 1992 reach age 18, their parents will have spent an average of $128,670 on them.

- In 1992, some 42% of all sneakers and gym shoes were purchased for kids under age 14, and 17% were bought for 14- to 17-year-olds.

- It cost an average of $8,562 to attend a 4-year public college in the 1993–1994 academic year, including tuition, fees, books, room and board, and other expenses. At private colleges, the average was $17,846.

- Tuition and fees at 4-year public colleges averaged $2,527 in 1993–1994; at private colleges, they averaged $11,025. At 2-year colleges, tuition averaged $1,229 and fees $6,175.

- The number of young people living with their parents has increased— 53% of 18- to 24-year-olds lived at home or in college dorms in 1993, up from 47% in 1970. Among persons 25 to 34, the percentage rose from 8% in 1970 to 12% in 1993.

- Between 1980 and 1993, the cost of a Super Bowl ticket rose by more than 550%.

PRICES AND INFLATION EASE, 1982–1993

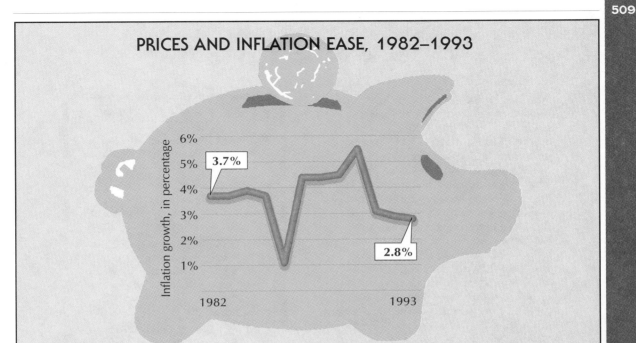

Inflation growth, in percentage

6%
5%
4%
3%
2%
1%

3.7%

2.8%

1982   1993

Source: U.S. Department of Labor

U.S. INFLATION IMPACT, 1980 vs. 1993

How costs have changed over the years for selected items, as a result of inflation:

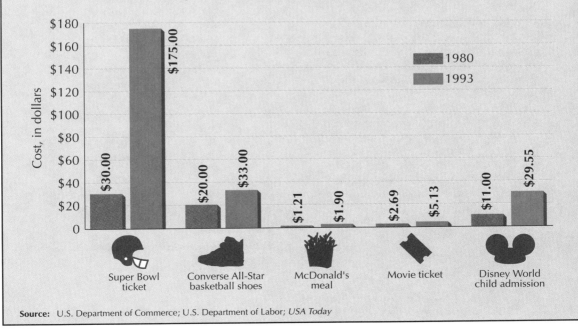

Cost, in dollars

$180
$160
$140
$120
$100
$80
$60
$40
$20
0

1980
1993

$30.00 $175.00 $20.00 $33.00 $1.21 $1.90 $2.69 $5.13 $11.00 $29.55

Super Bowl
ticket

Converse All-Star
basketball shoes

McDonald's
meal

Movie ticket

Disney World
child admission

Source: U.S. Department of Commerce; U.S. Department of Labor; *USA Today*

B A N K I N G

American taxpayers—who picked up the multi-billion-dollar tab for the savings and loan crisis of the 1980s—may be surprised to learn that the U.S. banking industry is no longer quite so rocky. It has enjoyed robust profits in recent years, thanks to the growth of loans, low loan losses, and healthy interest income. Indeed, more than 95% of banks were profitable in the third quarter of 1994. But the industry is not out of the woods. There are more than 10,000 banks in America, with a total of some 54,000 branches. Various changes in the banking industry are expected to cut these numbers and lead to significant layoffs among the nation's nearly 1.5 million bank employees.

The trend of recent years toward mergers and consolidations is expected to continue. The use of automated teller machines (ATMs) and personal-computer-based home banking is expected to rise. Brokerage houses and other financial institutions will become increasingly powerful competitors to banks—but banks are fighting back by adding the sale of annuities, mutual funds, and other financial products and services to their list of offerings.

Interstate banking is now allowed, though bank "holding companies"—companies with controlling stock holdings in one or more subsidiaries—have to maintain separate banks in each state. This requirement will end in June 1997; the resulting advent of "interstate branching" is expected to bring the industry's big players into many small markets now served by local banks.

FINGERTIP FACTS

- The U.S. has more than 10,000 commercial banks, with an average of 5.8 bank employees per 1,000 citizens.

- Federal Deposit Insurance Corporation (FDIC) insured banks had 1.48 million employees in mid-1994, the highest level since 1991.

- Of the world's 500 largest banks in 1992, the greatest percentage (24%) were Japanese; the U.S. came in second with 18%. The 500 banks had deposits of $17.00 trillion; the U.S. bank share was $1.31 trillion (8%).

- Citicorp is the largest U.S. commercial bank, with more than $200 billion in assets.

- In 1991, some 73.2% of U.S. households had interest-earning assets at financial institutions, including savings accounts (62.4%), interest-earning checking (37.8%), certificates of deposit (22.0%), and money market deposit accounts (14.9%).

- ATM transactions increased from 3.6 billion in 1985 to 7.7 billion in 1993. Point of sale, (POS) transactions rose from 14 million to 430 million.

- The number of monthly transactions per ATM terminal averaged 4,951 in 1985 and 6,772 in 1993. During that time, the number of terminals rose from 60,000 to 94,900.

- About 55% of all retail banking transactions take place at ATMs or via the telephone; only 43% occur at bank branches.

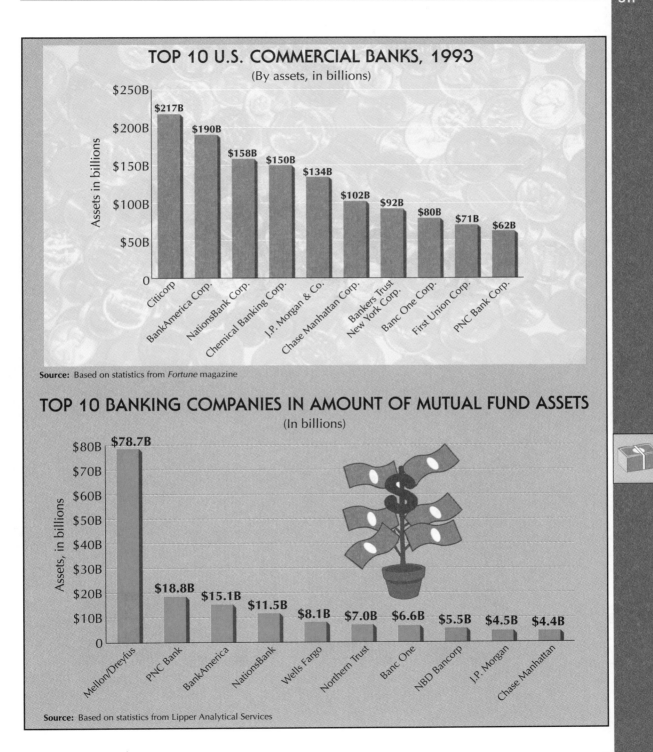

TOP 10 U.S. COMMERCIAL BANKS, 1993
(By assets, in billions)

Assets in billions

- Citicorp: $217B
- BankAmerica Corp.: $190B
- NationsBank Corp.: $158B
- Chemical Banking Corp.: $150B
- J.P. Morgan & Co.: $134B
- Chase Manhattan Corp.: $102B
- Bankers Trust New York Corp.: $92B
- Banc One Corp.: $80B
- First Union Corp.: $71B
- PNC Bank Corp.: $62B

Source: Based on statistics from *Fortune* magazine

TOP 10 BANKING COMPANIES IN AMOUNT OF MUTUAL FUND ASSETS
(In billions)

Assets, in billions

- Mellon/Dreyfus: $78.7B
- PNC Bank: $18.8B
- BankAmerica: $15.1B
- NationsBank: $11.5B
- Wells Fargo: $8.1B
- Northern Trust: $7.0B
- Banc One: $6.6B
- NBD Bancorp: $5.5B
- J.P. Morgan: $4.5B
- Chase Manhattan: $4.4B

Source: Based on statistics from Lipper Analytical Services

OFF-SITE BANKING

Less than half of all banking transactions are done at bank branch offices.
Automated teller machines (ATMs) are the most popular off-site option:

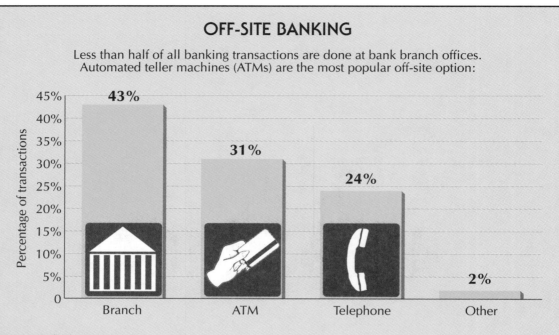

Percentage of transactions

Branch **43%** · ATM **31%** · Telephone **24%** · Other **2%**

Source: Bank Administration Institute

BANKING FEES RISE

Average bank service fees soared from 1990 to 1993. Here, some representative fee increases,
compared to the consumer price index increase during the same period:

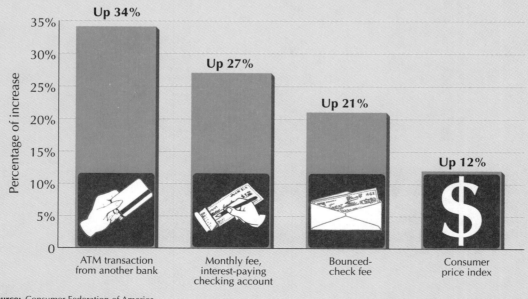

Percentage of increase

ATM transaction from another bank **Up 34%** · Monthly fee, interest-paying checking account **Up 27%** · Bounced-check fee **Up 21%** · Consumer price index **Up 12%**

Source: Consumer Federation of America

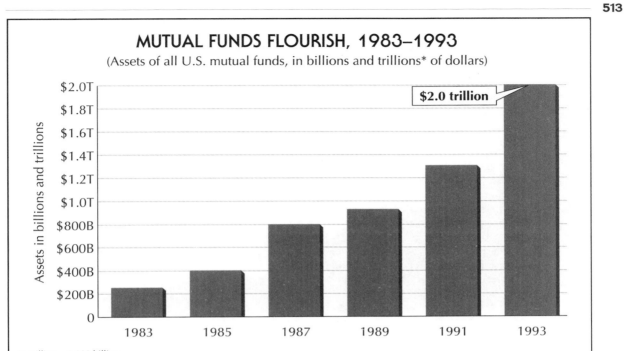

MUTUAL FUNDS FLOURISH, 1983–1993
(Assets of all U.S. mutual funds, in billions and trillions* of dollars)

$2.0 trillion

*1 trillion = 1,000 billion
Source: Based on statistics from Investment Company Inst.

THE AMERICAN CREDIT CRUNCH, 1980–1992
(Household debt as a percentage of personal income)

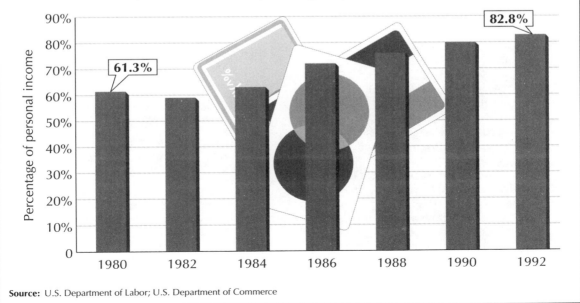

61.3%

82.8%

Source: U.S. Department of Labor; U.S. Department of Commerce

EXPORTS AND IMPORTS

International trade has a major impact on the U.S. economy and Americans' lives. Exports to Mexico alone supported more than 700,000 U.S. jobs in 1992. Workers at exporting firms have wages that average 15% higher than workers at non-exporting firms; their benefits are 33% higher.

Because the U.S. has been spending more for its imports than it has been receiving for its exports, it has had a trade deficit. In May 1995, for example, the nation had an $11.43 billion deficit, as exports reached $64.81 billion but imports climbed to $76.24 billion.

Governments have always imposed tariffs and other trade barriers, generally to protect local industries from foreign competition. But a move away from such protectionism and toward the free flow of goods and services has become a strong trend in recent years. For example, the North American Free Trade Agreement (NAFTA), concluded in 1992, will eliminate most trade barriers among Canada, Mexico, and the U.S. And this trade organization might grow in coming years—several Latin American countries have expressed interest in becoming part of an expanded NAFTA.

Exporting is not just for the large corporations. Twenty percent of U.S. companies with fewer than 500 employees exported products and services in 1994—up from 16% in 1993 and 11% in 1992.

The U.S. government would like to see more American companies prosper in international trade. It funds several trade-promotion programs that provide firms with business counseling, training, market research information, export subsidies, and export finance assistance.

FINGERTIP FACTS

☞ In 1992, U.S. exports totaled $726.9 billion, excluding goods and services under U.S. military grant programs. Merchandise accounted for the largest portion ($439.3 billion), followed by services ($178.5 billion) and income on U.S. assets abroad ($109.2 billion).

☞ Imports to the U.S. totaled $758.0 billion in 1992. Merchandise, excluding military-related items, accounted for the largest share ($535.5 billion), followed by services ($123.4 billion) and income on foreign assets in the U.S. ($99.1 billion).

☞ Coca-Cola sells 69% of its soft drinks outside the U.S. Latin America is its biggest customer, taking 2.4 billion cases a year.

☞ U.S. catalog companies took in $1.8 billion from sales to Japanese customers in 1994, up from $1.5 billion in 1992. Japanese postal officials said in mid-1995 that about 50,000 pounds of mail-order merchandise were arriving from the U.S. each day.

☞ In 1993, California was #1 in exports to other countries ($57.2 billion), followed by Texas ($45.3 billion) and New York ($28.4 billion).

☞ The U.S. imported $10.2 billion worth of footwear in 1992; South Korea ($1.5 billion) was the major source.

☞ In 1992, the U.S. exported $2.6 billion in furniture, with Canada importting nearly half of the total.

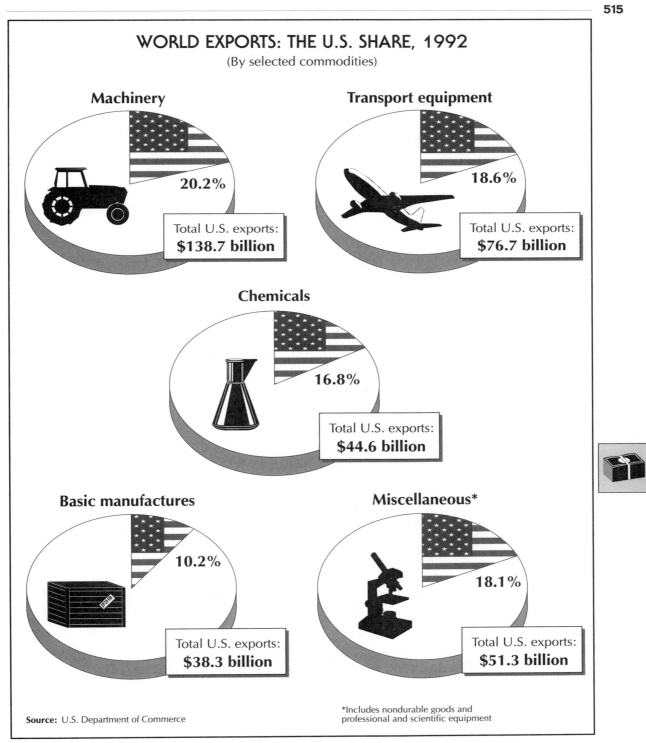

WORLD EXPORTS: THE U.S. SHARE, 1992
(By selected commodities)

Machinery
20.2%

Total U.S. exports:
$138.7 billion

Transport equipment
18.6%

Total U.S. exports:
$76.7 billion

Chemicals
16.8%

Total U.S. exports:
$44.6 billion

Basic manufactures
10.2%

Total U.S. exports:
$38.3 billion

Miscellaneous*
18.1%

Total U.S. exports:
$51.3 billion

Source: U.S. Department of Commerce

*Includes nondurable goods and professional and scientific equipment

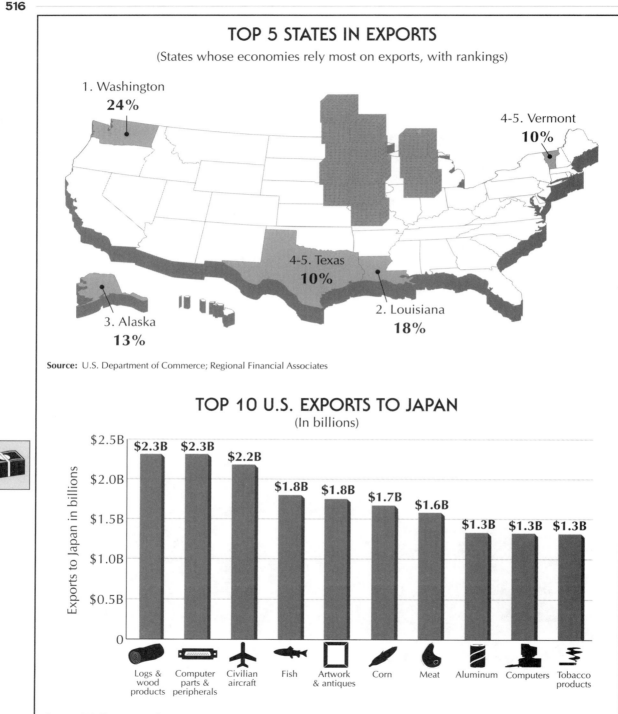

TOP 5 STATES IN EXPORTS
(States whose economies rely most on exports, with rankings)

1. Washington **24%**

4-5. Vermont **10%**

4-5. Texas **10%**

2. Louisiana **18%**

3. Alaska **13%**

Source: U.S. Department of Commerce; Regional Financial Associates

TOP 10 U.S. EXPORTS TO JAPAN
(In billions)

Exports to Japan in billions

- Logs & wood products — $2.3B
- Computer parts & peripherals — $2.3B
- Civilian aircraft — $2.2B
- Fish — $1.8B
- Artwork & antiques — $1.8B
- Corn — $1.7B
- Meat — $1.6B
- Aluminum — $1.3B
- Computers — $1.3B
- Tobacco products — $1.3B

Source: U.S. Department of Commerce

AMERICAN FOOD IS BIG BUSINESS OVERSEAS

Some U.S. food and beverages businesses earn a large portion of their profits through exports. Here, the foreign earnings of some top American companies, in percentages of sales:

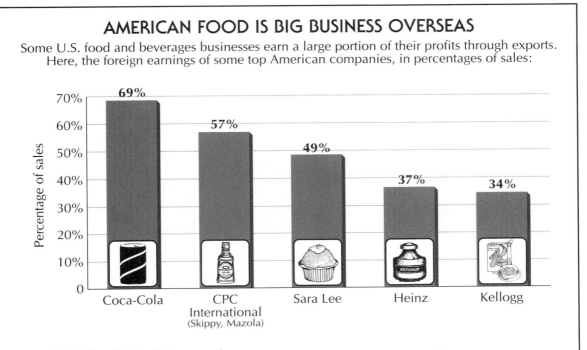

Source: Prudential Securities; *Food Business* magazine

NUMBER OF U.S. JOBS SUPPORTED BY EXPORTS TO MEXICO, 1986–1992

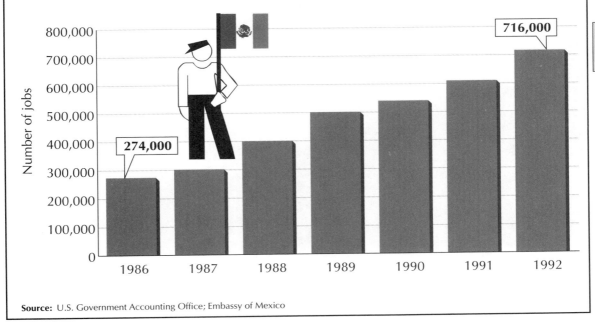

Source: U.S. Government Accounting Office; Embassy of Mexico

10

SCIENCE
AND
TECHNOLOGY

TECHNOLOGY

Throughout history, people have vastly underestimated the impact of new technologies. Never has this been more true than for semiconductors, which are used to form miniaturized electronic components and integrated circuits. The microprocessors of personal computers (PCs) are made up of semiconductors, as are the electronic components of many other pieces of equipment critical to today's world.

Indeed, semiconductors and related technologies—especially the integration of computers and telephones—have so dramatically changed the American home and workplace environments that they have made hundreds of other technologies and machines obsolete. Among many things, computers have made the process of creating and communicating information infinitely faster and easier.

Electronic mail (e-mail) and fax machines deliver messages and information around the world in seconds, while airplane telephones allow air-to-ground and ground-to-air calling. Cable services now enable people to shop, bank, and order movies from home. Desktop videoconferencing allows face-to-face meetings via PCs, saving time and money for busy executives.

An important result of these technological developments has been the growth of telecommuting—employees working at home or on the road, and communicating with their offices via computer and modem. Similarly, doctors in rural communities can consult instantly with medical experts and specialists at large urban hospitals, astronauts in space can beam photographs to Earth stations, and students in remote areas can review lessons with teachers at distant schools and universities.

FINGERTIP FACTS

- In 1980, the U.S. had 1.13 billion miles of telephone wire. By 1990, it had 1.53 billion miles.

- In 1980, Americans made 200 million overseas telephone calls. In 1992, with greater use of fiberoptic cables and computer technology, they made 2.72 billion such calls.

- In 1980, only 5 communications satellites were needed to carry telephone calls to and from the U.S.; by 1991, there were 16 such satellites.

- In the 5 years between 1990 and 1995, the number of people using pagers in the U.S. nearly tripled.

- In 1984, there were 91,600 cellular telephone subscribers in the U.S. By 1994, the number had jumped to 19.3 million.

- The telephone was invented in 1876, and 70 years passed before it was found in 50% of U.S. households. Television, introduced in 1946, took only 8 years to get into 50% of the nation's homes.

- In 1980, the U.S. Patent and Trademark Office received 104,300 patent applications for inventions, from both U.S. citizens and residents of other countries. In 1992, it received 173,100. It issued 61,800 patents for inventions in 1980 and 97,400 in 1992.

- Despite the great boom in the use and sale of fax machines, they are still utilized by less than 10% of Americans.

PROFILE: USE OF NEW TECHNOLOGY IN THE U.S.

(Percentage of Americans using new technology, by type)

VCR	
Cable TV	
ATM card	
Personal computer	
Premium cable TV	
Modem	
Fax machine	
Satellite dish	

0   20%   40%   60%   80%   100%

Source: U.S. Consumer Electronics data

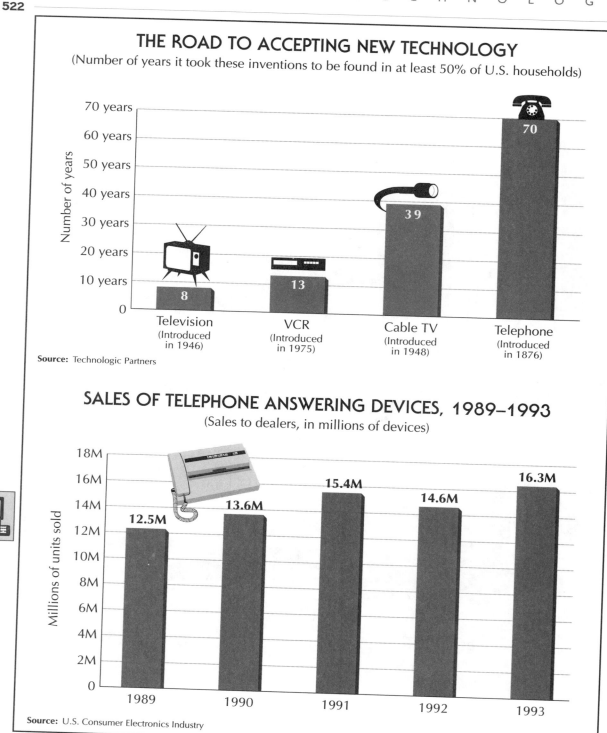

THE ROAD TO ACCEPTING NEW TECHNOLOGY

(Number of years it took these inventions to be found in at least 50% of U.S. households)

Number of years

| 70 years |
| 60 years |
| 50 years |
| 40 years |
| 30 years |
| 20 years |
| 10 years |
| 0 |

Television (Introduced in 1946) — 8

VCR (Introduced in 1975) — 13

Cable TV (Introduced in 1948) — 39

Telephone (Introduced in 1876) — 70

Source: Technologic Partners

SALES OF TELEPHONE ANSWERING DEVICES, 1989–1993

(Sales to dealers, in millions of devices)

Millions of units sold

| 18M |
| 16M |
| 14M |
| 12M |
| 10M |
| 8M |
| 6M |
| 4M |
| 2M |
| 0 |

1989 — 12.5M

1990 — 13.6M

1991 — 15.4M

1992 — 14.6M

1993 — 16.3M

Source: U.S. Consumer Electronics Industry

VIDEOCONFERENCING BOOMS, 1989–1995

(By number of teleconferencing systems sold)

Number of systems sold

100,000

80,000

60,000

40,000

20,000

0

92,000

1,113

1989   1990   1991   1992   1993   1994   1995
                                    (estimate) (estimate)

Source: The Yankee Group

CELLULAR PHONE USE SKYROCKETS, 1984–1994

An estimated 17,000 people per day are joining the ranks of cellular phone subscribers. The number of subscribers increased from fewer than 100,000 in 1984 to more than 19 million in 1994:

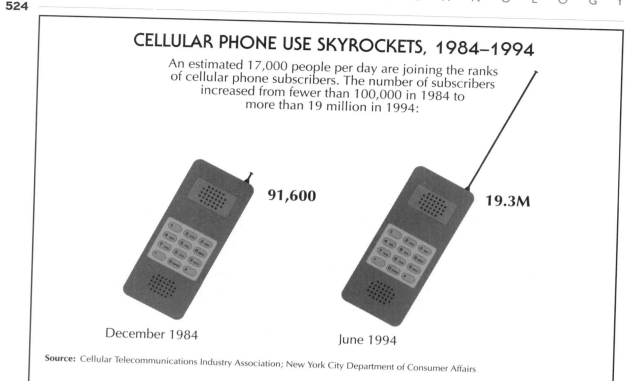

91,600

December 1984

19.3M

June 1994

Source: Cellular Telecommunications Industry Association; New York City Department of Consumer Affairs

PROFILE: MOST COMMON USES OF CELLULAR PHONES

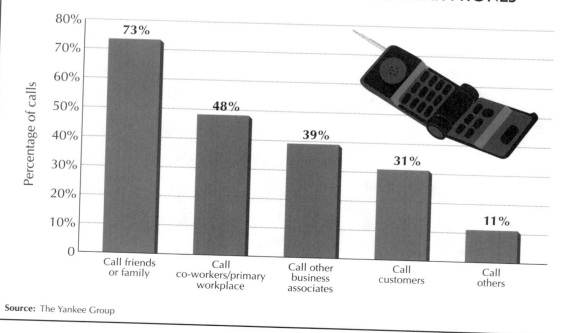

- Call friends or family — 73%
- Call co-workers/primary workplace — 48%
- Call other business associates — 39%
- Call customers — 31%
- Call others — 11%

Percentage of calls

Source: The Yankee Group

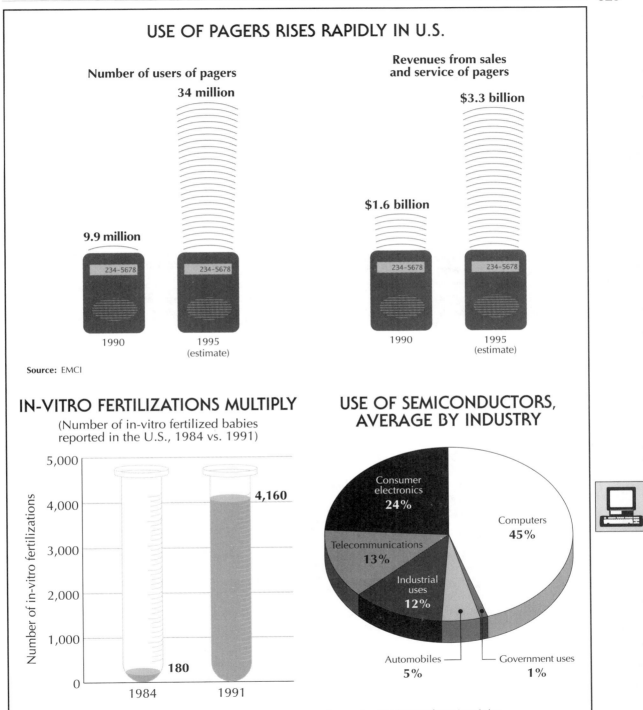

USE OF PAGERS RISES RAPIDLY IN U.S.

Number of users of pagers

34 million

9.9 million

1990

1995
(estimate)

**Revenues from sales
and service of pagers**

$3.3 billion

$1.6 billion

1990

1995
(estimate)

Source: EMCI

IN-VITRO FERTILIZATIONS MULTIPLY

(Number of in-vitro fertilized babies
reported in the U.S., 1984 vs. 1991)

Number of in-vitro fertilizations

5,000

4,000 — 4,160

3,000

2,000

1,000

180

0

1984   1991

Source: American Fertility Society

USE OF SEMICONDUCTORS, AVERAGE BY INDUSTRY

Consumer electronics
24%

Computers
45%

Telecommunications
13%

Industrial uses
12%

Automobiles
5%

Government uses
1%

Source: Semiconductor Industry Association

COMPUTERS

In the beginning, only some 50 years ago, there were mainframes—bulky computers so large they filled cavernous rooms. Today, personal computers (PCs) that sit on desktops or are carried in briefcases are commonplace, and their capabilities far outshine those of the first computers. There has also been an evolution in how computers are used. Originally viewed primarily as high-speed calculators and dedicated single-purpose data processing devices, they now are multipurpose tools that can be plugged into local and worldwide networks.

The PC market is more developed in the U.S. than anywhere else on the planet. Worldwide, 48.5 million PCs were shipped in 1994, while by 1995, some 90.0 million PCs were being used in the U.S. A survey of adults indicated that 83% used their computers for game-playing and other personal pursuits, 67% used them for work, and 46% for school. A 1995 survey of consumers found that 37% of U.S. households had one or more PCs, as compared to 28% in Germany, 23% in Great Britain, 15% in France, and 10% in Japan.

Technological development has been phenomenally rapid in the computer industry, providing users with ever faster and more powerful options. PCs have become smaller, lighter, more mobile, and more energy-efficient. CD-ROM and fax/modem hardware and software sales have soared. Going "on-line" and "surfing" the Internet attracts thousands of new participants daily. Even greater capabilities are predicted for PCs in the coming decade, including simple command and control voice recognition, miniature read-write CDs, and the ability to send and receive both voice and data simultaneously over wireless links.

FINGERTIP FACTS

- A typical 1995 desktop computer weighed about 25 pounds and had a processor about the size of a fingernail; it had 8 megabytes of internal memory plus a 1 gigabyte hard drive and 1.44 megabyte floppies for storage.

- Worldwide, the top computer vendors in 1994 were Compaq (10.0% market share), IBM (8.7%), Apple (8.5%), Packard Bell (4.7%), and NEC (3.5%).

- American consumers spent an estimated $8 billion in 1994 to buy 6.6 million PCs—almost as much money as they spent on television sets.

- The federal government buys some 20% of all PCs sold in the U.S.

- By the year 2000, PC penetration in U.S. homes is predicted to reach 62.8%, as compared to 52.4% in Germany, France, and Great Britain.

- In 1994, 22% of all new PCs were shipped with CD-ROM drives, up from 5% in 1993.

- In 1993, North American software sales totaled $6.81 billion. Word-processing software was the major category ($1.02 billion), followed by spreadsheets ($801 million), data bases ($476 million), and entertainment ($410 million).

- In 1994, software piracy cost the PC software industry more than $8 billion.

- An estimated 30 million people worldwide have access to the Internet and World Wide Web.

COMPUTER USE IN U.S. HOUSEHOLDS, 1994

(By characteristic, in percentage of households)

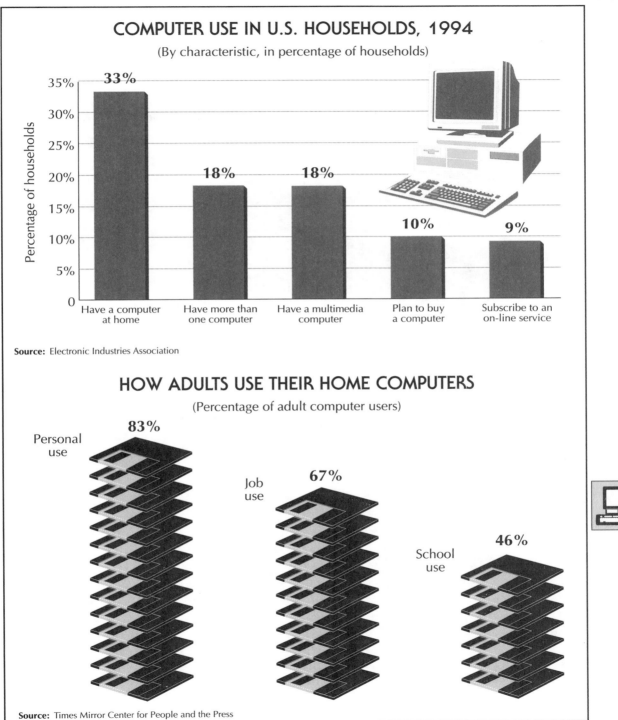

Source: Electronic Industries Association

HOW ADULTS USE THEIR HOME COMPUTERS

(Percentage of adult computer users)

Personal use — 83%

Job use — 67%

School use — 46%

Source: Times Mirror Center for People and the Press

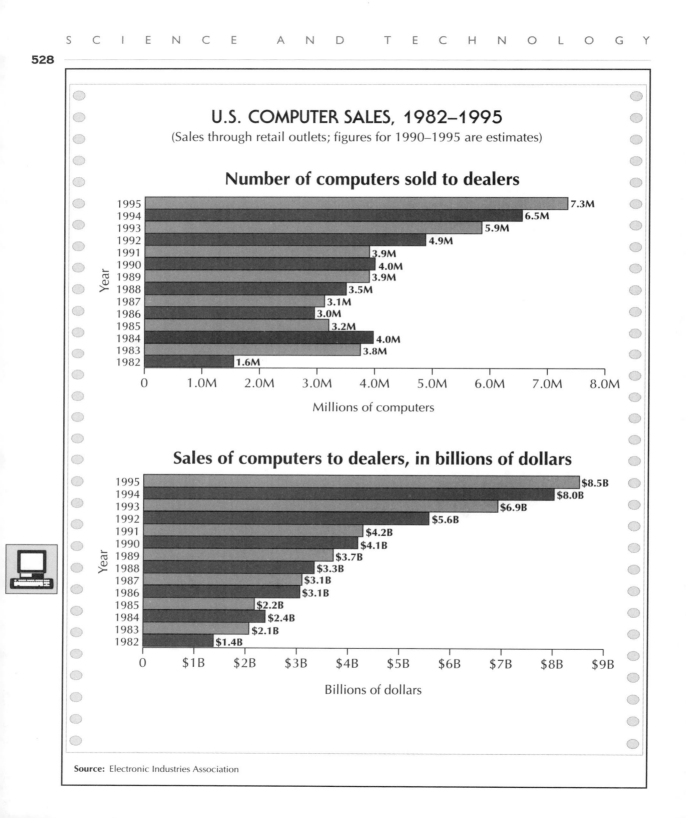

U.S. COMPUTER SALES, 1982–1995
(Sales through retail outlets; figures for 1990–1995 are estimates)

Number of computers sold to dealers

Year	Millions of computers
1995	7.3M
1994	6.5M
1993	5.9M
1992	4.9M
1991	3.9M
1990	4.0M
1989	3.9M
1988	3.5M
1987	3.1M
1986	3.0M
1985	3.2M
1984	4.0M
1983	3.8M
1982	1.6M

Millions of computers

Sales of computers to dealers, in billions of dollars

Year	Billions of dollars
1995	$8.5B
1994	$8.0B
1993	$6.9B
1992	$5.6B
1991	$4.2B
1990	$4.1B
1989	$3.7B
1988	$3.3B
1987	$3.1B
1986	$3.1B
1985	$2.2B
1984	$2.4B
1983	$2.1B
1982	$1.4B

Billions of dollars

Source: Electronic Industries Association

TOP SELLERS OF PERSONAL COMPUTERS IN U.S., 1992–1993

(As percentage of all personal computers sold in U.S.)

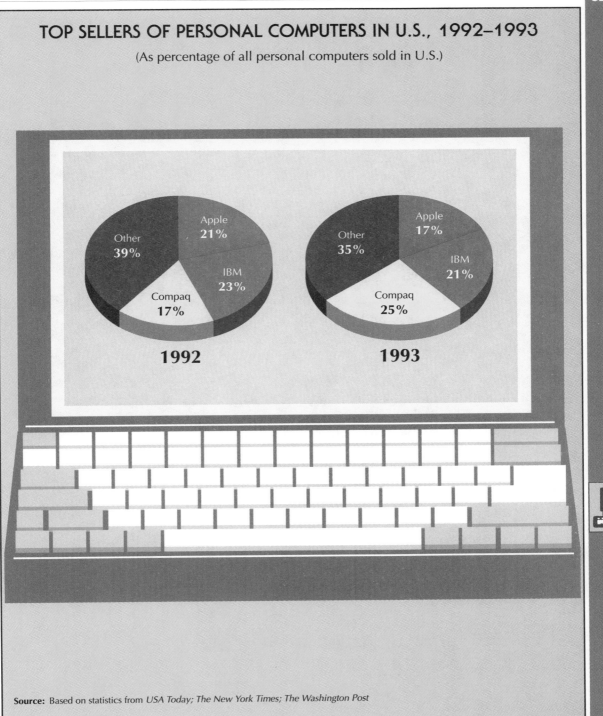

1992

Other **39%**
Apple **21%**
IBM **23%**
Compaq **17%**

1993

Other **35%**
Apple **17%**
IBM **21%**
Compaq **25%**

Source: Based on statistics from *USA Today; The New York Times; The Washington Post*

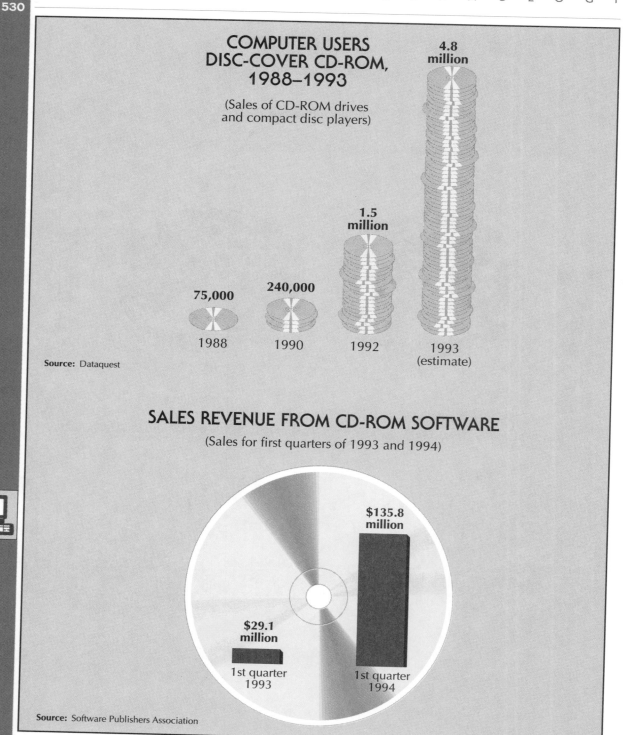

COMPUTER USERS DISC-COVER CD-ROM, 1988–1993

(Sales of CD-ROM drives and compact disc players)

4.8 million

1.5 million

240,000

75,000

1988

1990

1992

1993 (estimate)

Source: Dataquest

SALES REVENUE FROM CD-ROM SOFTWARE

(Sales for first quarters of 1993 and 1994)

$135.8 million

$29.1 million

1st quarter 1993

1st quarter 1994

Source: Software Publishers Association

U.S. HOUSEHOLDS WITH CD-ROM, 1993–1997

(U.S. households projected to have computer-installed CD-ROM drives, in percentage)

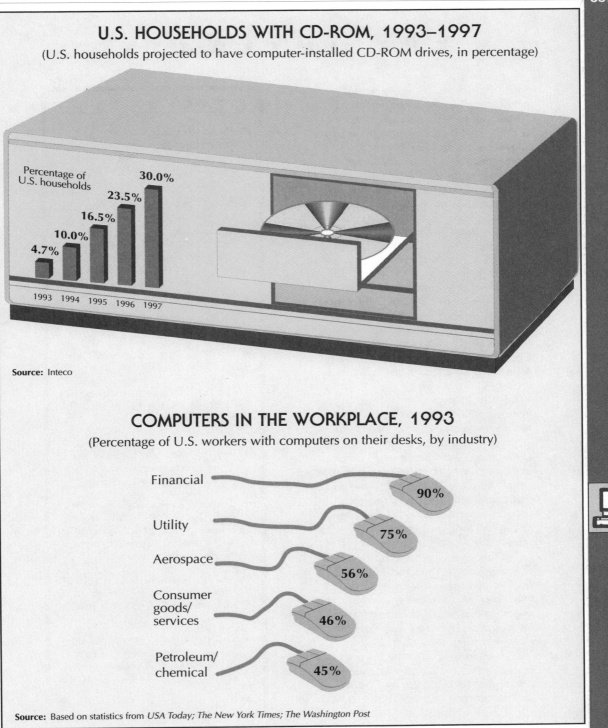

Percentage of U.S. households

4.7% 10.0% 16.5% 23.5% 30.0%

1993 1994 1995 1996 1997

Source: Inteco

COMPUTERS IN THE WORKPLACE, 1993

(Percentage of U.S. workers with computers on their desks, by industry)

Financial — 90%

Utility — 75%

Aerospace — 56%

Consumer goods/services — 46%

Petroleum/chemical — 45%

Source: Based on statistics from *USA Today; The New York Times; The Washington Post*

THE INTERNET

Each day, millions of people explore a new communications frontier called "cyberspace"— the term for the electronic world that spans the globe and allows people to send letters, pay bills, post messages on computer bulletin boards, transfer computer files, converse with friends and strangers, gain access to libraries and newspapers that have gone "on-line," and much more. Today, the world of cyberspace seems infinite.

At the center of cyberspace is the Internet, a network of networks. The Net links literally millions of computers around the world. By late 1994, some 13.5 million people worldwide were using the Internet. The largest on-line services by the middle of 1994 were CompuServe (3.2 million subscribers), America Online (3.0 million), and Prodigy (1.6 million).

Accessibility to the Internet has been simplified by the World Wide Web, a system of viewing information stored on tens of thousands of computers connected to the Internet. The function known as "hypertext" allows people to move quickly from one document to another related document within the system—even if the latter document is on a computer halfway around the world. Software programs called "browsers" make it relatively easy to maneuver the Web and, in turn, to explore and use Internet resources. Many browsers are being marketed, and major on-line information services have incorporated browsers into the services they offer subscribers.

Males in their 20s and 30s are the primary users of the Internet; male users outnumber female users by almost 20 to 1. Children under age 18 make up about 2.3% of users.

FINGERTIP FACTS

- Worldwide, as of October 1994, there were 2.5 million host computers on the Internet that provided interactive services of one type or another.

- In mid-1991, there were 144,000 U.S. companies on the Internet. By the beginning of 1994, that number had jumped to 568,000. Companies use the Internet primarily for communicating with colleagues (35% of their usage) and customers (26%).

- In 1994, the on-line information industry generated nearly $13 billion in revenue.

- In 1995, approximately 10,000 new subscribers were logging on to commercial on-line services every day. The subscriber total by the end of 1995 was projected to be about 10 million.

- By September 1995, the Internet was estimated to reach more than 30 million computers, a figure expected to double every year.

- By mid-1995, worldwide there were more than 60 "cybercafes"—cafes where customers can connect to the Internet while ordering cappuccinos and colas.

- American consumers spent $200 million on-line in 1994, compared to more than $1.5 trillion in retail stores.

- Analysts estimate that the potential market for "information highway" goods and services will be approximately $3 trillion by the year 2000.

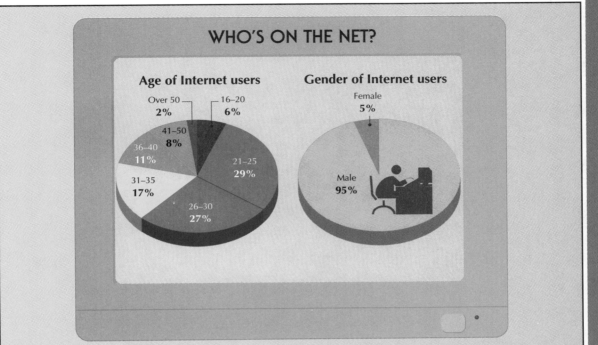

WHO'S ON THE NET?

Age of Internet users

Over 50 **2%**
16–20 **6%**
41–50 **8%**
36–40 **11%**
21–25 **29%**
31–35 **17%**
26–30 **27%**

Gender of Internet users

Female **5%**
Male **95%**

Source: Based on statistics from *Time* magazine

HOW THE INTERNET IS USED BY U.S. COMPANIES

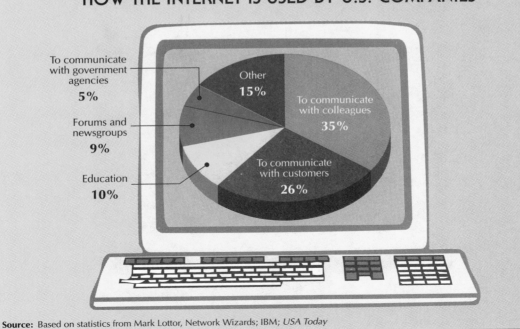

To communicate with government agencies **5%**

Forums and newsgroups **9%**

Education **10%**

Other **15%**

To communicate with colleagues **35%**

To communicate with customers **26%**

Source: Based on statistics from Mark Lottor, Network Wizards; IBM; *USA Today*

NUMBER OF U.S. COMPANIES ON THE INTERNET, 1991–1994

(Number of commercially registered computers on the Internet)

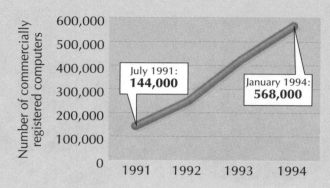

July 1991:
144,000

January 1994:
568,000

Source: Statistics based on IBM user survey; *USA Today* research

HOW USERS LEARN ABOUT WEB SITES

About 75% of people who use the World Wide Web say they browse it about once a day.
How they find out about Web sites:

Note: Many users get information from multiple sources
Source: Statistics based on Georgia Institute of Technology

COMPUTERS CONNECTED TO THE INTERNET, 1989–1995

(For selected years)

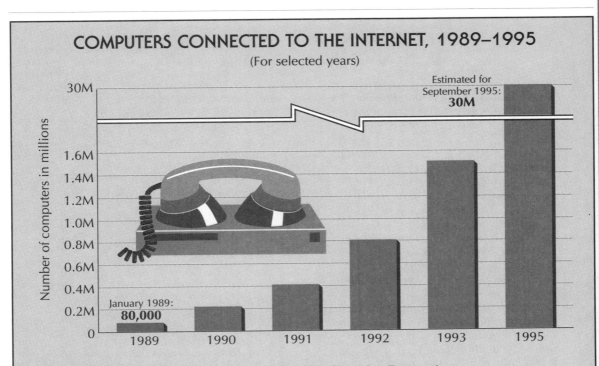

Estimated for
September 1995:
30M

January 1989:
80,000

Number of computers in millions

30M
1.6M
1.4M
1.2M
1.0M
0.8M
0.6M
0.4M
0.2M
0

1989   1990   1991   1992   1993   1995

Source: Based on statistics from *USA Today; The New York Times; The Washington Post; Time* magazine

FASTEST-GROWING ON-LINE SERVICES, 1995

(Percentage of growth in the first 6 months of 1995)

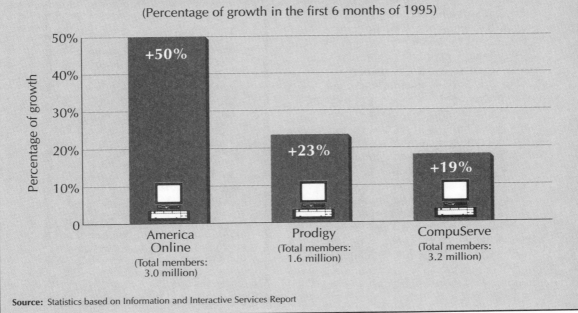

Percentage of growth

50%
40%
30%
20%
10%
0

+50%

+23%

+19%

America
Online
(Total members:
3.0 million)

Prodigy
(Total members:
1.6 million)

CompuServe
(Total members:
3.2 million)

Source: Statistics based on Information and Interactive Services Report

RESEARCH AND DEVELOPMENT

Scientific research and the development of technologies based on that research form the underpinnings of many modern societies. Without such work, the world would be lacking high-speed computers and telecommunications equipment, miracle medicines and diagnostic tools, efficient vehicles and appliances, and a host of other items that we take for granted today.

Each year, billions of dollars are spent worldwide on research and development (R&D). Although the percentage of Gross Domestic Product (GDP) devoted to R&D by the U.S. (2.7%) is similar to those of its main economic competitors (Japan, 2.0% and Germany, 2.8%) the U.S. devotes a large part of these funds to defense R&D, while the other two nations do not.

Federal funds traditionally have paid for a significant portion of research in the U.S.—of the $160.8 billion spent on R&D in 1993, 42% were federal funds. In recent years, however, Congress has cut such funding sharply, particularly in areas without immediately recognizable applications. Corporations and large universities, which have made major contributions to science, have also cut back on basic research. Some scientists approve of this focused direction of funding. Others, however, point out that most modern technology arose from research undertaken without any obvious practical applications.

In 1970, about 543,800 scientists and engineers were employed in R&D at corporations, universities and colleges, other non-profit institutions, and federally funded R&D centers. By 1989, that number had grown to 949,300. In the 1990s, though, funding cutbacks have resulted in reduced employment opportunities in some fields. In 1991, for example, an estimated 694,000 full-time R&D scientists and engineers were employed in industry—down 32,000 from 1989.

FINGERTIP FACTS

- In 1989, 76.5% of R&D scientists and engineers were employed by industry; 6.3% worked for the federal government; and the remainder were employed at universities and other institutions.

- In 1960, the U.S. spent $13.5 billion on R&D; about 56% ($7.5 billion) of this was defense- or space-related. In 1993, R&D expenditures were $160.8 billion, of which 30% ($48.2 billion) were defense- or space-related.

- In 1992, two-thirds of R&D expenditures in science and engineering at universities and colleges were spent on basic research, the remainder on applied R&D.

- Johns Hopkins University topped the list of university recipients of government R&D funding in 1991, receiving $490.9 million in federal R&D funds. The University of Washington was second, with $245.3 million.

- In 1993, the largest portion of federal R&D funding was devoted to life sciences (41%), followed by engineering (21%) and physical sciences (17%).

- The largest group of the 425 Nobel Prize laureates in chemistry, physics, and physiology/medicine from 1901 through 1992 came from the U.S. (173), followed by Great Britain (70), Germany (59), and France (24).

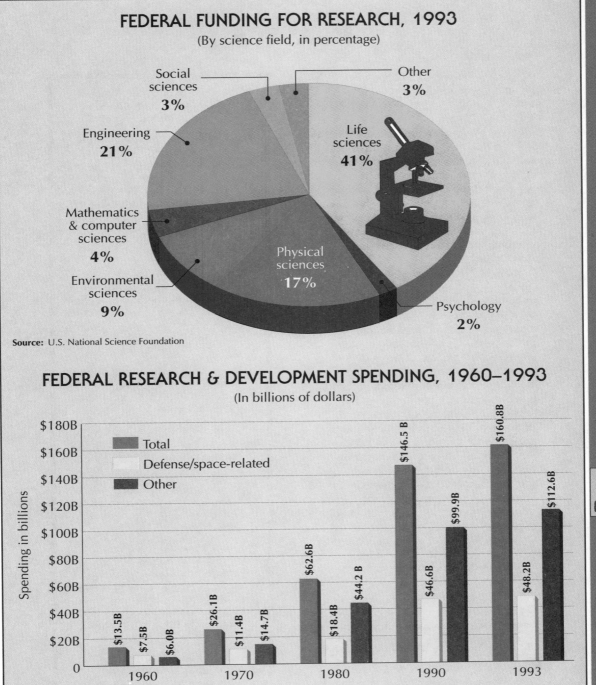

FEDERAL FUNDING FOR RESEARCH, 1993
(By science field, in percentage)

Social sciences **3%**

Other **3%**

Engineering **21%**

Life sciences **41%**

Mathematics & computer sciences **4%**

Physical sciences **17%**

Environmental sciences **9%**

Psychology **2%**

Source: U.S. National Science Foundation

FEDERAL RESEARCH & DEVELOPMENT SPENDING, 1960–1993
(In billions of dollars)

Spending in billions

- Total
- Defense/space-related
- Other

	1960	1970	1980	1990	1993
Total	$13.5B	$26.1B	$62.6B	$146.5 B	$160.8B
Defense/space-related	$7.5B	$11.4B	$18.4B	$46.6B	$48.2B
Other	$6.0B	$14.7B	$44.2 B	$99.9B	$112.6B

Source: U.S. National Science Foundation

NASA

The Space Age began on October 4, 1957, when the first satellite was launched—a metal ball named *Sputnik I*, owned by the Soviet Union.

The National Aeronautics and Space Administration (NASA) is the government agency in the U.S. responsible for space technology and exploration. It was created by the National Aeronautics and Space Act of 1958—though many people may be surprised to learn that its roots go back to 1915, when the National Advisory Committee for Aeronautics was created.

NASA has had many successes since its founding. Its *Apollo* flights landed men on the moon; probes have sent back photographs from distant planets; and dozens of complex space-shuttle missions have been successfully completed, with many more planned. A major project under development is *Alpha*, a multinational space station that is scheduled to be completed in the year 2002. Weighing 443 tons and able to house a crew of 6, it will orbit Earth at an altitude of about 250 miles.

Today NASA faces growing pressure to justify its existence. It is being asked to demonstrate social relevance, practicality, and affordability at the same time that it continues to provide a bold vision of the future. Its budget for fiscal 1995 was $14.3 billion, a reduction of $300 million from its 1994 budget. Particularly hard hit was the portion earmarked for human space flight.

☞ In fiscal year 1995, NASA spent $2.4 billion on space-shuttle operations, down from $2.9 billion in 1993.

☞ The U.S. space program is covered by several budgets. The two main components are NASA and the Department of Defense. In 1960, $1.1 billion was spent on the space program, with NASA providing 43.3% and Defense 52.6% of the total. In 1991, NASA provided 47.2% and Defense 51.4% of the $27.6 billion total.

☞ From 1957 through 1993, there were 3,569 successful space launches worldwide. The Soviet Union and its successor, the Commonwealth of Independent States, had 2,415 launches, followed by the U.S., with 1,004.

☞ Through 1993, a total of 308 people had traveled into space, including 195 Americans. The U.S. had launched 1,004 spacecraft, including 89 manned flights.

☞ The first space-shuttle flight began on April 12, 1981. Sixty-five flights had occurred by the end of 1994.

☞ In 1994, two Russian cosmonauts flew on U.S. space shuttles. In 1995, Norman E. Thagard became the first U.S. astronaut to travel into space aboard a Russian spacecraft.

☞ The U.S. Space Command uses radar to track some 7,000 pieces of orbiting debris that are softball-size or bigger, ranging from burned-out rocket boosters to spent satellites. Millions of other, smaller pieces also orbit Earth. The debris are a hazard to space shuttles and satellites.

☞ In 1994, NASA estimated a 10% risk of a catastrophic collision between the planned space station *Alpha* and space debris.

FINGERTIP FACTS

☞ In 1975, NASA spent $2.4 billion on research and development; in 1993, it spent $8.6 billion.

HOW NASA SPENDS ITS MONEY

In 1995, the National Aeronautics and Space Administration had a budget of $14.3 billion. Here, a breakdown of how NASA planned to distribute that money:

19%
Mission support*
Safety, reliability, and quality assurance, space communication services, research and program management, facility construction

41%
Science, aeronautics, and technology
Space science, life and microgravity sciences, mission to planet Earth, aeronautical research and technology, launch services, mission communication services, academic programs

40%
Human space flight
Space station, Russian cooperation, space shuttle, payload and utilization operations

* Less than 0.001% of the budget is allocated to the office of the Inspector General

Source: U.S. National Aeronautics and Space Administration

EARNINGS FROM SPACE, 1994

(Total commercial space revenues, by percentage)

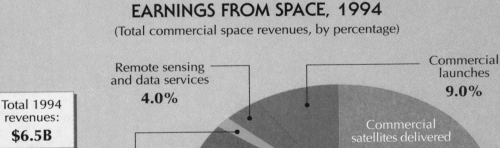

Total 1994 revenues: **$6.5B**

Remote sensing and data services **4.0%**

Commercial launches **9.0%**

Commercial satellites delivered **21.5%**

Commercial research and development structure **1.6%**

Satellite ground equipment **28.5%**

Satellite services **35.4%**

Source: U.S. Department of Commerce

WHAT THE NASA SPACE SHUTTLE COSTS, 1995

In 1995, the National Aeronautics and Space Administration was budgeted to spend $2.4 billion on the space-shuttle program. Here, a breakdown of how NASA planned to distribute that sum:

Mission & crew operations
$298.4 million
12%

Solid rocket booster
$144.9 million
6%

Launch & landing operations
$596.4 million
25%

Re-designed solid rocket
$373.1 million
15%

Orbiter
$292.8 million
12%

Main engine
$144.4 million
6%

System integration
$190.5 million
8%

External tank
$379.6 million
16%

Source: U.S. National Aeronautics and Space Administration

NASA's SPENDING SKYROCKETS, 1970–1994
(In billions of dollars)

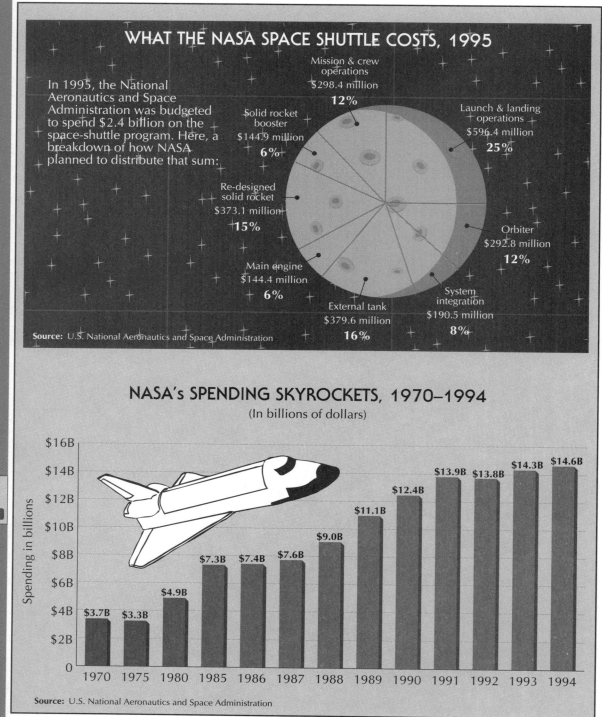

Spending in billions

Year	Spending
1970	$3.7B
1975	$3.3B
1980	$4.9B
1985	$7.3B
1986	$7.4B
1987	$7.6B
1988	$9.0B
1989	$11.1B
1990	$12.4B
1991	$13.9B
1992	$13.8B
1993	$14.3B
1994	$14.6B

Source: U.S. National Aeronautics and Space Administration

SPACE VEHICLE SYSTEMS TAKE OFF: NET SALES, 1965–1992

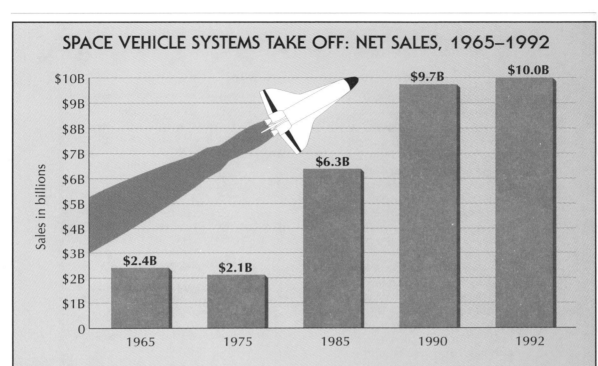

Sales in billions

$10B
$9B
$8B
$7B
$6B
$5B
$4B
$3B
$2B
$1B
0

$2.4B **$2.1B** **$6.3B** **$9.7B** **$10.0B**

1965   1975   1985   1990   1992

Source: U.S. Census Bureau

SPACE JUNK GROWS

(Comparison of number of working
satellites to pieces of "space junk")

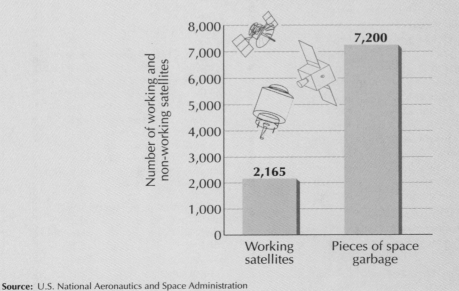

Number of working and
non-working satellites

8,000
7,000
6,000
5,000
4,000
3,000
2,000
1,000
0

2,165 **7,200**

Working
satellites

Pieces of space
garbage

Source: U.S. National Aeronautics and Space Administration

SCIENCE EDUCATION

Each year, about 650,000 students earn bachelor's degrees in science or engineering fields. An additional 135,000 master's degrees and 21,000 doctorates are awarded in these fields. Male degree recipients greatly outnumber females in agriculture, computer sciences, engineering, and physical sciences; females outnumber males in social sciences, health sciences, and psychology. In the life sciences, degrees are about evenly divided by sex.

Science education begins in kindergarten and continues through every level of primary and secondary school. Enrollment drops significantly in higher grades. About 85% of junior high school students are enrolled in science classes, compared to 75% of 10th graders taking biology and 20% of seniors enrolled in physics.

A certain degree of science literacy is important for all members of society. For most people, the foundations of this literacy are learned in primary and secondary schools. Critics have charged that science curricula at the primary and secondary levels have focused too heavily on the rote memorization of facts and figures, at the expense of teaching observation, problem solving, and the application of science to everyday live. In Benchmarks for Science Literacy, a 4-year study released in 1993, the American Association for the Advancement of Science (AAAS) advises that by teaching less material—but teaching it better—students will learn more and have greater understanding of facts and concepts.

FINGERTIP FACTS

☞ Foreign citizens received 31.5% of the science doctorates in 1992.

☞ In 1971, more than 50,000 bachelor's degrees in engineering were awarded, only 0.8% of them to females. In 1991, 3 times as many such degrees were awarded, 13.9% to females.

☞ In 1971, some 2,388 bachelor's degrees were awarded in computers and information sciences, 12.6% to females. In 1991, females earned 29.3% of the nearly 70,000 computer science degrees awarded.

☞ In health sciences, females earned 79% of the master's degrees and 57% of the doctorates in 1991.

☞ In mathematics, females earned 40.9% of the master's degrees and 19.2% of the doctorates awarded in 1991.

☞ Computer science garnered one-quarter of the master's degrees in science awarded in 1990, followed closely by life sciences and social sciences.

☞ Almost two-thirds of 1992 science doctorates were awarded to men.

☞ In general, the job market is better for young scientists who majored in fields with practical applications than for those in more theoretical fields. For example, the American Institute of Physics reported in 1994 that 75% of scientists with degrees in optics and lasers found jobs right after receiving their doctorates, as compared to only 14% of those with degrees in astrophysics.

☞ In 1993, male college-bound high school students averaged science-reasoning test scores of 21.5 on the American College Testing (ACT) program (maximum score 36.0); females averaged 20.3.

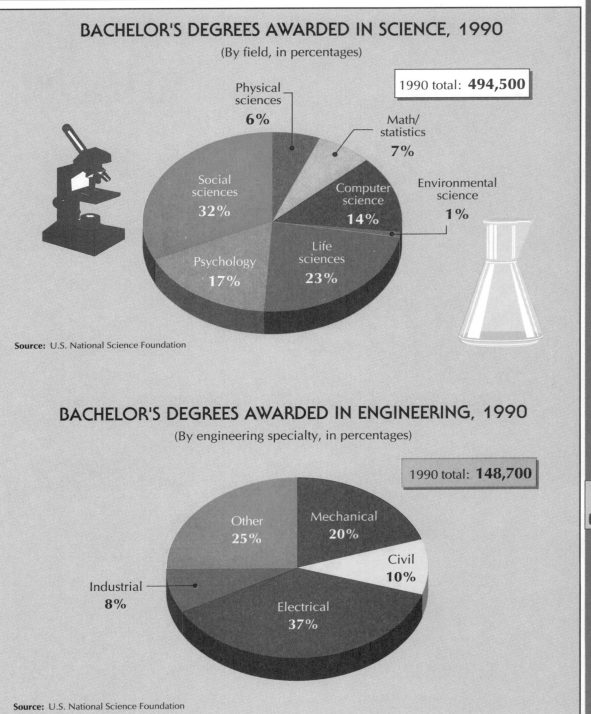

BACHELOR'S DEGREES AWARDED IN SCIENCE, 1990

(By field, in percentages)

1990 total: **494,500**

Physical sciences **6%**

Math/statistics **7%**

Social sciences **32%**

Computer science **14%**

Environmental science **1%**

Psychology **17%**

Life sciences **23%**

Source: U.S. National Science Foundation

BACHELOR'S DEGREES AWARDED IN ENGINEERING, 1990

(By engineering specialty, in percentages)

1990 total: **148,700**

Other **25%**

Mechanical **20%**

Civil **10%**

Industrial **8%**

Electrical **37%**

Source: U.S. National Science Foundation

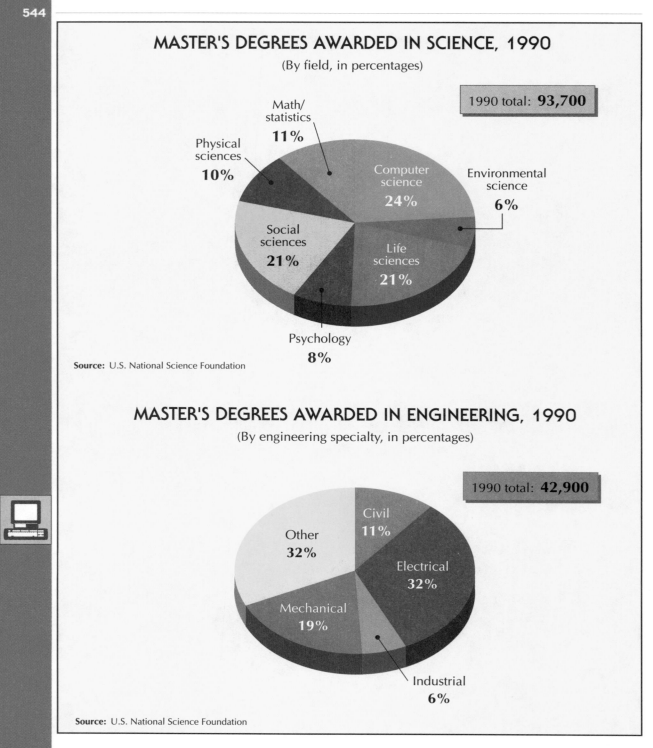

MASTER'S DEGREES AWARDED IN SCIENCE, 1990

(By field, in percentages)

1990 total: **93,700**

Math/statistics **11%**

Physical sciences **10%**

Computer science **24%**

Environmental science **6%**

Social sciences **21%**

Life sciences **21%**

Psychology **8%**

Source: U.S. National Science Foundation

MASTER'S DEGREES AWARDED IN ENGINEERING, 1990

(By engineering specialty, in percentages)

1990 total: **42,900**

Civil **11%**

Other **32%**

Electrical **32%**

Mechanical **19%**

Industrial **6%**

Source: U.S. National Science Foundation

WHO GETS THE DOCTORATES?

(Doctorates given in 1992 for engineering, physical sciences, earth sciences, mathematics, computer sciences, biological sciences, agricultural sciences, social sciences, and psychology)

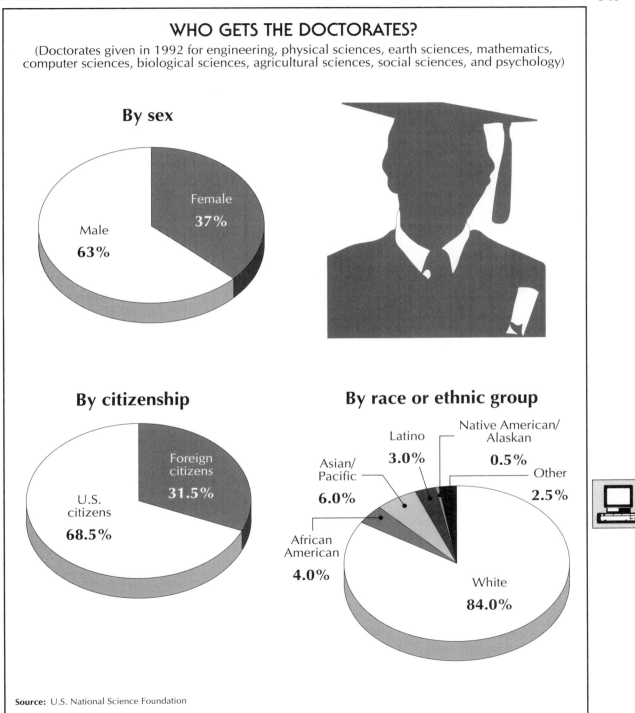

By sex

Female **37%**

Male **63%**

By citizenship

Foreign citizens **31.5%**

U.S. citizens **68.5%**

By race or ethnic group

Latino **3.0%**

Native American/ Alaskan **0.5%**

Asian/ Pacific **6.0%**

Other **2.5%**

African American **4.0%**

White **84.0%**

Source: U.S. National Science Foundation

11

SPORTS AND RECORDS

SPORTS IN AMERICA

Participating in and watching sports consumes a larger percentage of Americans' time than ever before. Children start swimming and throwing balls even before they start preschool, while increasing numbers of people in their eighties and nineties are walking and lifting weights. The volume of sports teams, from youth soccer leagues to tandem bicycling clubs, keeps multiplying. There is growing openness to new and less well known sports, plus a willingness to spend money on often-pricey equipment, memberships in gyms, and vacations in sports camps or distant scuba-diving havens.

Spectator sports—everything from local Little League games and college track meets to the Olympic Games and Monday night football—are a significant part of the nation's multi-billion-dollar entertainment industry. Professional sports keeps expanding at a rapid pace. Since 1945, major league baseball has added 12 new teams; since 1966, the National Hockey League has awarded 14 additional franchises; the National Basketball Association grew from 22 teams in 1980 to 27 teams by 1990; and so on. And the American thirst for sports seems only to intensify with each passing year.

FINGERTIP FACTS

- Some 15.2 million people ages 6 and older played soccer in 1992; fully 40% played 25 or more days a year.

- The most popular U.S. youth team sports are basketball (21 million participants in 1993), volleyball (13.1 million), softball (12.3 million), and soccer (12.2 million).

- The number of women participating in college sports increased about 8% from the 1984-1985 academic year (91,669 participants) to 1992-1993 (99,859).

- Basketball is played in the U.S. by 28.2 million males, but only by 12.2 million females.

- In 1975, about 308.6 million rounds of golf were played in the U.S., with 13 million golfers playing at least 1 round. By 1992, some 24.8 million golfers were on the greens, and 505.4 million rounds were played.

- Across the U.S., the number of bowlers increased from 62.5 million in 1975 to 82.0 million in 1992, but the number of bowling establishments fell from 8,577 to 7,250.

- Wisconsin and North Dakota have the largest percentages of golf-playing residents (20.2%); Louisiana (5.3%) and Arkansas (5.6%) have the lowest percentages.

- In 1973, only 5% of hockey pros were from the U.S.; 93% were from Canada. By 1993, 17% were from the U.S. and the Canadian portion had declined to 55%.

- Prior to the infamous 1994 "strike" season, attendance at major league baseball games topped 55 million annually.

- The number of professional rodeos rose from 631 in 1980 to 770 in 1992. During that period, membership in the Professional Rodeo Cowboys Association grew from 5,114 to 5,714.

- From 1980 to 1992, the number of pro basketball teams grew from 22 to 27, and average attendance per game rose from 11,017 to 15,689.

TOP 10 MOST POPULAR HIGH SCHOOL SPORTS, BY SEX, 1993–1994

(Numbers of students participating, by sport and sex)

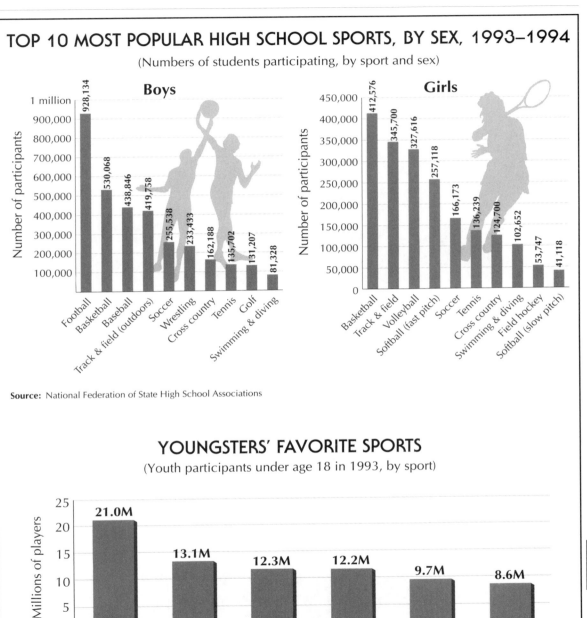

Boys

Number of participants

Sport	Participants
Football	928,134
Basketball	530,068
Baseball	438,846
Track & field (outdoors)	419,758
Soccer	255,538
Wrestling	233,433
Cross country	162,188
Tennis	135,702
Golf	131,207
Swimming & diving	81,328

Girls

Number of participants

Sport	Participants
Basketball	412,576
Track & field	345,700
Volleyball	327,616
Softball (fast pitch)	257,118
Soccer	166,173
Tennis	136,239
Cross country	124,700
Swimming & diving	102,652
Field hockey	53,747
Softball (slow pitch)	41,118

Source: National Federation of State High School Associations

YOUNGSTERS' FAVORITE SPORTS

(Youth participants under age 18 in 1993, by sport)

Millions of players

Sport	Players
Basketball	21.0M
Volleyball	13.1M
Softball	12.3M
Soccer	12.2M
Baseball	9.7M
Football	8.6M

Source: Based on *USA Today* Research statistics

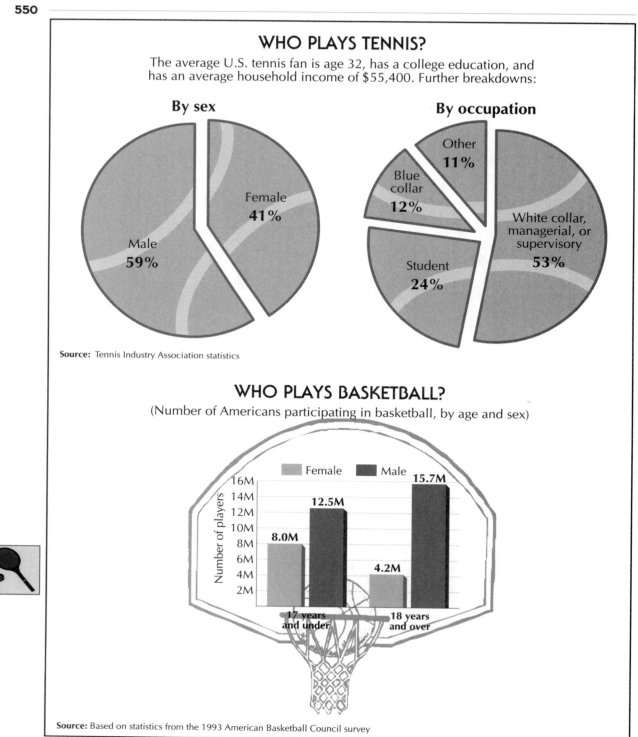

WHO PLAYS TENNIS?

The average U.S. tennis fan is age 32, has a college education, and has an average household income of $55,400. Further breakdowns:

By sex

Female
41%

Male
59%

By occupation

Other
11%

Blue collar
12%

White collar, managerial, or supervisory
53%

Student
24%

Source: Tennis Industry Association statistics

WHO PLAYS BASKETBALL?

(Number of Americans participating in basketball, by age and sex)

Female ▢   Male ▢

Number of players

16M
14M
12M
10M
8M
6M
4M
2M

8.0M   12.5M   4.2M   15.7M

17 years and under   18 years and over

Source: Based on statistics from the 1993 American Basketball Council survey

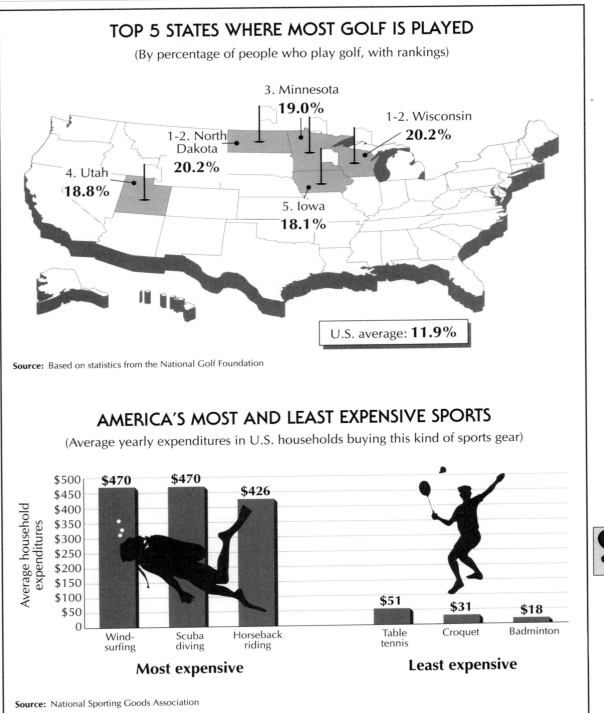

TOP 5 STATES WHERE MOST GOLF IS PLAYED

(By percentage of people who play golf, with rankings)

3. Minnesota
19.0%

1-2. Wisconsin
20.2%

1-2. North Dakota
20.2%

4. Utah
18.8%

5. Iowa
18.1%

U.S. average: **11.9%**

Source: Based on statistics from the National Golf Foundation

AMERICA'S MOST AND LEAST EXPENSIVE SPORTS

(Average yearly expenditures in U.S. households buying this kind of sports gear)

Average household expenditures

$500
$450
$400
$350
$300
$250
$200
$150
$100
$50
0

$470 Wind-surfing
$470 Scuba diving
$426 Horseback riding

Most expensive

$51 Table tennis
$31 Croquet
$18 Badminton

Least expensive

Source: National Sporting Goods Association

THE BIG BUSINESS OF SPORTS

It is not only the promise of fame that makes many high school athletes dream of playing professional sports; it is also the enticement of great wealth. They are spurred on by National Basketball Association and major league baseball salaries that, in the 1990s, average more than $1 million, coupled with endorsement contracts that may bring in additional millions.

Every aspect of professional sports is big business. Buying a pro team generally offers an excellent return on a person's investment. For example, the people who purchased the Baltimore Orioles for $70 million in 1989 sold the team just 4 years later for $173 million.

Fans spend billions of dollars annually not only to attend sports events but to wear team jerseys and hats, collect autographed memorabilia, and even buy cards and pogs featuring the images of their favorite players.

But fan loyalty is increasingly being soured by labor disputes, including the lengthy and bitter 1994-1995 baseball strike. Also bothersome to fans are the rising costs to attend games played by athletes who are already millionaires, playing for clubs owned by millionaires; and the all-too-frequent arrests of athletes for charges such as drug use, rape, and general mayhem. There are signs that the big business of sports will pay heavily if it continues to ignore the real interests of its fans.

FINGERTIP FACTS

- The top annual salary earned by baseball legend Babe Ruth was $80,000 in 1930. In 1993, San Francisco Giants outfielder Barry Bonds' salary was $7.29 million.

- In 1980, the average salary of a major league baseball player was $144,000. By 1994, it had jumped to $1.3 million.

- Following the 1994-1995 baseball strike, many free agents took pay cuts. Dave Stewart, whose 1994 salary with the Toronto Blue Jays had been $4.25 million, signed with the Oakland Athletics for $1 million.

- Basketball great Michael Jordan was the highest-earning athlete in 1994, with $30 million from product endorsements. Shaquille O'Neal was #2.

- Tennis player Steffi Graf was the highest-earning female athlete in 1994. She earned $1.5 million in salary and winnings, plus $6.5 million from endorsements.

- Commercial sports had revenues of $10.6 billion in 1992. Revenues from public recreation services included $3.3 billion at physical fitness facilities, $2.9 billion at bowling centers, and $2.6 billion at public golf courses.

- The month-long 1994 World Cup Soccer Tournament brought in more than $43 million in gate receipts.

- Television contracts are the major source of National Collegiate Athletics Association funds, providing 75% of revenues in 1991-1992.

- The NCAA women's basketball tournament took in $1.8 million in 1993—quadruple its 1982 receipts.

- The 107 franchises in professional baseball, football, basketball, and hockey are worth a total of $11.4 billion.

- The most valuable franchises are in the National Football League. In 1994, the Dallas Cowboys were estimated to be worth $190 million and the New York Giants $176 million.

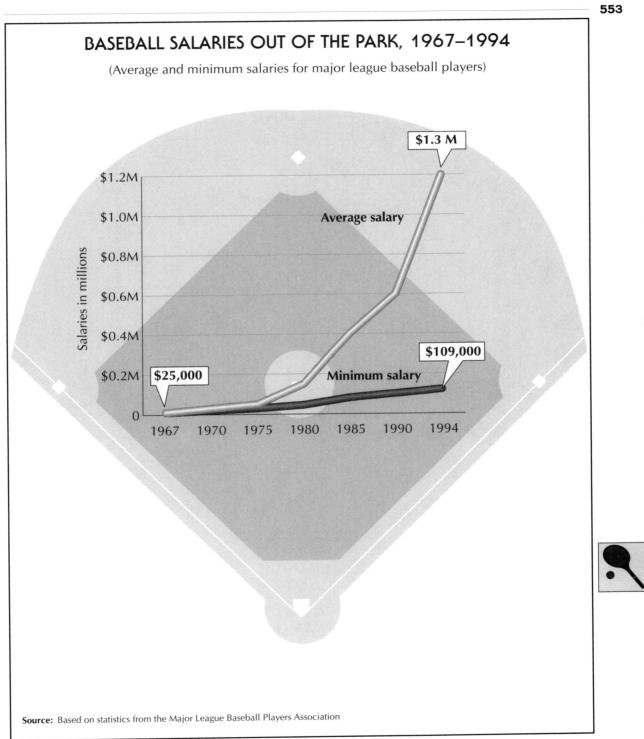

BASEBALL SALARIES OUT OF THE PARK, 1967–1994

(Average and minimum salaries for major league baseball players)

$1.3 M

$1.2M

$1.0M

Average salary

$0.8M

Salaries in millions

$0.6M

$0.4M

$109,000

$0.2M

$25,000

Minimum salary

0

1967   1970   1975   1980   1985   1990   1994

Source: Based on statistics from the Major League Baseball Players Association

FREE AGENCY SPIKES NFL SALARIES

In 1986, the average National Football League salary was under $200,000. Base salaries increased at an annual rate of 16.4% until the start of free agency. In the first year of free agency, 1993, the average salary jumped 51%:

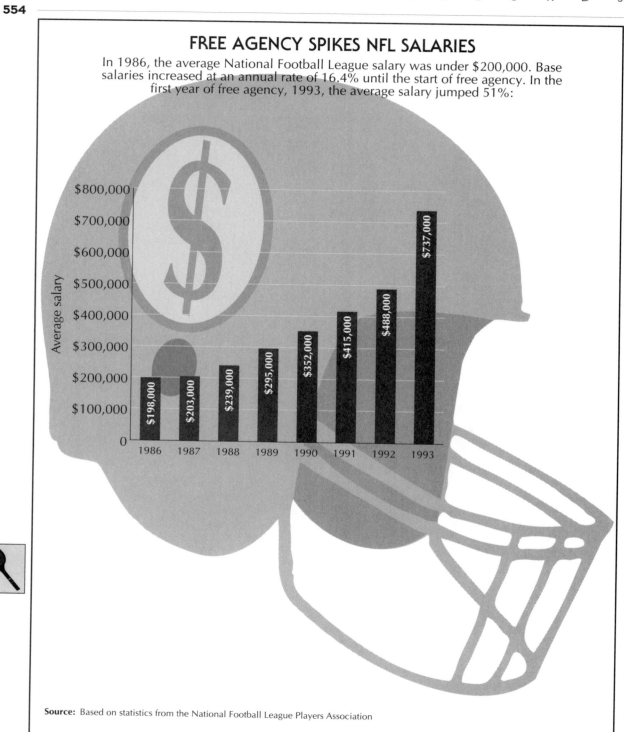

Average salary

Year	Salary
1986	$198,000
1987	$203,000
1988	$239,000
1989	$295,000
1990	$352,000
1991	$415,000
1992	$488,000
1993	$737,000

Source: Based on statistics from the National Football League Players Association

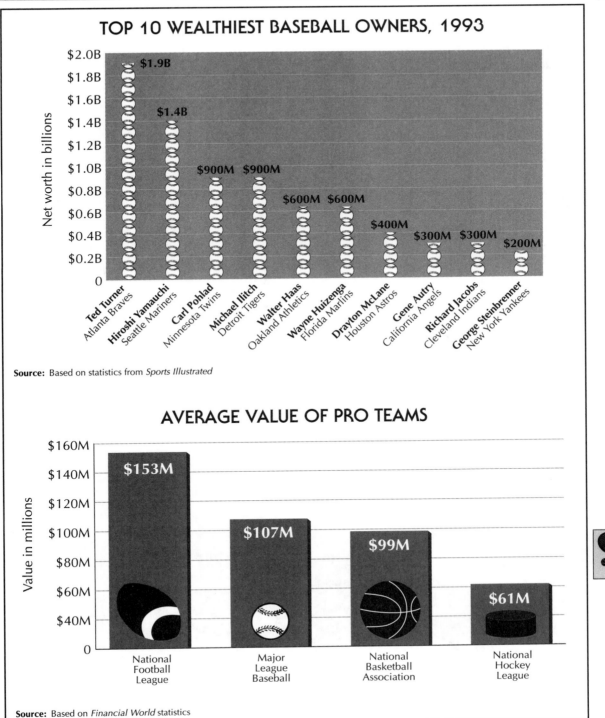

TOP 10 WEALTHIEST BASEBALL OWNERS, 1993

Net worth in billions

$2.0B
$1.8B
$1.6B
$1.4B
$1.2B
$1.0B
$0.8B
$0.6B
$0.4B
$0.2B
0

$1.9B — **Ted Turner** Atlanta Braves
$1.4B — **Hiroshi Yamauchi** Seattle Mariners
$900M — **Carl Pohlad** Minnesota Twins
$900M — **Michael Ilitch** Detroit Tigers
$600M — **Walter Haas** Oakland Athletics
$600M — **Wayne Huizenga** Florida Marlins
$400M — **Drayton McLane** Houston Astros
$300M — **Gene Autry** California Angels
$300M — **Richard Jacobs** Cleveland Indians
$200M — **George Steinbrenner** New York Yankees

Source: Based on statistics from *Sports Illustrated*

AVERAGE VALUE OF PRO TEAMS

Value in millions

$160M
$140M
$120M
$100M
$80M
$60M
$40M
0

$153M — National Football League
$107M — Major League Baseball
$99M — National Basketball Association
$61M — National Hockey League

Source: Based on *Financial World* statistics

NCAA WOMEN'S BASKETBALL REBOUNDS

The National Collegiate Athletic Association women's basketball tournament has grown in popularity in recent years. Here, the bottom line on attendance and gross receipts from 1982–1993:

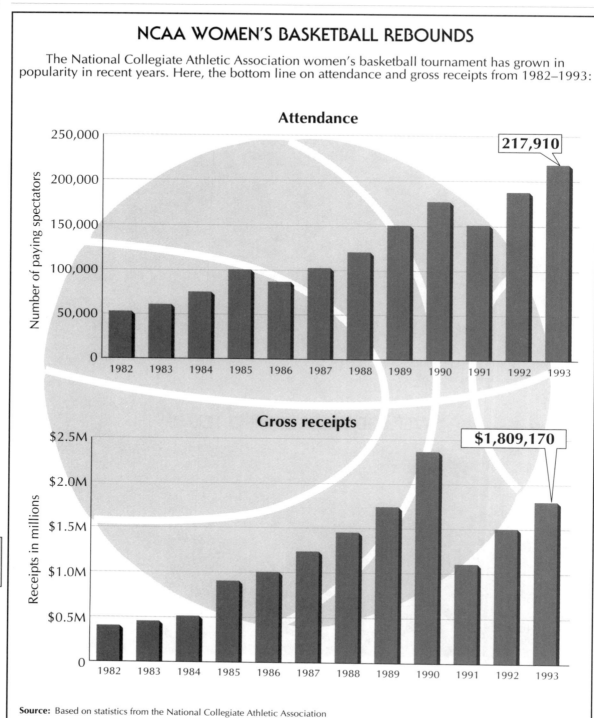

Attendance

217,910

Gross receipts

$1,809,170

Source: Based on statistics from the National Collegiate Athletic Association

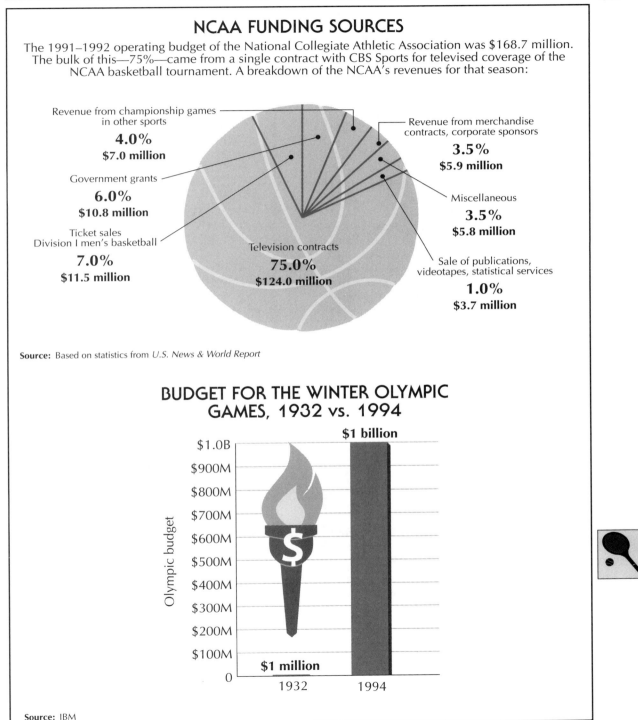

NCAA FUNDING SOURCES

The 1991–1992 operating budget of the National Collegiate Athletic Association was $168.7 million. The bulk of this—75%—came from a single contract with CBS Sports for televised coverage of the NCAA basketball tournament. A breakdown of the NCAA's revenues for that season:

Revenue from championship games in other sports
4.0%
$7.0 million

Government grants
6.0%
$10.8 million

Ticket sales Division I men's basketball
7.0%
$11.5 million

Television contracts
75.0%
$124.0 million

Revenue from merchandise contracts, corporate sponsors
3.5%
$5.9 million

Miscellaneous
3.5%
$5.8 million

Sale of publications, videotapes, statistical services
1.0%
$3.7 million

Source: Based on statistics from *U.S. News & World Report*

BUDGET FOR THE WINTER OLYMPIC GAMES, 1932 vs. 1994

$1 billion

Olympic budget: $1.0B, $900M, $800M, $700M, $600M, $500M, $400M, $300M, $200M, $100M, 0

$1 million

1932   1994

Source: IBM

SPORTS RECORDS

In 1954, when Roger Bannister became the first runner to break the 4-minute mile, the feat made headlines around the world. Since then, more than 700 athletes have run a mile in less than 4 minutes, and the record has been lowered by more than 15 seconds. In the 1970s, football professionals kicked field goals with 63.1% accuracy. Today, 80.1% of kicks are successful.

Clearly, athletes are getting swifter and stronger—routinely slamming tennis serves across the net at more than 100 miles per hour, vaulting over ever-higher bars, shaving seconds off records as they streak through swimming pools. Improved nutrition, more efficient training, and ever-more high-tech equipment are some of the factors in the never-ending breaking of records.

Still, some records have remained on the books for decades. For example, Ty Cobb's career total of 892 stolen bases was a major league record for almost half a century before being broken by Lou Brock in 1977. And Cobb's record of 3 season batting averages over .400 stands to this day.

FINGERTIP FACTS

- Brazil, Germany, and Italy have dominated World Cup Soccer since 1930, having won 3 championships each.

- In 1983, Australians became the first yachters to take the America's Cup out of U.S. hands since the event began in 1851. In 1995, New Zealanders became the second such victors.

- Ivan Lendl headed the men's tennis players ranking charts for a record 270 weeks, followed closely by Jimmy Connors at 268.

- In 1990, Pete Sampras became the youngest men's singles tennis champ in U.S. Open history. And Jennifer Capriati made her professional debut, becoming the youngest tennis player ever to play a pro title match.

- Through 1994, Martina Navratilova had the tennis world's best career-record totals, having won 167 singles and 162 doubles titles. Margaret Smith Court won the most grand slam titles—24.

- A.J. Foyt won the Indianapolis 500 a record 67 times. Mario Andretti holds second place, with 52 wins.

- Ray Floyd had the longest winning career in the PGA, with his first tournament win in 1963 and his last such win in 1992.

- Speed skater Bonnie Blair has 5 Olympic gold medals, more than any other U.S. female. Swimmer Mark Spitz won a record 7 gold medals in a single Olympics Games (1972).

- Wilt Chamberlain once amassed 55 rebounds in a game and led the NBA in rebounding for 11 seasons, but his career-points total of 31,419 was surpassed by Kareem Abdul-Jabbar, who hit 38,387.

- Baseball great Hank Aaron led the National League in home runs 4 seasons. He hit a career total of 755 homers, surpassing Babe Ruth's all-time record of 714.

- Ty Cobb, the first member of the Baseball Hall of Fame, batted over .400 an amazing 3 seasons in his career, and over .300 in 23 seasons.

- Cy Young won 511 games during his career, more than any other baseball pitcher. He also holds the records for most games completed (751) and most innings pitched (7,356).

TOP 10 MAJOR LEAGUE BASEBALL ALL-TIME CAREER PERFORMERS

(Figures calculated as of the end of the abortive 1994 baseball season)

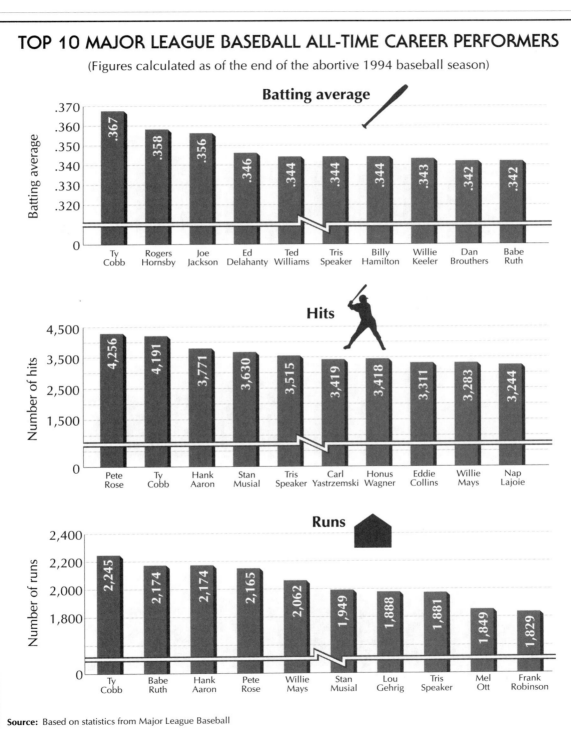

Batting average

Ty Cobb .367 | Rogers Hornsby .358 | Joe Jackson .356 | Ed Delahanty .346 | Ted Williams .344 | Tris Speaker .344 | Billy Hamilton .344 | Willie Keeler .343 | Dan Brouthers .342 | Babe Ruth .342

Hits

Pete Rose 4,256 | Ty Cobb 4,191 | Hank Aaron 3,771 | Stan Musial 3,630 | Tris Speaker 3,515 | Carl Yastrzemski 3,419 | Honus Wagner 3,418 | Eddie Collins 3,311 | Willie Mays 3,283 | Nap Lajoie 3,244

Runs

Ty Cobb 2,245 | Babe Ruth 2,174 | Hank Aaron 2,174 | Pete Rose 2,165 | Willie Mays 2,062 | Stan Musial 1,949 | Lou Gehrig 1,888 | Tris Speaker 1,881 | Mel Ott 1,849 | Frank Robinson 1,829

Source: Based on statistics from Major League Baseball

TOP 10 MAJOR LEAGUE BASEBALL ALL-TIME CAREER PERFORMERS

(Figures calculated as of the end of the abortive 1994 baseball season)

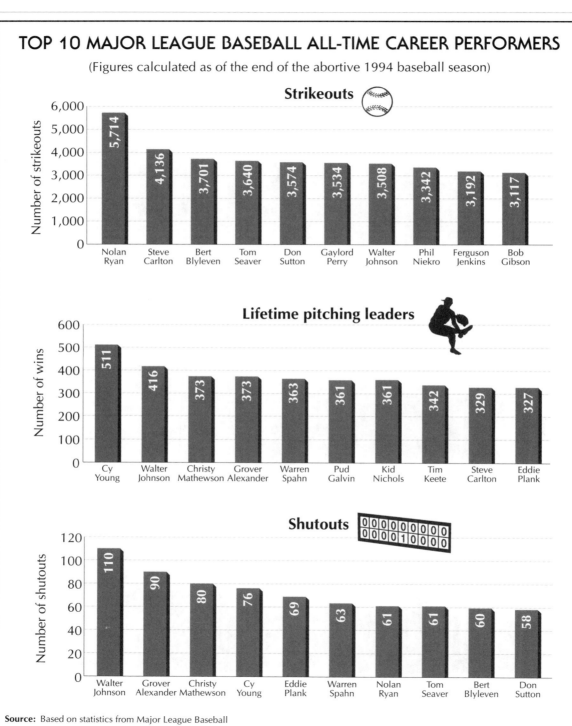

Strikeouts

Player	Number of strikeouts
Nolan Ryan	5,714
Steve Carlton	4,136
Bert Blyleven	3,701
Tom Seaver	3,640
Don Sutton	3,574
Gaylord Perry	3,534
Walter Johnson	3,508
Phil Niekro	3,342
Ferguson Jenkins	3,192
Bob Gibson	3,117

Lifetime pitching leaders

Player	Number of wins
Cy Young	511
Walter Johnson	416
Christy Mathewson	373
Grover Alexander	373
Warren Spahn	363
Pud Galvin	361
Kid Nichols	361
Tim Keete	342
Steve Carlton	329
Eddie Plank	327

Shutouts

Player	Number of shutouts
Walter Johnson	110
Grover Alexander	90
Christy Mathewson	80
Cy Young	76
Eddie Plank	69
Warren Spahn	63
Nolan Ryan	61
Tom Seaver	61
Bert Blyleven	60
Don Sutton	58

Source: Based on statistics from Major League Baseball

TOP 10 NHL GOAL-SCORING LEADERS
(National Hockey League figures as of the end of the 1993–1994 season)

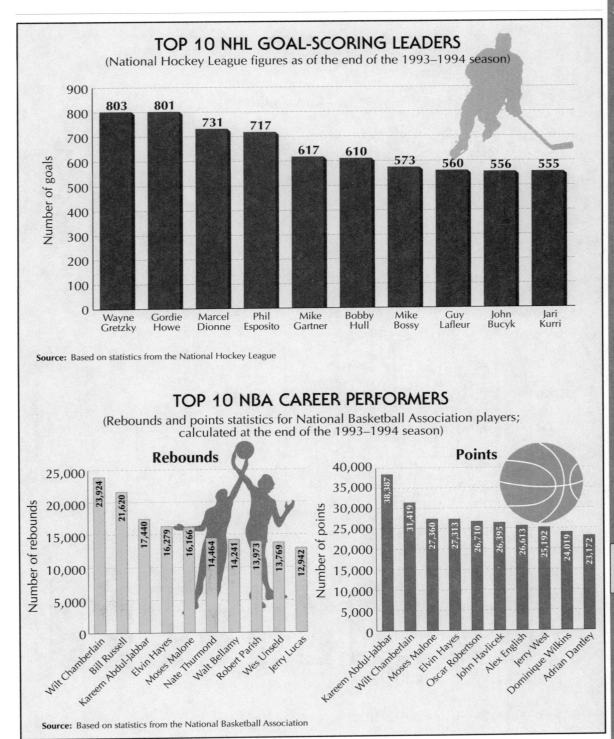

Number of goals

Wayne Gretzky	803
Gordie Howe	801
Marcel Dionne	731
Phil Esposito	717
Mike Gartner	617
Bobby Hull	610
Mike Bossy	573
Guy Lafleur	560
John Bucyk	556
Jari Kurri	555

Source: Based on statistics from the National Hockey League

TOP 10 NBA CAREER PERFORMERS
(Rebounds and points statistics for National Basketball Association players; calculated at the end of the 1993–1994 season)

Rebounds

Number of rebounds

Player	Rebounds
Wilt Chamberlain	23,924
Bill Russell	21,620
Kareem Abdul-Jabbar	17,440
Elvin Hayes	16,279
Moses Malone	16,166
Nate Thurmond	14,464
Walt Bellamy	14,241
Robert Parish	13,973
Wes Unseld	13,769
Jerry Lucas	12,942

Points

Number of points

Player	Points
Kareem Abdul-Jabbar	38,387
Wilt Chamberlain	31,419
Moses Malone	27,360
Elvin Hayes	27,313
Oscar Robertson	26,710
John Havlicek	26,395
Alex English	26,613
Jerry West	25,192
Dominique Wilkins	24,019
Adrian Dantley	23,172

Source: Based on statistics from the National Basketball Association

TOP 10 NFL PASSING LEADERS

(National Football League figures as of the end of the 1993 season)

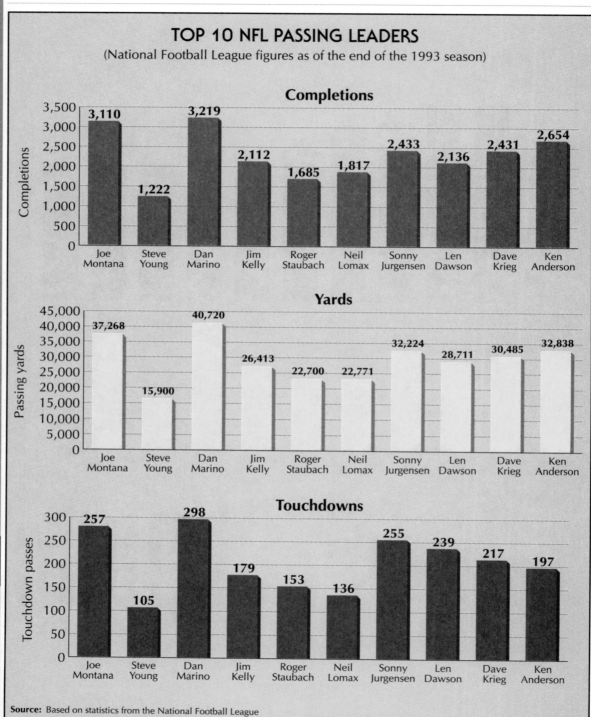

Completions

Player	Completions
Joe Montana	3,110
Steve Young	1,222
Dan Marino	3,219
Jim Kelly	2,112
Roger Staubach	1,685
Neil Lomax	1,817
Sonny Jurgensen	2,433
Len Dawson	2,136
Dave Krieg	2,431
Ken Anderson	2,654

Yards

Player	Passing yards
Joe Montana	37,268
Steve Young	15,900
Dan Marino	40,720
Jim Kelly	26,413
Roger Staubach	22,700
Neil Lomax	22,771
Sonny Jurgensen	32,224
Len Dawson	28,711
Dave Krieg	30,485
Ken Anderson	32,838

Touchdowns

Player	Touchdown passes
Joe Montana	257
Steve Young	105
Dan Marino	298
Jim Kelly	179
Roger Staubach	153
Neil Lomax	136
Sonny Jurgensen	255
Len Dawson	239
Dave Krieg	217
Ken Anderson	197

Source: Based on statistics from the National Football League

TOP 10 NFL RUSHERS

(National Football League figures as of the end of the 1993 season)

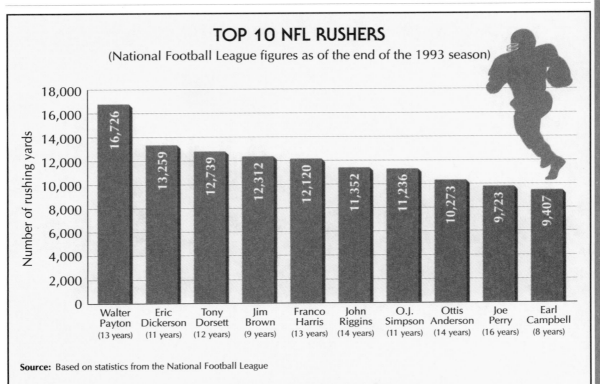

Number of rushing yards

Walter Payton (13 years)	16,726
Eric Dickerson (11 years)	13,259
Tony Dorsett (12 years)	12,739
Jim Brown (9 years)	12,312
Franco Harris (13 years)	12,120
John Riggins (14 years)	11,352
O.J. Simpson (11 years)	11,236
Ottis Anderson (14 years)	10,273
Joe Perry (16 years)	9,723
Earl Campbell (8 years)	9,407

Source: Based on statistics from the National Football League

WORLD CUP CHAMPIONS

Teams from 58 countries have played in the 14 World Cup soccer championships held since 1930. Winners and number of World Cup titles:

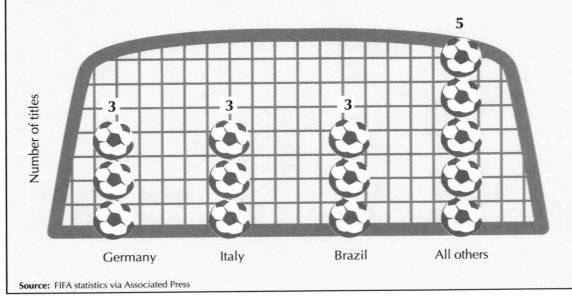

Number of titles

Germany **3** Italy **3** Brazil **3** All others **5**

Source: FIFA statistics via Associated Press

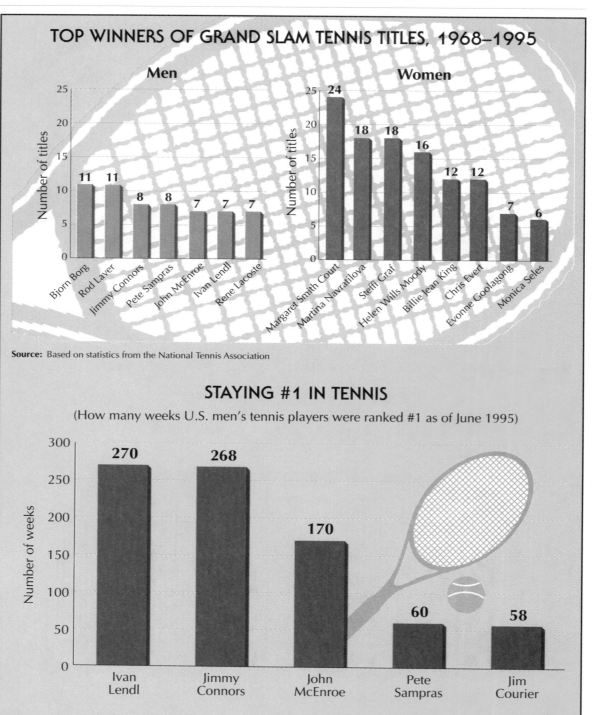

TOP WINNERS OF GRAND SLAM TENNIS TITLES, 1968–1995

Men

Number of titles

- Bjorn Borg — 11
- Rod Laver — 11
- Jimmy Connors — 8
- Pete Sampras — 8
- John McEnroe — 7
- Ivan Lendl — 7
- Rene Lacoste — 7

Women

Number of titles

- Margaret Smith Court — 24
- Martina Navratilova — 18
- Steffi Graf — 18
- Helen Wills Moody — 16
- Billie Jean King — 12
- Chris Evert — 12
- Evonne Goolagong — 7
- Monica Seles — 6

Source: Based on statistics from the National Tennis Association

STAYING #1 IN TENNIS

(How many weeks U.S. men's tennis players were ranked #1 as of June 1995)

Number of weeks

- Ivan Lendl — 270
- Jimmy Connors — 268
- John McEnroe — 170
- Pete Sampras — 60
- Jim Courier — 58

Source: Based on statistics from IBM/ATP Tour

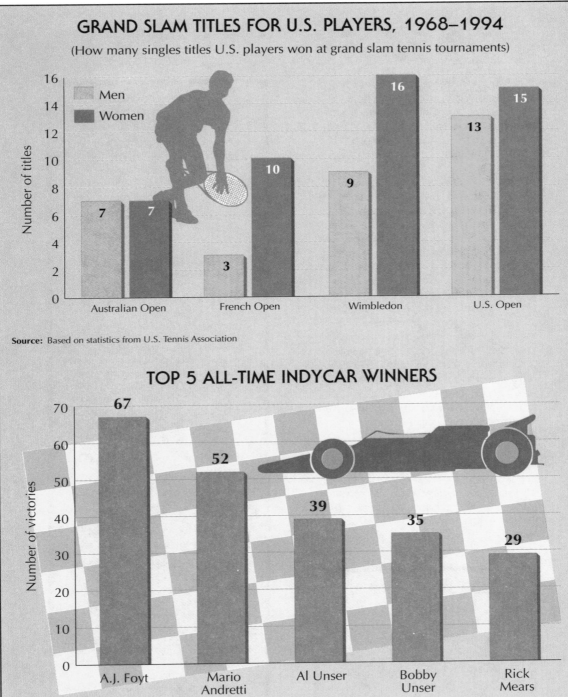

GRAND SLAM TITLES FOR U.S. PLAYERS, 1968–1994

(How many singles titles U.S. players won at grand slam tennis tournaments)

Men
Women

Number of titles

Australian Open: Men 7, Women 7
French Open: Men 3, Women 10
Wimbledon: Men 9, Women 16
U.S. Open: Men 13, Women 15

Source: Based on statistics from U.S. Tennis Association

TOP 5 ALL-TIME INDYCAR WINNERS

Number of victories

A.J. Foyt: 67
Mario Andretti: 52
Al Unser: 39
Bobby Unser: 35
Rick Mears: 29

Source: Based on statistics from CART

S P O R T S   T R E N D S

Skydiving and scuba diving, bungee jumping and shooting the rapids, rock climbing and rollerblading—these activities and sports trends are enjoying fantastic growth because adventurous athletes are seeking new challenges and thrills. The search for things new and different has affected spectator sports, too; soccer and jai-alai, for example, are pulling in ever-growing audiences. But what is trendy one year may be passé the next. For instance, the number of racquetball players has dropped steadily since 1985, and many courts have been converted to squash courts, aerobics facilities, and other uses.

Unfortunately, many amateur athletes resort to dangerous practices while pursuing their sports. They undertake activities without first getting proper training, preparation, or equipment. Too often, the result is serious injury, or even death. The majority of bicyclists do not wear helmets, for example, even though helmets reduce the risk of bicycle-related head injury by 85%.

Public and private groups are currently using various tactics to educate people about the risks of sports. In one Maryland county, legislation accompanied by an educational campaign increased bicycle helmet use from 4% to 47% within one year.

FINGERTIP FACTS

- One of the fastest-growing sports in the U.S. is rock climbing, with an estimated 500,000 enthusiasts.

- The number of in-line skaters increased from 3 million in 1989 to 14 million in 1994. Rollerblade, Inc., one of the leading manufacturers of in-line skates, sold 4.2 million pairs in 1992.

- Membership in the Tandem (bicycling) Club of America rose from just 11 teams in 1976 to more than 2,000 in 1991.

- An estimated 20,000 Americans participate in triathlons, which include a sequence of swimming, biking, and running.

- Americans owned 16.5 million recreational boats in 1992, up from 9.7 million in 1975. Boats with outboard motors made up the largest category (8.0 million in 1992), followed by canoes (2.4 million) and inboard boats (2.4 million).

- A worldwide TV audience of almost 2 billion soccer fans watched the 1994 World Cup final at the Rose Bowl in Pasadena, California, about 8 times as many people as watch the Super Bowl.

- Attendance at jai-alai games rose from 3.9 million in 1980 to 5.3 million in 1990.

- In 1995, the U.S. National Park Service began charging a $150 "user fee" for climbers of Mount McKinley, to help offset costs of rescuing people.

- Each year, bicyclists in the U.S. sustain injuries that result in 550,000 emergency room visits and nearly 1,000 deaths. Of the deaths, 52% involve head injuries.

- Sales of bicycle helmets jumped from 386,000 in 1985 to 10.8 million in 1993. Still, only about 15% of child bicyclists and 18% of all bicyclists wear helmets.

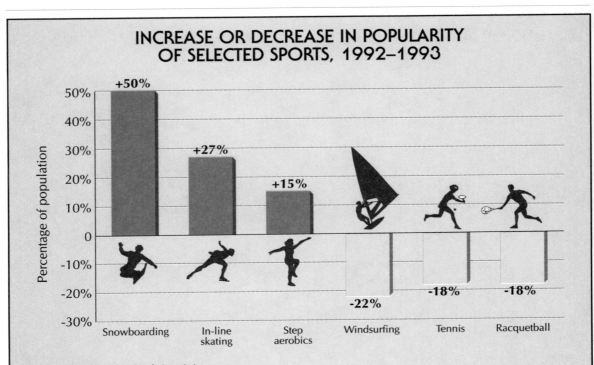

INCREASE OR DECREASE IN POPULARITY OF SELECTED SPORTS, 1992–1993

Source: National Sporting Goods Association

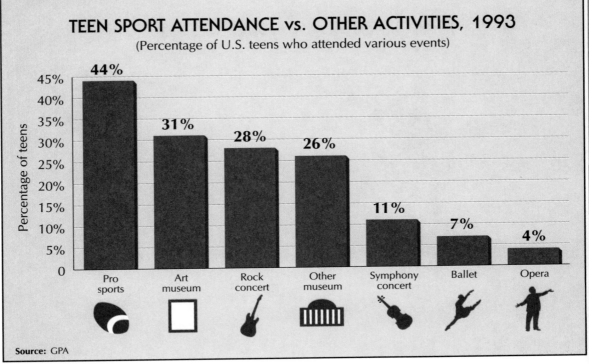

TEEN SPORT ATTENDANCE vs. OTHER ACTIVITIES, 1993
(Percentage of U.S. teens who attended various events)

Source: GPA

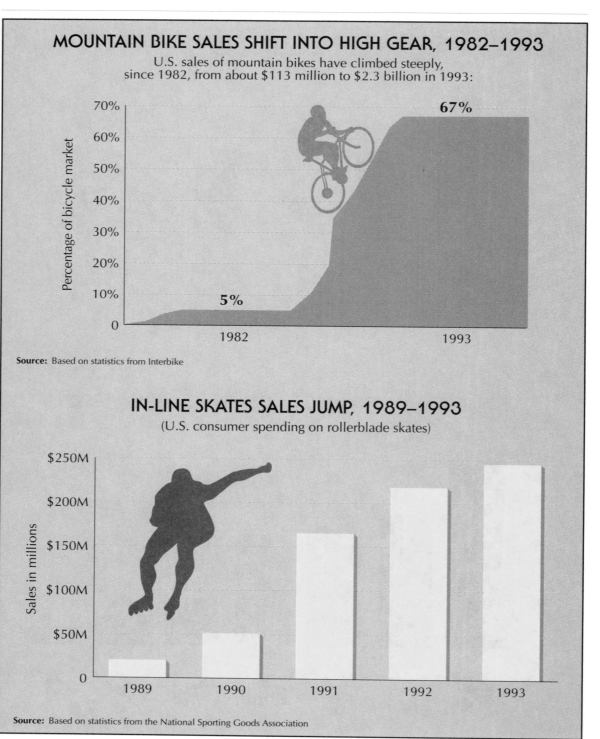

MOUNTAIN BIKE SALES SHIFT INTO HIGH GEAR, 1982–1993

U.S. sales of mountain bikes have climbed steeply,
since 1982, from about $113 million to $2.3 billion in 1993:

67%

5%

Percentage of bicycle market

70%
60%
50%
40%
30%
20%
10%
0

1982   1993

Source: Based on statistics from Interbike

IN-LINE SKATES SALES JUMP, 1989–1993

(U.S. consumer spending on rollerblade skates)

Sales in millions

$250M
$200M
$150M
$100M
$50M
0

1989   1990   1991   1992   1993

Source: Based on statistics from the National Sporting Goods Association

ROLLERBLADING ON A ROLL

Rollerblading is the fastest-growing sport in the U.S. Here is how the number of in-line skaters mounted from 1989–1993:

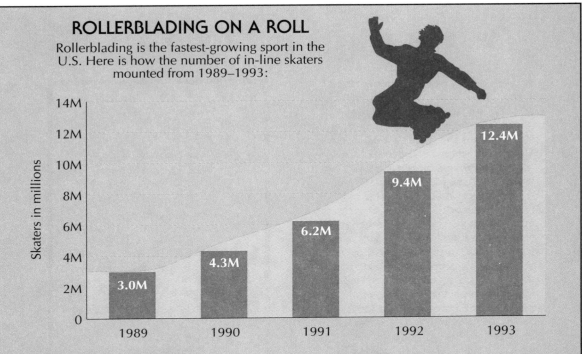

Skaters in millions

1989	1990	1991	1992	1993
3.0M	4.3M	6.2M	9.4M	12.4M

Source: Based on statistics from Rollerblade

CHESS POPULARITY RISING

Membership in U.S. Chess Federation after 1972, when Bobby Fischer beat Boris Spassky for the world championship:

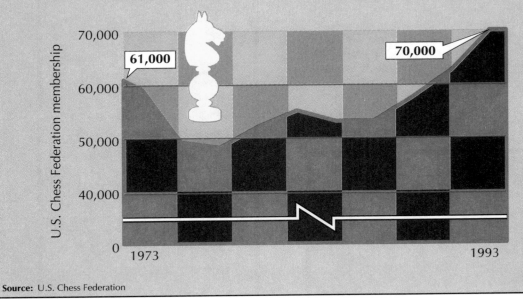

U.S. Chess Federation membership

61,000

70,000

1973   1993

Source: U.S. Chess Federation

WOMEN IN SPORTS

A revolution in women's sports began with passage of the U.S. Education Act of 1972. Its Title IX prohibits gender discrimination in sports at all educational institutions that receive federal funds. Since then, schools and colleges have moved to provide female athletes with facilities, coaching, and scholarships equal to those received by men. This has helped increase the number of women athletes; for instance, the number of girls involved in high school sports rose from 200,000 in the late 1970s to 2 million today. The impact has trickled down to elementary schools, and trickled up into professional sports. The paying public is also increasingly enthusiastic about women's sports, which has led to larger crowds—and hence greater earning potential—higher salaries and more endorsement opportunities for athletes.

Although female athletes enjoy more opportunities than ever before, and are receiving increasing respect for their athleticism, gender inequities continue to bedevil them. For example, a 1994 survey by the National Collegiate Athletic Association (NCAA) found that colleges award twice as much money in athletic scholarships to men as to women, and that female coaches earn much lower salaries than their male counterparts do.

FINGERTIP FACTS

- In 1992-1993, there were 7,137 high school soccer programs for boys, and 4,976 for girls.

- Female athletes graduate at higher rates (67% in 1987) than the general female college population (58%).

- During the 1970-1971 school year, 8% of high school athletes were girls. By 1993-1994, the figure had grown to 38%.

- During the 1992-1993 academic year, 149,053 girls nationwide played high school soccer, up from 11,534 in 1976-1977.

- According to the National Collegiate Athletic Association, 77 of its 752 member institutions in the 1981-1982 academic year operated soccer programs for women. In 1992-1993, there were 445 such programs at 895 institutions.

- Track is the most popular female varsity sport at NCAA colleges (23,119 participants in 1992-1993), followed by baseball (11,158), softball (10,356), and volleyball (10,241).

- In 1994, the U.S. Department of Education received 50 complaints nationwide alleging sex discrimination in various public school athletic programs.

- In 1992, some 84% of the aerobic shoes sold in the U.S. were for use by women, as were 64% of walking shoes, 48% of gym shoes and sneakers, and 41% of jogging and running shoes.

- Walking for exercise is the most popular sports activity among U.S. females (done by more than 44.6 million females in 1992), followed by swimming (33.3 million), bicycle riding (26.6 million), and aerobic exercise (22.8 million).

- Women comprise a significant portion of the professional sports audience; 35.1%, for example, say they are interested in the National Football League.

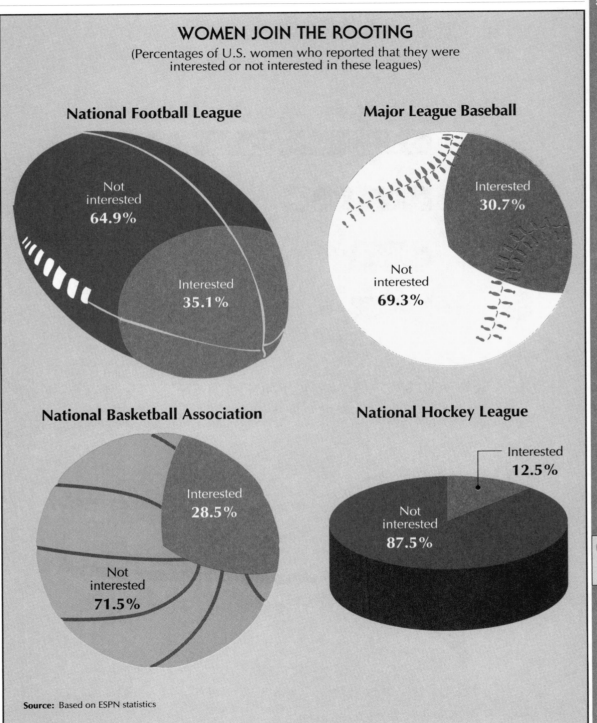

WOMEN JOIN THE ROOTING

(Percentages of U.S. women who reported that they were
interested or not interested in these leagues)

National Football League

Not
interested
64.9%

Interested
35.1%

Major League Baseball

Interested
30.7%

Not
interested
69.3%

National Basketball Association

Interested
28.5%

Not
interested
71.5%

National Hockey League

Interested
12.5%

Not
interested
87.5%

Source: Based on ESPN statistics

HIGH SCHOOL GIRLS IN MALE-DOMINATED SPORTS

(Number of U.S. high school girls who participate in male-dominated sports)

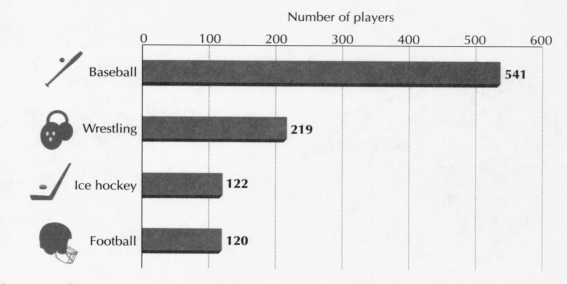

Number of players

Sport	Number
Baseball	541
Wrestling	219
Ice hockey	122
Football	120

Source: National Federation of State High School Associations

HIGH SCHOOL SPORTS PARTICIPATION TRENDS, 1971–1994

The number of boys participating in high school athletics slipped somewhat
in the period from 1971 to 1994, buts girls' participation increased significantly:

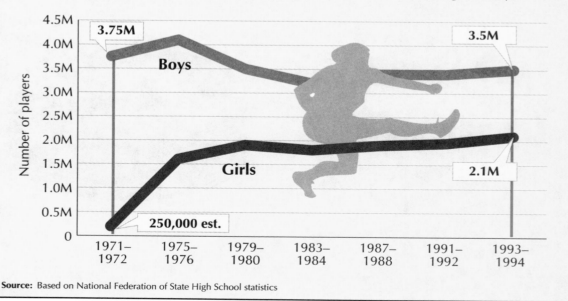

Boys: 3.75M → 3.5M
Girls: 250,000 est. → 2.1M

Number of players

1971–1972, 1975–1976, 1979–1980, 1983–1984, 1987–1988, 1991–1992, 1993–1994

Source: Based on National Federation of State High School statistics

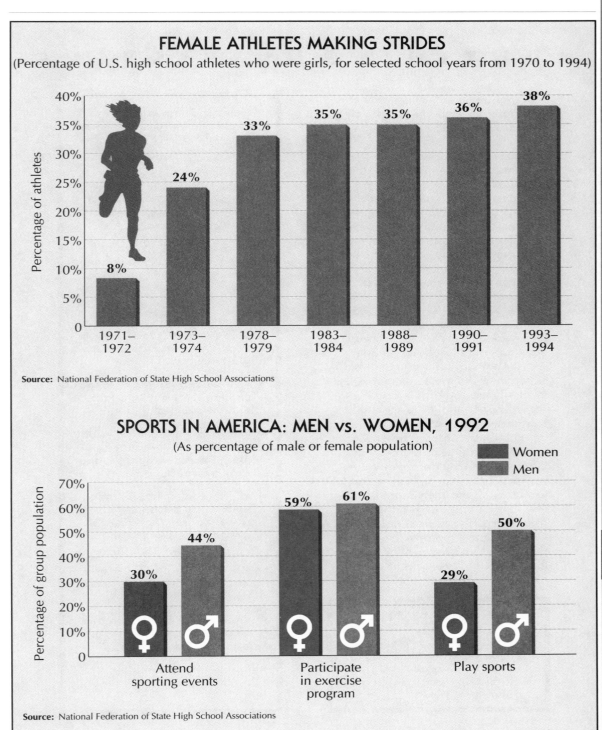

FEMALE ATHLETES MAKING STRIDES
(Percentage of U.S. high school athletes who were girls, for selected school years from 1970 to 1994)

Percentage of athletes

1971–1972	1973–1974	1978–1979	1983–1984	1988–1989	1990–1991	1993–1994
8%	24%	33%	35%	35%	36%	38%

Source: National Federation of State High School Associations

SPORTS IN AMERICA: MEN vs. WOMEN, 1992
(As percentage of male or female population)

Women
Men

Percentage of group population

	Women	Men
Attend sporting events	30%	44%
Participate in exercise program	59%	61%
Play sports	29%	50%

Source: National Federation of State High School Associations

HUNTING AND FISHING

Humans have hunted and fished since prehistoric times, but the purpose of these activities gradually shifted from survival to sport. Today's hunters and fishermen chase, catch, and kill more for excitement and pleasure than for the need to obtain a meal.

Some 35 million American adults (19% of the population) go fishing each year, and about 14 million (7%) go hunting. These activities are far more popular among males than females—87% of the fishing tackle bought in 1992 and 92% of the hunting equipment was purchased for use by males.

Various methods of hunting and fishing are used, depending on people's preferences and the species of animal being pursued. Most hunting is done with firearms: rifles for big game—such as deer, bear, and moose—and shotguns for small game and birds in flight. Trolling, casting, and still fishing are the basic methods of sport fishing.

Public lands, including national forests and areas administered by the U.S. Bureau of Land Management, are very popular hunting and fishing sites. Conservation and safety concerns, however, have led to growing restrictions on these sports. For example, in 1992, Colorado voters approved a measure restricting the hunting of black bears, and Iowa enacted a law protecting bats as a non-game species.

FINGERTIP FACTS

☛ In 1992, some 37.4 million fishing licenses and 31.3 million hunting licenses were issued in the U.S., at a cost of $398 million to anglers and $81 million to hunters.

☛ More than 31 million people ages 16 and older did some fresh-water fishing in 1991, and 8.9 million went salt-water fishing.

☛ Of the 14.1 million people who hunted in 1991, some 10.7 million pursued big game, 7.6 million small game, and 3.0 million hoped to shoot migratory birds.

☛ Hunters spent $12.3 million on hunting activities in 1991; fishermen expended $24.0 million on fishing. The bulk of their expenditures was for equipment.

☛ People in the U.S. spent an estimated $2.9 billion in 1993 on hunting equipment, including firearms—up from $1.4 billion in 1980.

☛ An estimated $685 million was spent on fishing tackle in 1993, up from $539 million in 1980.

☛ In 1992, some 11% of fishing tackle purchases and 5% of hunting equipment purchases were made for people under age 18.

☛ In 1992, people spent 287.7 million visitor days in national forests for recreational purposes. Hunting and fishing accounted for 33.2 million (11.6%) of those days.

☛ More than 50% of hunters travel at least 25 miles to reach their favorite hunting sites.

☛ Wyoming hosts the highest percentage of out-of-state anglers (64%), followed by Delaware (58%).

☛ Deer hunting is the most popular type of big-game hunting in the U.S.

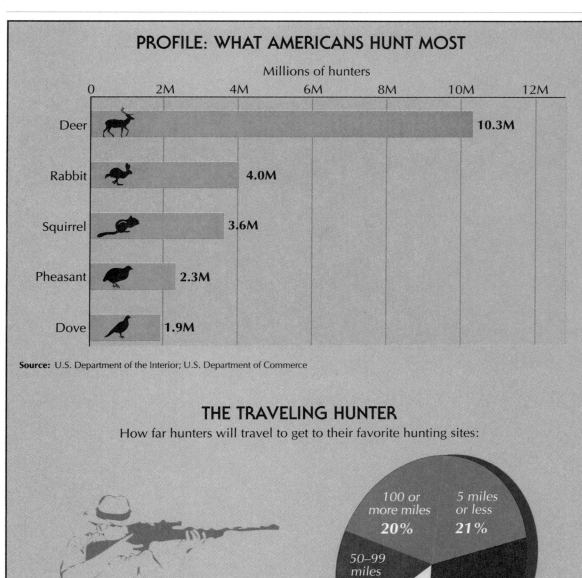

PROFILE: WHAT AMERICANS HUNT MOST

Millions of hunters

Deer	10.3M
Rabbit	4.0M
Squirrel	3.6M
Pheasant	2.3M
Dove	1.9M

Source: U.S. Department of the Interior; U.S. Department of Commerce

THE TRAVELING HUNTER

How far hunters will travel to get to their favorite hunting sites:

100 or more miles **20%**
5 miles or less **21%**
50–99 miles **15%**
6–24 miles **28%**
25–49 miles **16%**

Source: U.S. Department of the Interior; U.S. Department of Commerce

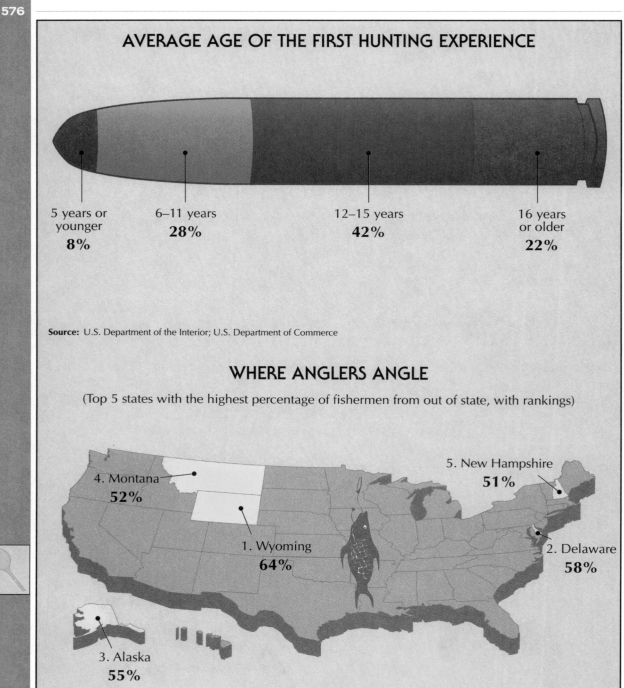

AVERAGE AGE OF THE FIRST HUNTING EXPERIENCE

5 years or younger **8%**

6–11 years **28%**

12–15 years **42%**

16 years or older **22%**

Source: U.S. Department of the Interior; U.S. Department of Commerce

WHERE ANGLERS ANGLE

(Top 5 states with the highest percentage of fishermen from out of state, with rankings)

4. Montana **52%**

5. New Hampshire **51%**

1. Wyoming **64%**

2. Delaware **58%**

3. Alaska **55%**

Source: U.S. Fish and Wildlife Service; U.S. Census Bureau

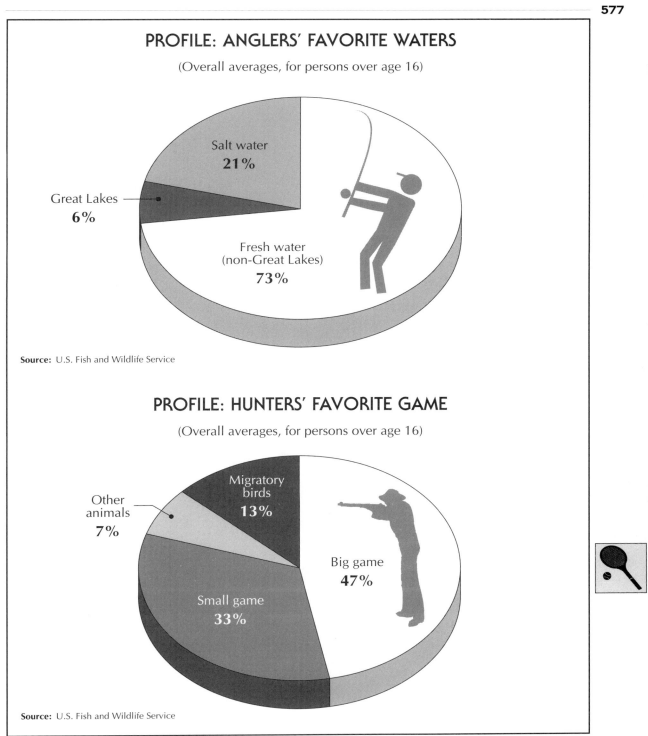

PROFILE: ANGLERS' FAVORITE WATERS

(Overall averages, for persons over age 16)

Salt water
21%

Great Lakes
6%

Fresh water
(non-Great Lakes)
73%

Source: U.S. Fish and Wildlife Service

PROFILE: HUNTERS' FAVORITE GAME

(Overall averages, for persons over age 16)

Migratory
birds
13%

Other
animals
7%

Big game
47%

Small game
33%

Source: U.S. Fish and Wildlife Service

12

EDUCATION AND LEARNING

PROFILE OF EDUCATION IN THE U.S.

Some 50 million children are enrolled in elementary and secondary schools in the U.S. An additional 15 million people are enrolled full-time in institutions of higher learning. The nation's educational system also encompasses millions of others from preschoolers to senior citizens—a majority of children ages 3 to 5 (56%) participate in preschool programs, and millions of people take courses in adult education programs, primarily to improve their job skills or for other personal and social reasons. In 1990-1991, some 57 million adults did so.

The majority of students attend public—that is, tax-supported—institutions. At the elementary and secondary levels, control of education is in the hands of the states, with local school districts charged with operating individual schools. Most schools, both public and private, teach a standard curriculum that focuses on language arts, mathematics, science, social studies, and health. The methods used to teach these and other subjects vary greatly, however, depending on school philosophy, student abilities, availability of teaching aids, and other factors.

Test scores are the most widely used indicator of what students have learned. On average, the more educated their parents, the higher students score on proficiency tests. Schools are increasingly developing programs to help parents and teachers work together, to ensure that children receive the education they need to succeed as adults—and that the nation's workforce needs—as the U.S. faces ever-tougher economic competition from other countries.

FINGERTIP FACTS

- More than 35 million U.S. children were enrolled in elementary school in 1995.

- In 1991, almost 4.7 million students were enrolled in private elementary and secondary schools. The majority of these attended Catholic schools.

- The average public elementary school has 458 students; the average high school has 678 students.

- In 1893, the average number of school days for U.S. students was 193.5. Today, it's 180.

- In the U.S., 5th graders were found to spend 46 minutes a day on homework as compared to 57 minutes in Japan and 114 minutes in China.

- In the 1984-1985 school year, 77.7% of public elementary and secondary schools had microcomputers, averaging 62.7 students per computer. By 1992-1993, 97.4% had them, with 12.2 students per computer.

- Only 47% of parents with young children read to them daily.

- Higher family income correlates with greater parental involvement in children's schooling—74% of parents in households earning $50,000 or more belong to parent groups at school, vs. 38% of parents in low-income households.

- The higher one's education level and income, the greater the likelihood of participating in adult education programs. In 1990-1991, 52% of people with college degrees took adult ed courses, as compared to 22% of high school graduates.

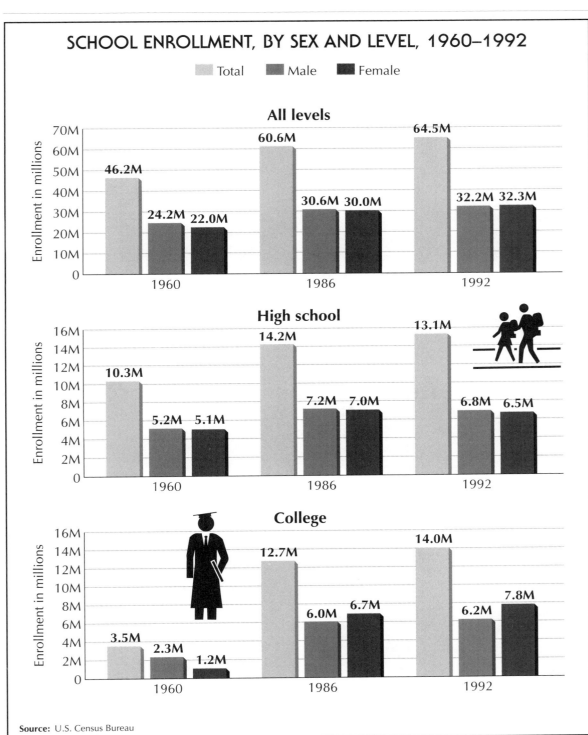

SCHOOL ENROLLMENT, BY SEX AND LEVEL, 1960–1992

Total   Male   Female

All levels

Enrollment in millions

1960: Total 46.2M, Male 24.2M, Female 22.0M
1986: Total 60.6M, Male 30.6M, Female 30.0M
1992: Total 64.5M, Male 32.2M, Female 32.3M

High school

Enrollment in millions

1960: Total 10.3M, Male 5.2M, Female 5.1M
1986: Total 14.2M, Male 7.2M, Female 7.0M
1992: Total 13.1M, Male 6.8M, Female 6.5M

College

Enrollment in millions

1960: Total 3.5M, Male 2.3M, Female 1.2M
1986: Total 12.7M, Male 6.0M, Female 6.7M
1992: Total 14.0M, Male 6.2M, Female 7.8M

Source: U.S. Census Bureau

U.S. SCHOOL ENROLLMENT, 1970–2000

(By grade level)

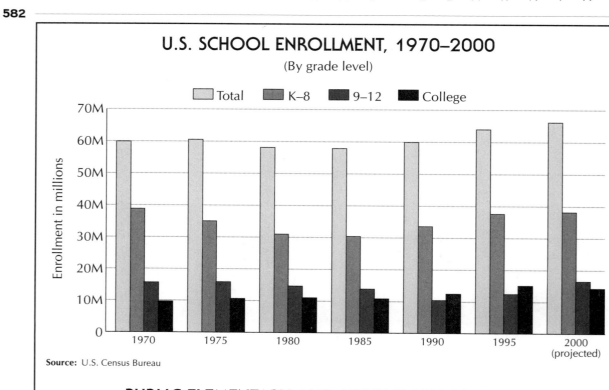

Total   K–8   9–12   College

Enrollment in millions

70M
60M
50M
40M
30M
20M
10M
0

1970   1975   1980   1985   1990   1995   2000 (projected)

Source: U.S. Census Bureau

PUBLIC ELEMENTARY AND SECONDARY SCHOOLS, BY SIZE, 1991–1992

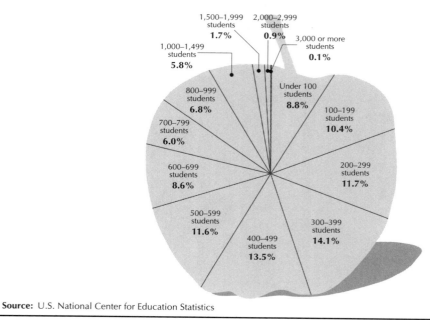

1,500–1,999 students **1.7%**
2,000–2,999 students **0.9%**
3,000 or more students **0.1%**
1,000–1,499 students **5.8%**
800–999 students **6.8%**
Under 100 students **8.8%**
100–199 students **10.4%**
700–799 students **6.0%**
600–699 students **8.6%**
200–299 students **11.7%**
500–599 students **11.6%**
300–399 students **14.1%**
400–499 students **13.5%**

Source: U.S. National Center for Education Statistics

AVERAGE VERBAL SAT SCORES, 1967–1993

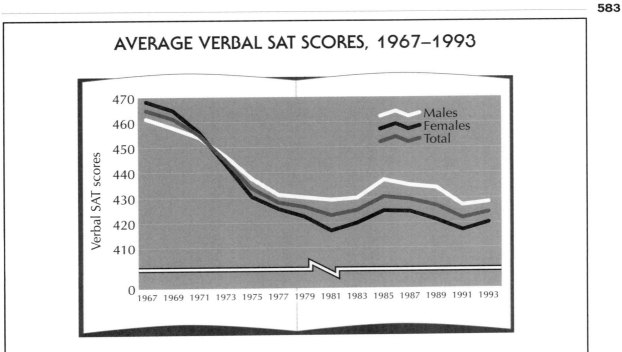

AVERAGE MATH SAT SCORES, 1967–1993

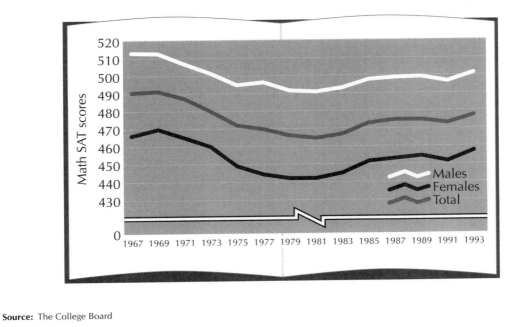

Source: The College Board

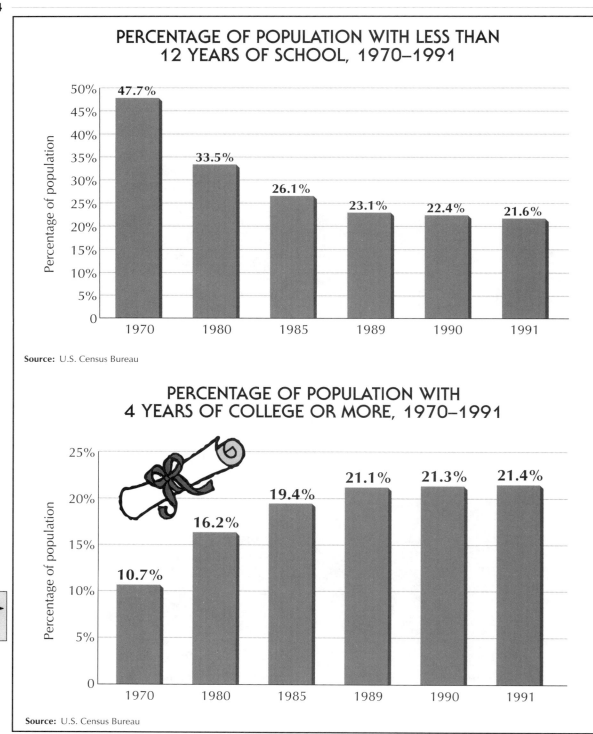

PERCENTAGE OF POPULATION WITH LESS THAN 12 YEARS OF SCHOOL, 1970–1991

Percentage of population

Year	Percentage
1970	47.7%
1980	33.5%
1985	26.1%
1989	23.1%
1990	22.4%
1991	21.6%

Source: U.S. Census Bureau

PERCENTAGE OF POPULATION WITH 4 YEARS OF COLLEGE OR MORE, 1970–1991

Percentage of population

Year	Percentage
1970	10.7%
1980	16.2%
1985	19.4%
1989	21.1%
1990	21.3%
1991	21.4%

Source: U.S. Census Bureau

HIGHEST EDUCATIONAL DEGREE EARNED, OF PEOPLE WITH SOME EDUCATION

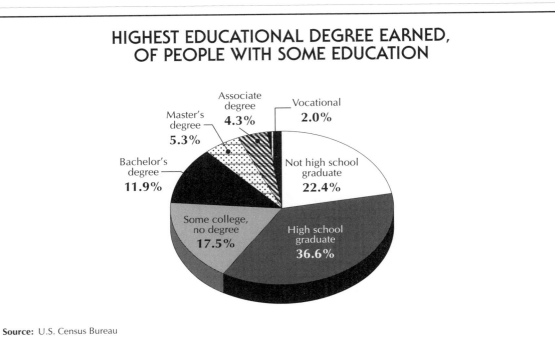

Source: U.S. Census Bureau

PROFILE: AVERAGE NUMBER OF YEARS OF EDUCATION, BY RACE OR ETHNIC GROUP

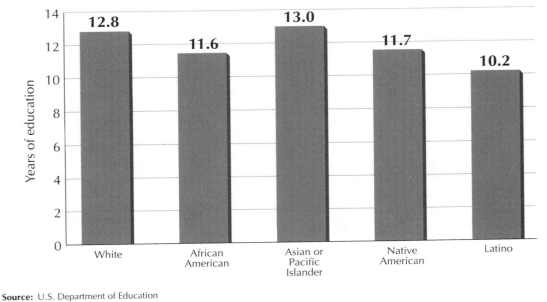

Source: U.S. Department of Education

HIGH SCHOOL AND COLLEGE

Four out of 5 adult Americans have graduated from high school. The Goals 2000: Educate America Act, originally adopted in 1989, calls for a 90% completion rate by the year 2000. Educators and the public, however, agree that competency is as important as completion. There is growing debate over educational standards and society's expectations of students—with good reason. For example, the failure of many graduating students to attain even basic language and math skills has forced colleges and universities to provide remedial courses for incoming freshmen. A 1993 study of literacy found that up to 47% of adult Americans do not know how to use a bus schedule or cannot distinguish between two employee benefits.

Another concern is preparedness for the labor force. Technological advances have reduced the number of well-paying opportunities for semi-skilled and un-skilled high school graduates. High school dropouts have an even harder time being hired for decent jobs.

In 1970, college enrollment was about 7.4 million; by 1995, about 15 million people were enrolled in U.S. colleges and universities. More people than ever before are also completing 4 or more years of college. For example, in 1960, only 7.7% of Americans age 25 or older had college degrees; by 1991, the figure had reached 21.4%.

As more Americans have gained access to educational opportunities, the college population has grown increasingly diverse. In 1960, there were almost 2 males for every female college student, and 92.2% of public college students and 96.3% of those in private colleges were white. By 1992, female students outnumbered men, and the percentage of white students had declined to 83.1% at public colleges and 84.5% at private colleges.

FINGERTIP FACTS

- Among Americans ages 25 and older in 1993, a total of 80.2% had completed high school—80.5% of males and 80.0% of females.

- In 1993, some 2,215,200 people in the U.S. graduated from high school. The greatest number (753,300) were in the South, the fewest (360,700) in the Northeast.

- Males are more likely than females to drop out of high school. Latinos have the highest dropout rates, followed by blacks, then whites.

- Scholastic Aptitude Test (SAT) scores have declined over the years. In 1970, verbal scores averaged 460; in 1993, the average was 424. In the same period, average math scores fell from 488 to 478.

- In 1993, fully 84% of college freshmen had A or B grade averages in high school.

- The South has the largest number of institutions of higher learning in the U.S. (1,148), followed by the Midwest (959).

- In 1993, the majority of college freshmen (53%) were female.

- In 1970, 4.4 million males and 3.0 million females attended college. In 1992, a total of 6.2 million males and 7.8 million females attended.

- In 1991, most male professors (69.7%) had tenure. Most female professors (51.5%) did not.

TOTAL U.S. PUBLIC HIGH SCHOOL GRADUATES, 1980–1994
(In millions)

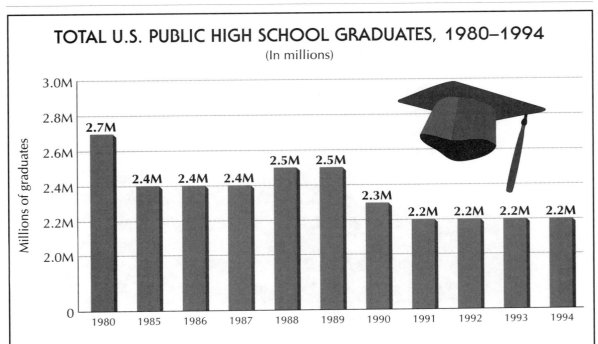

Source: U.S. National Center for Health Statistics

HIGH SCHOOL DROPOUT RATES, BY GENDER, 1967–1991

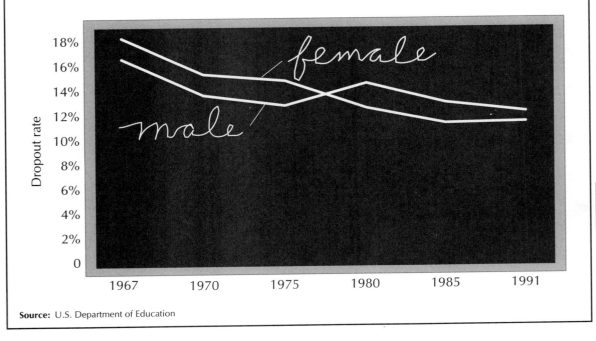

Source: U.S. Department of Education

HIGH SCHOOL DROPOUT RATES, BY RACE OR ETHNIC GROUP, 1983–1991

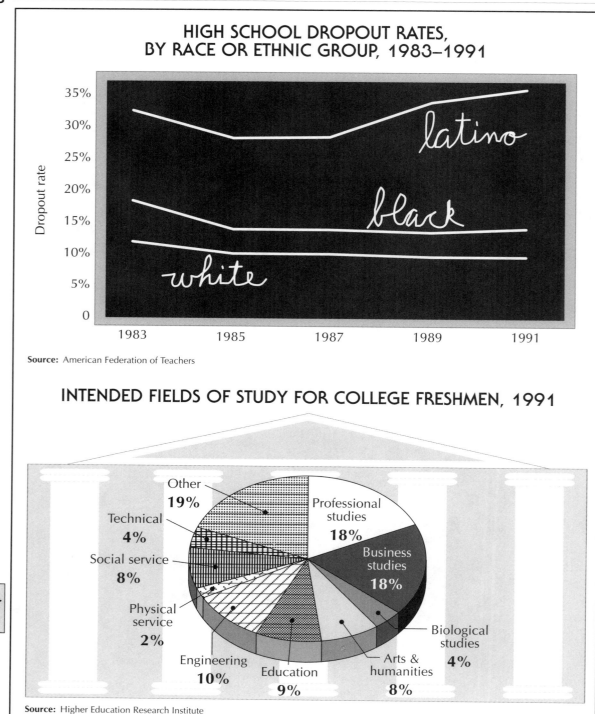

Source: American Federation of Teachers

INTENDED FIELDS OF STUDY FOR COLLEGE FRESHMEN, 1991

Other **19%**

Technical **4%**

Social service **8%**

Physical service **2%**

Engineering **10%**

Education **9%**

Arts & humanities **8%**

Biological studies **4%**

Business studies **18%**

Professional studies **18%**

Source: Higher Education Research Institute

COLLEGE ENROLLMENT, BY SEX AND RACE/ETHNIC GROUP, 1972–1992

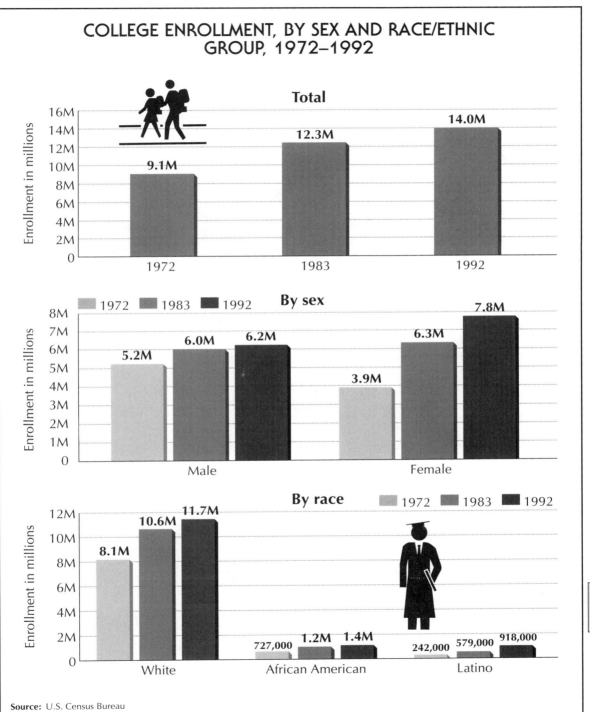

Total

Enrollment in millions

- 1972: 9.1M
- 1983: 12.3M
- 1992: 14.0M

By sex

1972 1983 1992

Enrollment in millions

Male
- 5.2M
- 6.0M
- 6.2M

Female
- 3.9M
- 6.3M
- 7.8M

By race

1972 1983 1992

Enrollment in millions

White
- 8.1M
- 10.6M
- 11.7M

African American
- 727,000
- 1.2M
- 1.4M

Latino
- 242,000
- 579,000
- 918,000

Source: U.S. Census Bureau

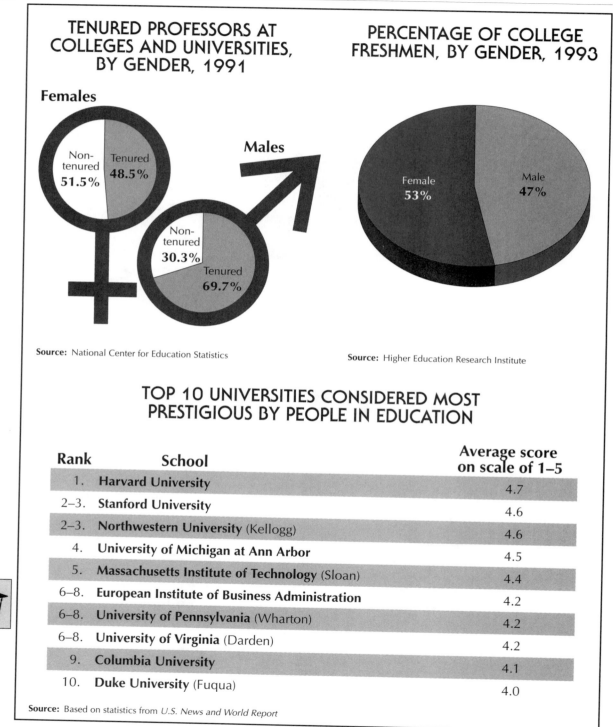

TENURED PROFESSORS AT COLLEGES AND UNIVERSITIES, BY GENDER, 1991

Females

Non-tenured 51.5%

Tenured 48.5%

Males

Non-tenured 30.3%

Tenured 69.7%

Source: National Center for Education Statistics

PERCENTAGE OF COLLEGE FRESHMEN, BY GENDER, 1993

Female 53%

Male 47%

Source: Higher Education Research Institute

TOP 10 UNIVERSITIES CONSIDERED MOST PRESTIGIOUS BY PEOPLE IN EDUCATION

Rank	School	Average score on scale of 1–5
1.	**Harvard University**	4.7
2–3.	**Stanford University**	4.6
2–3.	**Northwestern University** (Kellogg)	4.6
4.	**University of Michigan at Ann Arbor**	4.5
5.	**Massachusetts Institute of Technology** (Sloan)	4.4
6–8.	**European Institute of Business Administration**	4.2
6–8.	**University of Pennsylvania** (Wharton)	4.2
6–8.	**University of Virginia** (Darden)	4.2
9.	**Columbia University**	4.1
10.	**Duke University** (Fuqua)	4.0

Source: Based on statistics from *U.S. News and World Report*

ASIANS DOMINATE FOREIGN STUDENTS IN U.S. UNIVERSITIES, 1993

Two-thirds of the foreigners studying at American universities in 1993 were from Asia:

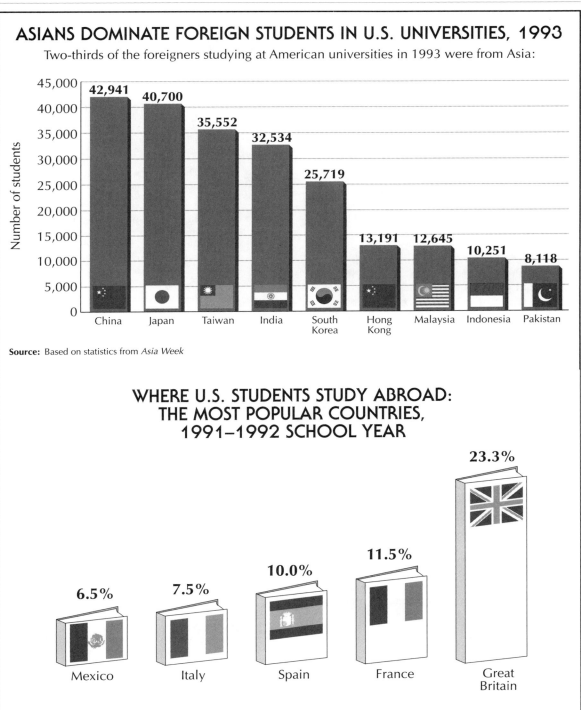

Source: Based on statistics from *Asia Week*

WHERE U.S. STUDENTS STUDY ABROAD: THE MOST POPULAR COUNTRIES, 1991–1992 SCHOOL YEAR

Source: Institute of International Education

TEACHERS

The United States has some 2.8 million elementary and secondary school teachers. Most of them are women, and the great majority are non-Latino whites. Increasingly, they are burdened by large classes, fearful of violence in the classroom, overwhelmed by the needs of children with social and emotional problems, discouraged by unrealistic community demands, and fed up with mediocre school bureaucracies. Frustrated and disillusioned, many quit their careers.

Although American society depends on teachers to educate its youth, it does not grant teachers a social and economic status that reflects that enormous responsibility. Average teacher salaries—from starting salaries to those of people with many years of experience—are lower than those in many other professions, though there has been significant improvement in teachers' wages during the past 2 decades. It is hoped that reforms in teacher training, including the establishment in 1987 of a National Board for Professional Teaching Standards, will improve public opinion of the teaching profession. By 1998, the board is expected to have standards and assessments in 33 certificate areas.

At the college and university level, there are some 890,000 professors and other faculty members. Typically, a beginning college instructor gradually advances through the ranks of assistant professor and associate professor to full professor. Advancement depends on a combination of teaching ability, research work, and publication of books and articles.

FINGERTIP FACTS

- In 1995, there were more than 2.8 million elementary and secondary school teachers, 87% in public schools.

- Most public school teachers (74% in 1992) are women.

- Most public school administrators are men—61% in 1992.

- Most public school principals and assistant principals (60% in 1992) are men.

- U.S. teachers spend more time in the classroom than their counterparts in other countries. U.S. elementary school teachers spend 1,093 hours teaching each year, compared to 624 hours in Sweden, 790 hours in Germany, and 944 hours in France.

- The two largest teachers' unions—the National Education Association and the American Federation of Teachers—have a combined membership of more than 2 million.

- In 1980, the average salary for classroom teachers was $15,970. By 1993, it had risen to $35,027.

- In 1993, Mississippi teachers earned the least in the U.S., an average of $24,400. Connecticut had the best-paid teachers, averaging $48,300.

- In 1993, the average starting salary of public school teachers was $22,505.

- Most elementary and secondary teachers over age 40 have master's or other advanced degrees. White teachers are more likely than their African American or Latino counterparts to have advanced degrees.

- Average salaries for full-time college professors vary enormously, and they are not always highest at the most prestigious schools. For the 1994-1995 year, these salaries were $104,200 at Harvard University, $79,900 at Nassau Community College (Long Island, New York), and $69,700 at Vassar College.

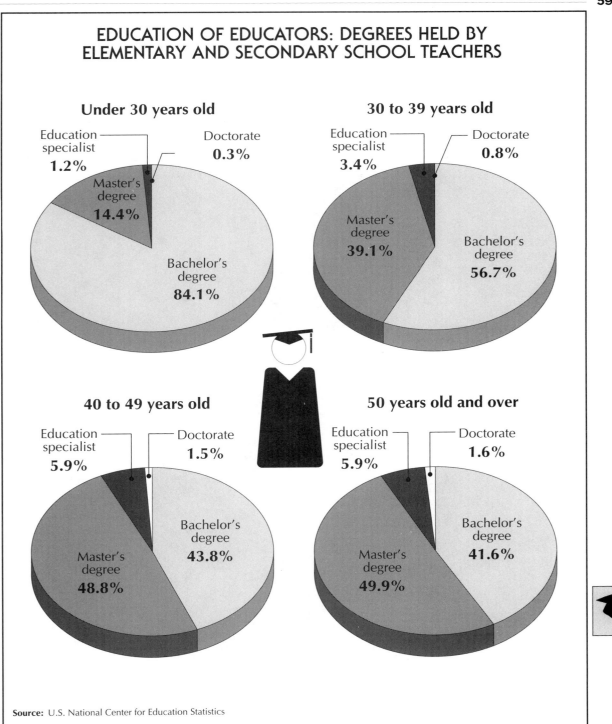

EDUCATION OF EDUCATORS: DEGREES HELD BY ELEMENTARY AND SECONDARY SCHOOL TEACHERS

Under 30 years old

Education specialist 1.2%
Doctorate 0.3%
Master's degree 14.4%
Bachelor's degree 84.1%

30 to 39 years old

Education specialist 3.4%
Doctorate 0.8%
Master's degree 39.1%
Bachelor's degree 56.7%

40 to 49 years old

Education specialist 5.9%
Doctorate 1.5%
Bachelor's degree 43.8%
Master's degree 48.8%

50 years old and over

Education specialist 5.9%
Doctorate 1.6%
Bachelor's degree 41.6%
Master's degree 49.9%

Source: U.S. National Center for Education Statistics

PROFILE: AVERAGE PAY FOR TEACHERS COMPARED TO OTHER PROFESSIONS

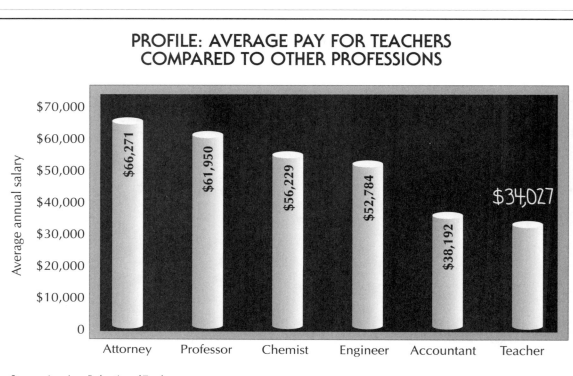

Source: American Federation of Teachers

WHO'S TEACHING U.S. STUDENTS?

(Number of elementary and secondary school teachers, by race or ethnic group)

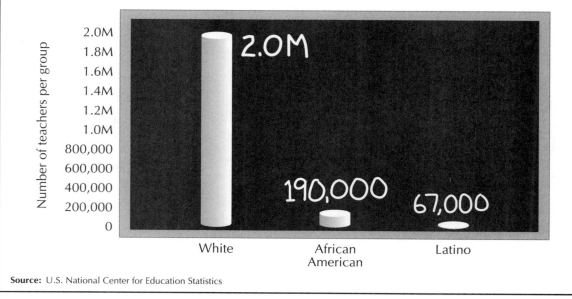

Source: U.S. National Center for Education Statistics

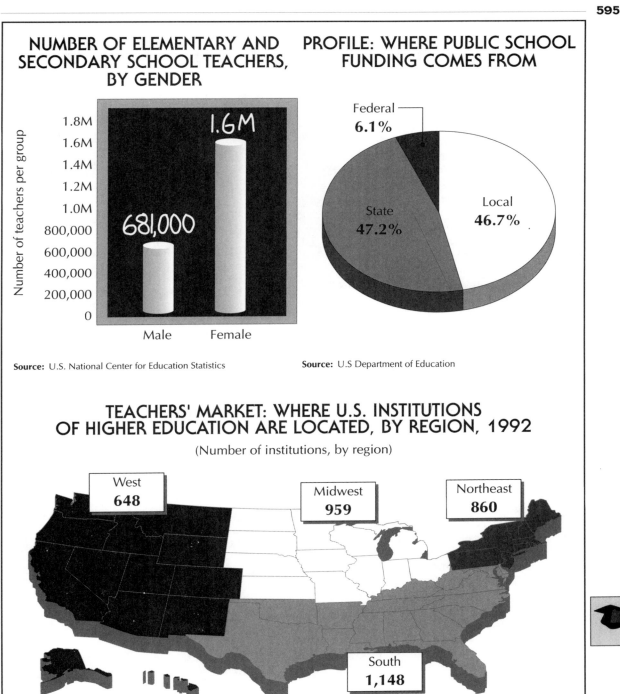

NUMBER OF ELEMENTARY AND SECONDARY SCHOOL TEACHERS, BY GENDER

Number of teachers per group

1.8M
1.6M
1.4M
1.2M
1.0M
800,000
600,000
400,000
200,000
0

681,000 — Male

1.6M — Female

Source: U.S. National Center for Education Statistics

PROFILE: WHERE PUBLIC SCHOOL FUNDING COMES FROM

Federal **6.1%**

State **47.2%**

Local **46.7%**

Source: U.S Department of Education

TEACHERS' MARKET: WHERE U.S. INSTITUTIONS OF HIGHER EDUCATION ARE LOCATED, BY REGION, 1992

(Number of institutions, by region)

West **648**

Midwest **959**

Northeast **860**

South **1,148**

Source: U.S. National Center for Health Statistics

THE COST OF EDUCATION

School costs are going up, up, up! While the general public focuses on salaries of teachers and administrators, and parents fret over college tuition payments, these are only part of the picture. Schools need to find millions of dollars to buy computers and other equipment. Insurance premiums have skyrocketed. Maintenance and repair expenditures, which have often been deferred for years, can no longer be delayed.

Yet school districts are under growing pressure to hold the line on budgets. State and federal governments have slashed aid to schools, and taxpayers are rejecting yearly jumps in local taxes (the large majority of school funding comes from local and state taxes). This has led to deep cuts in summer remedial programs, shortened kindergarten hours, ever-larger class sizes, the elimination of extracurricular activities, and other cost-saving moves.

In many U.S. school systems, teachers who want classroom supplies must often pay for them themselves. Even corporations—recognizing their need for a skilled workforce in the future—are getting into the act, donating money for scholarships, equipment, teacher training, and other programs.

Americans agree that spending money on education is of critical value to both society and the individual. Only with a solid education will today's students be able to survive in the increasingly complex and competitive global economy.

Educational accomplishment also contributes enormously to the development of positive self-esteem and greater control over one's life path. For example, spending more time learning translates into higher salaries and higher net worth.

FINGERTIP FACTS

- The bulk of public school funding comes from state (47.2%) and local (46.6%) monies; 6.1% comes from the federal government.

- Expenditures per student vary from state to state. In 1993, New Jersey spent an average of $9,712 per pupil; Utah spent $3,218.

- A 1995 government report projected that the nation's elementary and secondary schools need about $112 billion in repairs and upgrades to restore them to good condition.

- About 14 million students attend schools that need extensive repairs or replacement.

- In 1994-1995, federal student loans totaled about $23 billion.

- At private colleges and universities, a growing portion of tuition income is used to subsidize scholarships for needy students. A study of 31 institutions found that in 1995, 19.7% of the average $19,110 tuition and fees bill went for needs-based scholarships. This contrasted with 12.8% in 1985 and 9.1% in 1975.

- Men earn more than women. In 1993, salaries of men with high school degrees averaged $26,766; their female counterparts averaged $18,648.

- The higher the level of education, the greater the salary discrepancy between the sexes. In 1993, the average salary of men with master's degrees was $47,260; for women, it was $35,081.

- A household headed by a person with a high school degree has an average net worth of $33,254, while one headed by a college graduate has an average net worth of $72,373.

AVERAGE PUBLIC SCHOOL COSTS, PER U.S. PUPIL, 1983–1993
(In thousands of dollars)

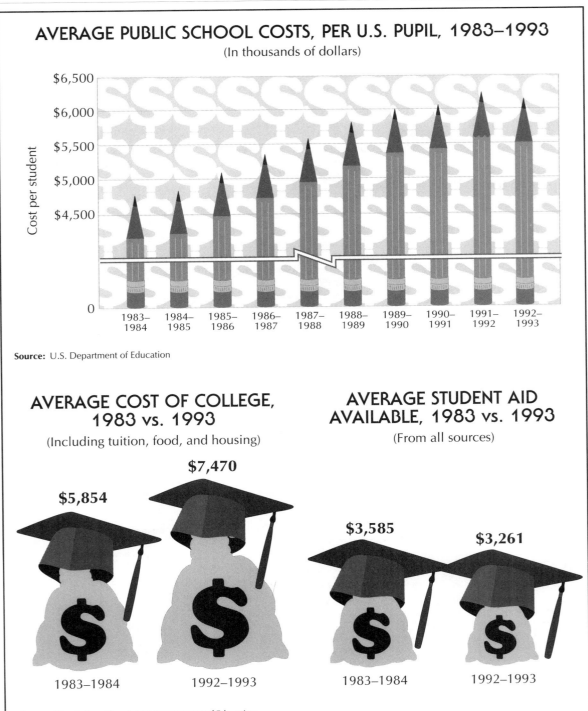

Source: U.S. Department of Education

AVERAGE COST OF COLLEGE, 1983 vs. 1993
(Including tuition, food, and housing)

$7,470

$5,854

1983–1984   1992–1993

AVERAGE STUDENT AID AVAILABLE, 1983 vs. 1993
(From all sources)

$3,585

$3,261

1983–1984   1992–1993

Source: The College Board; U.S. Department of Education

Index